RE-FRAMERS

170 ECCENTRIC, VISIONARY, AND PATRIOTIC PROPOSALS TO REWRITE THE U.S. CONSTITUTION

John R. Vile

 ABC-CLIO

Santa Barbara, California • Denver, Colorado • Oxford, England

To the Buchanan Family, the Martin Family,
members of the Board of Visitors, and other generous supporters
of the Honors College at Middle Tennessee State University

Library of Congress Cataloging-in-Publication Data
Vile, John R., author.
  Re-framers : 170 eccentric, visionary, and patriotic proposals to rewrite the U.S.
Constitution / John R. Vile.
    pages cm
  Includes bibliographical references and index.
  ISBN 978-1-61069-733-0 (hardback) — ISBN 978-1-61069-734-7 (e-book)
1. Constitutional history—United States. 2. Constitutional amendments—United States.
3. Law reform—United States. I. Title.
  KF4541.V55 2014
  342.7303—dc23   2014002092

ISBN: 978-1-61069-733-0
EISBN: 978-1-61069-734-7

18 17 16 15 14   1 2 3 4 5

This book is also available on the World Wide Web as an eBook.
Visit www.abc-clio.com for details.

ABC-CLIO, LLC
130 Cremona Drive, P.O. Box 1911
Santa Barbara, California 93116-1911

This book is printed on acid-free paper ⊗
Manufactured in the United States of America

Contents

Alphabetical Listing of Meetings and Authors of Plans Covered in This Book

Acknowledgments

Over almost 35 years of writing, I have accumulated numerous debts to individuals who have nurtured and instructed me, to the universities that have employed me, to a variety of editors and publishers who have shepherded my works into print, and to numerous colleagues and friends who have served as sounding boards and supports. I am especially proud of the support that I am currently receiving from my family, from administrators at Middle Tennessee State University, from my colleagues within the University Honors College, from the talented students who inspire me, and from the dedicated members of our Board of Visitors.

For this project, I owe special thanks to Professor Steven R. Boyd at the University of Texas at San Antonio, to Professor John Kaminski at the University of Wisconsin at Madison, and to Mayo Taylor, Mary Ellen Possebon, and Christy Groves at the reference desk of the Walker Library at Middle Tennessee State University. Jackie Dowdy and the Interlibrary Loan Office have also been helpful. I am particularly grateful to the late Dr. Everett Cunningham, a long-time member of the Department of Political Science at MTSU who willed me his books, many of which have been indispensable in my work on this one. I also consulted Dr. Mark Byrnes and Dr. Karen Petersen on a number of issues.

Denver Compton, Robin Tutt, and Kevin Hillstrom at ABC-CLIO have been particularly supportive of this book, and I especially appreciate their support as I do of Nicholle Lutz, the production editor. I dedicate this book to the families and members of the Board of Visitors who continue to support the University Honors College at Middle Tennessee State University.

Introduction

The Onion, which is notorious for its humor, published an article dated February 17, 2011, in which it announced the ratification of a new U.S. Constitution. It reported that a handful of businessmen and former congressmen stepped forward to write a new Constitution after the nation discovered that the previous one had expired. *The Onion* said that in less than five hours, they penned a document that was more than 500 pages long, but which was to be kept secret. After great effort, however, *The Onion*'s intrepid investigator reported locating the first page of the document, which began with pictures of the symbols of nine major corporations and was presented by AT&T.

Not to be outdone, Frank Lake reported in the November 12, 2012, issue of the supermarket tabloid *Weekly World News* that former law professor Barack Obama had decided to write a new constitution. Lake announced that the new constitution would resemble those of Kenya, France, and Soviet Russia. Some of the highlights of the new document would include appointing two more justices to the Supreme Court, giving the president complete financial powers, increasing representation for California, New York, and Illinois, and banning both guns and religion!

On September 18, 2013, Matt Rock reported on "Pardon the Pundit," a Web site devoted to political satire, that various groups had been busy redesigning the Constitution over the previous month. Democrats had come up with a constitution of 54,796 pages. It included free health care, amnesty for illegal aliens, and other matters, although no one had yet been able to read the whole thing. By contrast, Republicans had settled for a picture of "a bald eagle driving a monster truck over a hundred poor people" and various other nationalistic symbols. Libertarians wrote their proposals on a napkin with Ron Paul's picture on one side and an expletive on the other. The Tea Party had concentrated on declaring America to be Christian and requiring birth certificates and other documents from presidential candidates, while Green Party members were still debating over what kind of recycled paper to use and whether to replace the American Bald Eagle with "a bag of Tofurkey."

The authors of these three articles might have drawn inspiration from Nathaniel Whitten's satirical chapbook entitled *The Do-It-Yourself Constitutional Amendment Kit* (2008), which attempted to get citizens to think about constitutional amendments for which they might petition their legislators. Whitten included his own proposals for amendments 28 through 53. The first set the tone by requiring presidents who declare war "to physically lead the charge into battle." Similarly, his second proposal would automatically disqualify anyone from office who brought up religious issues. Although Whitten did include some serious proposals like eliminating the Electoral College, providing universal service for two years, mandating a 20 percent across-the-board "fair tax," and increasing representation for more populous states, other proposals include restricting the right to bear arms to carrying muskets and limiting political speeches to 14 minutes each.

After members of the 112th Congress began the session in 2011 by reading aloud the U.S. Constitution, David Cole of Georgetown University published an article in the *Washington Post* in which he claimed to have to have used WikiLeaks to discover "The Conservative Constitution of the United States," which included reference to "We, the Real Americans," the need for "a more God-Fearing Union," a "Right Not to Pay Taxes," a restriction on raising taxes on any day other than February 29, and constant references to opposition to national health care.

Kevin Bleyer joined the fun in *Me the People: One Man's Selfless Quest to Rewrite the Constitution of the United States of Americ*a (2013). Readers who may know Bleyer from his role on *The Daily Show with Jon Stewart* will be hard pressed to find much seriousness within the covers of his book.

Seventy years before any of these proposals, iconoclast journalist H. L. Mencken drafted a satirical version of a "Constitution for the New Deal," which was published in the June 1937 issue of *The American Mercury*. Provisions included making the president the "commander-in-chief of the Army and Navy, and of the militia, Boy Scouts, C.I.O., People's Front, and other armed forces of the nation"; allowing him to repeal "Gresham's law, the law of diminishing returns, and the law of gravitation"; requiring members of Congress to obtain presidential permission before introducing bills; preventing the Supreme Court from declaring any laws to be unconstitutional; and providing for "complete freedom of speech and of the press—subject to such regulations as the President or his agents may from time to time promulgate."

History of Past Treatments

As entertaining as such proposals are, the subject matter is important. Professor Walter Murphy of Princeton University, one of America's foremost constitutional scholars, devoted one of his last books to a discussion of how to create a just political order for a mythical nation he named Nusquam through deliberation and discussion (2007). So too, I have devoted much of my academic life to the study of the writing, ratification, and interpretation of the U.S. Constitution and to the history of attempts to amend or replace it.

Because proposals for rewriting the Constitution have been far more plentiful than commentaries that have sought to analyze those proposals, many have remained virtually unknown outside of a small circle of academicians. Praeger published my first book entitled *Rewriting the United States Constitution: An Examination of Proposals from Reconstruction to the Present* in 1991, which I followed up with an article in 1993. At the time I had identified about 40 proposals for significantly rewriting the Constitution that had emerged from the end of congressional Reconstruction in 1877 to the time of the book's publication.

Within a year, Steven R. Boyd, a history professor at the University of Texas at San Antonio, published his *Alternative Constitutions for the United States: A Documentary History*, which included the texts of 10 proposed new constitutions dating from 1861 to 1974, some of which I had not discovered. Since then, I have continued to locate proposals that we had missed, as well as a plethora of new proposals, many of which have been posted on the Internet or been published as e-books. I have included some entries on new finds in my *Encyclopedia of Constitutional Amendments, Proposed Amendments, and Amending Issues* (2010), which is now in its third edition. Although such entries can describe the substance of individual proposals, they cannot as readily capture the context of the time in which each proposal was formulated, its relationship to other proposals from the same or other time periods, and the wide sweep of American history from which each emerged.

I now know that the history of proposed constitutions is grander and more nuanced than I first imagined. Not only have I discovered several major rewriting proposals prior to Reconstruction, but I have drilled deeper into America's own founding period to illumine the constitutional-writing enterprise and the structure of the U.S. Constitution and provide a broader context for the proposals that I explore here. In addition to exploring its foundations, this book will treat more than 170 proposals to rewrite the U.S. Constitution. Although the book will therefore contain a significantly greater number of entries on rewriters than either of the two previous works, some passages dealing with the substance of individual proposals that I had identified previously will be similar to the descriptions that I included in *Rewriting the United States Constitution* and *Encyclopedia of Constitutional Amendments*.

Methodology

In a widely circulated theory of constitutional change in the United States, Yale's Bruce Ackerman argues that there have been three major "constitutional moments" in the nation's history, none of which has closely followed existing constitutional norms (1991, 1996). Ackerman observes that those who wrote and ratified the U.S. Constitution, thus inaugurating the "first constitutional moment," neither followed the mechanism for congressional proposal nor pursued state legislative ratification of amendments, as the Articles of Confederation had required. Congress later initiated a second constitutional moment when it would not seat representatives of Southern states until those states ratified post–Civil War amendments that radically altered existing understandings of federalism and the scope of national rights. Similarly, during the New Deal era, the president and Congress initiated a third constitutional moment of welfare state innovations in response to the crisis of the Great Depression. The Supreme Court, in time, affirmed these changes.

Ackerman's analysis raises the issue of how to determine inclusion criteria for this book. Apart from restricting this book (like Boyd's) to those who have actually proposed complete alternate documents, there is no easy answer. One can conceive of a single amendment (one, for example, providing for a hereditary king or abolishing the Supreme Court) that might be far more transformative than a series of minor emendations.

This book will focus on individuals who called for a new constitution or who advocated a multifaceted amendment or series of amendments that I believe would collectively represent a significant departure from, or addition to, existing constitutional norms. From time to time, I will also discuss individuals like John C. Calhoun, Woodrow Wilson, and Franklin D. Roosevelt, whose writings and speeches were catalysts for such proposals and provided the theoretical support for them. I will thus exclude consideration of proposals that call for reinterpreting existing constitutional provisions without adopting a new constitution or series of amendments. Similarly, I will exclude proposals that advocated a single amendment or reform (Henry George's proposal for a flat tax, for example); that proposed changes that could be adopted without changing the existing constitutional system; or that simply posed the question of how things would have been different had we had different constitutional arrangements (see Levine, et al. 1992). Especially in my coverage of America's earlier years, I will occasionally mention individuals whose proposals for a constitutional convention signaled that they thought the existing document was in need of serious reform, even though they did not specify an agenda. I will chiefly focus, however, on those who proposed a new constitution or a major series of amendments.

Organization, Scope, and Audience of This Book

I have divided this book into 14 chapters. The first examines some of the prequels to the U.S. Constitution, including colonial documents, early state constitutions, and the government under the Articles of Confederation. The second chapter explains how the writing and ratification of the U.S. Constitution emerged from various plans at the Constitutional Convention and includes a brief outline of the U.S. Constitution and its amendments. Chapters 3 through 11 examine proposals from the founding to the Civil War, Reconstruction to the turn of the century, the Progressive era and World War I, the Great Depression and World War II and beyond, the 1960s and 1970s, the Reagan and George H. W. Bush years, the Bill Clinton years, the George W. Bush years, and the years that Barack Obama has occupied the Oval Office up to the present. Chapter 12 examines proposals for constitutional reform that individuals have posted on the Internet. Chapter 13 provides a series of constitutional archetypes (key questions with respect to the current Constitution) by which to analyze all the previous proposals and summarizes the responses to those questions by reformers of every political persuasion. Finally, Chapter 14 provides further analysis of the proposers and suggests possible future courses of action. An index will supplement the list of individuals who have advanced key proposals that follows this essay.

This book reaches more than 200 years further back than my initial work on this subject, and it includes extensive coverage of developments since that work was published in 1991. I am almost certain that other scholars and I will continue to unearth other proposals from the past that have not yet received scholarly attention, and that individuals will continue to introduce new ones as well. Each proposed constitution or set of amendments provides a window on the politics of its day that illumines America's continuing dialogue on constitutional government.

Title and Pagination

I have titled this book to emphasize the colorful nature of the individuals and the eclectic proposals that they have advanced. I have attempted to portray each of them accurately and fairly. Similarly, I have included general references for those who would like to dig deeper into individual proposals while dispensing with long explanatory notes. Because this book covers such a broad expanse of proposals, many of which scholars have not treated elsewhere, I hope that it will provide grist for scholars from a variety of disciplines who are interested in performing additional qualitative and quantitative analysis.

I remain convinced that the U.S. Constitution is a wise and noble but imperfect document, and I believe that one of the best ways to understand it is to consider possible alternatives. I am particularly grateful to those who were courageous enough to risk their lives to secure our nation's liberties, wise enough to identify problems with the government that preceded our current one, bold enough to draft solutions for the most pressing of those issues, and prescient and humble enough to leave the door open for future constitutional changes. It is important to recognize that our Founders included not only those who drafted and ratified the U.S. Constitution but also those who extended full citizenship rights to African Americans and women and to those who have sought not only to preserve but also to improve upon the document that had been bequeathed to them.

To date, the Constitution has only been formally amended 27 times, each time through the method of congressional proposal and state ratification. This method seems likely to continue in the near future. Even if someday we the people of the nation find the need to replace the document or tinker with some of its institutions, however, I think that we will want to perpetuate many of its most basic principles. I certainly hope that we would not take such a step without understanding the document and its evolution or without a basic knowledge of the many alternative constitutions that have already been proposed.

References

Ackerman, Bruce. 2014. *We the People: The Civil Rights Revolution*. Cambridge, MA: Harvard University Press.

Ackerman, Bruce. 1996. *We the People: Transformation*. Cambridge, MA: Harvard University Press.

Ackerman, Bruce, 1991. *We the People: Foundations*. Cambridge, MA: Belknap.

Bleyer, Kevin, 2013. *Me the People: One Man's Selfless Quest to Rewrite the Constitution of the United States of America*. New York: Random House.

Boyd, Steven R., ed. 1992. *Alternative Constitutions for the United States: A Documentary History*. Westport, CT: Greenwood Press.

Cole, David. 2011. "The Conservative Constitution of the United States." *Washington Post*, January 6. http://www.washingtonpost.com/wp-dyn/content/article/2011/01/06/AR2011010602485.html. Accessed December 17, 2013.

Lake, Frank. 2012. "Obama to Write New U.S. Constitution." *Weekly World News*, November 12. http://weeklyworldnews.com/politics/35813/obama-to-write-new-u-s-constitution/. Accessed December 17, 2013.

Levine, Herbert M., et al. 1992. *What If the American Political System Were Different?* Armonk, NY: M. E. Sharpe, Inc.

Mencken, H. L. 1937. "Constitution for the New Deal," *American Mercury*, June.

Murphy, Walter F. 2007. *Constitutional Democracy: Creating and Maintaining a Just Political Order*. Baltimore: Johns Hopkins University Press.

"New Constitution of the United States Ratified." *The Onion*, February 17, 2011. Accessed June 14, 2013. http://www.theonion.com/articles/new-constitution-of-the-united-states-ratified.

Rock, Matt. September 18, 2013. "Major Parties, Movements to Propose New U.S. Constitutions during Academic Debates." "Pardon the Pundit" Web site (posting discontinued).

Vile, John R. 2010. *Encyclopedia of Constitutional Amendments, Proposed Amendments, and Amending Issues, 1789–2020*. 3rd ed. 2 vols. Santa Barbara, CA: ABC-CLIO.

Vile, John R. 1993. "The Long Legacy of Proposals to Rewrite the U.S. Constitution." *PS: Political Science and Politics* 26 (June): 208–11.

Vile, John R. 1991. *Rewriting the United States Constitution: An Examination of Proposals from Reconstruction to the Present*. New York: Praeger.

Whitten, Nathaniel. *The Do-It-Yourself Constitutional Amendment Kit*. 2008. N.p.: Vitally Important Books.

CHAPTER 1

American Constitutional Prequels

Although political observers dating back to the Greek philosopher Aristotle have written books on the constitutions of various governments (1964), it was not until the eighteenth century that the term became chiefly associated with the kind of documents that many contemporary Americans believe are essential to empowering, structuring, and limiting governments. The idea of written constitutions unchangeable by ordinary legislative means (if at all) arguably had roots in the examples of ancient lawgivers like Solon and Moses (Vile 1993). The idea further developed in the fertile soil provided by Protestant covenant theology by a people who settled in what to them was a "New World" (Moots 2010). They arrived under the authority and protection of charters issued by English monarchs and firmly rooted in rights that they associated with the Magna Carta, the English Bill of Rights, and other seminal documents that had outlined the rights of Englishmen (Lutz 1980, 1988, 1998).

Although it grew from the English constitutional tradition, the American model eventually departed from it. The British Constitution, which David Hume and Edmund Burke ably explicated and defended (see Vile 1992, 14–15), traced itself back to time immemorial and to the idea of accumulated wisdom rather than to a single document adopted at a particular point in time. As this tradition developed, it further came to emphasize the authority of Parliament over that of the monarch in a doctrine known as parliamentary sovereignty. Proponents of this view asserted that this legislative body could "do anything except make a man a woman or a woman a man" (quoted in Corwin 1955, 87). By contrast, the American colonists harkened back to an earlier tradition epitomized by Sir Edward Coke and echoed in John Locke's social contract philosophy. This tradition subjected both king and Parliament to higher law principles like the natural rights identified in the Declaration of Independence. These natural rights became enforceable civil rights when embodied in documents that eventually became identified as constitutions.

Most men (for males had a monopoly on power) who came from England to America continued to identify themselves as Englishmen. They believed that they had brought their rights with them, and they expected to pass them down to their descendants. The distance between England and the colonies and the long-standing British policy of "salutary neglect," which lasted until the French and Indian War, further contributed to the development of local colonial representative institutions. The first of these was the Virginia House of Burgesses, established in 1619.

The New England Body of Liberties

The New England Body of Liberties of 1642 is a particularly good example of the early development of a document within the colonies that would foreshadow later constitutions. Written largely by attorney and pastor Nathaniel Ward, it sought to summarize both biblical and British common law, which was largely based on judicial precedents that attempted to embody British liberties. The New England Body of Liberties consisted of 98 sections, many of which resemble provisions within modern bills of rights. In protecting men from deprivation of their lives, honor, and liberty, the very first section required that no punishments be carried out except "[b]y virtue or equitie of some expresse law of the Country warranting the same, established by a general Court and sufficiently published, or in case of the defect of a law in any particular case by the word of God" (Frohnen 2002, 15). In addition to describing the rights of freemen, the document went on to elaborate those of children, of servants, of foreigners and servants, and even of animals (prohibitions of cruelty). Perhaps not surprisingly given its Puritan context, it ended with "[a] declaration of the Liberties the Lord Jesus hath given to the Churches" (Frohnen 2002, 21).

Although the New England Body of Liberties had a primary author, it was adopted by the Massachusetts General Court (the legislature). By contrast, William Penn issued charters to the colonies he established. These served, like grants from the king to other colonies, as early constitutions. Scholars believe that these charters were the first "constitutions" that actually provided for their own amendment by supermajorities. Some rights, though, were viewed as so absolutely fundamental that they included entrenchment provisions that made them virtually irrevocable (Vile 1992, 11–12).

The colonists believed that the principle of "no taxation without representation" required actual representatives from the colonies in such legislative bodies. Not surprisingly, they developed greater loyalty to the legislators and members of Congress that they had elected in America than to members of Parliament across the ocean who claimed that they "virtually" represented the colonists, as they claimed to represent all Englishmen. Lingering in the background was the fact that the British king appointed colonial governors, who were thus accountable to him, and that Parliament could veto colonial acts of which British leaders disapproved.

The New England Confederation and the Dominion of New England

However they valued their individual identities, the colonists anticipated the advantages of a union—especially with regards to issues of defense—even before fissures developed with the British at the end of the French and Indian War. The first proposed agreements between colonies more closely resembled treaties than modern constitutions. Among the prototypes of the U.S. Constitution was the New England Confederation, into which four New England colonies (New Haven, Connecticut, Plymouth, and Massachusetts Bay) entered from approximately 1643 to 1686. Developed by delegates from these colonies at a meeting in Boston in 1643, the confederation was designed to present a united front against the Dutch in nearby New York and against Native American Indians, with whom the colonists had been in almost constant conflict. The confederation had powers to deal with matters of war and peace, to enact laws for the benefit of its members, to levy taxes for the cost of war to be defrayed on the basis of the number of male inhabitants, and to requisition additional troops if quotas for this purpose proved to be inadequate (Long 1926, 51–2).

In a provision that the Articles of Confederation later echoed, the agreement continued to recognize the sovereignty of each colony, each of which had two representatives. Six or more votes were binding on all member colonies. Other measures that passed by simple majorities required the approval of each colony's assembly, or general court. The New England Confederation prohibited states from combining without collective consent, allowed for the admission of new colonies by unanimous consent, recognized the superiority of collective decisions, and created mechanisms for extraditing criminals.

In 1686, England's King James II revoked the charters of the American colonies and replaced the largely homegrown product with the Dominion of New England, which he imposed, and which included New York and the two New Jerseys. The Dominion in turn came to an end after King James II was deposed in the Glorious Revolution of 1688 and replaced by a joint monarchy led by his daughter Mary and her husband, William of Orange. After the overthrow of James II, the individual colonies resumed their one-on-one relationships with Great Britain.

The Albany Plan of Union

As the French to the north replaced the Dutch as the chief threat, Benjamin Franklin, one of the colonies' most cosmopolitan citizens, authored the Albany Plan of Union in 1754. Franklin designed the Albany Plan to provide for greater coordination among colonies that had previously rested on their individual resources.

Delegates from seven colonies met at the Albany Congress in 1754 under encouragement from the British Board of Trade (Foner & Garraty 1991, 24) and, with Franklin's guidance, drew up a plan with a preamble and 23 sections (Matthews 1914). The preamble applied for an act of the British Parliament to form "one general government . . . in America, including all the said colonies, within and under which government each colony may retain its present constitution." This government would consist of a "President-General" appointed by the English crown and a "Grand Council" appointed by state legislatures. Council members were to serve three-year terms, with states being represented by from two to seven delegates according to the "proportion of money arising out of each Colony to the general treasury." A minimum quorum level of 25 members from a majority of the colonies was set for conducting legislative business. All acts of council would require the assent of the president-general and, in a mechanism that resembles the modern legislative veto, all acts so adopted would remain in force if not subsequently disapproved by the English King in Council within a three-year period.

The primary purposes of the union related to defense and security. The Albany Plan would have given collective authority to the colonies to make war and peace, enter into treaties, purchase land from the Indians, govern new settlements, support the military, levy taxes, etc. The articles also provided for replacing the president-general in case of his death and for allowing colonies to defend themselves in the case of sudden emergencies.

Even before the Albany Plan was received in England for consideration, however, the British government decided to pursue an alternate course and send regiments of Irish troops to defend the colonists. As one historian observed, "[A]pparently 1754 was a year in which English fear of an American revolt was enjoying one of its periodic revivals" (Olson 1960, 31). Although united colonies might have been more successful in offering collective resistance to the French and Indians under the Albany Plan, the English were aware that such an arrangement also would give the American colonies a greater capacity to resist the crown.

Continental Congresses and the Galloway Plan

In time, American colonies called congresses, like the one that had proposed the Albany Plan, to oppose British taxation. The Stamp Act Congress of 1765 set a precedent for the First and Second Continental Congresses, which began respectively in 1774 and 1775, to rally against parliamentary taxation. Although the latter of these is best known for issuing the Declaration of Independence, both congresses initially sought reconciliation.

To this end, Pennsylvania's Joseph Galloway proposed the creation of a "grand council," or colonial parliament. Galloway recommended that this council be composed of individuals that colonial legislatures elected to three-year terms to address issues, like commerce, that the colonies and Britain had in common (existing colonial governments would focus on purely local matters). A president general would head this council and serve "during the pleasure of the King" (Boyd 1970, 114), and Parliament would have ultimate authority to approve or disapprove all its measures. Opponents like Patrick Henry opposed a provision that referred to the president general and the grand council as "an inferior and distinct Branch of the British Legislature united and incorporated with it" (Boyd 1970, 114), and Congress tabled the plan by a 6–5 vote. Undaunted, the loyalist Galloway subsequently proposed an American branch of Parliament that would have included two houses. Under this proposal, the upper house was patterned after the British House of Lords, with members appointed by the crown for life (Schuyler 1942, 282).

William Smith, Jr., Proposes Creation of a Continental Parliament

Another alternative that emerged from the Stamp Act crisis was a proposal that William Smith, Jr., a lawyer, historian, and judge from New York, developed between 1765 and 1767. In his "Thoughts upon the Dispute between Great Britain and Her Colonies," which has been reprinted as an addendum to an article written by historian Robert M. Calhoon (1965, 11–118), Smith displayed a remarkable ability to understand both sides of the controversy. Smith believed that circumstances had already eroded the foundations of the existing constitutional system, and he appealed for the creation of a new American parliament that would work for the benefits of both the colonists and the crown. Smith's thoughts were not, however, widely circulated, although they received some attention as the Revolutionary War approached.

As Smith diagnosed the situation, the colonists had their own colonial legislatures and cherished their rights as Englishmen, including that of no taxation without representation. The colonists, then, would not recognize the authority of the British Parliament to tax them. Meanwhile, the British accepted the premise that Americans were entitled to rights. But they also believed that Parliament virtually represented the colonists, thus neutralizing American arguments about taxation without representation. Arguing that the division of America into colonies had not been planned, Smith thought that there should be "a Consolidation of all these little, continental Parliaments into *one*" (Calhoon 1965, 114). More specifically, he proposed that Britain should, as it had done in Ireland, create a lord lieutenant in America to serve as the crown's official representative. Smith also urged the king to appoint a legislative council of at least 24 members to form an upper house and a House of Commons chosen by colonial assemblies. In Smith's vision, the two houses would meet as the Parliament of North America in New York.

Smith wanted members of the council to be "Men of Fortune" (Calhoon 1965, 115) and family who would serve life terms. He suggested that the lower house consist of 141 members, with each colony receiving from 5 to 15 delegates depending on their respective populations. Under Smith's proposed system, the crown would continue to exercise its veto power over colonial laws, and the British Parliament would continue to be supreme, "in *all Cases* relative to *Life Liberty and Property*, except in the Matter of Taxation for *general Aids*, or the immediate, internal Support of the American Government" (Calhoon 1965, 115). The American Parliament would decide on the appropriate tax contributions for each state.

Smith suggested that if his proposal were implemented speedily, it would calm tensions on both sides and bring about greater prosperity for both America and Britain. The prosperity of one would benefit the other, perhaps much like the system of commonwealths that Britain later developed with many of its former colonies.

Early State Constitutions

Although it is common to focus on the U.S. Constitution and its regional and national predecessors, they are arguably what Donald Lutz has called "incomplete text[s]" (1980, 101) absent an understanding of state and colonial documents that preceded them. Lutz has identified 86 "constitution-like documents" that American colonists wrote prior to 1722, and another 42 such documents that were written in England for the colonies prior to 1735 (1980, 129–132). Lutz further counted 17 constitutions that were written prior to the U.S. Constitution (1980, 133; also see Fritz 1997).

The Second Continental Congress precipitated an intense period of constitution-making (although New Hampshire and South Carolina had already acted) when on May 10, 1776, it encouraged states to "adopt such Government as shall, in the Opinion of the Representatives of the People, best conduce to the Happiness and Safety of their Constituents in particular and American in general" (quoted in Adams 2001, 59). The state constitutions that subsequently emerged followed a general pattern. Most importantly, they specified a form of government, including an outline of its institutions and the fundamental principles underlying them (Lutz 1980, 103). These constitutions served as seedbeds of national reforms, and they and their successors are currently the recipients of increased scholarly attention (Levinson 2012; Zackin 2013).

Although state legislatures most frequently performed the task of writing these early constitutions, they were often guided by an overriding personal vision. In the case of Virginia, for example, Thomas Jefferson acted almost as an ancient lawgiver in preparing a draft of a constitution for his home state that would have provided for a bicameral legislature, imposed term limits, outlawed a standing army, and provided for slave emancipation (Lynch, 2007). The Virginia legislature, however, had nearly completed its work by the time Jefferson's version arrived. Virginia's George Mason, a planter without a law degree, nonetheless took the lead in creating the state's highly influential Declaration of Rights, which served in part as an inspiration for Jefferson's Declaration of Independence as well as for the U.S. Constitution's own Bill of Rights.

In 1780, John Adams, who spent much of his time during the Revolutionary War representing America abroad, took the lead in writing the Constitution for his home state of Massachusetts. By the time of the Constitutional Convention of 1787, the Constitution of New York, with its explicit incorporation of separation of powers, was also considered as a possible model for a new national government. By contrast, the Constitution of Pennsylvania was often considered by leaders of other colonies to be too democratic.

In his *Notes on the State of Virginia*, first published in 1785, Jefferson criticized the notion, which arguably came very close to the British idea of parliamentary sovereignty, that a legislature had power both to propose and to ratify a Constitution that was intended to be superior to other legislation. By what authority, Jefferson asked, should the lawmaker write the rules under which it operated? If one legislature could create a Constitution, what was to keep the next legislature from repealing it (Jefferson 1964, 118)?

Over time, the answer that emerged in America was that the Constitution needed a stronger foundation, which a convention of delegates called specifically for this purpose could best provide. In the emerging American mind, the conventions were (much like referenda of today) the embodiment of the popular will, the true foundation of republican, or representative, government (Wood 1969, 319–27). Whatever influence the primary author of the document might have or whatever wisdom he might embody, the authority of the document ultimately stemmed not from the prestige of the writer but from the authority of those who had ratified it. Arguing at the Constitutional Convention of 1787 for ratification of the proposed constitution by state conventions, James Madison thus observed:

The people were in fact, the fountain of all power, and by resorting to them, all difficulties were got over. They could alter constitutions as they pleased. It was a principle in the Bills of rights, that first principles might be resorted to. (Farrand 1966, II, 476)

By today's standards, these early state constitutions seem relatively crude. They typically vested almost all power in the legislative branch and gave governors, often elected for one-year terms, almost none. Legislatures often ran roughshod over civil rights and liberties, and they dismissed judges who opposed them. This was the context that led James Madison and other Federalist supporters of the new Constitution to question whether guarantees embodied in bills of rights could truly protect the public. In time, the discontents with the first set of state constitutions led to a new round of state constitution-making that put greater emphasis both on executive authority and on separation of powers. This shift further accelerated in the wake of the ratification of the U.S. Constitution.

Thomas Paine Appeals to Common Sense and for a Written Constitution

There is general agreement that the colonists initially sought to maintain their allegiance to the English monarch at the same time that they opposed the power of the British Parliament to tax them. Even after fighting developed between the colonists and the British, colonists continued to petition the king for redress of grievances. The king had issued colonial charters, under which colonists were now asserting their rights, and they believed that their common allegiance to him was the glue that held the British Empire together.

No one probably did more to undermine this understanding than Thomas Paine, the corset maker and gifted propagandist who emigrated to the United States from England in 1774. In January 1776 Paine published *Common Sense*, a famous pamphlet urging the American colonists to declare their independence from British authority. Paine's most notable accomplishment was that of questioning the value of monarchy. Arguing that no "natural or religious reason" could account for "the distinction of men into kings and subjects" (Paine 1953, 10), Paine went on to associate kingship with inequality, corruption, war, and oppression. He further pointed to what he considered to be the absurdity of basing succession on heredity rather than on popular choice.

In arguing for colonial independence, Paine recognized that it would be necessary to replace one national authority with another. Hiding the religious skepticism that would later alienate him from many more conventional believers, Paine claimed that, like the ancient Israelites, Americans should be content to have God as king, but that they could substitute a more democratic written constitution in place of all the customs and usages associated with the English monarchy:

Yet that we may not appear to be defective even in earthly honors, let a day be solemnly set apart for proclaiming the charter; let it be brought forth placed on the devine law, the word of God, let a crown be placed thereon, by which the world may know, so far as we approve of monarchy, that in America *the law is king*. (Paine 1953, 32)

Similarly, in declaring their independence from Britain and their belief that governments were designed to protect the unalienable rights of "life, liberty, and the pursuit of happiness," the one-time colonies would proclaim in July of 1776:

> That whenever any Form of Government becomes destructive of these ends [the securing of rights] it is the Right of the People to alter or to abolish it, and to institute new Government, laying its foundation on such principles and organizing its powers in such form, as to them shall seem most likely to effect their Safety and Happiness. (Solberg 1958, 34)

The Articles of Confederation

Just as states had to provide constitutional replacements for the charters that had preceded them, the allied states that declared their independence in 1776 needed a substitute for the direction that the government of Great Britain had provided on matters of commerce and foreign relations. This entity would not be approved directly by the people but by the states, which elected representatives to the body that had proposed it.

On the same day (June 7, 1776) that members of the Second Continental Congress voted to draft a Declaration of Independence and seek foreign aid, they decided to form a confederation. On June 12, they appointed a committee with one representative from each state. Just as Thomas Jefferson had taken the lead in drafting the Declaration of Independence, John Dickinson took the primary lead in authoring the Articles of Confederation. This "penman of the Revolution" was a reluctant revolutionary with Quaker leanings. He had refused to sign the Declaration of Independence, yet he volunteered to serve in the defense of the new nation.

The first draft of the Articles of Confederation was presented to the Continental Congress on July 12, 1776. Congress was, however, largely preoccupied with fighting a war against Britain and did not get to debating and altering these proposals until July 22. Debates followed on August 2, 6, 7, 8, and 20 and resumed on April 8, 1777 (by contrast, delegates would take four intensive months in the summer of 1787 to formulate and draft the U.S. Constitution in 1787), when Thomas Burke of North Carolina insisted on recognizing state sovereignty. Congress created yet another committee to add further amendments and put the document in final form, but it did not vote to recommend the articles for ratification until November 17, 1777. Although the articles embodied most existing protocols, they did not officially go into effect until May 1, 1781, when the last state (Maryland) finally gave its consent.

The Articles of Confederation were divided into a preamble and 13 articles. Unlike the current Constitution, which refers collectively to "We the People," the articles began with a listing of existing states. Article I further identified these states as members of a "confederacy" designated as "The United States of America." Despite this seeming unity, the most important provision of the Articles was Article II, which, in accord with Thomas Burke's wishes, provided that "Each state retains its sovereignty, freedom, and independence, and every Power, Jurisdiction and right, which is not by this confederation expressly delegated to the United States, in Congress assembled." Using language more reminiscent of a treaty than of modern constitutions, Article III (which resembles the current Constitution's preamble) referred to the states' "firm league of friendship with each other, for their common defence, the security of their Liberties, and their mutual and general welfare" (Solberg 1958, 42). Article IV further provided for privileges and immunities for all free citizens, for the extradition of fugitives, and for full faith and credit for acts and judicial proceedings of other states.

The articles centered national power in a unicameral Congress, which Article V described. State legislatures appointed two to seven members for one-year terms, renewable up to three successive years. States both paid members and could recall them at pleasure. Each state had a single vote. Article VI imposed various limits on states, most related to issues of foreign policy, in terms similar to those of Article I, Section 10 of the current Constitution. Article VII allowed states to appoint officers of their militia, while Article VIII provided for paying general defense expenditures out of the general treasury.

Article IX enumerated the rights of Congress, which largely centered on matters of foreign policy. It had power, through the creation of a fairly complicated procedure, to resolve boundary disputes between states and to regulate the value of coins, but it did not have power to control interstate or foreign commerce. Moreover, key decisions required the consent of nine or more states, not all of which were represented at any one time. As a confederal government, the Congress under the articles had to requisition states for tax revenues and troops. However, the early states were often jealous of their neighbors, and they were not always willing or able to meet these responsibilities. States with ports enacted tariffs on incoming and outgoing goods—including those going to fellow states. As a result, the potential advantages of a continental common market were largely lost. As dissatisfaction grew, it was unclear whether Congress could adequately protect states against domestic rebellion.

The articles did not have a permanent executive, but Article X specified that during congressional recesses, "A Committee of the States" had power to act in its name. Article XI made a fruitless provision for the possible future admission of Canada into the Confederacy, while Article XII provided that the Congress under the articles would assume the debts of the continental congresses that had preceded it. Article XIII, which initially served as an obstacle to effective reform, provided that congressionally proposed amendments would not go into effect unless the state legislatures unanimously consented to them. This part of the document also referred to God as "the Great Governor of the World" and was followed by signatures of 48 members of Congress who approved on behalf of their states.

Although Americans successfully prosecuted the war with Great Britain under the articles, and adopted the highly successful Northwest Ordinance during the time the Constitutional Convention of 1787 was meeting, it eventually became better known for its perceived failures than for its successes. Failures included its dependency upon the states in collecting taxes and raising armies; its lack of power to control interstate and foreign commerce or to protect states from taxing one another; its inability to enforce treaties into which it had entered; and its inability to provide adequate security to state governments. All of these failures led to economic stagnation. The current reputation of the articles is that of a transitional constitution, a placeholder that did more to reveal weaknesses of the confederal model than to provide a seedbed of principles and structures for the U.S. Constitution that would replace it.

Noah Webster on the Need for Constitutional Change

In 1785, Noah Webster, who later established himself as America's leading lexicographer, published his *Sketches of American Policy* (2008). Webster's work surveyed existing theories of government, examined existing state constitutions, and proposed a "Plan of Policy for improving the Advantages, and perpetuating the Union of the American States."

One of Webster's central conclusions was that the existing system of confederation in America was a mere "cob-web" (Webster 2008, 32). He asserted that "the idea of each state preserving its sovereignty and independence in their full latitude, and yet holding up the appearance of a confederacy and a concern of measures, is a solecism in politics that will sooner or later dissolve the pretended union, or work other mischiefs sufficient to bear conviction to every mind" (Webster 2008, 33). Pointing to the necessity of establishing a "general" government for the United States similar to that which states exercised, Webster proposed dividing powers so that "as towns and cities are, as to their small matters, sovereign and independent, and as to their general concerns, mere subjects of the state; so let the several states, as to their own police, be sovereign and independent, but as to the common concerns of all, let them be mere subjects of the federal head" (Webster 2008, 35). He suggested that such a system would resemble "the harmony of nature in the planetary system" in which "the earth and other planes govern their secondary planets and at the same time, are governed by the sun, the common center of our system" (Webster 2008, 35).

Webster argued that the existing states were "*not united*" but were "in a perfect state of nature and independence as to each other" (Webster 2008, 37). He contended that Congress should be given power not only to "enact laws," but also to "compel obedience throughout the continent, as the legislatures of the several states have in their respective jurisdictions" (Webster 2008, 38). He concluded that "either the several states must continue separate, totally independent, of each other, and liable to all the evils of jealousy, dispute and civil dissention . . . or they must constitute a general head, composed of representatives from all the states, and vested with the power of the whole continent to enforce their decisions" (Webster 2008, 38–9).

Although Webster did not propose a detailed plan, his ideas undoubtedly reflected the views of other individuals who saw flaws within the existing articles. Shortly after the Constitution was proposed, Webster wrote in favor of the document under the pseudonym "A Citizen of America."

Two Preludes to the Constitutional Convention: Mt. Vernon and Annapolis
After delegates from Virginia and Maryland met at George Washington's house at
Mt. Vernon, Virginia, in March 1785 to discuss mutual issues of navigation, they
issued a call for a convention at Annapolis to discuss issues of navigation and commerce involving all of the states. Although only five state delegations arrived for
this meeting in September 1786, leaders like John Dickinson, James Madison, and
Alexander Hamilton issued yet another call for a Constitutional Convention

> to take into consideration the situation of the United States, to devise such
> further provisions as shall appear to them necessary to render the constitution
> of the Federal Government adequate to the exigencies of the Union; and to re-
> port such an act for that purpose to the United States in Congress assembled,
> as when agreed to, by them, and afterwards confirmed by the Legislatures of
> every State, will effectually provide for the same. (Solberg 1958, 58–9)

They recommended that the convention be held the following May in Philadelphia, where past Congresses had assembled and where both the Declaration of
Independence and the Articles of Confederation had been approved. Moreover,
at the state level, "conventions" were recognized as the bodies that proposed new
written constitutions. The call for a convention served notice to the nation that far-
reaching changes were being considered. However, the language of this resolution,
and those that followed on the part of Congress, suggested something closer to
the formulation of constitutional amendments than the creation of an entirely new
document.

References

Adams, Willi Paul. 2001. *The First American Constitutions: Republican Ideology and the
Making of the State Constitutions in the Revolutionary Era*. Expanded ed. Lanham, MD:
Rowman and Littlefield Publishers.

Aristotle. 1964. *Aristotle's Constitution of Athens and Related Texts*. Translated and with
introduction by Kurt Von Fritz and Ernst Kapp. New York: Hafner Publishing Company.

Boyd, Julian B. 1970. *Anglo-American Union: Joseph Galloway's Plan to Preserve the
British Empire, 1774–1788*. New York: Octagon Books.

Calhoon, Robert M. 1965. "William Smith Jr.'s Alternative to the American Revolution."
The William and Mary Quarterly 22, Third Series (January): 105–18.

Corwin, Edward S. 1955. *The "Higher Law" Background of American Constitutional Law*.
Ithaca, NY: Cornell University Press.

Farrand, Max, ed. 1966. *The Records of the Federal Convention of 1787*. 4 vols. New
Haven, CT: Yale University Press.

Foner, Eric, and John A. Garraty, eds. 1991. *The Reader's Companion to American History*. Boston: Houghton Mifflin Company.

Fritz, Christian G. 1997. "Alternative Visions of American Constitutionalism: Popular Sovereignty and the Early American Constitutional Debate." *Hastings Constitutional Law
Quarterly* 24 (Winter): 287–357.

Frohnen, Bruce, ed. 2002. *The American Republic: Primary Sources*. Indianapolis, IN: Liberty Fund.

Isaacson, Walter. 2003. *Benjamin Franklin: An American Life*. New York: Simon & Schuster.

Jefferson, Thomas. 1964 [1785]. *Notes on the State of Virginia*. New York: Harper and Row, Publishers.

Levinson, Sanford. 2012. *Framed: America's 51 Constitutions and the Crisis of Governance*. New York: Oxford.

Long, Breckinridge. 1926. *Genesis of the Constitution of the United States of America*. New York: Macmillan.

Lutz, Donald S. 1998. *Colonial Origins of the American Constitution: A Documentary History*. Indianapolis, IN: Liberty Fund.

Lutz, Donald S. 1988. *The Origins of American Constitutionalism*. Baton Rouge: Louisiana State University Press.

Lutz, Donald S. 1980. "From Covenant to Constitution in American Political Thought." *Publius* 10 (Fall): 101–134.

Lynch, Jack. 2007. "'One of the Most Intriguing Might-Have-Beens in American History'; Jefferson's Tardy Constitution." *Colonial Williamsburg Journal* (Spring). Accessible online at http://www.history.org/foundation/journal/spring07/jefferson.cfm.

Matthews, L. K. 1914. "Benjamin Franklin's Plans for a Colonial Union, 1750–1775." *The American Political Science Review* 8 (August): 393–412.

Moots, Glenn A. 2010. *Politics Reformed: The Anglo-American Legacy of Covenant Theology*. Columbia: University of Missouri Press.

Olson, Alison Gilbert. 1960. "The British Government and Colonial Union, 1754." *William and Mary Quarterly* 17, Third Series (January): 22–34.

Paine, Thomas. 1953 [1776]. *Common Sense and Other Related Writings*. Edited by Nelson F. Adkins. New York: The Liberal Arts Press.

Schuyler, Robert Livingston. 1942. "Galloway's Plans for Anglo-American Union." *Political Science Quarterly* 57 (June): 281–85.

"The 1754 Albany Plan of Union." The University of Oklahoma Law Center, http://www.law.ou.edu/hist/albplan.html (accessed June 19, 2003).

Solberg, Winton U., ed. 1958. *The Federal Convention and the Formation of the Union of the American States*. Indianapolis, IN: Bobbs-Merrill Company, Inc.

Vile, John R. 1993. "Three Kinds of Constitutional Founding and Change: The Convention Model and Its Alternatives." *Political Research Quarterly* 46 (December): 881–95.

Vile, John R. 1992. *The Constitutional Amending Process in American Political Thought*. New York: Praeger.

Vile, John R. 1991. *Rewriting the United States Constitution: An Examination of Proposals from Reconstruction to the Present*. New York: Praeger.

Webster, Noah. 2008 [1785]. *Sketches of American Policy*. Introduction by John R. Vile. Clark, NJ: The LawBook Exchange, Ltd.

Wood, Gordon S. 1969. *The Creation of the American Republic, 1776–1787*. Chapel Hill: University of North Carolina Press.

Zackin, Emily. 2013. *Looking for Rights in All the Wrong Places*. Princeton, NJ: Princeton University Press.

CHAPTER 2

The Writing and Ratification of the U.S. Constitution and Its Emergence from a Number of Alternatives

The Constitution that emerged from the Convention of 1787 was not only an alternative to the existing Articles of Confederation but also to a variety of other complex proposals. The delegates to the convention rejected some of these other plans outright and incorporated provisions within others into the larger whole, but many of the ideas that the Framers of the Constitution ultimately rejected remained subjects of interest.

Most of the 55 delegates who arrived in Philadelphia for the Constitutional Convention probably believed that they were gathering to revise the Articles of Confederation, but Virginia's James Madison had other plans. He had spent months prior to the Constitutional Convention surveying and detailing the weaknesses of previous confederations and the central vices of the political system of the United States (Meyers 1973, 69–92). The fact that Governor Edmund Randolph's opening speech on behalf of the Virginia Plan presented many of these same arguments suggests that Madison was the primary mastermind behind the successful effort to divert the Convention's attention away from the confederal model and set a radically different agenda. Madison recognized, however, that a constitution would be a collective product that would require multiple compromises. His extensive notes, which form the basis of most of what we know about the Convention, confirm that the final product did so.

The Delegates to the Convention

As the author has explained elsewhere (Vile, 2005, 2012), delegates included leaders from throughout the colonies. They represented states from the East (today's Northeast), the Middle States, and the South, and delegations typically voted from North to South. Nicholas Gilman and John Langdon did not arrive from New Hampshire until relatively late in Convention proceedings and therefore had less influence than others who arrived early. The delegation from Massachusetts included Elbridge Gerry, Nathaniel Gorham, Rufus King, and Caleb Strong. Connecticut's astute and influential delegates included Oliver Ellsworth, William Samuel Johnson, and Roger Sherman.

New York was represented by Alexander Hamilton, John Lansing, Jr., and Robert Yates. The latter two left early, and Hamilton skipped about a month of the proceedings. New Jersey sent David Brearley, Jonathan Dayton, William Churchill

Houston, William Livingston, and William Paterson. Pennsylvania's delegation was second to none. It included George Clymer, Thomas Fitzsimons, Benjamin Franklin, Jared Ingersoll, Thomas Mifflin, Gouverneur Morris, Robert Morris, and James Wilson. Franklin was the best known of the Pennsylvanians, but Robert Morris had served as the financier of the American Revolution, Gouverneur Morris was the most loquacious delegate to the convention, and Wilson did much to create the modern presidency. Delaware sent Richard Bassett, Gunning Bedford, Jr., Jacob Broom, John Dickinson, and George Read.

Maryland delegates included Daniel Carroll, Daniel of St. Thomas Jenifer, Luther Martin, James McHenry, and John Francis Mercer. Virginia's delegation was almost as large, and equally distinguished, as that of Pennsylvania. Delegates included John Blair, James Madison, George Mason, James McClurg, Edmund Randolph, the incomparable George Washington, and George Wythe. North Carolina delegates included William Blount, William Richardson Davie, Alexander Martin, Richard Dobbs Spaight, and Hugh Williamson. South Carolina's delegates ranked among the young nation's firmest defenders of the institution of slavery. They included Pierce Butler, cousins Charles Cotesworth Pinckney and Charles Pinckney, and John Rutledge. Georgia's delegation rounded out the Convention and included Abraham Baldwin, William Few, William Houstoun, and William Pierce, the latter of whom is best known for writing character sketches of most of the delegates (Vile 2013).

Although delegates represented different states and regions, they shared much in common. All were white males. They were relatively young and highly educated, with the College of New Jersey (today's Princeton) supplying the most graduates and others having received higher education abroad. Most were native born, although some had been born in Britain or a British colony. The delegates were wealthier than average Americans, though a fair number would in time lose their fortunes in land speculation. Most delegates were Protestants, with some Deists and two Catholics. Most were committed to some variant of republicanism that valued patriotism, democratic deliberation, and accountability but that was wary of direct popular direction of day-to-day policies. Many had served in the American Revolution and most had a nationalist perspective. Perhaps most importantly, almost all the delegates to the Constitutional Convention were politically experienced. A large majority had served in the Continental Congresses, in the Congress under the Articles of Confederation, in their own state legislatures, and even on bodies that had written state constitutions. Some, like Roger Sherman of Connecticut, had experience serving in all three branches of government.

The Rules of the Convention

The experience of the delegates was reflected in the decisions and rules that they adopted at the onset of the Constitutional Convention. Even before they decided on them, they elected George Washington, who had patiently and successfully led American forces during the Revolution, to preside over the proceedings as convention president. Although Washington said very little during the formal proceedings, his presence had a sobering and salutary effect on the deliberations and encouraged members to pursue the common good.

The delegates adopted other rules at the outset to insure thorough debate. Most controversial to modern eyes is the requirement that all proceedings would be secret. Combined with rules permitting votes to be retaken and forbidding votes from being recorded under individual names, such procedures were designed to insure a maximum of deliberation and a minimum of grandstanding; they also made it less likely that mobs might form in the streets to influence convention deliberations. Although some of the more populous states wanted to insist at the outset on greater representation, they agreed to follow the Confederation Congress in allowing each state delegation to cast a single vote.

Each of the proposed constitutional outlines offered by the various state delegations had some influence on the emerging document. The final document further reflected a variety of compromises on issues as diverse as the length of congressional and presidential terms; the method of selecting members of each of the branches; how to represent, tax, and regulate the importation of slaves; and the majority requirements for approving amendments and other changes.

The Virginia Plan

The Virginia delegation introduced the plan that set the initial agenda and dominated discussion during the first two weeks of the convention. It presented a genuine alternative to the existing articles. Whereas the articles provided for equal state representation, the Virginia Plan proposed basing legislative representation on population. It further proposed substituting a bicameral for a unicameral national legislature. Under this proposal, the people would select the first house from individual districts. Members of this lower house would then select members of the upper house from nominees made by the states. The Virginia Plan proposed vesting Congress not only with the powers that the Congress had exercised under the Articles of Confederation but also with the power "to legislate in all cases to which the separate States are incompetent, or in which the harmony of the States may be interrupted by the exercise of individual Legislation" (Farrand, 1966, I, 29). The plan also proposed giving Congress the power "to negative all laws passed by the several States, contravening in the opinion of the National Legislature the articles of Union." The Virginia Plan further permitted Congress "to call forth the force of the Union" against states that did not fulfill their duties.

Whereas the closest the Articles of Confederation came to providing an executive was to authorize a committee to operate when Congress was in recess, the Virginia Plan called for the legislature to choose "a Magistry" for a single term of service. Another mechanism that did not make it into the final proposal, the Virginia Plan called for combining the executive with "a convenient number of the National Judiciary" to compose a "council of revision" with power to invalidate both state and national laws, unless the latter were adopted by an unspecified supermajority.

The Virginia Plan further departed from the system of state courts under the articles by allowing Congress to appoint members to one or more supreme and inferior tribunals, the judges of which would serve during good behavior (for life). Further provisions provided for the admission of new states, for congressional guarantees of "Republican Government" to the states, for the introduction of future amendments without requiring congressional consent, for binding all members of the new government by oath, and for ratification by assemblies called by the individual states.

Scholars characteristically describe the Virginia Plan as the "large state" plan, chiefly identifying how it would have weighted representation toward more highly populated states, the most populous of which was that of the delegation that introduced it. It is also common to recognize the plan as one that proposed significant increases in the power of the central government. The plan, however, was responsible for much more—a system of three distinct branches, a bicameral legislature, and new methods of constitutional amendment and ratification—as well as a number of mechanisms like the legislative veto and the council of revision that would not make it into the final document.

The New Jersey Plan

After about two weeks of discussion, New Jersey's William Paterson introduced a rival plan commonly named after his state. One Paterson biographer (O'Connor 1979) is convinced that the plan was largely "a stalking horse for equal [state] representation," and it is certainly chiefly remembered for attempting to restore this aspect of the Articles of Confederation. However, although it incorporated a number of aspects of the Virginia Plan, it also offered alternatives to a number of its provisions. Consistent with the original call for the convention, Paterson offered it as a revision and enlargement of the Articles rather than as a replacement.

Unlike the Virginia Plan, the New Jersey Plan did not seek to alter the unicameral structure of Congress or its system of equal representation. It did seek to enlarge its powers, including the power to levy goods on imports, and "to pass Acts for the regulation of trade & commerce as well with foreign nations as with each other." Although controversies over such acts were to originate in state courts, they would be subject to appeal to the national judiciary.

The New Jersey Plan favored congressional selection of a plural executive (the Virginia Plan was leaning in the direction of a singular executive) and for executive, rather than legislative, selection of judges. While omitting the legislative veto and Council of Revision mechanisms of the Virginia Plan, the New Jersey Plan not only called for the supremacy of federal law, but also allowed Congress to call out troops to make recalcitrant states comply.

The Hamilton Plan

The Constitutional Convention did not initially spend much time on the New Jersey Plan before returning to the Virginia proposals. Before it did so, Alexander Hamilton of New York gave a long speech in which he proposed a number of innovations. Although the majority of delegates do not appear to have taken the specific proposals particularly seriously—Samuel Johnson of Connecticut observed that "though he [Hamilton] has been praised by every body, he has been supported by none" (Farrand 1966, I, 363)—they remain as a possible direction that delegates could have taken had they been so inclined.

Hamilton favored vesting a bicameral Congress with the "Supreme Legislative power of the United States of America." He supported apportioning both branches according to population. The people would elect members of the first house to three-year terms, and electors would select members of the upper house "during good behavior," or for life. The upper house would have the "sole power of declaring war," advising on treaties, and confirming officers appointed by the chief executive, whom Hamilton chose to designate as a "governor." Like members of the upper house, the governor would serve during good behavior, with a veto, apparently absolute, "on all laws about to be passed, and the execution of all laws passed." He would have the sole power to appoint department heads of "the departments of Finance, War and Foreign Affairs" and issue pardons, except in cases of treason, where he would have to get Senate consent (all quotations from Farrand 1966, I, 291–2).

Hamilton outlined a "Supreme Judicial Authority" vested in judges serving "during good behavior" (Farrand 1966, I, 292). Not only would national laws be supreme, but the general government would appoint the governor or president of each state, who could veto any pending law. The national government would also have exclusive authority over state militia, including power to appoint and commission their officers.

Hamilton believed "the British government forms the best model the world ever produced" (Farrand 1966, II, 299). Although he did not think America was yet ready for a hereditary king, he thought a monarchy had distinct advantages. Notably, Hamilton proposed a plan whereby the upper house of Congress, the executive, *and* members of the judiciary would all serve for life terms (subject, however, to impeachment).

The British form of government was unitary, and it had no permanent states like those in the United States, which rested on their own constitutions for authority. Hamilton paid so little attention to the states that he subsequently had to explain (in words that probably did little to placate his opponents) that "[h]e had not been understood yesterday. By an abolition of the States, he meant that no boundary could be drawn between the Nation & State Legislature; that the former must therefore have indefinite authority" (Farrand 1966, I, 323). According to Madison's notes, however, Hamilton did say that "[a]s States, he thought they ought to be abolished. But he admitted the necessity of leaving in them, subordinate jurisdictions" (Farrand 1966, I, 323).

A Bundle of Compromises

During the time that the convention was comparing the Virginia and New Jersey plans, Delaware's John Dickinson apparently drafted a compromise plan that he did not introduce. So too, Charles Pinckney is believed to have introduced a plan at the beginning of the convention that was largely ignored. The Virginia and New Jersey plans remained the central alternatives. They presented relatively clear options between revising the articles or heading in a new direction; they presented a stark contrast between continuing to represent states equally in Congress and representing them according to population; and they offered different mechanisms for choosing federal judges.

The Great Compromise, also known as the Connecticut Compromise, largely resolved the issue of state representation by representing them according to population in the House of Representatives and giving each state equal representation in the U.S. Senate. Delegates also continually adjusted their understanding of what the powers of the new government would be and how its powers would relate to those of the states. They had to decide on term lengths for individual offices and how to appoint and confirm key officials. They had to come up with a model for selecting a president—they eventually settled on what they called the Electoral College—that would represent states appropriately, agree upon what powers the executive would exercise, and give this executive sufficient independence from Congress. They had to decide how to ratify and amend the new constitution.

The most troubling issue, apart from state representation, was slavery. There were at least three geographically based approaches to the problem. Although most Northern states continued to permit slavery, few had a significant interest in its continuing perpetuation. Middle and upper South states, most notably Virginia, which was serving as a slave breeding ground, were willing to give Congress immediate authority to stop the slave trade but wanted to count slaves toward the formula for representation in the House of Representatives. Representatives from the deep South, especially South Carolina and Georgia, wanted to keep prices of slave labor low by continuing the slave trade and requiring a two-thirds vote on the taxation of imports. Representatives from the deep South appear to have anticipated that slavery might long survive. The delegates resolved these issues through a series of compromises that continue to contradict the Founders' commitment to natural rights. Most notoriously, the delegates agreed to count slaves as three-fifths of a person for purposes of taxation and representation. Free states were obligated to return fugitive slaves. Congress would not have power to prohibit slave importation for another 20 years.

James Butzner (1941) has collected a whole book of what he called "constitutional chaff," or "rejected suggestions of the Constitutional Convention of 1787." These include the Virginia Plan's proposals for a Council of Revision and for vesting Congress with a potential veto of all state laws, Hamilton's proposals for service "during good behavior" (until they die, retire, or are convicted of crimes) for senators and the chief executive, and many others.

The Constitution as a Collective Product

Many ancient governments traced their origins to a single lawgiver, and it is particularly common to refer to James Madison as the "father" of the Constitution because of his deep involvement in the Virginia Plan and his steady contributions to debate throughout the course of the Constitutional Convention. However, when an admirer wrote to Madison in 1834 and referred to him as "the writer of the Constitution of the U.S.," Madison modestly responded, "You give me a credit to which I have made no claim." Continuing, he observed that the Constitution "was not, like the fabled Goddess of Wisdom, the offspring of a single brain. It ought to be regarded as the work of many heads & many hands" (Vile, Pederson, and Williams 2008, 41). Contemporary scholars note that Madison was particularly disappointed by the convention's rejection of the congressional veto and the Council of Revision (Hobson 1979). Others have observed how successful Connecticut's Roger Sherman and others were in pushing an alternate vision of state/national relations during the convention (Robertson 2005). Moreover, as Madison recognized, the authority of the Constitution rested not on the perspicuity or authority of himself but upon ratification in conventions called by the states.

In a notable speech that he delivered near the end of the deliberations, Benjamin Franklin observed that collective bodies brought not only their wisdom but also their prejudices to the table. He argued that the Constitution, while far from perfect, was the best that one could have expected from such a body. Proponents would also note that the new Constitution contained a far easier amending process than the one that had existed under the Articles of Confederation.

An Outline of the Document: Seven Articles

To understand the Constitution one needs to understand its alternatives. The Constitution that went into effect in 1789 replaced a weaker confederal system that the Articles of Confederation had established. But it did so without embracing a unitary system, like that of Great Britain, that dispensed with states. The Constitution also rejected: the idea of leaving the security of rights to customs and usages; the belief that parliament, or "the king, or queen, in Parliament," was sovereign; and the view that the executive should be a hereditary monarch. Because the new system incorporated separation of powers among three coordinate branches of the national government—and perhaps because the convention delegates did not fully anticipate the development of a political party system—it allowed for the possibility that the head of the government might be from a different party than that which dominated one or both houses of Congress.

The Constitution begins with a preamble with the elegant words (attributed to Gouverneur Morris of Pennsylvania) "We the People of the United States." It then proceeds to delineate a number of goals of the new government including—with a backward glance to the Articles of Confederation—the formation of a "more perfect Union."

Virginia's Governor Edmund Randolph served at the convention on a "Committee of Detail," which compiled resolutions into a document that would serve as the basis of discussion. His notes listed two principles that members of the convention largely followed with respect to the final document. These were:

1. To insert essential principles only, lest the operations of government should be clogged by rendering those provisions permanent and unalterable, which ought to be accommodated to times and events, and
2. To use simple and precise language, and general proposition, according to the example of the (several) constitution of the several states. (For the

construction of a constitution of necessity differs from that of law.) (Farrand 1966, II, 137)

The Framers divided the Constitution into seven articles (Vile 2011). The first
three articles embody the principle of separation of powers in the government. This
doctrine is, in turn, linked to the idea of checks and balances. Both articulate the
view that a government should be constructed in a way to balance the ambition of
those in one branch of government against the others in order to protect liberty for
the nation's citizenry.

Article I focuses on the legislative branch, which it divided into two houses.
Consistent with ideas of republican government, citizens from individual districts
elect members of the House of Representatives who are apportioned among the
states according to population. Under the original Constitution, state legislatures
appointed members of the upper house or Senate. Since the adoption of the Seventeenth Amendment in 1913, U.S. senators have been elected by popular vote.
Members of the House of Representatives serve for two-year terms, while senators
serve for six. Congress is responsible for adopting laws and declaring war. The
House originates all money bills, and the Constitution vests the Senate with special
powers to ratify presidential appointments and treaties.

Each house chooses its own officers, who are thus selected independently of the
chief executive. Unlike modern parliamentary systems, this can result in divided
governments where the party that has a majority in one or both houses differs from
the party of the president.

Article I, Section 7, outlines the law-making process. Majorities in both houses
must adopt bills, which the president signs, in order for them to become laws. If
a president exercises a veto, two-thirds majorities of both houses can override it.
Even then, courts can scrutinize laws to be sure that they are constitutional.

Article I, Section 8, lists, or enumerates, the specific powers of Congress, but
arguably undercuts the precision of such an enumeration by adding that Congress
shall have all powers "necessary and proper" to carry out those that are listed. This
"necessary and proper" phrase is the textual basis for the doctrine of implied powers. Article I, Section 9, further specifies certain limits on Congress, many similar
to those later incorporated into the Bill of Rights. Article I, Section 10 provides a
similar list of restrictions on the states.

Article II outlines the executive branch, which is headed by a single president
chosen by the Electoral College for four-year terms. Although Article I vests Congress with the power to declare war, Article II designates the president as commander-in-chief of the armed forces. The president has broad powers to execute, or
enforce, the laws and to make appointments, most of which are subject to senatorial confirmation. Subsequent judicial decisions have given the president authority
to fire executive officials without congressional approval, albeit not judges and
justices who serve life terms.

Article III creates a federal judiciary headed by the Supreme Court, over which a
chief justice presides. It may hear a limited number of cases of original jurisdiction

and a wide variety of cases related to the U.S. Constitution, federal laws, and treaties on appeal from either lower federal courts or from the states' highest courts. The president appoints judges and justices with the "advice and consent" of the Senate, and they serve "during good behavior." In addition to interpreting laws (a process sometimes called statutory construction), they also exercise the power of judicial review (although the Constitution does not use this term), which authorizes them to strike down laws found to be unconstitutional.

Article IV outlines a federal system of government that divides power between state and national authorities, each with their own constitutional foundations and each with power to operate directly upon individual citizens. It outlines obligations like extradition and honoring judgments of courts in other states. It also delineates obligations of the national government to the states, like protecting them and guaranteeing them republican governments.

Article V provides legal procedures for constitutional change. In a mechanism of potentially broad consequence that has yet to be utilized, two-thirds of the states can petition Congress to call a convention to propose amendments. In a more familiar route, two-thirds of the state legislatures can also propose individual amendments, which, like any convention proposals, do not become law of the land unless ratified by three-fourths of the states via legislative action or special ratifying conventions.

The best-known provision of Article VI is the supremacy clause, which affirms the superiority of the Constitution, federal laws, and treaties over state enactments. Article VII further provided that the new constitution would go into effect among ratifying states when conventions in nine or more states had approved—not when ratified by all the state legislatures. This article was followed by the signature of 39 of 42 delegates who remained present at the convention on September 17, 1787.

Debates over the Constitution and Adoption of the Bill of Rights
The Founders sought to be true to the Constitution's claim to be based on the consent of "We the people" by requiring the approval of specially called conventions in each state. Records of the debates at these state conventions over the proposed constitution have been the subject of increasingly detailed and perceptive analyses (Kaminsky 1976; Maier 2011; Heideking 2012).

Approval was far from certain. While Federalist supporters of the new document were well organized and had strong support among elites, Anti-Federalists were even less trusting of human nature than those who wrote the Constitution, and many worried that strong central government might result in a corresponding loss of their own political power back home. Some were also worried about what they considered to be aristocratic elements like the Senate, the presidency, and the federal judiciary within the new document and about certain powers that they believed to have been insufficiently cabined or limited.

Although it is common to focus on *The Federalist Papers*, which argued in favor of the Constitution, participants in the ratification contest published numerous works both advocating and opposing the new document (see Storing 1981, for the best collection of Anti-Federalist writings). Ultimately, the document was approved (just as it could have been defeated) not by a national vote but by contests within each of the states.

Federalists rejected the idea that states could conditionally ratify the Constitution, but they allowed state conventions to make recommendatory amendments. The key objection to the Constitution was that it did not contain a bill of rights. Delegates had included a number of such protections within the text of the document (most notably in Article I, Sections 8 and 9), but by the time the dyspeptic George Mason proposed that one should be added on September 12, most delegates were cooling their heels for a trip home after a long summer of deliberations. Perhaps more importantly, most delegates anticipated that the Constitution's enumeration of powers in Article I, Section 8, would leave the national government not only uninterested in, but largely incapable of, violating individual rights.

Despite initial arguments that such a bill was unnecessary, was likely to be ineffective, and could even prove dangerous (if, for example, individuals regarded the omission of a key right as evidence that the government could suppress it), key Federalists agreed in time to support the addition of a bill of rights once the document was adopted. James Madison took the lead in the first Congress in advancing the amendments through that body (for good accounts see Goldwin 1997 and Labunski 2008). Scholars still debate whether Madison was persuaded to take this role by correspondence that he received from his friend Jefferson advocating such a bill of rights, or whether Madison primarily did so to fulfill a campaign promise that he made when he ran against James Monroe for the first Congress (DeRose 2011). It has also been speculated that his primary motive was to take the initiative away from those who might seek to call a second convention that might undo the first (Weber 1989). Interestingly, Madison, who based the theory of factions that he presented in *Federalist* No. 10 on protecting civil liberties through creating larger legislative districts, was more concerned (albeit unsuccessful) with ratifying an amendment that would protect against oppressive state actions than in adopting amendments to prevent oppressive acts of the central government. The last of the 10 amendments to be ratified instead provided that "[t]he powers not delegated to the United States by the Constitution, nor prohibited by it to the States, are reserved to the States respectively, or to the people."

Scholars generally agree that the relatively quick adoption of the Bill of Rights by state legislatures increased faith that the new government was responsive to and would not oppress the people, and that it had an adequate mechanism for change. Still, the government adopted in 1789 was effectively the third national authority under which the colonies had been governed within a 15-year period, and no one could say how long the new one would last.

From the Bill of Rights to the Present

In the early years of the republic, Congress proposed and the states ratified two amendments. The Eleventh Amendment, which states ratified in 1794, limited judicial oversight over lawsuits that individuals initiated against the states without their consent. The Twelfth Amendment, ratified in 1803, modified the Electoral College to prevent ties between candidates running for the presidency and vice presidency. A hiatus followed until 1865, which marked the last year of the Civil War.

Although there were multiple causes for the war, many centered on the divisive issue of slavery. Building on Abraham Lincoln's 1863 Emancipation Proclamation, which freed all slaves within the "rebellious states," the Thirteenth Amendment (1865) prohibited slavery throughout the nation. The Fourteenth Amendment attempted to provide for those who had previously been held in slavery. It overturned the Supreme Court's notorious *Dred Scott* decision of 1857 and declared, "All persons born or naturalized in the United States, and subject to the jurisdiction thereof, are citizens of the United States and of the state wherein they reside." The first section of the Fourteenth Amendment further guaranteed privileges and immunities, due process, and equal protection to all. Section 2 reversed the notorious three-fifths clause and sought (unsuccessfully) to deprive states of representation if they did not extend voting rights to all qualified males. Section 3 further limited the offices that former members of the Confederacy could hold in the new government. Section 4 reaffirmed the validity of the debt of the United States while repudiating that of the Confederacy. Section 5 vested enforcement powers within Congress. The Fifteenth Amendment (1870) further prohibited discrimination on the basis of "race, color, or previous condition of servitude" with respect to voting.

The nation subsequently went more than a generation before adopting any new amendments. In the 1910s, however, the nation ratified four in short order in response to the demands of the Populist and Progressive movements. The Sixteenth Amendment (1913) overturned a Supreme Court decision to allow for a national income tax. The Seventeenth Amendment, also ratified in 1913, provided for direct election of U.S. senators. The Eighteenth Amendment (1919), later repealed by the Twenty-First (1933), outlawed the manufacture and sale of alcohol. Finally, the Nineteenth Amendment (1919) fulfilled the vision of the Seneca Falls Convention of 1848 by giving women the right to vote.

Most subsequent amendments have been less far-reaching. The Twentieth Amendment (1933) altered inauguration dates for incoming presidents and members of Congress. The Twenty-Second Amendment (1951) placed a two-term limit on presidents. The Twenty-Third Amendment (1961) provided for Electoral College representation for the District of Columbia. The Twenty-Fourth Amendment (1964) eliminated the use of the poll tax in national elections. The Twenty-Fifth Amendment (1967) clarified procedures in cases of presidential disability, and the Twenty-Sixth Amendment (1971) prohibited discrimination in voting to those who were 18 or older. The Twenty-Seventh Amendment (1992), which delays changes in congressional pay until an intervening election, is chiefly known for the fact that it was initially proposed (without a deadline) as part of the Bill of Rights.

Madison's Desire for Constitutional Stability

From 1789 to the present, then, there have only been 27 amendments. Is this a sign that the Constitution is too rigid? Many critics of the Constitution think so. Darren Patrick Guerra has, however, written a recent book (2013) in which he argues that the process has enhanced wisdom and justice while providing for needed changes.

There is good reason to believe that James Madison might have agreed. Although he had worked diligently on behalf of the Constitution and the Bill of Rights, Madison opposed frequent constitutional changes. In his *Notes on the State of Virginia*, Thomas Jefferson had proposed a draft of a constitution for his state stipulating that when two-thirds of two of the three branches of government should agree that a change in the constitution was necessary, they should be able to call a convention for that purpose. While Madison voiced a number of objections to this proposal in *Federalist* No. 49, his greatest concern was that "as every appeal to the people would carry an implication of some defect in the government, frequent appeals would, in great measure, deprive the government of that veneration which time bestows on everything, and without which perhaps the wisest and freest governments would not possess the requisite stability" (Hamilton, Madison, and Jay 1961, 314). Madison continued at considerable length:

> The reason of man, like man himself, is timid and cautious when left alone, and acquires firmness and confidence in proportion to the number with which it is associated. When the examples which fortify opinion are *ancient* as well as *numerous*, they are known to have a double effect. In a nation of philosophers, this consideration ought to be disregarded. A reverence for the laws would be sufficiently inculcated by the voice of an enlightened reason. But a nation of philosophers is as little to be expected as the philosophical race of kings wished for by Plato. And in every other nation, the most rational government will not find it a superfluous advantage to have the prejudices of the community on its side. (Hamilton, Madison, and Jay 1961, 315)

In the succeeding essay, Madison gave a similar thumbs down to yet another Jeffersonian idea—to mandate regularly scheduled conventions. Although Madison was not opposed to adding individual amendments when necessary, he wanted to keep wholesale revision to a minimum. While some might hail the Bill of Rights as such a revision, Madison believed the amendments simply affirmed principles of limited government that the Constitution already believed it articulated. Even at the state level, he arguably sacrificed democratic reform to the perpetuation of existing compromises (Dunn 2007, 163). Although they did not always agree on other matters, Chief Justice John Marshall undoubtedly captured the spirit of Madison's thoughts on the subject when, in establishing the principle of judicial review in *Marbury v. Madison* (1803), he observed that the creation of a new government "is a very great exertion, nor can it, nor ought it, to be frequently repeated."

References

Butzner, James. 1941. *Constitutional Chaff—Rejected Suggestions of the Constitutional Convention of 1787 with Explanatory Argument*. New York: Columbia University Press.

DeRose, Chris. 2011. *Founding Rivals: Madison vs. Monroe, The Bill of Rights, and the Election That Saved a Nation*. Washington, DC: Regnery History.

Dunn, Susan. 2007. *Dominion of Memories: Jefferson, Madison, and the Decline of Virginia*. New York: Basic Books.

Farrand, Max. 1966. *The Records of the Federal Convention of 1787*. 4 vols. New Haven, CT: Yale University Press.

Goldwin, Robert A. 1997. *From Parchment to Power: How James Madison Used the Bill of Rights to Save the Constitution*. Washington, DC: AEI Press.

Guerra, Darren Patrick. 2013. *Perfecting the Constitution: The Case for the Article V Amendment Process*. Lanham, MD: Lexington Books.

Hamilton, Alexander, James Madison, and John Jay. 1961 [1787–1788]. *The Federalist Papers*. New York: New American Library.

Heideking, Jurgen. 2012. *The Constitution before the Judgment Seat: The Prehistory and Ratification of the American Constitution, 1787–1791*. Charlottesville: University of Virginia Press.

Hobson, Charles F. 1979. "The Negative on State Laws: James Madison, the Constitution, and the Crisis of Republican Government." *William and Mary Quarterly* 36, Third Series (April): 214–35.

Kaminski, John P., et al., eds. 1976– . *The Documentary History of the Ratification of the Constitution*. 26 volumes to date. Madison, WI: Wisconsin Historical Society.

Labunski, Richard. 2008. *James Madison and the Struggle for the Bill of Rights*. New York: Oxford University Press.

Maier, Pauline. 2011. *Ratification: The People Debate the Constitution, 1787–1788*. New York: Simon & Schuster.

Meyers, Marvin, ed. 1973. *The Mind of the Founder: Sources of the Political Thought of James Madison*. New York: Bobbs-Merrill Company, Inc.

O'Connor, J. J. 1979. *William Paterson: Lawyer and Statesman, 1745–1806*. New Brunswick, NJ: Rutgers University Press.

Robertson, David Brian. 2005. "Madison's Opponents and Constitution Design." The *American Political Science Review* 99 (May): 225–43.

Storing, Herbert J. 1981. *The Complete Anti-Federalist*. 7 vols. Chicago: University of Chicago Press.

Vile, John R. 2013. *The Men Who Wrote the U.S. Constitution*. Lanham, MD: Scarecrow Press.

Vile, John R. 2012. *The Writing and Ratification of the U.S. Constitution*. Lanham, MD: Rowman & Littlefield.

Vile, John R. 2011. *A Companion to the United States Constitution and Its Amendments*, 5th ed. Lanham, MD: Rowman & Littlefield.

Vile, John R. 2005. *The Constitutional Convention of 1787: A Comprehensive Encyclopedia of America's Founding*. 2 vols. Santa Barbara, CA: ABC-CLIO.

Vile, John R., William D. Pederson, and Frank J. Williams, eds. 2008. *James Madison: Philosopher, Founder, and Statesman*. Athens: Ohio University Press.

Weber, Paul. 1989. "Madison's Opposition to a Second Convention." *Polity* 20 (Spring): 498–517.

CHAPTER 3

From the Founding through the Civil War

Many of the men who had united to create the Constitution soon found themselves on rival political sides. During George Washington's first term, proponents of what would become the Federalist Party united behind Secretary of the Treasury Alexander Hamilton to support creating a bank of the United States. Such a step required a relatively expansive view of federal powers. Federalists further followed Hamilton in being sympathetic to the British in foreign affairs and in being strong advocates for the development of a strong commercial republic. In opposition, Thomas Jefferson and James Madison emphasized a stricter construction of the Constitution that emphasized states' rights, a view reaffirmed by the Virginia and Kentucky Resolutions of 1787. Jefferson and fellow Democratic-Republicans also favored the development of an agrarian republic and a closer alliance with France over Britain.

Although George Washington professed to be above political parties, his policies inclined strongly in the Federalist direction. He ultimately sided with Alexander Hamilton on the creation of a national bank, supported a military expedition to face down frontiersmen who had opposed the Whiskey Tax, and issued a proclamation of neutrality that ended France's status as a cherished ally. His successor, John Adams, clearly identified with the Federalist camp. During Adams's presidency, however, deep fissures emerged among the Federalists between rival supporters of Adams and Hamilton. After the Federalists adopted the Alien and Sedition Acts of 1798, Democratic-Republicans viewed it as essential to put one of their own in the White House, and they hailed Jefferson's victory over Adams as the Revolution of 1800.

The most notable constitutional changes to emerge from the notorious election of 1800 were those that the Twelfth Amendment inaugurated. Electors were henceforth required to cast separate votes for president and vice-president, so that candidates from the same party would not tie, as Thomas Jefferson and Aaron Burr had in the election of 1800. Democratic Republicans became less wary about exercising national powers when they were in control. Indeed, leading critics claimed that they adopted many of the same constitutional policies in power that they had criticized when they were not (Adams 1974). Jefferson's failure to pursue an amendment giving the government direct authority to purchase the Louisiana Territory is a good example. Not everyone, however, was as content to rest on possibly transient majorities to insure the further perpetuation of constitutional liberties.

Federalists and Democratic-Republicans: Proposals from the First Party System

Two early sets of proposals for major constitutional changes were grounded in the partisan divisions of the day. The first was most concerned with trimming the powers of the new national government, while the second was especially concerned about perceived abuses on the part of the executive branch.

Edmund Pendleton Proposes Six Principles and Eight Amendments That Renew the Anti-Federalist Challenge

Virginia's Edmund Pendleton (1721–1803) had overcome childhood obstacles to become one of Virginia's finest lawyers. He had served as a member of Virginia's Committee of Correspondence, as a delegate to both continental congresses, as Virginia's de facto governor, as a member of the Virginia House of Burgesses, and as speaker of its House of Delegates, and he ended his career as chief justice of Virginia's high court of chancery, and later of its court of appeals. He also presided over the Virginia Convention that had ratified the Constitution before gravitating towards the Democratic-Republican Party (Vile 2001).

On October 5, 1801, Pendleton proposed a series of eight constitutional amendments in an article entitled "The Danger Not Over," which he first published in the Richmond *Examiner*. Lance Banning has observed that these reforms "would eventually flower into an Old Republican opposition to the more moderate course of Jefferson's and Madison's administrations" (Pendleton 2004). Although many Democratic-Republicans had heralded the election of 1800 as a revolution, Pendleton was among those who feared that this revolution might not go far enough in restoring what he considered to be lost principles.

Pendleton indicated that he did not intend "to damp the public joy occasioned by the late changes of our public agents or disturb the calm which already presages the most beneficial consequences." He thought, however, that it was time "to erect new barriers against folly, fraud, and ambition; and to explain such parts of the Constitution as have been already, or may be, interpreted contrary to the intention of those who adopted it" (Pendleton 2004). Many of Pendleton's principles reflected concerns that Anti-Federalists had raised when the Constitution was being ratified.

Pendleton outlined six principles, which he thought the federal government had violated. The first stressed that government was instituted for the common good and should not increase debt or multiply public offices. The second observed that "standing armies, fleets, severe penal laws, war, and a multitude of civil officers" could undermine "civil liberty." The third focused on executive powers to involve the nation in an undeclared war. The fourth warned against "a consolidated general government," and its power of taxation. The fifth focused on Pendleton's support of separation of powers and his fears that violation of this principle could lead to "a dangerous aristocracy." The sixth warned again about multiplying offices and patronage (Pendleton 2004).

Acknowledging that some of these concerns had been raised at the time the Constitution was ratified, Pendleton thought that the nation might now learn from subsequent experience. He accordingly offered eight amendments.

The first would make the president ineligible for reelection and transfer his power to make appointments to Congress. The second would trim the Senate "of all executive power" (possibly its power to ratify treaties), either by shortening its members' terms or by subjecting them to recall (as under the Articles of Confederation). The third would prevent federal legislators and judges from accepting offices within a specified period after leaving office. It also provided for "subjecting the judges to removal by the concurring vote of both houses of Congress." The fourth proposed "some check upon the abuse of *public credit*." The fifth favored "instituting a fair mode of impaneling juries." The sixth would prevent most treaties from becoming law until ratified by the legislature. The seventh proposed

> to interdict laws relating to the freedom of speech, of the press, and of religion, to declare that the common law of England or of any other foreign county in criminal cases shall not be considered as a law of the United States, and that treason shall be confined to the cases stated in the Constitution, so as not to be extended further by law or construction or by using other terms such as sedition, etc.

The eighth proposed "marking out with more precision the distinct powers of the *general* and *state* governments" (Pendleton 2004).

Pendleton's proposals and Madison's Report [on the Alien and Sedition Acts] of 1799 eventually became the "Old and the New Testaments" of the "political faith" of Thomas Ritchie, the influential editor of the Republican *Richmond Enquirer* (Mays 1984, vol. 2, 334). Pendleton's ideas also became prominent again when Andrew Jackson was elected president in 1828.

James Hillhouse Introduces Seven Amendments to Rein in Executive Power

James Hillhouse (1754–1832) introduced a series of transformative amendments in the Senate in 1808. Hillhouse was a Federalist lawyer who served in the Revolutionary War and in the U.S. House of Representatives (1791–1796) before being appointed to the Senate, where he served from 1796 to 1810. In addition, Hillhouse was the long-time treasurer of Yale College and served from 1810 to 1825 as the director of the Connecticut School Fund, which used earnings from the sale of Connecticut's western lands to support public education in the state.

The seven proposals that Hillhouse introduced in the U.S. Senate in 1808 called for changes in presidential elections, presidential powers, and presidential and congressional terms (1808a). Richard H. Hansen observed that Hillhouse was the first member of Congress to offer an amendment in Congress "to alter the method of nominating and electing the President" (Hansen 1962, 178). Hillhouse accompanied his proposals with a speech to the Senate in which he contrasted his own proposals, which sought "a radical cure," to some of the piecemeal proposals that had preceded it (Hillhouse 1808b, 4).

Hillhouse's first two proposals echoed Anti-Federalist concerns over the original Constitution by calling for shortening the terms of members of the House of Representatives to one year and of senators from six to three years. Hillhouse reasoned that "frequent elections are a complete antidote" to popular fears about entrusting legislators with power over sustained periods (Hillhouse 1808b, 12).

Hillhouse's third proposal was his most radical, and it shows that Federalist faith in executive power had begun to wane with the election of Democratic-Republicans to that office. Beginning in 1813—so as not to affect the scheduled 1812 presidential contest—Hillhouse proposed choosing the president by lot from among the class of senators who were serving in what would now be their last year. The resulting Senate vacancy would then be filled by the requisite state legislature via the same standard procedure used prior to adoption of the Seventeenth Amendment.

This proposal expressed great faith in the state legislatures responsible for selecting senators and discounted the need for extraordinary presidential leadership. Hillhouse reasoned that while it had taken genius "to organize and put in operation a new government . . . now that our government is *under way*, and furnished with *laws* and well digested systems, which are the *compass* and *charts* of the political pilots . . . a number of men may be found in every state fully competent to take the helm" (Hillhouse 1808b, 22). Taking a dig at Democratic-Republican leaders Thomas Jefferson and James Madison, Hillhouse further observed that the new system might be more likely to produce *"practical"* men rather than "men formed for *science* and abstruse learning."

Hillhouse's third proposal stemmed from his fear that the president was too powerful and that the contest for the office, and the hope of patronage that presidential appointments brought with it, inflamed party passions. He thus observed that "[p]arty spirit is the *demon* which has engendered the factions that have destroyed most free governments" (Hillhouse 1808b, 27). He opined that "state or local parties will have but a feeble influence on the general government. It is regular, organized parties, extending from the northern to the southern extremity of the U. States, and from the Atlantic, to the utmost western limits, which threaten to shake this UNION to its *centre*" (Hillhouse 1808b, 27).

Hillhouse observed that the existing Electoral College was working almost opposite to the Framers' intentions:

> And to secure his [the president's] election, it will be required that every person before he shall receive a vote or an appointment as an elector, shall pledge himself to support such nomination; and thus the *president* will in *fact* be made to *choose* the *electors*, instead of the *electors choosing the president*. (Hillhouse 1808b, 30)

He further observed that if the method of electing the president were not changed, it might be necessary "to strip the office of *royal* prerogatives" (Hillhouse 1808b,

31). This observation coincided with Hillhouse's fourth proposed amendment, to cap the president's annual salary (then $25,000) at $15,000.

With a president serving for such a shortened term, Hillhouse proposed to eliminate the vice presidency and to provide for the Senate to choose its own speaker. Hillhouse's sixth proposal was to subject presidential appointments to confirmation by both houses of Congress. His seventh proposal further advocated that presidents receive the consent of both houses before dismissing appointees.

Recognizing that some would think that a time during which the nation was facing "danger from abroad" and "party dissensions at home" (50) was inauspicious for amendments, Hillhouse argued that "the time of danger is the only time when public attention can be universally excited" (Hillhouse 1808b, 50).

Some 20 years after he proposed his amendments in Congress, Hillhouse corresponded with some notable statesmen to garner their opinions as to the merits of his proposals. James Madison opposed the changes as too sweeping, but Chief Justice John Marshall expressed support for "some less turbulent and less dangerous mode of choosing the chief magistrate." Similarly, New York's Chancellor Kent thought that popular election of the president "is that part of the machine of our government that I am afraid is doomed to destroy us." William Crawford of Georgia agreed with Hillhouse's contention that great talents were not necessary for a president, but he added that he was "not certain that the nation is prepared for such an amendment" as Hillhouse's proposal to fill the office by lottery (quoted in Bacon 1860, 27–8).

Simon Willard, Jr., Applies Clockmaking Sensibilities to Government

The next proposals to amend the Constitution emerged during the War of 1812. This war was precipitated in part by British attempts to impress U.S. seamen and in part by U.S. desires to capture Canada. Southerners and Westerners favored the war much more than those in the northeast, who had already suffered under various embargoes that the nation had adopted in futile attempts to forestall conflict.

It is difficult to identify Simon Willard, Jr. (1795–1874), with one or another side of this sectional divide. A Massachusetts native, graduate of West Point, and prominent clockmaker, Willard printed his reform proposals in New York in 1815 during the War of 1812 under the prolix title *The Columbian Union, Containing General and Particular Explanations of Government, and the Columbian Constitution, Being an Amendment to the Constitution of the United Sates: Providing a Yearly Revenue to Government of about Forty Millions of Dollars, and the Inevitable Union of the People by a Rule of Voting, and Exemption from Unnecessary Taxation, Consequently Their Permanent and Perpetual Freedom* (Willard 1815).

Willard was interested in both renaming and reforming the nation. He employed religious language and placed a fairly strong emphasis on the doctrine of original sin, which he associated in politics largely with the baneful influences of political parties, monarchy, and aristocratic language. Although he was from a state dominated by Federalists, Willard used highly republican language with roots in both the French Revolution and in Jeffersonian ideology. In a passage that resembles one from Jefferson's *Notes on the State of Virginia*, Willard thus observed that:

> The tiller's soul, forms the patriot of nature, but the civic minds of commodities invites the foreigner of wrong; the moveables of traffic, foreign to the fixidity of the soil.
>
> The fixed agriculturalists, are manufacturers most humble servants, and only guardian parent of all commerce. (Willard 1815, 12)

Unlike Jefferson and other contemporary American Republicans, however, Willard had little interest in federalism because he believed that rival governments disrupted civic unity. By contrast:

> A general constitution is an agreement, by which not a part, but all the people can understand each other, so as not only to keep out of war, but to direct each other in that kind of pursuit, the most common in society for the general happiness of all. (Willard 1815, 15)

Willard proposed a new constitution of 27 articles, many of which show a desire for order and precision that might come naturally to an individual engaged in clockmaking. Thus, Article I proposed renaming the nation "the Columbian Union," after Christopher Columbus, and dividing it into 34 geometrical units, each with populations that were approximately equal (but also allowing for the addition of Canada—a commonly entertained prospect during the War of 1812). Willard further proposed dividing districts into counties, each with its own capital, and its own towns and town houses, called "Temples" (Willard 1815, 30). Each county with 3,125 or more voters would select a representative to the Columbian Congress, with one representative in the upper house for each five in the lower.

Article II provided for nine annual meetings of states, designated as the May Election, the July Election, the September Election, the Vernal Council, the Summer Council, the Autumnal Council, the August Assembly, the New Year Assembly, and the Columbia Congress, the latter to meet from November through March (Willard 1815, 32–3).

Article III proposed annual elections for the legislative and executive divisions. Willard proposed creating six classes of legislators—actors, directors, commissioners, representers, legislators, and mediators—and dividing the executive office into minor presidents, major presidents, special presidents, and the general president. The Columbia Congress would be bicameral, with mediators serving in the higher branch and general legislators in the lower. Suffrage would extend "to every free male person of the Columbian Union, having attained to the age of twenty-one years." Stockholders, members of a "partial body politics" (presumably, political parties), and people still owning slaves at the end of the 1800s would also be prevented from holding office (Willard 1815, 34, 36, 37).

Article IV provided for other governmental offices. With no apparent concern for the First Amendment, it would have included a limitation on the kinds of information that could be introduced in campaign materials (Willard 1815, 43). With similar precision, Article V contained 11 sections that specified how and when various representatives would be elected. Article VI outlined elections for president, whom Willard portrayed as head of the respective legislative bodies.

Article VII specified the pay scale for public officials, which was to be paid in "talents," each worth 13 and one-third cents. The general president would receive 150,000 talents. The Columbian Congress would allocate monies from general revenues to the states to pay for the salaries of county officials.

Article VIII limited the authorization of public monies except through sovereign officials. Article IX also extended the "privilege against arrest" enjoyed by members of Congress going to and from work to such officials. Article X gave new names to various governmental bodies (such as the U.S. Senate, renamed the Mediation, and the House of Representatives, designated as the Grand Council) and specified that "[f]or the unity of general government all inferior legislative bodies shall be subservient to those of higher legislative powers" (Willard 1815, 59–60). Similarly, Section 3 of Article X voided all conflicting provisions of the current Constitution. Section 4 of this article allowed slavery to continue in states where it then existed while discouraging the slave trade and further growth of slavery. Willard also proposed a line, similar to that later enacted in the Missouri Compromise, north of which slavery would be prohibited.

Article XI allowed Congress to "make all laws necessary for carrying into effect the powers contained in this constitution" (Willard 1815, 52), without indicating whether he intentionally omitted the word "proper." Willard did favor vesting Congress with power to encourage internal improvements.

Willard's penchant for precision reemerged in Article XII, which authorized the production of Columbian maps with "an accurate projection of uniform points, relatively denoting the places of all capitols, and degree lines describing of Columbia the parallels of latitude, and meridians of longitude, representing oblong squares, in imitation of and equal to all the degrees of Columbia" (Willard 1815, 63). Article XIII further provided for subservient "military, judiciary and other necessary officers" (Willard 1815, 64).

Article XIV proposed dividing Columbian courts into four parts. In part tracking and in part elaborating the language of the Second Amendment, Article XV specified that

> [a] well-regulated militia under the general subordination and enfranchisement of all the people being required for their common freedom, the Columbian Congress . . . shall establish . . . a uniform military system of general order throughout the Columbian Union, for training, equipping, instructing, directing and governing the militia. (Willard 1815, 65–6)

This extensive article further delineated military organization and introduced the general president's executive council, or cabinet.

Article XVI extensively outlined plans for a general currency, with provisions protecting against counterfeiting and specifying the denominations of bills (including $3, $30, $200, and $300 bills). This article also set interest rates at 6 percent per year (Willard 1815, 78). Article XVII further specified the coins that would be used in the new union.

Article XVIII provided for revenue and taxation. It distinguished between "ratemen," who would be subject to taxation, and "freemen," who would not (Willard 1815, 84). To be considered a freeman, an individual:

> Shall not be a member privileged, or stockholder of any incorporated company, or partial body politic, or of any pursuit pernicious to the general obedience and welfare of the Columbian Union, who shall be the owner of and not exceeding the quantity of land of either of the following description, viz: an improved farm of one hundred acres of good feasible land. (Willard 1815, 85)

The constitution would set different standards for those pursuing "a necessary mechanical pursuit" (Willard 1815, 85). Taxes would apply to those who owned or hired slaves and on imported luxuries and gambling.

Article XIX provided for clarity in the conveyance of land titles and mortgages. According to Willard, all freemen "shall have an equal right to the common forest of Columbia," with protections provided for "obedient" Indian tribes (Willard 1815, 85). Article XX further provided for uniform weights and measures, while Article XXI provided for copyrights and patents.

Whereas the U.S. Constitution does not specifically mention schools, Willard provided in Article XXII that:

> The Columbian Congress shall establish and make all needful rules and regulations expedient for free schools throughout the Columbian Union under the direction of a general school office, to be kept in the vicinity of the Columbian Capitol: and which shall provide that the attention of orphans, and minors of poor parents (slaves excepted) shall be as constant and faithful at school, in acquiring a knowledge of government, and other essential advantages of society as those of the rich. (Willard 1815, 93)

Article XXIII further provided for "a general benevolent office" to provide for "the support of the needy" (Willard 1815, 93). Article XXIV granted Congress full power to regulate marriages and divorces, estates, criminal procedures, bankruptcies, and so forth.

Article XXV provided for the continuing validity of acts of the prior Constitution. Article XXVI permitted inducements to be given to English and Canadian officers who shall cease war against the United States. This novel provision further stated:

> The Columbian Union shall never assume the superior power and dominion of the seas, but the Columbian Congress shall cause to be kept dismantled, the guns of their vectored ships, so that Columbia shall never excel any combination of naval power. (Willard 1815, 96)

Article XXVII, the final article, provided for the Columbian constitution to go into effect when ratified in conventions "of three fourths of the compacts of the

United States called towns in this constitution, or of two thirds of the legislatures of the several states" (Willard 1815, 96).

After completing the outline of his proposed Columbian Constitution, Willard provided for the adoption of either of two additional provisions (both designated as Article I). The first was designed to repeal the three-fifths clause in 1830. The second would have prohibited individuals with direct financial interests in foreign trade from passing laws dealing with the same. Willard further printed the existing U.S. Constitution and specified that the existing Constitution "will remain in full force, and so far constitute a part of the Columbian Constitution" (Willard 1815, 97). Willard's proposed constitution combined a Hamiltonian irreverence for existing states and their boundaries, a Jeffersonian distaste for political parties and special interests, an abolitionist desire to eliminate slavery and reorder national institutions in a more systematic way, and a prolixity and attention to detail more characteristic of state constitutions and legal codes than of the U.S. Constitution.

The Hartford Convention Demonstrates That Sectionalism Was Not a Southern Monopoly

Madison and Jefferson had proposed the Virginia and Kentucky Resolutions to protect speech and oppose centralized power. In time, other Southerners transformed Madison's tentative suggestion for state "interposition" into the more virulent doctrines of nullification and secession (Powell 1897). But the Hartford Convention of 1815 demonstrated that neither advocacy of states' rights nor of constitutional innovations to enforce them was a Southern monopoly (Banner 1970).

Five New England states sent representatives to the Hartford Convention, which met from December 15, 1814, until January 5, 1815 (the Connecticut delegation included James Hillhouse, who had introduced to the U.S. Senate several wide-reaching proposals to amend the Constitution back in 1808). Although some states are believed to have arrived with the intention of seceding, the Convention ultimately proposed seven more moderate amendments. The first, which reflected the continuing split between Northern free states and their Southern slave counterparts, proposed eliminating the three-fifths clause, which, because of its effect on representation within the electoral college, had helped Southern states practically monopolize the presidency. A second proposal, a harbinger of the conflict that would later surround the Missouri Compromise of 1820, would have blocked further expansion of slave representation by requiring a two-thirds vote of both houses of Congress in order to admit new states.

At the Constitutional Convention, Southern states had been particularly adamant in opposing taxes on their exports. Stung by the dire economic consequences of the embargoes on goods leaving the nation for, or coming into America from, England, the New England states now proposed limiting the lengths of embargoes to 60 days and requiring that Congress adopt such measures by a two-thirds vote.

The fifth proposal would likewise have called for Congress to declare war by a two-thirds vote, absent the need for immediate defense. The sixth proposal, which hearkened back to Federalist concerns that had led to the adoption of the Alien Act of 1798, would have prevented foreign-born citizens from serving in Congress or holding other civil offices, while the seventh would have limited the president to one term. Ironically, the party that once favored strong national power now sought to restrain such powers through elimination of the three-fifths clause and the imposition of supermajority votes.

Delegates from the convention arrived in the nation's capital at the same time that people were celebrating Andrew Jackson's successes in the battle of New Orleans and the signing of a peace treaty with England. The Federalist Party died, but it had sown seeds for future controversies.

John C. Calhoun Articulates His Theory of Concurrent Majorities

In time, the mantle of state and regional rights would become most closely linked to the defenders of slavery within the South. States' rights was initially stimulated by opposition to tariffs, which Southerners believed benefited northeastern states at their expense. It gathered further strength throughout the ensuing decades as Southern fears increased that Northern states might not only prevent the spread of slavery into American territories but also seek to drive it from the South.

John C. Calhoun of South Carolina (1781–1850) was one of the strongest defenders of the Southern cause, and his works fill multiple volumes (Calhoun 1851–1856). Calhoun, who graduated from Yale and attended the Litchfield Law Academy, served as a member of the South Carolina legislature (1808–1809) and U.S. House of Representatives (1811–1817) before becoming secretary of state (1817–1825), vice president (1825–1832), and a U.S. senator from South Carolina (1832–1844, 1845–1850). Calhoun departed from the most articulate slave-owning American Founders (who had viewed slavery largely as a necessary evil) in arguing that slavery was a positive good, not only for the Southern economy but also for the enslaved, who Calhoun believed were incapable of taking care of themselves.

It is sometimes difficult to distinguish in Calhoun's writings when he was arguing for a particular interpretation of the existing Constitution and when he was advocating structural change. Calhoun outlined his theory of concurrent majorities in his *Disquisition on Government*, first published in 1851, a year after his death. Calhoun proposed to give each major interest or portion of the community "a concurrent voice in making and executing the laws or a veto on their execution" (Calhoun 1953, 20). Calhoun did not regard African Americans as part of this community, and he was chiefly interested in protecting majorities within each section, especially his own. In his *Discourse on the Constitution and Government of the United States*, also published posthumously in 1851, Calhoun argued that his theory was embodied in the constitutional amending process, with its requirements for supermajorities. As if to reverse the presumption of constitutionality, Calhoun argued that a state challenge to the exercise of federal power could only be overturned by constitutional amendment, although he believed that certain amendments went beyond constitutional capabilities (Vile 1992, 86).

Calhoun favored calling a constitutional convention to resolve the tariff controversy. Calhoun later advocated creating a dual executive representing the North and the South, with each executive required to approve acts of congressional legislation before they became law. This was similar to proposals by the Hartford Convention for supermajority requirements to enact embargoes and declare war. Ironically, the very amending supermajorities that Calhoun praised for representing diverse interests were obstacles to the adoption of this proposal.

Judge Augustus B. Woodward Expresses Concerns about the Cabinet System
In 1825, Augustus B. Woodward published *The Presidency of the United States*, a book that examined America's executive branch. Although Woodward was more intent on diagnosing perceived problems than making concrete proposals for reform, his critique reflected constitutional concerns that the contentious 1824 presidential contest had highlighted.

Woodward, who has been likened to Washington Irving's Ichabod Crane, was a tall man with a big nose who never married. Born in New York in 1774 and initially named Elias Brevoort Woodward, he changed his first name to Augustus. Educated at Columbia, he worked as a clerk in the Treasury Department in Philadelphia before moving to the nation's capital, where he became a member of the bar and a confidant of Thomas Jefferson. Jefferson appointed him as chief justice of the Territory of Michigan in 1805, where he served until 1824. President James Monroe then appointed him as a judge of the Florida Territory, where Woodward served until his death on July 12, 1827 (Sands, "Judge Augustus Woodward").

Woodward arrived in Detroit to assume his judicial duties shortly after the city had burned to the ground in June 1805. He proposed an elaborate scheme (never adopted) for rebuilding the city, based in part on Pierre L'Enfant's plans for the District of Columbia. Woodward laid the basis for a system of free public education and helped found the Catholepistemia, today's University of Michigan, which he patterned in part on Jefferson's plans for the University of Virginia.

Woodward's book on the U.S. presidency identified 20 problems with the institution, many of which centered on the cabinet. Although Woodward did not elaborate on how to solve these problems or provide language for constitutional amendments to adjust them, he did provide an outline for a Department of Domestic Affairs that would include branches for advancing sciences and the arts; for agriculture, commerce, and internal improvements; for preservation of public documents; and so forth. In what seems to have been a fairly far-sighted proposal, he also advocated dividing the Department of Foreign Affairs into eight bureaus, each dealing with a different area of the world.

Woodward identified the following problems:

1. Exclusion of the vice president from cabinet councils, where he might familiarize himself with the job that he could inherit;
2. Rivalry among members of the cabinet for the presidential post;
3. Difficulty for noncabinet members in becoming presidential candidates;
4. Misuse of patronage;
5. Problems caused by party opposition, often fueled by sectional divisions;

6. Variations in the methods of selecting presidential electors;
7. Problems arising when the House of Representatives has to choose among candidates who did not receive a majority in the electoral college;
8. Problems arising when states do not choose presidential electors on the same day;
9. Need for a presidential secretary;
10. District of Columbia's lack of representation in the electoral college;
11. Corruption within Congress fostered by insufficient attention to separation of powers;
12. Lack of constitutional authorization for providing the president with a residence—an apparent contradiction to provisions against additional emoluments for that office;
13. Need for a mechanism whereby the president can establish a committee of investigators;
14. Failure to standardize rules for presidential etiquette;
15. Need for a method whereby various regions of the country have an opportunity to fill the presidency;
16. Need to acquaint the vice president with presidential duties and relieve him of responsibility for presiding over the Senate;
17. Lack of a cabinet office relating to domestic affairs;
18. Concern that attending cabinet meetings could divert cabinet officers' attention from their respective departments;
19. Concern that the desire of cabinet officers to keep their jobs might keep them from providing the president with adequate counsel; and
20. Concern that the cabinet system lacks adequate constitutional sanction. (Woodward 1825, 43–67)

Although Woodward did not specifically call for a parliamentary system that would draw department heads from the legislative branch, a number of his proposals pointed in that direction. Woodward was anxious about sectional strife, and his concern about the constitutionality of providing the president with a residence indicated his narrow view of constitutional construction. His proposals for a Department of Domestic Affairs and for subdivisions of the Department of Foreign Affairs displayed a penchant for classification and systematization and resembled Simon Willard's plans for a new government.

Abel Upshur Advocates Measures to Tame the Presidency
Judge Abel Upshur (1790–1844) was a Virginia lawyer and politician who served as secretary of state during John Tyler's administration. He was tragically killed when the guns of the USS *Princeton* exploded during an official ceremony. Four years before his death, Upshur proposed major constitutional reforms in a work entitled *A Brief Enquiry into the True Nature and Character of our Federal Government*. As the subtitle of his work explained, his book was a series of reflections on Justice Joseph Story's *Commentaries on the Constitution of the United*

States (1833). Story argued that the Constitution was a creation of the people of the United States, rather than a compact among the states, and that its powers needed to be interpreted broadly, consistent with the necessary and proper clause.

Although Upshur spent most of his book explicating a view of strict constitutional construction that would honor states' rights, he introduced four reforms of the presidency that he thought would protect against excessive consolidation of power by the executive branch. The first reform was designed to limit the power of the president to remove individuals from office without the consent of the Senate, which had originally confirmed them. Although the Constitution had been silent on the subject, the president had assumed this power, which the Supreme Court would largely later confirm in *Myers v. United States*, 272 U.S. 53 (1926). Upshur observed, "Surely, it is a great and alarming defect in our Constitution, that so vast and dangerous a power as this should be held by one man" (Upshur 1863 [1840], 117).

Upshur's second proposed reform was to weaken the president's veto, which he viewed as an unwarranted barrier to legislation. Seeing "something incongruous in the union of legislative and executive powers in the same man" (Upshur 1863 [1840], 120), Upshur suggested that the Constitution should instead "authorize the President merely to send back to the legislature for reconsideration any law which he disapproved," thus "affording to that body time and opportunity for reflection, with all the additional lights which the President himself could throw upon the subject" (Upshur 1863 [1840], 120–1). Upshur's third proposal offered a similar fix for the trials of presidential impeachment. Believing that it was nearly impossible to muster a two-thirds majority among senators for this purpose, he thought the majority requirement should be reduced but was uncertain as to where it should be set.

Upshur foresaw a time when a president would serve for more than two terms and thought that it would be best to prepare for it. Upshur proposed limiting the president to one term, although he was willing to make it "a long term" as long as he was more accountable—presumably through the above impeachment mechanism—to the people (Upshur 1863 [1840], 122).

The Seneca Falls Convention Ends with a Declaration

One of the most consequential conventions of the nineteenth century was the Seneca Falls Convention of 1848. This women's rights convention of about 300 individuals led by Elizabeth Cady Stanton and Lucretia Mott was held on July 19 and 20, 1848, in Seneca Falls, New York. This gathering laid the groundwork for significant advances in the area of women's rights, including the right to vote.

The convention attendees did not express their desires and goals in the form of a new constitution specifying rights, but rather in the manner of the Declaration of Independence by focusing on grievances. They produced a Declaration of Sentiments asserting that "all men and women are created equal." The document then focused on a whole host of issues that its authors could have appropriately phrased as amendments. Grievances included the denial to women of "the elective franchise," their independent "right in property," "the guardianship of the children," and their exclusion from positions in both church and state. At one point, the document observed that men had withheld from women "her rights which are given to the most ignorant and degraded men—both natives and foreigners." The closest the document came to constitutional language was an insistence that women "have immediate admission to all the rights and privileges which belong to them as citizens of these United States" (Bernhard and Fox-Genovese 1995, 85–8).

The most controversial part of this declaration, as well as its most enduring legacy, was its insistence on women's suffrage. Suffragist Carrie Chapman Catt later observed that the Seneca Falls Convention initiated a total of:

> 56 campaigns of state referenda, 480 campaigns to convince state legislatures to submit suffrage amendments to voters, 47 campaigns attempting to get state constitutional conventions to write woman suffrage into state constitution, and 19 campaigns with 10 successive Congresses. (Palmer 2000, 429)

John Brown: An Abolitionist Fanatic with a Constitutional Plan

Tensions continued to rise between the North and South. Although Congress periodically papered over these controversies with legislative compromises, the momentum for war continued to build. The period thus became a seedtime for the development of radical proposals to alter or replace the Constitution.

One of these reformers was John Brown, who has been alternatively praised as an abolitionist savior and martyr and excoriated as a terrorist. Born in Torrington, Connecticut, on May 9, 1800, Brown spent much of his early life in Ohio and Massachusetts. Increasingly radicalized by the slavery controversy, he helped found the League of Gideadites in Springfield, Massachusetts, which sought to prevent the return of fugitive slaves. He then moved to Kansas, which was wracked by conflicts between pro and antislavery forces who were seeking to convert the territory into a state in their own image.

After proslavery forces sacked Lawrence, Kansas, in May 1856, Brown and his followers attacked homesteads along Pottawatomie Creek in southeastern Kansas and butchered five men with known proslavery leanings in front of their families. Brown subsequently directed military engagements against proslavery forces at Palmyra and Osawatomie before returning to the Northeast. In October 1859 he led an armed raid on the federal armory at Harpers Ferry, Virginia (now West Virginia), in the vain hope that it would trigger a slave revolt that would sweep the South. After federal forces captured Brown, he was tried in a state court and hanged, providing the antislavery cause with a martyr (Renehan 1995).

Prior to his famous raid on Harper's Ferry, Brown and 45 followers held a constitutional convention on May 8, 1858, in Chatham, Ontario, where they voted on a provisional constitution consisting of a preamble and 48 articles. It was designed to create an initial government for the free state that Brown anticipated establishing after slaves rallied to his cause (Oates 1970, 243), but it was a state that he apparently hoped would eventually include the entire South.

The constitution outlined a unicameral Congress consisting of 5 to 10 members serving three-year terms and elected by persons "connected with the organization" (Fogleson and Rubenstein 1969, 48). The president, vice president, and five members of the Supreme Court were to be selected in similar fashion, with the executive also serving a three-year term, and all subject to impeachment and removal. Members of the three branches were to choose the commander-in-chief for a three-year term, with a treasurer, secretary of state, secretary of war, and secretary of the treasury chosen in a similar manner. The constitution addressed recruiting for government posts and for the army and (in likely anticipation of conflict with existing slave states) dealt with court-martials, the treatment of prisoners, neutral parties, deserters, and captured property.

Brown's constitution required all to labor "for the common good," and prohibited "profane swearing, filthy conversation, indecent behavior, or indecent exposure of the person, or intoxication of quarreling" and "unlawful intercourse of the sexes" (Fogleson and Rubenstein 1969, 57). It also called for respecting "the marriage relation" (Brown's two marriages had produced 20 children) and for setting aside Sunday for rest and for "moral and religious instruction and improvement, relief of the suffering, instruction of the young and ignorant, and the encouragement of personal cleanliness" (Fogleson and Rubenstein 1969, 57–8).

Article 46 of the proposed constitution proclaimed its intention to "amend and repeal" rather than dissolve the Union. It further specified that "our flag shall be the same that our fathers fought under in the Revolution" (Fogleson and Rubenstein 1969, 59). Those who signed the document elected Brown as commander in chief, but the office of president remained unfilled after two black nominees both declined to serve (Oates 1970, 246).

The Peace Convention Seeks to Avert War by Making the Constitution More Slave Friendly

About the time that some Southern representatives were meeting in Montgomery in 1861 to draw up a Confederate constitution, the governor of Virginia called for a convention of Northern and Southern states to devise a plan of reconciliation (Crittenden 1964). The convention may have been patterned on the Nashville Convention of 1850, in which 176 delegates from nine Southern states had met for nine days in Nashville and adopted 28 resolutions affirming Southern rights, some of which were later incorporated within the Compromise of 1850 (Jennings 1998, 674).

Twenty-one of 34 states responded to the call for the Peace Convention. They sent a total of 132 delegates to the Willard Hotel in Washington, D.C., in early 1861 (Dumond 1973, 241). States sent from 5 to 11 delegates, who in turn created a committee consisting of one delegate from each state, headed by former secretary of the treasury James Guthrie of Kentucky. This committee reported seven proposals to the convention on February 15. These ideas were modified and presented collectively to Congress as a proposed Thirteenth Amendment. Many of the provisions resembled those of the Crittenden Compromise that Congress was hammering out at the time, and suggested the kind of changes that might have been needed to keep the Union together.

Section 1 of the amendment proposed reinstating the 36 degrees, 30 minutes line of latitude created under the Missouri Compromise of 1810 and extending it to the Pacific Coast. This provision would have permitted slavery south of the line and prevented it north of the line in all existing territories.

Section 2 prohibited the acquisition of new territory except by a majority vote of both free and slave states in the Senate and agreement by the requisite two-thirds majority required to approve a treaty. Section 3 prohibited Congress from interfering with slavery in those states where it existed or abridging slavery in the nation's capital without the consent of Maryland or without compensating slave owners. This section would also have permitted the continuing transport of slaves between slave states—but not through states that disapproved of that institution. The section did prohibit the transit of slaves to the capital for transfer to other states.

Section 4 was designed to enforce the fugitive slave law. Similarly, Section 5 prohibited the "foreign slave trade." Section 6 added an entrenchment clause to the Constitution by providing that Sections 2, 3, and 5 of the amendment, as well as other constitutional provisions relating to slavery (presumably including the notorious three-fifths clause), "shall not be amended or abolished without the consent of all the States." Section 7 further provided that the national government would compensate owners who lost their slaves as a result of "violence or intimidation from mobs or riotous assemblages," but such compensation would not preclude further attempts to secure such individuals. Finally, the proposal authorized Congress to "provide by law for securing to the citizens of each State the privileges and immunities of the several states." This proved to be an ironic provision, as the Fourteenth Amendment would later include a similar clause designed to protect the rights of former slaves (Gunderson 1961, 62, 86, 107–8). Some of these provisions, such as Section 1, barely garnered enough support for inclusion in the final Peace Convention document, while others received more widespread support. Section five, for example, was approved by a 16-to-5 vote.

The Peace Convention had no specific constitutional authorization, but it kept border states within the Union long enough for Lincoln to be inaugurated as president. Convention delegates appeared to hope that Congress would submit its proposals directly to the states for approval in special conventions called for this purpose. Although Congress failed to act by the requisite majorities on this measure, it did propose the Corwin Amendment, which would have protected states from amendments interfering with slavery. Instead, the next amendment to be adopted by Congress was an amendment outlawing the institution of slavery.

William B. Wedgwood Proposes Averting War by Uniting North and South in an Empire

In 1861, William B. Wedgwood (?–1888), proposed an alternative constitution of 22 articles in a book entitled *The Reconstruction of the Government of the United States of America*. A native of Maine, Wedgwood later moved to New York, where he joined the bar in 1841. He authored several books on the U.S. Constitution and the laws and constitutions of a number of New England states. He also helped found the City University of New York School of Law (Boyd 1992, 29).

Wedgwood published his 1861 volume in the hope that it might avert war. He proposed allowing the North and South to form two republics, joined together as the "Democratic Empire." Believing that the United States was heir to the blessings that God had once bestowed on ancient Israel, Wedgwood described his proposed plan as a "theocratic Democracy" (Wedgwood 1861, 15). Wedgwood included an acknowledgment of God in the preamble and stated that the primary purpose of government was to "develop and arrange" natural law principles into "a written code, under the sanction of legislative enactment" (Wedgwood 1861, 17). Early articles of Wedgwood's constitution elaborately described the flag and seal of the Democratic Empire. Wedgwood's flag, for example, was to contain seven colors and 13 stripes in a double rainbow that would also feature the otherwise unexplained symbolical letters W.C.P.P.

Wedgwood's constitution contained a number of novel features. In several places it went into detail about the relationship between natural rights and political rights. In a preview of later twentieth-century constitutions, Wedgwood guaranteed a good education to all and required that all citizens labor (Wedgwood 1861, 16). Although protecting the general right to worship, Wedgwood's constitution prohibited "the worship of idols and the sacrifice of human beings" (Wedgwood 1861, 17). In several places, the constitution sanctioned the government's right (specified indirectly within the Fifth Amendment) of eminent domain.

Wedgwood proposed setting up three levels of government—state, national, and imperial. Each level would consist of officeholders "of high moral and religious character" (Wedgwood 1861, 18). States would fall naturally into "Labor States" and "Capital States," with Wedgwood advocating extension of the Missouri Compromise line with respect to slavery "west until it reaches the Atlantic [sic] Ocean" (Wedgwood 1861, 19). Wedgwood proposed dividing each of the three levels of government into legislative, executive, and judicial branches, with terms in the respective Houses of Representatives of one, two, and four years and those in the respective Senates of two, four, and six years. Similarly, state governors would serve for two years, the president for four years, and the emperor for six years.

Wedgwood described the powers of state governments in considerable detail. State powers would include regulation of property, education, and highways; provision of employment for the needy; and enactment of laws for domestic relations. The national government would handle problems between and among the states. The imperial government (headquartered in New York) would deal with matters of defense and diplomacy, with the emperor serving as commander in chief of the army and navy.

Wedgwood believed that contemptuous statements from the pulpit and elsewhere about the Constitution and slaveowners had largely precipitated the impending Civil War. He thus proposed, with little apparent consideration of the First Amendment, that "slanderous words, coming from whatever source they may come, must be suppressed and punished." Almost as though he was addressing the school children for whom he sometimes wrote, he added that "all unkind language, by which the feelings of a fellow citizen may be injured, should be carefully avoided" (Wedgwood 1861, 26).

Wedgwood was advocating an empire, and he hoped that Canada, Mexico, and other Central and South American republics would eventually join and "triumphantly" vindicate the Monroe Doctrine, a U.S. policy introduced in 1823 that warned European nations against interfering in affairs in the Americas (Wedgwood 1861, 27). Perhaps as a warning, however, he ended his discourse with a reference to the four horses of the biblical book of Revelation. Wedgwood's fears prevailed over his hopes and war came apace.

The Confederate Alternative
The 11 states that joined the Confederacy approved a new constitution written by a Committee of Twelve and debated by a convention held in Montgomery, Alabama, in March 1861. This Confederate Constitution replaced a provisional constitution that had been adopted the previous month. Largely patterned after the existing national constitution, the Confederate Constitution was also heavily influenced by the philosophy that had guided the earlier Articles of Confederation. Reflecting the views of John C. Calhoun and other Southern constitutionalists (DeRosa 1991, 18–37), the document was built on the doctrine of state sovereignty (Lee 1963).

Fifty individuals from seven Southern states participated in the Provisional Congress/Convention, which began on February 4, 1861 (the Confederacy's four other member states did not secede until later that spring). The 50 delegates represented a remarkably talented and well-educated group, composed mostly of lawyers and planters. Nearly all of them were slaveowners with years of political experience. The most influential delegate was legal scholar Thomas R. R. Cobb of Georgia. Delegates appointed a 12-man committee, chaired by Robert Barnwell Rhett, Sr., of South Carolina, to draw up the constitution. The committee quickly adopted a constitutional draft that was presented to the full Congress of Delegates from the secessionist states. It was adopted on March 11 and sent to the states for approval.

Because the Confederate Constitution followed the general outline of its U.S. constitutional counterpart, it is common to focus on elements that were different. Whereas the U.S. Constitution omits such a mention, the preamble of the Confederate Constitution acknowledged God. Moreover, because the document embraced slavery rather than being ashamed of it, it explicitly referred to slaves rather than using euphemisms. It permitted two-thirds majorities of state legislatures to impeach judicial or other officials acting within a state. In imitation of parliamentary systems, it permitted Congress to grant a seat on the floor of Congress for members of the cabinet to discuss measures but did not allow members of Congress to hold other offices in the government.

The Confederate Constitution granted the president an item veto of appropriations bills and prohibited congressional appropriations for internal improvements other than aids to navigation and harbor improvements. Although the constitution prohibited slave importation, it explicitly affirmed the right to property in slaves. Appropriations required a two-thirds vote of both houses of Congress, with a clause providing that all appropriations bills "shall specify in federal currency the exact amount of each appropriation, and the purposes for which it is made." The constitution also limited bills to a single subject.

The Confederate Constitution provided that the president would serve a single six-year term. It gave explicit authority to the chief executive to remove department heads at his pleasure and others for specified grievances. It did not significantly alter the judicial system, but perhaps because they remembered the consolidating effect that federal courts had exercised, members of the Confederate Congress never established their equivalents.

Although it did not explicitly prohibit membership by free states, the Confederate Constitution seemed to provide a Southern echo to one of the proposals by the Hartford Convention by requiring a two-thirds vote of both houses of Congress to admit new states. The constitution also explicitly granted the government the right to acquire new territory where the right to own slaves would be protected.

The provisional Confederate Constitution had permitted amendments by a two-thirds vote in Congress (Urofsky 1988, 400). By contrast, the permanent constitution provided no method for Congress to propose amendments. It did, however, provide for Congress to call for a constitutional convention in the event of such a request from three states. Article VII of the Confederate Constitution provided that the document would go into effect when ratified by "conventions of five States" (Confederate president Jefferson Davis announced ratification on April 29, 1861). The provisions of the Bill of Rights were incorporated within the Confederate Constitution rather than listed at the end.

Robert E. Beasley Proposes Ending the War and Continuing Slavery

The author has been otherwise unable to identify Robert E. Beasley, who in 1864 introduced a proposed constitution in *A Plan to Stop the Present and Prevent Future Wars*. Beasley's central purpose was to stop the Civil War by requiring a popular referendum on the subject. Under his plan, nonvoters would be fined $1,000, and those who voted to continue waging war would be conscripted into the military. Beasley also crafted a proposed constitution for "the sovereign States of North and South America."

Under Beasley's constitution, each state would have two representatives in the House of Representatives and one senator, essentially restoring the equality of representation that states had exercised under the Articles of Confederation. The Senate would have to approve charges of impeachment by a three-fifths vote rather than a two-thirds vote, and members of Congress would receive $5 for each day of service plus expenses. Only Congress would have the power to suspend habeas corpus.

Under Beasley's constitutional framework, neither the president nor the vice president would be permitted to serve for consecutive terms. Each voter would write the name of his preferred candidate on the ballot, with the Senate deciding tie votes. The constitution would set the president's yearly salary at $40,000. The president's power to pardon would be restricted in cases of "lying, larceny, and impeachment," and he could be removed from office for "conviction of lying, larceny or other high crimes and misdemeanors" (Beasley 1864, 13–14).

Beasley's proposed constitution incorporated most provisions within the Bill of Rights. Government officials who were convicted of stealing were to be fined, with proceeds going to the construction of a national cemetery. Those stealing over $10,000 were to be "hung with a rope by the neck until dead" and denied burial in the aforementioned national cemetery (Beasley 1864, 16).

Under Beasley's proposed constitution, states would be prohibited from interfering in the domestic affairs of other states. Failure to abide by this rule would be punishable by a 50-year expulsion from the Union. Beasley would permit states to secede and keep governmental property within their borders. He also provided for the purchase of "white servants" from Europe who would become citizens after 14 years of service (Beasley 1864, 18). Beasley would further permit slaveholders to take their slaves into territories, thus affirming the Supreme Court's decision in *Scott v. Sanford* in 1857. Much as Stephen Douglas had advocated, Beasley would allow states to decide on slavery as a matter of popular sovereignty.

Another Beasley provision called for the national government to call upon states for quotas of troops. If the state failed to meet this quota, the national government was empowered to draft "all the males and half the females in his State" (Beasley 1864, 20). Neither slavery nor polygamy would exclude a state from the union. Office-holding and voting would be restricted to "white male citizens of the age of twenty-one years and upwards" (Beasley 1864, 20).

Beasley's constitution also officially adopted the Monroe Doctrine and authorized Congress to implement it. Under his scheme, Congress could admit adjacent islands into the Union after 1900, but states in Europe, Asia, and Africa would have to wait until after 2000. States would have the power to prohibit their citizens from interfering in the "domestic concerns" of their neighbors or "lying to their own or their neighbor's dumb brutes [presumably slaves], or unnecessarily abusing them in any way" (Beasley 1864, 21).

Beasley identified himself as one of the "sovereign people" of Rio Vista, California. Although he doubted that he was "a servant of God" (Beasley 1864, 3)—perhaps a dig at John Brown and other religiously motivated abolitionists—Beasley suggested that the people should consider four scriptures "as admonitions to all people" (Beasley 1864, 21). These involved the subjection of wives to husbands, instructions for familial relations, master-slave relations, and the proper allocation of responsibilities between Caesar and God.

Beasley proposed outlawing secret political parties and denying all parties the right to nominate candidates for office. He proposed allowing his government to go into effect when five states agreed to his proposed government. Once the new nation was established it would presumably attract other states. Subsequent amendments to the constitution would then have to be ratified by five-sixths of the states.

In an addendum, Beasley asserted that "whatsoever God has made inferior, man cannot make equal or superior" (Beasley 1864, 23). This statement, an apparent reference to slaves, stood in obvious contradiction to sentiments expressed in the Declaration of Independence. He further proposed a postwar census and the implementation of laws "that will give every one a chance to have a husband or wife"; he further suggested that the national seat of government should be "within one or two hundred miles of the 'Isthmus of Panama'" (Beasley 1864, 24).

Beasley's constitutional vision did not attract much attention, but echoes of his call for a popular referendum on the war were heard in later eras of American history. For example, Democratic representative Louis Ludlow championed a proposal for a referendum on war from 1914 to 1940 (Bolt 1977). Some opponents of the Vietnam War also called for a referendum on American involvement in that conflict.

E. L. Godkin Proposes Protecting Equal Rights
and Providing for Education and Marriage

Edward L. Godkin (1883–1899), the Irish-born founder of the *Nation* and editor-in-chief of the *New York Evening Post*, published "The Constitution, and Its Defects," in the July 1864 issue of the *North American Review*. Godkin opined that the reverence with which the document had been regarded for most of its history had retarded prospects for change. Saying that he doubted "if the worship of ancestors has ever been carried much further . . . even in China" (Godkin 1864, 126), he went on to argue that:

> There is not a mechanic in the United States who is not, or ought not to be, far wiser than either Sherman or Ellsworth, or Franklin or Hamilton, or any other man of the last century, concerning the merits and short-comings of the Constitution, concerning the advisability or unadvisability of acting under its permissory clauses, concerning the political needs and tendencies of this Union and of this age, and above all, concerning the nature and influence of negro slavery. (Godkin 1864, 126)

Godkin proceeded to anticipate both the Thirteenth and Fourteenth Amendments by suggesting that amendments were needed not simply to abolish slavery but to protect the "equal right" of blacks "to turn such faculties as God has pleased to give them to the best account" (Godkin 1864, 131–2). He further argued that "a Common regard for our own safety would seem to require, therefore, that the division of power between the State and central governments should now undergo careful revision, and that it should be redistributed under the guidance of that experience of our wants and dangers which we have derived from the history of the last eighty years" (Godkin 1864, 141). Perhaps further anticipating Reconstruction efforts to educate African Americans, Bodkin observed that "nothing can keep the national government together, but the general diffusion of education among those who live under it" (Godkin 1864, 143). He thought that the national government should have power to establish such schools "whenever the State governments through indolence or indifference, false economy or sheer malevolence, fail to do so" (Godkin 1864, 143). Godkin also pointed out that "there is no human relation which affects the distribution and transmission of property more powerfully than marriage" (Godkin 1864, 144). In light of this reality, Godkin asserted that the national government should establish "a uniform law of marriage and divorce" (Godkin 1864, 144).

Francis Lieber Foreshadows Coming Constitutional Changes

Some of the most significant provisions of the Thirteenth, Fourteenth, and Fifteenth Amendments to the U.S. Constitution were foreshadowed by Francis Lieber (1800–1862), a German-born immigrant who edited the 13-volume *Encyclopedia Americana*, which appeared from 1829 to 1833. Lieber had long served as a professor of history and political economy at South Carolina College, where he defended the Union against radical theories of states' rights and secession. In 1857 he left the South for a post at Columbia College in New York, where he taught until his death in 1872.

Lieber was a prolific scholar who wrote the *Instructions for the Government of the Armies of the United States* (1863), an influential text containing many proposals that were eventually adopted as international protocols. He also served as president of the Loyal Publication Society of New York, which sought to rally Northern support for the war by distributing pro-Union articles and editorials across the country.

In 1865, Lieber published a pamphlet in which he proposed a number of constitutional amendments. Lieber indicated that he favored a variety of significant reforms, including a six-year term for the president, a line-item veto, alterations in constitutional provisions relative to direct taxes, new antipolygamy laws, and a provision allowing cabinet officers to appear in Congress. However, he limited his specific proposals to seven presumably more-pressing amendments, some of which so clearly anticipated provisions in forthcoming amendments that they were probably not original to him.

The first, which resembled the privileges and immunities clause of the Fourteenth Amendment, required allegiance from each American native-born and naturalized citizen and a reciprocal guarantee by the national government of their "full protection." His second, third, and fourth proposals extended the definition of treason to include attempts to separate states from the Union, made armed resistance to the United States a "high crime," and permitted trials for treason outside a state or district during times of war and rebellion. His fifth and most critical amendment anticipated abolishing slavery and eliminating the three-fifths clause so that representation of the states within the House of Representatives would be based on the "respective number of male citizens of age." Lieber's sixth proposed amendment would classify those who participated in the slave trade as pirates, and his seventh guaranteed the "privileges" of all citizens, including those who had been recently freed. In elaborating on the last of these provisions, Lieber indicated that he was particularly interested in seeing that courts treated the testimony of blacks and whites equally.

Conventions Ignored, and the Constitution Retained and Amended

The proposals championed by Lieber and Godkin anticipated a number of provisions within the three amendments that Congress proposed and that states adopted between 1865 and 1870. The Thirteenth Amendment, which President Lincoln had vigorously supported, eliminated all involuntary servitude, except as punishment for crimes, when it was enacted in December 1865. After Lincoln's death, Congress proposed two further amendments. The Fourteenth Amendment, ratified in 1868, vested citizenship in all persons who had been born or naturalized in the United States and extended a number of rights to them, including privileges and immunities, due process, and equal protection. The Fifteenth Amendment, ratified in 1870, sought to outlaw discrimination in voting on the basis of race.

Although these amendments were far reaching, their full fruits would not be evident for almost 100 years. The nation had confronted its most divisive issue not by holding another Convention or adopting a new Constitution but by fighting a war and amending the existing one through established mechanisms. As they examined the language of these amendments, subsequent generations would argue about their intent and meaning. They would also have to decide whether to confront future crises by continuing to add amendments to the existing document or by proposing a constitutional replacement.

References

Adams, Henry. 1974. *The Formative Years*. Edited by Herbert Agar. 2 vols. Westport, CT: Greenwood Press.

Bacon, Leonard. 1860. *Sketch of the Life and Public Services of Hon. James Hillhouse of New Haven; with a Notice of His Son Augustus Lucas Hillhouse*. New Haven, CT: n.p.

Banner, James M., Jr. 1970. *To the Hartford Convention: The Federalists and the Origins of Party Politics in Massachusetts, 1789–1815*. New York: Alfred A. Knopf.

Beasley, Robert E. 1864. *A Plan to Stop the Present and Prevent Future Wars: Containing a Proposed Constitution for the General Government of the Sovereign States of North and South America*. Rio Vista, CA: Robert Beasley.

Bernhard, Virginia, and Elizabeth Fox-Genovese, eds. 1995. *The Birth of American Feminism: The Seneca Falls Woman's Convention of 1848*. St. James, NY: Brandywine Press.

Bolt, Ernest C., Jr. 1977. *The War Referendum Approach to Peace in America, 1914–1941*. Charlottesville: University Press of Virginia.

Boyd, Steven R., ed. 1992. *Alternative Constitutions for the United States: A Documentary History*. Westport, CT: Greenwood Press.

Calhoun, John C. 1953 [1851]. *A Disquisition on Government and Selections from the Discourse*. Edited by C. Gordon Post. Indianapolis, IN: Bobbs-Merrill.

Calhoun, John C. 1851–1856. *The Works of John C. Calhoun*. Edited by Richard K. Cralle. New York: D. Appleton and Company. Reprint, New York: Russell and Russell, 1968.

Crittenden, L. E. 1964. *A Report of the Debates and Proceedings in the Secret Sessions of the Conference Convention for Proposing Amendments to the Constitution of the United States held at Washington D.C., in February A.D. 1861.* New York: D. Appleton & Company.

DeRosa, Marshall L. 1991. *The Confederate Constitution of 1861: An Inquiry into American Constitutionalism.* Columbia: University of Missouri Press.

Dumond, Dwight L. 1973. *The Secession Movement, 1860–1861.* New York: Octagon Books.

Fogleson, Robert M., and Richard E. Rubenstein. 1969. *Mass Violence in America: Invasion at Harper's Ferry.* New York: Arno Press.

Godkin, Edward L. 1864. "The Constitution and Its Defects." *North American Review* 99 (July): 117–45.

Gunderson, Robert Gray. 1961. *Old Gentleman's Convention: The Washington Peace Conference of 1861.* Madison, WI: University of Wisconsin Press.

Hansen, Richard H. 1962. "Barriers to a National Primary Law." *Law and Contemporary Problems* 27 (Spring): 178–87.

Hillhouse, [James]. 1808a. *Amendments to the Constitution of the United States Submitted for Consideration by Mr. Hillhouse, April 12, 1808.* Washington, DC: U.S. Senate. 7pp.

Hillhouse, [James]. 1808b. *Propositions for Amending the Constitution of the United States Submitted by Mr. Hillhouse to the Senate on the Twelfth Day of April, 1808, with his Explanatory Remarks.* Washington, DC: U.S. Senate. 52pp.

Jameson, John A. 1887. *A Treatise on Constitutional Conventions: Their History, Powers, and Modes of Proceeding.* 4th ed. Chicago: Callaghan and Company.

Jennings, Thelma. 1998. "Nashville Convention." *The Tennessee Encyclopedia of History & Culture.* Edited by Carroll Van West. Nashville, TN: Rutledge Hill Press.

Lee, Charles Robert, Jr. 1963. *The Confederate Constitutions.* Chapel Hill: University of North Carolina Press.

Lieber, Francis. 1865. *Amendments of the Constitution Submitted to the Consideration of the American People.* New York: Loyal Publication Society.

Mays, David John. 1984. *Edmund Pendleton, 1721–1803: A Biography.* 2 vols. Richmond: Virginia State Library. Reprint of Harvard University Press edition of 1952.

Oates, Stephen B. 1970. *To Purge This Land with Blood: A Biography of John Brown.* New York: Harper and Row.

Palmer, Kris E. 2000. *Constitutional Amendments: 1789 to the Present.* Detroit: Gale Group.

Pendleton, Edmund. 2004 [1801]. "The Danger Not Over." In *Liberty and Order: The First American Party Struggle*, edited by Lance Banning, 422–5. Indianapolis, IN: Liberty Fund.

Powell, Edward Payson. 1897. *Nullification and Secession in the United States: A History of the Six Attempts during the First Century of the Republic.* New York: G. P. Putnam's Sons.

Renehan, Edward J., Jr. 1995. *The Secret Six: The True Tale of the Men Who Conspired with John Brown.* New York: Crown.

Sands, Richard H. "Judge Augustus Woodward: A Freemason and Founder of the First Complete Educational System in America." Online Bonisteel Masonic Library, http://www.bonisteelml.org/Judge_Woodward.htm (accessed May 27, 2013).

Upshur, Abel P. 1863. *A Brief Enquiry into the True Nature and Character of Our Federal Government: Being a Review of Judge Story's Commentaries on the Constitution of the United States*. Philadelphia: John Campbell Publisher. Reprinted from the original Petersburg Edition of 1840.

Urofsky, Melvin I. 1988. *A March of Liberty: A Constitutional History of the United States*. New York: Alfred A. Knopf.

Vile, John R. 2010. *Encyclopedia of Constitutional Amendments, Proposed Amendments, and Amending Issues, 1789–2010*. 3rd ed. Santa Barbara, CA: ABC-CLIO.

Vile, John R. 2001. "Pendleton, Edmund." In *Great American Lawyers: An Encyclopedia*, vol. 2., edited by John R. Vile, 548–52. Santa Barbara, CA: ABC-CLIO.

Vile, John R. 1992. *The Constitutional Amending Process in American Political Thought*. New York: Praeger.

Wedgwood, William B. 1861. *The Reconstruction of the Government of the United States of America: A Democratic Empire Advocated and an Imperial Constitution Proposed*. New York: John H. Tingley.

Willard, John Ware. 1911. *Simon Willard and His Clocks*. Reprint. New York: Cover Publications, 1911.

Willard, Simon, Jr. 1815. *The Columbian Union, Containing General and Particular Explanations of Government, and the Columbian Constitution, Being an Amendment to the Constitution of the United States: Providing a Yearly Revenue to Government of about Forty Millions of Dollars, and the Inevitable Union of the People by a Rule of Voting, and Exemption from Unnecessary Taxation, Consequently Their Permanent and Perpetual Freedom*. Albany, NY: Printed for the author.

Woodward, Augustus B. 1825. *The Presidency of the United States*. New York: J & J. Harper.

CHAPTER 4

From Reconstruction to the Turn of the Century

In surveying the amendments that members of Congress proposed during the United States' first 100 years of existence, Professor Herman Ames observed that in the fourth and last period that he studied, from 1870 to 1889, such proposals "more generally contemplated substantial alterations than confirmatory enactment" (Ames 1970, 24). So too, Amendments Thirteen through Fifteen may have served to stimulate thinking about further substantive changes. Certainly, the period from the end of the Civil War to the turn of the century witnessed a plethora of proposals to rewrite or substantially revise the Constitution.

Victoria Claflin Woodhull Seeks Greater Equality and Democracy

None of the three postbellum amendments addressed the issue of women's rights. Indeed, the Fourteenth Amendment was the first to introduce the word "male" into the document. In Section 2 it provided for the possible reduction of state representation for states that withheld the vote from "any of the male inhabitants of such state, being twenty-one years of age, and citizens of the United States." Still, the movement for women's rights continued to grow during this period.

In 1870 Victoria Claflin Woodhull (1838–1927) proposed a Constitution of the United States of the World in a speech that she gave before her first of five bids for the presidency as a member of the Equal Rights Party. Woodhull was alternatively a stockbroker and onetime protégée of Cornelius Vanderbilt; a reformer, lecturer, and spiritualist; a proponent of woman's suffrage who split with Susan B. Anthony's National Woman Suffrage Association; and an editor of *Woodhull and Claflin's Weekly* and later the *Humanitarian*. Woodhull was also a thrice-married member of an eccentric family; her sister was the vivacious Tennessee Celeste Claflin. Victoria also was the primary catalyst for charges of adultery against popular preacher Henry Ward Beecher (McHenry 1980, 451–2; Marberry 1967; Arling 1972).

Woodhull's proposed constitution, which consisted of 19 articles, was a unique blend of old and new proposals. Although she proposed continuing a bicameral congress, with senators serving terms of 10 years and representatives terms of 5 years, she proposed that all bills originate in the House of Representatives (Stern 1974, 6), and that three-fifths of the House would have the right to abolish the Senate if the American people concurred (Stern 1974, 22). Moreover, she favored giving the House the power to override presidential vetoes by a simple majority vote (Stern 1974, 76).

Woodhull proposed granting Congress authority to prescribe a common form of constitution for each state and guarantee equal rights. Woodhull also endorsed giving Congress expanded powers to establish a uniform criminal code, a common law, a system of welfare-workfare, prison discipline, inheritance and other progressive taxes, a system of national railroads, as well as to propose a world tribunal (Stern 1974, 7–11).

Under Woodhull's reforms, an electoral college would select the president and the president's ministerial cabinet of 16 designated officers, each of whom would serve 10-year nonrenewable terms (Stern 1974, 12–16). This electoral college would also select judges, with a judicial system consisting of district courts, a three-judge Supreme Court of the States, and a five-person Supreme Court of the United States (Stern 1974, 18).

Woodhull proposed extending the franchise to all 18-year-old citizens other than "idiots and the insane" (Stern 1974, 19), thus anticipating both the Nineteenth and Twenty-Sixth Amendments. Woodhull's constitution further provided for the recall, the initiative, and the referendum, with three-fifths of the voters permitted to adopt amendments either on their own or on the recommendation of a three-fifths majority of the House of Representatives (Stern 1974, 22–3). Woodhull did not include a bill of rights.

Although Woodhull anticipated a number of reforms that would become popular in the Progressive Era, her proposals received little publicity and "had little discernible impact on the American political process or the condition of women in American life" (Boyd 1992, 43). In 1893 Congressman Lucas Miller of Wisconsin offered a resolution to change the name of the United States to the United States of the World. It contained a number of other whimsical features, some of which resembled provisions of the Woodhull Plan (Musmanno 1929, 185–6). Oscar Crosby (1909) subsequently published *A Constitution for the United States of the World*, focused on creating an international organization.

Albert Stickney Proposes Relying on Nonpartisan Statesmen of Integrity

Boston lawyer Albert Stickney advocated major constitutional changes in a book entitled *A True Republic* in 1879. His central objective was to create a system to secure in each governmental department the "best men" and see that they gave "their best work" (Stickney 1879, 15). In Stickney's view, the primary obstacle to such objectives was the political party system, which he linked to a system of limited terms in office. He associated both parties and fixed terms with political corruption. In contrast to contemporary advocates of parliamentary systems, however, Stickney opposed both the fusion of the legislative and executive branches and the parliamentary mechanism calling for a vote of no confidence. His emphasis on service "during good behavior"—public service carried out responsibly and with integrity—resembled Alexander Hamilton's speech at the Constitutional

Convention recommending such standards for the president, for senators, and for members of the judiciary.

Stickney began describing his own proposed reforms by focusing on the judiciary. Convinced that voters would take their cues from legal practitioners—unlike Alexander Hamilton and the other founders—Stickney favored making its members elective.

Stickney advocated lodging executive power in one man with the power to appoint all heads of departments. These heads would, in turn, exercise authority over their subordinates. The president would serve during good behavior, and would be responsible to the legislature, which could remove him only by a two-thirds vote. Stickney proposed reviving the Electoral College, which would continue to choose the president, as a deliberative nonpartisan body.

Initially, Stickney indicated that the real work of the legislature should not be making and revising laws—in contrast to the Founders, he believed that lawmaking was a task for judges—but rather "supervision and control" (Stickney 1879, 214). Specialists within departments would submit spending plans, and the legislature would review, approve, authorize, and supervise them. Stickney favored a legislature (presumably unicameral) of 500 men who would devote their full time to their duties and would not have fixed terms. The legislature would have "absolute control of the money" and power to make "*all necessary laws*" (a provision closer to the language of the original Virginia Plan than to the Constitutional Convention's final product with its long enumeration of congressional powers). Stickney also favored giving the legislature authority to remove any governmental official by a two-thirds vote, but no power over appointments (Stickney 1879, 218). Stickney advocated granting Congress greater authority over areas like marriage and divorce. Stickney proposed eliminating the executive veto, but in its place, he proposed that all legislation would have to be adopted by a two-thirds majority.

Stickney favored eliminating the vice presidency. In cases of presidential vacancies, he would allow the senior cabinet officer to serve until the Electoral College could choose a new president. Believing that only men with established reputations would be selected to legislative office, he thought that the average member would serve about 12 years. Freed from party influence, such legislators would be better able to serve the public. Stickney expressed confidence that such legislatures would exercise greater wisdom than the people could exercise on their own behalf.

Stickney thus advocated an aristocracy based on talent rather than heredity. In seeking to use the size of districts and the interests of representatives to protect the nation against factions, James Madison had observed in *Federalist* No. 10 that "it is in vain to say that enlightened statesmen will be able to adjust these clashing interests and render them all subservient to the public good. Enlightened statesmen will not always be at the helm" (Hamilton, Madison, and Jay 1961, 80). By contrast, Stickney sought to find a system that would continuously select men of good character to govern (Stickney 1879, 258).

Woodrow Wilson Seeks Parliamentary Reforms

No critic of the U.S. Constitution has achieved greater station or been quoted more than Thomas Woodrow Wilson (1856–1924). Son of a Presbyterian pastor and a graduate of Princeton University, Wilson published his first critique of the constitutional system in an article that appeared in the August 1879 issue of *International Review*. While in law school at the University of Virginia, Wilson expanded his views into a book, unpublished in his lifetime, entitled *Government by Debate: Being a Short View of Our National Government as It Is and as It Might Be*. Wilson did publish a book, *Congressional Government* (1885), that he wrote while a student at Johns Hopkins University before going on to a career as a professor and president of Princeton University (1902–1910), Democratic governor of New Jersey (1911–1913), and twenty-seventh president of the United States (1913–1921).

Wilson was highly influenced by the English model of government. Michael Lind has observed that it was the "semidemocratic parliamentary monarchy of the British kind, not democratic republicanism of the French or American kind, that became the dominant form of representative government for most of the new countries created between the American Civil War and World War I" (Lind 2004, 304), and this trend influenced Wilson. He was familiar with contemporary criticisms of the Constitution by Americans like Charles O'Conor and Gamaliel Bradford, and by the English writer Walter Bagehot (1826–1866), who used *The English Constitution*, first published in 1867 and again in 1873, to stress the problems of a governmental system of checks and balances (Bagehot 1928).

In his *Constitutional Government*, Wilson faulted the American system of checks and balances for being based on an outdated mechanistic (Isaac) Newtonian model of the universe rather than on a more organic Darwinian scheme. As Wilson stated, "government is not a machine but a living thing. It falls, not under the theory of the universe, but under the theory of organic life. It is accountable to Darwin, not to Newton" (Wilson 1908, 56).

Wilson also pointed in his 1879 essay to a spreading "fear that grave, perhaps radical, defects in our mode of government are militating against our liberty and prosperity." In Wilson's view, the legislative power must necessarily dominate in a democracy. Wilson nonetheless focused special criticism on the operation of Congress and on the decline of "statesmanship," problems to be accounted for by legislative "irresponsibility" rather than, as some had suggested, the liberalization of the franchise. Wilson believed that instead of a grand deliberative assembly, Congress had become a den of irresponsible committees, meeting in private and manipulated by a Speaker and other powerful committee chairmen.

Wilson believed it was necessary to take a step that the Constitutional Convention had rejected, namely, *"allowing some of the higher officers of State to occupy seats in the legislature."* He asserted that this should be combined with another parliamentary mechanism, namely "the principle of ministerial responsibility—that is, the resignation of the Cabinet upon the defeat of any important part of their plans" (Wilson 1966, 498). Wilson explained:

For, if Cabinet officers sit in Congress as official representatives of the Executive, this principle of responsibility must of necessity come sooner or later to be recognized. Experience would soon demonstrate the practical impossibility of their holding their seats, and continuing to represent the Administration, after they had found themselves unable to gain the consent of a majority to their policy. (Wilson 1966, 498)

Under Wilson's proposed system, the president would select cabinet officers from among congressmen of the majority party. These officers would then support their party's programs. The resulting public debate would serve to suppress legislative support of special interests, educate the public, and act as a school for statesmen. Wilson did not follow others who blamed the decline in statesmanship to the passing of grand issues like slavery. He blamed the decline on a system in which no legislator could speak responsibly and effectively for anyone but himself. If cabinet officers had real authority to speak on behalf of their party, they would have to develop principles, and with principles would come leaders. The present system, by contrast, could be summarized as follows: "*No leaders, no principles; no principles, no parties.*"

In his unpublished *Government by Debate*, Wilson elaborated further on his proposed cabinet government. He indicated that such a system would work better if the legislators' terms were increased to "six or eight years." The president too should "hold his office for a long term, if not during good behavior." Wilson apparently did not think the president would necessarily have to be from the same party as the legislative majority, although his veto power would necessarily "fall into disuse" in order to avoid triggering constant governmental crises. Moreover, Wilson did not call for the abolition of the Senate, but he expected its members to fall in line and heed the election results in the lower house when that house was dissolved and reelected.

Encouraged by the acclaim that his article in the *International Review* received, Wilson believed that public opinion could trigger constitutional change: "The press and the platform must be the pulpits from which to preach this new crusade. . . . National opinion must be invoked and the people called upon to act. If they can once be brought boldly and unequivocally to declare their will, they must prevail. None can stand against them" ("Government by Debate," 1966 [1882], 258).

Wilson clearly favored changes to push the United States government in the direction of parliamentary government (Weatherman 1994, 43–56). As one who believed that government should be organic rather than mechanical, however, Wilson placed increased emphasis on the role that the president might play given "his conspicuous position and the fact that opinion will hold him responsible for use of his patronage" (*Constitutional Government*, 215). Wilson reintroduced the practice, which Thomas Jefferson had abandoned, of delivering his State of the Union addresses directly to Congress. He thus became something of an ambiguous figure in the battle for constitutional reform. Wilson was an advocate for constitutional changes, but he also attempted to use the presidency as a lever for progressive re-forms that fell short of changes in constitutional language.

William B. Lawrence Seeks Constitutional Changes
Based on the Swiss Model

William B. Lawrence (1800–1881) joined advocates of parliamentary reform, but sought to establish these reforms while still preserving states' rights. An American diplomat who specialized in international law, Lawrence published an article in 1880 in which he critiqued the American political system and advocated reform. A critic of both congressional and presidential actions toward the South during Re-construction, Lawrence believed that those who wrote the U.S. Constitution erred when they deviated from the proposal in the original Virginia Plan, which would have provided for congressional selection of the president. He explained:

> The advantage of that system would have been not only to introduce that accord between the executive and legislative departments, the absence of which, in certain contingencies, may be so deleterious to the public interest, but would have referred the choice to those whose acquaintance with the pub-lic men of the country might have been expected to insure a safe selection. (Lawrence 1880, 405)

Lawrence further objected to the office of the vice president, the power that a uni-tary president had to advance the interests of one region of the country over that of others, and the national nominating conventions. In regards to the conventions, in fact, he declared that "it is impossible to conceive of any worse political machin-ery" (Lawrence 1880, 407).

Because of his concern for states' rights, Lawrence offered a peculiar wrinkle on the parliamentary model. He expressed a preference for the lesser-known Swiss federal model over the British unitary system. Lawrence elaborated:

> I know of nothing more suitable . . . than the present Constitution of Swit-zerland. The Swiss Constitution provides for the exercise of the supreme ex-ecutive authority by a Federal Council, composed of seven members, only one of whom can be chosen from the same canton. They are named for three years by the two Houses of the Legislature (Federal Assembly), denominated the National Council and Council of States, the former corresponding to the House of Representatives, the latter to the Senate, of the United States. From this Federal Council the President and Vice-President of the Confederation are annually appointed by a vote, also of the two Houses; but their functions are not materially different from those of the other members, and four mem-bers are required to sanction every deliberation. The duties of the Federal Council consist especially in superintending the national relations of the con-federation. (Lawrence 1880, 408–9)

Although Lawrence referenced Switzerland, it is probably more accurate to iden-tify John C. Calhoun as the intellectual godfather of his proposal. Calhoun openly endorsed the idea of a plural presidency whose members would represent the nation's varied geographical districts.

Henry Lockwood Calls for Replacing the Presidency with a Council Appointed by Congress

Henry Lockwood (1839–1902), a New York lawyer and publicist, published a best-selling book in 1884 with the fairly straightforward title of *The Abolition of the Presidency*. Like Lawrence, Lockwood preferred a chief executive who was wholly responsible to Congress. Criticizing the current president as an anomalous "elective king in a republic" (Lockwood 1884, 22), Lockwood went on to attack: the country's method of presidential selection (chapter 3); the system of fixed terms of office (chapter 4); the president's power as commander-in-chief (chapter 5); the president's authority to issue reprieves and pardons and to negotiate treaties (chapter 6); the president's power of appointment and removal (chapter 7); the president's veto power (chapter 8); the weakness of the impeachment check (chapter 9); the subservience of the cabinet to the president (chapter 10); the president's power to make and execute policy independent of the legislature (chapter 22); and the weakness of the system used to nominate presidents (chapter 12). Lockwood believed that the Constitution of the Confederate States of America had shared similar faults.

Lockwood believed that America's experience with the presidency had ironically pointed the nation back in the direction of monarchy from which it had rebelled. He thus joined others who extolled the British Constitution over that of the American one, while questioning the typical distinctions that scholars had drawn between written and unwritten documents:

> We speak of the unwritten Constitution of Great Britain, and the written one of this country. Practically, ours is unwritten, while theirs is written. Theirs is stable and defined; ours unsettled and conflicting. Theirs is the growth of ages, with its experiences, facts and laws written in unambiguous terms; ours has been amended fifteen times, and there are as many different interpretations of it as there are parties and factions. No one disputes about the power and authority of the various branches of the British Constitution; everyone differs as to the interpretation to be put upon ours. (Lockwood 1884, 134)

Lockwood especially admired what he believed to be Britain's "complete and harmonious blending of the legislative and the Executive" (Lockwood 1884, 274). In a theme that would again become familiar at the end of the twentieth century, Lockwood extended his criticisms to the states and the U.S. Senate. Calling the Senate "the strongest fortress of the 'residuary sovereignty' of the States" (Lockwood 1884, 283), Lockwood indicted what he believed to be the unrepresentative nature of the institution, and its baneful influence on representation in the Electoral College.

Lockwood detailed his own plan in his concluding chapter. He proposed completely abolishing the presidency and vesting "[t]he supreme power of legislating and executing all laws of the United States" in a unicameral Congress "subject . . .

to the right of the Executive Council . . . at any time they shall elect, to dissolve Congress upon an issue framed and appeal to the people" (Lockwood 1884, 302). The council, or cabinet, appointed by Congress and headed by the Secretary of State, "shall be entitled to seats in Congress, have the right to debate, and also power to initiate legislation" and would be accountable to it (Lockwood 1884, 303). Similarly, a reconstituted judicial branch would be "confined and limited to defining, expounding, interpreting, and explaining the laws and intent of Congress" (Lockwood 1884, 304). If the legislature disapproved of council proposals, the council must either resign or appeal to the people, who would decide between them.

Although proposals for parliamentary government would continue to proliferate, the power of the presidency continued to grow rather than to shrink. In time the Seventeenth Amendment provided for direct election of U.S. senators, but few of Lockwood's other proposals prevailed.

Isaac Rice Advocates Vesting Primary Power in Congress and a Cabinet

Cabinet government continued to appeal to a number of Lockwood's educated contemporaries, including Isaac L. Rice (1850–1915). Rice was a Bavarian-born immigrant and graduate of Columbia Law School who became a librarian for its newly formed School of Political Science (he later became a successful lawyer, inventor, and businessman). In 1884, Rice published an article in *Century Magazine* in which he advanced his views on the need for constitutional revision. Rice thought that the existing government of separated powers was both "weak and irresponsible" (Rice 1884, 534). Checks on legislative power had led legislators to spend their time attempting to make money and perpetuate themselves in office. This, in turn, led to the dominance of special interests.

Rice traced these problems back to America's Founding Fathers and Montesquieu, the famous French political philosopher of the Age of Enlightenment. Whereas they had believed that concentrated power was the essence of despotism, Rice argued that the real distinction between despotic and nondespotic forms of government "is not the union of powers, but the fact that these powers united in a single person are exercised without any responsibility to the governed" (Rice 1884, 537). Further praising the British system, which Rice believed that Montesquieu had misunderstood, Rice continued:

Likewise, the conception of a government has grown from that of a class, depending on an individual sovereign, and consequently his tool, into the nobler conception of an agency entrusted with the expression of the general will, of servants under the duty to exercise it. And a fear of its servants is unworthy of a great people; nay, more, it is a factitious sentiment pernicious to the commonwealth. (Rice 1884, 538)

Rice believed that this more enlightened conception of government would weaken the influence of concentrated economic power over legislators, and their motivations for a life of public service would improve accordingly. With a renewed sense of responsibility, the government would be able to address problems of commerce, taxation, and the tariff as well as labor/management conflicts.

Rice advanced three measures to effectuate reform. The first would increase the power of Congress not only among the three branches but also within the federal system. "Congress must be enabled to settle all questions of national concern," he wrote, "and must have the range of the objects under its dominion extended sufficiently to prevent any petty local legislature from being able to thwart the will and endanger the welfare of the whole people" (Rice 1884, 540). Rice expressed specific concern that powerful industries were taking advantage of existing state boundaries to thwart effective national regulation of transportation and commerce.

Second, Rice proposed ending the separation of legislative and executive powers by making cabinet officers members of Congress and by selecting one such officer—presumably a prime minister or premier, though Rice did not use either term—and fixing upon him "the ultimate responsibility to the whole country for all the action and inaction of both Congress and the administration" (Rice 1884, 540). Third, Rice advocated allowing Congress to be the ultimate judge of the constitutionality of its actions. As the title of his article and the scope of his proposed reforms suggested, Rice thought that the reforms were appropriate work for a constitutional convention.

Caspar Hopkins Adds a Racial and Paranoid Dimension to Constitutional Reform Plans

Caspar Hopkins (1826–1896) advocated constitutional change in an article that he published in 1885 in *Overland Monthly*, a California-based magazine. A pioneer, businessman, author, and former president of the California Immigration Union, Hopkins proposed 10 eclectic changes to the U.S. Constitution. The first two called for expanding congressional jurisdiction and restricting existing state jurisdiction over a variety of civil matters, including marriage, education, and debt collection. Likewise, his third measure would extend judicial jurisdiction over all claims against the United States—but, perhaps with a view to reining in corruption, Hopkins proposed restricting congressional legislation to general matters rather than allowing for private bills, which addressed specific individuals.

Like Woodrow Wilson, Hopkins favored allowing cabinet members to be appointed from Congress and remain members of that legislative body. To further elevate the tone and quality of Congress, Hopkins endorsed provisions that would restrict immigrants from membership in the House and provide special education for newly elected members of Congress.

Lest it appear that Hopkins was simply parroting earlier reformers who favored expanded federal powers exercised through a parliamentary system, Hopkins advocated making the U.S. Senate a clear representative of the interests of wealthy Americans. He wanted to restrict voting for senator to men who earned more than $100,000 a year. Hopkins believed that a group that others would in time classify as a "millionaires' club" would be less corrupt if it were directly representing those of wealth rather than being influenced by bribes.

Hopkins further proposed to limit immigration to those with "a certain degree of education, and some art or profession, or sufficient property to insure them a living" and to restrict voting rights to men who were native born (Hopkins 1885, 388). Hopkins also favored abolishing programs that treated Native American Indians paternalistically. In typical Social Darwinistic language, Hopkins observed that "the best of them would hail such a change with acclamation, and would soon become good citizens; the worst would soon die out, as lazy whites and negroes perish, without exciting the compassionate sensibilities of Boston or Chautauqua," two late-nineteenth-century centers of progressive political reform (Hopkins 1885, 396).

Finally, Hopkins called for changing national terms of office. Under his proposals, members of the House would serve for 6 years, the president for 8, and senators for 10. Hopkins would further restrict the electoral re-eligibility of any elected official with the power of patronage. Hopkins also proposed to eliminate the Electoral College and create two or three vice presidents to deal with issues of presidential succession.

Like some Progressive spokesmen who would follow, Hopkins combined dreams of constitutional reform with paranoia about the unlikelihood of effectively assimilating and socializing foreigners. He also expressed fear that any effort to reform the Constitution would be hijacked by dangerous elements:

> The country is full of communists, socialists, advocates of woman suffrage, agrarians, and cranks, whose every effort would be concentrated upon such an opportunity to realize their peculiar views in the fundamental law. To attempt a revision, therefore, would be full of peril and probabilities of failure. (Hopkins 1885, 398)

Charles O'Conor Proposes a Rotating Presidency and Other Eclectic Constitutional Changes

Charles O'Conor (1804–1888) was a successful New York attorney and one-time defender of both the Southern cause and of Jefferson Davis. O'Conor called for sweeping constitutional change in a speech before the New York Historical Society (1877) and in a later encyclopedia article (1881).

O'Conor believed that modern government had bred both extensive corruption and redundancy of duties. O'Conor argued that both state and national legislatures should be limited to adopting general laws, that delegates should all be chosen from multimember districts, and that government debt should be prohibited. He further opposed governmental coining of money and issuing of currency, and he favored abolishing tariffs and duties and providing that "every governmental outlay" would be "immediately defrayed by the taxpayers" (O'Conor 1877, 1316). The attorney thought that these measures might reduce the nation's appetite for war and foreign conquest. O'Conor further claimed that reducing Congress and state legislatures to unicameral bodies might reduce the volume of needless legislation.

One of O'Conor's boldest proposals was to eliminate the office of the presidency as a source of national ambition by providing that the office should "be filled by lot every month from the representative body" of Congress (O'Conor 1877, 34). He also regarded the franchise—the vote—to be a "duty" to be borne rather than a "private right of personal privilege" (O'Conor 1877, 6). O'Conor's proposed reforms in this area included limiting the franchise, eliminating the secret ballot, and reducing the number of elected officials.

As a Roman Catholic, O'Conor feared that public schools were being used as tools of religious indoctrination. Like modern defenders of the separation of church and state, he favored keeping such matters private. He also believed that federal judges selected by states might better preserve state autonomy. O'Conor thought that the invention of the telegraph had made it possible to eliminate the diplomatic corps. He opposed laws that limited the working hours of employees, criticizing them as intrusions on "freedom of contract"—the right of individuals and corporations to negotiate contracts without governmental restrictions.

Although O'Conor's proposal to fill the presidency with rotating members of Congress suggested that he favored reforms in a parliamentary direction, he warned that "instead of adopting implicitly English forms, we should extract from them so much of their spirit as is appropriate to our situation" and that the United States should "drink charily at the fountains of European experience" (O'Conor 1877, 18). A sympathetic commentator observed that although O'Conor had identified many important problems, "when he comes to suggest the remedies for these evils, we are impressed by the conviction that the qualities that make a great lawyer do not necessarily make a statesman" (Daly 1885, 533).

Edward Bellamy Foresees a Socialized World without War

Few constitutional reform proposals were as widely read as the ones that Edward Bellamy (1850–1898) presented in an 1888 novel entitled *Looking Backward*. The son of a Baptist minister, Bellamy was a journalist and a cousin of Francis Bellamy, the Baptist minister and socialist who drafted the Pledge of Allegiance to the American flag. Bellamy's utopian novel was designed to portray a nation—and indeed a world—that had adopted a socialistic system, solved the problems of labor and management, and thereby created prosperity and peace. The novel sold more than half a million copies in the United States and was also popular abroad, where it was translated into numerous other languages.

The novel centered on a character named Julian West, who is hypnotized in a shelter in his Boston home in 1887 and is not awakened until 2000. Upon regaining consciousness, a doctor named Leete and his family update West on the tremendous progress that civilization had made over the past century. They attribute this progress to a peaceful governmental takeover of all industries and the establishment of an industrial army in which all men and women (who received generous maternity leaves) participated from ages 21 to 45. In this society, everyone capable of working begins with manual labor and then chooses occupations according to their desires and national needs. All wages are equalized in this world, but those in dangerous or otherwise undesirable jobs work fewer hours. Individuals receive credits through which they can purchase the goods they need in giant government stores. The system thus utilizes the benefits of economies of scale for public rather than private purposes. The family explains to West how the increased prosperity from these policies cut crime and reduced the desire for war. Bellamy's novel also anticipated continuing improvements in technology, such as telephone access in every home.

Although Bellamy did not include a sample constitution in *Looking Backward*, his novel did describe a number of features of the imaginary government. The nation's industries were divided into 10 great departments corresponding to groups of allied industries, the heads of which were considered to be "the agents and servants of the people" (Bellamy 1888, 193). The president was the head of the industrial army, which was organized by a series of ranks much like that of the military. Rather than being chosen by those who work under him, however, the president was chosen by those who had retired at 45. Generals below him were chosen in a similar manner. The president supervised an inspectorate entrusted with investigating "all complaints or information as to defects in goods, insolence or inefficiency of officials, or dereliction of any sort in the public service" (Bellamy 1888, 201). Bellamy anticipated that the president would typically be elected at the age of 50 (after retirement) and that a "national Congress" (Bellamy 1888, 201), otherwise undescribed, would either approve or disapprove of his work. If the former, he could be reappointed for another five-year term. Curiously, "the members of the liberal professions, the doctors and teachers, as well as the artists and men of letters" (Bellamy 1888, 202), who were exempt from the industrial army, were also ineligible for the presidency since they did not come up through the industrial ranks.

Criminals in Bellamy's future world were considered to be examples of atavistic behavior and were treated in hospitals. Since trials centered on ascertaining the truth, lawyers and juries were eliminated. Individuals without legal backgrounds were responsible for arguing both sides of cases and passing judgment. The president appointed judges from among retirees for single terms of five years (Bellamy 1888, 215). Lower judges selected members of the Supreme Court (Bellamy 1888, 215).

Since the national government administered the industrial army, state governments were eliminated. Municipal governments were maintained, however, to look after the interests of local communities. The socialist utopia imagined by Bellamy also dispensed with a military, bankers, and other financial specialists. Since there was little need for new legislation, Congress rarely convened—and when it did, it had to wait for action by the next session "lest anything be done hastily" (Bellamy 1888, 217–19, 238).

Bellamy's political system provided free universal education, and domestic tasks like preparing food and washing clothes were carried out by the industrial army. Although Bellamy's portrait of women was somewhat paternalistic, he described a society that treated women as men's equals. Moreover, he believed that the race would improve as individuals were able to choose mates based on love rather than on financial needs (Bellamy 1888, 279).

Doctor Leete did not explain to West in great detail how the new system was instituted except to say that it had been brought about peacefully by members of the National Party. He indicated that "followers of the red flag . . . had nothing to do with it except to hinder it" (Bellamy 1888, 264), and even suggested that corporate owners had paid such rabble-rousers to hide the real cause of industrial woes from the people.

Bellamy used millennial language and stressed the brotherhood of man and the fatherhood of God throughout his novel. If he did not present a blueprint for a new constitution, he did at least provide an outline of what a new government might resemble. The novel inspired more than 40 other novels in the United States and another dozen in Europe (Guarneri 2008, 4). In 1897, Bellamy himself published a sequel to *Looking Backward* entitled *Equality*, but it did not garner the same level of success as his earlier work.

James C. West Authors a Populistic Revision of the Constitution

James C. West (?–1946) of Springfield, Missouri, self-published a book proposing a new constitution in 1890. West followed the outline of the original document of 7 articles and 14 amendments while proposing a number of changes. Although the only known original copy was donated to the Library of Congress by West, it was later reprinted in Steven R. Boyd's *Alternative Constitutions for the United States* (Boyd 1992, 69–80).

West was a clerk, a newspaper editor, and a prosecuting attorney. His book reflected strong populist beliefs in its emphasis on democracy and its distrust of corporations and accumulated capital. In outlining the legislative branch, West proposed limiting members of the House to those who were native born and guaranteeing the appointment of at least one representative for every 175,000 persons. He proposed excluding individuals who were worth more than $25,000 from serving in the House and individuals who were worth more than $50,000 from serving in the Senate. Limiting senators to four-year terms, West also recommended that anyone serving in Congress first labor for at least five years as an adult in an agricultural or mechanical job. West specified that members of Congress take an oath to seek "the greatest good of the greatest number" and swear not to "approve of anything contrary to the spirit of the Constitution, either express or implied" or risk "the vengeance of God [who is not mentioned in the current U.S. Constitution] . . . and the universal detestation of mankind" (quoted in Boyd 1992, 74). West also endorsed limiting the wages of members of Congress to 15 times that of laboring farmhands, and permitted the House alone to override presidential vetoes of finance bills.

In enumerating the powers of Congress, West endorsed restricting the collection of surplus revenue but favored taxes on "the sumptuousness of the people," as well as taxes on land and income (the U.S. Supreme Court ruled taxation of income to be unconstitutional the same year that West published his book, but the passage of the Sixteenth Amendment in 1913 established Congress's right to levy a federal income tax). West also advocated maintaining circulating capital at $40 a person and making it a crime for persons or corporations to "engage in any pool, combine trust or rebate system" (Boyd 1992, 78). Like Hopkins, West wanted Congress to take a firmer hand in limiting immigration.

West sought to limit the president's salary to no more than 125 times that of the average wage for a laboring farmhand. He further hoped to entrench his own proposals by preventing them from being amended by anything less than a three-fourths vote of the entire House and ratification by a general election. Under West's reforms, by contrast, only the former mechanism would be required to amend the Constitution of 1787.

Populists Consider Calling Another Constitutional Convention

One of the strongest movements for reform from this era came from the Populists. This movement was concentrated among farming communities in the American Midwest, where many people believed that railroads and other monopolies had unfairly raised prices that were hurting family farms. In 1896, Populists and Democrats would join forces in nominating William Jennings Bryan for president.

Attendees at the Iowa Populist State Convention, which met in Des Moines in September of 1894, considered a motion for "a mass convention of the American people to assemble in . . . Des Moines on the first Monday in December, 1894, to consider the necessary amendment of the fundamental law of the land" (quoted in Haynes 1919, 358). Although the preamble to this resolution praised the original Constitution, it further stated that "it is now essentially a product of a by-gone age, too inflexible for the varied conditions of modern life, warped, blurred and burdened by judicial construction, and practically not open to amendment except as the result of war or supreme, universal and protracted effort" (Haynes 1919, 358). The resolution went on to propose:

> the adoption of a comprehensive amendment to the federal constitution, which shall reenact all valuable portions of the constitution of 1789 as subsequently amended and incorporate therein those necessary reforms which are not constitutionally impracticable, including elective United States senators, a single term of the presidency, determined by popular vote, an elective supreme court holding office for a defined term, with similar subordinate courts, direct legislation by the people through the initiative and referendum, and such broad extensions of popular rights as shall set the people absolutely free to govern themselves in their own way and to conduct in their national or local capacity such industries as may be withdrawn by monopoly from individual competition, and such other enterprises as may meet the public approval as properly subject to popular conduct. (Quoted in Haynes 1919, 357)

Although the resolution was favored by General James Weaver, who represented Iowa in the U.S. House of Representatives (1881–1889) and was the Populists' presidential nominee in 1892, the measure was tabled. However, the Progressive Party would call for many of these same reforms in the following two decades.

Frederick Upham Adams Presents His Populist and Socialist Ideas in a Novel

Frederick Upham Adams (1859–1921), an inventor, engineer, and labor editor of the *Chicago Tribune*, presented his proposed Constitution in a utopian novel, *President John Smith* (1896), which sold more than 750,000 copies. The protagonist of the novel was a one-time federal judge who ran for president as a populist, fell one vote short in the Electoral College, and then called a convention that met in Omaha, Nebraska, to write a new constitution under which he served as the first president. It was based on majority rule, socialism, and other populist themes.

Adams's constitution contained eight articles, the first of which called for a president selected by popular election (by men) and subject to recall. If the president died, he would be temporarily replaced by the secretary of state until a special election could be called.

Article II provided for a cabinet of 12 officers—including a superintendent of education—popularly elected and also subject to recall. This cabinet would take over some of the functions of the Senate (like ratifying treaties by a two-thirds vote), which would be eliminated.

Article III called for a unicameral congress of 200 members. Fifty members could submit legislation to the people for consideration through referenda.

Article IV outlined provisions for a Supreme Court of five members, appointed by the president, approved by the people, and subject to retirement by a popular majority vote. The justices would be required to advise Congress on how to make proposed legislation constitutional rather than relying on judicial review of national laws (judicial review would be preserved for state and local laws, however).

Article V granted Congress the power to value the dollar on "the average productivity of one hour's work" (Boyd 1992, 104). Articles VI and VII would allow the government to use its power of eminent domain to take over unoccupied land and to socialize basic industries.

Article VIII allowed the people to repeal, revise, or amend the constitution by majority vote. The constitution did not contain a bill of rights or the definition of citizenship that Section 1 of the Fourteenth Amendment currently provides.

Adams asked readers of his novel to consider forming a "Majority Rule Club" in their vicinity, and he further advocated his ideas in a socialist magazine that he renamed the *New Times*. By the turn of the century, however, he had apparently abandoned his efforts to garner support for such a constitution (Boyd 1992, 96).

Henry O. Morris Proposes a Populistic and Socialistic Constitution

In 1897 a socialist-leaning press published *Waiting for the Signal*, a novel by an otherwise obscure individual named Henry O. Morris. The characters in the novel, which went into at least three editions, included reporters Wesley Stearns and John McDermott and Chicago *Biograph* newspaper owner Adam Short, who is sympathetic to the working class and concerned about the moral degradation of the plutocrats.

Set immediately after William McKinley's election of 1896, workers initiate a revolution that results in little bloodshed except in New York City, which is almost completely burned by those trying to take advantage of the chaos. The people call a convention, where Ignatius Donnelly, a contemporary populist candidate, heads a committee that writes a new declaration of independence. The convention also produces a new constitution, under which William J. Lyon of Nebraska—a character very similar to the real-life Populist icon William Jennings Bryan—is nominated and elected president, replacing the military leader who oversaw the revolution. Adoption of the new constitution ushers in an era of peace and prosperity that haunts European plutocrats.

Although Morris's fictional constitution largely kept the structure of the existing government in place, he proposed numerous changes. He guaranteed each state at least three members in the House of Representatives and lessened the power of the Speaker of the House to retard the progress of legislation. He imposed 12-year term limits on members of Congress and allowed both houses of Congress to override presidential vetoes by majority vote. Morris also would allow Congress to impose income taxes and would provide for electing senators and the president by a popular vote, with the latter serving for a single eight-year term.

Morris's constitution embodied a number of socialist features. The national government would take over most of the means of production, destroy monopolies and trusts, and limit individual wealth.

Congress would establish uniform codes of civil and criminal procedure, and treat Native-American Indians like other citizens. In a theme that he might have borrowed from Caspar Hopkins (or simply been part of the climate of the day), Morris, who was suspicious of both Jews and foreigners, proposed restricting immigration privileges to "the healthy, moral, intelligent, and self-supporting" (Morris 1897, 344).

Morris favored expanding individual rights. He devoted special attention to freedom of speech and press. The fictional government he crafted limited the power of courts to issue injunctions, which were often used in the late nineteenth century to prevent strikes, and to imprison individuals who violated court orders without a jury trial.

Morris proposed allowing a majority of both houses of Congress to propose amendments or call a convention. He would further allow a majority of the state legislatures to ratify such amendments. In the preface to his third edition, Morris responded to letters he had received on the timing of his fictional revolution by saying that "the revolution is sure to come—it is on the way. I leave the reader to guess when the storm will burst" (Morris 1897, ix).

Goldwin Smith Proposes Changes to Tame "Bryanism" and Protect the Anglo-Saxon Heritage

Whereas numerous advocates of constitutional change from this period proposed parliamentary reform to initiate democratic reform, Goldwin Smith (1823–1910) suggested in an 1898 article called "Is the Constitution Outworn?" that such reform might actually help tame the threat of "Bryanism" (Populism). Born in England, Smith had served as a barrister and an Oxford professor before becoming a professor at Cornell. Although Smith was concerned about the growing gap between the rich and the poor, he believed that the forces that Bryan and Populism represented were a "socialist element . . . directly subversive of the principle of self-help and freedom of acquisition on which American institutions are founded" (Smith 1898, 257). He further observed that the nation was facing the challenge of revolutionary movements as well as "[s]exual revolution and political feminism" (Smith 1898, 258), which had arrived from Europe at a time of declining religious faith, and increased antagonism among classes.

Smith believed that presidential powers had grown "monarchical" and that this trend had raised the stakes in presidential contests that did not feature the best possible candidates. He thought that the Senate was abusing its power to confirm candidates, that Congress was admitting states into the union prematurely, that House terms needed to be lengthened, and that the power of the Senate to obstruct legislation should be restricted.

Consistent with his advocacy of a more parliamentary form of government, Smith wanted responsible cabinet officers to be represented within Congress. He thought that responsible party government would be better than vesting such power in the House Speaker and in congressional committees.

Smith feared that if populists were elected, they might appoint individuals to the Supreme Court who might undercut property interests. He thought that the power of the court was inadequately restricted because of the difficulty of the current constitutional amending process.

Smith also proposed repealing the Fifteenth Amendment, which granted African American men the right to vote. This position was not taken to disenfranchise African Americans, but rather a recognition of the fact that states in the South had effectively found ways to bypass its provisions and keep African Americans from voting. However, Smith's calls to reform the country's voting and immigration laws showed his strong prejudice in favor of what he considered to be America's Anglo-Saxon heritage. Smith also favored the adoption of constitutional provisions to limit tariffs, a reconsideration of congressional taxing powers, and provision for the government of U.S. dependencies.

Summary and Analysis

The proposals from this period present a deep and persistent apprehension over the quality of both state and national legislation, with special concerns raised about legislators' ties to interest groups and the increasing gap between the rich and the poor. Some reformers wanted to move the nation in a more socialistic direction, while others hoped to preserve the system of free enterprise. A number of the reformers who advocated an expansion of congressional powers also wanted to trim the powers of the states. Some reformers wanted the president to take the lead in initiating reforms. Others called for a plural executive, or for one or another variant of parliamentary government that would make the president the servant of

Congress and/or permit members of the cabinet to be drawn from, to serve in, or to appear before that body.

A number of reformers took special aim at the Senate, which they believed stood in the way of the popular will, and the national nominating conventions, which they connected to increased partisanship. Several reformers wanted to rein in excessive judicial power, taking special aim at the courts' existing power to invalidate legislation that judges considered to be unconstitutional. Although some reformers favored civil liberties and women's rights, others ignored or feared the latter movement. Some reformers even reflected an ugly underbelly of racist paranoia in their proposals regarding immigration policy and the enfranchisement of African Americans.

References

Adams, Frederick U. 1896. *President John Smith: The Story of a Peaceful Revolution*. Chicago: Charles H. Kerr & Company. Reprint. New York: Arno Press, 1970.

Ames, Herman. 1896. *The Proposed Amendments to the Constitution of the United States during the First Century of Its History*. Reprint, New York: Burt Franklin, 1970.

Arling, Emanie. 1972. *The Terrible Siren: Victoria Woodhull*. New York: Arno Press.

Bagehot, Walter. 1928. *The English Constitution*. London: Oxford University Press, World's Classics Edition.

Bellamy, Edward. 1888. *Looking Backward*. Reprint. New York: Magnum Books, 1968.

Boyd, Steven R., ed. 1992. *Alternative Constitutions for the United States: A Documentary History*. Westport, CT: Greenwood Press.

Crosby, Oscar T. 1909. *A Constitution for the United States of the World*. Warrenton, VA: n.p.

Daly, C.P. 1885. "Charles O'Conor, His Professional Life and Character." *Magazine of American History* 13 (June): 833.

Guarneri, Carl J. 2008. "An American Utopia and Its Global Audiences: Transnational Perspectives on Edward Bellamy's Looking Backward." *Utopian Studies* 19, 2 (June): 147.

Hamilton, Alexander, James Madison, and John Jay. 1961. *The Federalist Papers*. Reprint. New York: New American Library.

Haynes, Fred Emory. 1919. *James Baird Weaver*. Iowa City: State Historical Society of Iowa.

Hopkins, Caspar T. 1885. "Thoughts toward Revising the Federal Constitution." *Overland Monthly* 6 (October): 388–98.

Lawrence, William B. 1880. "The Monarchical Principle in Our Constitution." *North American Review* 288 (November): 385–409.

Lind, Michael. 2004. *What Lincoln Believed: The Values and Convictions of America's Greatest President*. New York: Doubleday.

Lockwood, Henry C. 1884. *The Abolition of the Presidency*. New York: R. Worthington. Reprint. Farmingdale, NY: Darbor Social Science Publications, 1978.

Marberry, M. W. 1967. *Vicky: A Biography of Victoria C. Woodhull*. New York: Funk and Wagnalls.

McHenry, Robert, ed. 1980. *Liberty's Women*. Springfield, MA: G. and C. Merriam.

Morris, Henry O. 1897. *Waiting for the Signal, a Novel*. Chicago: Schulte.

Musmanno, M. A. 1929. Proposed Amendments to the Constitution. Washington, DC: U.S. Government Printing Office.

O'Conor, Charles. 1881. "Democracy." In *Johnson's New Universal Cyclopaedia: A Treasury of Scientific and Popular Treasure of Useful Knowledge*. Vol. 1, Part 2. New York: A. J. Johnson.

O'Conor, Charles. 1877. *Address by Charles O'Conor Delivered before the New York Historical Society at the Academy of Music, May 8*. New York: Anson D. F. Randolph.

Rice, Isaac. 1884. "Work for a Constitutional Convention." *Century Magazine* 28 (August): 534–40.

Smith, Goldwin. 1906. "Chief-Justice Clark on the Defects of the American Constitution." *North American Review* 183 (November 2): 850.

Smith, Goldwin. 1898. "Is the Constitution Outworn?" *North American Review* 166 (March): 257–67.

Stern, Madeline B., ed. 1974. *The Victoria Woodhull Reader*. Weston, MA: M & S Press.

Stickney, Albert. 1879. *A True Republic*. New York: Harper and Brothers.

Weatherman, Donald V. 1994. *Endangered Guardians: Party Reform within a Constitutional System*. Lanham, MD: Rowman & Littlefield.

Wilson, Woodrow. 1966. "Cabinet Government in the United States." In *The Papers of Woodrow Wilson*, vol. 1, edited by Arthur S. Link. Princeton, NJ: Princeton University Press.

Wilson, Woodrow. 1908. *Constitutional Government in the United States*. Reprint. New York: Columbia University Press, 1961.

Wilson, Woodrow. 1885. *Congressional Government: A Study in American Politics*. Boston: Houghton Mifflin.

Wilson, Woodrow. 1882. "Government by Debate: Being a Short View of Our National Government as It Is and as It Might Be." Reprint. In *The Papers of Woodrow Wilson*, vol. 2, edited by Arthur S. Link, 149–275. Princeton, NJ: Princeton University Press, 1966.

Wilson, Woodrow. 1879. "Cabinet Government in the United States." Reprint. In *The Papers of Woodrow Wilson*, vol. 1, edited by Arthur S. Link, 493–510. Princeton, NJ: Princeton University Press, 1966.

CHAPTER 5

Proposals Occasioned by Progressivism and World War I

In 1898, America engaged in a war with Spain and acquired foreign territories around the globe. Despite Prohibition and movements on behalf of woman's suffrage and defenses of parliamentary democracy, the nation experienced a long period from 1865 to 1913 during which the states did not ratify any proposed amendments (Vile 1992, 137). This was, however, followed by the ratification of the Sixteenth through Nineteenth Amendments in relatively short order (1913–1919).

The years of the Progressive movement somewhat overlap with those of the Populist movement, and scholars differ on the exact dates the Progressive Era began and ended. The Progressive Era, though, is generally associated with the presidencies of Theodore Roosevelt (1901–1909) and Woodrow Wilson (1913–1921). World War I largely brought this movement to an end.

An Anarchist Constitution

A remarkable proposal for a new constitution from this time period is found in a book entitled *The Anarchist Constitution*, published in 1903, the same year that Congress banned immigrating anarchists under the Anarchist Exclusion Act (Goldstein 1974, 58). It was published by the Radical Publishing Company in San Francisco and attributed to "D. I. Sturber," which appears to be a word play indicating how the author thought he might be viewed. At several points in the narrative, he observed that anarchists felt that they were being unfairly tarnished as a group for the actions of Leon Czolgosz, the anarchist who assassinated President William McKinley in 1901.

If the title of the book seems oxymoronic, it also seems ironic that the anarchist constitution would contain 225 sections and run over 50 printed pages (with an additional chapter of explanation). The author begins with a parable of John Doe, an individual who continues to patch pants (meant to represent the existing U.S. Constitution) handed down by his male predecessors, all of whom have the same name. Reflecting the author's atheist perspective, it further attempts to trace the evolution of belief in God as an attempt to control the masses. The author claimed that anarchists were not opposed to a few laws that did not materially infringe on the rights of others, "provided that they are really *necessary*" (Sturber 1903, 24). He added that the entire anarchist constitution could be summarized as: "All law whatsoever is hereby repealed. But notwithstanding, the social structure for the execution of public policy and management of public affairs shall be continued as heretofore. But, notwithstanding . . . the rights of man shall not be materially infringed upon any more than is absolutely necessary" (Sturber 1903, 25).

The preamble of the anarchist constitution stated that the document's goals were to reach "a more advanced state of society," provide "a greater measure of justice and freedom," guarantee everyone "an opportunity to labor, and enjoy the fruits of their labor," and the like. Section 1 repealed all prior laws, but Section 2 reestablished a bicameral congress and a president and Section 8 provided for the continuation of local governing bodies (Sturber 1903, 26–7). Indeed, Section 8 went into great detail about the governance of local bodies, specifying duties for the county clerk, the county registrar of voters, the sheriff, the mayor, and other local officials.

A number of elements of the proposed constitution provided for public welfare. Section 19 provided that state legislatures "shall provide for the most efficient public school system possible and all books used therein shall be free of cost to the pupils" (Sturber 1903, 30). Sections 20 and 21 provided for the United States to engage in businesses that would benefit the public. Sections 30 and 31 provided for committees of Congress to decide on compensation for inventors and authors in place of the existing patent and copyright systems (Sturber 1903, 31). The constitution went into elaborate detail about jury trials, including payment to jurors, the size of juries, the majorities needed, and automatic appeals. Section 73 prohibited capital punishment and Section 74 outlawed the whipping post. Section 85 attempted to define the age of consent for females (no less than 14 years), while Section 89 provided that no children would be classified as illegitimate. Marriage was declared "to be for the purpose of giving paternity to children and not for the purpose of compelling people to live together against their will" (Sturber 1903, 45). Section 99 provided that the possessions of individuals who died without a living spouse or child would go into an "Orphans's Trust Fund" (Sturber 1903, 47). Section 102 further provided that each town and city would provide free medical care.

Section 108 provided religious freedom to those who did not receive gain from their work. Section 109 provided for payments for the support of children, while Section 114 outlawed corporations and Section 115 outlawed any franchises or special privileges. As if to complete state support from cradle to grave, Section 117 provided that towns and cities would pay for burial expenses.

Section 118 outlawed any titles to land or the natural elements while Section 119 eliminated all duties. Section 141 provided that the terms of members of the House would be for six years, and other sections set term lengths for state officials. Sections 158–62 outlined the powers of Congress, which included a provision whereby Congress would call a popular referendum to decide whether the nation should or should not engage in war. Section 169 authorized the president to dismiss cabinet officials with the exception of the postmaster general, who would remain under congressional supervision.

Section 173 provided for a Supreme Court of not more than 13 persons. Sections 180 through 188 largely reiterated existing provisions in the federal bill of rights. Section 205 required permission from the president from any individuals other than whites to "be admitted into the territory of the United States" (Sturber 1903, 65). It further provided that all "Mongolians" must register with the government or be deported within 60 days (Sturber 1903, 66).

Section 213 provided for an eight-hour working day. Section 221 limited all laws to a single subject, whereas Section 222 provided for a five-year automatic sunset provision for all U.S. laws. Section 224 provided for congressional proposals to be subject to presidential veto, but also gave Congress the authority to override such vetoes. Under the terms of Section 225, voters would decide every four years whether to perpetuate the constitution or not.

Some of the author's more interesting commentary included his declaration that most criminals could better be treated by hospitals than by prisons (Sturber 1903, 73); his notion that all should have the right to counsel regardless of ability to pay (Sturber 1903, 78); his concern over the abuse of vagrancy laws (Sturber 1903, 80–1); and his anti-Catholicism, which seemed largely based on his perception that "because it is the most powerful organization on the face of the earth," it was "therefore the most baneful" (Sturber 1903, 88). After referencing statements in the Declaration of Independence that declared that all were created equal, that government rested upon popular consent, and that people had a right to abolish or alter their government, the author observed that "the most anarchistic statements I have ever made have been simple quotations from this same Declaration of Independence" (Sturber 1903, 111).

In his concluding remarks, the author harkened back to the parable that he had used to introduce his anarchist constitution:

> Give the people a chance to vote on whether or not to do away with the old social compact and substitute therefor a better one, and they will demand it as vociferously as you, the reader, would clamor for a new pair of pants in place of ragged patches. (Sturber 1903, 181)

Walter Clark Presses for Democratization while Maintaining the Racial Status Quo

Walter Clark (1846–1924) was chief justice of the North Carolina Supreme Court when he presented a speech advocating constitutional reforms to the Law Department of the University of Pennsylvania in 1906. Clark was born in Halifax County, North Carolina, and graduated from the University of North Carolina. The son of a Confederate general, Clark rose to the rank of major fighting for the Confederacy. After the war, he began his legal career as an attorney for the railroads. He spent 40 years serving as a judge and was chief justice of the state's highest court from 1903 to 1924. Clark also served on the National War Labor Board, where he established a reputation for being particularly sympathetic to labor (Brooks 1944).

Clark's recommendations embodied the Progressives' faith in democracy, their distrust of corporate economic power, and their concerns about the dangers of plutocracy. Like some other Progressives, Clark believed that the Constitution was a reactionary document when compared to the Declaration of Independence. In his view, the Founders' failure to consult the people had necessitated the adoption of the Bill of Rights. Although the Founders designed the House of Representatives to be democratic, it was outweighed by the other institutions of government:

> The people's part in the Government in the choice of the House of Repre-sentatives even when reinforced by the Executive, whose election they have captured, is an absolute nullity in the face of the Senate and the judiciary, in whose selection the people have no voice. This, therefore, is the Government of the United States—a government by Senate and judges. . . . We know that is [sic] is not the American people. (Clark 1906, 559)

Clark offered a number of proposals, each discrete, but with a cumulative im-pact that would have significantly altered the Constitution. His first proposal—soon to be adopted through the Seventeenth Amendment—proposed direct popular election of senators. Clark also proposed altering the states' equal representation in the Senate, giving smaller states only one senator and larger ones an additional senator for each million inhabitants. Clark acknowledged that the selection of the president had become more democratic than the Framers of the Constitution had intended, but he still believed the existing system "left much to be desired." Re-jecting direct election for fear of magnifying the possible effects of voter fraud, Clark advocated preserving electoral votes but dividing them according to each state's popular vote, thus eliminating the undue influence of "pivotal" states. As-serting that the president possessed powers "greater than those of any sovereign in Europe," Clark advocated a single six-year term for the office (Clark 1906, 563). He apparently believed that the president's power would be reduced if he were ineligible for reelection.

Clark's criticism of the judicial branch was more intense and perhaps ironic, given his position as a state chief justice. He labeled "the appointment of judges for life, subject to confirmation by the Senate" as "by far the most serious de-fect and danger in the Constitution," and hoped to change this by constitutional amendment (Clark 1906, 563). Citing recent U.S. Supreme Court decisions that had invalidated the income tax and the New York law regulating the hours of bak-ers, Clark observed that "[i]f five lawyers can negative the will of 100,000,000 of men, then the art of government is reduced to the selection of those five lawyers" (Clark 1906, 566). He further argued that recent uses of the due process clause threatened "the preservation of the autonomy of the several States and of local self-government," which was "essential to the maintenance of our liberties" (Clark 1906, 566). Accordingly, he called for "the speedy repeal of the fourteenth amend-ment, or a recasting of its language in terms that no future court can misinterpret it" (Clark 1906, 567).

Clark recommended that Congress should abolish all federal judgeships below the Supreme Court and call for the election of new ones. He also favored curbing the jurisdiction of the Supreme Court, allowing postmasters to be filled through the civil service rather than by appointment, and inaugurating congressmen at an earlier date in the calendar year (the passage of the Twentieth Amendment in 1933 enshrined the last of these reforms).

Although Clark recognized that amendments could address specific issues and enact individual measures, he favored calling another constitutional convention. As he explained:

> The same reasons which have time and again caused the individual States to amend their constitutions imperatively require a convention to adjust the Constitution of the Union to the changed conditions of the times and to transfer to the people themselves that control of the Government which is now exercised for the profit and benefit of the "interests." (Clark 1906, 561)

Clark was a strong advocate of women's rights and women's suffrage, but he was less willing to acknowledge the rights of African Americans and immigrants. On May 26, 1920, for example, Clark delivered a commencement address at an African American school in Raleigh, North Carolina, in which he discussed his support for repealing parts of the Fourteenth Amendment. He also related a conversation in which he told a "northern man" that "there was no 'Negro Problem'" in the South:

> I pointed him to the fact that the north, where the immigration from the least advanced states in Europe for several years prior to the war had average [sic] over a million a year, they had millions speaking all languages, advocating all kinds of isms, and professing all kinds of religion, and many of them ignorant of our customs and our forms of government, there was perpetual hostility between the different races and towards the government, whereas down here the colored people were all native born, there was no diversity of languages, for they all spoke our own speech and they were 100 per cent loyal to the government. (Clark 1920)

Clark admitted that there was "no social equality between the races" but that "the colored people do not wish social equality, and the white people would not tolerate it, and there the matter ends." He furthered defended Jim Crow segregation laws in transportation, and he dismissed concerns over suffrage by noting that "I think that the wiser heads among the colored people have discouraged any attempt to intermeddle in politics and that the colored race has lost nothing but gained much by abstaining from doing so against the wishes of the white people." Clark clearly had a very narrow view of the rights to which African Americans or immigrants were entitled, and he was willing to accept their disenfranchisement.

J. Allen Smith Advocates a New Convention to Further Democratic Reforms

Like Clark, political science professor J. Allen Smith of Washington University was convinced that the United States needed serious democratization. In *The Spirit of the American Government*, first published in 1907, Smith helped lay the groundwork for later criticisms of the Constitution by Charles Beard and others. He suggested that the Framers had sought to reign in democracy and that the structures they bequeathed allowed special interests to flourish. "The distinguishing feature of the Constitution," he asserted, "was the elaborate provisions which it contained for limiting the power of the majority" (Smith 1965, 331). Smith acknowledged that informal changes had brought about some democratization but that the nation still had far to go. He leveled specific criticisms that the Electoral College sometimes elected presidents without majority support, that the Senate was malapportioned and too powerful, that the Supreme Court was undemocratic and upheld special interests, and that the amending process was too difficult.

Smith accordingly focused on the potential of the provision in Article V of the Constitution that provided for a new constitutional convention if two-thirds of the states called for one (Smith 1965, 346). Smith suggested that "a new Federal constitution might be framed which would eliminate the whole system of checks on the people and provide for direct ratification by a majority of the voters, as has already been done in the case of most of our state constitutions" (Smith 1965, 347). He seemed to hold out even greater hope for reform of states and municipalities. Like many other individuals in the Progressive movement, he favored expanded suffrage; use of secret ballots; expanded use of primaries to choose political candidates; and expanded use of the recall, the initiative, and the referendum.

Edward House Envisions a Parliamentary Democracy Led by a National Administrator

Edward "Colonel" House (1858–1939) was one of Woodrow Wilson's closest advisors and most influential diplomatic representatives. House was born in Houston, Texas, and attended Cornell University before dropping out to run his family's cotton plantation business after the death of his father. House became a leading advisor to Democratic politicians in the state, and in 1911 he met Wilson. After Wilson won the presidency in 1912, House became one of his most trusted advisors. That same year, House anonymously published a novel entitled *Philip Dru: Administrator*, which outlined his own views of government and proposed a new constitution for the United States.

The novel, which has been reprinted and is apparently still viewed by some on the political right as a blueprint for modern liberalism (Goldwag 2012), focused on a high-minded West Point graduate named Philip Dru, who uses military force to resist the plutocratic ambitions of a sitting president and then sets himself up as the nation's "administrator." As administrator, Dru creates a Council of Twelve (nine of whose members headed executive departments) and mandates needed reforms, including new state and federal constitutions. He then retires to a foreign land with a woman, Gloria Strawn, who shares his lofty ideals.

Dru was a socialist enamored with the altruistic ideals of Christianity and concerned that the profit motive in American capitalism had resulted in great inequality. The new federal constitution, which House introduced relatively late in his novel, contained a host of reforms associated both with parliamentary democracy and with the progressive era in U.S. history. The constitution was relatively brief and contained only four articles.

The first anticipated the Nineteenth Amendment. It provided for universal male and female suffrage, liberalized naturalization policies, and lowered the age of office-holding for all federal offices to 25. However, it prohibited individuals from serving if they had served as a senator or judge for the previous five years (House 1998 [1912], 191–2).

Article II focused on the House of Representatives, from which all legislation would originate. Each state would have one representative for every 300,000 residents. Members would serve six-year terms, subject to recall. In addition to choosing a speaker, House members would choose an executive, patterned after a prime minister in parliamentary democracies. The executive then selected cabinet members (House members were eligible), who served at the executive's pleasure. In conjunction with the cabinet, the executive was responsible for framing bills.

Article III outlined a Senate consisting of one member from each state "elected for life, by a direct vote of the people" (House 1998, 193) and subject to recall at the end of any five-year period of his term. The Senate had the power to approve legislation by majority vote or revise the legislation and send it back to the House for the latter body to accept or reject as it saw fit. If the Senate rejected a measure, the House could dissolve itself "and go before the people for their decision" in the form of new elections. Senators would have to retire by the age of 70.

Article IV limited the president, whose duties were described as "almost entirely formal and ceremonial," to a single 10-year term. Although it guaranteed voting rights, the Constitution did not contain a Bill of Rights, and the book offered no explanation for this omission.

The model the book provided for state constitutions specified that each should have a bicameral legislative body consisting of a House of Representatives and a Senate, with members of the former serving 2-year terms and members of the latter serving for 10. The House would have the main power and would have the authority to dissolve itself and appeal to the people. Governors would serve for six-year terms but have no veto power. Each state would have a pardon board and a civil service.

Although the proposed constitution did not reflect the change, Dru eliminated the courts' power to use judicial review to strike down legislation as unconstitutional. Lawyers were to be prevented from bring "suits of doubtful character, and without facts and merit to sustain them." In addition, attorneys and clients alike would be required "to swear to the truth of the allegations submitted in their petitions of suits and briefs" (House 1998, 136). Dru also implemented uniform divorce laws and an income tax graduated to take 0.5 percent from those earning less than $1,000 a year and establish a tax rate of up to 70 percent for individuals with incomes of 10 million dollars a year or more (House 1998, 145). He also implemented burial reform so that interments would be private and bodies would be cremated for sanitary purposes.

Dru provided for public service commissions to administer railroads. He wanted the Post Office Department to purchase telegraph and telephone companies "at a fair valuation" and for individuals to get messages "at cost" (House 1998, 154).

Just as President Wilson would later intervene in Mexico, so too Dru felt compelled to intervene in the country because of its "habit of revolutions without just cause" (House 1998, 227). After conquering Mexico, Dru announced that "it is not our purpose to annex your country or any part of it." However, he also specified that "in the future, our flag is to be your flag, and you are to be directly under the protection of the United States" (House 1998, 232–3).

With its mix of parliamentary and progressive reforms and its glorification of a leader who would decisively take matters in his own hands, it is easy to see how President Wilson would have been drawn to its author. Wilson continued to be the primary intellectual force behind many subsequent reformers who favored parliamentary reforms and/or strong presidential leadership.

Alan L. Benson Seeks to Undercut Plutocrats through Initiatives and Referendums

Alan L. Benson (1871–1940) published a scathing attack on the U.S. Constitution in his 1914 book *Our Dishonest Constitution*. Born in Plainfield, Michigan, Benson served briefly as a teacher before working as a machine hand, journalist, and editor of a monthly news magazine entitled *Reconstruction: A Herald of the New Time* from 1919 to 1921. Benson won the Socialist Party's presidential nomination in 1916, but he received only a little more than 3 percent of the vote.

Benson was heavily influenced by Charles Beard's *Economic Interpretation of the United States Constitution*, first published in 1913, which argued that America's Founders had been deeply influenced by economic interests. In contrast to those who suggested that the nation had outgrown a Constitution that was once good, Benson provocatively argued that "this observation is precisely as accurate as it would be to say that a dog suffering from fleas had outgrown its fleas. Fleas never fit dogs. The Constitution never fitted us. It never fitted us because it conflicts with the fundamental American ideal of majority rule" (Benson 1914, 54). Benson believed that the Constitution had been largely written by "grafters" as a way of protecting the interests of the wealthy.

Benson accordingly approved a number of majority reforms that would have come close to establishing congressional sovereignty. He favored a unicameral congress in which the only check on legislative power would be provided by popular initiatives. Like Robert E. Beasley, he also thought that popular referenda should be held before the nation committed to any war (Benson 1914, 75). Under Benson's reforms, members of Congress would be selected at large through a system of proportional representation, rather than from single-member districts. Stripped of veto powers and subject to popular recall, the president would act as the nation's "business manager" and would be "nominated and elected by the people at large, without the interference of a convention or an electoral college" (Benson 1914, 84).

Benson favored eliminating state lines and giving Congress the power to legislate on such issues as child labor, housing, adulterated foods, and business fraud without working through state intermediaries. Benson also believed that both men and women should be able to vote, and he favored eliminating the courts' authority to conduct judicial review of legislation or even "interpret the law" (Benson 1914, 87–8). Benson explained that "if the law be so obscure that men of average intelligence cannot understand it, no court should be permitted to hazard a guess as to what congress meant and give its guess all the force of law" (Benson 1914, 88). Benson also favored the repudiation of all national debts, which he believed provided support for war and aggression, and he advocated having the government buy all major industries.

Benson was highly critical of the U.S. banking system, but he expressed grudging respect for Henry Ford's efforts to give his employees a greater share of profits. Benson believed that money had corrupted the press. He did not think that the interests of capital and labor could be reconciled under a system of capitalism any more than could "the interests of burglars and householders."

Eustace Reynolds Proposes a Modified Constitution to Address Issues of Foreign Affairs

In 1915, Eustace Reynolds published a pamphlet entitled *A New Constitution: A Suggested Form of Modified Constitution*, which expressed populist views similar to those advanced by William Jennings Bryan. Reynolds presented his ideas in the form of a reprint of the existing U.S. Constitution with proposed changes highlighted in bold type.

Reynolds proposed eliminating "sex qualifications for voting" (as the Nineteenth Amendment would soon do), but he proposed increasing the voting age to 24 and limiting voting rights to those who could read and write (Reynolds 1915, 1–2). Under Reynolds's revised Constitution, the vice president would serve with the president for a single six-year term and represent the United States at a council of viceroys and vice presidents. With the approval of another international body consisting of "undersecretaries of state and deputy-ministers for foreign affairs," this council would have power to "make and promulgate decrees in all matters affecting international intercourse, commerce, affairs, or "relations"; to "regulate commerce with foreign nations"; and to punish "offenses against the law of nations" (Reynolds 1915, 2–3). With the creation of this new group, Congress would lose its power to "enter into any agreement or contract with another state, or with a foreign power, to engage in war," except in cases of "invasion" or "imminent danger" (Reynolds 1915, 7).

Reynolds proposed requiring the chief justice to appoint another Supreme Court justice to sit en banc with members of judiciaries from other nations "and pass upon international questions as they come properly before the court for adjudication" (Reynolds 1915, 10–11). In other words, this court would be empowered to hear and decide cases pitting the U.S. government or American citizens against foreign citizens or governments. The constitution would further give U.S. courts explicit authority to disregard unconstitutional laws and decrees.

Reynolds endorsed the civil liberties guarantees in the Bill of Rights, but he favored allowing a prosecutor to comment—and a jury to weigh the fact—when defendants chose to invoke their Fifth Amendment right against self-incrimination. He also proposed restricting the national government's right to collect tax on state securities.

A Flurry of Calls for Another Constitutional Convention

As the Progressive Era continued, a number of scholars called for a constitutional convention to reform the Constitution. Some of these calls were spurred by the rising demand for direct popular election of U.S. senators. The 1912 passage and 1913 ratification of the Seventeenth Amendment, which approved appointing senators by popular vote, was in part prompted by Congress's desire to avoid a new convention.

Walter Tuller (1886–1939), a California attorney, wrote a 1911 article in *North American Review* calling for a convention of "the strongest and ablest men in the nation" (Tuller 1911, 386). In addition to favoring the direct election of senators, Tuller wanted to make the Constitution more flexible by reducing the states required to call such a convention from two thirds to one half. He also endorsed granting the national government the power "to regulate corporations or monopolies in any form" (Tuller 1911, 385).

In 1913, Yandell Henderson (1873–1974) published another essay in favor of a new convention. A professor of physiology at Yale University and an active member and one-time unsuccessful congressional candidate of the Progressive Party, Henderson published his thoughts in the *Yale Review*. Henderson advanced three major reforms. The first called for fusing or bringing the legislative and executive branches closer together. At the state level, he thought that legislators might even be replaced by a board of directors, over which the governor might preside. The second called for empowering voters to "recall" judicial decisions that invalidated laws as unconstitutional. A third urged sublimating state authority to the federal government through the establishment of "a real union and a real national government instead of a Union of States and a Federal Government" (Henderson 1913, 89).

The nation entered World War I during Woodrow Wilson's second term. Socialist Bouck White (1874–1851) was among the individuals who considered the war as an opportunity for further social change. A graduate of Harvard and Boston Theological Seminary, White authored *The Book of Daniel Drew* (1910), a novel about a stock speculator, and *The Call of the Carpenter* (1911), which portrayed Jesus as a revolutionary. He was also the pastor of the Church of the Social Revolution, in which—according to White's *New York Times* obituary of June 9, 1951—he "baptized children of parents who pledged to raise their offspring in an atmosphere of social revolt." White burned an American flag during some of his speeches and served three jail terms for disrupting church services and participating in protests. After being repudiated by churchmen and socialists alike, he eventually became a potter.

In an article published in *Outlook* in 1917, White argued that the convention mechanism provided a revolutionary method for constitutional reform that would be particularly appropriate during a time of wartime disruptions. Although White clearly hoped that such a convention would result in a more socialistic system, he did not detail a specific agenda for its deliberations.

The following year, Lewis Mayers (1890–1975) added his voice to those who favored the calling of a constitutional convention. Mayers earned a PhD at Columbia in 1914 and an LLB from George Washington University in 1920. As an attorney and teacher of both law and political science, Mayers observed that the British Labor Party was far more successful in initiating its programs than was a U.S. party subject to such obstacles as federalism, the separation of powers, and "constitutional guarantees of private property." He advocated organizing a new convention to remedy "the inefficiency of our constitutional machinery" (Mayers 1918, 73). Mayers spent more time in his article touting the advantages of a convention—which he believed would transcend self-interests, be more focused and efficient, and "facilitate radical action"—than he did on selling specific provisions to move the U.S. political system closer to the British parliamentary model. In later years, however, Mayers authored a book in which he advocated alterations to the Fifth Amendment.

William MacDonald Advocates a Parliamentary System in Which the Cabinet Serves as Chief Executive

William MacDonald (1863–1938) wanted to call a convention and had plenty of ideas about what it should do. A journalist who also taught history and government at Brown, the University of California, and Yale, MacDonald supplemented ideas he presented in a 1921 article with a book entitled *A New Constitution for a New America*, which he published the following year.

The first two chapters of MacDonald's book expressed praise for the convention mechanism and a general critique of the federal system. Subsequent chapters indicated that MacDonald's model was that of parliamentary government, which he believed to be more "responsible," more majoritarian, and more "democratic" than that of the United States.

MacDonald favored significantly altering the presidency into a head of state who would designate a member of Congress as premier. The premier would subsequently form and lead a cabinet. Under this arrangement, the cabinet and the premier would exercise most governmental powers, but they would resign when they lost congressional support. If a new cabinet could not be formed, the president would dissolve Congress and call for new elections.

At a time when many native-born Americans feared immigrants, MacDonald favored ending the requirement that the president be born on American soil. He also called for electing presidents through the popular vote rather than the Electoral College. Perhaps taking a lesson from Wilson's failure to get Congress to endorse the League of Nations, MacDonald advocated transferring the directorship of the military forces and the negotiation of treaties to the cabinet, eliminating the president's power of appointment and removal, and taking away the president's power to recommend legislation. MacDonald also favored vesting the power to execute laws in the cabinet, elimination of the presidential veto, new elections in cases of presidential vacancy, and the formulation of a provision to deal with governmental operations during times of presidential disability (the latter concern may have arisen after Wilson suffered a stroke in his second term) (MacDonald 1922, 69–89).

MacDonald favored continuing the bicameral Congress, but with uniform four-year terms and a minimum age of 25 years for both houses. He favored eliminating the requirement that representatives be residents of their districts, abolishing secret congressional sessions, allowing both houses to ratify treaties, and creating a more structured budget system in which both bills raising revenue and those appropriating money would have to originate within the House. He advocated granting Congress expanded powers over corporations, immigration and naturalization, education, marriage and divorce, the budget, economic control (including possible nationalizations of industries), and internal improvements, with members being subject to recall (MacDonald 1922, 90–116). MacDonald also supported a system of uniform requirements for voting in federal elections and wanted the House to represent not only population but also occupations and professions.

In addition to increasing congressional powers, MacDonald wanted to delineate the respective roles of the state and national governments more clearly. He favored greater congressional attention to the issue of whether state governments were republican and would allow state citizens to petition Congress on the matter (155). Unlike some proponents of change from this era who largely ignored civil liberties, MacDonald actively sought to guarantee protections for freedom of religion, assembly, and petition, and for the right to bear arms, against abridgements by the states as well as by the national government. He also advocated eliminating state militias, which he considered to be outdated and anachronistic. Unlike some Progressives, MacDonald believed that the Eighteenth Amendment's imposition of national alcoholic prohibition unduly infringed on state police powers.

Under MacDonald's plan, the premier and the cabinet would be responsible for appointing judges who would be subject to removal, either by conviction for impeachment or by the request of both houses of Congress (MacDonald 1922, 181). MacDonald favored creating a system of administrative courts. He also endorsed other legal reforms aimed at controlling the exercise of judicial power over receiverships, reducing the use of injunctions, and—in another contrast to many other Progressive reformers—confirming the judicial branch's authority to declare laws unconstitutional. MacDonald proposed that Congress should pass a resolution favoring a constitutional convention and invite states to petition for one. Alternatively, he suggested that Congress might be able to call one on its own initiative.

Summary and Analysis

Most advocates of major constitutional reform during the first 25 years of the twentieth century wanted to make government more democratic, accountable, and responsive. Some were especially suspicious of corporations and other entrenched forms of economic power and favored nationalizing key industries and bringing the United States closer to socialism. The English parliamentary system continued to provide the primary alternate model, but proponents of change differed on whether to maintain a federal system.

Although Colonel House suggested a fictional scenario in which individuals seized power and initiated reform through military force, most other advocates of change continued to view the convention mechanism as the most effective means for reshaping the U.S. Constitution and the American system of government. Progressive reformers ultimately were unable to force such a convention into being. Nonetheless, they still managed to use the amendment ratification process to give women the vote and usher in the Prohibition era.

References

Beard, Charles A. 1949 [1913]. *An Economic Interpretation of the Constitution of the United States*. Reprint. New York: Macmillan, 1949.

Benson, Allan L. *Our Dishonest Constitution*. 1914. New York: B.W. Huebsch. Reprinted from the Harvard Law School Library under MOML (Making of Modern Law) Legal Treatises, 1800–1926.

Boyd, Steven R. 1992. *Alternative Constitutions for the United States: A Documentary History*. Westport, CT: Greenwood Press.

Brooks, Aubrey Lee. 1944. *Walter Clark: Fighting Judge*. Chapel Hill: University of North Carolina Press.

Clark, Walter. 1920. "The Negro in North Carolina and the South. His Fifty-five Years of Freedom and What He Has Done. Commencement Address at St. Augustine's School, Raleigh, N.C., May 26, 1920." Originally published in *St. Augustine's Record* 25, no. 5. Raleigh, NC: [St. Augustine's School?], 1920. Reprinted in *Documenting the American South*. http://docsouth.unc.edu/nc/staugust/clark.html (accessed November 27, 2013).

Clark, Walter. 1913. "Address by Chief Justice Walter Clark before the Federation of Women's Clubs, New Bern, NC. 8 May 1913." Reprinted in *Documenting the American South*. http//doesouth.unc.edu/nc/clark13/clark13.html (accessed November 27, 2013).

Clark, Walter. 1906. "Some Defects of the Constitution of the United States." In *The Papers of Walter Clark*, vol. 2., edited by Aubrey L. Brooks and Hugh T. Lefler. Chapel Hill: University of North Carolina Press.

Goldstein, Robert J. 1974. "The Anarchist Scare of 1908: A Sign of Tensions in the Progressive Era." *American Studies* 15 (Fall): 55–78.

Goldwag, Arthur. 2012. "The Century-Old Novel Right-Wingers Believe Guides Obama." *Salon.com* (January 3). http://salon.com/2012/01/03-the_century_old-novel_right-wingers_believe_guides (accessed November 27, 2013).

Henderson, Yandell. 1913. "The Progressive Movement and Constitutional Reform." *Yale Review* n.s. 3 (October): 78–90.

House, Edward Mandell. 1912. *Philip Dru: Administrator*. Reprint. Appleton, WI: Robert Welch University Press, 1998.

MacDonald, William. 1921. "A New American Constitution." *Proceedings of the American Antiquarian Society* 2 (October): 439–47.

MacDonald, William. 1922. *A New Constitution for a New America*. New York: B. W. Huebsch.

Mayers, Lewis. 1959. *Shall We Amend the Fifth Amendment?* New York: Harper & Brothers.

Mayers, Lewis. 1918. "Should We Remake the Constitution?" *The New Republic* 16 (August 17): 73–4.

McGerr, Michael. 2003. *A Fierce Discontent: The Rise and Fall of the Progressive Movement in America, 1870–1920*. New York: Free Press.

Reynolds, Eustace. 1915. *A New Constitution: A Suggested Form of Modified Constitution*. New York: Nation Press.

Smith, J. Allen. 1965 [1907]. *The Spirit of American Government*. Edited by Cushing Strout. Reprint. Cambridge, MA: Belknap Press of Harvard University Press, 1965.

Sturber, D. I. 1903. *The Anarchist Constitution*. San Francisco: Radical Publishing Company.

Tuller, Walter K. 1911. "A Convention to Amend the Constitution—Why Needed—How It May Be Obtained." *North American Review* 193: 369–87.

Vile, John R. 1992. *The Constitutional Amending Process in American Political Thought*. New York: Praeger.

White, Bouck. 1917. "Shall We Call a Constituent Assembly as Provided by the United States Constitution?" *Outlook* 116 (August 22): 613–15.

White, Bouck. 2009 [1911]. *The Call of the Carpenter*. Garden City, NY: Doubleday.

White, Bouck. 1910. *The Book of Daniel Drew*. New York: George H. Doran.

CHAPTER 6

Proposals from the Great Depression through World War II and Beyond

After World War I, national energies focused less on politics than on the quest for good times and prosperity. At home, the watchword was the malapropism "normalcy." On the world scene, the United States rejected membership in the League of Nations, hoping to pursue its own destiny without continuing European entanglements. In time, the Great Depression and the rise of Nazi Germany and Japanese imperialism reminded Americans that their fate was linked to the rest of the world. These developments, along with the sesquicentennial of the Constitution (1937), a series of judicial decisions voiding New Deal programs, Franklin Roosevelt's court-packing plan, and the Supreme Court's apparent shift in ideology, provoked renewed thinking about the United States' written charter of government.

Charles Merriam Outlines Areas of Conflict between the Constitution and the Party System

Charles Merriam, political science professor at the University of Chicago and president of the American Political Science Association in 1924–1925, developed his book *The Written Constitution and the Unwritten Attitude* (1931) from a series of lectures delivered at the University of Rochester. Merriam's plans to revise the Constitution provide insight into educated thinking of the day and, had they been adopted, they would have resulted in significant structural changes.

Impressed by the way that changing public attitudes and opinions could bring about changes in government short of constitutional amendments. Merriam saw the chief danger to U.S. government not in "lack of stability, but lack of mobility, failure to make prompt adjustments to the new era in industry and science" (Merriam 1931, 25). Merriam devoted attention to how changing demographics were fostering changes in the relationships between cities, states, and the nation. Countless overlapping governments had been formed, and Merriam observed—at a time before the Supreme Court required state legislative apportionment on the basis of one person, one vote—that cities often found themselves dominated by rural interests. Merriam suggested the idea of reorganizing certain cities as "independent states" (Merriam 1931, 48), and he was otherwise sympathetic to altering existing state boundaries.

Because many party institutions were extra-constitutional developments, Merriam believed that it would be possible to alter many of them without altering the Constitution. He listed five areas of potential conflict, however, in which constitutional changes might be needed:

1. The requirement that no United States official shall at the same time be a member of the Congress.
2. The requirement that laws could not be passed without the concurrence of both houses of Congress and the president.
3. The requirement that treaties be ratified by a two-thirds vote of the Senate.
4. The apparent barrier to congressional regulation of party primaries.
5. The relationship between the federal government and the states. (Merriam 1931, 72–3)

Merriam observed that "there is little probability of a modification of the Constitution either by amendment or custom in such a fashion as to permit the adoption of a parliamentary system" (Merriam 1931, 85), and he did not specifically call for another constitutional convention or for a more comprehensive reworking of the existing document.

John Piburn Proposes a Constitution That Elevates Education

John Logan Piburn (1872–?), a medical doctor, authored *A Constitution and a Code* in 1932. This work proposed the text of a new U.S. constitution of 64 sections and a revised code suitable for California and other states. In addition to rearranging provisions in the existing document, Piburn presented a number of quirky and highly prescriptive proposals.

His first proposal was to create an education department and educational college. This department would be led by five recent graduates elected by each college and initially governed by the first member to be selected from the University of Missouri (undoubtedly Piburn's own alma mater). Piburn favored granting the department extensive powers to promote and oversee all aspects of education, from setting tax rates for education and specifying criteria for grading to designating the size of diplomas. Piburn's constitution would prohibit "religious," "denominational," and "sectarian" schools, as well as night classes, the use of initials on diplomas (Piburn 1932, 16), and the issuance of any doctoral degrees other than in medicine; it further designated BS and MS degrees as outranking BAs or MAs.

Piburn proposed designating the House of Representatives as the House of Solons (Solon was an ancient Athenian statesman and lawmaker). He called for prohibiting the rewriting of laws, proposing instead that Congress adopt changes by passing new laws and repealing old ones. His prohibition against "sumptuary laws" (Piburn 1932, 46) appears to have been designed to abolish the Eighteenth Amendment, which he described in his introduction as "a crime." This same introduction identified the only good in the Nineteenth Amendment as the fact that "it will help to unChristianize women" (Piburn 1932). Piburn called for replacing the congressional power to declare war with the authority to call a popular election for declaring war. Passage would require approval by a majority of males under age 40—presumably those most likely to serve.

Piburn applied the restraints in the Bill of Rights directly to Congress, although he extended the establishment clause of the First Amendment to both the nation and the states. He further specified that "all the promoters of religion, and their followers, are jointly and severally liable for damages, libel, and slander for their utterances and practices" (Piburn 1932, 49–50). Piburn added prohibitions on civil and criminal libel. He also would have prohibited miscegenation laws "restricting the amalgamation of the races; or the mating of the sexes" (Piburn 1932, 50)—a position that the U.S. Supreme Court did not take until 1967 in *Loving v. Virginia*, 388 U.S. 1 (1967).

Piburn proposed eliminating the office of vice president and filling presidential vacancies with the oldest senator from the president's party. Piburn also included a provision for presidential disability similar to that now found in the Twenty-Fifth Amendment. He explicitly provided for the power of judicial review and would have imposed a one-term limit on all offices.

Piburn called for his constitution—and any subsequent amendments—to be ratified by the voters in three-fourths of the states. Piburn provided for a nine-member committee appointed by the Educational College, the Senate, and the House of Solons to consider revising the document in the year 2000 and "once every fifty years thereafter" (Piburn 1932, 71).

The Socialist Party Platform of 1932

Socialists favor adopting government ownership of major industries through peaceful means. Perhaps because of the crisis posed by the Great Depression, 1932 appears to mark the high point of Socialist proposals to promote change by constitutional amendments. The party offered seven proposals that may be grouped into three categories. In the first category are a group of four proposals designed to make the nation more democratic. The first three of these called respectively for "proportional representation," which is not further elaborated; "direct election of the President and Vice President"; adoption of "the initiative and referendum"; and (somewhat further afield) abolition of the power of the U.S. Supreme Court to invalidate legislation (quoted in Porter and Johnson 1966, 353).

A second class of proposals advocated economic reforms of the type more typically associated with the Socialist Party. Focusing on adoption of a "Worker's right amendment to the Constitution," the platform explained that such an amendment would empower Congress:

To establish national systems of unemployment, health and accident insurance and old age pensions, to abolish child labor, establish and take over enterprises in manufacture, commerce, transportation, banking, public utilities, and other business and industries to be owned and operated by the Government, and generally, for the social and economic welfare of the workers of the United States. (Quoted in Porter and Johnson 1966, 353)

A related proposal to repeal the Eighteenth Amendment proposed "government ownership and control with the right of local option for each state to maintain prohibition within its borders" (quoted in Porter and Johnson 1966, 353).

Yet another Socialist proposal, buried in the middle of the others, called for "[a]n amendment to the Constitution to make constitutional amendments less cumbersome" (quoted in Porter and Johnson 1966, 353). The platform did not call for a constitutional convention.

William Kay Wallace Proposes a Constitution to Advance "Scientific Capitalism"

William Kay Wallace (1886–?) was a U.S. diplomat, former war correspondent, and historian who worked with the Military Intelligence Division of the General Staff during World War I and helped negotiate peace at the end of the war. He presented his plans for a new constitution in a book entitled *Our Obsolete Constitution*, which he published in 1932. Much like Colonel Edward M. House, Wallace believed that government was largely a matter of good administration, albeit with special concern for social and economic rights.

Wallace believed it was time to replace "haphazard methods of ordering industrial life" with "[a] more efficient economy" that would put greater focus on the social as opposed to the individual point of view (Wallace 1932, 9). To this end, Wallace favored calling another constitutional convention to establish a system of "Scientific Capitalism," which he labeled as "*the one best way*, or the method of efficiency" (Wallace 1932, 104). This would replace earlier concepts based on natural rights, a social contract, and a "geographical national state system" (Wallace 1932, 118).

Focusing chiefly on economic rights over individual liberties, Wallace proposed a new constitution to make the state "the directive agency of social control, a clearing-house that will expedite and adjust public affairs" (Wallace 1932, 137). Industrial corporations would be nationalized "in the state" and "our first allegiance will be to the corporation which directly affords us the economic liberty and security we crave" (Wallace 1932, 138). In the new state, government would chiefly perform "an administrative function," and war "must be branded as a crime against the social order" (Wallace 1932, 146).

In his final chapter Wallace outlined five guarantees within his proposed constitution. The first was a guarantee of "economic liberty" that included "the right to the full fruits of one's labor," and full access to economic security, education, and leisure (Wallace 1932, 182). The second was a guarantee of social security designed to cover "all of the contingencies and possible caprices of fortune in the life of the individual." This included "social insurance" covering old age and unemployment, "child welfare and training," adjusted work schedules, and "adult education" (Wallace 1932, 183).

The third guarantee was for "more effective government." To this end, Wallace proposed replacing current states with nine regional states, each with four to six representatives. These representatives would form a national board of directors (presumably unicameral) that would select from its members a president, appoint all governmental officials from the civil service, and exercise legislative functions.

To implement his fourth guarantee of "personal liberty and property," Wallace advocated transferring all corporate enterprises from private to public ownership and paying current holders of such property in governmental bonds. The new industries would be "scientifically regulated," with the profit motive being replaced. Individuals would, however, still be able to own other forms of private property "in order to stimulate the creative ingenuity of all the citizens" (Wallace 1932, 188).

Wallace's fifth guarantee was for a "planned national economy" (Wallace 1932, 189). He favored making the state the "supreme economic arbiter," with power to conscript citizens in war and peace. The state would further coordinate economic activities and organize credit "as a public not a private function" (Wallace 1932, 191).

Whereas America's Founding Fathers—and their Anti-Federalist critics—focused on securing liberty by cabining power, Wallace sought an efficient government with expanded powers in order to enhance social and economic rights. Of all the plans to rewrite the U.S. Constitution, Wallace's was among the least democratic. It authorized representatives of the regional states to select—and perhaps control—the president, and it envisioned a system in which judges would be chosen from among members of the civil service.

Henry S. McKee Proposes a Parliamentary System with Increased Executive Power and Economic Regulation

Henry S. McKee (1868–1956) was convinced that American government had become a *Degenerate Democracy* (1933). A California businessman and banker who served for a time as a member of the Federal Reserve Advisory Council, McKee drew many of his political solutions from Woodrow Wilson and Gamaliel Bradford.

McKee identified three major problems in the United States: the organization of the national government, the "economic organization" of the country, and the failure to understand the causes of unemployment and to provide adequate remedies for them. McKee believed that the Constitution had vested too much power in congressional, or committee, government and too little in strong but accountable executive power. He thought such power could be created by adopting aspects of the British model that provided for the participation of cabinet officers in public debate before Congress. He also favored introducing a variant of the question hour, a British institution that requires the prime minister to appear before Parliament to answer policy questions posed by members. McKee asserted that these changes would encourage greater presidential initiative on budgetary and other policy matters, but would also subject such policies to public examination and accountability. McKee believed that such a system would expose what he considered to be the folly of the graduated income and inheritance taxes. He asserted that both of these forms of taxation undermined the ability of capitalists to invest in society. McKee also believed that the new system would make government by secret committee impossible, attract people of ability and character into public office, and heighten public attention to political issues.

McKee rejected schemes of public ownership of major industries, but acknowledged that the complexities of America's modern economy required a greater degree of control and planning. McKee thus proposed establishing "one central bank" and a "governor" of the Federal Reserve System who, like other cabinet officers, would be subject to increased public scrutiny. McKee also favored establishing ministers to oversee the rail and mining industries. The key was to create a system that centralized power but also made it more accountable. McKee believed this could be accomplished by establishing a "government by a responsible Executive" subject to a congressional veto in place of government "by a series of congressional committees without responsibility" (McKee 1933, 126).

McKee viewed the problems of poverty and employment as moral problems stemming from poor personal finance decisions. He accordingly proposed that public schools should teach children to keep expenditures within income and to save at least 10 percent of their income.

William Yandell Elliott Proposes a Variant of Parliamentary Government

In 1935, William Yandell Elliott (1896–1979), a Harvard historian and presidential advisor who had been among the Vanderbilt University poets known as the Fugitives, published a book entitled *The Need for Constitutional Reform*. It proposed a number of reforms that he hoped to initiate through a constitutional convention. Despite its subtitle (*A Program for National Security*) and a concluding chapter devoted to the rising threats posed by Germany and Japan, Elliott focused on the American economy and other domestic issues.

Convinced that the New Deal had already altered constitutional understandings, and that the Constitution was "in danger of being scrapped piecemeal and by indirection," Elliott argued that "if we are to save the Constitution we must amend it to fit the needs of a modern state; but we must amend it in an intelligent, coherent, and lawful manner, rather than by a hodgepodge of makeshift evasions" (Elliott 1935, 30). Moreover, because a number of changes that were needed involved Congress, Elliott favored using a mechanism like a constitutional convention that could largely bypass that body in implementing reforms.

Elliott thought that a number of small reform steps, like instituting a presidential item veto and prohibiting legislative riders that were not germane to the aims of a bill, could be initiated through individual amendments. The linchpin of Elliott's plan, however, was borrowed from parliamentary systems. It would have authorized the president, at least once during a term, to force members of the House of Representatives to stand for reelection. If such an election upheld Congress over the president, the president could resign (with Congress then choosing his successor), but the president would not be required to do so.

Elliott desired to trim the power of the Senate, which he associated with special interests, and he advocated taking from that body "the power over bills appropriating money or raising revenue" (Elliott 1935, 32). He further favored reorganizing states into districts designated as "commonwealths," similar to those used for the Federal Reserve System. Elliott suggested dividing the nation into 12 such regions, each electing eight senators. The president would be able to add 14 prominent individuals to the Senate, and losing presidential candidates would also serve there. A majority of both houses of Congress, rather than a two-thirds vote of the Senate, would be sufficient to ratify treaties.

Elliott would continue to base representation in the House of Representatives on population. In his scheme, however, the new commonwealths would elect members from multimember districts. Elliott believed that this system would tame the power of interest groups. He also called for a continuing committee of both houses to be in "perpetual residence" in Washington, D.C. (Elliott 1935, 37).

Consistent with a parliamentary system, a joint House and Senate committee would nominate presidential candidates under Elliott's system. The House would then choose two of the nominees to run in a national election. The president would be selected by a majority popular vote and would choose an executive vice president or assistant president who would also head the administrative cabinet.

Elliott believed that the system of judicial review was needed in the United States' existing political system, but that such power might be modified if the legislative and executive branches were given greater responsibilities. Under his proposed system, then, the Supreme Court would be required to vote by a two-thirds majority or better to invalidate legislation. With an undoubted view toward the escalating conflict between the Court and President Roosevelt in the mid 1930s, Elliott suggested that battles "over social reform should be fought out in party politics, not in the courts" (Elliott 1935, 179). He feared that existing protections for criminal defendants—such as the prohibition on double jeopardy—were working to "aid gangsters and racketeers" (Elliott 1935, 204). He also suggested that the Supreme Court should choose the attorney general.

Elliott called for strengthening the positions of governors in the new commonwealths on the order of the national parliamentary model. He wanted to grant governors the power to dissolve the legislature (now to be unicameral) once during their four-year terms, and to create governors' councils and legislative steering committees. As with the president, state governors in Elliott's system of governance would originate the budget and would be subject to override on money bills only by a two-thirds majority.

Elliott advanced a number of administrative reforms as well. He wanted to create a civil service head for each department and a permanent cabinet secretariat "to propose and document Cabinet meetings" (Elliott 1935, 203). He also proposed adding an advisory committee to each department consisting of "all the great interests with which it comes into normal contact" (Elliott 1935, 203), and he favored allowing cabinet members to have seats in the Senate and to appear before the House.

Malcolm Eiselen Proposes That a Convention Consider a Potpourri of Changes

Historian Malcolm R. Eiselen (1902–1965) used the sesquicentennial of the U.S. Constitution to write an article calling for a new constitutional convention. He followed with an additional article arguing for making the constitutional amending process easier in 1941.

Although Eiselen called for a convention, his proposals were designed not so much to reorient the direction of government along new lines as to correct a variety of perceived defects, any one of which could be addressed by an individual amendment. His proposals thus called for: abolishing the Electoral College; reconsidering the presidential term of office; adopting a national initiative and referendum; providing for seating members of the cabinet in Congress; nominating presidents more democratically; providing a clearer set of processes to follow when presidential disability occurred; making the amending process easier; eliminating the requirement that the Senate ratify treaties by a two-thirds vote; limiting federal spending; consideration of longer terms of office; initiating an item veto and an executive budget; and redrawing the boundaries between state and national powers (Eiselen 1937, 29–33).

Eiselen proposed that members of the convention include a mix of elected and appointed delegates. He included the American Bar Association, the American Political Science Association, and the American Economic Association among the organizations that should be involved in the delegate selection process.

Architect Ralph Cram Seeks to Restore a "High" Form of Democracy Based on Associational Representation

Ralph Cram (1863–1942), a prominent church architect who designed the Cathedral of St. John the Divine in New York, cofounded *Commonweal*, and admired the Middle Ages, published *The End of Democracy* in 1937, the sesquicentennial year of the Constitution. Cram was troubled by what he perceived to be the decline of Western civilization, and he drew from such prominent European intellectuals as José Ortega y Gasset and Salvador de Madariaga in making his case.

Cram believed that the modern harnessing of nature and subsequent development of capitalism had created a proletariat wage-earning class at one extreme and financiers and capitalists at the other. He felt that the rise of universal suffrage had further combined with the rise of politicians, political parties, and the popular press to undermine the middle class and contribute to spiritual decline. Cram sought to restore "true" or "high" democracy—an "aristocratic republic"—which he associated with the high Middle Ages and the era of the United States' founding, as well as with the quest for spiritual liberty (Cram 1937, 19).

Although all previous amendments on the subject of suffrage had sought to remove barriers to voting, Cram wanted to impose restrictions and thus elevate it. He sought to deprive those convicted of "moral turpitude" from voting and to reestablish the link between voting and property rights. Absent this, he favored longer residence requirements, stricter naturalization laws, and the possibility of tying voting to participating in "voluntary associations" or "functional groups" (Cram 1937, 153–5).

In order to restore the middle class, Cram favored replacing the existing "*political* organization" with a new "*functional* organization" (Cram 1937, 120). He asserted that his corporate state would result in "the substitution for professional politicians chosen on a partisan [sic] or territorial basis" with "nonpolitical, non-partizen [sic] delegates or representatives made up of voluntary associations of the functional factors in society" (Cram 1937, 122). Individuals would associate in largely autonomous units of 500 families, each with their own farms, gardens, town halls, and professional personnel (Cram 1937, 201–22). Cram believed such associations would help eliminate issues of overproduction and unemployment that had caused the Great Depression.

In addition to rearranging Congress along functional representative lines, Cram wanted to establish a legislative budget that would produce greater cooperation between the legislative and executive branches. Consistent with his earlier critique of expanded voting rights, Cram wanted to repeal the Seventeenth Amendment so that the Senate would become known as "a body of men of high character, noble intelligence and wide vision; men of mature judgment, of scholarly attainments and knowledge of the world" (Cram 1937, 166). Cram thought that such a body would be a "mixed tribunal, partly chosen by direct election, partly filled by appointment" (Cram 1937, 167), with major secular and religious interests performing the latter function. Much as in the plan proposed by Alexander Hamilton at the Constitutional Convention of 1787, members would serve terms of from 10 years to life.

Cram favored designating the president as "His Highness the Regent of the Republic of the United States"—and allowing him to serve for life (Cram 1937, 187). In a variant on the original Virginia Plan, he suggested that the House of Representatives choose the regent from among members of the Senate. This regent would have the power to appoint a prime minister, who would in turn choose a cabinet. The regent also would be authorized to call a vote to dissolve the House of Representatives and undertake new elections. If the House vote went against him, however, he would have to choose a new prime minister.

Cram expressed admiration for William Yandell Elliott's proposal that laws only be invalidated by a court with a two-thirds or greater voting majority (rather than simple majority). He also believed that the Supreme Court should be able to issue advisory opinions. Still drawing from Elliott, Cram advocated dividing the nation into five or six provinces or commonwealths and decentralizing administration. As a further means of recognizing a natural aristocracy, he proposed creating an order of nonhereditary knighthood, with recipients being designated as "Sir." In a proposal that goes all the way back to some of the Founding Fathers (Vile 2010, I, 155), he also favored creating a "Civilian West Point" (Cram 1937, 218).

Cram feared that citizens were abusing freedoms of speech, press, and religion, but he concluded that "the dangers of suppression are greater than the dangers of license" (Cram 1937, 238). Almost as though he were echoing Albert Stickney,

Cram thought the key to real progress was that of placing "men of character, capacity, and intelligence in all positions, social, economic, political" (Cram 1937, 237).

Hugh L. Hamilton Offers a Constitution with an Eclectic Set of Proposals

Hugh L. Hamilton, whose occupation was unknown, was the elusive author of *A Second Constitution for the United States* (1938), which Professor Steven Boyd discovered when searching for proposed constitutions. Comparing the Constitution of his day to a jigsaw puzzle, Hamilton observed that "thirty-one pieces are rotted and have to be thrown away; forty-four of them are badly in need of repair; thirty-seven of them have to be repainted; and we have to make eighteen new pieces to complete the picture. Only thirty-seven of the original pieces are left intact" (Hamilton 1938, 5).

Whereas Cram was concerned about "low" democracy, Hamilton appeared to accept it. He suggested that his contemporaries sought "contentment—congenial occupation, adequate leisure, an absorbing hobby, a pleasant home, and wholesome recreation"—and he did not indicate that his own proposed constitution would aim for anything different (Hamilton 1938, 102).

Hamilton proposed a constitution of 10 articles. Article I addressed general provisions. Innovations included allowing adjustments to state boundaries, with a provision setting the lower number of states at 30. Hamilton also proposed limiting travel on ships of belligerent nations and restricting loans to or trade with such countries. Another provision specified that most government jobs would be filled through a civil service commission.

Article II consisted of a bill of rights. Contrary to Section 1 of the Fourteenth Amendment, which extends citizenship to all persons born or naturalized in the United States, this article would deny citizenship "to the insane, the criminal, the illiterate, the non-English speaking and those who fail to comprehend the nature of our government" (Hamilton 1938, 112). Freedom of the press would include a provision "prohibiting control of the press in any part of the United States by individuals or groups which tends to abridge their freedom" (Hamilton 1938, 113). A revised version of the Fourth Amendment would have made governmental officials responsible for unreasonable searches and seizures or from publicity, initiated by their order or performed by them (Hamilton 1938, 113). Hamilton further proposed accepting the sworn testimony of witnesses who later died, outlawing capital punishment, and eliminating the due process clause, which he considered to be too ambiguous.

Article III outlined states' rights and limitations and included a provision requiring state governors to extradite criminals who had fled to their states. Articles IV through VII dealt with the framework for a National Assembly, to be divided into a Senate and a Congress. Under Hamilton's plan, Congress would consist of from 100 to 200 members chosen for a maximum of two six-year terms, and the Senate would be of similar size. Setting forth an idea that he may have borrowed from Cram, Hamilton provided that senators would be chosen by "representatives of the professions, finance, service, agriculture, manufacturing, construction, trade, communication and transportation, apportioned according to the census" rather than by states (Hamilton 1938, 122). Senators would serve for a single 12-year term. The National Assembly would have power over child labor, with a provision allowing those over the age of 13 to be employed in work that was not injurious to their health or schooling. In language that mirrored some Supreme Court decisions of the day, the National Assembly would have power over commerce, but not over manufacturing. Hamilton would further have required all laws mandating expenditures to "specify the method of raising said funds" (Hamilton 1938, 120).

Article VIII outlined the executive branch. The people would directly elect the president to a single six-year term for a salary of $75,000 a year. One unusual feature of Hamilton's design was to also designate the vice president as the postmaster general and to make him a member of the presidential cabinet.

Article IX outlined judicial powers. Perhaps with a view toward Roosevelt's court-packing plan, Hamilton proposed setting the number of Supreme Court justices at nine and establishing a mandatory retirement age of 80. Hamilton's constitution recognized judicial review but specified that when the Supreme Court invalidated legislation it would have to "include the wording of a Constitution Amendment which would validate the legislation" (Hamilton 1938, 132). Hamilton favored elimination of the Eleventh Amendment (which limited suits against states) and allow a two-thirds majority of the Supreme Court to impeach the president "for non-adherence to this Constitution" (Hamilton 1938, 133).

Article X spelled out an amending process, which required passage of proposals by two-thirds of both houses of the National Assembly and ratification by the people. Hamilton also suggested an idea similar to one once espoused by Thomas Jefferson, empowering the president to call a constitutional convention every 25 years. He added that "no amendment which would prohibit the electorate from changing any part of this Constitution by methods prescribed therein shall ever be proposed or ratified" (Hamilton 1938, 134).

Charles Coleman Proposes a Modest Rewrite

Dr. Charles Coleman (1900–1971), who taught history and social studies at Eastern Illinois University, offered a modest proposal for constitutional reform entitled *The Constitution Up to Date* in a 1938 publication of the National Council for the Social Studies. Coleman proposed five guiding principles for reform, only the last of which appeared to call for major change:

(1) The original text should be disturbed as little as possible—unnecessary changes or "tinkering" should be avoided; (2) obsolete provisions should be eliminated; (3) the subject matter of the amendments should be incorporated in the body of the document; (4) certain changes in arrangement should be made to bring together related provisions; (5) and, finally, certain changes should be made so that the document will conform to modern conditions, and

so that a definite constitutional basis can be provided for various phases of our "unwritten constitution." (Coleman 1938, 17)

Coleman's proposed constitution contained nine articles in all. Article I drew from the Fourteenth, Fifteenth, and Nineteenth Amendments to set rules of citizenship. Article II dealt with the legislative branch. Because Coleman proposed eliminating the vice president, the Senate would elect its own president. Simple majorities of both houses would approve treaties, and congressional powers were specifically expanded to authorize the regulation of corporations and the conditions of labor, conservation, and agriculture. Article III provided for the elimination of individual electors but made no change in the allocation of electoral votes.

The only addition to Article IV (the judiciary) barred those convicted of treason from holding office, and changes in Article V (federal relations) were insubstantial. Article VI (prohibitions) more clearly applied the limits contained within the Bill of Rights to the national government. The article specifically prohibited states from seceding. Article VII altered the amending process by specifying that two-thirds (rather than three-fourths) of the states could ratify amendments, provided that the ratifying states contained at least three-fourths of the overall national population. Article VIII contained the supremacy clause, which confirmed that the constitution and federal statutes remained the law of the land. Article IX provided that the new constitution go into effect when ratified by conventions in 36 of the states.

Thomas Carlton Upham Calls for a More Democratic and Socialistic Society

The first half of the twentieth century was turbulent. Although Americans initially seemed isolated from German aggression in Europe and Japanese expansion in the East, in time they too became entangled in a second world war. Although most of the nation's energies were directed to that conflict, at least five individuals formulated or published plans to rewrite the Constitution during World War II.

Thomas Carlton Upham (1894–?) was born in Massachusetts and earned a master's degree in 1918 from the University of Illinois. In *Total Democracy: A New Constitution for the United States* (1941), he said that he hoped to "retain much of the framework, some of the contents, and all of the spirit—plus—of the old constitution," but he advanced a number of socialistic ideas as well, many of which were concerned with promoting greater equality. His proposed preamble thus lists, among other objectives, that of forming a society "of mutual cooperation, human brotherhood, general kindliness, common welfare, equal rights, economic security, material prosperity, and universal peace" (Upham 1941, 67).

Upham's proposed constitution began with the executive branch, consisting of a president nominated by petition and elected by a plurality of voters for a single six-year term. A senator would succeed the president in case of vacancy or incapacity. A three-fourths vote of Congress would be able to override the president's power as commander in chief. The president would have the right to submit legislation directly to Congress or to the people for approval. He would in turn be subject to recall by petition and a vote of two-thirds of the population.

Upham's Senate would consist of 17 nonpartisan citizens, elected for a maximum of two six-year terms. Each would also head one of 17 departments, including one dealing with "cultural security" and another with "private relations" (Upham 1941, 77). Members of the House would be chosen from 24 newly created districts that would take the place of the existing state and local governments. Upham advocated subjecting congressional laws to an item veto and granting people the right of petition, referendum, and recall.

Although Upham favored retaining the Supreme Court, he favored setting a mandatory retirement age of 75. He also provided for district courts and criminal boards. Petit (trial) juries would consist of six local citizens with six citizens from another part of the country. Upham called for taking the guarantee that defendants be tried by a jury of one's peers to a whole new level by asserting that at least one juror would be "of the same race, color, sex, and religious persuasion as the accused" (Upham 1941, 91). Government attorneys would serve both as defense counsel and as prosecutors.

At age 18 every citizen would be obligated to register for citizenship, which would carry the responsibility of working from age 21 to 70. Citizens could not be required to work, however, for more than five days and 35 hours a week, and they would be guaranteed two-week paid vacations. All would be paid according to a standard wage ranging (for those aged 25 to 60) from $1,000 to $10,000 annually. Although individuals would be permitted to own small businesses, the government would own major industries and individuals would be limited to owning $100,000 of private property. Upham's constitution included provisions to outlaw strikes and guarantee medical care and education to all. Other provisions forbade charity and required all citizens to learn English. A "work and wages" standard would replace the gold standard (Upham 1941, 113). Rights would be protected against both governmental and private action, with existing rights preserved and occasionally expanded.

Upham proposed to outlaw wars, but he made exceptions for defense and for actions within the Western hemisphere. He called for the United States to seek to form an international union that would work for "the attainment of Christian or other good ideals in the world" (Upham 1941, 114). Upham favored calling a convention of 84 individuals to write the new constitution, which would become effective when ratified by the people. Future amendments would be proposed by two-thirds of both houses of Congress and ratified by two-thirds of those voting. The president would also have the right to take proposed changes to the people through national referendums.

Henry Hazlitt Issues an Urgent Call for Parliamentary Government

Journalist Henry Hazlitt (1894–1993) published *A New Constitution Now* in 1942, and reissued it in 1974. Hazlitt was convinced that the U.S. Constitution was an inflexible document that contributed to many of the nation's ills. He stated in 1942 that U.S. adoption of a new parliamentary political system was not "a diversion from the war effort, any more than reform of military organization or personnel at such times is a diversion from the war effort. It is, on the contrary, one of the most essential things we must now do to organize our government properly to conduct a war" (Hazlitt 1942, 98).

Drawing from a deep vein of criticism by parliamentary advocates, Hazlitt characterized the U.S. government as irresponsible; subject to deadlocks brought about both by the separation of the legislative and executive branches and by the division of the former into two houses; and undemocratic. In his view, the existing U.S. system alternated between periods of presidential and congressional dictatorship and was so rigid that it encouraged governmental officials to "'interpret' the existing Constitution to mean that these officials already have the new powers they are looking for" (Hazlitt 1942, 13).

Hazlitt favored a parliamentary system incorporating three major changes: elimination of the relative equality of the two houses of Congress; changes in fixed congressional terms of office; and alterations to the presidential veto and other executive powers. Hazlitt wanted to reexamine voting qualifications, reduce membership in Congress, and allow Congress to choose a premier (separate from the president) to select a cabinet. The cabinet and a legislative council would have increased power over legislation, with the powers of the Senate reduced so that it became "a delaying and revising chamber" (Hazlitt 1942, 166). Hazlitt further advocated having senators appointed by state legislatures. He envisioned a Congress with authority to elect the president for five- to ten-year terms, and he favored the introduction of a new voting mechanism in which voters would rank candidates. Both the premier and the Congress would be subject to votes of no confidence, which could trigger new elections.

Other reforms advocated by Hazlitt included eliminating the Electoral College; limiting the president to two terms; vesting the president with an item veto; removing the residency requirements for members of Congress; fixing the membership of the Supreme Court; providing for the retirement of justices at age 70 or 75 and other means to remove them from the bench; permitting a majority vote of both houses of Congress to approve treaties; limiting the Senate's ability to add to appropriations bills; abolishing the vice presidency; and reforming the rules of Congress.

Convinced that the most urgent priority was to liberalize the amending process, Hazlitt favored adoption of the so-called Australian model, whereby amendments proposed by majorities of both houses of Congress would become law when ratified by "a majority of the voters in a majority of the States" (Hazlitt 1942, 261). He also favored allowing Congress to present more technical amendments to the state legislatures and leaving open a path for states to propose amendments. He did not think it was necessary to maintain the convention mechanism, since Congress could propose wholesale changes if it chose.

Herbert Agar and the Twelve Southerners Advance
More Philosophical Considerations

Herbert Agar (1897–1980) was an historian and editor for the *Louisiville Courier-Journal* who in 1942 authored *A Time for Greatness*, in which he called for national spiritual and political renewal to save civilization. One of the chapters in this book asked "Can We Make Government Accountable and Understandable?" Agar contrasted the "multiple-agency system" in the United States that separates governmental powers in order to keep them in check with a system like that in Great Britain that "concentrates power in an executive, and sets up a representative body whose sole task is to watch and criticize the executive" (Agar 1942, 83–4).

Although Agar did not advocate for strict American emulation of the British system, he believed that the chief executive should be responsible for formulating the budget, with the legislature serving in a strictly advisory capacity. More generally, Agar believed that it was the responsibility of the executive to prepare all needed measures and the function of Congress to act on them, "rejecting them, refining them, proposing alternatives, or accepting them as they are" (Agar 1942, 261).

Agar argued that the American Founders had actually intended for the system to be more accountable than it had become. He specifically criticized the Senate's unwillingness during President Washington's administration to serve as a type of privy council in formulating treaties, as well as Congress's refusal to allow Alexander Hamilton to appear on the House floor and "establish direct relations between the heads of Cabinet departments and Congress" (Agar 1942, 265). Concluding that "constitutional reinterpretation" might solve key problems, Agar was willing to use a convention mechanism if necessary (Agar 1942, 278).

Agar's emphasis on both spiritual and political reform resembled that of the Twelve Southerners, a group of intellectuals from Vanderbilt University in Nashville, Tennessee, who authored a book entitled *I'll Take My Stand* in 1930. The group, consisting of Donald Davidson, John Gould Fletcher, H. B. Kline, Lyle H. Lanier, Stark Young, Allen Tate, Andrew Nelson Lytle, H. C. Nixon, F. L. Owsley, John Crowe Ransom, John Donald Wade, and Robert Penn Warren, are associated with the Southern Agrarian tradition, which challenged modern industrialization and consumerism.

Two members of this group, Donald Davidson and Frank Owsley, advocated establishing regional governments, which they thought would be more capable of preserving regional identities, in place of existing states (Davidson 1936, Owsley 1961). Less concerned with competent administration than with drawing from deeper wells of wisdom and insight, Davidson envisioned a constitutional convention led by men who,

> like the fathers of the original Constitution, believe in the power of humanity over circumstances, and can bring to the task of constitution-making something more than the statistical and technical knowledge of the modern expert, and a great deal more than the sleek political knowingness which is the

average American politician's substitute for statesmanship. (Davidson 1936, 128–9)

Davidson believed that each regional commonwealth should have a veto power relative to tariff matters similar to "Calhoun's principle of nullification" (Davidson 1936, 130–1).

Alexander Hehmeyer Advocates for Cabinet Reform and Legislative/Executive Cooperation

Attorney Alexander Hehmeyer (1910–1993), a Chicago lawyer, hoped to use the sense of urgency that World War II had generated to stimulate interest in governmental reform. As the title of his 1943 book, *Time for Change: A Proposal for a Second Convention*, suggested, he wanted Congress to propose a constitutional convention for this purpose.

Hehmeyer favored a convention of 97 members. He thought the states should appoint 48 delegates, while Congress, the president, and the chief justice would each appoint 16 delegates. Congress would also appoint a chair—the ninety-seventh member—to oversee the convention. Hehmeyer further thought the convention should concentrate its attention in four areas: relations between the president and Congress, the balance between the nation and the states, liberalization of the amending process, and a reexamination of the Bill of Rights.

Hehmeyer thought that plans for parliamentary government were impractical, but he did seek "to make Congress more responsive to the President and to make the President more responsive to Congress and to do this without departing radically from existing institutional forms" (Hehmeyer 1943, 64). Although he toyed with the idea of a three-year presidential term, Hehmeyer suggested that terms for members of the House be extended to four years. Hehmeyer also advocated extensive cabinet reform, including reorganizing the cabinet to create the following eight members: a "Secretary Without Portfolio, Secretary for Administration, Secretary for Legislation, Secretary for International Affairs, Secretary for National Defense, Secretary for Law, Secretary of the Economy, [and a] Secretary for National Welfare" (Hehmeyer 1943, 77). Unlike current cabinet officers, however, most cabinet officials in Hehmeyer's government would allow their departments to be run by full-time administrators appointed through the civil service. The secretary of legislation would have the power to initiate legislation in Congress and participate in debates. The president could make changes in the cabinet on the basis of midterm elections.

Hehmeyer also proposed a number of congressional reforms, including the establishment of automatic vote recorders, more efficient parliamentary procedures, better staffing, and a joint legislative council. Consistent with his desire to streamline presidential-congressional relations, the aforementioned legislative council would include three presidential representatives to coordinate legislation between the two houses. Hehmeyer also favored reducing the number of standing committees, eliminating the seniority rule, and altering the system of appropriations. Like many other proponents of change during this period, he favored allowing majorities of both houses of Congress to ratify treaties. Hehmeyer believed that there was considerable room to develop regional authorities and consolidate local governments. He also favored eliminating tax duplication and resolving conflicts between state and national taxing authorities.

Hehmeyer admired the Bill of Rights and wanted to expand it by including economic and social rights. He also favored a more liberalized amending process. He proposed five different ways of proposing amendments: by majorities of both houses of Congress; by a two-thirds majority of either house in two or three consecutive sessions; by a majority of state legislatures proposing identically worded reforms within a five-year period; by a convention called either by Congress or by a majority of state legislatures; or, in a mechanism reminiscent of one that Thomas Jefferson had advanced, by a convention called every 30 years by the president (Hehmeyer 1943, 163–7). Hehmeyer further provided for ratification by two-thirds of the state legislatures acting within a four-year period or "[b]y a majority of the voters in two-thirds of the States and a majority of all those voting in the nation at a special election held within two years from the date of the proposal or at the next succeeding election for Representatives" (Hehmeyer 1943, 169).

Hehmeyer admired the work of the Supreme Court in protecting rights and favored allowing it to render advisory opinions. He wanted to fix the number of justices at nine and eliminate federal jurisdiction in diversity of citizenship cases. Under miscellaneous reforms, Hehmeyer proposed allowing the ex-president to serve for life in the Senate, granting the president an item veto, allowing for the postponing of national elections in times of national emergency, abolishing the electoral college and the vice presidency, and abolishing state residency requirements for members of Congress.

Thomas Finletter Advances Proposals for a More Unified Government

As World War II drew to a close, Thomas Finletter (1893–1980), an attorney and special assistant to the secretary of state, authored a book entitled *Can Representative Government Do the Job?* He wanted a government capable of creating "a peaceful world" and providing "substantially full and steady employment and social, economic, and personal security for our people" (Finletter 1945, 192). He feared, however, that the separation of powers and the conflicts that it was engendering between Congress and the Oval Office were creating obstacles to both goals:

> The general line which should be taken is, I think, reasonably clear. It is to change the procedures of the federal government so as to eliminate the causes of conflict between the two branches, to centralize the affirmative powers of government in the executive, and to do so in a way as to preserve the authority of Congress. (Finletter 1945, 67)

Finletter proposed a mix of measures, not all of which would require constitutional changes. He favored amending house rules to permit cabinet officers to appear before Congress to answer questions. He wanted to alter the seniority system in Congress; reduce the number of congressional committees; create more joint House and Senate committees; allow majorities of both houses to ratify treaties; and create "a joint Executive-Legislative Cabinet" of 18 people, all from the majority party.

To reduce the chance of divided government, Finletter favored making the terms of the president and members of Congress the same length. He suggested terms of six years for each. He further favored allowing the president to dissolve Congress and call a general election whenever a deadlock arose between Congress and the joint cabinet. Finletter believed that this system would restore unified government, strengthen party discipline, and make parties more responsible. He further favored eliminating the residency requirement for members of Congress so that parties could run candidates for office outside their districts.

Finletter framed his proposals as "a natural development of the American form of government" (Finletter 1945, 130) and emphasized that his reforms preserved federalism and bicameralism but also called for popular election of the president. Finletter recognized that formidable forces of "inertia and of satisfaction with things as they are" blocked the path to reform. However, he believed that barring major reforms, the conflict between the legislative and executive branches would eventually destroy self-government in the United States (Finletter 1945, 145–7).

Franklin D. Roosevelt's Proposed "Second Bill of Rights" and Huey Long's Share Our Wealth Program

The Depression-fighting New Deal programs of President Franklin D. Roosevelt (1882–1945) brought new understandings of the powers and responsibilities of the national government. It brought the initiation of the Social Security program, the creation of numerous regulatory agencies, and an assumption by the national government of responsibility for addressing economic problems that had previously rested largely on state and local authorities. Although much of the impetus for reform was spent during the first 100 days of Roosevelt's administration and later dissipated by the war effort, Roosevelt continued to articulate a vision whereby government would supplement existing political rights with social economic rights. Notably, in presenting his historic address on the Four Freedoms on January 6, 1941, Roosevelt included "freedom from want" among traditional freedoms of speech and expression, freedom to worship, and freedom from fear.

In his 1944 State of the Union Address, Roosevelt further elaborated on what he described as "a Second Bill of Rights." These rights, which were designed to secure "economic security and independence," were as follows:

- The right to a useful and remunerative job in the industries or shops or farms or mines of the Nation;
- The right to earn enough to provide adequate food and clothing and recreation;
- The right of every farmer to raise and sell his products at a return which will give him and his family a decent living;

- The right of every businessman, large and small, to trade in an atmosphere of freedom from unfair competition and domination by monopolies at home or abroad;
- The right of every family to a decent home;
- The right to adequate medical care and the opportunity to achieve and enjoy good health;
- The right to adequate protection from the economic fears of old age, sickness, accident, and unemployment; [and]
- The right to a good education.

Despite the nomenclature ("a second Bill of Rights"), Roosevelt did not propose these as constitutional amendments but as items of legislative action.

Almost a decade before Roosevelt unveiled his Second Bill of Rights, Louisiana senator Huey P. Long (1893–1935) had advanced a Share Our Wealth Program that had an even greater redistributionist focus. Long's program was based on the idea that those who owned wealth had effectively stolen it from those who did not have it. In a speech published in the *Congressional Record* of May 23, 1935—the same year he was assassinated—Long outlined an eight-point plan.

The first provision called for the government to furnish every family with a homestead allowance of $5,000 to $6,000 and limit the highest fortune to no more than 300 times that of the lowest. A second provision guaranteed annual family incomes at $2,000 to $2,500 and limited individual incomes to no more than $1.8 million annually. A third provision provided for the regulation of work hours and a fourth established old-age pensions for individuals over 60. The fifth provision provided for governmental storage of surplus agricultural production, and a sixth mandated care for veterans and for the disabled. Long's seventh proposal called for providing universal education and training for all children, while the last explained that the aforementioned social programs would be funded by reducing "swollen fortunes from the top." Long did not believe that constitutional change would be needed to implement his reforms. Instead, he argued that the principles he advocated were already embodied in American documents, including the Mayflower Compact of 1620 and the U.S. Constitution.

C. Perry Patterson Calls for Readjusting the Balance between President and Congress

Constitutional reformer C. Perry Patterson obtained a law degree from the University of Texas and a PhD from Columbia before becoming a professor of government at Texas. In 1947, he published *Presidential Government in the United States: The Unwritten Constitution*, in which he proposed a plan to significantly impact the way that the Constitution would operate.

In the book's preface, Patterson explained his belief that American "constitutional democracy" has been changed "into a political democracy" and his conviction that the United States has "converted a limited into an unlimited democracy and, thereby, substituted an unwritten for a written constitution and a government of laws for a government of men" (Patterson 1947, v). In Patterson's view, the president had established virtual "hegemony," and the cure for such "irresponsible executive government" was "a modified form of responsible cabinet government" (Patterson 1947, v–vi). Although America had been premised on the idea that fundamental law would control government, practice had overcome such restraints, and it was time to substitute political controls.

Patterson believed that U.S. history had witnessed "the drifting of the powers of the Congress into the hands of the President with the approval of judicial review and the American people" (Patterson 1947, 239). Although Congress was supreme in theory, the president was wielding primary power in practice. Patterson joined Harold J. Laski and others in arguing that it was time to take action against what they saw as a dangerous development. Patterson believed that the attempt to separate legislative and executive powers had been flawed from the start and that the development of unwritten constitutional practices had simply confirmed this: "The Constitution, like the English Crown, is the source of authority but no longer governs" (Patterson 1947, 254). The two alternatives were "a dictator" or "responsible party government" (Patterson 1947, 254). According to Patterson, the nation had already tried reliance on the congressional caucus, the speaker of the House, the committee system, and the presidency, only to find that none of these options worked. In his view, it was impossible to make the president the head of the government in a system of fixed terms. Better, then, to separate the presidential functions as head of state from those as head of the government:

> Responsible government requires that both leadership and the opposition come from the same body and that the opposition, as a matter or right and fair play, be allowed to succeed to the position of governing when it defeats the Government of the Day. (Patterson 1947, 258)

He added that attempts to duplicate "the English form of cabinet government" would be "beyond the realm of probability and in some respects is not desirable" (Patterson 1947, 259).

Patterson explained that the executive could be made responsible "only by making the ministers responsible to the Congress and by forcing the President to act through ministers chosen from the Congress" (Patterson 1947, 260). This, in turn, required

> that the Congress . . . be organized on a party basis by the creation of a body of political leaders who will be responsible to the party system and who will initiate legislative policy, and, thereby, serve as a check upon the President by means of the party system in the Congress. They cannot be presidential puppets subject to his dismissal at will. (Patterson 1947, 260)

Such party leaders would be separated from "the bondage of the committee system" (Patterson 1947, 260), which relied chiefly upon seniority. According to

Patterson, these reforms would foster meaningful debates within Congress and encourage leaders to show their worth through oratory, much as they do in sessions of Parliament in Britain.

Because the existing cabinet system had largely grown up outside the Constitution, Patterson anticipated that it could be changed without requiring constitutional amendments. He proposed that Congress select a prime minister "by a caucus composed of the members of the Congress of the majority party" (Patterson 1947, 261). He anticipated that members of both houses would participate in the selection, thus largely making bicameralism "a constitutional formality" (Patterson 1947, 262), but that the prime minister would almost always be a member of the House. The prime minister would then select the cabinet with approval of the party caucus. The opposition party would be similarly organized. The cabinet would exercise collective responsibility, and the prime minister would fall when defeated on a major measure. Two cabinet officers (one for each house) would be connected to each major department of government, serving as their "political heads," while "the President's secretaries would be their legal heads" (Patterson 1947, 269). Patterson explained that "this proposal leaves the President with an administrative council composed of these legal appointees but places it under the political supervision of the responsible representatives of the party or coalition in power" (Patterson 1947, 270). Patterson suggested that judicial review would play a minor role in this system. After each congressional election, the cabinet would be dissolved as some members were voted out of office. Patterson thus thought he had provided "within the Constitution . . . for a more ideal and responsible cabinet system than has yet been constructed" (Patterson 1947, 271). He described his reforms as "not revolutionary but restorative in character" and "involv[ing] no constitutional changes or statutory enactment" (Patterson 1947, 273).

In a final chapter, Patterson asserted that his plan would strip the president "of the powers of an English Cabinet," convert "the political executive into a plural executive," simplify the legislative process, unify legislative and executive powers, provide "for capable and responsible supervision of the bureaucracy," permit "a real merit system and a career service for the national service," and bring about numerous other advantages (Patterson 1947, 277). He did not, however, provide a timetable for implementing his plan.

The New York Bar Association Proposes Amendments and a Law to Defend the Supreme Court

In the wake of his reelection in 1937, President Franklin D. Roosevelt proposed a plan to add one justice to the Supreme Court for each sitting justice who, having served at least 10 years, did not resign or retire within six months after reaching the age of 70. Roosevelt announced that he would add no more than six additional justices to the court under this plan. Initially proposed as a way to help the Supreme Court handle its heavy workload, it became apparent that the plan was motivated by Roosevelt's frustration with the Supreme Court's hostility to many of his proposed New Deal programs (Somin and Devins 2007, 984). Congress ultimately defeated Roosevelt's "court-packing" proposal and the Supreme Court gradually became more receptive to his policies. Nonetheless, Roosevelt's gambit exposed possible vulnerabilities of the third branch of government.

In 1948, the Special Committee on the Federal Courts of the New York City Bar Association proposed four constitutional amendments and a law designed to protect the Supreme Court from future political maneuverings and attacks. The first proposed amendment would have altered the U.S. Constitution specifically to indicate that the Supreme Court would consist of a chief justice and eight associate members. A second would have provided that justices would have to retire at age 75 (it was unclear whether this amendment would have required immediate resignations of those already over this age or not). A third proposed amendment would have added a sentence to the existing language of Article III, Section 2 of the Constitution (immediately after the sentence delineating the original jurisdiction of the Supreme Court) providing that "[i]n all Cases arising under this Constitution the supreme Court shall have appellate Jurisdiction both as to Law and Fact." The section then continued with a provision granting Congress the authority to make exceptions to other cases, thus presumably protecting core Court functions against judicial tinkering. A fourth proposal would have made any justice or chief justice eligible for president or vice president. The committee also proposed a law that would forbid sitting justices from holding any other governmental posts. These proposals did not attract sustained political support, but they attracted high-profile commentary from legal scholars ranging from former Supreme Court Justice Owen Roberts (1949) to distinguished attorney Frank Grinnell (1949), who served as secretary of the Massachusetts Bar Association from 1915 to 1960.

A Note on Internationalism

World War II stimulated renewed thinking about world alliances and world governments. Journalist Clarence K. Streit advanced what he called a proposal for a "Federal Union of the Leading Democracies" in *Union Now: The Proposal for Inter-democracy Federal Union*, with its own "illustrative constitution" (1940, 201–11). Similarly, a prestigious group of scholars called the Committee to Frame a World Constitution and headed by Robert M. Hutchins, president of the University of Chicago, issued a *Preliminary Draft of a World Constitution* in 1947. John Francis Goldsmith published a novel entitled *President Randolph as I Knew Him* in 1935. Set in the 1950s and 1960s, it follows the title character as he moves from being U.S. president to president of the United Nations of the World. Notably, Goldsmith's novel included a draft of the Constitution of the United Nations of the World, which consisted of nine articles patterned after the U.S. Constitution (Randolph 1935, 421–48).

Instead of following either of these routes, the United States established a series of post-war alliances, including the North Atlantic Treaty Organization (NATO), to contain Communist expansion around the world. Whereas the U.S. Senate refused American entry into the League of Nations at the end of World War I, it approved American entry into the United Nations after World War II. The UN charter and a number of subsequent human rights conventions have helped proclaim the ideals of human rights, which were already deeply embedded in the U.S. Declaration of Independence and the U.S. Constitution, throughout the world.

Summary and Analysis

During the period covered in this chapter, advocates of major constitutional reforms introduced myriad plans. Ideas of parliamentary government and socialism continued to provide alternate models to the U.S. Constitution, as did an eclectic mix of other proposals, including associational representation and individual adjustments to the existing branches of government. Several proposals advocated redrawing or eliminating existing state lines and consideration of statehood for some municipalities. Finally, some reformers openly wondered whether the kind of confederation that had once provided an umbrella for 13 colonies to oppose the British Empire might serve as a model for ending the wars engendered by a multiplicity of nations.

References

Agar, Herbert. 1942. *A Time for Greatness*. Boston: Little Brown.

Coleman, Charles. 1938. *The Constitution Up to Date*. Bulletin No. 10. Cambridge, MA: National Council for Social Studies.

Cram, Ralph. 1937. *The End of Democracy*. Boston: Marshall Jones Company.

Davidson, Donald. 1936. "That This Nation May Endure—The Need for Political Regionalism." In *Who Owns America? A New Declaration of Independence*, edited by Herbert Agar and Allen Tate, 113–34. Boston: Houghton Mifflin.

Eiselen, Malcolm R. 1941. "Can We Amend the Constitution?" *South Atlantic Quarterly* 40 (October): 333–41.

Eiselen, Malcolm R. 1937. "Dare We Call a Federal Convention?" *North American Review* 244 (Autumn): 27–8.

Elliott, William Yandell. 1935. *The Need for Constitutional Reform: A Program for National Security*. New York: Whittlesey House.

Finletter, Thomas K. 1945. *Can Representative Government Do the Job?* New York: Reynal and Hitchcock.

Goldsmith, John Francis. 1935. *President Randolph as I Knew Him*. Philadelphia: Dorrance & Company.

Grinnell, Frank W. 1949. "Proposed Amendments to the Constitution: A Reply to Former Justice Roberts." *American Bar Association Journal* 35 (August): 704–6.

Hamilton, Hugh L. 1938. *A Second Constitution for the United States of America*. Richmond, VA: Garrett and Massie.

Hazlitt, Henry. 1974 [1942]. *A New Constitution Now*. New York: Whittlesey House.

Hehmeyer, Alexander. 1943. *Time for Change: A Proposal for a Second Constitutional Convention*. New York: Farrar and Rinehart.

Hutchins, Robert M. et al., eds. 1947. *Preliminary Draft of a World Constitution*. Chicago: The University of Chicago Press.

Long, Huey P. May 23, 1935. "Statement of the Share Our Wealth Movement." *Congressional Record*, 74th Cong., 1st sess., 79: 8040–3.

McKee, Henry S. 1933. *Degenerate Democracy*. New York: Thomas Y. Crowell.

Merriam, Charles. 1931. *The Written Constitution and the Unwritten Attitude*. New York: Richard R. Smith.

Owsley, Frank L. 1961. "Democracy Unlimited." *Georgia Review* 15 (Summer): 140.

Patterson, C. Perry. 1947. *Presidential Government in the United States: The Unwritten Constitution*. Chapel Hill: The University of North Carolina Press.

Piburn, John L. 1932. *A Constitution and a Code*. San Diego: Bowman Printing Company.

Porter, Kirk H., and Donald B. Johnson. 1966. *National Party Platforms, 1840–1964*. Urbana: University of Illinois Press.

Roberts, Owen J. 1949. "Now Is the Time: Fortifying the Supreme Court's Independence." *American Bar Association Journal* 35 (January): 1–4.

Roosevelt, Franklin D. January 11, 1944. "State of the Union Address." http://www.heritage.org/initiatives/first-principles/primary-sources/fdrs-second-bill-of-rights.

Roosevelt, Franklin D. January 6, 1941. "The Four Freedoms." http://www.americanrhetoric.com/speeches/fdrthefourfreedoms.htm.

Shand-Tucci, Douglass. 1995. *Ralph Adams Cram: Life and Architecture*. Vol. I. Amherst: University of Massachusetts Press.

Somin, Ilya, and Neal Devins. 2007. "Can We Make the Constitution More Democratic?" *Drake Law Review* (2006–2007): 971–1000.

Streit, Clarence K. 1940. *Union Now: The Proposal for Inter-Democracy Federal Union*. New York: Harper & Brothers Publishers.

"Supreme Court of the U.S.: Amendments of the Constitution Are Proposed." 1948. *American Bar Association Journal* 34 (January): 1–3.

Twelve Southerners. 1930. *I'll Take My Stand*. New York: Harper & Brothers. Also see Baton Rouge: Louisiana University Press, 1977.

Upham, Thomas C. 1941. *Total Democracy: A New Constitution for the United States. A Democratic Ideal for the World*. New York: Carlyle House.

Vile, John R. 2010. *Encyclopedia of Constitutional Amendments, Proposed Amendments, and Amending Issues, 1789–2010*. 3rd ed. Santa Barbara, CA: ABC-CLIO.

Wallace, William Kay. 1932. *Our Obsolete Constitution*. New York: John Day.

CHAPTER 7

Proposals from the Tumultuous 1960s and 1970s

No major constitutional reform proposals emerged during the 1950s. In 1950, the American Political Science Association (APSA) did release a report from its Committee on Political Parties advocating a more responsible two-party system. The APSA report did not, however, suggest any constitutional amendments, and it even warned that a cabinet system might not result in more effective political parties (1950, 35–7).

The 1960s and 1970s witnessed the flowering of the civil rights movement; the assassinations of John Kennedy, Martin Luther King, Jr., and Robert Kennedy; rising casualties and increasing protests over the Vietnam War; and the Watergate crisis. As in past periods of turbulence in American society, a variety of individuals responded to these events by proposing constitutional changes. In 1976, however, the nation celebrated the bicentennial of the Declaration of Independence. This milestone, along with the subsequent celebration of the bicentennial of the U.S. Constitution in the following decade, affirmed to many Americans that the nation had successfully weathered the storms of the 1960s and 1970s without having to significantly amend the U.S. Constitution.

Herman Finer Advocates Reform of the Presidency

Political scientist Herman Finer (1898–1969) presented far-ranging reforms of the U.S. government in his 1960 book *The Presidency, Crisis and Regeneration: An Essay in Possibilities*. Although Finer believed that the job of president had become too big for any single individual to handle, he also believed that differing terms of office for the president and members of Congress contributed to the problem. Most of his reforms pointed to a constitution closer to that of a parliamentary system.

Finer offered nine major reforms to the existing system. His first reform proposed that the president run for office on a ticket with 11 vice presidents selected by national nominating conventions. All elected nominees would have four-year terms. The vice presidents would, like current members of the cabinet, head executive departments, although some might also serve solely as policy advisors and counselors. Finer's second proposal called for extending four-year terms to members of both the House and Senate. He believed this change would encourage them to promote a common platform and strengthen existing parties.

Finer's third proposal called for limiting the presidency and vice presidency to individuals who were either currently serving in Congress or who had done so for four years. Members of Congress who were elected to the cabinet would be replaced through special elections, and nominees on the losing ticket would still serve in the house of Congress of their choice.

Finer's fourth proposal called for the president to name his top vice president and to designate an order of succession among the others. His fifth proposal called for the president to set general policy but empowered each vice president to "conduct the business of his department independently and on his own responsibility" (Finer 1960, 314).

Finer's sixth proposal gave the president authority to dismiss and replace vice presidents. It also contained provisions giving the president and cabinet members the right to participate in debates in the House of Representatives and answer questions posed to them. Another provision reduced the Senate's power by removing its authority to confirm appointments, ratify treaties, and participate in the overriding of presidential vetoes. The seventh proposal set forth by Finer would allow the House to override such a veto by a 55 percent vote.

Finer's eighth proposal would allow the president and his cabinet to resign and call for new legislative and executive elections, but he did not think that Congress should be able to oust the president and his cabinet on its own. His ninth proposal would eliminate patronage and spoils by allowing civil servants to continue in office, regardless of party affiliation, as long as they served the government faithfully and competently. In *Cracks in the Constitution* (1980), economist and journalist Ferdinand Lundberg wrote in positive terms about a number of Finer's proposed reforms.

The Council of State Governments Responds to Warren Court Reforms

Several U.S. Supreme Court decisions of the 1950s and early 1960s established state legislative apportionment as "justiciable"—subject to Court review—and required state legislatures to be apportioned according to the "one person, one vote" standard. These rulings prompted the National Legislative Conference of the Council of State Governments in September 1962 to direct its Committee on Federal-State Relations to consider proposing amendments to strengthen the power of states within the federal system (Committee on Federal-State Relations 1963, 10). It submitted its report to the December 1962 meeting of the General Assembly of the States, sponsored by the Council of State Governments. The committee asserted in its report that decisions by the Warren Court were undercutting the powers of the states. The committee also echoed Anti-Federalist concerns about the impartiality of an unelected branch of the *national* government—the Supreme Court—empowered to rule on the constitutionality of *state* actions:

> While the founding fathers fully expected and wished the words of the Constitution to have this degree of finality, it is impossible to believe that they envisaged such potency for the pronouncements of nine judges, appointed

by the President and confirmed by the Senate. The Supreme Court is, after all, an organ of the federal government. It is one of the three branches of the national government, and in conflicts over federal and state power, the Court is necessarily an agency of one of the parties in interest. . . . There is need for an easier method of setting such decisions straight when they are unsound. (Committee on Federal-State Relations 1963, 10)

The committee decided to recommend three constitutional changes, which it wanted state legislatures to present in identically worded "memorializing" resolutions to Congress, to call a constitutional convention.

The first called for making the constitutional amending process easier by eliminating the convention mechanism altogether (presumably as a way of safeguarding state legislatures). This proposal further provided that passage of identically worded resolutions from two-thirds of the state legislatures would automatically trigger the ratification process (in which the amendment would come into force if approved by three-fourths of the states). The Council of State Governments adopted this resolution by a vote of 37 to 4, with four states abstaining.

The second amendment, which passed by a 26 to 10 vote, contained language overruling the Supreme Court decision in *Baker v. Carr*, 369 U.S. 186 (1962). In this ruling, the Supreme Court had declared congressional apportionment issues to be within its jurisdiction by providing that "[n]o provision of this Constitution, or any amendment thereto, shall restrict or limit any state in the apportionment of representation in the legislature" (Committee on Federal-State Relations, 1963, 10). The Supreme Court further specified that "[t]he judicial power of the United States shall not extend to any suit in law or equity, or to any controversy, relating to apportionment of representation in a state legislature" (Committee on Federal-State Relations 1963, 10).

The third amendment, adopted by a razor-thin 21 to 20 majority, with five states abstaining, was the most radical of all. It proposed creating a "Court of the Union" consisting of the chief justice of each state's highest court. When duly petitioned by "the legislatures of five states, no two of which shall share any common boundary," this Court of the Union would review any Supreme Court decision "relating to the rights reserved to the states or to the people by this Constitution." This court would have the power to reverse Supreme Court decisions. The proposed amendment further provided that "decisions of the Court of the Union upon matters within its jurisdiction shall be final and shall not thereafter be overruled by any court and may be changed only by an amendment of this Constitution" (Committee on Federal-State Relations 1963, 14).

Of the three proposals, the one that came closest to calling for another constitutional convention was the one calling for a repeal of *Baker v. Carr*. The other two proposals, however, elicited significant scholarly commentary, much of it negative. Professor William Swindler of the College of William and Mary called them a throwback to the Articles of Confederation (Swindler 1963); Professor Charles Black, Jr., of Yale called them "a threatened disaster" (Black 1963); and Professor

Alpheus T. Mason of Princeton referred to them as "'DisUnion' Amendments" (Mason 1964). Other voices also weighed in with critical responses. Journalist Thomas B. Morgan published an article on the proposals in *Look* under the title "Seventeen States Vote to Destroy Democracy as We Know It" (Morgan 1963), and the American Bar Association also expressed its disapproval (Swindler 1963, 11–12).

H. Wentworth Eldredge Calls for Developing an Aristocracy of Talented Elites

In 1964, Dartmouth College sociology professor H. Wentworth Eldredge (1910–1991) authored a book entitled *The Second American Revolution*. The book was based on his view that every nation was ruled by elites, and that if America were to win the Cold War, it needed to do more to cultivate such elites and to organize its government in a more rational system.

Eldredge believed that separation of powers and federalism were impeding prompt and effective governmental actions. He favored strengthening executive powers and suggested that "a happy functional design might well be the British parliamentary system as basic design leavened with the American spirit" (Eldredge 1964, 293). He disdained the idea of allowing common people to make governmental decisions and thought it was important to identify individuals with "IQ, aptitude, and creativity" (Eldredge 1964, 300), train them, and put them in governmental positions. As he explained: "the United States requires for this dangerous world a centralized government of top-notch professionals tightly organized and tightly [run]; it has instead a passel of amateurs—sometimes gifted, sometimes not" (Eldredge 1964, 331).

Eldredge believed that the United States had outgrown the antiquated government of the Founding Fathers and that modern citizens were "less interested in the powers of government than in the results" and would welcome elites who were able to deliver (Eldredge 1964, 334). He was contemptuous of efforts to get ill-informed citizens to the ballot booth, and he referred to such voters as "demagogue-bait" (Eldredge 1964, 370).

Eldredge further asserted that federalism was an anomaly in the modern world. He suggested that "the internal civil service, the career foreign services, and the military arm of the federal government are adjuncts of the Executive Branch" should "be the natural habitat of an American aristocracy of talent" (Eldredge 1964, 339). Summarizing his position, he described his book as "a plea for the granting to an enlarged, elegantly staffed, professional administered executive branch of the government massive grants of power commensurate with the human and social realities of our time." Whereas the Founders had concentrated on "anchors," it was now time to concentrate on "navigation" and "propulsive power" (Eldredge 1964, 343).

Eldredge believed that judicial review further hindered effective governmental action, and likened adherence to the institution to the Hindu worship of sacred cows. He was even more contemptuous of Congress, which he called a "futilitarian anachronism" (Eldredge 1964, 346). He criticized many of the institution's practices and folkways, including the power wielded by committee chairs and the seniority system. Eldredge suggested both term limitations and a presidential item veto as antidotes to reduce Congress's influence.

Elredge was similarly dismissive of state and local governments, describing them as "a mudbank left by the receding tides of history" (Eldredge 1964, 353). He also expressed contempt for municipal governments, which he thought were inadequate to deal with major metropolitan areas. Eldredge favored applying the managerial revolution to governments. In his view, the cure for democracy was not "more democracy" but more effectively organized government with greater executive authority. He recommended greater long-range planning for conservation; "a reasoned plan for national urbanization"; "the enhancement of higher culture"; "a rational agricultural policy"; "a fundamental revamping of the control, ownership, and use of mass media so that in addition to amusing for profit they might also enlighten"; a more coherent science policy; more effective investment for economic growth; an "expanded program of social welfare from the 'cradle to the grave' including medical care"; a way to lever private resources to pay for public sector services; greater attention to producing useful rather than useless goods; separation of the capital budget from the operating budget; and a more rational model of foreign policy-making. If all of these changes are made, wrote Eldredge, "the executive part of the federal government will be in effect *the* government" (Eldredge 1964, 365–8).

Further Calls for a Convention by Carl B. Swisher and Mario Pei

Despite negative responses to the constitutional revisions it had proposed in 1963, the Council for State Governments reopened consideration of another constitutional convention. The CSG proposals prompted Carl B. Swisher (1897–1968), a political scientist at Johns Hopkins University, to reflect on whether the time had arrived for "a 'convention' of thought and speculation about the underlying assumptions of our constitutional system" (Swisher and Nelson 1968, 725). He observed that:

> We shall be better served by overcoming our aversion to bold, broad, hard thought in the tradition of the Founding Fathers than by merely considering adoption, by any means whatever, of constitutional amendments dealing narrowly and specifically with legislative apportionment, or prayer in the public schools, or the scope of Supreme Court jurisdiction. (Swisher and Nelson 1968, 725)

Among the topics that he thought were ripe for reconsideration were such concerns as the relation between the people and their leaders; problems connected with "the proper flow of information"; leadership; the role of business corporations; relations between the military and the people; industry; the presidency, Congress, and the judicial branch; the role of the states; and the commitment to the rule of law (Swisher and Nelson 1968, 724–31).

Mario Pei (1901–1978), an Italian-born professor of romance language, added his own call for a convention in the 1967–1968 issue of the conservative journal *Modern Age*. Pei endorsed a convention to review such issues as prayer in school, the Supreme Court's decisions on reapportionment and the rights of the accused, and executive powers over "taxation, public welfare, and foreign relations" (Pei 1967–68, 10–11). He further suggested that a convention could decide whether to lengthen terms of members of the House of Representatives to four years; whether to clarify congressional and presidential war powers; whether to continue the Electoral College; whether there was a better way to select Supreme Court justices; whether the president might run on a ticket with his cabinet; whether the establishment clause should have the meaning the Court had given to it; how to interpret the guarantee of "liberty" in the Fifth Amendment; whether the Sullivan Law (a New York gun control law) violated the Second Amendment; how to define state and federal powers; and how to apportion taxes between the state and national governments (Pei 1967–68, 10–12). Pei suggested selecting delegates to a convention on a nonpartisan basis and requiring agreement on proposals by a two-thirds vote.

Michael Oliver Proposes a New Constitution for a New Country

In 1968, a Lithuanian-born Nevada businessman named Michael Oliver published *A New Constitution for a New Country*. Oliver wrote the book after becoming convinced that the U.S. government was becoming increasingly totalitarian and that its policies were "raising generations of beggars" (Oliver 1968, 12). He believed that forces were in place to burn down U.S. cities and proclaimed "that the United States no longer can be saved from severe crisis" (Oliver 1968, 16). He further asserted that it was important for him and others to pursue their own self-interests, even if this meant abandoning their native land. He cited the philosophy of Ayn Rand and Ludwig Von Mises, which held that "man's pursuance of his rational self-interest is fully moral."

Oliver had concluded that the only sensible thing for rational citizens to do, given the declining state of America, was to create a new country. *A New Constitution for a New Country* contained his proposed constitution for that nation. In an opening Declaration of Purpose, Oliver discussed his proposal to create a corporation to purchase and settle a new country in which individuals would buy stock and where they would settle. Once 500 settlers arrived, they would create a local government. Once eight or more local governments had been established, they would be organized into counties. Once the population reached 40,000, these counties would then be organized into a nation.

Oliver believed that one of the problems of the U.S. Constitution was that it omitted details, thus allowing "an array of clauses open to interpretation; thereby making willful debasement of Constitutional intent easy to accomplish" (Oliver 1968, 43). With this perceived shortcoming in mind, he preceded his constitution with a glossary emphasizing the rights of "life, property, and freedom" (Oliver

1968, 45). He further defined government as "an entity hired by participating persons and entities" to protect such rights (Oliver 1968, 46). His preamble, printed in all caps, provided that "This Constitution is founded on the principle that the only true and proper function of government is to protect persons and entities from force and fraud, and that this government is to be limited to this function only" (Oliver 1968, 49).

Article I outlined the structure of a national government, which was to be divided into a legislative branch, a judiciary branch, and an executive, or "Ready-Alert Branch" (Oliver 1968, 51). Congress would consist of a House and a Senate, the former to be capped at 75 people who would serve three-year terms, and the second to consist of two representatives from each county serving six-year terms. Oliver's judiciary was divided into a House Judiciary Board, selected from among judiciary supervisors from the counties serving four-year terms, and a Senate Judiciary Board selected from the former, with two additional years of service. The Ready-Alert Branch was a plural executive of from 7 to 10 individuals who would serve two-year terms, and the chairman of which would chair the National Security Council.

Article II provided for "Time of Assembly, Quorums, Procedures, Rules and Impeachments" (Oliver 1968, 57). Some of these elements were taken from the existing U.S. Constitution, with ample provisions for impeachment and removal from office. Article III outlined limited duties for the government, mostly in the realm of national defense and related matters. For example, it stipulated that the Ready-Alert Panel could repel immediate attacks, but most defense matters would be decided by the Congress. Article III further provided that the House and Senate Judiciary Boards would advise as to the constitutionality of legislation before it was passed.

Article IV outlined the structure of local and county governments, the latter of which would have their own constitutions. Article V further outlined the function and organization of military forces. It prohibited involuntary conscription and relied on liberal pay and benefits to attract recruits. The military could help during domestic natural emergencies, but would be reimbursed by insurance companies.

Article VI prohibited any treaties with foreign nations or the creation of embassies. It also included a provision requiring immigrants to pay for governmental services. Article VII prohibited any government-issued money; private entities would issue money but would have to show sufficient collateral for doing so. The government would get all its money from the voluntary payment of premiums or reimbursements for services, with minors being charged less than adults.

Article VIII outlined Oliver's proposed judiciary system, which included local civil and criminal courts, county courts, and the National Judiciary Boards. All persons would be guaranteed equal protection "regardless of race, religion, origin, wealth, or influence" (Oliver 1968, 83). The government would appoint defense attorneys for those who needed them, but those found guilty would have to reimburse the government. Special provisions also were made for combatting organized crime and treason.

Article IX expanded the personal rights included within the current Bill of Rights. These rights included prohibitions on any governmental interference with marriages or other voluntary associations, as well as protections for privacy and "freedom of movement" (Oliver 1968, 92). The government was prohibited from supporting education, aiding religious organizations, or building roads and post offices, all of which would instead be undertaken by private enterprises. This article also prohibited the government from providing "any sort of insurance, compensation, pension, or retirement services" (Oliver 1968, 93).

Article X outlined activities permitted to government, including service as a voluntary registration agency. Other services included securing right-of-ways, formulating a National Legal Code to protect patents, prohibiting the importation of dangerous products, preventing fraud, and the like. Other responsibilities included protecting access to waterways and requiring owners of roads and utilities to keep them adequately maintained. The final article provided further commentary on the preceding provisions.

Oliver and his allies and supporters moved to make this nation a reality in the early 1970s. Oliver formed a corporation to build a 400-acre island on an atoll south of Fiji and Tonga in 1971. After months of construction activity on the atoll, known as Minerva Reef, a flag was raised and independence was proclaimed in 1972. The king of Tonga reclaimed the atoll in September of that year, however, and Oliver's project collapsed.

Dwight Macdonald Proposes Moving the U.S. Closer to a Parliamentary System

In 1968, journalist Dwight Macdonald offered a set of 10 proposed amendments in response to a request by the editors of *Esquire* "to bring the Constitution up-to-date" (Macdonald 1968).

Macdonald's first two proposals would have moved the nation closer to parliamentary government by replacing the president with a chairman elected by the majority party in Congress and giving this chair a term of six years. The chair, however, was subject to a vote of no confidence, which would trigger new elections in both branches. He further proposed eliminating the vice presidency and extending the terms of House members to four years.

Macdonald's next four proposals called for conscripting all male citizens for military or social service; a negative income tax "without regard to Work, Moral Character or any other Consideration except Need" (Macdonald 1968, 146); the appointment of ombudsmen, called "tributes," in each congressional district (Macdonald 1968, 238); and the establishment of commissions with power to preserve historical buildings and protect the natural environment (Macdonald 1968, 240).

Two other proposals were designed to restrain the U.S. military. The first would limit the number of U.S. service members overseas (except in emergency situations requiring a four-fifths vote of both houses of Congress) to one-fourth of 1 percent of the population, while the second would cap military expenditures at 3 percent of the gross national product. Macdonald's penultimate proposal would halt funding of the space program until the percentage of poor people living in America was less than 1 percent, while his final amendment would redraw the states in accord with "the present economic, social and political Geography of the North American Union." He tentatively proposed the establishment of nine regional subdivisions and 20 to 30 "city states" that would provide a better urban-rural balance in Congress (Macdonald 1968, 243–6).

The Black Panthers Hold an Unconventional National Convention

Although mainline civil rights groups followed Dr. Martin Luther King, Jr., in pursuing desegregation through nonviolent means, others heeded Malcolm X's exhortation to defend their rights "by any means necessary." African American college students Bobby Seale and Huey Newton founded the Black Panther Party in Oakland, California, in October of 1966. Admirers of such revolutionary thinkers as Karl Marx, Mao Tse-Tung, and Che Guevara, Black Panther leaders (who later came to include Eldridge Cleaver) pursued a strategy of "armed self-defense" that led them into frequent and often bloody conflicts with the police. These violent clashes and the group's revolutionary rhetoric heightened the group's profile and enabled it to establish chapters in cities across the country.

On June 19, 1970, representatives of the group appeared at the Lincoln Memorial and announced its plans for "a Revolutionary People's Convention" to be convened on Labor Day in Philadelphia. Panther Chief of Staff David Hilliard announced the meeting's rather conventional-sounding (if a pun may be permitted) hope to prepare a "constitution that will guarantee and deliver to every American citizen the inviolable human rights to life, liberty, and the pursuit of happiness" ("Panther Conference" 1970, 683).

Almost 6,000 Panther supporters attended the convention on the campus of Temple University from September 5–7, 1970, against a "backdrop of violence, rumors of violence, and a raging war of words" (Moore 1970, 1298). In his address to the participants, Newton—whose formal title was Minister of Defense of the Party—focused on the gap between the rhetoric of the founding Americans and the treatment of minorities by a nation that had "become an imperialist power dedicated to death, oppression, and the pursuit of profits" (quoted in Heath 1976, 380). Newton called for "freedom and the power to determine our destiny . . . full employment for all our people . . . [and] an end to capitalist exploitation of our community," as well as improved housing, exemptions from military service, a crackdown on police brutality, and the release of all political prisoners. Other demands included "fair trials for all men by a jury of their peers" and "a United Nations plebiscite to determine the will of the black people as to their national destiny" (quoted in Heath 1976, 380–1). Continuing, Newton explained his aims:

> [W]e assemble a Constitutional Convention to consider rational and positive alternatives. Alternatives which will place their emphasis on the common man. Alternatives which will bring about a new economic system in which the rewards as well as the work will be equally shared by all people—a

Socialist framework in which all groups will be adequately represented in the decision making and administration which affects their lives. Alternatives which will guarantee that all men will attain their full manhood rights, that they will be able to live, be free, and seek out those goals which give them respect and dignity while permitting the same privileges for every other man regardless of his condition or status. (Heath 1976, 381)

The Panthers barred members of the media from attending, but a participant recorded that the convention broke into 15 discussion groups to examine such issues as "homosexual liberation; distribution of production, goods and services; artists' contributions to the new society; women's liberation; international relations; the military; the family and the state; and . . . religious oppression and the new humanism" (quoted in Heath 1976, 381).

An article in the September 21, 1970, issue of *U.S. News & World Report* called "Rising Clamor for Black Separatism" reported that the following proposals were considered:

- Abolishment of present political boundaries; creation of independent, self-governing communities from which political power would flow upward
- A rotating police force of volunteers, under community control, with community councils instead of courts to deal with criminals
- A national defense force of volunteers, trained in guerilla warfare
- Free housing, health care, education and day care centers for children
- U.S. support of the Communist Viet Cong in South Vietnam and the Communist Pathet Lao in Cambodia; return of Taiwan to Red China; "liberation" of Palestine from "Zionist colonialism"

These discussions were intended to lay the groundwork for yet another Black Panther convention in Washington, D.C., in November. When some 4,000 persons gathered in November for what they hoped would be a meeting at Howard University, however, the university withdrew its offer of support and the plan for the meeting fizzled.

P. G. Marduke Proposes Using Technology to Enhance Democracy

In 1970, P. G. Marduke, whom the author has not otherwise identified, published a hand-typed brochure titled *The CASCOT System for Social Control of Technology*. It argued that technology could be used to enhance democratic processes and to change the current political system from a "system of 'power politics' to a system of 'people politics'" (Marduke 1970, 37).

Marduke favored initiating a system of touch-tone voting whereby citizens could vote on pending legislation. He also favored abolishing the Senate and granting public officials "a lifetime salary" while prohibiting them from receiving any other income or engaging in any investment activity (Marduke 1970, 43). Marduke wanted to conduct nominations through telephone computer systems, require the media to give candidates the opportunity to communicate with the public, and place caps on campaign spending. He also favored eliminating independent regulatory agencies and expanding the congressional representatives' roles as ombudsmen. In addition, Marduke proposed replacing the presidency with an elected national council of five officials, each heading an agency with distinct responsibilities (international affairs, environment, commerce, public welfare, and administration).

Marduke believed that technology also needed to be applied to the U.S. economic system. He thus favored replacing currency with electronic transactions, recording all capital assets over $25 in value, imposing limits on individual net worth, establishing a minimum net worth below which no one should be permitted to fall, and redistributing the nation's wealth according to public vote. The system would provide "whatever amount of credit the people wanted" (Marduke 1970, 70–1).

Marduke favored establishing parallel public and private health systems. He also advocated hiring a network of foreign agents pledged to stop their nations from "the first use of atomic, biochemical or other mass-murder weaponry" (Marduke 1970, 94). His ultimate goal was the creation of a "cosmopolitan system where people, not nations or institutions, are the essential ingredients," and where both economic resources and political ideals would be shared. Marduke proposed opening the doors of this system "to any and every other nation that cares to enter" (Marduke 1970, 95, 98).

Convinced that technological advances made traditional prohibitions against premarital sex outdated, Marduke favored establishing a fairly permissive code "for what is legally and morally prohibited," as well as a nonbinding code for "what is socially encouraged and discouraged." The latter would involve polling the public on attitudes about "dating, drinking and drugs; fashion, fads and fornication." Marduke further suggested "random-sample-censorship" for media producers and the establishment of social centers to distribute drugs to addicts (Marduke 1970, 110–12).

Marduke favored creating a mass-transit system in order to deal with environmental problems. He also advocated banning all chemicals "applied to soil or vegetation for any purpose" (Marduke 1970, 126), creating sewage treatment plants in every city, ending offshore oil drilling, declaring minerals to be the property of all the people, and making birth control available on a voluntary basis, with a compulsory system as a backup. Marduke also endorsed replacing the existing welfare system with social centers for mass feeding and care. He also advocated more extensive consumer education and examinations for workers in the repair business. He favored extensive education reform divided into four levels, the first of which was oriented toward practical training and consumer education. Marduke criticized the legal system for being preoccupied with money and called for the establishment of a tripartite system consisting of a public arbitrator, three-person investigatory boards, and an appeals advisory board. Criminal sanctions would be designed chiefly to motivate better behavior or isolate criminals from the rest of society.

Marduke's proposed changes involved not only the constitutional system but society as a whole. He accordingly recognized that "the most difficult problem will be to keep the change on an evolutionary, rather than a revolutionary scale" (Marduke 1970, 163). He planned to begin by running CASCOT candidates in the 1972 elections—with nominees running for the Senate pledged to eliminate that body. He further planned to modify the amending process sometime before 1980 so that a majority of the House could propose amendments that would go into effect when approved by popular majorities. This change would be followed by "the chain of amendments necessary to establish the popular voting system and the economic system and the form of government that can effectively deal with the world's crisis" (Marduke 1970, 170).

Leland Baldwin Offers a Modified Form of Parliamentary Government

In 1972, Leland Baldwin (1897–1981), emeritus professor of history at the University of Pittsburgh, presented his views of constitutional revision in *Reframing the Constitution: An Imperative for Modern America*. Baldwin feared that without constitutional changes, the nation would be unable to meet looming challenges in the areas of environmental pollution, overpopulation, youthful disillusionment, violence and rebellion, and problems generated by modern science. In advancing such change, he advanced two theses:

> First, the electorate does not have the expertise to propose the details of legislation or administration, or to serve as constant and informed guardians of the public welfare. Therefore some provision should be made in the Constitution for such guardians and at the same time for a greater degree of legislative and administrative flexibility. On the other hand, and second, neither legislators, administrators, nor guardians should be allowed to operate in disregard of the public will; therefore the electorate should have more effective power than it has at present to force the government to take notice of its will. (Baldwin 1972, xii)

Baldwin identified key constitutional problems as stemming from federalism, separation of powers, a weak party system, and misconceptions of majority rule.

In describing existing states, Baldwin claimed that they "have no real viability, are bogged down by antediluvian constitutions, hopelessly fragmented and expensive local governments, and systems of taxation that are universally on the verge of breakdown" (Baldwin 1972, 23). Baldwin proposed consolidating states into regions. His final proposal called for 15 states (with names like Deseret, Erie, Savanna, and Sierra), with Alaska to become either a commonwealth or to join with the new state of Oregon. Although the national government would have more powers than it does under the current system, it could delegate the administration of certain programs to these new states.

Baldwin was less interested in abolishing than in making existing aspects of separated powers more "flexible and constructive" (Baldwin 1972, 74), although he did refer to his proposals as "a modified version of the Cabinet or Parliamentary form" (Baldwin 1972, 96). He proposed granting the president and the new unicameral Congress five-year terms, with provisions for the president to dismiss Congress (although not simply for partisan advantage) and for Congress to oust the president. Although the president would be nominated in convention, he would be a "member of Congress, its presiding officer, and *chief of the executive arm of Congress*" (Baldwin 1972, 93, emphasis in original). Under Baldwin's plan, Congress would be composed of 200 regular members selected from multimember districts and a number of pro-forma members, such as defeated presidential candidates. The vice presidential office would be abolished and Congress would fill presidential vacancies.

Baldwin favored placing the Senate in charge of the judicial system. The Senate's one hundred members would include 50 "Law-Senators" and 50 "Senators-at-Large" selected by the president and Congress from nominees submitted by the states. Senators would serve for life or until the age of 70 and would have power to decide on the constitutionality of laws, "suspend Presidential orders or Congressional legislation for six months," "introduce legislation," propose amendments, "serve as a national ombudsman," and, in some cases, to dissolve Congress (Baldwin 1972, 89). The chief justice, elected by the Senate for a five-year term, would assume the president's current duties as chief of state and would live in the White House.

Baldwin proposed strengthening political parties not only by making the system more parliamentary but also by explicitly recognizing the parties within the Constitution. He called for Congress to be responsible for legislation governing national campaigning, conventions, and elections. He also included a provision stating that the president had the right to a 55 percent majority within Congress.

Baldwin consolidated most civil liberties within the Constitution. He proposed making the amending process easier. Under his plan, two-thirds majorities of Congress or the Senate could propose amendments, which could in turn be ratified by three-fourths of the state legislatures or a majority of the popular vote. One-half of the states could call for such a plebiscite. A two-thirds vote of the Congress, the Senate, and the states could call a convention, as could two-thirds of the states acting within a five-year period.

Baldwin suggested that Congress could call a constitutional convention to initiate such changes, but he thought it would be more realistic "for professional and legal organizations to advance their proposals for Constitutional reform and bring pressure on Congress and the States to launch them either as amendments or to call a Constitutional Convention" (Baldwin 1972, 116). The last article of the proposed constitution that closed Baldwin's book proposed:

On its own volition or on petition of the legislatures of one-half of the present States, Congress shall set a date about one year in advance, at which time the people shall vote their choice: (1) to accept this Constitution; or (2) to call a Constitutional Convention to amend or revise the Constitution of 1787. (Baldwin 1972, 142)

William Gardiner Argues for Modifying Existing Guarantees of Civil Liberties

William Gardiner was born in Missouri in 1885, and worked as a teacher and department store credit supervisor before earning his EdD in 1942. He published *A Proposed Constitution for the United States of America* in 1973. His plan included a mix of prescription and commentary that sought to blend existing constitutional provisions with innovations.

Under his plan, the House would consist of 200 members serving for four-year terms. They would elect the president and vice presidents, who would serve as cabinet members. State legislatures would select senators to eight-year terms. Legislators would have to pledge not to consult in advance when choosing executive officials. Page-boys and -girls would keep attendance, and legislators who missed more than twice a month or three times in a year could be removed. The president and eight vice presidents would serve for four-year terms, and the Justice Department would be elevated to serve a more prominent watchdog function. The Supreme Court would consist of 11 members serving to age 70. Other governmental officials would be required to attend special academies.

Gardiner outlined the organization of state governments at great length. In his proposed framework, all counties would have to adopt a commissioner form of government. Gardiner listed specific state officials and their methods of selection. Under his plan, parent-teacher associations would replace local school boards. Schools would work with industries to provide minors with jobs to keep them from sliding into delinquency. Gardiner also proposed prohibiting political parties and lobbying and eliminating campaign managers, speechwriters, and most congressional staff.

Gardiner outlined four ways for proposing constitutional amendments and five avenues by which they could be ratified, albeit under a five-year deadline. Gardiner suggested that a president might make himself a temporary dictator to implement his plans.

Gardiner's boldest innovations concerned civil liberties. He would permit a speaker to lecture or pray in public schools, "provided he does not boost or condemn any church organization, or question the validity of the Bible." He would eliminate freedom of the press so that "spoken or printed words that have a deteriorating influence on the morals and stability of the people shall be prohibited. He also specified that "any mawkish person or news medium that criticizes an apprehending officer for a justifiable killing shall be prosecuted" (Gardiner 1973, 9, 15, 17).

Gardiner proposed to eliminate both grand and petit juries and replace trials with "criminal proceedings" without Fifth Amendment guarantees against self-incrimination or the right to confront witnesses. He also favored banning private defense attorneys from these proceedings. Capital punishment would be prescribed for a litany of offenses. Individuals who had received "free food" or other relief over the past four years would be prohibited from voting (Gardiner 1973, 27). Guns and other concealed weapons would be registered but not prohibited. In place of the current Bill of Rights, people would be assured of being "treated fairly and squarely" (Gardiner 1973, 43).

Bill Strittmatter Models a New Constitution on the Ten Commandments

Puritans came to America with the intention of creating a Christian Common-wealth. Although the First Amendment of the U.S. Constitution prohibited an establishment of religion and guaranteed its free exercise, the twentieth century witnessed the birth of Christian Reconstructionism, or Theonomy. The movement was founded by Rousas John Rushdoony (1917–2001), the son of Armenian immi-grants and the founder and president of the Chalcedon Foundation (named after an early Christian creed). Rushdoony was deeply influenced by Professor Cornelius Van Til of the Westminster Theological Seminary, who urged Christians to base their defense of their religious beliefs on the Bible rather than on human reason.

Rushdoony was a prolific writer who set forth detailed views of governance in *The Institutes of Biblical Law* (1973). Many of Rushdoony's followers believe that the American Framers intentionally created a Christian constitution in which laws upholding Christianity were to be left to individual states (see Edgar 2001). A stu-dent of the movement observes that in his *Theonomy in Christian Ethics*, Recon-structionist Greg Bahnsen advocated capital punishment for 15 crimes, including "not only murder and rape, but sodomy, Sabbath breaking, apostasy, witchcraft, blasphemy and incorrigibility in children" (Clapp 1990, 1415).

In a similar vein, Bill Strittmatter authored a pamphlet entitled "A Christian Constitution and Civil Law for the Kingdom of Heaven on Earth," which attempted to base a national constitution around the Ten Commandments. At the time he au-thored the undated pamphlet (probably the early 1970s), he was the pastor of the Church of Jesus Christ in Lakemore, Ohio, a church with possible ties to the Ku Klux Klan. The cover of the work pictures an early American flag and translates the word America with "Ameri" meaning heavenly and "rica" (reich) meaning kingdom."

In the unpaginated introduction, Strittmatter asserted that:

1. The United States was founded as a Christian Nation.
2. Article I of the Constitution of The United States of America DOES NOT SAY "separation of Church and State." Read it for yourself.
3. The Supreme Court of the United State has declared that America is A Christian Nation (Holy Trinity Church vs. United States, 143 U.S. 471). (Strittmatter, n.d.)

Strittmatter further asserted that "civil Rules are God's Ministers," and presented a diagram of an open Bible in which he identifies 71 percent of the material as relat-ing to government and 29 percent as relating to "personal" matters (Strittmatter n.d., 1).

Like the Ten Commandments, the first articles of Strittmatter's constitution con-cerned individuals' relations with God. Article One thus began with the declara-tion, "I AM THE LORD THY GOD, THOU SHALT HAVE NO OTHER GODS

BEFORE ME" (Strittmatter n.d., 4). This article identified God as Jesus Christ, and provided the penalty of stoning for those who worship others. It further identified Christ as the nation's Commander and Chief, and vested all citizens with the responsibility of receiving military training. Under specified "rules of war," Strittmatter wrote that all enemies who did not surrender as tributaries should be slaughtered, and that covenants with "heathen people" were forbidden (Strittmatter, 6). This article also contained admonitions to maintain cleanliness, limited citizenship to "the Christian Race," denied citizenship to persons of "mixed race," and prohibited terminology like "German-American," "Italian-American," and "Mexican-American" that created "hyphenated citizens." Strittmatter also indicated that only members of the "Christian Race" could hold church offices, and he endorsed the burning of the writings of "the children of Belial" (Strittmatter n.d., 7).

Article Two of Strittmatter's constitution prohibited the worship of "graven images," and Article Three prohibited the taking of God's name in vain. The penalty for blasphemy against Jesus Christ was death (Strittmatter n.d., 9). Article Four provided for the keeping of the Sabbath, with "those rendering essential services" on the Sabbath taking their day of rest on Wednesdays. Again, the penalty for violating the Sabbath was death. Feast days and holidays included Pentecost, Thanksgiving, the Passover, and the Year of Jubile[e] in which every man's lands would be returned.

The rest of the proposed constitution dealt with individuals' relations with their neighbors, again following the outline of the Ten Commandments. Article Five focused on honoring one's parents, with penalties of death for those who smite or curse them. Civil power was to be committed to "a[n] elder . . . whom Jesus Christ your King shall choose" (Strittmatter n.d., 13), and who would subsequently base decisions on the Bible. "Judges, elders and officers" were also created, with people further divided into tens, fifties, hundreds, and thousands, and "priests" making final judgments in difficult cases (Strittmatter n.d., 16). Punishment would be by "stripes," or whipping. This article further specified that "[o]nce elected, selected or appointed, elders, officers, and ministers have absolute authority under and within law, likewise the principle of absolute responsibility" (Strittmatter n.d., 17). Tithes would be collected for the support of both church and state.

Article Six dealt with murder. Like the Old Testament, it provided for the establishment of cities of refuge for those who commit involuntary manslaughter. The inclusion of matters of criminal law in this national constitution suggests that Strittmatter was not particularly committed to a division of power between state and federal authorities. He also included a section on liability based on Old Testament passages relating to damage done by animals owned by others.

Article Seven prohibited adultery, which it defined to include "interracial marriage and miscegenation" (Strittmatter n.d., 19). Violators were subject to the penalty of death by stoning. Strittmatter also handed down rules indicating which plants, animals, and foods were to be considered unclean. One prohibition included that of plowing "with an ox and an ass together" (Strittmatter n.d., 20). Article Eight prohibited theft and dealt with weights and measures, restitution, lost and found articles, confessions of guilt, usury, and wages. Usury (excessive interest on financial loans) was permitted to strangers but not to fellow citizens. The spoils of war were to be divided between Jesus and those who fought in a war, with "the five hundredth part" going to the "National Cathedral." The latter stipulation meant that one five-hundredth of the value of wartime seizures would go to support the National Cathedral (Strittmatter n.d., 23). Article Nine dealt with bearing false witness. It also committed individuals to keeping vows.

Article Ten dealt with coveting. This section of Strittmatter's constitution included explicit instructions about the obligations of husbands and wives and sexual relations. It permitted divorce in certain cases but prohibited incest. A welfare provision was included for "the stranger, the fatherless, [and] the widow." It also provided for gleaning, whereby individuals in need were permitted to follow behind harvesters and appropriate any remaining food (Strittmatter n.d., 28).

Article Ten was followed by a specific prohibition against adding amendments to the Constitution: "Ye shall not add unto the word which I command you, neither shall ye diminish ought from it." Although officials were permitted to settle controversies under the law, their decisions "shall not become case law to base further decisions thereon" (Strittmatter n.d., 28). The section further specified that "[t]he rest of the Bible not mentioned herein is made a part hereof" (Strittmatter n.d., 28).

Rexford Tugwell Authors 40 Drafts of a New Constitution

Few Americans since James Madison have taken the task of constitution writing more seriously than Rexford Tugwell (1891–1979). One of three original members of Franklin D. Roosevelt's "brain trust," Tugwell worked during World War II with Robert Hutchinson and others on the preliminary draft of a "World Constitution." He also served as a college professor and governor of Puerto Rico (1941–1946) before joining the Center for the Study of Democratic Institutions. During his years at the Center, Tugwell drafted multiple proposals for a new U.S. Constitution. He published the fortieth of these drafts in *The Emerging Constitution* (1974), a somewhat repetitive 600-page book that reflects a number of New Deal themes, including persistent criticism of the courts for altering the Constitution through judicial review.

Consistent with his New Deal work, Tugwell's proposed reforms emphasized the benefits of government planning and called for the addition of numerous new boards, commissions, and positions. He also believed that many state governments were antiquated and needed to be radically altered, but while he favored the inclusion of additional social and economic rights, he favored maintaining the present system of separated powers and did not advocate for a parliamentary system, unlike many other twentieth-century reformers.

Tugwell's fortieth version consisted of 12 articles. Article I dealt with rights and responsibilities. In addition to most guarantees now found within the Bill of Rights and other amendments, this section contained protections for individual privacy; guarantees against discrimination based on "race, creed, color, origin, or sex"; prohibitions against any public support for religion; a guarantee that those unable to "contribute to productivity shall be entitled to a share of the national product"; and a guarantee of education "at public expense" for all eligible people (Tugwell 1974, 595–6). Responsibilities of citizenship included respecting the rights of others, participating in democratic processes, and avoiding violence. To promote the latter goal—and in marked contrast to the Second Amendment of the existing Constitution—Tugwell called for reserving the bearing of arms to "the police, members of the armed forces, and those licensed under law" (Tugwell 1974, 597).

Tugwell designated the government under his fortieth constitution the "Newstates of America" (the thirty-seventh version referred instead to the "United Republic of America"). Article II dealt with these "newstates," none of which was to contain less than 5 percent of the existing population. Each would have its own constitution as well as its own "governors, legislatures, and planning, administrative, and judicial systems" (Tugwell 1974, 598). Like present states, they would exercise "police powers"; all rights and responsibilities applied at the national level would also apply to them.

Article III established an "electoral branch" of government supervised by an "overseer" selected by the Senate. The overseer would "supervise the organization of national and district parties, arrange for discussion among them, and provide for the nomination and election of candidates for public office" (Tugwell 1974, 599). Duties would include assisting in the nomination of candidates and in arranging and supervising elections. All costs would be paid from public funds, and all private personal expenditures would be prohibited.

Article IV delineated a planning branch headed by a national planning board of 15 members. This board would be responsible for submitting 6- and 12-year plans. Article V designated the president as "the head of government, shaper of its commitments, expositor of its policies, and supreme commander of its protective forces" (Tugwell 1974, 604). The president would serve a nine-year term, subject to recall by 60 percent of the voters after three years. The president would be served by two vice presidents, one for internal affairs and the other for general affairs. The latter would supervise "chancellors of External, Financial, Legal, and Military Affairs" (Tugwell 1974, 604). Treaties that the president negotiated would go into effect unless rejected by a majority vote of the Senate. The president would appoint a public custodian in charge of governmental property and an intendant to supervise intelligence and investigation offices.

Article VI described a drastically altered Congress. Various groups and individuals would appoint a Senate of 70 to 80 members who would serve for life terms. The Senate could consider—and at times delay—but not initiate legislation. It would also select a three-person national security council to consult with the president about the deployment of U.S. troops abroad. The Senate would also select the national watchkeeper, or ombudsman.

Members of the House of Representatives would be selected from 100 districts, each of which would select three members for three-year terms. In an effort to give the body a more national orientation, Tugwell called for filling out the House membership with another 100 at-large members. Tugwell designated the House as "the original lawmaking body of the Newstates of America" (1974, 609). Tugwell's document outlined the selection of committees and their chairs and included a much longer list of congressional powers, including powers over banking, insurance, communications, transportation, space exploration, welfare, education, libraries, the conservation of natural resources, and civil service.

Article VII established a regulatory branch headed by a national regulator to be selected by the Senate. This official would head a regulatory board of 17 members. The regulator would charter corporations, regulate industrial mergers, and supervise the marketplace. Article VIII described a judicial branch with considerable more complexity than the language of the current document. Section 2 thus specified, "There shall be a Principal Justice of the Newstates of America; a Judicial Council; and a Judicial Assembly. There shall also be a Supreme Court and a High Court of Appeals; also Courts of Claims, Rights and Duties, Administrative Review, Arbitration Settlements, Tax Appeals, and Appeals from Watchkeeper's Findings" (Tugwell 1974, 614). The principal justice would preside over the system and appoint all members of the national courts; the justice would serve an 11-year term and would share with the president the power to grant reprieves and pardons. Under Tugwell's plan, the Supreme Court would continue to exercise its powers of judicial review.

Article IX dealt with general provisions, Article X with governmental arrangements, and Article XII with transition to the new government. Article XI provided for an amending process in which the judicial council would formulate amendments to be approved by the Senate and president, submitted to the people, and adopted by majority vote. Every 25 years the overseer would conduct a referendum on whether a new constitution was needed. If the referendum was approved, the judicial council would draw up a constitution to go into effect, provided it was not disapproved by a majority. Tugwell's various proposals generated considerable discussion and criticism (Kelly 1981, 650), some of it fanatical (Preston 1972).

Charles Hardin Calls for the Institution of Party Government

Political scientist Charles Hardin (1908–1997) introduced his plans for governmental reform in the midst of the Watergate crisis in *Presidential Power and Accountability* (1974). Hardin viewed the Watergate scandal as part of a larger structural problem:

> Presidential abuse of power, though seriously worsened, had been visible for decades; the inadequacy of Congress to provide an alternative to presidential government had been shown from the close of the Civil War . . . and the malaise of public opinion had appeared in the late 1960s. In other words, the problems were long-standing and were rooted in structural faults; they were not associated with one administration or one series of events. (Hardin 1974, 2)

Hardin believed that the solution was to institute a system of party government that would both grant powers to the president and subject such power to greater control. Such a system, which would incorporate major elements of the parliamentary model, would also vest voters with a greater "share in both political power *and* responsibility" (Hardin 1974, 12).

Hardin devoted much of his book to historical analysis. In his second chapter, he argued that the president was often surrounded by aides who failed to question his judgments, resulting in what he labeled in chapter three as "government by presidential instinct" (Hardin 1974, 46). Bureaucracies, especially those connected to the military, exploited separated powers and took advantage of weak political parties. Stronger parties were needed to "improve governmental resistance to private pressures, increase the coherence of related policies, and encourage government to concert its policies on the great economic issues" (Hardin 1974, 139). After completing his historical review, Hardin advanced nine specific reform proposals.

First, Hardin proposed that the president and members of the House and Senate should be elected simultaneously to four-year terms, although these terms could be terminated if the government dissolved and new elections were called. Second, he proposed supplementing existing single-member House districts with at-large seats. Under his plan, the party winning the presidency would get an additional 100 seats and the losing party 50, provided that the winning party retained a majority. Party committees would select the at-large members, with the minority "shadow cabinet" having input into its party's slate of candidates.

Third, Hardin proposed that members of the House nominate presidential candidates and replace presidents who are killed or disabled, thus eliminating the need for a vice president. Fourth, Hardin advocated a significant reduction in the powers of the Senate. It would no longer confirm nominees to office or ratify treaties. Moreover, after a 60-day waiting period, the House could re-pass a bill rejected by the Senate and send it to the president for approval. Hardin's fifth proposal authorized a majority of the House to override a presidential veto.

Sixth, Hardin endorsed giving members of Congress the freedom to serve simultaneously in other offices, including the cabinet. His seventh proposal was to give the defeated presidential candidate a seat in the House and various other privileges, although the candidates could be removed by the party committee that nominated them. Hardin's eighth proposal eliminated the Electoral College and provided for the presidency to go to the party winning the national voting plurality. His ninth proposal repealed all conflicting laws, including the two-term presidential limit in the Twenty-Second Amendment.

Hardin wanted to leave a number of mechanisms for governance loosely structured, so that they could develop naturally through time and experience:

The ideal is to create conditions so that the conduct of government itself will be ruled largely by conventions rather than by fixed laws. It will be better to let the precise means of replacing presidents or leaders of the opposition develop by convention than to stipulate them in advance; the same is true for the means of enforcing party discipline and even for the use, devoutly to be wished, of dissolution as the sovereign means by which governments end and new governments are created. (Hardin 1974, 182)

Hardin did not call specifically for another constitutional convention, but he renewed his call for reform in 1989, when he reiterated his belief in the need to replace "the separation of powers between the executive and the legislature by a separation between the government and the opposition" (Hardin 1989, 201).

Michael Novak and George Reedy Call for Reassessing the Presidency

In *Choosing Our King* (1974), scholar, speechwriter, and journalist Michael Novak (1933–) analyzed the symbolic role of the president in American life and suggested four reforms of the office, some of which would have moved the U.S. system closer to a parliamentary model. He believed that the abuses of the Nixon presidency demonstrated that the office had grown to the point where it needed serious reconsideration.

Novak called first for the selection of a spokesman to represent the opposition party in Congress. Elected annually or biennially and subject to recall, the opposition spokesman would represent the majority view of his party rather than his own personal views. Unlike the head of the party opposition in parliamentary democracies, however, Novak preferred that this individual not be a candidate for the presidency.

Novak's second proposed reform resembled the British "question-hour." Novak proposed that "the president should be obliged on a biweekly basis to come before leaders of the opposition for a public hour-long accounting of his policies" (Novak 1974, 261). Novak hoped that such sessions would not only elicit important information from the chief executive but also symbolically "equalize the presidency and Congress" (Novak 1974, 262). Novak's third proposal deviated from the parliamentary model in suggesting that "the president's cabinet should always, perhaps by force of law, includ[e] a proportion of members of the opposition party" (Novak 1974, 262). Novak thought this would assure that the president had individuals around him who would challenge presidential initiatives of dubious value.

Novak's fourth reform called for dividing the presidency into a head of state and chief executive. This proposal was designed to eliminate some of the symbolic aura around the presidency—an aura that, according to Novak, sometimes allowed presidents to advance policies without having to show their merits. Novak proposed that the chief of state be elected at the beginning of each decade. He, rather than the chief executive, would occupy the White House, receive foreign dignitaries, and perform ceremonial duties.

There are similarities between Novak's proposals and those that George Reedy (1917–1999), a former aide to President Lyndon Johnson, sketched four years earlier in *The Twilight of the Presidency* (1970). Reedy suggested a plan for parliamentary government with simultaneous terms for the parliament and the head of government, a mechanism for dissolving the government, and a separate chief of government and chief of state, the former to be chosen by parliament and the latter to be elected for a ten-year term.

Conley Dillon Proposes Creation of a Constitutional Commission

In 1974, the American Society for Public Administration (ASPA) proposed establishing a Permanent Commission for Constitutional Review consisting of 15 members appointed by the president, the president pro tempore of the Senate, and the speaker of the House of Representatives. Political scientist Conley Dillon (1906–1987) was a moving force behind this proposal. He sought to justify such a commission on a wide variety of grounds:

> The two action branches of our national government, the Congress and the Executive, are at great odds and are not successful in responding adequately to the needs of our situation. Our plight is not the product of any one incident or series of incidents, but is the latest stage of a far-reaching and dynamic interaction involving many environmental, technological, social, political, economic, and other variables. In these circumstances, the traditional forms of our Constitutional and legal concepts may well be acting as constraints on our capacity for adjustment to the contemporary demands. (Dillon 1977, 8)

Dillon proposed a number of topics for the commission to address. They included: (1) possible "adjustments" to the "federal structure"; (2) the "selection, removal, . . . succession" and "accountability" of the executive branch; (3) "the method of selecting and removing the members of Congress, their terms of office, and the organization and procedures by which the Congress performs its roles"; (4) the method of judicial selection; (5) the "distribution and sharing of the powers of government" among the three branches; (6) the "constitutional status and the role of political parties"; (7) the scope "of individual and group freedoms and rights"; (8) the suitability of a constitutional convention for initiating changes; and (9) the "loss . . . of confidence" of Americans in their government (Dillon 1977, 13–14). Dillon added his hope that presidential powers in foreign affairs—especially relative to war powers and treaty-making—might be clarified, and that the issue of judicial activism be examined.

Dillon favored entrusting the commission with power "to take testimony, hold hearings, subpoena materials and witnesses, and other powers that are customary for conducting business" (Dillon 1977, 14). Dillon expressed doubts about the efficacy of the amending process and about constitutional reform proposals such as the one advanced by Tugwell. Dillon considered such proposals to be elite products unlikely to receive public or congressional report. He acknowledged, however, that he had little more hope for his own plans.

Theodore L. Becker Attempts to Reorganize Presidential Elections

Theodore L. Becker was a professor of law and political science at the University of Hawaii when he offered a series of proposed constitutional reforms in in a textbook entitled *American Government: Past—Present—Future* (1976).

Becker favored a national presidential primary (NPP) as a vehicle for increasing governmental responsiveness and accountability, but his ultimate aim was to institute a presidential election tournament (PET). Similar in framework to organized athletic tournament brackets, PET candidates would first face off at state and regional levels. The East and West would then conduct semifinal elections, with the two candidates that emerge from those contests vying for the presidency. Becker also favored instituting a vote of no confidence as a means of executive recall and suggested that voting should be a compulsory, perhaps even a paid activity, with citizens having a "no preference" option (1976, 459).

Becker favored converting Congress into a unicameral body and establishing an "executive Committee, Council, or Cabinet" to run its affairs (1976, 467). In an unusual twist, he anticipated a legislature of 500 to 1,000 members in which at least half of the representatives would be selected at random. He also favored creating a national initiative and referendum process that might be implemented through home cable television or computer hookups.

Becker wanted presidents to run for office on a ticket that included members of his or her proposed cabinet. He also thought that the president should need 60 percent approval of Congress before being able to fire a cabinet member, and he stated that members of Congress and ombudsmen should form a "countergovernment" to provide greater administrative oversight (Becker 1976, 509).

Becker favored establishing a national appeals court to ease the Supreme Court's workload or an expansion of the Court to 18 members who would work on nine-judge panels. He thought that judges should have 12- to 15-year terms and retire at the age of 70. Becker also favored the selection of many judges by lottery from bar associations. Individuals selected in this manner would receive at least six months' training at a judicial academy before assuming their duties. Further reforms of the criminal justice system suggested by Becker included allowing members of the public to preside in many state trials, eliminating the state's peremptory challenges for jurors, widening jury pools, and increasing jurors' pay. Becker also favored the repeal of all so-called victimless crime laws.

In 1992, Becker—who by that time had joined the faculty at Auburn University—worked with Barry Krusch to develop a national network of individuals interested in a second constitutional convention. Becker became a supporter of the National Initiative for Democracy, or Philadelphia II, which was designed to amend the U.S. Constitution by referendum. In 2000, he coauthored a book (with Christa Daryl Slaton) touting the advantages of citizen participation online, or what he called teledemocracy.

Summary and Analysis

This period demonstrated continuing fissures in American political thinking. Attempts to rally support for single-issue amendments or constitutional conventions to repeal the Supreme Court's reapportionment decisions stimulated thoughts of constitutional reform that might be applied to other problems. Reformers expressed fears of an overly strong presidency, concerns with American racism, the desire to apply modern technology to democracy, and discomfort with Supreme Court decisions that were perceived as overly permissive.

References

American Political Science Association, Committee on Political Parties. 1950. "Toward a More Responsible Two-Party System: A Report of the Committee on Political Parties." *APSR* 44, no. 3, Part 2, Supplement.

Baldwin, Leland. 1972. *Reframing the Constitution: An Imperative for Modern America.* Santa Barbara, CA: ABC-CLIO.

Becker, Theodore L. 1976. *American Government: Past—Present—Future.* Boston: Allyn and Bacon.

Becker, Theodore Lewis, and Christa Daryl Slaton. 2000. *The Future of Teledemocracy.* Westport, CT: Praeger.

Black, Charles Jr. 1963. "The Proposed Amendment of Article V: A Threatened Disaster." *Yale Law Journal* 72 (April): 957–66.

Bloom, Joshua. 2000. "Black Panther Party." In *Civil Rights in the United States*, vol. I, edited by Waldo E. Martin Jr. and Patricia Sullivan, 84–5. New York: Macmillan Reference USA.

Clapp, Rodney. 1990. *The Reconstructionists.* Downers Grove, IL: Intervarsity Press.

Committee on Federal-State Relations. 1963. "Amending the Constitution to Strengthen the States in the Federal System." *State Government* 10 (Winter): 10.

Committee on Political Parties, American Political Science Association. 1950. *Toward a More Responsible Two-Party System.* Supplement to the *American Political Science Review* XLIV (September).

Dillon, Conley. 1977. "American Constitutional Review: Are We Preparing for the 21st Century?" *World Affairs* 140 (Summer): 5–24.

Dillon, Conley. 1974. "Recommendation for the Establishment of a Permanent Commission of Constitutional Review." *Bureaucrat* 3 (July): 211–24.

Edgar, William. 2001. "The Passing of R. J. Rushdoony." *First Things: A Monthly Journal of Religion and Public Life* (August): 24.

Eldredge, H. Wentworth. 1964. *The Second American Revolution.* New York: William Morrow.

Finer, Herman. 1960. *The Presidency, Crisis and Regeneration: An Essay in Possibilities.* Chicago: University of Chicago Press.

Gardiner, William. 1973. *A Proposed Constitution for the United States of America.* Summerfield, FL: William Gardiner.

Hardin, Charles M. 1989. *Constitutional Reform in America: Essays on the Separation of Powers.* Ames: Iowa State University Press.

Hardin, Charles M. 1974. *Presidential Power and Accountability: Toward a New Constitution.* Chicago: University of Chicago Press.

Heath, G. Louis, ed. 1976. *The History and Literature of the Black Panther Party.* Metuchen, NJ: Scarecrow Press.

Kelly, Frank K. 1981. *Court of Reason: Robert Hutchins and the Fund for the Republic.* New York: Free Press.

Krusch, Barry. 1992. *The 21st Century Constitution: A New America for a New Millennium*. New York: Stanhope Press.

Lundberg, Ferdinand. 1980. *Cracks in the Constitution*. Secaucus, NJ: Lyle Stuart Inc.

Macdonald, Dwight. 1968. "The Constitution of the United States Needs to Be Fixed." *Esquire* 70 (October): 143–6, 238–46, 252.

Marduke, P. G. 1970. *The CASCOT System for Social Control of Technology*. Silver Spring, MD: Citizens' Association for Social Control of Technology.

Mason, Alpheus T. 1964. *The States Rights Debate: Antifederalism and the Constitution*. Englewood Cliffs, NJ: Prentice-Hall.

Moore, Trevor W. 1970. "A Rumbling in Babylon: Panthers Host a Parley." *Christian Century* 87 (October 28): 1298.

Morgan, Thomas B. 1963. "Seventeen States Vote to Destroy Democracy as We Know It." *Look* 27 (December 3): 76–88.

Novak, Michael. 1974. *Choosing Our King: Powerful Symbols in Presidential Politics*. New York: Macmillan.

Oliver, Michael. 1968. *A New Constitution for a New Country*. Rev. ed. Reno, NV: Fine Arts Press.

"Panther Conference." 1970. *Facts on File Yearbook*, 683. New York: Facts on File.

Pei, Mario. 1967–68. "The Case for a Constitutional Convention." *Modern Age* 12: 8–13.

Preston, Robert L. 1972. *The Plot to Replace the Constitution*. Salt Lake City, UT: Hawkes Publications.

Reedy, George. 1970. *The Twilight of the Presidency*. New York: World Publishing.

Rushdoony, Rousas John. 1973. *The Institutes of Biblical Law*. Phillipsburg, NJ: Presbyterian and Reformed Publishing.

Strittmatter, Bill. N.d. "A Christian Constitution and Civil Law for the Kingdom of Heaven on Earth." Lakemore, OH: N.p.

Swindler, William. 1963. "The Current Challenge to Federalism: The Confederating Proposals." *Georgetown Law Journal* 52 (Fall): 1–41.

Swisher, Carl B., and Patricia Nelson. 1968. "In Convention Assembled." *Villanova Law Review* 13 (Summer): 711–31.

Tugwell, Rexford. 1974. *The Emerging Constitution*. New York: Harper and Row.

CHAPTER 8

The Reagan and George H. W. Bush Years

In the 1980 presidential election, Republican nominee Ronald Reagan defeated Democrat Jimmy Carter, who had served as president for four years. During Reagan's two full terms in the White House, America celebrated the bicentennial of the U.S. Constitution. This milestone stimulated renewed thinking about possible constitutional changes, and calls for reforms and revisions continued into the presidency of George H. W. Bush.

Lloyd Cutler Proposes Adoption of Parliamentary Changes

In 1980, Lloyd N. Cutler (1917–2005), a Washington attorney and advisor to the Carter administration, published an article urging constitutional reforms in the prestigious *Foreign Affairs* journal. It was later republished in 1986 in a collection of essays on separation of powers in a book edited by Robert A. Goldwin and Art Kaufman.

Comparing the difficulties that President Carter had experienced with the successes of leaders in parliamentary systems characterized by greater party discipline, Cutler believed that Carter's problems showed the need to create a system that could govern more efficiently. He pointed out that despite occasional periods in U.S. history when a president like Franklin D. Roosevelt or Lyndon Baines Johnson achieved extraordinary consensus, most of the time the nation was likely to be "divided somewhere between 55–45 and 45–55 on each set of a wide set of issues," making it almost impossible for presidents to carry out their programs (Cutler 1986, 11). Cutler believed that the only way to form effective governments during such periods was to amend the Constitution. He offered a set of seven proposals, most of which would have moved the system closer to the parliamentary model.

The first proposal called for increasing the terms of members of the House of Representatives from two years to four and requiring voters to cast straight-ticket votes for their representative, president, and vice president. He further advocated decreasing the terms of senators to four years and including them in the straight-ticket package.

Second, Cutler proposed requiring the president to select half of cabinet members from the president's party in the House and Senate. He believed that this "would tend to increase the intimacy between the executive and the legislature and add to their sense of collective responsibility" (Cutler 1986, 14). Cutler's third proposal would allow presidents the option at least once a term "to dissolve Congress and call for new congressional elections" (Cutler 1986, 14). A fourth proposal further suggested that two-thirds of both houses should be able to call for new presidential elections.

Cutler's fifth proposal suggested a six-year presidential term. Alternatively, Cutler proposed combining his third, fourth, and fifth proposals so that the president and all members of Congress would serve six-year terms, with the president having power to dissolve Congress at least once a term and Congress having its own powers to call a new election within 30 days. In either circumstance, Cutler would require that the entire cycle of state primaries and conventions, national nominating conventions, and elections take place within a 120-day period.

Cutler's seventh proposal provided that "Congress would first enact broad mandates, declaring general policies and directions and leaving the precise allocative choices, within a congressionally approved budget, to the president," to whom all such agencies would be responsible (Cutler 1986, 16). Presidential actions would then become law unless both houses of Congress vetoed them.

Cutler was skeptical that the public would support a constitutional convention to enact such measures. He thus favored appointing "a bipartisan presidential commission to analyze the issues, compare how other constitutions work, hold public hearings, and make a full report" (Cutler 1986, 17) that might then be incorporated in the Constitution through amendments. Cutler subsequently served on the Committee on the Constitutional System, which issued a report in January 1987 that called for less-sweeping changes than those that he had advocated. Cutler also later served on the Continuity of Government Commission, which sought to formulate plans for continuing government in the event of a catastrophic attack on the United States.

Robert Shogan Suggests Reforms to Increase Presidential Success

In 1982, a national political correspondent for the Washington Bureau of the *Los Angeles Times* named Robert Shogan published *None of the Above: Why Presidents Fail—And What Can Be Done about It*. Shogan argued that an increasing gap between government and politics was making the job of the president too difficult. He believed that future presidents would be aided by revitalized political parties, but he was convinced "that if the parties are to be brought to life the Constitution must be changed. . . . The restraints which have crippled party development should be removed and replaced with machinery that grants the parties expanded responsibility and the authority to match" (Shogan 1982, 23). According to Shogan, "the ultimate objective should be to shift the burden of national leadership from the personality of the president to the collective authority of the executive and legislature, bound together by clear policy goals and a vigorous majority party" (Shogan 1982, 24).

Shogan offered several constitutional proposals that he thought might be more effective. The first called for combining presidential and congressional elections and requiring voters to support all candidates from a single party. This would require reducing the terms of U.S. senators to four years and making one-party control of both the presidency and Congress more likely. Shogan borrowed a second proposal from Charles Hardin. This provision called for each party to run 100 at-large candidates for the House, with the winning majority being guaranteed a majority in the House. He also mentioned, without endorsing, Hardin's further proposal to reduce the powers of the Senate.

Shogan suggested two methods to move the nation closer to a parliamentary system. The first called for "lifting the ban on members of Congress serving in the cabinet," and the second empowered the president or Congress to issue one call within a four-year period for midterm elections. Shogan also favored eliminating the vice presidency. He believed that such alterations would make the government "more cohesive, more accountable, and more responsive." Shogan also called for "creating a coordinating party council," for "nominating by party caucus," and for "institutionalizing the opposition party" (Shogan 1982, 271–2).

Shogan observed that "the impetus for change must come from outside the political establishment" and suggested it might be desirable to establish a "national commission" (Shogan 1982, 276–7). He also attempted to address fears connected to any change in the current system of separation of powers, asserting that "such alarms ignore the fact that the separation of powers can be modified while still preserving the integrity of state governments and the existence of the Senate" (Shogan 1982, 279).

Joseph Church Proposes a Libertarian/Parliamentary/Socialist Alternative

Psychologist Joseph Church (1918–2003) advanced what the cover of his 1982 book, *America the Possible: Why and How the Constitution Should Be Rewritten*, described as "An Iconoclastic View of the Social, Political, and Economic Order in the U.S.—With Some Startling Suggestions for Change." Educated at the New School for Social Research, Cornell University, and Clark University, Church subsequently taught at Vassar College and the Brooklyn College of the City College of New York, where he developed his expertise in child development.

Church was disturbed by what he considered to be the myths generated by religion and Victorian sexual morality and sought greater human fulfillment, greater egalitarianism, and a way for America to withdraw from its foreign military alliances. He also thought that a new constitution should reflect advances in thinking:

> We have learned a great deal about how societies work in the nearly 200 years that our present Constitution has been in effect. It would be foolish or insane not to incorporate that learning into a new document. We do not want to accord the people in power great flexibility in decision making. They have all too consistently made the wrong decisions, sometimes out of avarice and self interest, but often out of sheer stupidity. (Church 1982, 81)

Church's ideas on the family stemmed from "the libertarian premise that the states should interfere as little as possible in the private lives of individuals" (Church

1982, 87). He was willing to permit consensual living arrangements among both heterosexual and homosexual couples and opposed laws against prostitution or bestiality except in cases where the latter resulted in animal suffering. Although he would continue laws against rape, he favored lowering the age of consent and would not prohibit "noncoercive sex with children" (Church 1982, 94) or abortion on demand, at least during the early stages of pregnancy. Church favored allowing teens irrevocably to declare their independence, which would permit them to drive, access pornography, consume alcohol or drugs, choose what schools to attend, engage in sexual relations, and qualify for his proposed "universal living-allowance program" (Church 1982, 119). Research institutes would replace high schools and colleges. Church called for equally far-reaching reforms of the economic system.

Church proposed abolishing the presidency, which he associated with war and with aggrandizement of power, and replacing the office with a chief administration (CA), selected by Congress. With the CA doing congressional bidding, the new balance of power would not consist of "the legislature, the judiciary, and the electorate" (Church 1982, 244).

Church also advocated replacing existing states with new arrangements, perhaps allowing for divisions into an urban and a rural America. He favored funding programs like education and health care through imposition of a progressive income tax on personal (but not corporate) income, but would enable local groups to maintain authority over their daily operations. The people would exercise their authority through the referendum, initiative, and recall.

Church anticipated an expansive preamble. He would, respectively, "make explicit that ours is a pluralistic society and that the rule of the majority must not work hardships on any minority or group of minorities" (Church 1982, 249); affirm electoral supremacy through referendums, initiatives, and recall mechanism that would go so far as to allow voters to accept or reject budgets on a line-by-line basis; include provisions for universal voting and "fulltime polling sites" (Church 1982, 253); proclaim peaceful coexistence, dissolve foreign alliances, and commit the nation to work through the United Nations and support free trade; limit arms sales; set a figure for "the maximum desirable population size of the nation," which he estimated would be about 200 million; and "establish that the foundation of our society is the rights set forth in the various amendments to the original Constitution" (Church 1982, 258).

Church expressed concerns about American political parties. Although he favored the continuation of a bicameral Congress that would provide health care and a universal living allowance for all, he wanted to replace the Senate with a "House of Delegates" representing various special interest groups, with delegates being selected through a system of "preferential balloting of the kind used in many nongovernmental organizations" (Church 1982, 263). Members of both houses would serve five-year terms but be subject to recall. Although Church would eliminate the states, he provided for the right of secession for any part of the country that so chose. Such a decision would be "irrevocable for a period of fifty years" and would have to provide for free migration for a period of five years (Church 1982, 267).

Church wanted all courts to operate "with a uniform system of laws" (Church 1982, 268). He favored establishing a "second system of courts of legislative review, culminating in a second Supreme Court" (Church 1982, 268). The new courts would review all acts of legislation at the times of their passage, without waiting for legal challenges to arise. Judges would be elected and would campaign for office.

Church wanted to draw a clear line between legality and morality. He favored spelling out the exclusionary rule, limiting grants of immunity, and nationalization of key industries and of "our national resources" (Church 1982, 275). He opposed capital punishment but endorsed establishment of "right to die" laws, including provision of "the means of suicide" for prisoners who requested it (Church 1982, 279).

Church also expressed concern about "antiquated" provisions in the First Amendment. He proposed eliminating tax exemptions for churches and government support for chaplains, and favored changing the national motto to "In Humankind We Trust" (Church 1982, 282). He thought the Government Printing Office should "grant to every citizen the right to publish, at public expense, a pamphlet of up to ten pages a year, to be distributed through the same channels as other government publications" (Church 1982, 284). He also thought the Constitution should recognize the right of citizens to travel abroad.

Church was somewhat vague as to how he would implement his suggested reforms, indicating that he was primarily interested in "consciousness raising" (Church 1982, 287). He later elaborated:

> My primary hope lies not in economic, legal, and political revolution, but in a psychocultural revolution, whereby we come to realize that we have built our social institutions in a quicksand of false assumptions and that these illfounded institutions needlessly deform our humanity. From this sort of awareness, institutional changes could flow quite readily—not necessarily painlessly, but in a manageable way. (Church 1982, 294)

Thomas Brennan Urges a Reassertion of the Integrity of the Written Constitution

Thomas Brennan (1929–), former chief justice of the Michigan Supreme Court and president of the Thomas M. Cooley Law School, called for a constitutional convention in the inaugural issue of the *Cooley Law Review* in 1982. He issued this call for two purposes. The first was "to reestablish the integrity and primacy of the written constitution as the charter of our national government, and to preserve the rights of the American people as defined and guaranteed in the plain written words of the Constitution." Second, he wanted to reassert "the sovereignty of the people of the several states of the American Union, to reestablish the federal system of government, and to insure the inviolability of the institution of state government" (Brennan 1982, 7).

Brennan also favored constitutional revision to modernize constitutional language. He supported a convention to eliminate anachronistic words and phrases, clarify existing ambiguities, and redirect attention from "indifferent matters" to "affairs of great consequence" (Brennan 1982, 29). The issue, as Brennan viewed it, was "whether it is better to alter our fundamental law through a process of judicial interpretation and legislative and executive encroachment, combined with popular acquiescence, or whether it is better to change the Constitution through a process of formal amendment, ratified by the legislatures or conventions in three-fourths of the states as specified in Article V" (Brennan 1982, 46).

Consistent with his hopes to reinvigorate state sovereignty, Brennan favored equally representing states at the constitutional convention. As he envisioned it, the Convention should be "a convention of the *people of the respective states of the United States*" (Brennan 1982, 65).

Donald L. Robinson Seeks to Generate Discussion of Constitutional Reform

Donald L. Robinson (1936–), a professor of Political Science at Smith College, has been closely associated with the bipartisan Committee on the Constitutional System (CCS) and authored two books (in 1985 and 1989) designed to elicit discussion about reforms that the CCS had considered and proposed.

In an article articulating his own views, Robinson advocated three specific constitutional reforms. These called for lengthening the terms of members of the House of Representatives to four years and senators to eight; allowing members of Congress to head executive agencies; and allowing the president and one-third of both houses of Congress or a majority of either house to call for new presidential and Congressional elections (Robinson 1987).

James L. Sundquist Proposes Amendments to Overcome Governmental Deadlock

James L. Sundquist (1915–) is a political scientist and one-time deputy undersecretary of the U.S. Department of Agriculture who in 1986 published *Constitutional Reform and Effective Government*. After referring explicitly to critiques of the U.S. system by Woodrow Wilson, William MacDonald, William Yandell Elliott, Henry Hazlitt, Thomas Finletter, Charles Hardin, and Rexford Tugwell, he concluded that the American Founders had solved the problem of tyranny by creating a system that resulted in excessive deadlock and stalemate. Sundquist examined specific proposals to forestall divided government (chapter 4), lengthen terms of office (chapter 5), reconstitute a failed government (chapter 6), further inter-branch collaboration (chapter 7), and alter the present system of checks and balances (chapter 8).

Sundquist ultimately recommended nine constitutional changes. These included combining presidential and vice presidential candidates on a team ticket with members of the House and Senate so that voters would be unable to split their votes; raising the terms of members of the House to four years and those of the Senate to eight; allowing the president or a majority of either house of Congress to call special elections in which members of both the legislative and executive branches would be up for election; removing the constitutional prohibition against members of Congress simultaneously serving in the executive branch; creating a limited presidential item veto, subject to an override by a majority of both houses of Congress; restoring the legislative veto, albeit only when both houses of Congress concur; incorporating the provisions of the War Powers Resolution of 1973 (providing for presidential consultation and notification before committing troops abroad) into the Constitution; allowing majorities of both houses of Congress to approve treaties; and providing for a national referendum to break deadlocks between the legislative and executive branches (Sundquist 1986, 241–2).

Sundquist was not particularly hopeful that these proposals would ever be adopted, although he discussed the options of having amendments either approved by state conventions (rather than by state legislatures) or through a new constitutional convention. Ultimately, he hoped that further reflection on the subject might result in action.

The Committee on the Constitutional System Proposes to Strengthen Parties and Enhance Legislative-Executive Cooperation

The Committee on the Constitution System (CCS) was a bipartisan group co-chaired by Lloyd Cutler, Senator Nancy Landon Kassebaum of Kansas, and C. Douglas Dillon, a former secretary of the treasury. In January 1987, the CCS issued a 20-page report calling for reforms to address sources of strain in the American political system. The report identified the system of checks and balances and the weakness of political parties as root causes of five specific problems: the brevity of the honeymoon period between a new president and Congress; the "inconsistency, incoherence and even stagnation" of "divided government"; the "lack of party cohesion in Congress"; the "loss of accountability"; and the "lack of a mechanism for replacing failed or deadlocked government" (Committee 1987, 5–8).

The committee proposed a number of recommendations by majority vote. It decided not to tamper with the Bill of Rights and its enforcement by an independent judiciary, but it favored three proposals designed to strengthen political parties. These included modifying party rules to seat all nominees for House and Senate seats (as well as Senate holdovers) as uncommitted delegates at national nominating conventions; requiring all states to "include a line or lever" permitting straight-ticket voting in all federal elections; and providing public funding of congressional campaigns, with much of the money to be channeled through party organizations so as to increase party "loyalty and cohesion" (Committee 1987, 8–9).

The committee advanced three additional proposals to ensure legislative-executive coordination. These included lengthening the terms of members of the House to four years and those of senators to eight; allowing the president to appoint sitting members of Congress to the cabinet; and permitting the ratification of treaties by simple majorities of both Houses. The committee also proposed an amendment limiting campaign spending.

The committee offered other proposals for further consideration. These included allowing the president to appear before congressional committees; encouraging the congressional opposition to form a shadow cabinet; requiring mandatory straight ticket voting; scheduling president and vice presidential elections before those for Congress; permitting the calling of new elections to break governmental dead-locks; and calling a "special convocation" every 10 years to reexamine federal, state, and local governmental relations (Committee 1987, 14–17). The committee's report drew a flurry of criticisms (Vile 1991, 134–7).

Arthur S. Miller Favors Increased National Powers and Parliamentary Reforms

Arthur S. Miller (1917–1988), a professor emeritus of law at George Washington University, advanced a number of ideas for changing the Constitution in the 1980s. He presented these reforms in a 1984 article in the *Washington and Lee Law Review* and in a 1987 book called *The Secret Constitution and the Need for Constitutional Change*. An advocate of judicial activism (Miller 1982), Miller believed that the nation was governed by informal rules that privileged economic elites. Miller thus attempted to debunk popular beliefs in democracy, in the efficacy of the Bill of Rights, in a system of checks and balances, and in individualism (Miller 1987, 36–8). Citing problems of overpopulation, nationalism, injustice, nuclear power, environmental degradation, technology, loss of personal privacy, and automation, Miller asserted that it was imperative to create a "sustainable society" that "satisfies human needs and fulfills human desires within environmental constraints" (Miller 1987, 77).

Miller ultimately supported five reforms. First, he wanted to vest Congress with the power to make all laws needed "to provide for and maintain an environment conducive to the attainment of a sustainable society." This would include the power "to achieve an optimum population, to control and diffuse the threat of nuclear war, and to control environmental degradation." Second, Congress should have authority "to provide for and maintain the reasonable satisfaction of human needs and fulfillment of human desires." Specifically, Miller wanted Congress to be responsible for providing "sufficient meaningful job opportunities for all who are able to work." Third, Congress should be able to check excessive presidential and bureaucratic powers. Miller favored establishing a council of state with whom the president would have to discuss decisions, and Miller endorsed increased congressional use of the legislative veto (since deemed unconstitutional). Fourth, Miller wanted to expand the original jurisdiction of the Supreme Court so that any voter could bring a suit to "determine the validity of allegations that congress had failed in any of its duties." Fifth, Miller proposed rewriting the Constitution so that it applied not only to governmental action but also "to any societal group that exercises substantial power over individuals." This would include "the supercorporations, the major trade unions, churches, farmers' leagues [and] professional associations" (Miller 1987, 105–6).

Miller offered six other proposals, the first three of which aimed to bring the nation closer to the parliamentary model. These included making Congress a unicameral body of 100 members; dividing the presidency into a separate head of government and head of state; and strengthening political parties so that they would have greater control over members of Congress. He also favored substituting 10 or 12 regional governments for the existing 50 states; recognizing "supercorporations" in the Constitution and bringing greater regulatory powers to bear against them; and expanding the role of the Supreme Court to take cases against both the two political branches and "private governments" (1987, 123). Miller hoped to transform the Constitution from a collection of negative prohibitions into a set of more affirmative guarantees.

Jeremy M. Miller Proposes Greater Protections for Natural Rights

Jeremy M. Miller (1954–), a professor at Western State University College of Law, also used the bicentennial of the constitution to advocate reform by proposing the text of a new constitution. He designed it to further the values of truth, dignity, equality, and fundamental fairness while forestalling "paternalistic legislation" (J. Miller 1987, 221).

Miller's expanded preamble sought to tie his document to the natural rights principles of the Declaration of Independence and specifically invoked "the Supreme Judge of the World" (God) (J. Miller 1987, 226). Consistent with such a focus, Article I of Miller's proposal was an expanded version of the Bill of Rights that applied limits to all three levels of government. His provision for religious freedom specifically prohibited either the use of "government monies for" or "government endorsement of" any religion (J. Miller 1987, 227). It also distinguished between religious belief and religious conduct and specified that "a short prayer to God as 'God,' is not a government endorsement of religion" (J. Miller 1987, 227). Similarly, Miller's provision for freedom of speech and press prohibited "prior licensing" but allowed reasonable "time, place, and manner restrictions" (J. Miller 1987, 227). The right to bear arms would include the right to own and carry "knives, swords, non-automatic pistols and non-automatic rifles" (J. Miller 1987, 228). Miller's proposed constitution would entrust traffic regulations to unarmed personnel and limit most abortions, dissections of the dead, and mechanical organ transplants. It provided detailed requirements for issuing warrants and provided for seven-person juries.

Article II outlined citizen duties. These include the duty of males age 17 and older to be subject to the military draft, of families to find "gainful employment" (J. Miller 1987, 232), and of losing plaintiffs to pay double a defendant's attorney's fees. This article also stipulated that the exclusive method of constitutional amendment would be for two-thirds of the states to call conventions (each state supplying a single delegate) whose proposals would become law if ratified by a majority of voters in two-thirds or more of the states.

Article III outlined three branches of government, which Miller identified as "executive, parliamentary, and judicial" (J. Miller 1987, 233). The president would serve a three-year term, to be followed by possible reelection to a six-year term and subsequent two-year terms. The president would be elected by a popular vote (with a runoff required when no one received a majority) and would share the power to nominate federal judges with the two houses of Congress and a constitutional court. The president would have increased powers over the budget, including an item veto, power to hold a national lottery when bankruptcy threatened, and instructions to keep income taxes from 2 to 15 percent of individual income.

The parliament, like the current Congress, would consist of a house and a senate. Each state would be represented by one senator and one to three representatives, depending on its population. Members of the house would serve a maximum of two three-year terms. A fourth-fifths vote of both houses of Congress could overturn decisions by the constitutional court on matters of constitutional interpretation, and majorities of both houses would ratify treaties.

Miller's proposed constitutional court would consist of nine judges who would serve 12-year terms and were to be bound by both the letter and the spirit of the constitution. Miller did not include federal protections for voting rights or an equal protection clause. A fellow scholar criticized what he thought to be "the undue specificity of some sections" and said that the end result was that the plan "looks like a patchwork quilt, not a balanced, patterned tapestry" (Knipprath 1987, 153–4, 256).

Marcia Lynn Whicker, Ruth Ann Strickland, and Raymond A. Moore Propose Major Congressional Reforms

Political scientists Marcia Lynn Whicker, Ruth Ann Strickland, and Raymond A. Moore also authored proposed constitutional changes during the bicentennial celebration of the Constitution. They presented their proposals in *The Constitution under Pressure: A Time for Change* (1987). The work opened with an examination of the U.S. Constitution, discussed various proposals for change, and ended with a chapter in which they detailed their own proposals to change the workings of Congress.

This chapter outlined five criteria by which to judge the existing system. They focused on whether the system allowed for the articulation and advancement of the national interest; fostered efficiency and responsibility; approximated citizen preferences; fostered accountability; and encouraged citizen participation (Whicker et al. 1987, 180–2). Concluding that there were obstacles to each of these objectives within the current organization of Congress, the authors proposed a series of REFORMS, an acronym standing for "Representational Efficient Functional Open Responsive Multi-cameral System" (Whicker et al. 1987, 192).

The first reform called for increasing the number of members in the House of Representatives. Although they suggested that this could be done by making existing districts smaller, they favored electing multiple representatives from the same districts and allowing those representatives to specialize. Their second proposal called for selecting senators on the basis of representation. They favored choosing senators from a series of shifting regions rather than from states. Their third proposed reform was to create a minimum of four specialized houses of representatives, each dealing with a different policy area. If there were four houses, voters in each district could select one such representative to a different house each year. A single specialized house of Congress would adopt most legislation, subject to "an internal legislative veto of the Senate" (Whicker et al. 1987, 199) and the possibility of overriding a senate veto by a three-fourths vote (the executive veto would also apparently remain in place). Under this proposed system, the senate would retain hierarchical authority over the houses of representatives, thus providing coordination and accountability.

The political scientists argued that their plan would better equip the government to meet important policy goals and address pressing issues. Larger senatorial districts would direct greater attention to national issues. Functional specialization of the Houses of Representatives would promote efficiency and responsibility. The "super Senate" would help promote accountability, and the greater number of representatives would open up greater opportunities for citizen participation. The authors observed that their reforms would not "alter relationships between branches or levels of government" but "restructure the national legislative branch to restore some of its lost power and make Congress simultaneously more efficient and more responsive to the people" (Whicker et al. 1987, 203).

Cornelius F. Murphy, Jr., Calls for a Convention
to Reassert the Authority of the People

Cornelius F. Murphy, Jr. (1933–), a professor of law at Duquesne University, published an essay in 1988 arguing for a new constitutional convention to reaffirm the American people's place as the document's constituent authority. Murphy seemed more interested in the positive effects of popular input into such a convention than in the results of its deliberations, but he did make a number of reform suggestions.

Murphy thought that the convention might seek to "delineate the boundaries between personal freedom and social order" and favored adding "economic, social and cultural entitlements," like those recognized in the Universal Declaration of Human Rights. He wanted to combine states into more functional regional units. Murphy also thought that a new convention should address problems created by the separation of legislative and executive powers and the "fractionalism of power." He did not believe these reforms could be adequately addressed "within the inherited constitutional structure" or by "piecemeal amendment" (Murphy 1988, 70).

Paul Fisher Proposes an Elaborate Amendment
to Advance Scientific Capitalism

Paul Fisher (1913–2006), the founder and owner of the Fisher Pen Company, published a book in 1988 entitled *The Plan to Restore the Constitution and Help Us All Get Out of Debt*. It proposed a constitutional amendment of 15 sections that he believed would address major economic and structural issues facing the nation.

The opening sections of Fisher's proposals dealt with taxes. Section 1 would apply all tax laws "uniformly to all individuals, partnerships, trusts, clubs, foundations, corporations, churches, unions, schools, and all other organizations including all governments and their agencies" (Fisher 1988, 331). Section 2 would repeal the Sixteenth Amendment and "all income, payroll, inheritance, gift and sales taxes (except Federal excise taxes)" (Fisher 1988, 331). Section 3 would provide for a tax on "all assets in excess of $100,000 which are owned or controlled by any individual or by any organization" (Fisher 1988, 331). Rates would vary from 0.5 percent on assets from one hundred thousand to one million dollars to 1.2 percent on assets in excess of five billion dollars. Fisher also included elaborate provisions whereby state and local governments could "levy a graduated tax on all assets, provided the state and local governments' total combined taxes on any asset does not exceed 60% of these initial federal rates" (Fisher 1988, 332). Section 4 called for creating a cabinet-level controller of the budget who would be charged with reducing the federal debt "to less than $200 billion," with balancing the federal budget, and with reducing federal expenditures to "less than 10% of the nation's Gross National Product" within three years (Fisher 1988, 333). Section 5 would require the treasury secretary to purchase the Federal Reserve System and regulate "all financial institutions, including insurance companies, with over $50 million in total assets" (Fisher 1988, 333). Section 6 would further vest the secretary of state with power to maintain a "fair balance of trade and credit with each foreign nation" (Fisher 1988, 334). The secretary would have power to raise and lower tariffs and interest rates to accomplish this objective.

The next sections proposed structural changes in government. Section 7 called for all new legislation to be written and endorsed by the cabinet, recommended by the president, and adopted by two-thirds majorities. Four-fifths majorities of Congress could replace the president, vice president, and cabinet members. Section 8 further proposed repealing the Seventeenth Amendment and choosing members of the House for four-year terms that corresponded with those of the president.

Section 9 required 12 or more citizens to endorse an individual before that person could vote. Section 10 attempted to control constitutional interpretation by providing that "no decision nor opinion by any court may be used to justify alternation of the literal, accurate meaning of the Constitution or any other governmental law."

Section 11 would limit governmental licensing, with exceptions for transportation that resulted in pollution. Section 12 would, in possible tension with the First Amendment, limit the dissemination of untruths or harmful services. Section 13 would mandate that courts settle cases within a year. Section 14 would require governments to subsidize private schools to the same extent that they did public schools.

J. William Fulbright Advocates a Parliamentary System

J. William Fulbright (1905–1995), a Democratic senator from Arkansas from 1945 to 1974 and one-time chairman of the Senate Foreign Relations Committee, advocated constitutional changes in an extended essay in a book that he published in 1989. He indicated, however, that he had first advocated such changes as far back as 1946, and that in the Eightieth Congress (1947–1948) he had proposed allowing either the president or Congress to dissolve the government and initiate elections for six-year terms.

Fulbright's primary interest lay in making the office of the president more accountable. He associated the existing constitutional system with "acute bickering,

polemical stalemate, and governmental paralysis" (Fulbright 1989, 55). He attributed this state of affairs to branches of government headed by different parties, a
decline in accountability, and the excessive influence of special interests. Under
a system of divided powers, claimed Fulbright, "presidential agreements" with
foreign governments are "tentative and provisional" (Fulbright 1989, 58). The
members of the legislative and executive branches had no real respect for, or accountability to, one another, and "without a parliamentary vote of no confidence"
(Fulbright 1989, 60), there was no real occasion for direct confrontation. Drawing from George Reedy's earlier critique of the presidency, Fulbright portrayed
American presidents as isolated individuals who, having rarely risen through
the legislative ranks, lacked understanding of the legislative process and rapport
with members of Congress. Fulbright also decried the constitutional provision requiring members of Congress to resign a seat before accepting appointment to a
cabinet post.

John Mertens Advocates an Intrusive Socialist Government
to Protect the Environment

The author has been unable to further identify John Mertens, the author of *The Second Constitution for the United States of America* (first printed in 1990 and subsequently reissued in 1991 and 1997), other than to note that he authored a 1998
novel titled *The Fall of America*. Although the title page of the 1997 edition of *The
Second Constitution* described the constitution as "a fantasy of which some should
not be taken too seriously," the publishers stated that they "believed that some of
the propositions and ideas put forth in the Second Constitution will become realities at some time in the future."

Mertens patterned the book along the lines of the U.S. Constitution, with six
articles and multiple sections. It combined such diverse ideas as population limitation, concern about the environment and dependence on foreign resources, a desire
to limit government to those of European descent, sexual equality, limitations on
wealth, and massive governmental involvement into many areas currently left to
private enterprise.

Article I of Mertens's imagined constitution would establish a legislative department consisting of an altered house and senate. Nominees for both houses would
initially be selected at random from among previous state legislators and would
have to be "third-generation citizens" (Mertens 1997, 2–3). The House would consist of 300 members and the Senate of one from each state. House members would
serve four-year terms while senators would only serve for three years. During their
time in office, members would be granted leave from their regular jobs and receive
similar compensation. All bills would be voted on in joint session. Budgets would
be strictly limited, and a one-time tax on assets and incomes would be used to
pay off the national debt within three years (perhaps that is the part designed to
be fantasy?). Congress would be empowered to use the armed forces to eradicate
drug trafficking. State officials would be selected much like federal officials, with
state legislatures nominating candidates for governor. Election seasons would be

significantly shortened, and all campaign contributions would be forbidden, with states reimbursing candidates for "reasonable travel expenses incurred during the campaign" (Mertens 1997, 2).

Article II proposed to divide the presidency into three parts. The executive president would command the military, with co-presidents supervising foreign and domestic affairs. Presidents would serve six-year terms and would rotate offices every two years. All three would have adjoining offices and live within a short distance of the White House.

Like other branches, the judiciary would be split equally between men and women. Supreme Court justices would serve ten-year terms. Each of six identified regions would have an appellate court. The Supreme Court would have the power to grant pardons, but they would only be granted with a unanimous vote. The Court would also appoint an ad hoc commission to create a uniform code of laws, "which the Supreme Court shall review, amend, or change as they deem proper" (Mertens 1997, 19). Mertens moved provisions in the current Constitution relative to the rights of criminal defendants to this section of his proposed constitution. One provision required that prisoners "shall work for their keep, at hard labor, and be incarcerated in remote areas at minimum comfort" and called for more serious offenders to be sterilized (Mertens 1997, 21). Section IV proposed dividing states into six designated regions. U.S. territories would become independent nations. No new states could be admitted into the union.

Section V combined the treatment of rights, privileges, and responsibilities. Mertens would set the voting age at 21, and ensure that voting and "equality of rights" would not be abridged "on account of race, color, or sex." Indeed, Mertens stipulated that "men and women shall be equal in all respects." Citizens would be guaranteed free health care as well as a right of privacy. Duties of citizenship would include one year in a National Labor Service, another year in the military, and the maintenance of "personal and family health." Mertens also called for limiting offspring to no more than two per family and banning unmarried couples from reproducing (Mertens 1997, 23).

Section VI of the *Second Constitution* set forth 17 "critical goals" for the United States, including reducing the population to 200 million and distributing it equally among 58 states, "eliminating the causes of inflation," "reducing oil consumption to three million barrels a day," building "a national electrified rail transport system," eliminating welfare, establishing national health care and "an effective national education system," and preserving the environment (Mertens 1997, 26–7). Many of these tasks would be the responsibilities of councils and sub-councils.

Attempts to control and relocate populations would include compulsory sterilizations and the provision of "minimal health care for illness caused by consumption of tobacco, drugs, alcohol, and overeating" (Mertens 1997, 28). Mertens would limit population density to "two hundred persons per square mile" (Mertens 1997, 30), with those in cities and states with higher densities encouraged or forced to relocate. A proposed "Council for an Integrated Economy" would limit an individual's accumulation of wealth to $5 million, although a subsequent amendment appears to raise this amount for those engaged in production. Corporate bonds would be exchanged for U.S. stocks, with the national government either taking over or directing most major industries.

A "Council for the Conservation, Generation, and Consumption of Energy" would abolish busing in favor of neighborhood schools of no more than 300 students, build windmills for the milling of grain, and replace fossil fuel plants with nuclear reactors. A "Council of Transport" would plan and build electrified mass-transit systems and consolidate and operate airlines "as a single national fleet" (Mertens 1997, 37). A "Council for Education" would limit or reduce college enrollments to no more than 5,000 students while increasing the number of doctors. A "Council for Production and Distribution of Food" would be authorized to outlaw fast foods that lacked adequate health and nutritional benefits (Mertens 1997, 41). A "Council for Healthcare and Care for Senior Americans" would take control of all hospitals and nursing homes and establish new care facilities for orphans. A Council for the Protection of the Environment would establish a 200-mile offshore fishing limit, abolish clear-cutting of forests, phase out "internal combustion engines running on fossil fuels or their derivatives," and set aside half of the U.S. land area as national parks, on which environmentally friendly farming could be conducted (Mertens 1997, 49).

A "Council for Racial Affairs" would offer "immigrants of non-European origin who have entered the United States of America since 1945" incentives to "return to the country of their origin with their descendants." In Mertens's scheme, the United States would buy property from South African whites so that American blacks could migrate there. Meanwhile, South African whites would be encouraged to relocate to the United States. A "Council for Religious Affairs" would assure that churches were independent of foreign control and monitor church affairs "for deliberate acts of mismanagement, embezzlement or fraud involving their organizations' assets" (Mertens 1997, 54–5).

Three amendments round out the document. One is a $750 million limit on individual accumulations. The second would provide for distributing $50 million each year to 100 of the nation's best scientists and teachers. The third would establish two kinds of juries, the first of which would monitor television advertising and the second of which would monitor other types of advertising.

Mertens did not indicate how his constitutional document would be implemented, and his only comment regarding the amending process was an endorsement of the Supreme Court's authority to amend the code of laws. Many of his provisions were aspirational, and those that stated specific goals did not specify how they would be implemented other than through massive new assumptions of governmental powers.

Bruce E. Tonn Seeks to Incorporate a Futurist Perspective within the Constitution

Futurists Alvin and Heidi Toffler are well known for their works on technology and American society, including the books *Future Shock* (1970) and *The Third Wave*

(1980). Although they did not write a proposed constitution, they did outline some principles that government should follow in their 1995 book *Creating a New Civilization: The Politics of the Third Wave*. These included the principles of "minority power," "semidirect democracy," and "decision division"—the latter of which called for the devolution of some powers long held by the national government (Toffler and Toffler 1995, 91, 96, 99).

Futurist Bruce E. Tonn (1955–), a researcher at the Oak Ridge National Laboratory in Tennessee, subsequently wrote articles in 1991 and 1996 applying a futurist perspective to the U.S. Constitution. His first article proposed and described what he dubbed the "Court of Generations" amendment, but it was divided into four sections.

Section 1 of the proposed amendment created a "Court of Generations, which shall be an adjunct of the judicial department of the national government" (Tonn 1991, 483). Sections II and III indicated that this court would consist of a grand jury composed of the Supreme Court and one representative from each of the U.S. states and territories. Its function would be to "return a bill of indictment to the members of the Supreme Court if evidence suggests an intolerable threat to the security of the blessings of liberty to our posterity" (Tonn 1991, 483). Members of the Supreme Court would then decide whether the extant generation was in contempt. Section IV further provided that the first Court of Generations would meet within five years after the adoption of the amendment and every five years thereafter.

Tonn wanted this new court to exist outside partisan structures and receive the "same stature and visibility" as the U.S. Supreme Court. As a grand jury, the Court of Generations would have subpoena power and would meet in secret. It would serve to "create a dialogue between living generations" (Tonn 1996, 490, 496).

In Tonn's second article, he expressed concerns about the lack of long-term vision shown by most legislators. Employing language reminiscent of the Twelve Southerners, he observed that:

> People of wisdom are not self-selected or self-centered. That is, they do not normally declare to the world that they are the wisest, because that would violate their values. Wisdom cannot be conveyed via twenty-second commercials. It can be recognized by others only through close association in various difficult and trying contests. Current processes tend to drive people of wisdom away from the fray, do not hold wisdom as a central characteristic for political office, and are, in any case, incapable of identifying people of wisdom and nurturing their growth over the years. (Tonn 1996, 415)

Tonn supplemented his earlier proposal for a Court of Generations with a proposal for a "Futures Congress" and a "Futures Administration" that would "build and administer (1) a Diagnostic and Decision Support System; (2) the Futures Congress Management System; and (3) systems that integrate with other national and global information systems" (Tonn 1996, 424). His Futures Congress would consist of four chambers composed of "Elders," "Visionaries," "Realists," and

"Decision Makers." Citizens would choose two million Decision Makers, each of whom would have to be 30 years or older, garner support from 100 to 200 individuals, and use "moral and ethical judgment" to "choose among future-oriented decision alternatives." The Decision Makers would also choose approximately 20,000 Realists (with a minimum age of 40), whose function would be to evaluate "future-oriented decision alternatives." Realists would in turn choose 200 Visionaries (50 years of age or older) to create "future-oriented decision alternatives." Finally, a group of 20 elders (60 years of age or older) would set "criteria to guide the creation and evaluation of future-oriented decisions" (Tonn 1996, 420).

Barry Krusch Introduces a Plan That Would Multiply Governmental Agencies

Barry Krusch (1958–) is a Web designer with degrees in psychology and education who offered an ambitious plan for a new U.S. Constitution in a book entitled *The 21st Century Constitution* (1992). Krusch blamed a litany of problems in America on the separation of powers, the writing of the Constitution prior to the modern information age, and disparities between constitutional language and actual practices. Krusch wanted the constitution to be more responsive to public wishes and more adaptive to modern technologies, but he also expressed faith in the power of experts to guide legislative decision making and identify national interests. His reform proposal followed the general outline of the existing U.S. Constitution.

Krusch planned to keep a bicameral Congress, but members of both houses would be prohibited from membership in political parties and limited to eight total years of service. The new House of Representatives would have a minimum of 1,000 members serving for one-year terms. Members would be required to graduate from a federal academy. States would continue to be represented by two senators who would serve two-year terms and be chiefly responsible for governmental oversight. A committee of 50 senators would administer "the National Database, the National Poll, the National Objectives, the National Initiative, the National Referendum, and the National Recall" (Krusch 1992, 128). The committee would also nominate candidates for the House of Representatives and the presidency in a way that fairly represented "sex, race, national origin and other factors" (Krusch 1992, 129). The Senate would create a legislative review board of nine members, serving for single three-year terms, who would compile "performance ratings" for representatives according to the degree to which they voted for bills that served the national interests. The Senate would also commission polls to ascertain the public will.

The assessment by the legislative review board would determine whether particular bills required the consent of one or both houses of Congress and signature by the president. Any income taxes would have to apply to at least three-fourths of the population; the highest tax bracket would be limited to 50 percent and the lowest would be at least half of that. Borrowing would require a vote by two-thirds of both houses and the voters. Krusch would restore the legislative veto. Congress would create and regulate a national academy, a department of rights enforcement, and a federal election commission, with all electoral campaigns to be publicly financed.

Krusch's constitution would guarantee a right to education. A national database would disseminate information to the citizens, and a national television channel would educate people (who would help shape programming through participation in national polls). His constitution also would set forth principles regarding freedom of speech, religion, and other provisions of the Bill of Rights in greater detail. One provision would impose penalties for those distorting "those aspects of reality which have been or can be objectively verified as true" (Krusch 1992, 183).

The president and vice president would be selected by majority vote, and a national recall would replace the current impeachment mechanism. The constitution would limit presidential powers to commit troops without congressional authorization. Nine nonpartisan judges representing the population would serve staggered nine-year terms. Although they would no longer exercise the power of judicial review, they would not be required to enforce laws that they considered unconstitutional.

Krusch provided that two-thirds majorities of both houses would be able to propose amendments to the constitution. A vote of two-thirds of the people or two-thirds of the state legislatures could also bring about a constitutional convention. Amendments would be ratified by two-thirds votes of the state legislatures or conventions, or by approval from three-fifths of the electorate. The new government would ask the people every 25 years whether they wanted to call another convention.

Krusch favored augmenting the main articles of the new constitution with supplements that could be more easily altered. Krusch also proposed a rule of constitutional construction ensuring that "strict terms such as 'no' or 'all' shall be strictly construed, and broad terms such as 'liberty' and 'justice' shall be broadly construed" (Krusch 1992, 247). A second federal convention act would provide the rules for constitutional ratification. Krusch anticipated a convention of 1,200 delegates to write or affirm the constitution, with members of no single profession to compose more than 5 percent of its members. Voters would choose from among three to six such documents.

Summary and Analysis

Most of the period from 1980 through 1992 featured divided government in which Republicans controlled the White House and Democrats controlled one or both houses of Congress. This dynamic may explain why so many proposals from this period either explicitly favored parliamentary government or sought greater cooperation between the legislative and executive branches. As Bruce E. Tonn explained his futurist perspective on the Constitution, others expressed more traditional concerns over the preservation of natural rights and federalism. Barry Krusch and John Miller, meanwhile, proved that some reformers continued to advocate for a more complex and prescriptive national constitution than the one that the American Founders had bequeathed to their posterity.

References

Brennan, Thomas, 1982. "Return to Philadelphia." *Cooley Law Review* 1: 1–72.

Church, Joseph. 1982. *America the Possible: Why and How the Constitution Should Be Rewritten.* New York: Macmillan and Company.

Committee on the Constitutional System. 1987. "A Bicentennial Analysis of the American Political Structure." Report and Recommendations of the Committee on the Constitutional System.

Cutler, Lloyd N. 1986. "To Form a Government." In *Separation of Powers—Does It Still Work?*, edited by Robert A. Goldwin and Art Kaufman. Washington, DC: American Enterprise Institute for Public Policy Research.

Fisher, Paul. 1988. *The Plan to Restore the Constitution and Help Us All Get Out of Debt.* Boulder City, NV: Paul Fisher Campaign for Scientific Government.

Fulbright, J. William (with Seth P. Tillman). 1989. *The Price of Empire.* New York: Pantheon.

Knipprath, Joerg W. 1987. "To See the Trees, but Not the Forest in Constitution Making: A Commentary on Professor Miller's Proposed Constitution." *Southwestern University Law Review* 17: 239–56.

Krusch, Barry. 1992. *The 21st Century Constitution.* New York: Stanhope Press.

Mertens, John. 1998. *The Fall of America.* N.p.: Gazelle Books.

Mertens, John. 1997. *The Second Constitution for the United States of America.* Cottonwood, CA: Gazelle Books.

Miller, Arthur S. 1987. *The Secret Constitution and the Need for Constitutional Change.* Westport, CT: Greenwood Press.

Miller, Arthur S. 1984. "The Annual John Randolph Tucker Lecture: Taking Needs Seriously: Observations on the Necessity for Constitutional Change." *Washington and Lee Law Review* 41 (Fall): 1243–1306.

Miller, Arthur S. 1982. *Toward Increased Judicial Activism: The Political Role of the Supreme Court.* Westport, CT: Greenwood Press.

Miller, Jeremy. 1987. "It's Time for a New Constitution." *Southwestern University Law Review* 17: 207–37.

Murphy, Cornelius F., Jr. 1988. "Constitutional Revision." In *Philosophical Dimensions of the Constitution*, edited by Diana T. Meyers and Kenneth Kipnis. Boulder, CO: Westview Press.

Robinson, Donald. 1989. *Government for the Third American Century.* Boulder, CO: Westview Press.

Robinson, Donald. 1987. "Adjustments Are Needed in the System of Checks and Balances." *Polity* 19: 660–6.

Robinson, Donald. 1985. *Reforming American Government: The Bicentennial Papers of the Committee on the Constitutional System.* Boulder, CO: Westview Press.

Shogan, Robert. 1982. *None of the Above: Why Presidents Fail—And What Can Be Done about It.* New York: New American Library.

Sundquist, James L. 1986. *Constitutional Reform and Effective Government.* Washington, DC: Brookings Institution.

Toffler, Alvin, and Heidi Toffler. 1995. *Creating a New Civilization: The Politics of the Third Wave*. Atlanta: Turner Publishing.

Tonn, Bruce E. 1996. "A Design for Future-Oriented Government." *Futures* 28 (June): 413–31.

Tonn, Bruce E. 1991. "The Court of Generations: A Proposed Amendment to the U.S. Constitution." *Futures* 21 (June): 482–98.

Vile, John R. 1991. *Rewriting the United States Constitution: An Examination of Proposals from Reconstruction to the Present*. New York: Praeger.

Whicker, Marcia Lynn, Ruth Ann Strickland, and Raymond A. Moore. 1987. *The Constitution under Pressure: A Time for Change*. New York: Praeger.

CHAPTER 9

The Clinton Years: Approaching a New Century and a New Millennium

In the 1990s, the approach of the new century and new millennium worked in combination with fierce partisanship and political warfare to generate numerous new proposals to rewrite the Constitution. Perhaps the most famous of these proposals came in 1994, when Republicans unveiled an ambitious reform agenda they called a "Contract with America" (Gillespie and Schellhas 1994). This agenda included support for constitutional amendments to require a balanced federal budget and impose term limits.

Many advocates of constitutional change from this period specifically referred either to the year 2000 or to the twenty-first century in their proposals. They used these upcoming milestones to underscore their belief that America needed a new constitution to meet the challenges of the next century. A number of these proposals were originally posted on the Internet, which seemed to replace the early American pamphlet as the preferred means of political communication and persuasion. Chapter 12 will cover these and later online proposals.

Michael Noah Mautner Offers a Constitution of Direct Democracy

In 1992, Dr. Michael Noah Mautner (1942–) published *A Constitution of Direct Democracy: Pure Democracy and the Governance of the Future, Locally and Globally*. Born in Budapest, Hungary, during the Holocaust, Mautner grew up under Stalinist rule before moving to Israel, the United States, and New Zealand. He earned a PhD in chemistry from the Rockefeller Institute in New York, served in academic positions, and became active in the Nuclear Freeze Movement. Mautner tailored his proposed constitution for a direct democracy so that it would function under either a presidential or a parliamentary system.

Mautner's proposed constitution consisted of five sections—preamble, principles, institutions, principles of competent justice, and procedures and institutions. The last section contained six articles detailing public decision making, expert management, the judiciary, election and removal of officials, checks and balances and stability, and amendments.

Mautner's preamble stated that "all people share the basic needs of survival and the social drives basic to human nature." It further proclaimed that "Direct Democracy is based on the decency, goodness and common sense of most people."

Mautner believed that the transition from representative democracy to direct democracy could be peaceful. Mautner argued that the central problem with representative democracy is that individuals could rarely find candidates who agreed with all their views and often became sidetracked by the personalities of political figures, rather than their positions on matters of public policy.

Mautner believed that these problems could be remedied through the creation of new institutions. He planned to extend direct democracy by allowing citizens to send requests for referendums to a body called a National Proposal Bank. A "Debates Agency" would then create issue panels, which would formulate specific referendums (subject to oversight by referendum juries). Once the people adopted referendums, they would be administered by "Expert Agencies." Policy juries and policy ombudsmen would, in turn, oversee the work of the expert agencies, with the former deciding when polls were sufficient to ascertain popular will and when referendums would be required. An executive council composed of the heads of expert agencies would handle special emergencies, while the legality of their activities would be overseen by expert courts and by a Supreme Court. Individuals in most of these agencies would be selected at random. The public would choose high-ranking executive officials based solely on their qualifications, because information about their "race, gender, age, physical appearance and personal charisma" would be withheld. The anonymous candidates would be represented by "professional stand-in advocates" (Mautner 1992, 36). Individuals would serve 10-year terms, subject to recall. Amendments would have to be approved by 60 percent in a national poll and pass by a 70 percent majority in a national referendum.

Mautner illustrated how his system would work through a series of hypothetical studies involving gene therapy, arms reduction, and national budgets. He suggested that public debates could be linked to entertainment. He believed a nation might transition to such a system if candidates ran on a "Direct Democracy" platform requiring them to vote on every major issue according to majority decisions by their constituents. In an appendix to the book, the author's wife, Helene D. Mautner, described how she had conducted the first such campaign for Maryland's sixth congressional seat. Mautner suggested that implementation of direct democracy might be "particularly easy to introduce in new pioneering societies" like Israeli kibbutz settlements or space colonies.

Mautner argued that social progress "does not require centralized leadership" (Mautner 1992, 114), and he expressed his belief that majority rule would be unlikely to result in suppression of minority rights. Mautner asserted that the United States Constitution was insufficiently flexible, and that interpretations of the First and Second Amendments had adversely impacted campaign finance and violence in society, respectively. He believed it was possible to move from direct democracy within individual nations to direct democracy throughout the world and even into outer space. He cited Switzerland as an example of a nation that had already successfully incorporated a number of aspects of direct democracy into its political system.

Bernard H. Siegan Uses the U.S. Constitution as a Model for Other Nations

The year 1989 marked the fall of the Communist Iron Curtain and the emergence of new governments throughout Eastern Europe. As these emerging nations turned to crafting constitutions for themselves, legal scholar Bernard H. Siegan bucked the trend of criticizing the U.S. Constitution. Instead, he published a 1992 book in which he cited the U.S. Constitution as a model for these new governments to follow (a second edition was published in 1994). But Siegen's outline of the essentials of a constitution for emerging nations did differ from the American Constitution in some ways, and many of his ideas resurfaced in later proposals to rewrite the U.S. Constitution.

Siegan (1924–2006) attended the law school at the University of Chicago and spent most of his career at the University of San Diego School of Law, during which time he served on the National Commission on the Bicentennial of the Constitution. In 1987, President Reagan nominated Siegan to serve on the U.S. Ninth Circuit Court of Appeals, but Siegan eventually withdrew after failing to receive a positive vote from the Democratic-controlled Senate Judiciary Committee because of concerns about his conservative views on economic matters and civil rights.

In his book, Siegan concentrated on how a constitution could protect economic and other rights. He believed that constitutions should largely outline "negative rights"—rights against governmental action—and direct the legislature (albeit within strict constitutional limits) to deal with social and economic rights. Siegan was a strong proponent of separation of powers and judicial review, which he believed should extend both to enumerated and unenumerated rights. He criticized court decisions that gave greater protection to noneconomic than to economic rights and believed that free enterprise systems were more prosperous than socialist or welfare-oriented policies. Siegan specifically favored constitutional provisions that limited property taxes to a fixed percentage of their value, limited taxes to a fixed percentage of the gross national income, prevented deficit spending without a supermajority vote, set aside budget surpluses for years with debt, and authorized the chief executive to exercise a line-item veto on spending bills.

Siegan embodied these and other ideas in his "Suggested Model Constitution for Emerging Nations and Republics," which consisted of nine articles. The first provided for a tripartite government of separated powers. Article II further designated a national assembly as the major legislative body, with members to be elected to four-year terms. Legislation was required to proceed through a committee system, to be limited to a single subject, and to be subject to presidential veto. In contrast to the U.S. Congress, the national assembly appears to have been unicameral.

Perhaps because the model constitution had so many restrictions, Article III extended to the national assembly wide powers over "all subjects of legislation not herein forbidden, restricted or otherwise constitutionally protected" (Siegan 1994, 83). Within constitutional limits, the assembly was authorized to "seek to improve and elevate the people's health, safety, well being and living condition, advance and encourage education and culture, tax and spend for the common good and public interest, protect and preserve personal security and family life, enhance the environment, and safeguard the people from their domestic and foreign enemies" (Siegan 1994, 84). Siegan proposed seriously limiting government ownership of commercial enterprises, and he forbade "any special preference or exclusive right, privilege, or immunity" to business interests (Siegan 1994, 85).

Article IV outlined the powers of a president who would also serve four-year terms. The president would be both head of government and head of state. Although the president could respond to immediate military threats, the president had to seek approval of his action from the national assembly within five days. Article V provided for two kinds of national courts. The "Constitution Court" would exclusively review the constitutionality of legislation, whereas the "Supreme Judicial Court" would handle other appeals. The national assembly and the president would appoint its members.

Article VI consisted of 20 sections providing for rights, including those contained in the U.S. Bill of Rights and the post–Civil War amendments. Such rights specifically extended to corporations and to the protection of unenumerated rights. Article VII further detailed the rights of individuals accused of crimes. Article VIII left blanks to designate the official language, the flag, the national hymn, the national coat of arms, and the location of the capital. Article IX provided for ratification by a two-thirds vote of the national assembly, and by more than 50 percent of the voters. It provided similar mechanisms for the passage of constitutional amendments.

Roderick Long Proposes a New System Based on Virtual Cantons

Roderick Tracy Long (1964–), a Harvard- and Cornell-educated professor of philosophy at Auburn University, is associated with the Ludwig von Mises Institute. A libertarian anarchist, Long sought to unite anarchists (who think the state is unnecessary) and minarchists (who favor a minimal state). He authored an article in the Autumn 1993 issue of *Formulations*, published by the Free Nation Foundation, entitled "Virtual Cantons: A New Path to Freedom?" In this article, Long suggested that the nation could best preserve its freedom by decentralizing. He imagined dividing the nation into 500 states, similar to the Swiss system of cantons. Long anticipated that these entities would be based on common interests rather than geography, thus allowing people to switch from one canton to another without physically moving.

Long likened this system to the Icelandic Free Commonwealth, which operated from 930 to 1262 and used "the Thing system." The national assembly, or "Thing," was divided into four Quarter-Things, which were in turn divided into Varthings. Such a system, as he envisioned it, would move representation from the national to the state level, which would in turn be represented in the national legislature. The national government would coordinate policies among the cantons, but its powers would be severely restricted.

Long subsequently elaborated on this idea in an article (originally published in the Summer 1994 issue of *Formulations* and now available online) proposing an actual constitution, which he divided into three parts and modeled in part on the proposed island government of Oceania. The first part, which would be amendable, outlined the government of the Free Nation (a placeholder for whatever name was chosen for the new nation). It would create a government consisting of a "Federal Administration and a number of Virtual Cantons," all of which would be voluntary. Each individual citizen would have to consent to this government, and all citizens would have the right to vote and run for office. They would be taxed only so long as they remained citizens. Citizens had the right to launch national referendums to recall members of the federal administration, which would consist of three branches. The federal legislature would be a bicameral parliament. One legislative body would be composed of a representative from each canton, who would serve seven-year nonconsecutive terms. The other, called a "Negative Council," would consist of councilors, half chosen on the basis of population and half randomly, also for seven-year terms. Passing legislation would require supermajorities of two-thirds of each house and four-fifths majorities to overturn executive vetoes. Legislation would be limited to a single subject and would be subject to line-item executive vetoes, and the total word length for all federal laws would be restricted to one million words. The Negative Council could repeal any existing law by a one-third-plus-one vote. The power of both houses would be restricted largely to matters of foreign policy. The necessary and proper clause was revised in Long's constitution, both to eliminate the word "proper" and to provide "that no law imposing greater restrictions on the people than needed for the attainment of this end shall be regarded as necessary."

Long called for establishing a plural executive consisting of the president of the parliament, the president of the Negative Council, and the president of the Free Nation to be elected by a plurality of the people. No one could serve for more than five years, and all could be recalled. Although the executive would be commander in chief of the military, the executive could not initiate military action.

The judiciary would consist of a Supreme Court whose members would serve indefinite terms until they retired. The Supreme Court would receive appeals from an independent judiciary consisting of "private judicial service or services." Long's constitution contained numerous provisions for due process, including most within the current Bill of Rights. Not only would the nation rest on a plethora of cantons, but individuals would be permitted to join more than one. Canton taxation rates would be limited, as would those of the national government.

Long favored a constitutional amendment process that would require approval by four-fifths of both houses, and by both four-fifths of the cantons and two-thirds or more of the citizens. Laws would apply "equally to all persons regardless of gender, ethnicity, opinions, religion, national origin, or peaceful lifestyle." The constitution would outlaw "victimless" and "consensual crimes." It would also prohibit the government of the Free Nation from supporting any schools or

religion, regulating currency, or engaging in occupational licensure. Long's constitution also guaranteed the right to secession. Addendums included protections for
animals above specified intelligence levels, a right to abortion, the imposition of
retributive punishments, and laws protecting copyrights or patents.

George Kennan Proposes Creation of a Permanent Advisory Body

George Kennan (1904–2005), an American diplomat who authored the Cold War
doctrine of containment and served as an ambassador to the Soviet Union, wrote
a book in 1993 examining challenges faced by the United States. Within the book,
he suggested that European parliamentary systems were preferable to those in the
United States. He did not advocate changing the current U.S. government structure, however. Kennan recognized that the people accepted the current system and
he feared that changing the Constitution could lead to "unpredictable dangers"
(Kennan 1993, 66).

Kennan argued that politicians find it difficult to devote time to long-term problems. In a chapter entitled "What Is to Be Done?" Kennan suggested that numerous
people who had retired from public life or professional careers might be recruited
to serve their country in a long-range planning capacity. Kennan developed six
criteria for membership for such a group. It should be drawn exclusively from
individuals without current involvement in government; be purely advisory; be approved by existing authorities, perhaps through an act of Congress approved by the
president; be by presidential appointment; be permanently endowed; and

> occupy itself only with long-term questions of public policy, avoiding matters
> of current contention, restricting itself to the identification of the preferable
> principles and directions of action, and refraining from involvement, either
> by prior suggestion or by ex post facto comment, with the implementation of
> the judgments it might offer. (Kennan 1993, 237)

Kennan recommended calling this group a "Council of State" and suggested that
it be comprised of nine members. The council could either initiate its own subjects
of investigation or pursue studies at the request of the two elected branches. Members could hold hearings but not subpoena witnesses. He suggested that members
be drawn with input from state governors, judicial officers, and other public officials. Although their recommendations would be advisory only, "they should make
a deep impression on public opinion, and should come with time to constitute a
factor which . . . the president and the legislators would feel a certain pressure to
treat with some consideration and respect" (Kennan 1993, 247).

Malcolm R. Wilkey Calls for a Second Constitutional Convention to Overcome Gridlock

During a long career as a judge and diplomat, Malcolm R. Wilkey (1918–2009)
served in such positions as judge on the U.S. Court of Appeals for the District of
Columbia and ambassador to Uruguay. In 1993, he delivered a series of lectures
at Brigham Young University on the U.S. political system. These lectures—and

responses to them from a number of scholars and political figures—were published in a 1995 book called *Is It Time for a Second Constitutional Convention?*

Wilkey based his lectures on the premise that "the performance of the federal government has become a great disappointment to most Americans." He viewed the central problems as "gridlock, perpetual incumbency, and total unaccountability" (Wilkey 1995, 11, 19). According to Wilkey, these problems stemmed from the excessive size of the House of Representatives, inter-branch conflict, and the growing practice of ticket-splitting. Wilkey was especially concerned with increasing budget deficits and the inability of Congress to control them. He further tied inaction by the two elected branches to increased judicial activism. Wilkey based much of his diagnosis on the analysis of the 1987 Report of the Committee on the Constitutional System.

Wilkey proposed two overall solutions to the problems he identified. One was to accept the idea of career politicians and seek to bring more accountability to the system, as in parliamentary systems. The other was to recognize the failure of both career politicians and the political party system and move to what he described as a "Cincinnatus" model of government that would rely less on experts. He preferred the second option, which would prevent individuals from serving consecutive terms, but he thought that some reforms would be useful whichever option was chosen.

Specifically, Wilkey favored six-year terms for the president and for members of both houses of Congress; allowing nonpartisan commissions to reapportion House districts, thus reducing the membership of the House of Representatives to 250 members; fixing the salaries of members of Congress and justices; and reducing the length and costs of political campaigns. He also favored adopting a presidential line-item veto; a balanced budget amendment; and the elimination of Senate confirmation for most offices other than Supreme Court justices. To reduce deadlock, he would permit the president to dissolve Congress and call a new election or permit Congress to take a vote of no confidence in the president. He would also permit the president to choose cabinet members from Congress and to answer questions directly before it. Wilkey also wanted to facilitate straight-ticket voting and hold the vote for Congress after that of the president to help strengthen political parties. He would limit terms of Supreme Court justices to 15 years, provide for public participation in a constitutional convention every 20 years, and allow voters to cast a vote for "none of the above"—a choice that could, if it received enough support, trigger a new election with a new slate of candidates (Wilkey 1995, 52–3). Wilkey favored allowing the president to establish national referendums, albeit on policy issues rather than constitutional issues. He also endorsed a revision to the Tenth Amendment to identify "specific" duties for the states (Wilkey 1995, 107).

Wilkey anticipated that term limits would bring a wider range of people into the government. He also wanted to rethink the division of powers between the legislative and executive branches relative to foreign policy. He favored either junking the War Powers Resolution and vesting "full military responsibility in the President" or requiring "prior congressional approval of any troop deployment above a certain size" (Wilkey 1995, 96, 97). Wilkey's approach to party reform included allowing party elders to hold conventions, where nominees would be selected for primary elections. He also proposed campaign reforms, including the provision of free or subsidized airtime for candidates.

Wilkey suggested that most of these reforms would never be adopted by a modern Congress due to the influence of entrenched special interests. He therefore favored calling a second constitutional convention for this purpose. He thought that it might be preceded by a commission that could study and recommend reforms.

Walter Berns and Phyllis Schlafly both opposed Wilkey's suggestions for another convention. Terry Eastland and former attorney general Edwin Meese III largely agreed that federal powers had grown inordinately. Michael E. Debow and Dwight R. Lee also believed that the central problem facing the U.S. political system had been the growth of the national government, but they expressed doubts about the capacity of a second convention to solve this. They subsequently proposed what they called an "Article I, Section 8 Pledge," whereby "members of Congress should be asked to pledge publicly not to vote for any new government program or activity that cannot be squared with the enumerated powers of Congress set out in Article I, Section 8—*read as of the time of the Founding*" (Wilkey 1995, 198).

Jim Davidson Proposes a Libertarian and Democratic Constitution for a New Nation-State

In 1994 a man named Jim Davidson, whose publications did little to describe him, proposed a new constitution for a "floating" concrete nation, which he dubbed "Oceania," that would be placed in the Caribbean Sea. This proposal was published in *The Atlantis Papers* (1994), coauthored by Eric Klien, Norm Doering, and Lee Crocker. Unlike architects of utopian schemes, Davidson designed his proposals for what he hoped would become a real country. In constructing his constitution, Davidson charged that the U.S. Constitution was so "vague" as "to allow its government to pass laws clearly at odds with the spirit of liberty in which that once-free nation was founded."

The constitution of Oceania began with "A Partial Listing of Rights." Rights could not be removed without a 95 percent vote, and new rights would not be enshrined without approval from 66 percent or more of voters. Davidson classified rights under the headings of life, liberty, property, and privacy. The right to life included the right of a hospital to turn off life support for individuals whose families can no longer afford such care. This right would also encompass "the Right to keep and bear Weaponry," and even to set booby traps, for those who posted proper warnings. It included a "Right to Self Sovereignty" that encompassed what individuals put into their bodies—such as drugs—or wore on their bodies—like seat belts and helmets. This self-sovereignty provision also applied to all kinds of consensual sexual conduct and participation in dangerous sports. The right to life also included broad protections of free speech, employment, and religious liberty.

The right to liberty included a prohibition of slavery, a right to travel, a right to assemble, a right to associate and discriminate, and a right to knowledge. This latter right included being able to engage in insider trading. The right to travel would provide that all land in Oceania "contain eight-meter-wide and eight-meter-high easements in a grid format of squares with eight kilometers wide on which there is an Entitlement to travel."

The constitution based the right to property on the proposition that "taxation, civil forfeiture, [and] eminent domain" are all "forms of theft." Individuals would be permitted to sell body parts, engage in sex or medical experiments for money, and operate businesses without licenses. The constitution would prohibit "minimum wage, family leave benefits, medical insurance, disability benefits, unemployment insurance, or workers' compensation." The right of property would further include the right to negotiate contracts, including same-sex unions. The right to privacy included protections against warrantless searches, the "Right to Self-Identity," the "Right to Financial Privacy," the "Right to Encryption," the "Right to Secure Conversations," and privacy rights on government property and in the workplace.

Article II of the constitution dealt with "Government Agencies and Power Structures." It began with the judiciary. The proposed constitution would outlaw victimless crimes and abolish the distinction between civil and criminal law. Judges of the nation's Supreme Court and lower bodies would serve two- or four-year terms, and judges would not require licenses. Individuals would obtain court membership—expected to be widespread—in order to bring suits. Membership would bring the "Right to Fair Prosecution," the right to a jury, "The Right to a Level Playing Field," the "Right to Fair Bail and Fines," the "Right to Presumption of Innocence," and other rights currently designated within the U.S. Bill of Rights. The constitution would create a statute of limitations of 10 years for all crimes, and would require prisoners to either engage in labor to support themselves or live off private charity.

The delineation of the executive branch began by specifying that all major laws must "be decided by referendum." Presidents and vice presidents would serve for four-year terms and could put referendums on the ballot and "sign minor Contracts and legislation." The president could sign treaties to which 75 percent or more of Oceania voters had previously agreed. Directors of the various departments of war would be selected through popular election and would contract for services with private militia. An "Anti-Law Department" would help repeal unwanted laws.

Direct popular legislation would take the place of a legislature, thus eliminating lobbying. The areas in which the people could legislate were, however, restricted. The constitution expressed the hope that "Whenever a need or a problem arises . . . Oceanians will not ask 'What law can we pass?' but 'What Business can we create?'" Elections would include designations for "None of the Above" and "Remove This Office."

A section of the constitution focusing on "The Power Structures of Oceania" dealt primarily with the rights of restricted and unrestricted businesses. The constitution would strip governments of their powers to "issue or control currency," to generate power, to run a postal service, to finance art, to engage in traffic control, to inspect foods, to provide job training, or to finance scientific research or tourism. The constitution tersely noted, "Governmental charities are compassion at gun-point."

Article III further listed powers denied to government. It forbade government from levying taxes; establishing businesses; running embassies; owning property or streets; regulating banking; operating schools; engaging in "Welfare and Humanitarian Activities," including Social Security; or funding police, fire protection, garbage, disposal, public transit, or other services.

Article IV dealt with national security. All wars, other than those in direct response to attack, would be declared by referendum. If Oceania decided to join the United Nations, the membership would be privately funded. The right to free trade would not include the right to export mind-altering drugs or weapons to nations on forbidden lists.

Article V allowed the people to regulate abortion by referendum after the first trimester. Article VI dealt with budgeting and required agencies to publish a list of donors each year. It provided for some agency budgets to be funded by fees levied against losing parties in court cases.

Article VII identified a housing development as "the most powerful governmentlike structure in Oceania." Such developments would be subdivided once they reached 5,000 persons. Article VIII would permit a county or local government to secede if 75 percent of the population voted for such a measure. Article IX provided constitutional ratification "by unanimous consent of the original Land Owners of Oceania." Article X ended with a list of nonbinding suggestions that included permitting animal rights groups to be plaintiffs in animal rights' cases, allowing armed forces to challenge one another in games of skill, and establishing English as the nation's official language.

Herbert C. Kirstein Proposes a More Democratic and Complex Government

Herbert C. Kirstein identified himself as a former employee of the Central Intelligence Agency, the staff of the U.S. Senate, and the U.S. Department of Health and Human Services. Like Davidson, Kirstein published his plans on a Web site and in book form. Kirstein's *U.S. Constitution for the 21st Century and Beyond* (1994) sought to democratize the current Constitution, but whereas Davidson aimed to keep government lean, Kirstein multiplied proposed agencies.

Kirstein listed 10 objectives of government, comprising a

stronger "voice" for citizens; knowledgeable national-global leadership; effective management of government; futurized Congress for the 21st Century; law enforcement, security, and justice; tax laws to accelerate economic progress; monetary policy to finance future; stewardship of national resources; accelerated science and technology; and [a] new "Voice of USAMERICA."

He accompanied these objectives with sharp criticism of contemporary examples of governmental corruption and inefficiency.

Kirstein's proposed constitution of eight articles is considerably more complex than the U.S. Constitution. Article I described the "Powers of the Citizens," including the right to "enact laws by national referendum" and "to instruct, remove, or impeach" elected officials (Kirstein 1994, 14). Citizenship would require an oath or affirmation to abide by the document. Voting would be both a right and a duty, and citizens could be fined for not participating. The article also provided for a "Universal Academy for Freedom and Democracy" to educate all candidates.

Article II outlined legislative powers. In addition to the existing two houses, it proposed an "Office of the Premiere Legislative Coordinator of Congress" (Kirstein 1994, 16). Elected by the people from among those who scored highest on a "National Knowledge Examination," this individual would establish legislative goals and priorities, enhance legislative management, and exercise veto powers over legislation. The coordinator would serve for renewable six-year terms. Senators and members of the House of Representatives would also be expected to pass national exams, and House terms would be increased to four years. Kirstein listed 43 separate powers that congress would exercise (Kirstein 1994, 24–8).

Article III described executive and administrative powers. Under Kirstein's constitution, the president would become the "Chief Executive Officer of the National Executive and Administrative Service." Like members of Congress, the president would have to attain a certain score on the National Knowledge Examination. The president could serve a maximum of two six-year terms and would direct the "National Council for Progress and Security," which Kirstein divided into a number of departments. These included a Department for Legislative Affairs; a Department of National Economic Development and Progress (along with a Directorate for a National Monetary System, a Directorate for a National Banking System, a Directorate for National Value and Pricing Systems, a Directorate for National Investment Policy and Systems, and a Directorate for Market Economy and Enterprise Systems); a Department for National Human Work Force and Automated and Robotic Systems (the former Department of Labor, which will in turn be divided into a number of directorates); a Department for Agriculture, Aquaculture, and Other Food-Production Systems; a Department for Natural Resources; a Department for Environmental Protection, Preservation, and Enhancement; a Department for Advancing Science and Technology; a Department for International Policy and Global Affairs; a Department for Extraterrestial and Outer Universe Exploration and Developments Programs (formerly NASA); a Department for Advancing the Status of Citizens (with numerous subdirectorates); a Department for National Intelligence and Citizen-Information Systems; a Department for Natural Disaster-Recovery Systems; as well as a number of existing departments. All told, Kirstein proposed a total of 20 main departments with many subdirectorates.

Article IV would create a "National Judicial System for Law and Justice" that would be headed by a "Supreme Judicial Minister" who, like other officeholders, would only be seated after passing an examination and winning a plurality of votes in a national election (Kirstein 1994, 52–3). This minister would serve renewable six-year terms and would nominate members of the judiciary for Senate confirmation. The judicial branch would include a "Ministry for Law Enforcement and Citizen Security" that would replace the current Department of Justice. The ministers would be nominated by the Supreme Judicial Minister and confirmed by a majority of Supreme Court justices so that the individual would be less partisan than the current attorney general. The constitution specified that the minister "shall be a permanent, career appointment" (Kirstein 1994, 44).

The constitution would also establish a "National Societal-Clone Prison System," which would mirror the institutions of the larger society and would be expected to be self-supporting. The judicial branch would also include a Ministry of Justice composed of members of the U.S. Supreme Court and other courts. The minister of justice would be nominated by the "Supreme Judicial Minister for Law and Justice" and confirmed by majority vote of U.S. Supreme Court justices. In addition to passing tests confirming their legal knowledge, most judges would be required to have at least 10 years of experience in the judicial system. The supreme judicial officer of the National Judicial System would nominate U.S. Supreme Court justices, who would be confirmed by the Senate for service up to 30 years. Kirstein would further establish special exams before individuals could serve as jurors. A "National Council for Constitutionality of Law" would review congressional laws prior to their implementation and force their reconsideration if it believed them to be unconstitutional.

Article V contained an equivalent of the supremacy clause, while Article VI provided for ratification of the constitution by a two-thirds vote of the electorate. Article VII discussed the issue of constitutional amendments. Such amendments could be proposed either by congressional legislation or by legislation or referendum passed by two-thirds of the states. Like the constitution itself, amendments would be ratified by a two-thirds vote of the citizenry.

Article VIII dealt with "Citizen Rights, Obligations, and Rewards." Citizens would pledge to obey the law, vote, respect the rights of others, and serve their nation for one or two years upon reaching the age of 18. An accompanying "Golden Chronicle of Citizen Rights" included some protections in the current Bill of Rights and some additional ones. These included freedom; democracy; entitlements to basic needs like "food, housing, health and medical care, education, and acceptable standards of living"; the right to own property, including firearms; freedom to communicate; freedom of assembly; equal status under law "without regard to race, creed, nationality, ethnic origin, gender, ideology, religion, economic status, or other factor or value"; due process of law; protections for private life; protections against exploitation and economic servitude; protection against discrimination; the right to worship; the right to present grievances to government without the improper use of money to influence politicians; the sharing of resources; separation of religion and government; human rights; "truth in public communications"; and a provision guaranteeing "general rights and privileges" (Kirstein 1994, 63–5).

Chester Antieau Proposes Revisions to Social and Economic Rights

Chester Antieau (1913–2006), a long-time professor of constitutional law at Georgetown University, proposed three types of desirable constitutional changes in *U.S. Constitution for the Year 2000* (1995). The first set proposed to explicitly recognize certain rights identified by the U.S. Supreme Court but not contained within the existing text. The second dealt with current constitutional provisions that the author wanted to amend. The third highlighted additional rights that should be added to the document.

The four rights that courts currently recognize and that Antieau thought should be formally incorporated into the Constitution were freedom of association, freedom of enterprise, freedom of movement, and the right to privacy. Although he mentioned that the right to privacy could conflict with the right to life, he did not indicate how he would resolve that issue.

Antieau's proposed changes to existing amendments included expanding Eighth Amendment guarantees specifically to protect "the inherent dignity of the human person, to outlaw torture, and to stipulate a right to bail" (Antieau 1995, 37). He wanted to change existing grounds of impeachment to "serious misconduct to the harm of the nation" (Antieau 1995, 56) and proposed establishing special non-legislative tribunals to try such impeachments. Antieau favored modifying the Seventh Amendment to eliminate jury trials in civil cases. He further advocated allowing the president to exercise a line-item veto, elimination of the pocket veto, and authorizing Congress to override presidential vetoes by less than a two-thirds majority. He favored authorizing the Supreme Court to issue advisory opinions and withdrawing federal diversity jurisdiction from federal courts. He endorsed state-appointed counsel for indigents in civil as well as in criminal cases. Antieau wanted to allow naturalized citizens to be eligible for the presidency and to permit the use of popular initiatives to introduce constitutional amendments. He would also have expanded the First Amendment to require a right of the public and the press to have access to information.

Antieau also called for adding several social and economic rights to the Constitution similar to those contained in some other nations. These included the right to an education; a healthy environment; and adequate social services, such as housing, health care, employment, food, clothing, and social security. He also favored recognizing the importance of a number of interrelated rights of movement, including the rights of asylum, departure, emigration, voluntary expatriation, and entry and return, and the freedom from exile and deportation. He also discussed miscellaneous proposals to give citizens the right to recall members of Congress, register as conscientious objectors to military service, and outlaw capital punishment.

A Pseudonymous Virginia Vanguard Advocates Greater Democracy and Discourages Paternalism

Pseudonyms were quite common in early American history, and a 1995 book entitled *The Populis: A Draft Constitution for a New Political Age* revived this technique to "focus attention on arguments versus personalities." As the title suggests, the chief desire of the author (or authors) was to enhance direct democracy in the United States.

The book presented a draft of a proposed constitution consisting of a preamble and 12 articles followed by a brief description of how the constitution would work. The preamble, otherwise similar to that of the current Constitution, omitted the words "of the United States" and was relatively vague as to what role, if any, states would play in the new system.

Article I identified five elements of the new national government. The "Populis" would determine basic policies and select office holders. The "Caucis" would select and present policy issues and candidates to the voters. The "Legis" would translate public decisions into law. The "Executis" would implement and enforce such laws, and the "Judicis" would interpret the laws and attempt to assure fair treatment for all.

Article II stipulated that citizenship would be limited to individuals born to a citizen parent or naturalized. Individuals could forfeit citizenship upon "accepting the citizenship of another nation, upon conviction of a serious criminal act, or upon death." Citizens were charged with gaining adequate education and training and would be required to "possess sufficient financial insurance against personal calamity." Citizenship carried with it, as a birthright, "all freedoms," which could only be abridged "with the explicit consent of the Populis," which had the right "to directly and collectively determine all national policy" as "indelible" (Virginia Vanguard 1995, 19–20).

The constitution provided that citizens 18 years and older could join the Populis. Only such citizens could hold office or participate in national elections and referenda. Such citizens would be required to perform at least four years of military and civilian service. Individuals who failed to join the Populis within four years would permanently lose the opportunity to do so, although they would continue to be bound by the laws if they stayed.

The Caucis was patterned after the grand jury and would consist of "seven willing persons, selected randomly and secretly from the rolls of the Populis." Chosen every two months, members "will be sequestered at a central location, along with their immediate families, to allow full concentration on their tasks" (Virginia Vanguard 1995, 22). This body would identify issues of national importance, frame issues for the National Policy Referendum, and present candidates for high office. It would also oversee the "Civis," or national service board.

Article V described the unicameral Legis, which would be chiefly responsible for incorporating the will of the people. The next lower governmental entities, whether "state, province, or territory" (Virginia Vanguard 1995, 24), would select two representatives to the Legis to serve single three-year terms. The Legis would "formulate national laws that faithfully implement the policies of the Populis, as reflected in the results of National Policy Referenda" (Virginia Vanguard 1995, 25). These laws would be known as the "National Code of Justice." The Legis would have some additional powers in times of national emergency. Each year the Legis would select a chief legislator.

Article VI outlined the duties of the Executis, who would have the duty "to faithfully and efficiently implement, administer, and enforce the laws as codified by the Legis" (Virginia Vanguard 1995, 27). It would consist of a chief executive, a deputy executive, and administrators of civilian and military programs. Much like the current U.S. president, the chief executive would sign treaties, appoint ambassadors, and serve as commander in chief of the armed forces. The chief and deputy would serve for a single five-year term, with the chief legislator designated as following next in succession.

Article VII outlined the Judicis, which would "rule on the correctness of conflicting interpretations of the law, develop consistent guidelines for punishment and awards, and render timely judgments" (Virginia Vanguard 1995, 29). The Populis, however, would be empowered to overrule the Judicis. The Populis would elect a high court consisting of seven judges serving seven-year single terms. The chief justice would serve for a single nonrenewable term.

Article VIII outlined the duties of the Civis—civil servants. All civil servants would be paid on a consistent scale that limited the chief executive to no more than 20 times the salary of the lowest full-time employee of the national government. All new members of the Populis would serve in the Civis for at least four years, with "Boards of Inquiry" established to hear charges against members accused of failure to fulfill their duties.

Article IX outlined the processes for making, amending, and repealing laws. The Caucis would present new laws for consideration after each meeting, initiating a two-month referendum during which each member of the Populis was expected to vote. If the law passed with a majority vote, the Legis would have 120 days to implement it. All laws and policies would be required to adhere to 10 principles stipulating that they "perpetually strive for Justice, by ensuring equal protection under the law and equal application of the law"; "be applied universally"; be national in scope; not address "infrequent events"; not be ex post facto (retroactive); not include unrelated clauses; have benefits that outweigh costs; only regulate personal behavior "where significant harm or risk to self or a fellow Citizen is inevitable"; and expire within 25 years. The Legis also would review existing laws and assure that "the nation's Code of Justice will be subjected to a general revalidation at least once per century" (Virginia Vanguard 1995, 36–7).

Article X provided for the election of national representatives. The Caucis was charged with screening all such candidates and presenting from two to five candidates to the Populis for each position. Nominees would be required to receive at least 3 percent more of the vote than the next most popular candidate before they could take office. Otherwise, the Caucis would make the choice.

Article XI covered the issue of governmental financing. All revenues would be raised by a personal income tax that would exclude any "deduction, allowance, or exemption." The government would be forbidden from "incurring any long-term indebtedness or credits." Likewise, it "may neither borrow money from nor lend money to another government, organization, financial institution, or person without the consent of the Populis" (Virginia Vanguard 1995, 40–1). The Executis, with Legis approval, would determine the amount of money in circulation, but it would not be permitted to artificially manipulate its value without the consent of the Populis.

Article XII described other governmental entities. The national government was to be carefully circumscribed: "It shall provide no service that can reasonably and more efficiently be made available through a non-governmental entity or a lower government entity." The Populis might create "the permanent or temporary formation of such states, regions, provinces, territories, etc., as may be necessary." The structure of subgovernments would complement those of the national government and could be dissolved. All polices of subgovernments would have to conform to those of the national government. Although the nation was encouraged to join "benevolent international organizations," the document specified that "any surrender of national prerogatives to such an organization must be explicitly approved by the Populis" (Virginia Vanguard 1995, 42–3).

Designed both to enshrine popular sovereignty and to end governmental paternalism, the constitution specified that "[i]n the POPULIS, Citizens will conditionally relinquish to government only those powers they deem absolutely necessary and retain the right to reclaim even those" (Virginia Vanguard 1995, 56). This may be the reason that the document listed very few rights.

Edwin Lee Wade Proposes 10 Amendments to Strengthen the Presidency

Edwin Lee Wade (1932–) published *Constitution 2000: A Federalist Proposal for the Next Century* in 1995. The flyleaf of his book described him as "a businessman, lawyer, writer, lecturer, and former public official" with a law degree from Georgetown University who worked as a foreign service officer. Wade proposed 10 amendments, most of which would strengthen the national government and the presidency. He wrote, however, that none of them would become operative unless ratified by conventions in three-fourths of the states by December 31, 2000.

Wade's first amendment called for cutting the size of the House of Representatives to 225 members, apportioned according to population. Wade further proposed cutting the number of House committees to 12 and limiting the number of subcommittees on any committee to five. He would further restrict the total number of House employees to no more than 20 times its membership, and curtail expenditures for "partisan or religious" activities (Wade 1995, 292).

Wade's next provision also proposed cutting the number of senators in half, limiting the U.S. Senate's total number of committees to eight, and capping the number of its employees at 2,500. A provision subjecting Senate debate to "reasonable limitations" was probably designed to limit filibusters.

Wade's third proposal altered congressional terms. Members of both houses would serve four-year terms, with members of the House being selected in presidential election years and members of the Senate in off years.

Wade directed his next three proposals to the executive branch, which he believed had been severely weakened over time. Wade proposed allowing presidential and vice presidential tickets to be placed on the ballot if they presented petitions "equal to or greater than two percent of the total popular vote cast in the immediately preceding [presidential] election" (Wade 1995, 294). These officers would be selected directly by "either a plurality or a majority of the national popular vote" (Wade 1995, 295). The president would select a cabinet officer to serve as a personal chief of staff, thus helping to assure access of cabinet officers to the president. Wade would have further limited the presidential staff to no more than twice the size of Congress. A separate amendment would repeal the two-term limit in the Twenty-Second Amendment. Although Wade wanted to strengthen the presidency, he did not favor giving the office the line-item veto.

In examining the judicial branch, Wade expressed particular concern about pretrial discovery procedures, which he believed were more frequently used to embarrass litigants than to get to the truth. He thus provided in his next amendment that no persons in civil cases be compelled to give testimony "except before or under the supervision of a judge or other officer or officers of the United States as provided by law" (Wade 1995, 196–7). Wade proposed establishing and maintaining "a system of pretrial court-annexed mandatory arbitration" to most civil cases (Wade 1995, 297). Wade further favored limiting the employment of retired judges to employers and interests that had not benefited from their rulings during their time on the bench.

Wade believed that the Federal Reserve System was exercising powers that properly belonged to Congress. He accordingly called for an amendment stipulating that:

Congress shall make no law which delegates any power it possesses pursuant to Article I, Section 8 for the purpose of regulating banks and the banking system or credit and money in its several forms to any department or agency of the government of the United States unless such delegation is based on a clear statement of legislative policy and contains a system of precise, objective standards for application to specific cases, and in no case shall such delegation be made to any private persons, firms, partnerships, corporations, or to any other private enterprises or privately owned organizations. (Wade 1995, 299)

Wade's last proposed amendment would allow Congress to limit expenditures for elections and forbid "federal general revenue of any nature of description" from being "used to finance or otherwise assist any political campaign for any elective office anywhere in the United States of America" (Wade 1995, 300).

Wade also favored a number of changes in constitutional interpretation. He argued, for example, that the Second Amendment was designed to maintain state militias rather than to guarantee a personal right to own guns. Although he opposed Supreme Court decisions on abortion, he also opposed a human life amendment since "neither the decision nor the Amendment belong in the Constitution. Our Constitution again is about the way our federal government is *constituted*. It is not about social policy" (Wade 1995, 259). In a similar vein, Wade asserted that it was up to Congress, rather than an amendment, to attempt to solve the issue of unbalanced budgets.

An appendix included a "Proposed Uniform Application from the Several States to Congress Requesting and Requiring That a Constitutional Convention Be Called" (Wade 1995, 287). Scheduled to meet in Philadelphia no later than January 6, 1999, the convention was to consist of "no more than two hundred twenty-five delegates, to be apportioned among the several states in proportion to the total number of Representatives and Senators possessed by each state" (Wade 1995, 287). Wade wanted to limit the convention to issues raised in his book, with the proposals to be ratified by conventions within the states. He would forbid current officeholders from service and mandate that the convention establish a nine-member Committee on Consolidation and Restatement, which would "prepare a Consolidation and Restatement of the Constitution as then in effect" (Wade 1995, 290).

A. R. Adams Proposes to Guarantee Social and Economic Rights

A. R. Adams, whom the author has otherwise been unable to identify, authored *The Fourth Constitution* in 1996 as a successor to the Declaration of Independence, the Articles of Confederation, and the current Constitution. The back cover of this book proclaimed Adams's desire to create "an egalitarian, merit-based democracy that adds economic and social rights to the political rights of all citizens."

Adams called for establishing a unicameral Congress of 600 representatives who would be limited to three three-year terms and to $3,000 in campaign expenses. The people would select the chief executive from among seven candidates nominated by Congress. Twenty-one justices, serving 10-year terms, would head the Supreme Court.

Consistent with his desire for social and economic rights, Adams sought to guarantee full employment, "egalitarian, managed health care," "universal higher education," and national military training and public service duty for all (Adams 1996, ix). He further hoped to provide a balanced federal budget, eliminate the debt, and punish environmental polluters. Adams favored replacing states with 600 congressional districts, each containing 100 wards further subdivided into 10 precincts.

Adams believed that the current constitution had created "a plutocracy," or government by and for the wealthy (Adams 1996, 2). He took 83 pages to describe the new legislative branch he proposed. His detailed blueprint included an order of chapel services for Congress that included singing "My Country 'Tis of Thee" and reciting the Gettysburg Address, the Three Parts of the Tenets of American Citizenship, and the Desiderata.

Adams favored making lobbying a felony and making omnibus bills illegal. He wanted to institute a progressive income tax that took up to 70 percent of upper incomes and further supplement this revenue with a 99 percent inheritance tax and with sumptuary taxes, which would exempt "vegetarian diet controlled cafeterias" (Adams 1996, 17). Property owners would pay a tax on all space above 970 square feet. Wade would further limit upper incomes to 25 times that of the lowest.

Article I of Adams's proposed constitution outlined a variety of compulsory measures to improve the environment, including mandatory organic farming. It would also provide for balancing trade with foreign nations. Individuals convicted of sexual crimes would be neutered, and tobacco and alcohol would be heavily regulated.

Health care would include the right to assisted suicide. The government would limit health services for individuals who were obese or practiced unhealthy lifestyles. A "Department of Rehabilitation" would closely supervise and regulate unwed mothers. Couples would be limited to two children and could not divorce as long as they had children under the age of 18. Adams would further mandate abortions and birth control for unwed mothers and sterilize individuals who might pass on hereditary diseases.

Adams called for an expansion of government in other areas as well. Under his constitutional framework, the government would maintain youth rehabilitation centers and issue its own pension to replace all existing private pensions. The government would mandate English as the official language and increase supervision of education to include provision for school uniforms and a daily chapel call. Although he affirmed freedom of speech, Adams called for increased governmental controls over electronic media, including advertising.

Article II outlined the responsibilities of the president and vice president. His provision for their election was similar to that which prevailed prior to the adoption of the Twelfth Amendment, with the top vote getter becoming the president and the runner-up assuming the vice presidency.

Article III provided that members of the Supreme Court would select their chief justice. Local courts would take cases against

> Scolds (those troublesome and angry persons who, by brawling and wrangling among his or her neighbors increased discords) and against Common Nuisances (those disturbers of the peace who interrupt the peace, quiet, and good order of the neighborhood by unnecessary and distracting noises, such as keeping dogs that bark by day and night, playing radios and sound systems at a volume that can be heard outside the house or vehicle, and any conduct which tends to annoy all good citizens). (Adams 1996, 93–4)

Article III also contained provisions currently found in the Fourth, Fifth, Sixth, Seventh, and Eighth Amendments, sometimes modified by accompanying case law.

Article IV abolished state lines and provided for national referendums. It also modified the First Amendment to provide for limiting freedoms that "in any manner or degree infringe upon the rights of others to their privacy, to their tranquility, to their peace and quiet of mind and body or to the public peace and quiet" (Adams 1996, 106). Article V provided for "The Tenets of American Citizenship." These included "Duties or Legal Obligations," "Moral Obligations," and "Values or Personal Obligations."

Article VI provided for congressional districts to play the role that states currently do in ratifying amendments. Article VII dealt with miscellaneous matters, while Article VIII provided for ratification of the document "[i]n a concurrent referendum with the first election of Representatives to the first congress" (Adams 1996, 111).

Kenneth Dolbeare and Janette Hubbell Take Aim at the Two-Party System and Propose "Economic Nationalism"

Kenneth Dolbeare (1930–) and Janette Hubbell (1948–) advanced their proposals for constitutional change in a novel entitled *USA 2012: After the Middle-Class Revolution* (1996). They described themselves as "an eastern iconoclast who teaches politics at a small college and a southwestern populist who left elementary school teaching to launch a successful small business" (Dolbeare and Hubbell, 1996, ix). In their book, a college student reviews with his parents the developments that led to a successful middle-class revolution based on the concept of "economic nationalism" (Dolbeare and Hubbell 1996, xiii).

The authors described a world in which economic deterioration and middle-class outrage prompted the creation of a new Declaration of Independence on July 4, 2000. The novel targeted the two-party system, large corporations and banks, the media, special interests, and the bureaucracy. The book also expressed concern over the effects on workers of free trade policies such as the General Agreement on Tariffs and Trade (GATT) and the North American Free Trade Agreement (NAFTA).

After adopting the new Declaration of Independence, the people agreed to four amendments. The first provided for quarterly popular referendums on major issues of public policy, which neither the president nor the Congress could veto (Dolbeare and Hubbell 1996, 118–19). This was designed to convert members of Congress into delegates of the people rather than independent decision makers. The second amendment capped campaign contributions at $100 for any individual or group while mandating that television and radio stations make free time available to candidates. It also limited campaigning to 60 days prior to a primary election or 90 days prior to a general election. The third amendment provided for proportional representation within Congress and the Electoral College. The amendment lifted restrictions on third parties to encourage a multiparty system and sought to enhance voting by lifting registration requirements, extending voting to a two-day weekend, and allowing voters to cast their ballots for "None of the Above (NOTA)." The fourth amendment dealt with the judicial system and attempted to balance individual rights against public concerns. It mandated consideration of "comparative liability and contributory negligence," allowed judges to review jury awards, and attempted to reduce litigation (Dolbeare and Hubbell 1996, 134).

Daniel Lazare Proposes a System of Parliamentary Sovereignty

Freelance journalist Daniel Lazare authored a stinging critique of modern American government in *The Frozen Republic: How the Constitution Is Paralyzing Democracy* (1996). He believed that many American social problems resulted from an antiquated Constitution that stresses checks and balances and separation of powers and produces gridlock rather that accountability. In almost every area that he examined, he found European parliamentary systems to be superior.

Lazare was particularly critical of the difficulty of amending the current Constitution but imagined a scenario whereby California threatened to secede unless equal state representation was ended in the U.S. Senate. He suggested that the House of Representatives could respond by abolishing such equal representation and then getting this action affirmed by a popular referendum.

Lazare did not draw up a proposed constitution, but he said that it would elevate the status of the newly apportioned Congress, "reduce the president to semi-figurehead status," and "effectively rob the judiciary of much of its power." He noted that

> not just the Constitution would be toppled, but so would checks and balances, separation of powers, and the deeply inculcated habit of deferring to the authority of a group of eighteenth-century Country gentlemen. Instead of relying on previous generations' judgment and analysis, the people would have no choice than to rely on their own. (Lazare 1996, 293–5)

Lazare extended his criticism of the U.S. Constitution in another book that he published in 2001.

Thomas H. Naylor and William H. Willimon Advocate "Downsizing the U.S.A" and Permitting Secession

Long after the Civil War, some individuals continue to fear rather than celebrate an extended republic such as the one James Madison defended in Federalist No. 10. One expression of these views can be found in *Downsizing the U.S.A.* (1997), which was authored by Thomas Naylor (1936–2012), an economist and professor at Duke University, and William H. Willimon (1946–), a prominent Methodist theologian and longtime professor of Christian ministry at Duke.

Advocating the principle that "small is beautiful," and viewing the state of Vermont as an ideal, the authors asserted that modern corporations, cities, schools, states, and the United States as a whole had all grown too large. They devised strategies for downsizing each of these institutions and eliminating the federal agencies that they believed had encouraged their growth. They sought to downsize corporations, for example, by abolishing the U.S. Departments of Commerce and Labor; encouraging corporate downsizing; buying locally; and avoiding large chain stores (Naylor and Willimon 1997, 77). They favored downsizing cities by abolishing the U.S. Department of Housing and Urban Development; eliminating most federal subsidies; allowing cities to limit their growth; and permitting cities to secede from states and form their own city states (Naylor and Willimon 1997, 75). Rural America could be revitalized by abolishing the U.S. Department of Agriculture; subsidizing family-owned farms; revoking federal aid for interstate highways; and patronizing local merchants (Naylor and Willimon 1997, 93). Naylor and Willimon called for downsizing education by eliminating the U.S. Department of Education; using educational vouchers; limiting individual schools to 300 students; dividing universities with more than 10,000 students into colleges of 3,000, with residential colleges of about 300 students; reducing federal aid to colleges and universities; and replacing tenure with long-term contracts. The authors argued that religious organizations should "decentralize decision-making power" to "the local congregation," reduce denominational central offices, and cultivate small groups within congregations (Naylor and Willimon 1997, 154).

Naylor and Willimon also called for reducing the size of the welfare state by abolishing Medicare and Medicaid; closing the U.S. Department of Health and Human Services; practicing holistic medicine; and using more resources to teach people "how to live healthy, meaningful lives and how to die happy" (1997, 171). Superpowers could be brought to heel by substituting "constructive engagement, tension reduction, and power sharing for military confrontation"; reducing troop commitments abroad; resigning from the United Nations and the World Bank; and substituting voluntary for compulsory alliances (Naylor and Willimon 1997, 202). States could be empowered and downsized by reducing federal regulations, allowing large states to split, and authorizing large cities to establish themselves as separate states (Naylor and Willimon 1997, 236).

Naylor and Willimon made four arguments on behalf of the right of secession, which they anticipated would occur through conventions. Secession would involve an allocation of existing national wealth and debt. Once states seceded, however, they anticipated a continuing system of "free trade and free travel among states having a single currency and a common economic system. Member states might form a mutual defense alliance"; states would, in turn, "have complete responsibility for and total control of their own taxes, schools, social welfare, health care, law enforcement, highways, airports, housing, and physical environment" (Naylor and Willimon 1997, 278). The authors suggested certain regional and state groupings, including a black nation in the Mississippi Delta. They observed, however, that they had "no grand scheme for downsizing America, for such a plan would be antithetical to what we are trying to accomplish" (Naylor and Willimon 1997, 284).

Naylor headed a movement for a Second Vermont Republic—an independent republic of Vermont—and has further advanced his ideas in a book entitled *Secession: How Vermont and All the Other States Can Save Themselves from the Empire* (2008). Philosophy scholar Donald Livingston and author Bill Kauffman have expressed similar views favoring state secession in their books entitled, respectively, *Rethinking the American Union for the Twenty-First Century* (2012) and *Bye Bye, Miss American Empire* (2010).

Steven G. Calabresi Urges Greater Implementation of Separation of Powers

In 1998, William N. Eskridge, Jr., of Georgetown and Sanford Levinson of the University of Texas at Austin edited a book that originally began as a symposium in *Constitutional Commentary*, entitled *Constitutional Stupidities, Constitutional Tragedies*. In the first part of the book, more than 20 participants were asked to name the "stupidest" provision in the U.S. Constitution, excluding superseded provisions related to slavery.

The provisions that the participants suggested indicated areas for possible reform, most of which have been previously mentioned in this book. Akhil Reed Amar questioned provisions in the Electoral College. Prior to the 2000 presidential election, he innacurately predicted that another minority vote winner would likely lead to change. William N. Eskridge, Jr., questioned the provision giving senators from sparsely populated states the same voting power as senators of high-population states, and Suzanna Sherry focused on state equality in that body. Mark Graber focused on the lack of welfare protections and the ambiguity of the necessary and proper clause; Stephen M. Griffin targeted the difficulty of the amending process; Randall Kennedy questioned the provision requiring the president to be native born; L. H. LaRue and Michael Stokes Paulsen focused on life tenure for judges in separate essays; Sanford Levinson expressed concern over lame-duck presidents; Matthew D. Michael criticized the minimum age requirement for the presidency; Robert F. Nagel focused generally on states' rights; Michael Stokes Paulsen cited constitutional provisions that might allow a vice president to preside over his own impeachment trial; Jeffrey Rosen identified the Constitution's division of power to set voting requirements between the nation and the states; Frederick Schauer focused more generally on what he considered to be constitutional miscalibrations regarding the protection of rights; Louis Michael Seidman criticized the provisions respecting the rights of criminal defendants within the Fourth through Sixth Amendments as contributors to unacceptable rates of incarceration; Laurence H. Tribe thought the Twenty-First Amendment improperly made carrying liquor into a dry state a constitutional offense; and Mark Tushnet, who thought the whole document needed reworking, focused on the difficulty of the procedures for amending the Constitution.

Another contributor, a law professor at Northwestern University named Steven G. Calabresi, praised the U.S. Constitution as "the best constitution human beings have ever devised." Despite such accolades, however, he asserted that "the famous Madisonian system of checks and balances does not go far enough" (Eskridge and Levinson 1998, 22–3).

Calabresi thus offered a variety of mechanisms that he thought were necessary to rein in each of the three branches of the national government. In attempting to tame congressional powers, he proposed a balanced budget amendment, a spending limit, a congressional term limit amendment, and a line-item veto amendment. He further proposed that Congress be prevented from delegating its legislative powers to other areas of government, and that Congress approve all agency rule-making before such rules went into effect. Fearing the further "growth of raw, unchecked judicial power," he favored amendments directing courts to enforce federalism and separation of powers "as vigorously as any other part of the Constitution"; requirement of a three-fourths majority before the Court could invalidate a state law or executive regulation; mandatory confirmation of all Article III judges by a majority of state governors; reduced appropriations for law clerks; limited injunctive powers and facial challenges to laws; alteration of justiciability requirements; and an end to the use of "head-swelling aristocratic forms in federal court, like the wearing of black robes, the title 'Your Honor,' and the designation 'The Honorable'" (Eskridge and Levinson 1998, 26).

Michael Marx Combines Laissez-Faire Economics with Strict Moralism

Michael Marx, a California filmmaker, wrote and marketed a novel entitled *Justus—A Utopia* (1999). The work included a constitution of 40 articles. Marx's proposed constitution combined laissez-faire economics and moralism with proposals to abolish nuclear weaponry.

The novel centers on the life of Michael Justus, a child who appeared on the doorstep of Professor Eric Greenfield wrapped in a priceless Renoir painting. Fearful of a nuclear attack, the professor takes the child, a prodigy, to a remote area of Mexico, where they protect themselves against radioactivity, invite others to join, and figure out how to get static energy from the air to produce power. After a nuclear attack that wipes out 95 percent of the world's population, Justus leads an army to eliminate nuclear weaponry but is lost at sea. He leaves behind a state—also called Justus—and a government designed to last for 1,000 years or more.

The constitution that provides the framework for this nation provides for the adoption of laws through petitions, with amendments requiring 80 percent or more of the popular vote. "Since every citizen can vote for or against (by not signing) every petition of law in the State of Justus, there is no need for legislative or executive branches" (Marx 1999, 184).

Article 2 of the constitution was premised on the idea that "there is no such thing as a good tax" (Marx 1999, 187). By contrast, property and ownership are sacrosanct—"In Justus, the property owner is king" (Marx 1999, 189). Individuals and not corporations will own property. Article 6 observed that "contracts of all types . . . shall be enforced to the letter" (Marx 1999, 194). Under Justus's free market framework, minimum or maximum wage laws do not exist, and gold and silver constitute the only currency. Each citizen retains "the right to be paid in gold and/or silver coin at the end of each work day for that day's labor" (Marx 1999, 195). English is the official language, nuclear weapons are prohibited, and citizenship is limited to individuals 18 or older who own at least 20 ounces of gold, are disease free, and can pass a test on the new constitution.

Although Marx's novel stated that the gods had abandoned the earth, Justus both prohibited religious establishments and permitted free exercise of religious belief. Churches and private individuals provided all education, and individuals who did not set aside money for their own retirement or medical care risked destitution.

Marx's constitution provided for free speech, but it included punishments for lying, filthy language, and pornography. It prohibited children under the age of 18 from all sexual activity, including that which is "self-induced" (Marx 1999, 215). Individuals were expected to protect themselves by owning firearms. Those caught using drugs would be exiled to "a neutered sexual existence on Violent Criminal Island" (Marx 1999, 217).

Individuals could walk off their jobs, but unions and collective bargaining would be prohibited. Citizen-elected judges would oversee search warrants and would be paid through fines. There would be one elected police officer for every 200 citizens. All criminals would be punished in the same manner that they treated their victims (Marx 1999, 237).

Since Justus applied "universal moral law," ignorance would be no excuse for violations (Marx 1999, 245). Those who burned the flag would be exiled. Human rights would be placed above animal rights, and medical doctors would take the original Hippocratic Oath. All children would be raised in two-parent heterosexual homes, and if parents divorced, their children would be put up for adoption. Unwed mothers could not keep their children unless the mothers got married before childbirth. Abortion would be considered as murder and punished by death. Homosexuals would be prohibited from visiting or attaining citizenship. Those committing rape or having sex with children would be castrated.

Rodney Scott Proposes a More Complex Constitution with a Parliamentary System

Rodney D. Scott (1949–) of Fort Wayne, Indiana, offered a discursive proposal for a new constitution in a book entitled *The Great Debate: The Need for Constitutional Reform* (1999). A social worker and adjunct professor of political science at the University of St. Francis in Fort Wayne, Scott discussed the U.S. Constitution for 276 pages before proposing a new constitution consisting of a preamble and 73 articles. He concluded the work with another 200 pages of commentary and appendices. Scott's discussion of the current Constitution focused on sections that are "not being followed," sections that "are no longer needed," and those that "are confusing or contradictory." His plan often departed from existing constitutional language. Thus, one of the goals of the preamble was to "verify axioms of law."

Article 1 of Scott's constitution specified that his proposal "be considered a continuation of the rights, and responsibilities of the current Constitution" (Scott 1999, 77). Article 2 announced an intention to create a parliamentary system, and Article 3 provided for record keeping. Articles 4 through 7 dealt with Congress. Scott proposed creating at least one representative for every 77,000 citizens, or more than 3,000 people. Members would operate from home districts and do most of their work through teleconferencing, meeting together only two weeks a year. Each state would continue to elect two senators, with the Senate acting much like the British House of Lords. It would vote on acts of the House, but not amend House legislation or create legislation of its own. Scott's version of the Senate would retain its current power to ratify appointments and treaties.

Article 8 outlined the responsibility of the prime minister, chosen by the House to serve as the head of government. Although Scott said that the nation would not have a head of state, he would invest the prime minister with power as commander in chief and other powers that the president currently exercises. Scott also provided that the president would engage Congress in question and answer periods. Articles 10 and 11 addressed the cabinet, which would be appointed by the prime minister and confirmed by the Senate.

Articles 12 through 21 addressed governmental duties and powers. Article 12 thus declared the supremacy of federal law, and Article 13 vested Congress with the power to declare war. Article 14 provided for balanced budgets, except in time of declared war, and Article 15 vested the power of adjusting congressional districts to the General Accounting Office. Article 16 made English the official language of the federal government. Article 17 granted Congress the power to tax, and Article 18 compelled the government to release information upon request. Article 19 limited the duration of treaties to 99 years. Article 20 provided for a census every 10 years, and Article 21 granted Congress power over commerce, bankruptcy laws, copyrights and patents, and weights and measures.

Articles 22 through 24 dealt with the political process. Article 22 recognized political parties and gave them the responsibility of formulating platforms. Article 23 guaranteed free elections, and Article 24 sanctioned universal suffrage.

Articles 35 through 41 addressed the judicial system and established various rights, many of which expanded on protections currently found within the First Amendment. Scott offered specific protections for a "right to privacy," "[f]reedom of movement," and provisions against discrimination based on "race, creed, color, gender, age, national origin, economic status, physical capacity, handicaps, or sexual orientation." The "inherent rights" that he listed included "liberty, life, acquiring possessions, being productive, and seeking happiness and security" (Scott 1999, 294–5).

Articles 41 through 47 listed various judicial entitlements, including elaborations of various provisions in the Bill of Rights related to the rights of defendants. Article 44 prohibited torture and Article 47 provided for victims' rights.

Article 48 prohibited titles of nobility; Article 49 provided for the right to an education, Article 50 for academic freedom, and Article 51 for the Federal Reserve System. Articles 52 through 55 dealt with the military. Article 53 allowed for conscription after a declaration of war, and Article 54 constitutionalized the system of military justice. Articles 56 through 62 dealt with state directives. One provision allowed states to establish "a Rite of Passage" into adulthood.

Articles 63 through 65 dealt with the family. The first article provided that "it is the natural right of parents to care for, support, and direct the upbringing of their children," but specified that "the state has an equal responsibility to supervise this exercise" (Scott 1999, 302). Article 69 dealt with the relation between the national government and the states and territories.

The last four articles dealt with modification and termination of the Constitution. Amendments could be proposed by a two-thirds vote of the Senate and a majority of the House and ratified by two-thirds of the states within seven years. A vote by three-fourths of the states also could mandate a constitutional convention or conference. The new constitution would go into effect when ratified by two-thirds of the states and would become "null and void" after 200 years (Scott 1999, 305). Scott favored use of the constitutional convention system and ended on the hope that "great nations do great things" (Scott 1999, 521).

Paul Christopher Manuel and Anne Marie Cammisa
Consider a Parliamentary System

In 1999, Paul Christopher Manuel and Anne Marie Cammisa, a married couple who taught government at St. Anselm College in New Hampshire and Suffolk University in Boston, Massachusetts, respectively, published *Checks & Balances? How a Parliamentary System Could Change American Politics*. (As of 2013, Manuel was director of the Institute of Leadership at Mount St. Mary's University in Maryland and Cammisa was a member of the Georgetown University faculty in Washington, D.C.) The scholars traced the failure of the Republicans' Contract with America, budget impasses, and other political stalemates to the American system of checks and balances. Although they were designed to serve as checks on tyranny, the authors believed that these measures also stymied democratically generated reform proposals.

Manuel and Cammisa devoted much of their book to explaining and comparing the U.S. system of checks and balances with the system of fused powers in Great Britain and other parliamentary democracies. In their first chapter, they attempted to counter six misperceptions about government. They dealt successively with the idea that "The American Constitution defines modern democracy"; that democracies require a federal system; that such democracies require a bicameral legislature; that the head of government and head of state must be combined; that each election and each district must have one winner; and that the U.S. system would work anywhere. Citing political scientist Robert Dahl, who had noted that the United States had come close to adopting a parliamentary system, Manuel and Cammisa considered how a parliamentary system might have worked during various crisis points in American history. Although the authors explicitly stated that their book "does not argue that the American government should adopt a British-style parliamentary system" (Manuel and Cammisa 1999, 37), most of the reforms that they proposed for consideration in their fifth and final chapter were based on mechanisms borrowed from such a system.

That concluding chapter identified three central problems with the American system: "divided government," which they associated with unaccountability; "gridlock," which they largely associated with the system of checks and balances; and the "lack of any mechanism for quickly replacing a failed or deadlocked government" (Manuel and Camissa 1999, 145). The authors proposed three corresponding solutions. The first called for merging executive and legislative powers and increasing communications between them. They suggested repealing Article I, Section 6, Paragraph 2 of the Constitution, so that cabinet officials could also serve in Congress. A second solution called for "restoring governmental accountability" by mandating "team-ticket reform," which would prevent individuals from splitting their tickets when voting. They also proposed "the d'Hondt system of proportional representation for national elections," which would allocate votes to parties based on "the highest average of votes cast per party." They further favored lengthening the terms for members of Congress and considering "a line-item presidential veto, a change in the Senate's filibuster and hold rules, the restoration of legislative veto, and a redefinition of governmental 'powers.'" Manuel and Cammisa's third solution called for abandoning fixed terms. This proposal authorized "the president to dissolve Congress and call for new elections if, in his view, Congress had lost the support of the people." It also subjected the president to a Congressional vote of no confidence "if, at any time, the legislature seriously doubted the continuing ability of the president to lead." The authors framed these suggestions as "the start of a dialogue" and expressed hope that "these reforms could, perchance, permit governmental leaders to quickly adopt new laws and adapt the government to the changing times" (Manuel and Camissa 1999, 148–54).

Frederick Ellis and Carl Frederick Endorse Voting Reforms and Employee-Owned Enterprises

Frederick Ellis and Carl Frederick introduced their ideas for constitutional change in an adventure novel called *The Oakland Statement* (2000). Ellis had left a brokerage firm to work for the presidential campaigns of Eugene McCarthy in 1968 and George McGovern in 1972, and Carl Frederick was a retired businessman and novelist. After meeting in the mid 1990s in Costa Rica, where they had both retired, they collaborated on *The Oakland Statement*.

The volume's inside back cover described the novel as presenting "a progressive vision for *real solutions* by creating two new constitutional amendments to the Bill of Rights, resulting in a *popular political economy* for all the people." The authors also noted that "our citizens are voting less and less, while our economic wealth is being concentrated rapidly into the hands of fewer and fewer people" (Ellis and Frederick 2000, 3). They cited two primary goals for their amendments. The first would "guarantee the absolute right of the people to enjoy the most equitable methods of a representative electoral system," including "proportional representation, preference voting, cumulative voting, and referendums at every level of government." The second was to "guarantee the absolute right of the people to participate in the creation of the national wealth . . . primarily through the establishment of majority employee owned enterprises and progressive labor organizing" (Ellis and Frederick 2000, 4).

The book begins by describing a leaderless revolution in which patriotic terrorists blow up power stations throughout the country. Their actions spark a limited constitutional convention that proposes two very detailed amendments to the Bill of Rights that are subsequently ratified by state conventions, which the states then ratify in conventions. The authors further anticipated that the nation would add Puerto Rico, the Virgin Islands, and the District of Columbia as states, and make overtures to Caribbean and Central American nations, including Haiti and Cuba, to join.

The first provision, presented as a Twenty-Eighth Amendment, proposed major reforms to the American electoral system. The provision stated that "if the various branches of government failed to change the electoral process to what citizens believed to be 'most equitable,' then suits could be filed in various courts, challenging the process and at the same time demanding specific remedies" (Ellis and Frederick 2000, 93–4). The amendment had eight sections in all. The first provided for mandatory voting for all, except for those with conscientious objections to the practice. Section 2 provided that elections "shall be conducted using the most equitable methods as determined by each level of state, district, territory, and local governments utilizing the process of referendums" (Ellis and Frederick 2000, 224). Section 3 provided for the election of the president through preference voting and abolition of the Electoral College. Section 4 further provided for an open referendum process. Section 5 increased the number of U.S. representatives by assuring that no district had more than 250,000 individuals, and Section 6 guaranteed that each state had at least three House members. Section 7 provided for the public financing of elections, except for individual contributions of up to $250 each. Section 8 allowed local, state, and federal governments to limit the length of campaigns, but gave citizens the right to challenge those limitations in court.

The Twenty-Ninth Amendment featured several sections advocating economic arrangements that General Marshall Tito employed in Yugoslavia after World War II. Section 1 guaranteed all citizens age 18 or older the right "to participate in the creation of the national wealth." Section 2 specified that they would do so "by the majority-employee ownership of conditional and certified enterprises," the categories being determined by the number of employees. Section 3 provided for governmental charters and licenses for all "private, conditional, and certified enterprises as businesses for profit." Section 4 guaranteed the right to organize "democratic labor unions, supervisor and management employee organizations," and Section 5 provided that the federal government "shall be the employer of last resort for able-bodied and mentally capable citizens under retirement age." Section 6 proceeded to guarantee "the right to free education to the highest levels available, based on scholastic qualification." Section 7 further provided all citizens with "the right to free complete medical and mental health insurance coverage" (Ellis and Frederick 2000, 235–6).

David B. Jeffs Proposes an Amendment
for Direct Representative Democracy

David B. Jeffs outlined his views on direct democracy and direct education in his book *America's Crisis: The Direct Democracy and Direct Education Solution* (2000). This work was a follow-up to an earlier pamphlet "The Truth: the 28th Amendment," published under the name "John Citizen," in which he advocated installing interactive television features in voters' homes (Jeffs 2000, 36–7). Jeffs identified himself as the founder of the Direct Democracy Center, which maintains a Web site at www.realdemocracy.com.

All 12 sections of Jeffs's proposed amendment can be found on the Direct Democracy Center Web site. Although he preferred a more simple amendment that would say "[t]he government of the United States, and the several states, shall be a nonpartisan direct democracy through established voting networks connected to voters' homes," he observed that "if left to the Congress, the Presidency, and the Supreme Court, they would soon dilute it out of existence in the same ways they have perverted the U.S. Constitution."

Jeff labeled his amendment the "Nonpartisan Direct Representative Democracy Government Electorate Voting Networks and Education Networks." Section 1 of the amendment would provide for "nonpartisan direct representative democracy government" based on the equality of citizenship. This would require "truth and accountability to the electorate from all elected representatives and all government employees."

Section 2 would provide that within four years of representation, a system of "direct representative democracy" would be established using "electorate voting networks of interactive electronic devices between elected representatives of all levels of government and the homes of the electorate." The section further provided that "all elected representatives shall be nonpartisan," and it provided for annual confirmation or rejection "by majority vote of the electorate." Section 3 sought further to enhance democracy by allowing the electorate "to instruct, direct and control all levels of government through their elected representatives by majority vote," with "all elections, recall elections, initiatives and referendums . . . conducted by means of the electorate voting network."

Section 4 further extended direct democracy to members of all U.S. courts, cabinet posts, and agency heads at both state and national levels. Section 5 repealed the current Electoral College and replaced it with annual direct confirmation or rejection of the president and vice president. Section 6 repealed the national income tax, which Jeffs identified in *America's Crisis* as "the gravest mistake the American people every made" (Jeffs 2000, x).

Section 7 provided a two-thirds vote of the majority of the electorate for "all matters of public policy and taxation." It would also vest the electorate with the power to recall judges and amend both state and national constitutions by a two-thirds majority.

Section 8 called for providing all citizens with "direct education by interactive electronic devices" in their homes. Section 9 further provided that this education, initially conducted by the government, would subsequently be contracted out to private institutions. It also provided for educational vouchers and provided that "no student shall be excluded for lack of funds" from education through the first four years of college. Section 10 vested the federal Department of Education with setting minimum national standards, which states could raise if they chose. Jeffs would entrust the Federal Communications Commission with "the public communication function of direct education."

Section 11 provided for the amendment to supersede existing constitutional provisions. Section 12 further specified that within four years of establishing voting networks, the government must give the people of opportunity of either confirming or repealing "each law, or group of laws, by majority vote" (Jeffs 2000, 304–7).

Jeffs's Web site contains links to the Web site "Philadelphia II." This organization favors the National Initiate for Democracy, a proposal advanced by former Alaskan senator Mike Gravel in which voters would be empowered to adopt constitutional amendments and accompanying legislation through initiative and referendum mechanisms (Vile 2010, II: 332–3).

Richard Labunski Advocates a Second Constitutional Convention and 10 Proposed Amendments

Richard Labunski (1952–), a journalism professor at the University of Kentucky, published *The Second Constitutional Convention* in 2000. He divided the book into four parts. The first discussed the current Constitution and perceived abuses of its provisions, particularly in the areas of campaign financing, congressional resistance to term limits, and the limits to judicially initiated reforms, which he thought necessitated a second constitutional convention. The second section of the book discussed how meetings could be organized for a national "preconvention" to pressure states to call a new convention. The third section described a set of 10 amendments that he thought a constitutional convention should consider, and the fourth attempted to show how his proposals square with the eight guidelines for amendments previously advanced by the Citizens for the Constitution (1999).

In sketching out his plan to convince states to call for a constitutional convention, Labunski drew in part from the unsuccessful Peace Convention that preceded the Civil War, as well as from the National Issues Convention held in 1996 in Austin, Texas. He envisioned meetings beginning at the county or congressional district level that would 1) stimulate interest in reform and 2) elect representatives to state conventions (each with 52 or fewer delegates), which would take place roughly at the same time. Each convention would then select two delegates to a national preconvention in the nation's capital that would specify "the *problems* that will be addressed by constitutional amendments"; identify "the specific *sections* of the Constitution that will be considered for revisions"; and suggest "in *general terms* language that may be appropriate for the new amendments" (Labunski 2000, 220–1). After such a meeting, Labunski believed that individuals could use the Internet to generate further pressure on the states to call a convention.

Labunski labeled his 10 proposed amendments from "A" to "J." He phrased each proposal as a legislative petition, each with a built-in seven-year ratification requirement and a provision for ratification by state conventions.

Amendment A, which dealt with campaign finance reform, proposed to overturn parts of the U.S. Supreme Court decision in *Buckley v. Valeo*, 424 U.S. 1 (1976), so as to permit greater regulation of both campaign contributions and expenditures. It would require candidates to raise at least half their funds from within their districts. Limits would apply both to the candidates' expenditures of their own money and to soft money contributions, and the amendment would require comprehensive disclosure of expenditures.

Amendment B was an expanded version of the Equal Rights Amendment. Addressing an issue that initially divided supporters of the amendment, Labunski specifically provided that "this amendment shall not be construed to invalidate legislation, administrative regulations, or other acts of Congress or the states that have benign effects on the economic or political status of women." With a view to the precedent in *United States v. Morrison*, 529 U.S. 598 (2000), he also specified that the commerce clause should not be interpreted in ways that would inhibit congressional authority to regulate "gender-motivated violence" (Labunski 2000, 314, 316).

Amendment C advanced the cause of victims' rights. These included

> the right to be present in all public proceedings to determine release from custody, acceptance of a plea agreement, or a sentence; the right to be informed of and to offer written or oral testimony at parole hearings; the right to reasonable notice of release or escape from custody of the defendant; and the right to compensation for crimes in amounts fixed by federal and state law. (Labunski 2000, 338)

It also extended a "civil right of action" against criminals and waived state immunity (thus presumably modifying existing interpretations of the Eleventh Amendment) in cases where the conduct of public officials resulted "in gratuitous harm to the crime victim, and where the conduct of such officials is reckless or malicious" (Labunski 2000, 338).

Labunski grouped Amendments D through F together. The first would limit members of the House to four two-year terms and senators to two six-year terms, with similar overall limits in effect if the terms of senators were reduced to four years, as Amendment E proposed. Amendment F would allow the Senate to ratify treaties by majority vote.

Amendment G proposed to replace the Electoral College with a system of direct election in which voters would designate their top three choices for president. If, when adding second- and third-choice votes, no candidate got 40 percent or more of the electoral vote, then an assembly of both houses of Congress would resolve the issue. Labunski designed Amendment H to protect the judiciary. It provided that Congress "shall not have the power to alter, modify, restrict, or enhance the appellate jurisdiction of the federal courts" (Labunski 2000, 377).

Amendment I proposed three methods for adopting amendments. The first would allow for 60 percent majorities in Congress or the states. The second would require Congress to call conventions within 90 days of receiving petitions from 50 percent or more of the state legislatures. The third would require such a convention after Congress received petitions from 50 percent or more secretaries of state affirming that they had received petitions from 10 percent or more of the voters in the last general election. The people would elect delegates, and states would be unable to rescind ratifications. Labunski's final proposal called for repealing the Second Amendment.

Patrick J. McGrath Advocates Responsible Parliamentary Government

Patrick J. McGrath (1960–) published *The Way to Responsible Government* in 2000 to advocate for major changes to the U.S. Constitution. According to the back cover of his book, McGrath works in public relations for a small nonprofit company in New York City. In explaining why he proposed a new constitution, McGrath identified the current American constitutional structure as "the worst possible imaginable," and pointed to a "better way" based on the idea that "responsibility is singular. Division of responsibility results in no responsibility." Here, and in the introductory chapters that followed, McGrath quoted extensively from Woodrow Wilson's *Congressional Government* to support his positions. McGrath's book included an appendix containing his proposed U.S. Constitution as well as another appendix laying out a model state constitution.

McGrath's preamble is almost identical to that of the existing Constitution. Article I of the new constitution outlined its "structure and functions," focusing on Congress, defined as consisting of "the President of the United States, the College of States' Legates, and the House of Representatives." It began with a quotation from the Declaration of Independence affirming a right "to institute new government . . . as to them shall seem more likely to effect their safety and happiness" (McGrath 2000, 38).

Article I designated the president as the head of state; every seventh year, lawmakers known as legates would select from two to five presidential candidates, and the people would choose among them in a popular election. Candidates were to be forbidden from being members of a political party, from ever having been a party committee member, from being lobbyists, from having contributed more than $500 to any candidate, or from holding political office. Candidates would be limited to spending $500,000 each on their campaigns. The president would be the commander in chief, "but will act in this capacity only on the advice of the appropriate Minister of State." The president was vested with power to "ratify Treaties, upon the advice of the appropriate Ministers of State," and to make appointments. The president may also dissolve the House on the advice of the prime minister. The president was also designated as "Grand Commander of the Order of Honor," as "Grand Commander of the Order of Freedom," and as "Grand Commander of any order of Honor" that Congress might establish (McGrath 2000, 40–2).

The "College of Legates" was to be organized like the current senate, with members serving five-year terms unless previously dissolved. Such legates would be nominated by state legislatures, which would also pay them. Members would be forbidden from being members of parties. Candidates could spend no more than $20,000 each. The college would nominate presidential candidates, appoint members of "Boundary Commissions" to draw up nonpartisan House districts, and make a number of appointments. It could pass resolutions, but they would not have the force of law.

The House of Representatives would serve much like the House of Commons in England, with 625 to 650 members. Its members would serve for four-year terms unless dissolved earlier. McGrath provided that "it shall not be lawful for the House to adopt or pass any Vote, Resolution, Address, or Bill for Appropriation of any Part of the Public Revenue, or of any Tax or Impost, to any purpose that has not been recommended by Message of the President in the Session" (McGrath 2000, 49). The House would have the powers that Article I, Section 8 currently vests in Congress as a whole.

The executive power of Congress was to be vested in an administration that would consist of "the Prime Minister and such other Ministers of State as the President, on the advice of the Prime Minister, shall appoint" (McGrath 2000, 53). The head of the administration would be designated as the prime minister. The "Leader of the Loyal Opposition" would have power to propose a vote of no confidence in the administration, which would trigger another election.

Article II of the proposed constitution dealt with "restrictions upon government," and celebrated "the self-evident truth that all human beings are endowed by their Creator with certain inalienable rights" (McGrath 2000, 54). It compiled and listed restrictions on governments currently found within Article I, Section 9 and 10, and the Bill of Rights.

Article III outlined the judicial branch, which would be structured much as it was in the existing constitution. The courts would have the power to examine a law before the president signs it to determine whether it is constitutional, but it must speak with one voice, and may publish no dissents.

Article IV provided that the president could propose amendments on the advice of his administration, on recommendations by the College of Legates, or on the application of two-thirds of the state legislatures. Amendments would require ratification by a majority of voters and "majorities of the votes cast in more than one-half of the states" (McGrath 2000, 63).

Article V provided for miscellaneous matters, most reaffirming existing obligations of the states to one another. The article further provided that the document would come into force "on the second January 2 or July 1 following approval of this Constitution by the people, whichever is the later of the two" (McGrath 2000, 65). It also provided for transitory laws to assist in the transition from one constitution to the other.

Summary and Analysis

Never within the space of less than a decade had so many different individuals from so many different backgrounds offered such diverse proposals for rewriting the U.S. Constitution. Proposals included plans to bring the system closer to parliamentary democracy, to include more social and economic rights, to seek a more libertarian government, and to downsize the nation. Others took diametrically opposed positions. In 1987, for example, novelist Gerald Lund published a book—*The Freedom Factor*—asserting that parliamentary democracy might produce tyranny rather than freedom and prosperity.

References

Adams, A. R. 1996. *The Fourth Constitution of the United States of America*. Salt Lake City, UT: A. R. Adams Publishing.

Antieau, Chester J. 1995. *A U.S. Constitution for the Year 2000*. Chicago: Loyola University Press.

Citizens for the Constitution. 1999. *Great and Extraordinary Occasions*. New York: Century Foundation, Inc.

Committee on the Constitutional System. 1987. "A Bicentennial Analysis of the American Political Structure." Report and Recommendations of the Committee on the Constitutional System. Washington, DC: Committee on the Constitutional System.

Davidson, Jim, with Eric Klien, Norm Doering, and Lee Crocker. 1994. *The Atlantis Papers*. Houston, TX: Interglobal Paratronics Inc.

The Direct Democracy Center. http://www.realdemocracy.com. Accessed December 6, 2013.

Dolbeare, Kenneth, and Janette Hubbell. 1996. *USA 2012: After the Middle-Class Revolution*. Chatham, NJ: Chatham House Publishers.

Ellis, Frederick, with Carl Frederick. 2000. *The Oakland Statement: A Political Adventure Novel*. Miami, FL: Synergy International of the Americas, Ltd.

Eskridge, William N., Jr., and Sanford Levinson, eds. 1998. *Constitutional Stupidities, Constitutional Tragedies*. New York: New York University Press.

Gillespie, Ed, and Bob Schellhas, eds. 1994. *Contract with America: The Bold Plan by Rep. Newt Gingrich, Rep. Dick Armey and the House Republicans to Change the Nation*. New York: Random House.

Jeffs, Daniel B. 2000. *America's Crisis: The Direct Democracy and Direct Education Solution*. Amherst Junction, WI: Hard Shell Word Factory.

Kauffman, Bill. 2010. *Bye Bye, Miss American Empire: Neighborhood Patriots, Backcountry Rebels, and Their Underdog Crusades to Redraw America's Political Map*. White River Junction, VT: Chelsea Green.

Kennan, George F. 1993. *Around the Cragged Hill: A Personal and Political Philosophy*. New York: W. W. Norton & Company.

Kirstein, Herbert C. 1994. *U.S. Constitution for the 21st Century and Beyond*. Alexandria, VA: Realistic IDEALIST Enterprise. http://www.newusconstitution.org/usc21a.html (accessed December 6, 2013).

Labunski, Richard. 2000. *The Second Constitutional Convention: How the American People Can Take Back Their Government*. Versailles, KY: Marley and Beck Press.

Lazare, Daniel. 2001. *The Velvet Coup: The Constitution, the Supreme Court, and the Decline of American Democracy*. New York: Verso.

Lazare, Daniel. 1996. *The Frozen Republic: How the Constitution Is Paralyzing Democracy*. New York: Harcourt Brace & Company.

Livingston, Donald, ed. 2012. *Rethinking the American Union for the Twenty-First Century*. Gretna, LA: Pelican Publishing Company.

Long, Roderick T. 1994. "Imagineering Freedom: A Constitution of Liberty." *Formulations*, Summer.

Long, Roderick T. 1993. "Virtual Cantons: A New Path to Freedom." *Formulations*, Autumn.

Lund, Gerald N. 1987. *The Freedom Factor*. Salt Lake City, UT: Bookcraft.

Manuel, Paul Christopher, and Anne Marie Cammisa. 1999. *Checks & Balances? How a Parliamentary System Could Change American Politics*. Boulder, CO: Westview Press.

Marx, Michael. 1999. *Justus—A Utopia: Formation of a Tax Free Constitutional Democracy*. Flat Rock, IL: Marx & Marx.

Mautner, Michael Noah. 1992. *A Constitution of Direct Democracy: Pure Democracy and the Governance of the Future, Locally and Globally*. Christchurch, NZ: Legacy Books.

McGrath, Patrick J. 2000. *The Way to Responsible Government: The Constitutional Re-Structuring America Needs*. San Jose, CA: Writer's Showcase.

Naylor, Thomas H. 2008. *Secession: How Vermont and All the Other States Can Save Themselves from the Empire*. Port Townsend, WA: Feral House.

Naylor, Thomas H., and William H. Willimon. 1997. *Downsizing the U.S.A.* Grand Rapids, MI: William B. Eerdmans Publishing.

Scott, Rodney D. 1999. *The Great Debate: The Need for Constitutional Reform*. Chicago: Rampant Lion Press.

Siegan, Bernard H. 1994. *Drafting a Constitution for a Nation or Republic Emerging into Freedom*. 2nd ed. Fairfax, VA: George Mason University Press.

Strauss, Erwin S. 1979. *How to Start Your Own Country*. Boulder, CO: Paladin Press.

Vile, John R. 2010. *Encyclopedia of Constitutional Amendments, Proposed Amendments, and Amending Issues, 1789–2010*. 3rd ed. 2 vols. Santa Barbara, CA: ABC-CLIO.

Virginia Vanguard. 1995. *The Populis: A Draft Constitution for a Political New Age*. Brentsville, VA: The Wingspread Enterprise.

Wade, Edwin L. 1995. *Constitution 2000: A Federalist Proposal for the Next Century*. Chicago: Let's Talk Sense.

Wilkey, Malcolm R. 1995. *Is It Time for a Second Constitutional Convention?* Commentary by Walter Berns et al. Washington, DC: National Legal Center for the Public Interest.

CHAPTER 10

The George W. Bush Years

As the nation prepared to celebrate the arrival of the new millennium, the presidential election of 2000 raised serious questions about the Electoral College. After weeks of legal battle and controversy, the U.S. Supreme Court issued a decision that stopped vote counting in Florida where Republican George W. Bush was ahead, resulting in his election even though Democrat Al Gore, Jr., had received a greater number of nationwide popular votes. Less than nine months after he was sworn into office, Bush was confronted by the terrorist attacks of September 11, 2001, against the World Trade Center in New York and other American targets. As Bush's presidency continued, the nation became engaged in wars in Iraq and Afghanistan and took national security steps that sparked fierce debates about constitutionally guaranteed civil liberties.

Martin J. Bailey Applies Public Choice to Constitutional Construction
In 2001, a book entitled *Constitution for a Future Country* by Martin J. Bailey (1927–2000) was posthumously published. Bailey was an advocate of public choice economics that concentrates on the ties between economic choices and political institutions. Proponents often favor one or another variant of a balanced budget amendment (Vile 2010, II, 392–3). Bailey believed that governments were riddled with inefficiencies brought about because special interests organize and lobby for legislation to grant themselves benefits. Since individually, these benefits have only minimal costs to the public at large, the public incentive to organize against them remains limited. Bailey estimated that close to 50 percent of governmental spending was wasteful and could be sharply reduced if governments had fewer monopolies and if individuals could express their true preferences when it came to what programs they were willing to support through taxation.

Bailey thought that his model had a better chance of success in a new nation with fewer vested interests. It would probably also have a better chance of thriving among economists familiar with such mechanisms as "a Lindahl tax" (designed so that citizens favor taxes that benefit them and oppose those that are overly costly), the "Thomson Insurance Mechanism," and the "Vickrey-Clarke-Groves, or VCG mechanism," all of which his book features prominently.

Bailey identified the seven prime characteristics of his arcane proposal. They were:

1. Stratified random selection of official legislators
2. A demand-revealing process in each official legislature
3. Estimated Lindahl taxes
4. Potentially generous compensation for legislators based on all relevant outcomes, combined with competition among legislatures
5. Protection from bribery and extortion
6. Referenda with combined demand-revealing mechanisms
7. Monitoring and enforcement of the performance of approved programs (Bailey 2000, 51)

Bailey's model called for randomly selecting legislators and sealing off their communications with constituents. Bailey would further encourage competition among courts, which would have to support themselves through user fees, and legislatures, but the people would ultimately settle almost every question through the use of referenda. Bailey proposed strictly limiting the judiciary:

> The courts shall interpret the law as it [was] meant when enacted, and shall not amend or modify the law. The only law, in addition to this constitution, shall be statute law. The courts shall interpret the constitution in terms of the meaning it had at the time it was ratified and similarly for the interpretation of each constitutional amendment and of each law. (Bailey 2000, 110)

Although Bailey's proposed constitution emphasized freedom of contract and property-related rights, he devoted significantly less attention to traditional civil liberties. In a section that he may not have been able to complete before his death, Bailey wrote:

> Bill of rights. Standard stuff, including strict prohibition of retroactive laws. Strict prohibition of involuntary servitude in any form, except that in the case of foreign invasion or an imminent threat of same, the government may use emergency powers to compel military service for up to a maximum of sixty days by citizens represented in official legislatures and qualified to vote, whose compensation shall be provided by law. Freedom of association and of political expression shall not include freedom to form coalitions or conspiracies by voters having the purpose of misrepresenting the harms to them of legislative proposals on the ballot. (Bailey 2000, 99)

Hans-Hermann Hoppe Calls for a Hierarchical Society
That Prioritizes Property Rights

Born in West Germany in 1949, Hans-Hermann Hoppe was a one-time associate of libertarian economist Murray Rothbard and taught business at the University of Nevada in Las Vegas until he retired in 2008. In his book *Democracy: The God That Failed* (2001), Hoppe argued that monarchy was more effective at stemming the tide of statism than democracy. He also asserted that the U.S. Constitution, rather than being regarded as "a legitimate source of pride, represents a fateful error" (Hoppe 2001b, 271). Hoppe celebrated the idea of a natural order based on property.

Hoppe believed that rather than destroying royal institutions with powers to "tax and legislate" (Hoppe 2001b, 272), Americans had simply transferred them—first to state governments and then to the national authority. Instead of a single heredi-tary family regarding the nation as property, all politicians came to feel that way. They subsequently used their positions to earn the favor of constituents who failed to realize that with governmental largesse comes increased governmental power. Although defenders of the U.S. system point to separation of powers as a protec-tion, Hoppe felt that this system led to "the proliferation, accumulation, reinforce-ment, and aggravation of error" (Hoppe 2001b, 276). Governmental policies have accordingly leaned ever more strongly to "protectionism, militarism, and imperial-ism." Ironically, "the Constitution is itself unconstitutional, i.e., incompatible with the very doctrine of natural human rights that inspired the American Revolution" (Hoppe 2001b, 279).

Hoppe wanted to replace the coercive apparatus of government with a system providing for "the provision of law and order by freely competing private (profit and loss) insurance agencies" (Hoppe 2001b, 280). Since agencies would not have the ability to tax or legislate, all transactions would therefore be consensual. Com-petition would drive down prices, companies would have incentives to be efficient, and insurers would respect property rights in a way that current governments do not. Whereas governments discourage gun ownership, insurance companies would encourage such self-defense. Similarly, insurance would not provide immunity from criminal or negligent behavior.

Hoppe anticipated that secession might bring about a second American Revolu-tion resulting in a transition from compulsory government to voluntary insurance. Rather than attempting to do this through a sectional strategy, Hoppe proposed establishing hundreds of "free" cities throughout the United States, what he called "a multitude of Hong Kongs, Singapores, Monacos, and Liechtensteins strewn out over the entire continent" (Hoppe 2001b, 291) that would bring about such a tran-sition. He asserted that the establishment of such free cities could bring about the withering away of the state—and the imperialism that went with it.

Hoppe thought that the exercise of property rights and the right of association included the right to exclude others. Indeed, he described such a system as "decid-edly nonegalitarian, hierarchical, and elitist" (Hoppe 2001b, 71). Hoppe explained that:

> There would be signs regarding entrance requirements to the town, and, once in town, requirements for entering specific pieces of property (for example, no beggars, bums, or homeless, but also no homosexuals, drug users, Jews, Moslems, Germans, or Zulus), and those who did not meet these entrance requirements would be kicked out as trespassers. Almost instantly, cultural and moral normalcy would reassert itself. (Hoppe 2001, 211)

He further asserted that:

> Left-libertarians and multi- or countercultural lifestyle experimentalists, even if they were not engaged in any crime, would once again have to pay a price for their behavior. If they continued with their behavior or lifestyle, they would be barred from civilized society and live physically separate from it, in ghettos or on the fringes of society, and many positions or professions would be unattainable to them. (Hoppe 2001b, 212)

In light of these penalties, Hoppe speculated that a version of "don't ask, don't tell" might take hold, in which individuals choose to keep their behavior "in the closet, hidden from the public eye, and physically restricted to the total privacy of one's own four walls" (Hoppe 2001b, 212).

Robert A. Dahl Calls for a More Democratic Constitution

In 2001, Robert A. Dahl (1915–), the Sterling Professor Emeritus of Political Science at Yale University and the past president of the American Political Science Association, authored a book entitled *How Democratic Is the American Constitution?* He concluded that the document had fallen far short of this objective. Although he began his first chapter by saying that his aim was "not to propose changes in the American Constitution but to suggest changes in the way we *think* about our constitution" (Dahl 2001, 1), Dahl's critique of the Constitution has served as the launching pad for others to level criticisms and propose changes.

Dahl acknowledged that many Americans revered the Constitution, but he argued that "the legitimacy of the constitution ought to derive solely from its utility as an instrument of democratic government—nothing more, nothing less" (Dahl 2001, 39). Although Americans thought that their Constitution was a model for the rest of the democratic world, Dahl argued that the U.S. system was more federal; more strongly bicameral; more unequally represented (Dahl was especially critical of representation in the Senate); relied more heavily on judicial review; and was more heavily two party than most other democracies. Moreover, he observed that the Electoral College left open the possibility that a president could be chosen without a majority, or even a plurality, of the popular vote.

After examining each of the ways in which Dahl believed that the U.S. Constitution fell short, he presented a very pessimistic assessment of the likelihood for change:

> The likelihood of reducing the extreme inequality of representation in the Senate is virtually zero. The chances of altering our constitutional system to make it either *more clearly consensual or more definitely majoritarian* are also quite low. The likelihood is very low that the Supreme Court will refrain from legislating public policies, often highly partisan ones, and instead focus its power of judicial review strictly on the protection of fundamental democratic rights and issues of federalism. The combination of chief executive and monarchy in the American presidency is not likely to change. Finally, the

probability that democratic changes in the electoral college will occur appear to be inversely related to their desirability, with the most desirable having the lowest probability of occurring. (Dahl 2001, 154–5)

Dahl did make two suggestions. The first pointed to the need "to invigorate and greatly widen the critical examination of the Constitution and its shortcomings" (Dahl 2001, 155–6). He envisioned "a gradually expanding discussion that begins in scholarly circles, moves outward to the media and intellectuals more generally, and after some years begins to engage a wider public" (Dahl 2001, 156). Second, he advocated a strategy designed "to achieve greater *political* equality within the limits of the present American Constitution" (Dahl 2001, 156).

Jesse L. Jackson, Jr., and Frank Watkins Propose to Expand Constitutional Protections for Social and Economic Rights

Jesse L. Jackson, Jr., is the eldest son of veteran civil rights activist Jesse Jackson, Sr., who waged two unsuccessful campaigns for the Democratic presidential nomination in the 1980s. Jackson graduated from North Carolina A & T State University and earned a degree from the Chicago Theological Seminary and from the Illinois College of Law at Champaign-Urbana. He represented Illinois's Second Congressional District from 1995 until his resignation in 2012. In February 2013, he was sentenced to two and a half years in prison after pleading guilty to charges that he had misused campaign funds for personal use.

Years before his resignation from office, Jackson penned *A More Perfect Union: Advancing New American Rights* (2001) with assistance from his press secretary, Frank Watkins. Within this work, Jackson analyzed American history from the dual perspectives of race and federalism. Jackson further proposed eight constitutional amendments, which he also introduced in Congress. Most of Jackson's proposals centered on economic and social rights.

Jackson regarded his proposal for a full-employment amendment to be both his "most controversial" and "most important" reform (Jackson 2001, 253). It was based on the twenty-third article of the United Nations Universal Declaration of Human Rights. The amendment contained five sections. The first provided that "every citizen has the right to work, to free choice of employment, to just and favorable conditions of work, and to protection against unemployment." The second section focused on nondiscrimination and on "equal pay for equal work." Section 3 was designed to see that each citizen received fair remuneration that provided for both the worker and the worker's family; Jackson believed that this would require raising the minimum wage. Section 4 provided for an explicit right to form and join trade unions (Jackson opposed "right to work" laws), and Section 5 was a congressional enforcement mechanism that Jackson attached to each of his proposed amendments.

Jackson's second proposal called for provision of "health care of equal high quality" for all American citizens (Jackson 2001, 285). Jackson believed the government should be willing to commit substantially more resources to health care than it was doing. Jackson thought the details of this and other amendments would have to be left to political processes, but his next proposal for "decent, safe, sanitary, and affordable housing without discrimination" did not contain a similar equality clause (Jackson 2001, 300). The proposal for a "right to a public education" did specify that it should be "of equal high quality" (Jackson 2001, 330), although Jackson suggested that the amendment would provide for "a high minimum state floor" rather than a ceiling (Jackson 2001, 348).

Jackson proposed an equal rights amendment, to go into effect two years after being ratified (Jackson 2001, 350). Jackson also favored an environmental amendment that would guarantee each citizen the right to enjoy "a clean, safe, and sustainable environment" (Jackson 2001, 371), and he included a copy of the People's Earth Charter as an appendix to his book.

The Sixteenth Amendment to the U.S. Constitution permits an income tax, but does not require that it tax higher incomes at higher percentages. Jackson's next proposal would have changed this. It provided that "the Congress of the United States shall tax all persons progressively in proportion to the income which they respectively enjoy under the protection of the United States" (Jackson 2001, 385). Jackson believed that this amendment might remedy some of the disparities in income and wealth in the United States. Jackson's commentary suggested that the amendment would also apply to state taxation, which he regarded as more regressive than that at the federal level (Jackson 2001, 403).

Although a number of constitutional amendments relate to voting rights, Jackson stated such provisions affirmatively rather than negatively. His longest amendment, with five sections, was his proposed voting rights amendment. The first section would guarantee everyone age 18 or older the right to vote in all public elections. The second section provided that Congress would establish electoral standards to be reviewed each year. Section 3 would guarantee "the opportunity to register and vote on the day of any public election." Section 4 would provide for election by majority vote within each state or district, and Section 5 was the familiar enforcement provision (Jackson 2001, 425).

Jackson thought that a system of proportional representation, giving representation to minor parties, would be preferable to a system, like that utilized in the U.S. House of Representatives, of single-member districts. He also favored instant runoff voting (IRV), in which individuals would indicate their second and third choices for office, allowing votes cast for third and fourth party candidates to be aggregated with those for those at the top of the ticket. Jackson expressed concern about the large number of ex-felons excluded from voting in many states, and he asserted—seven years before Barack Obama's candidacy for the presidency—that the Democratic Party would benefit if it selected an African American candidate for vice president.

Mary Becker Offers a Progressive Bill of Rights
In the wake of the 2000 presidential election, Mary Becker, a professor of law at DePaul University, published a 2001 article in the *Fordham Law Review* entitled

"Towards a Progressive Politics and a Progressive Constitution." Becker identified the two central obstacles to the progressive political movement as an "archaic electoral system" built around winner-take-all districts and the United States Constitution. Admitting that the time did not seem particularly propitious for constitutional change, she observed that political winds often changed quickly and seemed to want to get her own proposals on the table in the event that momentum for progressive reforms increased in the future.

Becker devoted the initial part of her article to describing pressures (mostly on families) that she thought called for changes in line with those adopted by other Western democracies. Such pressures included the need for greater support of working parents; increased incarceration rates, income disparities, issues (including drug use) related to poverty; societal tolerance of guns, violence, and hatred; the U.S. failure or unwillingness to sign international agreements relative to human rights; and the failure of representation within the United States to keep up with demographic changes. She showed how other nations provided greater social services; focused less on punishment than on care; instituted restrictions on hate speech; provided for more accountable electoral systems (including proportional representation and cumulative voting); and provided quotas to assure political representation for women and other minorities. In her judgment, American society needed to balance its current concerns with justice with greater emphasis on "care," which she thought was just as implicit in human nature (Becker 2001, 2038).

Becker believed that most of the problems that she identified in current voting arrangements could be accomplished short of constitutional change. She therefore recommended that for all legislative elections other than those for the U.S. Senate, "we should . . . shift to a system of at-large cumulative voting in districts with at least seven seats in order to realize the many benefits of proportional representation while retaining the ability of voting for specific candidates" (Becker 2001, 2049). She further thought that it would also be desirable to enact "campaign finance reform, votes for children to be exercised by parents, and reform to maximize voter turn out" (Becker 2001, 2049).

Becker thought that constitutional reforms should be reserved for two areas— limitations on judicial review and adoption of a progressive bill of rights. Charging that judicial review had largely served conservative causes, she wanted either to explicitly "indicate what level of judicial review is appropriate for various specific provisions of the Constitution," or to "provide for only very limited judicial review as other constitutional democracies do" (Becker 2001, 2051).

Becker designed her proposed progressive bill of rights to move from negative to positive rights and to embody the "politics of care" that she had elaborated earlier. She suggested that positive rights could include "a commitment to afford individuals and families the conditions necessary for their nurture and development; a right to health care; a right to education; a right to employment; and a right to affordable, quality day care for all children over the age of three months" (Becker 2001, 2051–53). She also favored a second provision to prohibit discrimination "on the basis of race, class, religion, national origin, or sexual orientation" along with specific protections for the use of affirmative action (Becker 2001, 2053). A proposed amendment designed to promote sexual equality would require each state to have at least one woman senator.

Becker also favored a constitutional requirement assuring that news media would be independent of one another; constitutional protections against gun violence; a constitutional right to ensure that public defenders received "adequate funding" and "reasonable case loads"; protections against hate speech and portrayals of violence in the media; a commitment to the environment; a guarantee that "[t]hose who work should have the right to a decent living, with government support . . . of wages to reach this level where necessary"; stronger protections of religious freedoms for "non-mainstream religions"; and a provision stating "that free trade is a goal subordinate to human needs." She cited Jesse Jackson, Jr.'s, proposed amendments as an example of "the kind of thinking progressives need to be doing and the kind of platform progressives should be developing and advocating" (Becker 2001, 2054–6).

Cass R. Sunstein Takes Another Stab at a Second Bill of Rights

In 2004, Cass R. Sunstein (1954–), then a professor at the University of Chicago Law School (subsequently a professor at Harvard and head of the White House Office of Information and Regulation Affairs–OIRA), authored a book entitled *The Second Bill of Rights* in which he lauded President Franklin D. Roosevelt's call for a "second bill of rights" in a speech on January 11, 1944.

Sunstein devoted much of his book to explaining why the United States had never chosen to incorporate guarantees of social and economic rights into the U.S. Constitution. He acknowledged that one issue was that the United States regards constitutional guarantees as enforceable in courts rather than as mere aspirational statements, but he thought that it might be possible to follow the example of the South African Constitution and vest primary responsibility for such rights in Congress. Although he believed that the nation should commit itself to guaranteeing basic economic rights, he ultimately agreed "that Roosevelt was correct to contend that the second bill should be taken not as part of the written constitution, but as embodying principles to which the nation is fundamentally committed" (Sunstein 2004, 207).

Moreover, after reviewing Roosevelt's proposals as well as a proposed amendment to guarantee jobs introduced in the U.S. House of Representatives in 2003, Sunstein proposed an alternate amendment of six sections:

Section 1. Every citizen has the right to a good education.
Section 2. Every citizen has the right to adequate protection in the event of extreme need stemming from illness, accident, old age, or unemployment.
Section 3. Every citizen has the right of access to adequate food, shelter, clothing, and health care.
Section 4. Every citizen has the right to a chance at remunerative employment.
Section 5. Every citizen has the right to freedom from unfair competition and domination by monopolies at home or abroad.

Section 6. Congress and state governments must take reasonable legislative and other measures, within available resources, to achieve the realization of these rights. (Sunstein 2004, 183)

At one point Sunstein contrasted his proposals with those of Roosevelt by asserting that Roosevelt's plan to guarantee every farmer a return that would provide a decent living no longer made as much sense, given that the nation was not as dependent on agriculture and that "some farmers should go out of business" (Sunstein 2004, 183). Sunstein stated that the work of Roosevelt's generation—often called the Greatest Generation—remained "radically incomplete," and that "the second bill of rights should be reclaimed in its nation of origin" (Sunstein 2004, 234).

Sanderson Beck Proposes a More Democratic and Less Militaristic Constitution

In 2005, Sanderson Beck (1947–) published a book entitled *BEST FOR ALL: How We Can Save the World* in which he included a chapter entitled "Reforming the US Constitution." Beck has described himself as a graduate of the University of California at Berkeley (BA in dramatic art) and University of California at Santa Barbara (MA in religious studies) who earned a PhD in philosophy from an institution called the World University in 1980. He has also been a self-described conscientious objector and antiwar activist; author of more than 25 books, mostly on issues related to philosophy and history; one-time presidential candidate; and founder and president of World Peace Communications, described as a nonprofit educational and charitable corporation.

Beck's proposed constitution of eight articles, which is available on the author's Web site (www.san.beck.org), followed much of the outline of the current document (with Article VII incorporating most provisions of the Bill of Rights and the three post–Civil War amendments), but also included a number of innovations. Many of these were designed further to democratize the document and move the nation away from what he considered to be militaristic and imperialistic policies.

Although Article I retained the current size of Congress, it guaranteed the District of Columbia a voting representative in the House of Representatives, provided for instant runoff voting for the House (designed to aid third parties), and reallocated representation in the Senate. Beck thus proposed providing proportional representation for four regions of the nations—East, South, Central, and West— each of which would choose 25 senators. The U.S. Supreme Court could reallocate states to different regions to balance their populations. Senators would be selected in nonpresidential election years and serve four-year terms, with candidates being chosen in regional primaries held from March through June. Article IV further prohibited the United States from occupying any foreign territory. Beck would thus allow Puerto Rico and other island territories to determine their own status.

Beck would remove congressional powers to declare war and raise armies but retain militia. He would require members of the House to be citizens for 10 years, senators for 15, and the president for 20. States would be empowered to admit immigrants without hindrance from the national government.

Beck would provide for instant runoff voting for primary and general elections for the president. He also proposed a system for electing the heads of 15 executive departments who would serve for six-year terms and could only be forcibly removed by impeachment and conviction. Beck would further limit the length of presidential recess appointments.

Beck proposed specifying the establishment of three U.S. appellate courts in each of the five regions (he did not explain the disparity between this and the four regions he outlined earlier) and at least one district court per state. Judges would serve for ten-year renewable terms, and confirmations would require the advice and consent of three-fifths of the Senate.

The rights that Beck listed in Article VII no longer included the right to bear arms that is found in the current Second Amendment, but it would outlaw the death penalty as a form of cruel and unusual punishment. It also provided for the right to attend free public schools and use public libraries and for the right to receive "free health care." Beck would further limit officials of the national government from accepting any other income during their terms of service. His proposed constitution also provided for free public financing of elections and prohibited individuals from contributing more than $100 to any candidate in a primary or general election.

Although Beck mentioned that the current Constitution prohibits states from being deprived of their equal suffrage in the Senate, he did not explain how he would attempt to bypass this entrenchment clause. He proposed that the new constitution be ratified either by three-fourths of the state legislatures or by a majority vote in three-fourths of the states.

After explaining each of these changes, Beck observed that "adopting a new constitution such as this is not absolutely essential to most of the reforms discussed in this book, but I do believe that these political reforms would substantially improve our system of constitutional government."

James Buchanan Proposes Three Amendments to Bring About Fiscal Responsibility and Moderate Federal Regulations

Dr. James M. Buchanan (1919–2013), a Nobel laureate in economics, was one of the founders of public choice, an approach to politics and economics that analyzes the manner in which individuals, interest groups, and elected officials seek to use their positions for personal gain. In 2005 the Cato Institute, a libertarian think tank, asked Buchanan and several other scholars to respond to the question, "If you could add any three amendments to the Constitution, what would they be?" Buchanan's answer was produced as an e-book that also featured responses to Buchanan's proposal from Akhil Reed Amar of Yale, Judge Alex Kozinski, and William A. Niskasen, the Chairman of the Cato Institute.

Buchanan chose to advance all but the first of three proposals in fairly general language. He respectively called for a balanced budget amendment to promote fiscal responsibility, an amendment requiring generality of laws, and an amendment providing for natural liberty. All three amendments were predicated on Buchanan's belief that "fiscal irresponsibility stares us in the face and cries out for correction." The problem stemmed from the incentives for Congress "to advance popular spending programs separately from the imposition of taxes needed to finance them."

Buchanan's proposed balanced budget amendment specified that "in its final budget resolution, Congress should restrict estimated spending to the limits imposed by estimated tax revenues." Three-fourths majorities of both houses could waive this limit in extraordinary circumstances like war. A second amendment, which had been suggested by economist F. A. Hayek, would provide that "Congress shall make no law authorizing government to take any discriminatory measures of coercion." Buchanan believed that Congress had abused its powers under the general welfare clause and the commerce clauses to expand its powers unduly. He thus likened his second proposal to the equal protection clause. The main objective of the amendment would be to ensure that any governmental benefits were distributed on generalized principles; he hoped it would disqualify all programs that relied upon identification based on "ethnicity, location, occupation, industry, or activity." Similarly, Buchanan's third proposal would prohibit all governmental interference with voluntary exchanges, both within the nation and outside its political jurisdiction.

Akhil Amar largely questioned the language and effectiveness of the proposals, while suggesting three proposals of his own. One, which Amar advanced somewhat tentatively, called for congressional term limits in hopes that this might increase the number of people who served in both Washington, D.C., and the states. He also suggested that Senate malapportionment be remedied and that naturalized citizens be permitted to run for president.

Judge Kozinski concluded that "a body politic that needs Dr. Buchanan's amendments is a body politic that won't adopt them in the first place." He thought that the repeal of the Sixteenth Amendment would be as effective as the measures that Buchanan proposed, presumably by taking away the source of funds for Congress to distribute.

Niskasen's responses, like those presented by Amar, ultimately ended up including his own reform proposals. Niskasen expressed great concern over the delegation of legislative powers to regulatory agencies. Legislatively, he wanted to delay implementation of all laws for 60 days to allow members of Congress to introduce floor votes on them. He also introduced three amendments. The first would repeal the Seventeenth Amendment to restore power to the states to choose their representatives in the Senate. The second would permit states to nullify congressional laws within a year of their passage. Niskasen said that the problem with the current Constitution was that it did "not establish an adequate procedure for forcing a constitutional test of the assertion of undelegated powers by the federal government." Finally, he proposed a secession amendment, although he noted that he no longer believed that the major issues in U.S. government continued to correspond to state boundaries.

Dick Formichella Advances a Possible Mechanism
for Reengineering America

In 2005, Dick Formichella, who identified himself as a chief information officer, college professor, and expert on applied technology, advanced ideas of constitutional change in a novel entitled *Reengineering America*. The hero of the book is John Payton, who after becoming wealthy in the computer business decides to devote his life to reengineering the Constitution to bring it up to date. With the sponsorship of Senator Jacques Lagrande from Rhode Island, the two seek adoption of a Twenty-Eighth Amendment, which would instruct the National Archivist to call a Constitutional Convention within six months "for the purpose of revising, updating, and modernizing the original document" to a "2.0" version. Each governor would appoint two delegates, one of which would be a senator (if the senator were willing to resign his/her seat in order to serve). The delegates would in turn propose a constitution that would go into effect when ratified by two-thirds or more of the people voting in all 50 states.

Much of the book centered on how such a movement might begin. The novel anticipated that young people would be most supportive. It was based on the idea of pressuring Congress to propose such an amendment by holding a national referendum, in which the entire population (biometrically verified) would cast ballots through computers. It also suggested that individuals could post possible revisions on the Web. Such postings actually occur in the novel. As Formichella writes, "many of them were on the wacky side but just as many were thoughtful, insightful and potentially useful if and when the constitutional convention were to begin" (Formichella 2005, 290).

Formichella never presented a draft of the constitution that he hoped would emerge from the convention, but the book expressed concerns about the wisdom of altering the first four articles to address ineffectiveness and inefficiency. He suggested at other points that Congress was too large, that states need to be restructured and local government consolidated, that the president could be reduced to more of a figurehead, and that Congress could be "disintermediate[d]," meaning that citizens could vote on most measures directly, with the Senate remaining as a check against precipitous measures. The House of Representatives, meanwhile, would be abandoned:

> The House would be replaced by Internet-based popular voting, however, unlike voting for public offices, the legislative voting privilege would not be automatically extended to anyone who had attained adulthood and took the time to register. Instead, people wishing to participate in the legislative process would need to obtain and maintain a voter's certification. (Formichella 2005, 290)

Formichella likened this certification to a license that would "require the holder to demonstrate a basic level of understanding and proficiency not only of how the government functioned but also of the issues under consideration" (Formichella

2005, 291). Despite such a qualification, he likened this new voting system to "the referenda you find on state ballots" (Formichella 2005, 291).

Somewhat later, Formichella described the aim of the proponent of change as that of "restructuring the House and the Senate and reconsidering the separation of powers between federal and state governments" (2005, 297). Although the novel's hero appeared to want additional requirements to assure "truth and impartiality in news coverage" (Formichella 2005, 326), it was not clear that he was willing to amend or replace the First Amendment in order to bring this about.

Formichella never explained why he did not recommend the traditional Article V mechanism for calling a constitutional convention, but it would appear that his proposal provided that the results of such a convention could be ratified by supportive votes from two-thirds of the voters in the states.

William S. Field Issues a Strong Call for Parliamentary Government
William S. Field (1929–2013) was a pioneering insurance industry executive and noted venture capitalist with the insurance giant Prudential for more than 40 years. In 2006, though, Field strayed from the world of insurance and high finance to publish a book entitled *Why America Needs Parliamentary Government*. The book was divided into four chapters. The first described what Field believed to be "America's Political Malaise"; the second detailed defects in the American political system; the third described how a parliamentary system could correct them; and the fourth discussed implementation of his plans.

Field believed that the American system was "mired increasingly in a paralytic gridlock of confrontation, polarization and self-gratification" (Field 2006, 1). These problems had been exacerbated by the proliferation of primaries, initiatives, and referenda, and were manifested in excessive debt, increased permissiveness, and decreasing public faith in governmental institutions.

Field believed that although America's Founding Fathers had improved on the Articles of Confederation, the compromises that they incorporated into the Constitution contained a number of flaws. These included the exercise of judicial review (which had not been outlined in the document); the conflict between the supremacy clause and the Tenth Amendment; the Electoral College system; equal state representation in the Senate; state control over congressional elections; the system of separated powers; lack of controls on congressional delegations of power; and the eventual rise of presidential supremacy (Field 2006, 38–9). Field observed that when the Framers wrote the Constitution, modern parliamentary democracies with responsible political parties did not exist to provide appropriate models. In time, presidents stepped in to fill leadership voids in the United States, and unwritten constitutional practices, including modern interest-group politics, overwhelmed the guarantees of the written document.

Although proponents of presidential systems touted their stability, democracy, and limits on government, Field expressed skepticism about each of these claims and asserted that modern parliamentary democracies were not only far more pervasive but also far better at overcoming partisan gridlock. He believed that such a government would better "achieve results efficiently, assign accountability unambiguously, better control abuses of powers, produce more stable executive tenure, be more democratic, rely on strong political parties, [and] be superior based on objective empirical evidence" (Field 2006, 121).

Although he did not propose a formal constitutional document, Field outlined the central aspects of the new system in America as he envisioned it. He favored abolishing the Senate and creating a unicameral Congress of 700 members, chosen under uniform voting procedures established by a national Electoral Commission "staffed by judges of diverse political persuasion" (Field 2006, 131, 137). He further favored reducing the number of states, and, in a near reversal of the Tenth Amendment, more clearly delineating their powers so that "all powers not specifically delegated to the states are reserved to the federal government" (Field 2006, 137). Congress would choose the chief executive officer, or prime minister, from among its members and grant the individual "broad authority to organize and reorganize the executive branch" (Field 2006, 137). Parliament would be supreme. Congressional elections, held at least once every five years, would be organized on the basis of proportional representation. Although courts would continue to exercise judicial review, actual exercises of that power would probably decrease since they would advise parliament on the constitutionality of pending legislation. Amendments would require the votes of two-thirds of the members of Congress representing two-thirds of the population, although amendments relating to federalism would require approval of 75 percent of the states. Field would further prohibit state initiatives and referenda and establish a "codified, more detailed Bill of Rights" similar to the Canadian Charter of Rights and Freedoms (Field 2006, 138). He also wanted to require unicameral state legislatures, with state governors wielding powers similar to those of the prime minister. Field endorsed establishing an advisory panel of "retired judges, law school professionals and lawyers appointed by Congress" that might propose a list of judicial nominees, which Congress could amend and from which the prime minister would make appointments (Field 2006, 140). He thought the Supreme Court might be expanded to include 15 justices.

Field believed that a constitutional convention was the best mechanism to implement his plan. He thought that it might in turn be implemented by creating a grassroots "Parliamentary Party" to draft and advocate such reforms. He also emphasized the importance of attracting more talented and knowledgeable people into government, endorsing guarantees of full-time employment, higher pay, and the introduction of "undergraduate and postgraduate degree programs in politics in at least our major universities" (Field 2006, 152). He specifically envisioned "comprehensive, integrated degree programs that combine these two disciplines [politics and law] in ways that are most suitable to holding elective office and infusing the degree program with healthy doses of courses in economics, economic and business history, economic development, history, comparative government, ethics, psychology, sociology, comparative religion, and science" (Field 2006, 152).

Steven Hill Offers a Variety of Reforms to Voting and Government

Steven Hill (1958–) is a long-time political analyst and reformer who formerly directed the Political Reform Program of the New America Foundation and co-founded the Center for Voting and Democracy. In 2006 he published *10 Steps to Repair American Democracy*, which was reissued in a 2012 election edition. A foreword by Hendrik Hertzberg likened American veneration of the Founding Fathers to "ancestor worship" and the Constitution and *The Federalist Papers* to "the Pentateuch and Talmud of our civic religion" (Hill 2012, ix), but Hill's book included a mix of proposals to update the work of those Founding Fathers—some of which would require constitutional amendments.

In a chapter titled "Secure the Vote," Hill suggested six reforms. These included hiring "impartial election officials," professionalizing "election administration," establishing a "national elections commission," mandating a paper trail for all votes, developing "public-interest voting equipment," and committing to "adequate funding of our elections" (Hill 2012, 23). A second chapter on the need to "Expand Voting Participation" advocated implementing "universal/automatic voter registration," establishing "a national voting holiday," passing "a right-to-vote constitutional amendment," establishing voting rights for members of the District of Columbia, enfranchising ex-felons and prisoners, preventing voting suppression, providing election monitors, enfranchising overseas voters, and increased ballot access for third-party candidates (Hill 2012, 39).

A third chapter focused specifically on wider adoption of instant runoff voting (IRV) for all single-winner elections at all levels of government. This move away from plurality or run-off elections would allow voters to indicate second and third preferences on their ballots. A complementary fourth chapter called for scrapping all winner-take-all elections and recognizing that simply providing for nonpartisan redistricting would not accomplish all the goals that its advocates anticipated. Hill also called for the establishment of randomly selected "citizens' assemblies" to overcome partisan hurdles to reform.

Chapter 5 focused on Hill's desire for direct election of the president, for which he advocated adoption of a constitutional amendment. Short of this, however, he favored a plan whereby states would agree to award their votes to the winner of the national vote. Chapter 6 further called for an overhaul of the U.S. Senate. Recognizing that Article V of the Constitution prohibits states from being deprived of their equality in this body without their consent, Hill favored abolishing "the filibuster, Senate holds, and other anti-majoritarian parliamentary procedures," reducing the Senate's power to confirm judicial appointments (giving this instead to the House), or passing a constitutional amendment to abolish the Senate and create a unicameral House.

Chapter 7 focused on reclaiming the airwaves, which Hill believed were too subject to the control of a few corporations. In addition to using antitrust laws to break up current monopolies, Hill favored a restoration of the fairness doctrine, subsidies for daily magazines and newspapers, expansion of public broadcasting, and expanded access to broadband Internet (Hill 2012, 130). In chapter 8, Hill condemned U.S. Supreme Court decisions relative to the role of money in elections and called for reforms to reduce the role of money in campaigns. He wanted to institute public funding of all elections, require free media time for candidates, and impose limits on donations and campaign spending caps (Hill 2012, 147).

Hill proposed a number of reforms to the U.S. Supreme Court in chapter 9. He favored limiting the terms of justices to 15 to 18 years; setting a retirement age of 70 or 75 for the justices; setting a higher threshold (perhaps 60 percent) for confirmation, with the intention of weeding out partisan appointments; designating multiple appointing authorities; vesting confirmation in the House of Representatives rather than the Senate; and televising hearings before the Court (Hill 2012, 163). Hill also favored trimming the power of the chief justice by removing most of the position's administrative responsibilities.

Hill's tenth chapter called for greater reliance on "smart government" rather than "limited government." He also wanted to promote awareness of the good things that government does through advertising. A concluding chapter imagined how things could be different if the nation adopted his reforms versus what might happen in future elections if it refused to do so. Ultimately, Hill believed that "America will change because it has to" (Hill 2012, 191).

Floyd Wynne Seeks to Check Unwarranted Federal Assumptions of Power

Floyd Wynne (1918–2008) was an Oregonian who worked in radio and newspapers and served as a city councilman, county commissioner, and leader of several civic organizations in the Klamath Falls region. In 2006, he published a novel entitled *Saving Our Constitution* that had distinctly Southern roots, including a picture of the Confederate Stars and Bars on the cover.

The plot of this 118-page book begins with federal courts telling citizens of South Carolina that they may not fly the Confederate flag. It continued with a challenge before the U.S. Supreme Court on the constitutionality of the Fourteenth Amendment, which its challengers believed was not properly ratified. The Court refuses to strike down the amendment but suggests that it has been misinterpreted. The novel then ends with a constitutional convention.

Wynne was chiefly concerned with what he believed to be the unwarranted assumption of state powers by the federal government. The proposals that emerged from his fictional convention, however, consisted of a potpourri of proposals to reform all three branches of the national government.

Suggested reforms of Congress included limits on campaign contributions and expenditures; state approval of federal purchases and uses of land within their jurisdictions; closer congressional monitoring of departmental decisions; separation of Social Security funds from general revenues, raising the retirement age and limiting Social Security payments; prohibiting punitive damages in lawsuits; enacting cost controls on drugs; reform of Medicare; and scrutiny of the Endangered Species Act. Proposed executive reforms included mandating that all federal agency directives comply with constitutional authority; prohibiting civil rights charges for crimes of which citizens have previously been found not guilty; and greater protection for private property. Judicial reforms included greater scrutiny of actions for unconstitutionality; limiting the interpretation of the General Welfare Clause; and further limiting remedies that judges can impose when they find legislation to be unconstitutional.

Wynne anticipated that the convention would operate according to the "one-state, one-vote rule" (Wynne 2006, 105). Ultimately, the novel suggested that the convention would have to complete its work behind closed doors. Wynne devoted relatively little attention to the mechanics of how to call or operate a convention or how it would work.

Robert F. Hawes, Jr., Proposes a Twenty-First-Century Bill of Rights

Robert F. Hawes, Jr., is a native Virginian who graduated from Pensacola Christian College in 1995 and later settled in South Carolina. A self-described "Jeffersonian," Hawes is the author of *One Nation Indivisible? A Study of Secession and the Constitution* (2006), which examined the doctrine of secession and concluded, contrary to Lincoln's thinking, that states have a right to secede from the Union.

Concerned that the nation was becoming increasingly divided and that it was denying civil liberties because of fears of terrorism, Hawes proposed 14 "potentially helpful constitutional amendments" that might be considered to be "a 21st Century bill of rights" (Hawes 2006, 295). The first would limit presidential war powers by providing that the president obtain the consent of two-thirds of Congress before employing "armed forces in any purely offensive, pre-emptive, 'peace-keeping,' or punitive operation on foreign soil." The second was designed to limit the time during which citizens could be imprisoned without a suspension of the writ of habeas corpus for such citizens. The third limited the use of martial law, the fourth prohibited suspension of the Constitution, and the fifth curbed the use of executive orders outside the executive department. The sixth would tighten search and seizure requirements; the seventh would provide greater security against invasions of privacy; and the eighth would allow one half of the state legislatures to invalidate any act of the president, Congress, or the Supreme Court.

The ninth proposal would prohibit the U.S. Supreme Court from considering foreign law when making its rulings, and the tenth would require three-fourths of the state legislatures to ratify treaties. The eleventh would prohibit international bodies from adopting laws or regulations for the states. The twelfth would amend congressional powers under the commerce clause "to actual exchanges of goods and services and related monies between persons and/or entities of differing states." The thirteenth would forbid inheritance taxes, and the fourteenth would prohibit Congress from "regulating the private or public behavior of individuals; domestic institutions and civil unions; reproductive concerns; minor child rights and status; or private business contracts and practices, where interstate commerce is not involved" (Hawes 2006, 295–9).

Sanford Levinson Seeks a Convention to Democratize the Constitution

Sanford Levinson (1941–) is a law professor who has published thoughtful commentaries on the U.S. Constitution and the amending process. In 2006 Levinson published *Our UnDemocratic Constitution: Where the Constitution Goes Wrong (And How We the People Can Correct It)*, in which he called for a new constitutional convention to ratify perceived defects in the Constitution. Concerned that the U.S. Constitution was too undemocratic, Levinson wanted the American people to vote on the following proposal:

> Shall Congress call a constitutional convention empowered to consider the adequacy of the Constitution and, if thought necessary, to draft a new constitution that, upon completion, will be submitted to the electorate for its approval or disapproval by majority vote? Unless and until a new constitution gains popular approval, the current Constitution will continue in place. (Levinson 2006, 11)

Levinson began his critique of the current constitutional system with the legislative branch. He believed that the system had overemphasized bicameralism, and he was especially critical of equal state representation in the Senate and the denial of voting representation to the District of Columbia. Levinson thought that the presidential veto granted the president too much power in the legislative process and he raised objections to the length of time between elections and the seating of new members of Congress.

The subtitle of Levinson's next chapter encapsulated his critique of the presidency: "Too-powerful presidents, chosen in an indefensible process, who cannot be displaced even when they are manifestly incompetent" (Levinson 2006, 79). Levinson was particularly critical of the Electoral College. He also believed that too much time elapsed between presidential elections and inaugurations. He expressed additional concerns over recess appointments, presidential exercises of the pardon power, the rigidity of presidential terms of office, and the office of the vice president.

In examining the judiciary, Levinson questioned life tenure for Supreme Court justices. Levinson further argued that the age requirements for public office-holders "are indefensible in our contemporary world" (Levinson 2006, 143). He argued that residency requirements provided a "*bias toward localism*" (Levinson 2006, 147), and he thought that it was unfair to require that presidents be native-born citizens. Levinson also objected to the two-term limit for presidents.

Levinson believed the Article V amending processes constituted "an iron cage with regard to changing some of the most important aspects of our political system" (Levinson 2006, 165). He argued that the article stunted constitutional imagination: "Because it is so difficult to amend the Constitution—it seems almost utopian to suggest the possibility, with regard to anything that is truly important—citizens are encouraged to believe that change is almost never desirable, let alone necessary" (Levinson 2006, 165).

What then should be done? Levinson acknowledged that some amendments, such as ones providing for the continuity of government after an attack on the United States or permitting immigrants to run for president, could be adopted through the amending process. He believed, however, that others might need to be initiated through a constitutional convention. Echoing the sentiments of Akhil Reed Amar, Levinson stated that "a new convention could legitimately declare that its handiwork would be binding if ratified in a national referendum where each voter had equal power" (Levinson 2006, 177). He favored the use of "deliberative polling," whereby people would discuss issues for several days before deciding what to do about them, and thought that such polling might be a way to get such a convention off the ground. He opined that "if a critical mass does indeed agree that our Constitution is seriously defective, then a campaign would have the potential to capture national attention and forge a new consciousness" (Levinson 2006, 180).

Levinson reiterated his call for a convention in a 2012 book, *Framed*, that focused chiefly on state constitutions. Arguing that the national constitution is far less democratic than those of the 50 states, he repeated his call for "a new constitutional convention, one that could engage in a comprehensive overview of the U.S. Constitution and the utility of many of its provisions to twenty-first century Americans" (Levinson 2012, 391). He proposed that states be represented in such a convention according to "overall population" and be chosen "by lottery, with very limited restrictions on selection (the most obvious one being age)" (Levinson 2012, 391). He further proposed that they serve with a salary for two years and have the right to conduct hearings. Levinson defended his relatively novel idea of selection by lottery on the basis that it "would protect us against takeovers of a constitutional convention by single-issue zealots who might, with the support of generous financing, prevail in election" (Levinson 2012, 392). Affirming his belief in the people, he further denied that either "legal interpretation" or "constitutional design" required knowledge equivalent to that for "rocket science." To the contrary, Levinson asserted that such issues "involve basic value choices that ordinary Americans are capable of making" (Levinson 2012, 393).

Larry J. Sabato Advances Reforms to Democratize the Constitution and Clarify Party Politics

Larry J. Sabato (1952–) is a professor of government who directs the Center for Politics at the University of Virginia, where he received an undergraduate degree before earning a graduate degree from Oxford. Sabato is one of the most widely quoted political scientists in the nation. More known for his political punditry than for constitutional analysis, in 2007 Sabato published a book entitled *A More Perfect Constitution*, in which he made the case for a series of 23 constitutional reforms. Sabato thought that Congress could propose these reforms, but he anticipated that they would more likely be the product of a constitutional convention. A number of Sabato's proposed reforms involved issues relative to political parties and the nomination of candidates that the Constitution does not currently address.

Although Sabato's proposals were far reaching, he did not regard them as radical. Constitutional reform should be consistent with American principles of idealism, pragmatism, fairness, and "the needs of the present and future" (Sabato 2007, 13). He further said that any proposals should honor the idea of a written constitution, republicanism, separation of powers, federalism, and the rule of law. He thus specifically rejected the adoption of a parliamentary system or nationwide initiative and referendum ideas; getting sidetracked by hot-button issues like abortion, capital punishment, and gay rights; or altering the existing Bill of Rights (Sabato 2007, 13–14).

In examining Congress, Sabato proposed adding two additional senators for states with the greatest population and one for the next 15. He would also award representation in the Senate to the District of Columbia and to former presidents and vice presidents. He did not initially note that Article V prohibited states from being deprived of their equal representation in the Senate without their consent, but he did acknowledge later in the book that this might be a problem. Sabato was quite concerned about the lack of competitive districts in the House of Representatives and proposed changing this by providing for a system of nonpartisan redistricting. He favored expanding House terms from two years to three and aligning Senate terms so that they coincide with presidential elections. He advocated expanding the House of Representatives to 1,000 members who would, like members of the Senate, be subject to unspecified term limits. Sabato also supported a balanced budget amendment, with 55 percent being permitted to override the requirement, and he favored allowing for gubernatorial appointment of members to the House in cases of mass catastrophe.

Sabato argued for a modified six-year term for the president, which would allow the president in his fifth year to seek an additional two-year extension to his term. Sabato also favored institutionalizing provisions of the War Powers Act of 1973 by expanding congressional oversight of the president's war powers. He favored granting the president a line-item veto and allowing non-native born citizens to run for the presidency if they have been U.S. citizens for at least 20 years.

In dealing with the judiciary, Sabato sought mandatory retirement ages and 15-year term limits on all federal judges, although he would allow lower judges to apply for five-year extensions. He also favored increasing the number of Supreme Court justices from 9 to 12. He believed that the possibility of tie votes might reduce judicial powers and reduce the likelihood of justices becoming "swing" votes. Sabato further thought that federal judges and justices should receive automatic cost of living adjustments without having to depend on Congress to enact them.

Sabato proposed "a new, separate constitutional article specifically for the *politics* of the American system" (Sabato 2006, 227). He argued that the current presidential nominating system gave undue influence to states like New Hampshire, which conducted the first primary, and Iowa, which conducted the first caucus. He proposed dividing the nation into four regions and determining which sections would vote on the basis of a lottery. The nominating process would be limited to the four months immediately preceding national nominating conventions in August.

Consistent with his proposed increase in the size of both houses of Congress, Sabato would add electors to the Electoral College and eliminate the possibility of "faithless electors" who do not vote for their party's designated candidate. He also favored "reasonable limitations on campaign spending by [candidates who use] the wealth from their family fortunes" as well as partial public financing for general election House and Senate campaigns (Sabato 2006, 228). He would encourage voting by having an "automatic registration system for all qualified American citizens" (Sabato 2006, 228).

Although acknowledging that such a proposal would probably cost about $65.7 billion annually, Sabato favored requiring all Americans to give two years of national service between the ages of 18 and 26. He observed, "This universal civic duty would be, in essence, a Bill of Responsibilities to accompany the Bill of Rights" (Sabato 2006, 228–9).

Finally, Sabato proposed convening an Article V Constitutional Convention for the purpose of making such proposals. Taking some comfort from a poll that he conducted that suggested that Americans favored many of his proposals, he recognized that the process could take some time. He thought that delegates to such a convention should be elected by the people according to the "one person, one vote" principle and that a convention of 436 delegates (the current number of House districts plus one for the District of Columbia) would be ideal. He thought that members of Congress should be excluded from participating and envisioned that the chief justice of the United States might preside over the initial meetings. Although he did not include it in his later list of proposals, he suggested that future conventions be convened at the turn of each century.

In a fairly clever move, the back flyleaf of the book included "endorsements" for "a more perfect constitution" in the form of quotations from Thomas Jefferson, James Madison, George Washington, and George Mason.

Joseph F. Coates Proposes a Bill of Rights for Twenty-First-Century America

In 2007, Joseph F. Coates (1929–), a professional futurist who has worked in research and development and in think tanks, published *A Bill of Rights for 21st Century America*. Coates apparently first delivered a talk on the future of the Constitution in 2005 and then found a benefactor who was willing to finance a shorter study on possible revisions of the Bill of Rights. Coates divided the resulting book into three parts. The first described the existing Bill of Rights and how he thought it should be changed. The second proposed 10 additional amendments, and the third discussed how such changes might be implemented.

After discussing existing provisions of the Bill of Rights, Coates made the following suggestions. He proposed to add the Ninth and Tenth Amendments to the First, as well as provisions found in Article I, Section 9, relative to the writ of habeas corpus, bills of attainder, and ex post facto laws. He favored rethinking the Second Amendment to permit reasonable limits and to divorce the right to bear arms from that of being in the militia, and he thought the Third Amendment could be dropped as antiquarian. Coates advocated revising the Fourth Amendment "to accommodate the complex new world of information technology" (Coates 2007, 30). He believed the Fifth Amendment should include definitions that included both substantive and procedural due process and should be altered to put jury selection in the hands of judges and "forbid extra courtroom jury selection advice to attorneys." He further favored adding the Sixth, Seventh, and Eighth Amendments to the Fifth, modifying the clause in the existing Sixth Amendment with respect to confronting witnesses, and providing limits on appeal, with appropriate penalties for those who abuse the privilege. He also proposed combining Amendments Thirteen, Fourteen, Fifteen, Nineteen, Twenty-Four, and Twenty-Six into a single amendment relative to voting rights.

In part II of his book, Coates proposed an additional 10 amendments. The first called for legitimizing and licensing heterosexual, homosexual, transsexual, polygamist, group, and trial marriages, with due "access to governmental programs, benefits, support, subsidies and payments" (Coates 2007, 52).

The second would entitle all citizens to "employment up to age 70." The government would provide work for those who could not get jobs in the private sector, although it would pay 10 percent below market rates. The amendment would also recognize the right to join labor unions.

Coates's third proposed amendment would entitle all capable citizens to up to 16 years of "work-oriented education" (Coates 2007, 55). Institutions that failed to do so would be "open to collective and individual losses, dissolution of the institution, replacement of its management by an appropriately trained and designated panel." They would also be required to provide refunds (Coates 2007, 55–6).

Coates's fourth proposed amendment would provide a "governmentally assured baseline of reasonable quality healthcare" to all (Coates 2007, 58). It would not only inform citizens about how to improve their health but ensure "that the actions that would improve the quality of life are taken" (Coates 2007, 58). A "uniform nationwide code" would also provide for voluntary euthanasia.

The proposed fifth amendment dealt with privacy. It would provide protections for securing health and other personal information, for preventing hacking, scamming, unauthorized videos, unauthorized selling of mailing lists or use of social security numbers, limits on workplace data collection, and restricting information gathering except during wartime.

The proposed sixth amendment, designed to promote voter equality, would replace the Electoral College with direct voting, limit campaigns to five months, and prevent candidates from campaigning until 45 days before elections. It would further prohibit businesses and corporations from participating directly in the process.

Coates's proposed seventh amendment called for replacing the current adversarial legal system with a nonadversarial process that would utilize experts to judge complex cases. The proposed eighth amendment would provide for relatively free movement of U.S. citizens to other countries.

The ninth proposed amendment was designed to provide for more open government. It included provisions for opening most meetings to the public and for an Information Release Officer who would work to reduce over-classification of governmental documents. A final, tenth proposal would ban torture "including beatings, degradation and sexual, social, or religious humiliation" and would end the practice of extraordinary rendition to nations that engaged in torture.

Coates indicated that he had rejected other proposals because he considered them to be either legislative rather than constitutional in nature; "too vague and uncertain"; inapplicable to the United States; or involving situations involving discrete minorities within an otherwise homogeneous society (Coates 2007, 78–9).

In the last section of his book, Coates described how the "sluggish" amendment process would make implementation of his proposed changes difficult. He suggested creating a Bill of Rights Web page, a series of blogs, and recruitment of news media. He further recommended that the three branches of the national government form a national commission on the Bill of Rights, filled with 25 "people of genius." Coates suggested that the president of the American Political Science Association designate the first member of this commission, who would then designate a second, and so forth. As an alternative, he suggested that state legislatures organize consortia on the subject or that Congress propose such amendments as a package. Finally, following a proposal by Professor Emeritus Richard Pierre Claude of the University of Maryland, he suggested that such rights be incorporated into a binding treaty that the United States would sign. Ultimately, Coates favored calling a constitutional convention to do the job.

References

Bailey, Martin J. 2001. *Constitution for a Future Country*. New York: Palgrave.

Beck, Sanderson. 2005. *BEST FOR ALL: How We Can Save the World*. Santa Barbara, CA: World Peace Communications.

Beck, Sanderson. 2005. "Reforming the US Constitution." http://www.san.beck.org/BFA5=ReformingUSConst.html (accessed July 25, 2013).

Becker, Mary. 2001. "Towards a Progressive Politics and a Progressive Constitution." *Fordham Law Review* 69: 2007–56.

Buchanan, James M., et al. 2005. *The Living Constitution: Amendments for the 21st Century*. Washington, DC: The Cato Institute.

Coates, Joseph F. 2007. *A Bill of Rights for 21st Century America*. Washington, DC: Kanawha Institute for the Study of the Future.

Dahl, Robert. 2001. *How Democratic Is the American Constitution?* New Haven, CT: Yale University Press.

Field, William S. 2006. *Why America Needs Parliamentary Government*. Baltimore, MD: Gateway Press.

Formichella, Dick. 2005. *Reengineering America*. New York: iUniverse.

Hawes, Robert F., Jr. 2006. *One Nation, Indivisible? A Study of Secession and the Constitution*. Palo Alto, CA: Fultus Books.

Hill, Steven. 2012. *10 Steps to Repair American Democracy: A More Perfect Union*. 2012 Election Edition. Boulder, CO: Paradigm Publishers.

Hoppe, Hans-Hermann. 2001a. "On the Impossibility of Limited Government and the Prospects for a Second American Revolution." In *Reassessing the Presidency: The Rise of the Executive State, and the Decline of Freedom*, edited by John V. Denson, 667–710. Auburn, AL: Ludwig von Mises Institute.

Hoppe, Hans-Hermann. 2001b. *Democracy: The God That Failed; The Economics and Politics of Monarchy, Democracy and Natural Order*. New Brunswick, NJ: Transaction Publishers.

Jackson, Jesse L., Jr., with Frank E. Watkins. 2001. *A More Perfect Union: Advancing New American Rights*. New York: Welcome Rain Publishers.

Levinson, Sanford. 2012. *Framed: America's Fifty-One Constitutions and the Crisis of Governance*. New York: Oxford University Press.

Levinson, Sanford. 2011. "So Much to Rewrite, So Little Time. . . ." *Constitutional Commentary* 27 (Winter): 515–26.

Levinson, Sanford. 2006. *Our UnDemocratic Constitution: Where the Constitution Goes Wrong (And How We the People Can Correct It)*. New York: Oxford University Press.

Sabato, Larry J. 2007. *A More Perfect Constitution: 23 Proposals to Revitalize Our Constitution and Make America a Fairer Country*. New York: Walker and Company.

Sunstein, Cass R. 2004. *The Second Bill of Rights: FDR's Unfinished Revolution and Why We Need It More Than Ever*. New York: Basic Books.

Tushnet, Mark. 2011. "Abolishing Judicial Review." *Constitutional Commentary* 27 (Winter): 581–8.

Vile, John R. 2010. *Encyclopedia of Constitutional Amendments, Proposed Amendments, and Amending Issues, 1789–2010*. 3rd ed. 2 vols. Santa Barbara, CA: ABC-CLIO.

Wynne, Floyd. 2006. *Saving Our Constitution*. Bloomington, IN: Author House.

CHAPTER 11

The Barack Obama Years

As George W. Bush's second term came to a close, the nation faced war weariness, expanding debt, and a recession. The Democrats nominated Barack Obama, the party's first African American presidential candidate, who captured the presidency and secured adoption of a national health care plan that continues to stir both hopes of increased health protection and fears of over-assumptions of federal power. In 2012, he won reelection over Republican nominee Mitt Romney. The Tea Party movement, born early in Obama's first term, continues to articulate concerns, especially strong among conservatives and libertarians, about governmental deficits and the growth of government in general. Meanwhile, the so-called Occupy movement directed attention to an increasing income gap between the wealthy and the rest of the nation.

In the volatile Middle East, the Arab Spring brought both the promise of democratic reform and the threat of increased turmoil. Although the tone of the new administration was quite different from the one that preceded it, Obama faced many of the terrorism issues of his immediate predecessors, and civil libertarians continued to raise concerns about the role of the government in gathering data and in interfering with individual privacy.

Paul R. Heim Calls for a Second American Revolution

In 2009, Paul R. Heim published a book entitled *Second American Revolution: Change You Really Want*. Heim, a retiree from the energy industry, filled his book with an unlikely mix of Bible commentary and the justification for—and texts of—53 proposed constitutional amendments. Heim hoped to initiate these reforms by passing referenda for a new constitutional convention within three-fourths or more of the states.

Although the opening chapters of Heim's book put forth arguments for term limits, regulation of short selling in the stock market, and an end to mandatory teaching of evolution in public schools, the author quickly turns to attempting to prove that the biblical account of creation actually described two creations of man, one on the sixth day and another on the eighth, after God "realized He did not have a farmer, someone who would till the soil" (Heim 2009, 22). By this account, Cain was the fruit of a sexual union between Eve and Satan, while Abel was the son of Adam and Eve. Heim further believed that there had been two major floods in world history, and that America was founded by the 10 lost tribes of Israel, who settled in the Caucasus before moving to Great Britain and the United States (Heim 2009, 136–7).

Heim listed his proposed amendments in chapter 26. The amendments, labeled "People's" amendments, called for a virtual smorgasbord of proposals, including the following: 1) limiting short selling in the stock market; 2–4) providing one 4-year term for members of the House; one 8-year term for senators; and a 10-year term for the president, with the latter subject to impeachment "for any reason, by referendum vote with a majority vote in at least 3/5's of the States" (Heim 2009, 156); 5–6) limiting Supreme Court justices to two nine-year terms, with impeachments to be initiated by the chief justice of any state Supreme Court; 7–8) providing that elected officials have the same Social Security payments as other citizens; 9) preventing lawyers from running for the House of Representatives more than once in every four elections and limiting the role of lobbyists to that of providing information; 10–11) allowing states to permit religious exercises that acknowledge the United States' place as a Christian nation, but preventing the national government from engaging in such activities; 12–13) recognizing that life begins at conception and providing the death penalty for rape in hopes of deterring such pregnancies; 14–17) reinstituting the death penalty for a variety of crimes, including nine successive misdemeanors or three felonies, or the manufacture or transport of drugs for resale; 18) prohibiting federal funding for research or teaching on evolution; 19) making English the official language; 20) requiring illegal immigrants to register within 90 days or face deportation; 21) limiting marriages to those between one man and one woman and limiting federal benefits for gay couples; 22) providing a single appeal for death penalty cases; 23–25) limiting pro bono, tort, and contingency fee awards; 26) limiting entitlements of atheists; 27) limiting governmental control of the media; 28) allowing Web sites to serve limited constituencies; 29) rooting out pornography on Web sites; 30) preventing video games from killing the same person over and over again; 31) paying down the debt and requiring 80 percent supermajorities to raise it; 32) instituting a line-item veto; 33–34) requiring zero-based budgeting and identifying members of Congress who insert particular earmarks; 35) instituting a tax on petroleum products; 36) extending freedom of speech to collective bodies like churches; 37) permitting individuals who attempt to enforce "political correctness" to be charged with blackmail; 38) putting an end to affirmative action programs; 39) preventing teachers from using tenure to avoid tests of their abilities; 40) limiting compensation for supervisory positions; 41) providing penalties for defamation of character and pornography; 42) encouraging gun ownership for protection, except for felons; 43) preventing socialistic governmental ownership; 44) instituting campaign finance laws; 45) instituting a "Fair Tax" (probably a flat tax); 46) replacing the Electoral College with either a popular vote of a majority of the people or a majority of the states; 47) limiting international agreements that would interfere with U.S. sovereignty; 48) guaranteeing the secret ballot; 49) providing time for minority party members to speak before adoption of a law that they oppose; 50) preventing individuals from receiving more than one federal pension; 51) instituting a "Make My Day" self-defense of one's home amendment; 52) distinguishing non-state terrorist enemy combatants from enemy soldiers of a formal military; and 53) clarifying that the right to bear arms does not apply to members of street gangs, members of the Ku Klux Klan, or to paramilitary groups that do not support capitalism, "the American way of life," and religious tolerance (Heim 2009, 154–71).

Heim hoped to stimulate what he described as a silent majority of moderate Democrats and Republicans to call a convention to consider his and other proposals using the Article V convention process, but with a twist. By his analysis—which is in tension with *Hawke v. Smith*, 253 U.S. 221 (1990), which prohibited states from substituting *approval* of amendments by referendum rather than through state legislatures—a state "legislature" could consist either of a state's elected representatives *or* of the people acting through referendums (Heim 2009, 152). He hoped to invoke the latter mechanism.

A. Hines Presents Two Constitutions

An otherwise unidentified A. Hines published a book in 2009 entitled *An Informal and Unauthorized Proposition* that is perhaps most interesting for offering two updated constitutions of the United States. One version simply presents the current Constitution using updated grammar and language. The other incorporated the author's suggestions for substantive changes. Most of the initial part of the book is a review of U.S. and Western history and their moral foundations, but with expressions of fear that current rights are in jeopardy. The author is an individual of faith who observed early in the first chapter that he "holds to the same opinion as our founding fathers, that we have been given supernatural, absolute, and eternal truth in Holy Scriptures." Much of the book consists of a review of the current document and its foundations. Almost as though the author were offering a new translation of the document, chapter 5 presents "The Constitution in Modern Language" with the observation that:

> Our law is showing its age, not only in obsolete spelling, but also in grammar, words no longer in common use, as well as in many repealed and expired portions. These marks hinder comprehension and must, at the very least, be recast in modern language so that we may successfully permeate our society with it.

The result is a clearer, if otherwise fairly unremarkable, version of the current document.

Chapter 9 proceeds to present "A Christian Ideal for a Christian Nation." It contains a number of premises, however, that some Christians will likely contest. The author asserts, for example, that governmental charity should be illegal because the money used will not be spent uniformly. The author observes that the lesson of the Great Depression was that "the most carefully controlled economy is weaker than an uncontrolled economy," and that "we have learned that the cost and regulation of medical care must always and only be handled directly by the private sector."

Chapter 11 of the book presents Hines's own recommended constitution, which largely follows the existing constitutional outline while incorporating the author's suggested changes. It would significantly expand the Bill of Rights, while omitting its current numbering.

Article I, Section 3 returns to the original constitution by providing that state legislatures choose U.S. senators, thus nullifying the Seventeenth Amendment. Section 4 states that the National Treasury should only provide $1,000 a year for the salaries of members of Congress, with states deciding (as under the Articles of Confederation) what supplemental income they will provide.

Article I, Section 7 provides that bills that Congress adopts without the president's signature or over the president's veto will be sent to the U.S. Supreme Court for review. In delineating the powers of Congress, Article I, Section 8 further alters the current naturalization provision so that:

> [Congress shall have power] to determine minimal requirements for national citizenship, but each state shall determine the requirements for its own citizenship, and no one shall be a citizen of these United States who shall not be a citizen of at least one state, and in no case may United States citizenship be granted without a demonstrated knowledge in, and record of adherence to, this constitution.

Article IV included a section, later affirmed elsewhere, permitting states to withdraw from the Union. Hines, however, did not provide any specific guidelines for this process.

Article V revised the amending process to provide for a convention to enact "proper amendments to or retractions from the Constitution" on the application of three-fourths of the states. Amendments would become law when ratified by four-fifths of the states. This article also provided a sunset clause for all legislation at the end of six years.

Hines made his most extensive changes to the Bill of Rights. Hines's version began by stating that "the People or the States shall retain every right not explicitly granted by this Constitution to the National Government." His rewrite of the Second Amendment provided that "the individual and corporate right of the people to keep and wield lethal force in the protection of their person, property, family, district, or state shall not be abridged nor questioned, nor shall their right to employ them in the defense of the nation and principles thereof be infringed." Another provision provided that "the sovereignty of parents over their children, the proprietor over his business, the people over their possessions, or the individual over his own person shall never be abridged or questioned." Further proposals called for the imposition of the death penalty, reiterated the ban on the exercise of unenumerated powers, limited taxation, and specified the level of reimbursement required for certain crimes. Another provision specified that "each state shall preserve the right to refuse federal mandates by withdrawing from this Union."

Rick Sirmon Proposes a Twenty-Eighth Amendment
with a Provision for Free Enterprise Towns

In 2009, Rick Sirmon published a novel entitled *In Search of George Washington (The Story of the 28th Amendment)*. Biographical information on Sirmon is sparse, but the back cover of this work described the author as a grandfather from Alabama, and he clearly identified himself as a conservative/libertarian.

Sirmon's novel imagines a "Prairie Fire"—a political movement—that sweeps the nation in 2012 and 2013 and creates support for a constitutional convention in accordance with Article V provisions. The convention subsequently proposes a Twenty-Eighth Amendment to the Constitution to restore the economy and repair the political system. The novel imagines George Washington, James Madison, Thomas Jefferson, Benjamin Franklin, Alexander Hamilton, Patrick Henry, Roger Sherman, and other founding luminaries returning to Philadelphia, analyzing the current system, and affirming the wisdom of some of the initial Anti-Federalist critiques of the document. Hamilton is among those whom Sirmon presents as now realizing the dangers of governmental consolidation, while Patrick Henry and Thomas Jefferson are among those who are able to say "I told you so."

Sirmon repeats and explicates his proposals for change throughout the book. The most transformative is the first section of the amendment (patterned after an idea by former congressman Jack Kemp), which called for creating Free Enterprise Towns (FETs) and Social Enterprise Towns (SETs), where businesses are able to operate tax free for 25 years, except for a 5 percent Social Security tax, for which they will not qualify for benefits (Sirmon 2009, 218).

A second provision called for limiting members of the House to three terms and members of the Senate to two, and applying this limitation to those currently in office (Sirmon also proposed an 18-year limit for Supreme Court justices). It specified that members of Congress would provide for their own retirement, Social Security, and health benefits like everyone else. It further limited the length of bills and restricted them to a single issue, prevented excessive amendments, required a statement of the specific constitutional authority for each bill, and outlawed "any new open-ended mandatory spending programs" (Sirmon 2009, 220).

A third provision designed as a substitute for a balanced budget amendment would specifically limit powers of Congress to those that were enumerated, provide "a 10-year moratorium" on the creation of new governmental agencies, and a 1 percent reduction for each of the next 10 years, which Sirmon expected to save almost two trillion dollars (Sirmon 2009, 222). A fourth provision called for restoring federalism by repealing the Seventeenth Amendment, and a fifth called for reaffirming "In God We Trust" as the national motto.

Sirmon decried Supreme Court decisions relative to religion and marveled "at the miracle of a nation founded on Divine Providence" (Sirmon 2009, 18). He thus proposed changing the First Amendment to read:

Congress shall make no law establishing a government sponsored religion or prohibiting the free exercise of religion, or overturning or limiting the original traditions, heritage and history of religion as intended to be observed and passed on to posterity by the founders at America's founding the original intent of which is further found in the words of the national motto: "In God We Trust." (Sirmon 2009, 222)

Provisions six and seven called respectively for defining marriage as "the traditional union between a man and a woman" and making English the official language. The eighth would specifically repeal Obamacare, Dodd-Frank, and Sarbanes Oxley legislation. The ninth targeted the Environmental Protection Agency and the Departments of Education, Energy, Transportation, Labor, Agriculture, Commerce, and Interior for elimination. The tenth section would further prohibit earmarks and other practices associated with pork-barrel spending.

Sirmon's eleventh proposal called for expediting the path to citizenship through a guest worker program that would have special application within his Free Enterprise Towns. A twelfth proposal for tort reform would cap awards and penalize losing parties in cases found to be frivolous or malicious.

The thirteenth section eliminated "federal powers in all matters of interstate commerce and the national economy" (Sirmon 2009, 224). Twelve regional associations of states would handle such matters on their own. The fourteenth provision would prohibit any branch of the government from subordinating national sovereignty to international agreements, while the fifteenth would lift limits on the private ownership of gold and silver.

Section 16 would set four income tax rates of from 5 to 18 percent. This would be accompanied by the elimination of all deductions and credits, federal rebates to states of 25 percent of the taxes they collected, and limitations on new federal mandates or welfare payments.

The concluding sections called for a one-time audit of the Federal Reserve, changes in the system of budgeting, clarification of the Second Amendment right to bear arms that would limit licensing and permitting, and defining human life as beginning at conception. Sirmon drew his final chapter largely from Og Mandino's *The Greatest Salesman in the World* (1968), a self-help and inspirational book for salespeople.

Paul Antinori Seeks to Trim Federal Assumptions of Power

Paul Antinori (1934–) graduated from Georgetown Law School in 1959 and has been a trial lawyer in Florida for more than 50 years. He published *A Modest Proposal to Amend the U.S. Constitution* in 2010. The book reflected many of the themes behind the Tea Party movement, including concerns over adoption of a national health care plan and rising deficits. Antinori thus sought to "restore our original Constitution and thereby preserve its textual application as our Founders intended" (Antinori 2010, 3). He was particularly concerned about restoring the meaning of the Tenth Amendment and reserving nondelegated powers to the states. He described the Tenth Amendment as "not just a potted plant in the nation's living room but a critical and important part of the Bill of Rights without which the Constitution would never have been ratified" (Antinori 2010, 13).

Antinori believed that federalism was the lynchpin of the current system but that Congress had undermined state powers through use of several clauses within the Constitution that need to be clarified. Much of Antinori's book reviewed the cases through which he believed advocates of the living Constitution had undermined the original intentions of the document's framers and ratifiers. The specific clauses that most concerned him were the commerce clause, the general welfare clause, the necessary and proper clause, the supremacy clause, and the Eleventh Amendment.

Antinori proposed adding language to the commerce clause requiring that activity must "directly" affect or interfere with interstate or foreign commerce, and not that which has "only an incidental or indirect effect" (Antinori 2010, 208, underlining in original), thus reducing decisions by the Supreme Court under what is known as the dormant commerce clause. Similarly, he thought the general welfare clause needed to be modified so as to prevent "pork barrel" spending and other aid of "particular or private entities" (Antinori 2010, 209; underlining in original). He would further prohibit congressional regulation through conditional funding and would extend judicial standing to lawsuits that challenged such spending.

Antinori's concern over the necessary and proper clause stemmed in part from the Supreme Court's decision in *United States v. Comstock*, 560 U.S. 126 (2010), which upheld a law granting Congress power to continue to incarcerate individuals who had served their time for sexual offenses. He suggested rephrasing the clause to grant Congress power "to make all laws which shall be necessary and proper as essential means for directly carrying into execution the foregoing powers, but not so as to enlarge upon the powers delegated herein, nor as to infringe upon any other right or power preserved in this Constitution" (Antinori 2010, 209–10). Antinori would effectively limit the supremacy clause to direct, rather than presumed, conflicts. He further proposed adding a sentence making it impossible to abrogate or suspend "fundamental unalienable rights" through the treaty-making process (Antinori 2010, 210). In addition, Antinori proposed adding a sentence to the Eleventh Amendment providing that "any suit in law or equity commenced or prosecuted by the United States against a State shall be by original action in the Supreme Court of the United States" (Antinori 2010, 210).

Antinori favored calling a constitutional convention to bypass Congress. He thought a convention should have between 150 and 200 delegates but would leave it to Congress as to how to apportion them. States would decide how to choose delegates, who in Antinori's view should include "constitutional scholars from legal and academic backgrounds, economists, historians, industrial and small business entrepreneurs, and a cross section of citizens" (Antinori 2010, 204). He further hoped that "the Convention will be attended by all sides of the ideological spectra" (Antinori 2010, 205). In addition to the amendments that he proposed, Antinori suggested that the convention consider congressional term limits, a balanced budget amendment, and an amendment to deal with the establishment clause of the

First Amendment. Antinori included a "Sample Petition to Initiate a Constitutional Convention" (2010, 219–20) as well as a "Sample Letter to Accompany Petition" (2010, 221–3). Antinori published yet another book, *Convention: To Resurrect the U.S. Constitution*, in 2012.

The Revolutionary Communist Party Constitution

In 2010, the Revolutionary Communist Party (RCP), USA, published a draft proposal for a *Constitution for the New Socialist Republic in North America*. The document was 90 pages long and offered a fairly radical alternative to the current Constitution. On a number of occasions, the proposal mentioned party chairman Bob Avakian (1943–), who may have been the author of the document (it may also have been a collective—pun intended—product).

The RCP constitution was divided into a preamble and six articles. The preamble consisted of eight pages that described how the RCP, serving as "the vanguard of the revolutionary process," arose "to defeat, abolish and dismantle the imperialist system in the former USA" (RCP 2010, 1). It further announced the internationalist orientation of the new "multi-national and multi-lingual state" (RCP 2010, 5), the constitution of which will work in conjunction with the Constitution of the RCP Party.

Article I outlined the powers of the central government, beginning with a central legislature of 300 to 500 members chosen by an apportioned popular vote for five-year terms, unless elections are called earlier. Twenty percent of the seats would be determined through votes "cast by the organs of government at workplaces, neighborhoods, educational institutions, and other basic institutions." Another 20 percent of seats would be filled by organs of government in local areas and regions, while 30 percent of the legislators would be chosen by direct popular election in districts created by the national legislature. The remaining seats would be filled from a group of candidates nominated by the RCP (RCP 2010, 12). The executive would consist of an executive council selected by the legislature from among its members; however, the members would not continue to serve simultaneously in the legislature, which retained the power to recall or impeach them. The government was to be funded by "the initiative and work, physical and intellectual" (RCP 2010, 27) of the people.

A subsection of Article I on the economy explained that it would be organized "along socialist lines" with the power to "buy out" private corporations (RCP 2010, 18, 20). Another subsection on the environment explained the concern for the new government about this issue. A subsection on defense and security "renounces all wars of aggression and domination," announced a new "internationalist orientation," and repudiated nuclear weapons and weapons of mass destruction. Volunteers would be used for self-defense prior to the use of conscription, again with help from the RCP. The military would be based on gender equality and would minimize "saluting and 'yes-sir-ing'" (RCP 2010, 27).

Section 1 further outlined a Department of Legal Defense and Assistance, described the nation's new role in international relations, and provided that all education would be public. Where possible, "education at all levels shall combine intellectual pursuits with various kinds of physical labor" (RCP 2010, 32). It will aim for "the pursuit of the truth" (RCP 2010, 33), albeit from a "dialectical materialist understanding that all of reality consists of matter in motion, of various kinds, and nothing else" (RCP 2010, 34). Educational efforts would particularly focus on the "promotion and support of science and scientific endeavor" (RCP 2010, 35). The government would also seek "to promote the all-around health and well-being of the people" (RCP 2010, 36). The government would own the media but would apparently allow for the operation of some independent groups.

A section on culture quoted Jesus (without attribution) as observing that humans "cannot live simply by 'bread' (the basic material requirements of life) alone" (RCP 2010, 40). It proceeded to outline how the new government would promote culture, the arts, sports events, national parks, and the like. Section 3 created a judiciary headed by a Supreme Court of between 9 and 15 justices nominated by the executive council of the central government. The constitution specifically provided for trying former capitalist leaders for war crimes.

Article II outlined regions, localities, and basic institutions, the structures and selection of which would be similar to those of the central government (the section does not mention state governments). Minorities and formerly oppressed nationalities would be able to govern themselves autonomously. African Americans would be given the option of concentrating themselves in the nation's southern region and seceding, provided that two successive votes registered more than 50 percent approval for such a step (RCP 2010, 55). Mexican Americans and Native Americans would also have greater autonomy. Puerto Rico would establish its own socialist republic, and Hawai'i could do the same. The new nation would welcome immigration.

Article III dealt with the "Rights of the People and the Struggle to Uproot All Exploitation and Oppression" (RCP 2010, 63). It described civil rights and liberties in detail. It anticipated the release of many criminals from jail and projected that many would be saved from a life of crime by economic and social reform. The new constitution would specifically protect freedom of speech, the right to strike, the right to travel, and due process of law. Religious exercise would be permitted, but Article III also specified that "religion and religious practice may not be used to carry out exploitation and to accumulate private capital, in violation of the law" (RCP 2010, 70). The constitution would seek to eradicate oppression against women, guarantee the right to abortion and birth control, and overcome the "longstanding and deeply-rooted division between intellectual and physical work" (RCP 2010, 77).

Article IV described the relationship between "The Economy and Economic Development in the New Socialist Republic in North America" (RCP 2010, 78), which essentially consisted of advancing world revolution and "socialist sustainable development" (RCP 2010, 79). It would also emphasize central planning. Article IV would guarantee the right to employment and income and would be based on the principle of "from each according to her/his ability, to each according to her/his work." It would seek to minimize wage and salary disparities. Article V provided for adoption of the constitution by the "Provisional Governing Council." Article VI specified that three-fourths majorities of the legislatures would be necessary to initiate amendments, and that these proposed amendments would have to be affirmed by two-thirds or more of the voters.

Ted Aranda Calls for Replacing Representative Institutions with a True Democracy

Ted Aranda, a former community organizer who earned a PhD from the University of Illinois at Chicago, is the author of *The Racket and the Answer: The Representative System and the Democratic Alternative* (2010). Explaining his title in a short preface, Aranda indicated that "the American system of government is a racket"; indeed, the same could be said of "all nations with a presidential or a parliamentary political system" (Aranda 2010, 2). According to Aranda, such systems were better than the systems of hereditary monarchy that often preceded them, but they failed to measure up to the direct democracy of ancient Athens. Aranda proceeded with a 40-page discussion of ancient Athenian democracy, followed by a 150-page discussion of English history. He then turned his attention to American Populists and Progressives, paying particular attention to single-tax proponent Henry George (1839–1897), novelist Edward Bellamy (1850–1898), muckraking icon Henry Demarest Lloyd (1847–1903), Ohio political reformer Frederic C. Howe (1867–1940), and William U'Ren (1859–1949), an Oregonian who devised the "Oregon System" with its commitment to the initiative and referendum and other democratic reforms, including that of "occupational representation" (Aranda 2010, 239–40).

Aranda argued that the only times that representative governments are free are on election days. As he explained, "democracy is the exercise by the people of their own power; representation is the alienation of this power" (Aranda 2010, 243). Aranda observed that only a minority of states adopted Populist and Progressive reforms, the initiative and referendum were never adopted at the national level, and "even where they were established, the haphazardly operating initiative and referendum did not supplant the extant, full-time representative institutions" (2010, 244). Asserting that it was impossible "to separate democracy from community," he wrote that "we can no longer afford to rejoice in the wonders of our 'free' governments, wherein—glory of glories!—we get to elect our masters and send them supplicating emails. There is nothing wondrous or glorious about the representative system in the twenty-first century" (Aranda 2010, 245, 248).

Aranda favored replacing the Constitution in order to fix the U.S. system. He proposed his own plan in the page-and-a-half Appendix A, which described how he would replace all three branches of the current government at local, state, and national levels. Under his plan, all adult citizens would constitute the legislature. They would gather "in Primary Assemblies at the community level twice per month at scheduled meetings and at other times if necessary" (Aranda 2010, 249). They would discuss issues established by various councils and make decisions by

majority vote. Aranda did not indicate how many of these assemblies he anticipated or how large they would be.

A "Council of Five Hundred" would replace the current executive branch. As
befits a true democracy, its members would be selected "annually and randomly
from among all citizens in the polity at the given level" (Aranda 2010, 249). A
"Committee of Fifty," selected randomly from council members, would in turn
organize its proceedings. It would, in turn, be chaired by a "Board of Five," whose
chief would also be selected randomly, albeit subject to the approval of the other
four board members.

Each council would have up to five functions: discussing issues, deciding agenda,
and calling additional meetings; presiding over meetings; executing decisions and
policies with the assistance of the bureaucracy; serving through the Board of Five
at the national level as the head of state; and running the court system. The court
system would, in turn, consist of "201-member to 501-member juries of randomly
selected citizens hearing and deciding criminal and civil cases, with the assistance
of legal professionals as necessary" (Aranda 2010, 250).

Robert R. Owens Resurrects Anti-Federalist Concerns and Calls for a Second Constitutional Convention

In 2010, Dr. Robert R. Owens published a book entitled *The Constitution Failed*.
Owens, who was a one-time entrepreneur and pastor, is affiliated with the Richmond (Virginia) Tea Party and teaches at Southside Virginia Community College.
The Constitution Failed is organized as a series of 52 numbered "dispatches," or
articles, and three final chapters.

Owens expressed particular concern about the rising power of the national government and attempts to bypass existing checks and balances. He believed that
taxes had become oppressive, regulations were strangling competition, foreign entanglements had become too numerous, government spending was out of control,
and leaders were dividing rather than uniting the nation. He cited the passage of the
Alien and Sedition laws, the purchase of the Louisiana Territory, and the presiden-
tially formulated and issued Monroe Doctrine as early examples of a government
that exercised powers that Federalists had denied that it would. He further thought
that Lincoln aggravated the situation by interpreting the Constitution to forbid the
right of secession. He directed some of his strongest ire against current Democrats,
including House Speaker Nancy Pelosi and President Barack Obama.

Owens offered a detailed critique of constitutional development and indicated
that he thought the amending process was the only legitimate way to bring about
constitutional change. Owens portrayed his central object as that of restoring the
original Constitution, but he also seemed to agree with those who believed that
Federalists originally joined in a kind of conspiracy to increase the powers of the
national government. Still, he expressed a strong sense of nostalgia:

Our nation has inexorably grown from the vision of Jefferson for a commonwealth of freemen into what is rapidly being revealed as a statist express

highballing on its way to the gulag of collectivist uniformity and shabby mediocrity. Gone is the meritocracy of the young Republic. Gone is the equality of opportunity smothered in the cold dead grasp of the equality of outcome. Gone is the blind justice of a nation of laws devoured by the politically correct insanity of social justice. (Owens 2010, 221)

Owens concluded that "it is time to think the unthinkable and to embrace the abhorrent conclusion that the Constitution has failed" (2010, 222). He supported this assertion by pointing to the Tenth Amendment, which he felt had failed to limit governmental power. Concluding that it was time to call a second constitutional convention, he provided only broad outlines of its agenda:

> In a Second Constitutional Convention we could advocate for either a return to the document as written and amended with the inclusion of even stricter controls upon the power of the Federal Government. We could even offer the proposal that we return to the Confederation concept and reconstitute our nation as it was originally born: a league of independent States held together by mutual heritage and self-interest. (Owens 2010, 230)

In his judgment, "we have got to either change the game or change the rules, because this deck has been stacked and the fix is in" (Owens 2010, 230).

John Médaille Calls for a More Distributist and Monarchical Constitution

In 2010, John Médaille, a businessman, author, and adjunct instructor of theology at the University of Dallas, wrote a series of three articles in *The Distributist Review*, a journal published by the (G. K.) Chesterton Society that is devoted to the promotion of Catholic social thought, favoring monarchy and outlining other changes that he favored in the U.S. Constitution.

In his first article, "Why I Am a Monarchist," Médaille likened democracy to a religion, with its sacrament being the voting booth, its liturgy the election campaign, and its dogma "that the election will represent the will of the people." Convinced that society was an organic unity of past, present, and future, he argued that elections gave inadequate attention to the sacrifices and wishes of past generations. He also charged that political campaigns, and the excessive money they required, turned the political arts from "deliberation and persuasion" to "manipulation and propaganda." Instead of furthering democracy, the result has been to support oligarchy.

In a second article, entitled "A Real Catholic Monarchy," Médaille distinguished the monarchy that he advocated from what he called "regalism." The former was limited, whereas the second, like some forms of democracy, attempted to dominate the whole of society without due regard for the principles of subsidiary and solidarity. The principle of subsidiary, wrote Médaille, "states that the higher levels of government exist only to serve the lowest," while solidarity evaluates all actions of government with respect to how they affect the poorest citizens. A monarch thus needed to have real authority, and his or her own source of revenue, without dominating the entire society. Such a monarch would be balanced in part with an aristocracy, one not chosen by birth or wealth but rather with some attention to virtue.

In his third article, entitled "Monarchy and the American Constitution," Médaille outlined a number of constitutional changes that he thought would achieve his objectives. Despite the article's title, it was as much about making the nation more aristocratic as it was about making it more monarchical. Arguing that the adoption of both the Sixteenth (income tax) and Seventeenth (direct election of senators) amendments had been mistakes, Médaille suggested that the House of Representatives should be a sufficient institution to adopt laws. He believed that the way to increase the authority of the Senate was to decrease its actual power. He proposed vesting this body with nine powers: auditing; appointing inspector generals; investigating crimes by members of Congress or the king's ministers; possessing exclusive subpoena powers; ascertaining judicial qualifications and exercising impeachment powers; authorization to vacate orders by the U.S. Supreme Court; controlling monetary policy; exercising supermajority veto power over acts of Congress; and investigating and reporting on long-term problems. He likened the role that he envisioned for the Senate to that of "the National Nanny." Médaille further proposed that governors would select members of the Senate and that their minimum ages should be raised to 40 or 45 (he did not indicate whether their current terms should be changed).

Médaille thought the best way to tame the influence of money on congressional campaigns was to double or triple the number of members of the House of Representatives. Alternatively, one might use a system of indirect election whereby groups of from 5 to 10,000 people "would then meet in an assembly to choose the congressman for their district."

Médaille's proposed monarchy was somewhat less radical that the name might suggest, largely because he believed that "we already have an imperial presidency." Médaille thus proposed first to devolve most authority back to the states (the principle of subsidiary). If it were more efficient for the national government to collect revenues, "[they] should speedily be disbursed back to the states, with only such funds remaining with the federal government which are absolutely necessary for its essential operations." Médaille further proposed doubling the presidential term. He did not offer specific proposals for changing presidential elections.

Médaille ended his essay by suggesting that:

> I am a monarchist because I am a democrat (small 'd'"): that is, I believe governance is by consent of the governed. But this consent cannot be reduced to the fashionable passions of the moment; rather it must respect both the past and the future, and this respect is best expressed in proper aristocratic and monarchical institutions.

He further argued that the United States has a "more stable Constitution" than that of Great Britain because Americans do not recognize parliamentary supremacy.

James Schmitendorf Proposes Regular Conventions and Modifications to the Existing Constitution

James Schmitendorf (1933–) has described himself as a retired pilot and engineer who taught engineering at a small university in the Midwest for 15 years. He appears to have been the guiding force between Abe's Indignation League, a bipartisan organization named after Abraham Lincoln that favors a new constitutional convention. Schmitendorf also appears to have been central in the crafting of a online petition posted by the organization in 1999. This petition asserted rights under Article V and the First Amendment to request states to call a constitutional convention. In 2011 Schmitendorf published a book entitled *Lex Ferenda* (meaning "what the law should be") to again press for a new constitutional convention. The back cover of the book has a color photo of the author standing beside a statue of James Madison in Rapid City, South Dakota.

Largely drawing from this author's first book on the subject (Vile 1991), Schmitendorf reviewed previous proposals for rewriting the Constitution. He then presented an up-to-date version of the Constitution that clarified existing language, modernized spellings, and incorporated existing amendments within the text (Schmitendorf 2011, 31–68). He followed with a review of six changes that he thought were generally accepted among constitutional critics and added an additional suggestion for promoting governmental ethics.

Schmitendorf's first proposal called for lengthening terms of the members of the House of Representatives to four years and placing elections midway between presidential elections. His second called for limiting consecutive years of congressional service to 12 years. A third proposal would require the president to concur with another top official, perhaps the secretary of defense, before responding to an attack with nuclear force. Schmitendorf's fourth proposal, aimed at achieving campaign finance reform, called for banning political action committees (PACs) and prohibiting all television campaign advertising except for debates. His fifth proposal would set a retirement age for each judge "at least one year prior to the statistical longevity age for his or her gender" (Schmitendorf 2011, 77). A sixth proposal for a balanced budget amendment would limit congressional spending to "90 percent of the estimated revenues" while the seventh proposal, aimed at presidential ethics, required the presidential oath to include a pledge "to set an example of honesty, ethics and morality for our citizens" (Schmitendorf 2011, 77).

Schmitendorf followed with two more proposals designed to address what he perceived as the excessive size of American businesses and labor groups. The first would add a provision limiting the size of the workforce or membership of any corporation or union to "10% of the smallest States' population" (Schmitendorf 2011, 104–5). A second would limit the assets of "corporations of mining, manufacturing and commercial banking" to "no greater than one percent of the average last five years of positive real GDP," and the assets of other corporations to half of that.

Schmitendorf then analyzed 20 additional areas in which elites had called for constitutional reform, most of which he thought were appropriate subjects for a constitutional convention. Schmitendorf believed that conventions should review the Constitution at least once every 50 years. He envisioned staffing such conventions by lottery from native-born citizens ages 40 to 75 who were also physically fit, college educated, had IQs over 120, and had built a career as an "Academic, Scientist or Engineer, Business Manager, Entrepreneur or Self-Employed, [or a] State or Local Politician" (Schmitendorf 2011, 119). He further provided that convention delegates would be sequestered for three months, study basic founding documents, and then present their proposed revisions to a majority vote, which, if approved, would be confirmed by three-fourths of the state legislatures. Alternatively, he suggested that one might "assign the project to the military and see what they come up with" (Schmitendorf 2011, 119).

Daryl Lloyd Davis Seeks to Establish Direct Democracy and Abolish Congress

Daryl Lloyd Davis, who did not otherwise identify himself, published a book in 2011 entitled *New American Democracy: A Direct Democracy Alternative*. Davis observed that the nation had changed significantly since the time of the Founding Fathers and that "limitations on swift travel and communications that then *necessitated* a government-by-proxy approach to law-making no longer impede our high-tech society." Davis accordingly sought a government in which, according to Article I, Section 2, of his proposed constitutional model, "all non-regulatory, legislative powers herein granted shall be vested in the People, whose will shall be represented by electoral initiative within the voting precincts of each State."

Under Davis's system, candidates and issues would qualify for a place on the ballot with the signatures of no more than 5 percent of registered voters. Once the document was ratified, the power of all members of Congress, of city councils, and equivalent bodies would be revoked. Periodically, the voters would participate in referendums to elect candidates and decide on proposed legislation. Article I, Section 6 specified that "boundaries between voting precincts shall be redrawn or withdrawn only with the consenting signatures of all adults whose residency shall have changed."

A revised Article II specified that the president, vice president, and attorney general would be elected by plurality vote to two-year terms. The president would retain powers as commander in chief but declarations of war and peacetime commitments of troops would require the consent of two-thirds of the state governors and the unanimous consent of a number of specified cabinet officers. Section 3 further required the consent of two-thirds of the governors to ratify treaties and three-fifths of them to confirm presidential appointments of judges and ambassadors.

Article III of Davis's constitution was much like that of the current document except that in his version, the Supreme Court would possess the power to impeach and try the president. A conviction would require the consent of six of the nine justices.

Davis expanded the full faith and credit clause in Article IV to include "those public records designating the identification, property, debt, divorce, child custody, and criminal history of a person, and to those licenses and contracts without which interprecinct, interstate, or international commerce, transportation or communication would be substantially hindered or barred." The admission of new states would require a two-thirds aggregate vote of those within 95 percent of U.S. precincts. Without a Congress, "the President, with a unanimous vote of the Cabinet and a two-thirds vote among the Governors of the States, shall have the power to make rules and regulations respecting the territory of other non-military property belonging to the United States."

Article V provided for amendment by two-thirds vote of those in 95 percent or more of the precincts. Article VI appeared to call for renegotiation of existing federal debts. Article VII further provided for ratification of the constitution by 67 percent of the voters.

The most expanded portion of Davis's document was a proposed Bill of Rights that set explicit limits on Congress's power to infringe on civil liberties. The proposed Fourth Amendment asserted that "no citizen shall be deprived of life, liberty, privacy or property without a reasonable, impartial application of the law." A revised Fifth Amendment proposed special penalties for adults who harmed minors. A revised Tenth Amendment would limit the right of voters to accrue debts to be paid by future generations. It further listed governmental sources of revenue, including a variety of user fees and annually authorized income deductions to which voters would have to agree.

The proposed Eleventh Amendment vested "the exercise of oversight, investigative and regulatory power formerly delegated to the United States Congress" in the attorney general and his appointees. It further outlined duties for the postmaster general and the secretaries at the helms of the Treasury, Commerce, Homeland Security, State, and Defense departments.

The proposed Twelfth Amendment guaranteed adults the right to enter into contracts, while the Thirteenth allowed workers to form unions. Businesses that failed to earn a profit would be forbidden to give bonuses or raises to top executives "without the express, contemporaneous assent of all its owners." Businesses with governmental licenses would be limited to paying no more than twenty times the minimum wage to any employees.

The proposed Fourteenth Amendment would further limit citizenship to immigrants who learned English. No one would be allowed to pass the sixth grade without passing a citizenship test. Finally, the proposed Fifteenth Amendment would permit adults to use intoxicants but heightened the penalty for crimes involving them and provided that the use of such intoxicants by parents could result in the loss of child custody.

John F. Naglee, Sr., Writes a Constitution That Restrains Activist Judges and Eases the Amending Process

John F. Naglee, Sr., who retired from the Bell System and previously wrote on climate change, published *Our New Constitution: Conceived by Citizens Determined to Restore Their Nation* in 2011. It offered a new constitutional text containing a variety of proposals, many designed to facilitate constitutional change and to combat an activist judiciary.

Naglee proposed electing members of the House of Representatives (each representing 50,000 or fewer voters) every four years. They would be paid by the state and reside in the districts they represent. Each group of 10 would elect one to go to the federal House, but most business would be conducted electronically. He would restore state legislative selection of senators. A majority plus one member of each house would be able to override presidential vetoes. Borrowing would be limited to 1 percent of the federal budget and would have to be paid back within 10 years. Congress would have the "sole" power to declare war and deploy troops. It would only be able to enact income taxes in "account-in-trust," as in the Social Security system. Rights were incorporated into the text of the Constitution, with some existing ones modified. Members of Congress would be responsible for libels committed during their service.

Naglee would replace the Electoral College with a scheme in which the most populous state would vote first and the rest would be awarded the same number of votes, which would be split proportionally among the candidates. The minimum age for public office would be raised to 45, and the salary would be on a par with that of other CEOs. State governors would be named in the line of secession behind the president and vice president, and the words "so help me God" would be added to the presidential oath. According to Naglee, "if the candidate doesn't want to swear before God, they do not need the job" (Naglee 2011, 57). Justices and judges would be confirmed by state governors, two-thirds of whom would be required to transfer territory from states to the national government. Naglee favored establishing restitution as punishment for nonviolent crimes.

Every 20 years, Congress would forward no more than two amendments for consideration by a Convention, whose work would require confirmation by two-thirds of the states. The United States would invalidate debts to any foreign sponsors of terrorism. The new constitution, which he envisioned emerging from a convention called by three-fourths of the states, would go into effect two years after being ratified by the same majority. Naglee also included a new Declaration of Independence and a copy of the Constitution of the Confederate States of America in his book.

C. Earl Campbell Favors Expanding Social and Economic Rights and Legalizing Marijuana

In 2011 C. (Charles) Earl Campbell published an e-book entitled *The Revised Amended Constitution for the United States of America for the 21st Century*, which is available for sale online. Campbell earned a bachelor's degree in social work from Jackson State University and a master's in social work administration from Ohio State University. He has described himself as "an author, poet, inventor, entrepreneur, innovator and humanitarian" who is "dedicated to the uplift and empowerment of all human and universal beings."

The title page of Campbell's book of proposed constitutional reforms highlighted such features as "D.C. Voting Rights," "Ex-Felons' Voting Rights," and "Universal Bill of Human Rights." His proposed constitution followed the outline of the current document and did not, apart from some of the issues identified on the title page, distinguish the original from the new. The preamble added insuring health care, housing, and "the common equitable education of all" to the goals of the document.

Article I of Campbell's revised constitution lowered the minimum age for members of the House of Representatives to 18 and of Senators to 21. The general welfare clause in Article I, Section 8 also granted Congress power to "provide for the common Education, Health Care, Defense and general Housing and Welfare of the Citizens of the United States." The section further amended the copyright clause to promote the progress not simply of science but also of "Math, History, Music and Arts." He also included a provision referencing letters of marque and reprisal, which were papers described in the original Constitution that authorized individuals to attack foreign shipping. Campbell's particular reference was used to justify a power "[t]o declare Moral and Just Peace." Section 9 expanded provision for the writ of habeas corpus even in cases of rebellion or invasion.

Article II incorporated the provision in the Thirteenth Amendment forbidding slavery. It specifically designated the president as commander not only of the army and navy but also of the "Air, Peace, [and] Space Force." The impeachment provision extended to murder and genocide and substituted the word "felonies" for "misdemeanors." Although Article III appeared substantively unchanged, Article IV again repeated the prohibition on slavery. It also provided that the national government would guarantee "a Democracy [rather than Republican] Form of Government" to the states.

Article V authorized the people "with a majority vote in each state" to require Congress to propose constitutional revisions and amendments (these would be ratified under the same guidelines provided for in the current U.S. Constitution). This section also included provisions relative to the Electoral College. Article VI appears unchanged, while Article VII required ratification by 39 states.

Campbell referred to the amendments he proposed as a "Universal Bill of Rights." Under his Second Amendment, the right to bear arms was limited to the possession of "non-lethal ammunition." The Third Amendment guaranteed health, medical, housing, education and job training to veterans regardless of their ability to pay. The Fourth Amendment specifically covered electronic communication and provided for the restoration of search sites to their original condition and the return of seized materials that are not illegal within 30 days.

The Fifth Amendment further prevented detentions of more than 24 hours and questioning for more than two consecutive hours. It also provided that a jury of one's peers should consist "of fifty percent of the same race, gender and geographic location of the accused," and cited the due process clause to prevent deprivation of food, water, sleep, income, and family responsibilities. The takings clause would require "compensation at fair current and future market value." The

Sixth Amendment further defined a speedy trial as one that takes place within thirty days of indictment. The Eighth Amendment attempted to define cruel and unusual punishments with similar specificity.

The revised Fourteenth Amendment would protect voting rights of anyone over 18 or to anyone 16 or older who was "employed and paying taxes." Provisions for voting in the Fifteenth Amendment further prohibited denials on the basis of "race, species, gender, color, criminal incarceration or criminal history or income," while his revamped Nineteenth Amendment (originally passed to give women the vote) guaranteed voting rights regardless of "sex, gender, sexual orientation, race, or species." The revised Sixteenth Amendment specified that government funds would be used for investments in education, health care, job training, renewable energy, senior services, human development, transportation, and space research. A replacement for the Eighteenth Amendment would allow for "the growth, manufacture, sale, or transportation of marijuana as a legal agriculture crop." Other amendments in Campbell's constitution remained largely the same as under the current document.

Uldis Sprogis Proposes a New Constitution That Eliminates States and Preserves Biodiversity

In 2011, Uldis Sprogis, who identified himself as having a master's degree in science, published an e-book entitled *New Constitution of the United States*. In this work, Sprogis proposed a new constitution for the United States. He summarized 16 key points of his plan and then printed two copies of his proposed constitution—one without commas and a second version in which they were included. Sprogis's constitution also included an amended and abbreviated edition of the Declaration of Independence for the United States and the World.

The constitution proposed by Sprogis consisted of nine articles, 24 amendments, and a prologue, which, fairly curiously, comes at the end of the document. Article I delineated a unicameral Congress consisting only of a house of representatives. House members were to be chosen every 10 years from individuals who were at least 18 years old and had been citizens for five years or more. Congress's borrowing authority would be capped at 10 percent of the gross national product (GNP), and such funds could only be used to build rail systems between cities of two million people or more. Its authority to declare war would be limited to wars of self-defense. Congress would have no power to provide money for the teaching of liberal arts, which would instead be the responsibility of "private institutions of learning with private funds." Congress would institute a national sales tax "to pay for all the unemployed and destitute citizens and discourage the consumption of goods and services." Sprogis altered the wording of the necessary and proper clause by omitting the term proper, but he did not say whether the omission was intentional or not.

Articles II and III dealt respectively with the executive and the judicial branches. Like members of the House, the president and vice president would serve ten-year terms. Presidential nominations would be subject to the advice and consent of the house. The judiciary would remain largely as it is, with the provision for treason providing punishment by exile to the nation for whom the treason was done.

Section IV provided for the addition of new countries "through purchase or voluntary political union." Section V indicated that two-thirds majorities of the house could propose amendments but did not specify how they would be ratified. Section VI included a supremacy clause, and Section VII dealt with ratification. Sprogis was not particularly hopeful about the adoption of his system. Recognizing that the ratification of a new document would be "in the hands of the seriously handicapped legal authority of the United States," he suggested that it could be adopted either in whole or in part. Section VIII provided for conserving wilderness by allowing the government to buy land "at fair market value." Section IX spelled out "a secular moral code," the chief tenet of which was to preserve biodiversity. Other guidelines provided: "don't lie and don't be inefficient and don't steal and don't commit adultery if married and don't murder."

The 24 amendments featured in the Sprogis book were a blend of old and new. A revised First Amendment provided for separation of church and state but tasked religious institutions with providing medical insurance and retirement benefits for employees. Sprogis would limit the right to bear arms to "working citizens without criminal records." The revised Fourth Amendment provided for constant eavesdropping of "convicted repeat felons." The minimum financial amount for civil lawsuit claims would be raised from $20 to $20,000 in Sprogis's revamped Seventh Amendment. A revised Eighth Amendment would eliminate the death penalty. The Thirteenth Amendment continued to prohibit discrimination on the basis of race. Sprogis's Fourteenth Amendment no longer included the equal protection clause but described taxation for monopolies and polluting industries. The Fifteenth Amendment continued the antidiscrimination provision of the current Nineteenth Amendment.

The proposed twenty-first amendment asserted that "every citizen should have the right to pursue a job which is based on merit." It further provided for water, food, basic clothing, shelter, medical care, computer access and "basic toiletries"—but no money—for individuals who were unemployed and destitute. The twenty-second amendment reiterated that "the most important moral code which will be practiced is don't destroy biodiversity but conserve and expand it," and a twenty-fourth amendment provided for the rights of individuals who had been arrested and/or were in custody. The twenty-third amendment reworded the introductory paragraphs of the Declaration of Independence. It began by observing that "we hold these truths to be obvious that all humans are created different that they are endowed by their genetic inheritance with certain unalienable rights that among these are life and the pursuit of a job which is rewarded based on merit and a right to be helped with free basic needs."

Sprogis favored abolishing all state governments. He observed that "the major problem with the government of the United States today is that it is too large and the state governments are almost all alike and doing a lot of paperwork and making government very inefficient." Sprogis thought the nation could save money by cutting the size of the House to about 300 members. He also hoped that his plan would encourage people to move to big cities, which he thought were more efficient.

Constitutional Commentary Sponsors a Symposium on Rewriting the Constitution

In 2011, the University of Minnesota law journal *Constitutional Commentary* devoted an issue to what it described as "The United States Constitution (Rev. Ed.)." It then printed responses to the question "How would you rewrite the United States Constitution?" by leading professors. Although lacking the unity of proposals offered by a single individual or organization, the issue highlighted areas of modern constitutional concern.

Although he did not offer the text of a specific amendment, Professor Michael C. Dorf of Cornell said a basic issue involved determining what new groups should be included or denied representation within the polity. He suggested that "non-citizens outside the United States; future generations of citizens; and non-human animals" should be considered, even suggesting at one point modifying the supremacy clause so that it would incorporate international law (Dorf 2011, 500). He also suggested restricting the rights of corporations and making the constitution easier to amend so as to decrease the influence of dead generations on current constitutional structures.

Allison L. LaCroix of the University of Chicago proposed an amendment that would more explicitly link judicial powers in Article III with the Supremacy Clause in Article VI. Specifically, she wanted to clarify the right of federal courts to have appellate jurisdiction over constitutional issues adjudicated in the states. University of Texas law professor Sanford Levinson largely repeated proposals he had made elsewhere (Levinson 2006). He favored eliminating life-tenure for Supreme Court justices and substituting a system of 18-year terms; abolishing equal representation in the U.S. Senate; organizing the Senate so that its members transcended state boundaries and so they would take a wider view of national interests (he suggested a system of proportional representation by party to facilitate this); exploring the benefits of a parliamentary system and, at a minimum, providing for a vote of no confidence in the president; moving inaugurations closer to elections; eliminating or at least reducing the possibility of deadlocks in the electoral college; eliminating the office of the vice president, or moving the vice president's selection until after the president's election; adding a provision to provide for emergency powers; and making the amending process easier.

Jenny S. Martinez of Stanford University favored an amendment that specified that "when acting outside the sovereign territory of the United States, the U.S. government, its officials, employees, and agents shall not deprive any person of life, liberty, or property without due process of law. The federal courts shall have jurisdiction to enforce this provision" (Martinez 2011, 527). Michael Stokes Paulsen of the University of St. Thomas used irony to suggest that the current Constitution was "perfect," then proposed 20 amendments that would update the

Constitution in accord with current judicial interpretations. His proposed amendments would, for example, repeal the Tenth Amendment, describe "the doctrine of stare decisis [adherence to precedents] as fundamental to the rule of law . . . except when it [the Supreme Court] decides not to do so" (Paulsen 2011, 536). He further proposed specifying that people had the right "to kill living human embryos or fetuses," to use racial qualifications in university admissions, to infringe on freedom of religion through neutral-sounding laws, to "portray sexual sadism involving the killing of animals," and to recognize the right of men "to engage in anal sex with one another" as "a transcendent dimension of liberty" that "shall not be infringed" (2011, 539–40).

In separate articles, Girardeau A. Spann of Georgetown and Mark Tushnet of Harvard both argued for the abolition of judicial review of Congressional legislation. Spann portrayed such reviews as simple exercises of political power dressed in the hypocritical guise of natural law. Tushnet, meanwhile, said that he did not intend for his amendment—"The constitutionality of acts of Congress shall not be reviewed by any court in the United States" (Tushnet 2011, 581)—to preclude judicial review of executive actions; prevent Congress from enacting the Constitution as statutory law, which federal courts would review; or limit judicial review of state or municipal laws.

Tom Hopper Proposes to Fix Government, Starting with Congress

In 2011, Tom Hopper, a World War II veteran and retiree from the field of information technology, published the third edition of his book *USGOV.FIX: Fixes for a Failing Government* to address what he believed to be serious flaws in the U.S. economy and government. He believed that Congress had essentially defaulted to the executive branch of government, to the detriment of the American people. Although he questioned bicameralism, he was more concerned with excessive legislative fragmentation, the influence of lobbyists, and seniority rules. He charged that the executive branch had become "pseudo-monarchical" (Hopper 2011, 34) and the judiciary had connived with lawyers to obscure the law. Instead of providing leaders, the political system had corrupted the governmental system, as was evident in the public's excessive "hysteria over taxes" (Hopper 2011, 40). Hopper argued that these trends have taken a toll on America's economic health.

Hopper urged citizens to mobilize in order to fix the situation. He believed that a flat tax could bring in substantial new revenue and that currency reform was also needed. Most of all, he thought it was essential to create a new national database that could handle both private and public issues, including the census. Other reforms included rewriting legislative procedures, adopting legislative term limits, establishing "financial responsibility," developing "a more precise legal language," eliminating lobbyists, and staggering national elections for the legislative and executive branches so as to minimize their disruptive impact on society and business (Hopper 2011, 80–1).

Hopper wanted presidents to win elections by acquiring a majority of congressional districts rather than by focusing on Electoral College votes from a few key states. He also wanted to limit the president to a single seven-year term and make the salary more attractive. In addressing the judiciary, he recommended "replacing 'legalese' with Boolean logic, which would provide a high level of precision" (Hopper 2011, 87). Hopper favored adopting an amendment prohibiting politicians from pledging not to raise taxes. He thought the prospects for such change would be enhanced by a bipartisan movement, which he hoped to generate with a Web site named after his book.

Lawrence Lessig Proposes a Convention to End the Corrupting Influence of Money in Politics

Harvard law professor Lawrence Lessig authored a book in 2011 entitled *Republic, Lost: How Money Corrupts Congress—And a Plan to Stop It*. Lessig argued that campaign contributions corrupt the judgment of American politicians, and he asserted that the best way to address this issue was to create a system of public financing for political campaigns. He supported what he called "The Grant and Franklin Project" (Lessig 2011, 265), under which each taxpayer could convert the first 50 dollars of taxes into a voucher for whatever candidate or candidates he/she chose. If the voter made no such choice, the money would go to the political party in which the voter was registered. Voters could further add up to $100 per candidate. No candidates would receive any funds unless they agreed to use such taxpayer funds exclusively.

Lessig discussed three different ways to initiate such a reform. One was for private citizens to challenge incumbents in primaries. Since the Constitution does not specify that a member of Congress has to be from a particular district, he believed that such challengers might run in several elections at once. Another possibility was for a presidential candidate to run for office on a reform platform and agree immediately to step down once it was adopted—an appendix to Lessig's book refers to this individual as a "regent president" (Lessig 2011, 323). Lessig believed that it would be difficult for Congress to resist the platform of a candidate with such an electoral mandate.

Lessig, however, devoted the greatest attention to the constitutional convention option. He believed that such a convention could be organized from the grass-roots up and that Congress would have adequate authority under the necessary and proper clause to set appropriate rules. Lessig commended legislation that Senator Orrin Hatch of Utah introduced to govern a constitutional convention. Lessig further argued that states had the right to call for a limited convention. He also stated that the dangers of a "runaway convention" had been exaggerated, noting the constitutional requirement that three-fourths of the states ratify a convention's proposals.

Lessig believed that such a movement might begin "beneath the radar at first." While the American people were "ignorant" about a number of political matters, he did not believe they were "stupid"; they were capable of proceeding with "the right incentives, and the right opportunity" (2011, 300–2). Lessig was particularly hopeful about the possibility of establishing "shadow conventions" at the state

level and implementing "deliberative polls," where individuals were provided sufficient information to enable them to form reasonable decisions.

Whereas most previous proponents of conventions have thought of them as representatives of state interests, Lessig stressed that the constitutional convention he
proposed would be different: "It should not be a convention of experts. Or politicians. Or activists. Or anyone else specific. It should be a convention of randomly
selected voters called to a process of informed deliberation, who would concur
on proposals that would be carried to the states" (Lessig 2011, 303). He further
proposed that:

> The Convention would convene in a remote place, far from Washington, and
> maybe far from the Internet. And delegates would then be charged with the
> duty the law had placed upon them: to propose amendments to the Constitu-
> tion. (Lessig 2011, 303)

On September 24 and 25, 2011, Harvard University sponsored a conference
designed to highlight Lessig's book and discuss the constitutional convention option (Rice 2011). The convention mustered proponents of conventions from both
the right and the left of the political spectrum. Numerous scholars discussed this
mechanism, but they do not appear to have reached a clear consensus.

Lessig argued in an appendix to the paperback edition of his book that the central problem with the American constitutional system was that the Founders had
failed to anticipate political parties: "Like molasses poured into the gearbox of a
sports car, political parties have jammed the functioning of the machine our framers designed." Instead of the legislative and executive branches checking one another, parties try to secure control of both branches and thus fail to hold either to
account (Lessig 2011, 322). Lessig suggested that the "regent president," rather
than a second convention, might hold the key to effective reform.

John B. Miller and Four Anonymous Writers Propose Amendments That Express Tea Party Concerns

John B. Miller is an engineering professor at the Massachusetts Institute of Technology who specializes in soil mechanics. In 2012 he edited a series of 50 essays
under the title *The Second Bill of Rights & the New Federalist Papers*, in which
he and four other individuals writing under the names of Amicus, Atticus, Pros-
perus, and Valerius described and defended a series of 11 proposed constitutional
amendments (Amendments 28 through 39) designed as a second Bill of Rights.
Their amendments were sympathetic to concerns about federal taxes and spending
expressed by the modern Tea Party movement. Miller and his colleagues likened
the U.S. Constitution to a mighty ship that had acquired unsightly barnacles from
factions over the years. They called for scrubbing off these barnacles with a re-
commitment to founding principles. Many of the essays quoted *The Federalist*
to demonstrate the original commitment of the Constitution to civil liberties and
to a more balanced concept of federalism that allowed the people themselves and

the states to make many decisions that the national government has subsequently sought to control.

Miller identified the first four amendments as "The Liberty Rights Amendments." The first amendment had two sections. Section one indicated that "The Rule of Law" allocates power "among the people, the states, and the national government," allowing broad liberty rights to remain with the latter. Section two indicated that the Preamble to the Constitution and the general welfare clause in Article I, Section 8 were not designed to vest the national government with additional powers, and it instructed the judiciary to interpret the Constitution according to "the publicly known meaning of the words . . . at the time such words were adopted" (Miller 2012, 1).

The proposed second amendment had four sections. The first called for repealing Section 1 of the Fourteenth Amendment, for Miller did not believe that its authors intended to confer citizenship rights on individuals born in the United States to noncitizen parents. Section 2 sought to reserve all "privileges and immunities" to the people. Section 3 explained that these "include, but are not limited to" a variety of rights, some of which are already listed in other amendments. Miller's list was especially notable for its list of economic rights. These rights included:

> the rights to life, liberty, and pursuit of happiness; to property in one's own labor and industry; to preserve and secure personal health and safety; to keep and bear arms; to acquire, inherit, purchase, lease, sell, hold, convey, and enjoy real and personal property; to religious liberty; to freedom in matters of conscience; to freedom in making and enforcing lawful contracts of all kinds (including freedom not to contract); to establish a family, to care for and to raise children, and to secure the health, education, and safety thereof; to freedom of press, speech, assemblage, and petition; to pursue any lawful livelihood or avocation; to engage in a profession, trade, business, or calling; and to privacy in one's person, effects, papers, preferences, and affairs. (Miller 2012, 2)

Section 4 further extended the presumption of validity to the exercises of such rights and specifically limited exercises of congressional powers under the necessary and proper clause to cases where such power "(i) is plainly necessary in the exercise of an enumerated power; (ii) could not achieve the purpose of an enumerated power by other means not so restrictive of liberty rights; and (iii) is consistent with the Rule of Law" (Miller 2012, 2).

Miller's third amendment would extend due process and equal protection provisions to both state and national governments and prohibit discrimination "on the basis of race, color, national origin, or gender, or on the basis of belief or non-belief in any creed or religion" (Miller 2012, 2). His fourth amendment reinforced the Tenth Amendment by reserving powers to the states "to promote the health, good order, morals, peace, and safety of citizens residing therein through laws of general application that preserve the common exercise of liberty rights" (Miller 2012, 3).

The amendment would further prevent the national government from using aid to entice or coerce states to follow federal policies, and it would allow all cases arising under the amendment to originate in state courts, subject to review by the Supreme Court, "with due deference to each State's exercise of the police power."

Miller identified his fifth and sixth proposals as "Finance and Revenue Amendments." The first required the national government to issue standardized financial statements by October 1 of each year and to establish the number of grains of gold by which to anchor the dollar. The second proposed substituting "a uniform consumption tax" for the income tax and prohibiting the implementation of any future value-added taxes. As an alternative proposal, Miller proposed limiting the national government to a single tax on income not to exceed 30 percent of income, with the highest rate being no more than twice that of the lowest. This would be accompanied by personal exemptions for each individual that would be distributed in the form of rebates.

Miller's seventh and eighth proposals dealt with naturalization and residence. The first specified that the government establish clear rules for naturalization applications and for their prompt review. The second, Miller's response to gerrymandering, specified a mathematical formula for redistricting after each census with the intention of establishing "district boundaries for the House of Representatives that are substantially different from the preceding Enumeration, without regard to race, color, gender, creed, religion, or party affiliation" (Miller 2012, 6). It also called for retrocession of most of the District of Columbia to Maryland.

Miller identified his last three proposals as federalism amendments. The first would limit the current definition of interstate commerce and forbid Congress from requiring "any citizen, resident, or legal entity to participate in or contribute to any retirement, annuity, insurance, medical, disability, or similar plan established, managed, or controlled by the United States." The next amendment would repeal the enforcement clauses of a number of amendments, require the president and Senate to consider the experience in the common law of judicial nominees, and withdraw most judicial jurisdiction over military justice (Miller believed that the Constitution vested the latter authority in Congress). The final amendment partly allowed for transition to the new system by allowing individuals from ages 45 to 64 to decide whether to continue in the present Social Security system or turn to private investment. Miller's book included a printing of the Constitution appending the new amendments and marking out sections of the document that would be repealed under his revisions.

Marty Piatt Proposes Constitutional Change
as Part of a Presidential Platform

In 2012, a Californian named Marty Piatt (1958–), who identified himself as a registered architect employed by the Department of Defense in San Diego, wrote a book entitled *If I Was President . . . My Blueprint for America*. It offered a platform for a presidential run that he hoped might be affected through write-in votes. The book, which featured a portrait of Piatt on the cover against the backdrop of an American flag, covered a wide-ranging number of topics, many of which relate to current legislation and to executive orders that Piatt intended to offer in his first 100 days in office. The opening chapters, however, focus chiefly on constitutional issues, which Piatt not only draws up as amendments but also incorporates into a revised constitution that he includes toward the end of his book.

Piatt's central concern was with congressional abuses. He referred to current members as a "corrupt gang of criminal racketeers" (Piatt 2012, 13). He believed that they had ceased representing their constituents and were instead representing private interests. Under his proposed reforms, the House of Representatives would expand to 500 members. He proposed eliminating the U.S. Senate and replacing it with a "Committee of the States" to which each state would send a single individual. Under his plan, a two-thirds majority of the states would have the power to repeal congressional laws. He would further restrict congressional legislation to five goals that he found articulated in the current Preamble, and he would attempt to tame self-interested congressional behavior—in part by stripping Congress of the power to set its own pay.

Piatt also wanted to replace the Electoral College with a nonpartisan election system in which individuals would cast separate votes for the president and vice president. He would further use uniform primary and general elections to take away the current advantages of states that held their contests earlier than others. Piatt favored vesting the president with a line-item veto. One of his more curious proposals called for removing "the influence and expense of the President's spouse or partner from Executive partner" (Piatt 2012, 21).

Piatt thought the structure of the judicial branch should be outlined in the Constitution rather than supplemented with congressional legislation. He favored creating a Supreme Court of six men and six women, any of whom the president could remove with two-thirds support from Congress.

Piatt did not think Congress should have a role in the amending process. He favored a system wherein a two-thirds majority of the state legislatures could call for a convention, amendments from which would go into effect when ratified by a three-fourths vote of the people. He included a provision, however, that would prohibit amendments from undermining "any previous enumerated Article of this Constitution hereafter."

Piatt offered numerous other reforms, such as eliminating the federal minimum wage; abandoning federal prevailing wage standards; taking measures to avoid U.S. dependency on oil; eliminating a wide variety of existing governmental agencies; creating a single "Americare" health system (he disliked Obamacare); imposing "a fair and reasonable flat rate Gross Income Tax (GIT)," which he estimated might be 10 percent and which would be applied to nonprofit organizations (including churches) as well as to individuals; transferring the responsibilities of the Federal Reserve System to the Treasury Department and nominating television financial analyst Suze Orman to be its secretary; withdrawing from the North Atlantic Treaty Organization; establishing a "Libra Colony" at the libration point between the earth and the moon; creating a lunar outpost and a colony on Mars (he suggested that some explorers be left there to save the cost of bringing them back to earth); creating a war tribunal to try members of the Bush administration for their incursions into Iraq (though he would, by executive order, pardon those who served in the conflict); halting immigration and allowing states to exercise concurrent powers in this area; allowing abortion (which he personally opposed) and gay marriage while focusing on reducing divorce and infidelity; and an executive order, patterned after the Emancipation Proclamation, to create equal rights for men and women.

After his election, Piatt planned to call a Second Constitutional Convention on March 1, 2013. He wanted the convention to create the "2013 Articles of Federation." This document would consist of the original preamble and 10 revised articles, which three-fourths or more of the states would ratify as the Twenty-Eighth Amendment. He patterned the first seven articles after the current ones. Articles VIII, IX, and X would respectively include the Bill of Rights, an Equal Rights provision, and his proposals for birthright and citizenship. Piatt called for making Pepsi, Apple, Hershey, Whole Earth Farms, and the Chevrolet Silverado official trademarks of the Office of the President. Piatt's proposed constitution contained an expanded First Amendment that included dicta from court decisions and other documents, and specifically referenced a wall of separation between church and state.

Robert M. Hinkelman Proposes a Constitution 2.0
Featuring a Plural Executive

In 2012, Robert M. Hinkelman, who said he had spent four decades working for AT&T and Lucent Technologies, published a 110-page novel entitled *America 2.0: The Amendment*. The title belies the scope of the work. Although it only calls for a single new amendment, it would actually redesign much of modern politics.

In Hinkelman's story, America adopts an amendment making the 2016 election a milestone. According to the terms of the amendment, the 2016 incumbent faces a troika of opponents. If the incumbent wins, America's system of government remains unchanged, but if the troika wins—as it did in the novel—then executive power becomes vested in those three individuals, with one executive concentrating on governmental affairs, another on the economy, and the third on science. Under the amendment's provisions, each serves for nonconsecutive five-year terms, and different voting criteria are required for different issues. Nominations to the Supreme Court, declarations of war, and pardons, for example, require unanimous agreement from the three executives, whereas a majority can approve or veto legislation.

Hinkelman had great faith in expertise. Candidates within each of the three groupings would thus be nominated by "established, certified organizations in each grouping chosen by the Congress." Such organizations would include the National Academy of Science, the Social Sciences Institute, and the American National Standards Institute. Candidates would, in turn, be tested by qualifications compliance evaluators (QCEs) before being placed on the ballot.

The three candidates who won in the 2016 election ran on "America 2.0," which the novel described as a "Platform for Restorative Initiatives." The first plank of this platform called for "A Return to Responsible, Adam Smith Framed Capitalism," and included corporate tax reductions for businesses that agree not to inject money into political campaigns. A second plank for "A Restoration of Responsible Fiscal Governance" called for budget reductions, the closing of foreign military bases, and lower capital gains taxes. Plank three favored improving national infrastructure and stimulating jobs. Other planks called for creating a "National Water Resources Optimization Commission," a health care "retrofit" and entitlement reform, and reforms of education.

James R. "Chip" Downs Proposes a Constitutional Convention to Adopt Six Complex Amendments

James R. "Chip" Downs III, who has described himself as a formal naval officer and full-time software programmer, published a book in 2012 entitled *United Once More: Balanced Change through Constitutional Reform*. Published under the name "Chip Downs," the work features a series of paired chapters. The opening chapter in each of these pairings outlines a perceived problem in the United States, while the second provides extended descriptions and texts of amendments designed to solve the problem.

The first amendment called for amending citizenship, the second for amending marriage, the next three for amending prosperity (by securing incomes, checking monopolies, and unleashing prosperity), and the last for amending health care. A subsequent chapter described how these amendments, as well as others addressing "a federal balanced budget, war powers, and education" (Downs 2012, 268), might be proposed by a convention of 536 delegates. A subsequent chapter described the prosperity that was likely to result from these changes. In an epilogue, Downs suggested that the United States' main problems were spiritual, and that God might punish the nation if its people did not repent.

The proposed amendments all had multiple sections. Downs apparently considered the citizenship amendment (proposed as the Twenty-Eighth Amendment) to be the most important. It contained eight sections. The first would provide for national registration of everyone born or residing within the United States within six months. Each individual would be classified "as a citizen, resident, or alien," and no one would be able to aid or deal with anyone not so registered (Downs 2012, 38). Section 2 provided that all citizenship would be provisional and would be rescinded at the age of 25 for individuals who did not qualify. Citizenship would require understanding the Constitution, taking an oath to defend it, knowledge of English, and optional service in "military, civil, or humanitarian service" for two or more years (Downs 2012, 41). Section 3 grandfathered in those who were already citizens. Section 4 doubled penalties for any citizens serving in political office who committed crimes. Section 5 provided for loss of citizenship for native-born and loss of residence for naturalized citizens convicted of "treason, felony, or other high crimes" (Downs 2012, 48). Section 6 provided simplified eligibility for individuals who had been physically present within the United States for four years prior to adoption of the amendment. Section 7 provided simplified eligibility for residence status for individuals who had been registered aliens for two years, provided they had not been convicted of any crimes. Section 8 further provided "conditional amnesty" for individuals who met residency requirements and did not have criminal records (Downs 2012, 53).

Downs's second proposed amendment (which would be the Twenty-Ninth) had three parts. The first would keep the definition of marriage out of the hands of the national government and make it a religious or cultural practice subject to state regulation, while "excluding polygamy, bigamy, adultery, incest, molestation of minors, bestiality, or racial bias" (Downs 2012, 82). Section two provided for "a Writ of Potestas Familiaris" in which two guardians vowed to protect children under the age of 18 (Downs 2012, 84). Section 3 prevented modification of this writ except by due process of law.

The proposed Thirtieth Amendment on securing income contained eight sections. The first, entitled "The Right of Basic Subsistence," provided that registered citizens and residents incapable of supporting themselves would receive "food, water, shelter, and clothing, at least equal in value to one-tenth more than a certain measure of poverty, which shall be determined by Congress" (Downs 2012, 120). Section 2 gave individuals "the Right to be Uninsured" (Downs 2012, 124). Section 3 provided for minimum incomes for full-time laborers equivalent to one-tenth or more of the definition of poverty. Section 4 provided for privatizing Social Security while still providing governmental oversight. Section 5 further outlined issues connected to "Appropriation, Revenue, and Outlays" of this privatization program (Downs 2012, 131). Section 6 provided that seven or more insurance carriers would be chosen to administer such programs. Section 7 further outlined the right of individuals to resign from the Social Security program while Section 8 covered distribution of benefits.

The proposed Thirty-First Amendment to check monopolies contained seven sections. The first section sought to counter the Supreme Court decision in *Kelo v. City of New London* by preventing governmental seizures of property absent specified exigent circumstances (Downs 2012, 166). Section 2 limited U.S. senators and representatives to two and four terms, respectively. Section 3 prevented officials from giving themselves special benefits. Section 4 limited income taxation to one-fourth of income and sales-related taxes to one-twentieth of the value of transactions. Section 5 prevented the incorporation of companies in the United States that did not employ at least half their workers in America. Section 6 would divest companies of any more than a 65 percent market share, while Section 7 provided a temporary exemption from the requirements of Section 6 in times of national emergency.

The Thirty-Second Amendment proposed by Downs contained six sections designed to unleash economic prosperity. The first would end "non-Legislative Legislation" by limiting presidential orders and regulations issued by independent regulatory agencies. Section 2 would forbid trade with nondemocratic nations.

Section 3 provided for the "Separation of Business and State" by divesting the government of enterprises, like the post office, that private enterprises could administer. Section 4 provided for public and private employees to voluntarily join unions but prohibited compulsory membership. Section 5 limited bailouts and governmental loans, while Section 6 again provided an exception for these rules in times of national crisis. Finally, the proposed Thirty-Third Amendment contained eight complex sections for securing health (Downs 2012, 210–14).

Downs doubted that Congress would propose such amendments on its own and favored having the states petition for a convention to do so. He called this "*our* constitutional 'nuclear option'" (Downs 2012, 284).

Payne Edwards Proposes Five Amendments to Overcome Gridlock

Gridlock: Why We're In It and How to Get Out (2012) was written by Payne Edwards, who described himself on the book's back cover as "a writer and consultant with experience in the federal government." Edwards believed that while reformers of the Progressive era had identified and corrected problems chiefly in state governments, the time had come to correct problems resulting from the overexpansion of the national government. Reforms were necessary both to "rebalance" powers between state and national authorities and "to refocus the federal government on its core Constitutional responsibilities in a fiscally sound construct" (Edwards 2012, 8). Criticizing the "myth" that state governments were necessarily oppressive and regressive, Edwards claimed that these governments were actually closer to the people than their federal counterpart.

Edwards devoted the first part of his book to describing the consequences of an over-expansive national government and the constitutional loopholes—most notably overly expansive interpretations of the commerce clause—and political incentives that had allowed this to happen. He identified the obstacles to reform as both "practical" and "attitudinal." The former chiefly consisted of the special interests that were benefiting from the existing system while the latter stemmed from widespread beliefs that only the national government could address complex problems. Edwards pointed out, however, that many U.S. states were larger than smaller countries that governed themselves quite effectively. He further attributed some of the problems facing the nation to the fact that the meanings and understandings of words in the Constitution had changed since the nation was founded.

Edwards proposed a series of five amendments. The central purpose of all but one of them was not to "take away any power of authority from government" but to "transfer some power to state governments, and enumerate some powers to the federal government that it is already exercising (e.g., regulating the airways and the airwaves)" (Edwards 2012, 58). The fifth one was a proposed budget amendment that would eliminate the federal government's power to establish the national debt. Edwards suggested constitutional language for each of these proposed amendments in an appendix.

Edwards believed that the primary purpose of the commerce clause in Article I, Section 8 had been to create a "'Free-Trade Agreement' among the states"

(Edwards 2012, 59). Instead, Congress had used it as a vehicle to control the entire economy. He accordingly proposed modifying the clause so that "Congress shall have the Power to establish uniform regulations to ensure the free-flow of goods, services and information among and between the states, territories and possessions; to exercise exclusive legislation over the airways, the airwaves, and interstate waterways; to regulate industrial airborne emissions and waterborne emissions that enter interstate waterways" (Edwards 2012, 79). He would further forbid Congress from erecting any company or corporation engaged in commerce.

Edwards drew from documents that states had drafted when ratifying the Constitution for his second proposal, which would replace the current Tenth Amendment. It provided:

> THAT each state in the union shall, respectively, retain every power, jurisdiction and right, which is not by this Constitution delegated to the Congress of the United States, or to the departments of the Federal Government; that the President shall not issue any order or regulation except as necessary for the administration of Federal Departments; that the Supreme Court or its lower Courts may render no opinion which has the effect of granting a power or right to the Federal Government which is not by this Constitution delegated to it. (Edwards 2012, 80–1)

Edwards distinguished his finance amendment from a balanced budget amendment. He proposed dividing the budget into three parts—an "Operating Budget, a Capital Budget, and Special Budgets for specific activities whose revenues are derived from specific sources" (Edwards 2012, 82). The capital budget would include all expenditures funded by debt. It further provided for balanced operating budgets and five-year budget plans. If Congress failed to approve the budgets within two months of the beginning of the fiscal year, the president's budget would become law. The amendment further provided that the capital budget "shall not exceed 50% of the total Operating Budget appropriations," and that any surpluses would be applied to the national debt (Edwards 2012, 84). Edwards modeled this proposal on Virginia budget rules.

Edwards' next proposal would repeal the Seventeenth Amendment and return the selection of senators to state legislatures. Edwards also sought to add provisions to Article I, Section 9 (limiting Congress) so as to prevent any federal transfers of funds (revenue sharing) to states, "except pursuant to treaties, or in time of national emergency or in response to natural disaster" (Edwards 2012, 86). The amendment would further prevent federal tax credits or other "exceptions to the general rules for the collection of revenues" (Edwards 2012, 86) as well as any federal laws "concerning education, except as necessary for the support of the armed forces and of diplomatic missions" (Edwards 2012, 86–7).

Edwards listed a number of other changes that he thought would be desirable. These included simplifying state and federal tax codes; state adoption of unicameral and nonpartisan legislatures; adopting language to clarify the meaning of the Second Amendment right to bear arms; greater protection for Fourth Amendment rights related to automobiles; providing a specific definition for speedy trials in the Sixth Amendment; changing the dollar amount for jury trials in civil cases in the Seventh Amendment; more specifically defining "cruel and unusual punishments" in the Eighth Amendment; more clearly defining what "privileges and immunities" the Fourteenth Amendment was designed to protect; granting Congress specific powers to regulate air traffic, wireless communications, industrial emissions, and the like; and more clearly defining the respective roles of the national government and the governing bodies of Puerto Rico and other U.S. territories. He also believed that an apportionment amendment could reduce the partisanship surrounding the current process of legislative apportionment.

Keith B. Anderson Proposes Semi-Socialism as an Alternate Governmental and Economic System

In 2013, Keith B. Anderson of West Virginia self-published a book entitled *Semi-Socialism: An Alternative Government and Economic System.* Anderson described himself as "a craftsman, amateur writer, and part-time whatever-else" and defined semi-socialism as "the hybrid merging of capitalism and communism into a more beneficial structural order for man." Anderson expressed particular interest in making certain that the elite from one generation not be able to pass on their "inordinate wealth" to "future soles [sic] yet to be born."

Anderson apparently designed his entire proposal of about 30 single-spaced pages as a new constitution. The document began by listing a multiplicity of governmental departments and agencies, but it was not divided into separate articles. The "National Directive Conglomerate" apparently included the legislative branch, the executive branch, the National Reserve, and the National Reserve's Bureau of Distribution. The legislative branch consisted of a "House of Provincial Senators" selected from a single party by "individual provinces." It would be led by a "Chief Senator," and could override the president by a 60 percent vote. The president would supervise all department heads and direct foreign policy. Departments under the president's supervision would include the Department of Sustenance, the Department of Livelihood, the Department of Population Control, and several others.

The Official Citizens' Conglomerate would allow "the citizenry to explore the more intriguing aspects of life" and included a Council of the People, or Congregational Branch, elected by individual provinces with "the power to initiate progressive national programs which do not interfere with essential official action," and an Interactive Branch consisting of a "Prime Councillor" responsible for the Office of Human Relations, the Office of Human Advancement, the Board of Holistic Incorporators, etc. Its Master Documented Program would be "one part of the plan to unify mankind," while its Collective Earth Organization would serve to promote a common world language.

A conglomerate of "Commercial and Industrial Operations" would "function as the heart of the nation's production base," according to Anderson. "Its main purpose was to provide small but creative entrepreneurs with an alternative outlet for the production and marketing of their creations." Additional "Citizens' Independent Agencies" included an Office of Economic Balance and a Resource Allotment Agency. The National Judiciary System would consist of a Supreme Court of Governmental Affairs, whose members would be elected by the people, and a Supreme Court of Civil and Criminal Affairs. "Judicial Commissioners" would appoint "all judges below the supreme court." Individuals would be educated to serve as Commissioners of Trial Jurors.

The constitution proposed by Anderson allowed for abortion during the first trimester, and would work to create "substitute wombs" for those who did not want to carry children to term. Alcohol, tobacco, and drugs would be regulated, as would the media. The government would have "one national TV network, one national newspaper, and one FM radio network accessible to all areas of the nation." Government would assume full control of banking, and civil servants would regulate banks. The constitution would restrict capital punishment but give criminals the option of committing suicide. The government would provide universal free day care and cremation. It would provide free education through four years of college for individuals who showed themselves capable of such training.

Each citizen would be allocated two "granted property lots (GPLs)," each of which would be large enough "for a reasonably sized house." The government would control all gambling, prohibit all handguns, and limit other weapons to those suitable for self defense. Health care would be free, and government would provide housing for those who could not afford it. Courts would focus on "finding truth" and would consist of inquiry panels, which "shall be used in lieu of the defense and prosecuting attorney." Government would enforce a minimum wage and would set a strict population limit. Regulations to restrict population growth would be initially based on monetary incentives, but would also include provisions for the forced sterelization of "over-productive parents," and of "all children born above the limit." The government would raise revenue through "its marketing of goods and services (sustenance, utilities, resources and fuels, transportation, rent, postal services, production and marketing services, bank loans, bonds) and from fines and penalties." It would also supervise all sports, with governmental contributions to coaches' salaries not to "exceed that of the average salary of a teacher or professor of equal seniority."

Anderson was much more concerned with the government and the security of "the masses" and did not mention a bill of rights. He believed that equalizing land would make it more difficult for one generation to pass down wealth to another. He thought that those who favored pure socialism were too idealistic, that they did not fully appreciate the advantages of private enterprise, and that his system might provide a proper transition to a more purely socialistic model.

William Wilson Proposes a Christian Constitution for a New America

In 2013, William Wilson published an e-book called *New America: A National Renaissance*. Wilson, who is not otherwise identified in the book, relates biblical prophesies of Isaiah against a people that had turned against God. He also includes a new version of both the Declaration of Independence and the U.S. Constitution. Wilson stated that the people of the United States were not "the chosen people of God," like those to whom Isaiah prophesied, but he asserted that there were significant parallels in the way that God had blessed both. The American Founders had started well, according to Wilson, but "the worm of Progressivism invaded the tree early in the 20th Century and has eaten its way *progressively* through the tree, rotting it from within, causing it to slowly die, and readying it for the axe." He claimed that God would judge people responsible for Progressivism harshly, but that hope for salvation remained for some. Wilson further outlined what he considered to be the evils of abortion, homosexual practice, divorce, violence, gay marriage, and governmental paternalism, all of which he thought were leading to decline and to God's judgment.

Wilson formulated "The Constitution of New America," which he described as "the United States of America reborn." He further indicated that this nation would initially "exist peacefully side-by-side" with the existing government until such time as God judged the existing government. In rephrasing the Declaration of Independence, Wilson observed that "the history of the United States this past century is a history of ever increasing permissiveness and licentiousness, and of ever increasing laws and regulations, all having in direct object the establishing of an absolute secular state that controls all aspects of society." Wilson's reworked declaration ended with the statement that "these states are, and of right ought to be, free and independent; that all political connection between them and the United States of America is and ought to be totally dissolved."

The Constitution of New America contained six articles. It followed the general outline—and repeated much of the same language—of the current document. The preamble began with the words, "In the name of Almighty God, from whom all rights are bestowed" and ended with the goal of securing "the blessings of God to ourselves and our posterity." Article I and other portions of the document provided for raising the voting age to 21. Districts for the House would be "divided by strict rectangular geographic boundaries" and states would be re-divided in areas of 30,000 to 100,000 square miles for more equal representation. Wilson's constitution would prohibit political parties, limit every congressional bill to a single topic, and restrict the general welfare clause "solely to financial provisions for the limited powers specifically delegated to the national government," and "for the benefit of the *whole.*"

Wilson incorporated a revised First Amendment in Article I, Section 8 and provided that "Congress shall make no law prohibiting the free exercise of peaceful religion, or establishing any denomination or organization as the official national religious body; or abridging freedom of wholesome speech, particularly religious speech, or of a free and fair press." Wilson anticipated outlawing religious groups that were not committed to peace and censoring unwholesome speech and unfair stories in the press. Wilson indicated that "while no religious denominational or organizational test shall be required of public officials in New America, it will be required that each clearly state his faith in God."

Article I, Section 9 continued with specific protection of life in the womb and stated that "no person . . . shall be denied the liberty to do the right, nor given license to do the wrong." It further provided that individuals living in the United States could become citizens by pledging allegiance to America. Wilson mandated capital punishment for murder and rape, but would ban guns from nonmilitary personnel "for non-hunting purposes." Article I, Section 9 also provided that "marriage in New America shall consist solely of the union of one man and one woman, and neither marriage nor any legal incidents thereof shall be conferred upon any other union." A "New America Safety Net" would require individuals to set up personal trust funds "for their own benefit." The government would only be permitted to borrow money in times of crisis and would be forbidden from raising the national debt above 10 percent of the gross national product (GNP). The dollar would be replaced with "a cashless instrument, the value of which will remain valid due to its national budget being balanced." Corporate and business taxes would be eliminated and a "New America Health Service" would be funded by real estate taxes and co-pays. Physicians would have their way paid to medical school and would be paid a salary. The income tax would be a flat 10 percent up to $100,000 and 30 percent above $100,000, with no taxable deductions except for credits to charities. Businesses that paid top employees more than 20 percent more than the wages earned by their lowest-paid employees would also be taxed at 50 percent.

Article II provided for the electronic conveyance of electoral votes to the capital and included the same provisions for presidential succession as found in the current Twenty-Fifth Amendment. Wilson wanted members of the Electoral College to exercise their judgment as to the best candidate without regard to party affiliation. Members of the judiciary would serve for ten-year renewable terms. The convention method of revising the Constitution, which Wilson considered to be too dangerous, would be eliminated.

Wilson believed that the American people had fallen into such a depraved state that they were unlikely to adopt his constitutional plan. He thus viewed his plan not so much as a document for the present as one for a chastened America of the future.

Tom Green Proposes a Simple Plan to Fix Congress, the Bureaucracies, and the Debt

In June 2013, Tom Green (otherwise unidentified) published an 11-page book entitled *A Simple Plan* that reflected libertarian ideas for reforming the U.S. political system. The book began with a fable that featured characters like Membrants (human beings), Nimrods (hunters who rule over others), Esquandelera (Alexander the Great), the Lupines (Romans), the Yahwets (Jews), and the development of republican government. It was followed by a speech that the author had apparently presented in a class about voting. The speech posed the question, "At what point do you have too much democracy and not enough republic?" It then proceeded to describe three distinct 12-step programs to fix Congress, the bureaucracies, and the debt.

Green did not include texts of possible amendments, but his central aims were fairly clear. His reforms of Congress included limiting members to three terms, preventing external funding of elections, eliminating congressional pensions, preventing gerrymandering, establishing a voter ID system, moving members of Congress to the veterans' health care system, adding sunset provisions of three years to all laws, prohibiting lobbyists, requiring members of Congress to write their own laws, requiring that they follow the Constitution, and preventing off-budget expenditures.

Green proposed a similar plan for fixing bureaucracies. His proposals would abolish guaranteed jobs, prevent unionization of governmental employees, abolish budget tricks, abolish governmental hiring and mandate a 30 percent reduction in the federal work force over five years, eliminate duplicative agencies, enact a flat tax, prohibit lawmaking by regulatory agencies, remind employees that they serve the taxpayers, mandate the purchase of goods from private enterprises, eliminate governmental pensions, and tie governmental salaries to "industry standards"— then reduce them by 3 percent.

Debt solutions proposed by Wilson included an opening provision to "QUIT SPENDING MORE THAN YOU MAKE." Other proposals included trimming governmental operations "to only constitutionally allowed areas," eliminating subsidies for domestic and foreign companies, stopping foreign aid, eliminating trade with repressive regimes, limiting the export of raw materials, requiring prisons to be self-sufficient, getting government out of private markets, requiring recipients of welfare to work, and resolving that it was not always necessary for the government to do something. Green concluded his book with an appeal to vote for the Libertarian Party.

Thomas Dahlberg and Erick Kaardal Propose a Postmodernist Constitution Designed to Promote Christianity

In July 2013, Thomas Dahlberg and Erick Kaardal published *The Rebirth Constitution*. They did not identify themselves other than by indicating that they had published two previous "Neopopulist" books, one entitled *Neopopulism as Counterculture*, and the other *The Problem with Wheaton: A Postmodern Analysis of the Christian Academy's Failure to Challenge the Culture. The Rebirth Constitution* opened with an extended philosophical analysis, followed by the text of a proposed constitution consisting of a preamble and 21 articles.

Dahlberg and Kaardal asserted that those who love freedom know that "democracy requires the separation of the government from all of the means of cultural production enforced by the military might of the people themselves" (Dahlberg and Kaardal 2013, 3). The authors were particularly concerned about governmental provision of education. Their introductory analysis contained many philosophical references, but the authors described three core propositions as the foundations of their neopopulist agenda:

1. There is no such thing as universal reason.
2. All human thought and action is tradition-bound—rooted in an integrated web of belief about Reality, including an account of reason, which cannot be verified or falsified.
3. Democracy is itself a tradition rooted in a view of Reality in which (1) and (2) are true and in which people are ends in themselves, not the tools of any state. (Dahlberg and Kaardal 2013, 12)

The authors believed that both liberalism and conservatism were on the verge of collapse and that Christianity would emerge from American society if the means of cultural production were decentralized. In their view, "the salvation of human freedom is postmodernism without post-structuralism" (Dahlberg and Kaardal 2013, 35). They further proclaimed that "the Rebirth Constitution preserves the American tradition while initiating a whole new government. *It is the tradition which is to be preserved. Not the government. Not the old constitution*" (Dahlberg and Kaardal 2013, 27).

The authors associated Abraham Lincoln, whom they variously call "a brilliant tyrant," one of the "clever snakes," and "the American Stalin," with the development of a superstate over people "including many if not most of the slaves" who "just wanted to be left alone" (Dahlberg and Kaardal 2013, 38, 29, 40). They end their narrative with the phrase "sic semper tyrannis," a Latin phrase meaning "thus, always, to tyrants." John Wilkes Booth famously shouted these words after assassinating Lincoln at Washington, D.C.'s, Ford Theatre in 1865 (Dahlberg and Kaardal 2013, 68).

The preamble to the authors' "Rebirth Constitution" began by "invoking the favor and guidance of Almighty God," and included a recognition that "government is inherently untrustworthy" (Dahlberg and Kaardal 2013, 69). Article I articulated "Basic Principles, Processes and Methods of Reforming Government." It indicated that the limited purposes of government did not include guaranteeing "any kind of positive freedom," regulating commerce, or engaging in licensing. It provided for a plebiscite on foreign aid every two years, for nullification of laws and declarations of war, and for the right of the citizens of a state to secede by a popular vote. It further authorized state militia to resist any efforts to prevent such secession, including imposition of the death penalty on offending officials. The constitution would forbid governments from engaging in most business regulations, setting "wages or prices," or requiring one citizen to subsidize another (Dahlberg and Kaardal 2013, 70–3).

Article II outlined provisions for "Separating the Government from the Means of Cultural Production" (Dahlberg and Kaardal 2013, 77). It began with part of the First Amendment and explained how "no unit of government shall be required to deny the Christian roots of this constitution and its system of government" (Dahlberg and Kaardal 2013, 77). It also prohibited government from adopting an immigrant policy that would allow non-Jews or non-Christians to exceed "15% of the citizenry" (Dahlberg and Kaardal 2013, 77). It would forbid governments from running schools, defining marriages, requiring pledges of allegiance, or regulating "what a citizen eats or drinks nor the risks to which he submits his body where such behavior does not physically coerce others" (Dahlberg and Kaardal 2013, 79).

Article III outlined provisions for "Constraining the Government's Military and Police Power." It included the right of citizens who were not convicted felons to bear and carry arms and their right to participate in militias, which would share in the military arsenal of the entire nation. Each state militia would further elect five representatives to a national assembly, where they could adopt bills of attainder for any governmental officials guilty of "crimes against this constitution" (Dahlberg and Kaardal 2013, 84).

Article IV limited the government's right to tax by preventing such taxes on individual or corporate income or capital gains. It identified property taxes as illegal, and prohibited the use of tax money to construct sporting facilities or to incentivize some behaviors above others. Sales taxes were to be limited to 8 percent in ordinary times and up to 15 percent during times of war. Governments would be prohibited from raising money through gambling. Article V would replace state and national currencies with privately issued currencies. Article VI would limit legal grounds for declaring or waging war, but it also authorized state militia to make war against the federal government "for cause" (Dahlberg and Kaardal 2013, 92).

Article VII limited the government's ability to define the meaning of law by providing that all judges be elected and subject to recall. It also provided that "State Militias have coequal authority with the U.S. Supreme Court and the State Supreme Courts in interpreting this constitution" (Dahlberg and Kaardal 2013, 95).

Article VIII dealt with freedom of speech and encouraged "the open and public discussion of the overthrow of the government, whether state or federal" (Dahlberg and Kaardal 2013, 98). Article IX dedicated all Social Security and Medicare funds and turned them over to the states. Article X prohibited abortion except when necessary for "the physical survival of the mother" (Dahlberg and Kaardal 2013, 101). Article XI prohibited punishing crime on the basis of the emotion that animated the criminal behavior, while Article XII limited the power of international organizations.

Article XIII limited the role of the national government in regulating pollution, while Article XIV dealt with "The Conditions of Citizenship, the Age of Majority, and the Right to Vote." It defined a native-born citizen as one with at least one biological parent who was a citizen (Dahlberg and Kaardal, 2013, 105). Article XV further limited information that the government could collect on censuses while reaffirming existing Fourth Amendment rights.

In outlining the legislative branch, Article XVI provided for three-year terms for members of the House and for repeal of the Seventeenth Amendment. It also limited senators to a single term. It prohibited the use of congressional appropriations for internal improvements but retained the necessary and proper clause. The article further provided for a nonrenewable presidential term of six years and retained the Electoral College. Under the "Rebirth Constitution," the Senate would retain its current power to give advice and consent to ambassadorial appointments. Article

XVII did not introduce significant innovations into the judicial branch other than a provision providing for direct election of judges.

Article XVIII largely reiterated provisions with respect to states that are within Article IV of the current U.S. Constitution. Article XIX empowered a third of the states to convene a convention, proposals from which would become part of the constitution when approved by two-thirds of the states. Article XX dealt largely with housekeeping matters, while Article XXI provided that the new government would go into effect among ratifying states when 30 or more states approved the constitution.

Mark R. Levin Proposes 11 "Liberty Amendments"

In August 2013 syndicated talk-radio host and author Mark R. Levin (1957–) published a book entitled *The Liberty Amendments: Restoring the American Republic*. His primary concern centered on "statism"—a condition in which the state wields excessive centralized control over a nation's economic and social affairs—and on redressing, through constitutional restoration, what he perceived to be the imbalance between state and federal authorities. Using commentary that he laced with long quotations from the Founding Fathers, Levin justified the addition of 11 "liberty amendments" to the U.S. Constitution. The book included the full text of these proposed amendments, many which are similar to those advanced on the Internet by Professor Randy Barnett.

Levin's first proposal would limit all members of Congress (including incumbents) to 12 years of service in one or both houses of Congress. Levin believed such an amendment would help mitigate the role of "professional politicians who operate at an increasing distance from their constituents" (Levin 2013, 32). Levin's second proposal called for the repeal of the Seventeenth Amendment. State governors would appoint individuals to replace senators unable to fill their terms. State legislatures would further be able to remove sitting senators by a two-thirds vote. Levin believed that this amendment would help restore states' rights and make Congress once again "a true bicameral institution" (Levin 2013, 48).

Levin's third proposal imposed 12-year term limits on members of the U.S. Supreme Court, although justices would continue to be appointed and confirmed in the current manner. Levin would allow three-fifths of the House of Representatives or three-fifths of the votes of the several state legislatures to override Court decisions, as long as such overrides took place within 24 months.

Levin's fourth and fifth proposals related to federal taxes and spending. The first called for automatic 5 percent across-the-board cuts when Congress failed to adopt and the president failed to sign a budget by October 1 of any year. Further provisions would limit spending to 17.5 percent of the gross domestic product and require three-fifths of both houses of Congress to consent to any increase in the debt ceiling. The proposed amendment on taxing would limit it to 15 percent of individual income, set the deadline for filing tax returns the day before elections, and prohibit congressional estate or value-added taxes.

Levin's sixth proposal required Congress to reauthorize all federal departments and agencies every three years. It would also create a "Congressional Delegation Oversight Committee" to review any executive branch regulation that imposed a burden of $100 million or more. Failure of the committee to act within a six-month period would automatically void such regulations.

Levin's seventh proposed amendment was aimed squarely at the Supreme Court's decision in *Wickard v. Filburn*, 317 U.S. 111 (1942). This decision authorized the government to regulate the intrastate growing of grain that it thought affected U.S. commerce. Levin's amendment stated that the congressional right to regulate commerce was "not a plenary grant of power to the federal government" but a means of keeping states from impeding it. It would further limit congressional authority to regulate intrastate commerce. Levin aimed his eighth proposed amendment at Supreme Court decisions that liberalized governmental takings of property. It would provide compensation any time that the financial cost of a taking or regulation exceeded $10,000.

Levin's ninth proposal would supplement the current amending process by allowing two-thirds of the state legislatures to adopt amendments, provided that all the amendments used identical language and were adopted within a six-year period. It prohibited states from rescinding or modifying their proposals during this time. Levin's tenth proposal provided for bills to wait 30 days before being finalized and adopted (except when the bill passed by a two-thirds vote of both houses). If these bills contained federal statutes or executive branch regulations that imposed financial burdens of $100 million or more, they could be overridden by votes from three-fifths of the state legislatures, provided those votes took place within 24 months. The amendment would further insulate such overrides from litigation or review in any courts.

Levin's eleventh and final proposal would require individuals to show "valid photographic identification documents demonstrating evidence of their citizenship" (Levin 2013, 183) to vote in any election. It would also limit early voting to within 30 calendar days of an election. The amendment would apply to those voting by mail, and would prohibit any electronic voting unless accompanied by such photographic validation. In his final chapter, "The Time for Action," Levin commended the Article V convention mechanism as the most likely way to initiate such constitutional reforms.

Sam Carr Polk Seeks to Dethrone King Money

Sam Carr Polk (1919–) published *Dethroning King Money by Re-Forming Uncle Sam* (2013) as a follow-up to his 1989 book *CORFA: Constitutional Rebirth for America*. A retired municipal attorney with a master's degree in political science, Polk served a term in the Colorado State House of Representatives in 1957–1958.

Polk was convinced that bribery—"King Money"—posed the greatest threat to American democracy. However, he also blamed shortcomings in the Constitution on slavery; the inability to ratify the League of Nations; the Great Depression; the most recent recession; and the politicization of the Supreme Court, especially with respect to the 2000 presidential election. He further cited a litany of issues, including pollution, illegal immigration, crime, drugs, and racism, that the current system had proven unable to solve.

Polk urged progressive reform associations to join together to call a new constitutional Convention (NewCon), which could "appoint a convention of experts to draft a new constitution," which he dubbed a ConvEx for "Convention of Experts." It could sponsor an unofficial ratification election in which two-thirds of the voters could either consent to the alternative, agree to keep the current document, or ask the convention to "Try Again!" Although it would have no legal force, he believed that the new constitution would be accepted under the Supreme Court's political questions doctrine, which left the elected branches to determine which government was republican.

In his third chapter, Polk outlined the need for four changes, most of which would move the nation in a more parliamentary direction. One would unify Congress into a unicameral body. The second would allow it to choose its head CEO, or chief executive officer, now designated as "Chief." The third would limit the Supreme Court's power of judicial review, and the fourth (more tentative than the first three) would abolish state governments but guarantee the continued employment of state employees during the transition. Polk envisioned a congress of 400 members, 300 of which would be elected from single-member districts and 100 of which would be elected at large (the latter would be designated as senators). Each district would elect two members whose votes in Congress would be weighted according to the number of votes that they received. In addition to containing information about party affiliation, ballots would list the candidate's income, education, and their score on S.T.O.C.K., the "*S*tandard *T*est *O*f *C*andidate *K*nowledge," administered by the Political Guardians, a group of officials charged with overseeing America's affairs. Polk further called for eliminating primary elections and providing public funding and free airtime for others. Any other contribution to a candidate or lawmaker would be considered a bribe.

The 100 at-large senators would be elected through an "Adjustable P.R." (proportional representation) system. Much as in parliamentary democracies, however, the majority party would always be given sufficient votes to carry its programs through Congress. Polk provided for four kinds of voting, each of which would be assisted by computers that would also ascertain tentative rankings of items of legislation during congressional debates. Polk asserted that these measures would be sufficient to eliminate the need for congressional committees or secret party caucuses.

Polk's plan called for the creation of 50 to 70 nonpartisan "Political Guardians." He further suggested dividing them into six categories—financial guardians, military guardians, news guardians, law guardians, administrative guardians, and political guardians. They would initially be appointed by the ConvEx, their pay would be guaranteed, and they would serve life terms. In some cases they would have the right to raise taxes.

News guardians would have "the job of riding herd on the news media and the administration's abuse of its secrecy powers." Law Guardians would issue advisory opinions on the constitutionality of legislation and would appoint lower court judges. Political guardians would act as referees over "nominations, elections, and campaigns."

In cases where two successive bimonthly polls showed that faith had waned in this document, the political guardians would be tasked with calling a new convention and new ratification elections. Terms would be based on continued voter approval rather than fixed terms. The head of the political guardians would serve as the chief of state. Political guardians would also conduct investigations, which Polk did not think were being adequately conducted at present:

> Isn't it peculiar that almost all of the 'accidental deaths' of political leaders have been Democrats, in office or ahead in the polls before an election? Or important witnesses like the eighteen who saw mishandling of evidence of the John Kennedy assassination, and who *all* met "accidental" deaths within two years after the Warren Commission reports. We need to put a stop to that vicious corruption of our public life.

In his final chapter, Polk called for changes in the Bill of Rights, which he wanted to incorporate within the body of the Constitution. Some of his proposals would clarify existing amendments, others would update them, and others would add social and economic rights based on Franklin D. Roosevelt's Second Bill of Rights. Polk favored deleting the Third Amendment and stated that the Second Amendment should provide for "the right to be free from ever present fear of robbery by armed thieves, and from mayhem and murder by armed crazies with automatic weapons." He thought it was time to declare capital punishment and life without parole to be cruel and unusual punishments. Polk believed it might be necessary to include an amendment to provide for raising revenues to guarantee the social and economic rights that he favored. An appendix includes a song entitled "People Power," set to the music of La Marseillaise, and an additional stanza for "America the Beautiful."

Stravo Lukos Proposes a Libertarian Confederacy That Emphasizes Peace and Environmental Protection

Stravo Lukos, who is retired and lives in the state of Washington, published an e-book in 2013 entitled *A New Nation Conceived: The Call for a New Constitutional Convention*. Written with considerable passion, the preface states the need for friendship and fairness and proclaims that "either we'll have a new Constitution or a new revolution." Lukos believes that the current document was founded by elites and has become even more corrupted by corporate and political interests who are creating environment pollution at home and fomenting wars abroad. He constantly invites readers to examine various YouTube videos that he believes prove his point. The first chapter proclaims that one can no more clean up the current government than one can "polish a turd." He subsequently declares that it is time to "flush the toilet" and start over to prevent the continuing "swindle." Specifically, Lukos wants governors to initiate a new convention that will reestablish the United States as a confederacy in which states exercise primary powers.

At the end of his discussions of various social problems, Lukos includes both a Declaration of Independence, which he asks voters to send to their representatives, and what he calls "A New Constitution by and for the People." The declaration refers to the "stolen Convention" of 1787, excoriates the national banking system, lists a variety of ills, and says that under the present circumstances, "disobedience to government" is both a "civic duty" and a "moral obligation."

Lukos's proposed constitution follows the general outline of the current document but introduces considerable innovations. Article I creates a lower house consisting of one representative for every 1,000 residents, but indicates that with television there is no need for "physical attendance by congressional members." Members of the lower house will be elected each year. The upper house will consist of three senators from each state chosen by popular vote "and then approved by the representatives of that state." Most states would be required to have at least one African American or Hispanic senator. A chief justice would preside over the Senate and state supreme courts would judge the elections to Congress. The supreme justice would have the power to veto, as would the president. A "Council of Governors," consisting of all state chief executives, could convene Congress. Lukos's constitution would give Congress specific authority to establish up to six wilderness corridors up to 10 miles wide throughout the contiguous United States, as well as general authority over environment protection issues.

Article 1 would prohibit states from obstructing travel, and Congress would establish a federal certificate for individuals to drive (this certificate would include seatbelt and helmet regulations). A flat tax of 10 percent on incomes would cover pay for governmental officials, with a "graduated or stepped-fee on all assets." Congress would not establish school curricula except to provide 12 years of liberal arts education and eight years of "military science and training." The right of states to rise up against the national government would be specifically recognized, as would their right to secede. States would, however, be prohibited from legislation not "upon moral principles, but rather upon demonstrable harm, restriction of rights, trespass of person or property, or the criminal degradation of the environment."

Voting would be extended to individuals who are 20 years old or older and also citizens (which in turn requires completion of at least 12 years of schooling and public service and an absence of felony convictions). The Constitution would guarantee universal health care except in some cases of self-inflicted harm. Individuals would be able to use drugs that are currently illegal, but licensed physicians would not issue them. Each state would have its own "Public Communications System," which would have to grant each religion an opportunity to make a presentation once a week. Religious and nonprofit organizations would be exempt from taxes, and unfunded mandates and filibusters would be prohibited. Lukos further provided for the safe transportation of sewage, for the reuse of gray water in flush toilets, and for the construction of at least one public toilet in every three blocks of a city. States would be prohibited from utilizing the death penalty, although individuals could voluntarily accept up to 30 lashes in exchange for reduced sentences.

Lukos would share executive power in "the President, the Vice President, the Chief Commander, the Lieutenant Commander, the Supreme Justice, and the Chief Justice of the Senate." The president and vice president would be selected by the governors and two senators from each state, but only the former would have to vote with the majority.

All campaigns would be publicly funded. Presidents could serve two successive three-year terms and one additional term after an intervening presidency. The chief commander would be selected from the armed forces and confirmed by two-thirds of the Senate and state legislatures. Military alliances and sales of arms would be limited.

The judicial branch would consist of a "Supreme Court of the Senate" comprising 13 justices of the Senate, the chief justice, and the supreme justice, for a total of 15 members. Lukos does not mention lower federal courts.

Article 4 prohibited the incorporation of "political entities or agencies." Article 5 added a provision to the current amending process that would require a new convention every 75 years, with candidates chosen through popular ballot. From these candidates, each state legislature would appoint one delegate. Articles 5 and 6 were similar to those of the current Constitution.

Amendments were generally kept but sometimes expanded or elaborated. Lukos's second amendment allowed for gun control. The fourth prohibited warrantless "use of cameras, recorders, or other technical devices." The fifth would prohibit the release of the names of suspects until they were convicted. A twelfth amendment would prohibit abortion and euthanasia. The fifteenth amendment would expand existing voting rights and provide a procedure to impeach and remove governmental officials afflicted with "illness or mental degeneration." The proposed nineteenth amendment provided that "all longstanding human rights such as personal relationships and choices, unobstructed movement, familial bonds, recreation, and self-defense, among others, are recognized as inalienable and beyond the jurisdiction of any government." The twentieth amendment would require two years of service from every graduate, while prohibiting women from being drafted or engaging "other than defensive and logistical services in the militias or armed forces."

The twenty-second amendment went into great detail about the environment. It prohibited "land, water, and air" from being sold, required that all the people profit from minerals that were mined, and prohibited the importation of exotic animals. The twenty-fourth amendment provided further monitoring of credit bureaus and financial institutions, and the twenty-fifth (the last of Lukos's proposed amendments) clarified the provisions of the current Freedom of Information Act.

Summary and Analysis

In August 2013, Richard Morgan wrote an article for the *New Republic* in which he reviewed sixteen recent ideas for a Twenty-Eighth Amendment. These included an equal rights amendment, an amendment to restrict marriage to heterosexual couples, a balanced budget amendment, an amendment defining embryos as persons, a proposal to strip corporations of personhood, one to outlaw flag desecration, another to redefine congressional powers, a campaign-finance reform amendment, an amendment allowing naturalized citizens to run for president, a proposal to bypass the Electoral College, one providing for replacement of governmental officials during times of emergencies, one to make the District of Columbia a state, another to repeal the limit on presidential terms, one to impose limits on congressional terms, one to make voting a positive right, and one that would repeal the existing Constitution and replace it with a new one.

Plans to rewrite the Constitution from the last dozen years have been as eclectic as those of any past period, but they appear to have fewer unifying themes. Only Sam Polk called for the adoption of something akin to parliamentary democracy. None of the proposals advocated socialism, although a number did focus on what they perceived to be undemocratic features of the current system. A number of proponents of change, including reformers with Tea Party and libertarian roots, were concerned about what they believed to be increased federal intrusiveness, and only Jesse Jackson, Jr., and Sam Polk called for the recognition of new social and economic rights. Despite the publicity achieved by the Occupy movement and a conference held at Harvard University to discuss the possibility of another convention, support for another constitutional convention appeared no greater at the end of this period than at its beginning.

References

Anderson, Keith B. 2013. *Semi-Socialism: An Alternative Government and Economic System.* Bluefield, WV: self-published.

Antinori, Paul. 2012. *Convention: To Resurrect the U.S. Constitution.* N.p.: Ludvik Books.

Antinori, Paul. 2010. *A Modest Proposal to Amend the U.S. Constitution.* N.p.: Ludvik Books.

Aranda, Ted. 2010. *The Racket and the Answer: The Representative System and the Democratic Alternative.* http://democracyfortheusa.org/docs/Racket1original_350pgs.pdf.

Barnett, Randy. 2009. "A Bill of Federalism." Forbes.com. May 20. http://forums.anandtech.com/showthread.php?t=2139696 (accessed December 17, 2013).

Campbell, C. Earl. 2011. *The Revised Amended Constitution for the United States of America for the 21st Century.* http://www.mymoneybudget.com.

Dahlberg, Thomas, and Erick Kaardal. 2013. *The Rebirth Constitution: A Whole New Constitution for the Freedom Loving People of the United States.* Lexington, KY: Create Space Independent Publishing Platform.

Davis, Daryl Lloyd. 2011. *New American Democracy: A Direct Democracy Alternative.* E-book.

Dorf, Michael C. 2011. "The Constitution and the Political Community." *Constitutional Commentary* 27 (Winter): 499–506.

Downs, James R. "Chip." 2012. *United Once More: Balanced Change through Constitutional Reform.* Create Space Independent Publishing Platform.

Edwards, Payne. 2012. *Gridlock: Why We're In It and How to Get Out.* Kissimmee, FL: Signalman Publishing.

Green, Tom. 2013. *A Simple Plan.* N.p.: Ugly Books.

Guerra, Darren Patrick. 2013. *Perfecting the Constitution: The Case for the Article V Amendment Process.* Lanham, MD: Lexington Books.

Heim, Paul R. 2009. *Second American Revolution: Change You Really Want.* Charleston, SC: BookSurge.

Hines, A. 2009. *An Informal and Unauthorized Proposition.* Bloomington, IN: Author House.

Hinkelman, Robert M. 2012. *America 2.0: The Amendment.* E-book.

Hopper, Tom. 2011. *USGOV.FIX: Fixes for a Failing Government.* Lexington, KY: N.p.

LaCroix, Alison L. 2011. "On Being 'Bound Thereby.'" *Constitutional Commentary* 27 (Winter): 507–14.

Lessig, Lawrence. 2011. *Republic, Lost: How Money Corrupts Congress—And a Plan to Stop It.* New York: Twelve.

Levin, Mark R. 2013. *The Liberty Amendments: Restoring the American Republic.* New York: Threshold.

Levinson, Sanford. 2006. *Our UnDemocratic Constitution: When the Constitution Goes Wrong (And How We the People Can Correct It).* New York: Oxford University Press.

Lukos, Stravo. 2013. *A New Nation Conceived: The Call for a New Constitutional Convention.* Spokane, WA: Cincinnatus Club.

Martinez, Jenny S. 2011. "The Extraterritorial Constitution and the Rule of Law." *Constitutional Commentary* 27 (Winter): 527–29.

Médaille, John. 2010. "Monarchy and the American Constitution." *The Distributist Review* (December 6). http://distributistreview.com/mag/2010/12/monarchy-and-the-american-constitution/ (accessed December 14, 2013).

Médaille, John. 2010. "A Real Catholic Monarchy." *The Distributist Review* (December 1). http://distributistreview.com/mag/2010/12/a-real-catholic-monarchy/ (accessed December 14, 2013).

Médaille, John. 2010. "Why I Am a Monarchist." *The Distributist Review* (November 18). http://distributistreview.com/mag/2010/11/hy-i-am-a-monarchist/ (accessed December 14, 2013).

Miller, John B., ed. 2012. *The Second Bill of Rights & The New Federalist Papers: Eleven Amendments to the United States Constitution and Fifty Papers That Present Them.* Arlington, MA: The New Federalism.

Morgan, Richard. 2013. "Sixteen Good, Bad, and Insane Ideas for a Twenty-Eighth Amendment to the Constitution." *New Republic,* August 22. http://www.newrepublic.com/article/114337/28th-amendment-what-should-our-next-amendment-be.

Naglee, John F., Sr., 2011. *Our New Constitution: Conceived by Citizens Determined to Restore Their Nation.* Shelbyville, KY: Wasteland Press.

Owens, Robert R. 2010. *The Constitution Failed: Dispatches from the History of the Future.* Maitland, FL: Xulon Press.

Paulsen, Michael Stokes. 2011. "Our Perfect, Perfect Constitution." *Constitutional Commentary* 27 (Winter): 531–40.

Piatt, Marty. 2012. *If I Was President . . . My Blueprint for America.* Bloomington, IN: Author House.

Polk, Sam Carr. 2013. *Dethroning King Money by Re-Forming Uncle Sam.* E-book.

Polk, Sam Carr. 1989. *CORFA Constitutional Rebirth for America.* Santa Monica, CA: CORFA Books.

Revolutionary Communist Party, USA. 2010. *Constitution for the New Socialist Republic in North America.* Chicago, IL: RCP Publications.

Rice, Lewis. October 6, 2011. "Tea Party and Liberals Convene at HLS to Discuss Constitutional Convention." http://www.law.harvard.edu/news/spotlight/constitutional-law /conference-on-the-constituti.

Schmitendorf, James M. 2011. *Lex Ferenda: We the People.* Lexington, KY: N.p.

Schmitendorf, James. N.d. "Abe's Indignation League: Petition for a Constitutional Convention." http://www.abesindignationleague.org/petition.html (accessed December 14, 2013).

Schmitendorf, James. N.d. "Abe's Indignation League: Questions & Answers." http://www .abesindignationleague.org/qanda.html (accessed December 14, 2013).

Schmitendorf, James. 2008. "Justifying a Constitutional Convention for the 21st Century (Plain Talk and Common Sense." http://www.abesindignationleague.org/justification .html (accessed December 14, 2013).

Sirmon, Rick. 2011. *In Search of George Washington (The Story of the 28th Amendment).* Bloomington, IN: Xlibris.

Spann, Girardeau A. 2011. "Constitutional Hypocrisy." *Constitutional Commentary* 27 (Winter 2011): 557–80.

Sprogis, Uldis. 2011. *New Constitution of the United States.* E-book.

Tushnet, Mark. 2011. "Abolishing Judicial Review." *Constitutional Commentary* 27 (Winter): 581–88.

Vile, John R. 1991. *Rewriting the United States Constitution: An Examination of Proposals from Reconstruction to the Present.* New York: Praeger.

Wilson, William. 2013. *New America: A National Renaissance.* E-book.

CHAPTER 12

Constitutional Reform in Cyberspace

When the author published his first book on constitutional reform in 1991, every such proposal that he examined was advanced either in a book or an article. Since then the Internet has filled a role once met by multivolume encyclopedias, and most Americans have at least some acquaintance with online resources. A Web site entitled "Constitutional Topic: Rewriting the Constitution," by an unidentified individual who relied largely on the author's first book, observed that since its publication, "the Internet exploded onto the scene." That Web site identified seven such proposals, which are among many more that this chapter includes.

The Internet has not only dispersed information but opened up new avenues to those who could not previously publish articles or books. As a partial consequence, discourse on constitutional issues has become democratized. Individuals with a Web site or other access to social media can now easily post their views on constitutional reform, and many who have done so advocate incorporating such democratic mechanisms within their proposed constitutions.

Web technologies pose special problems for academic researchers. Authors may or may not disclose their affiliations. One cannot always determine when postings were first made. Moreover, many sites are fairly transitory. Today's post may or may not be there tomorrow, and past postings are not archived in libraries like books and published articles. Whereas books can be judged by their sales and magazines by the number of their subscribers, it is not always possible to determine how many visitors a site has had, and such sites are not likely to be the subject of scholarly reviews and commentaries. Moreover, unlike books that are issued in new editions, it is not always possible to know whether materials are original or whether they are subsequent additions. Finally, Web sites do not typically have page numbers, making it difficult to direct others to specific passages that are cited or quoted.

Given these unique challenges, the author has devoted this chapter to a potpourri of proposals that he has located exclusively on the Internet. The author has presented these in rough chronological order, but it is not always possible to ascertain when postings were first made, and authors may have further revised their proposed reforms even prior to publication of this book.

L. Henry Platt, Jr., Revises the Constitution to Encourage Free Enterprise

L. Henry Platt, Jr., posted "The Revised Constitution of the United States of America" on a Website titled DarkHorseCandidate.com. According to Platt, the constitution was originally published on July 4, 1972, and has since undergone minor revisions. Platt has apparently run a number of unsuccessful political campaigns over the past 40 years for state and local offices. His proposal largely follows the existing document, with a total of eight articles (existing amendments are absorbed within the document). The revised preamble, which consists of four paragraphs, states that Platt's proposed constitution was designed to "secure the Blessing of Liberty and Prosperity." It further indicated that the latter is best promoted "through individual initiative and contribution to the common cause."

Article I of the proposed constitution provided that the House of Representatives have from 350 to 435 members, with districts drawn by the upper house of each state. Elections of members of Congress would be by "all intelligent, adult, bona fide inhabitants, who are citizens of the United States, and all members of the armed Forces." The powers of Congress in Article I, Section 8 would include the power to punish piracies "on the high seas, in the air, or in outer space," and the power to support armed forces would include the Air Force.

Platt incorporated most provisions within the current Bill of Rights in Article I, Section 9, which limits Congress, but ended the section by saying that "restrictions on the Congress providing protection for the people shall be extended to the States as well." The equivalent of the First Amendment provided that

> Congress shall make no law respecting an establishment of religion, and all persons shall be free to practice their own religion or philosophy so long as it doesn't tax or restrict the freedoms of others. Germane to this section, religion shall be recognized by its content and not by its parentage.

The right to freedom of speech referred to "the rights of persons to speak respectfully on any matter." Platt's substitute for the Second Amendment permitted "any honest, sane, intelligent, capable, and responsible citizens the right to own and bear appropriate weapons and firearms." A provision designed to protect privacy prevents warrants authorizing secret observations for more than 180 days and requires replacing or compensating for items that the government takes. Another guarantee protected against "confiscatory taxation," and provided for taxation "on a pro rata basis to support the exigencies of government." Noting that "respect is the cornerstone and foundation of an orderly society," Platt's constitution provided for punishments but limited the crimes for which capital punishment may be applied. A provision provided that "neither Congress nor any State shall make any law which recognizes or distinguishes between people on the basis of race, skin color, ancestry or religious affiliation; but Congress may enact legislation on request of certain sociological groups from participation in government programs of enumerated contributions and rewards." A provision prohibiting sex discrimination provided for "physical needs and decent privacy."

Article II created an elaborate electoral mechanism in which representatives and senators would vote for the individual who got the greatest number of votes within their district or state. Platt stated that this mechanism would better combat fraud than a system of direct election. Article III provided for jury trials but allowed for juries of six in cases involving less than $1,000. It also provided "guaranteed legal counsel" in criminal cases involving fines of $250 or more.

Article IV supplemented Article I, Section 9 by articulating personal rights and liberties. Section 4 included a provision that "no minor child may be taken from his domestic setting without his consent except to protect either the child or society." Section 6 protected the rights of fetuses beginning at 17 weeks of gestation. Section 7 provided that all citizens "shall enjoy the right to speak and worship, with due courtesy to others, as they desire; and no acts between consenting adults shall be questioned." Section 8 provides that "in criminal protection, the intended victim shall always enjoy prior right."

Article V articulated the state obligations currently found in Article IV. Article VI provided that the people of two-thirds of the states could apply within a seven-year period for a convention that "a majority of the people in three-fourths of the States" could ratify. Article VII provided for honoring past laws while Article VIII established what was called a "Tradition." Platt explained:

> Upon ratification of this Constitution, a suitable large ornamental copy shall be made of this Constitution on high quality parchment. This copy of the Constitution will be placed on display in a place in the White House where the public visitors might see it, and each succeeding new President of the United States will affix his signature to it confirming the traditional constitutional form of government of the United States and affirming his pledge to support this Constitution as the supreme law of the land superseding the Constitution of September 17, 1787 and all other laws.

Kirk Brothers Posts a Libertarian Constitution Based on 12 Propositions

Kirk Brothers was the pen name for Wilburt J. Richter (1929–2006). He posted "Propositions for a Libertarian Constitution" as the last two of 13 essays that he began writing in "late 1996 and mid-1997," and which he had unsuccessfully attempted to publish in a book entitled *The Revolutionary Right*. At the end of the last essay, Brothers self-identified himself as having been "born both gifted and gay" in 1920. He confessed that he "had never been able to relate to mental mediocrities for long, and I am afraid it shows." He indicated that he had written under a pen name in part because he was involved in a Social Security test case *Richter v. United States*. He further said that he had served at various times as "a college professor, TV news writer/editor, actor/singer, and finally a health consultant practicing homeopathic medicine in New York City." At the time of the post, he was living in Florida as a retiree.

Brothers thought that civilization was headed for a collapse that would result in armed warfare, martial law, and declining birth rates. In Malthusian fashion, however, Brothers hoped that societal collapse and martial law would prompt the formation of a plebiscite in which his own proposals, which were only in draft form, might be considered.

His first proposition, divided into five parts, focused on original intent. It indicated that the proposed constitution was designed to correct the corruption of the current Constitution. The new document was to be ratified by popular vote, with votes taken every seven years on possible amendments. The proposition noted that "government is not a party to this contract" in which the people would be sovereign, and indicated that his constitution superseded all existing state constitutions.

Brothers's second proposition would recognize English as the official U.S. language and mandate strict construction of the proposed constitution. Proposition Three indicated that executive and judicial officials could be subject to civil suit for disregarding the constitution, and could be removed from office if found to have abused their discretion. Proposition Four affirmed the need for law and order and for an unwritten social contract "based upon natural law," including the rights articulated in the opening sentences of the Declaration of Independence.

Proposition Five included a list of 11 powers that government (including state government) would exercise. These included national defense, disaster relief, environmental protection, and police and fire protection. Among the more unusual powers he proposed were ones establishing "rural communes of agricultural and/or other self-supporting nature for able-bodied persons who are indigent and unemployed," creating a new monetary system, instituting ombudsmen to investigate cases of alleged child abuse, and the right to establish ghettos for prostitutes and "special beaches for nude swimming or sun-bathing."

Proposition Six included sanctions on government involving religious neutrality, balanced budgets, taxing powers, social welfare, education and health care, sexual privacy, common law and other specific rights, and the division of governmental powers. A provision extended religious neutrality to all religions, but bestowed special favors to none. Brothers indicated that "the United States shall NOT be held to be a Christian or Jewish nation, and the Bible shall be of no legal interests. Neither the Bible nor the word 'God' shall be used in any legal ritual" nor would any national symbol be deemed sacred. The provisions for balanced budgets required repaying of existing debts within 50 years. Federal taxes would be capped at 10 percent for individuals and 15 percent for corporations, and states would rely upon real estate and retail taxes and lotteries for revenue.

The government would have "no legal interest in the economic welfare of any citizens" except for bankruptcy. It would be permitted to serve meals, but not issue checks, to disaster victims. Although government could require safe working conditions and provide information about infectious diseases, both education and health care would become purely private responsibilities. All private consensual sexual acts would be legal. The proposed constitution also stipulated that "natural and common law rights shall in each and every case be construed as intentionally broad and general—vague as vague or imprecise." The most preeminent rights would be "(1) the right of self-determination in each and every decision; and

(2) the right to be left alone" except in cases where behavior caused actual injuries to others. A section on specific rights incorporated most provisions of the Bill of Rights, although it omitted Third Amendment protections against quartering troops in private houses because Brothers viewed the provision as anachronistic. Innovations included mandating uniform criminal and civil codes throughout the nation and providing for capital and corporal punishments, as well as "medical sterilization of genetically defective persons, habitual violent criminals, or unfit parents" and "castration of violent sexual criminals."

The most novel aspect of Brothers's proposal was a provision to divide most existing federal legislative powers among the states, thus eliminating the House of Representatives but leaving the Senate (apparently as currently configured, albeit with state lieutenant governors serving as ex officio members) to affirm or reject presidential nominees to the judiciary and cabinet posts. Brothers's proposed Senate would also affirm or reject legislation proposed by the state legislatures, all of which would be unicameral and all of whose members would serve seven-year terms. Sections on the federal judiciary further provided for a separate court to deal with questions related to the constitutionality of legislation. All elected officials would be subject to popular vote, and they and members of the federal judiciary would be required to have IQs of 130 or higher. In addition, judges would be expected to "demonstrate superior scholarship in matters of natural and common law, and the history and philosophy of jurisprudence." After a year and a day of service, the president and vice president would be subject to votes of no confidence, but their terms would not otherwise be fixed. The U.S. Senate would have to concur to proposed legislation by a vote of 60 percent or higher for a bill to become law, but the president would be stripped of veto power.

Brothers would not allow parties to nominate candidates or candidates to run under party labels, although they could endorse them and engage in educational activities. Brothers observed that "political parties are the greatest enemy of equality under law." Proposition Seven limited voting to individuals over age 18 with an IQ of 100 or higher. All elections would be by direct popular vote, with run-offs provided when no candidate won a majority of the vote.

John VanSickle Applies the Principles of Ayn Rand to the Constitution

John VanSickle (1965–) began posting proposals for constitutional change on his Web site, which no longer appears operative, sometime in 1998. VanSickle proposed five amendments, most of which were fairly complex. In personal e-mail correspondence with the author, VanSickle observed that he was influenced by Ayn Rand, but did not agree with all that she or her followers espoused.

VanSickle's proposed twenty-eighth amendment would have prohibited Congress or the states from making laws "respecting an establishment of production, trade, employment, education, medicine, culture, or charity, or restricting the free exercise thereof." It would further repeal the congressional power to levy income taxes, "to borrow or lend money," or to "consider any bill to reverse any part of this amendment."

VanSickle's proposed twenty-ninth amendment contained 18 sections devoted primarily to the criminal justice system. It would prohibit fines or forfeitures except for a crime of which an individual had been convicted (Section 1); compensate individuals for property damaged during governmental seizures (Section 2); require unanimous jury verdicts and limit their application to crimes involving an "identifiable harm to a specific person or party of persons" (Section 3); eliminate "peculiar courts" (Section 4); provide for the selection of jurors by lottery while excluding individuals in law enforcement or with personal interest in the case (Section 5); allow jurors to judge matters of law and fact "independent of the instructions of the court" (Section 6); prohibit convictions based simply on the testimony of governmental officials or individuals engaged in plea-bargaining (Section 7); prohibit the use of testimony "obtained by coercion or fraud" (Section 8); separate individuals whose crimes involved bodily harm to others from those who were incarcerated for nonviolent offenses (Section 9); reserve the death penalty for specified crimes (Section 10); limit the definition of cruel and unusual punishment of prisoners to the infliction of "injury or illness" (Section 11); hold officials liable for abridging the "rights, privileges, or immunities" of persons under guise of their authority (Sections 12 and 13); prohibit punitive damages (Section 14); specify the presumption of innocence and sanity and provide that the "beyond a reasonable doubt" standard be applied in both criminal and civil cases (Section 14); distribute fines to individuals harmed or to taxpayers (Section 16); make it a crime for governmental officials to cover up evidence that might help exonerate a defendant (Section 17); and criminalize "entrapment" by law enforcement officials (Section 18).

VanSickle's proposed thirtieth amendment contained 13 sections limiting perceived governmental abuses. Section 1 would apply all laws that Congress passed to itself. Section 2 would require all regulations to be "expressly worded." Section 3 would require all governmental representatives and appointees to divest themselves of "commercial interests" and prohibit pensions to them. Section 4 would require elected officials to take an oath to tell the truth and make them impeachable for violating this oath. Section 5 would enable each individual to place bills before Congress. Sections 6 and 7 would permit the nomination of presidents and vice presidents by petitions of 2 percent or more of the voters. Section 8 would prohibit monies from the treasury from being spent on petitions, and Section 9 would prohibit felons or ex-felons from serving in office. Section 10 would specify that any crime for which an individual could be incarcerated would be considered to be an impeachable offense. Section 11 would prevent the federal government from using expenditures to induce state behavior. Section 12 would limit congressional powers to regulate trade only when such trade "transacts state borders," and Section 13 would provide an automatic sunset for any law on its tenth anniversary, although new laws could replace them.

VanSickle's proposed thirty-first amendment related to the military. Section 1 would eliminate the draft. Section 2 would limit the stationing of troops abroad "except in prosecution of a war declared by Congress." Sections 3 and 4 would prohibit the United States from entering into treaties abridging citizens' "rights, privileges, or immunities."

VanSickle's proposed thirty-second amendment limited state and federal powers. Section 2 limited the power of licensing and limited such fees to a minimum. Section 3 affirmed the right to bear arms without being "subject to any system of governmental consent or license" except for those who used weapons to cause or threaten harm. Section 4 mandated that child welfare would be the basis of "all custody decisions." Section 5 allowed states to prohibit governments within their jurisdiction over matters that states had reserved to themselves. Section 6 limited restrictions over individual rights to those that were specifically enumerated within the constitution. Section 7 limited the information that governments could collect on private individuals. Section 8 provided for a referendum initiated by 1 percent or more of the voters of any state and enacted into law when favored by "a majority of voters," and entrusted such referendum with broad powers. The final section limited U.S. governmental ownership to "only those lands used in the exercise of the powers reserved to it in this constitution."

VanSickle also borrowed a copy of "the No Bill of Rights" from an unknown Web site. It informed individuals that they are entitled to opportunities—but not to government largesse to obtain food, housing, health care, or other such services.

Jack Durst Presents a Variant of Parliamentary Government

In 2000, a young man named Jack Durst posted a proposed constitution on the Internet. Durst listed a variety of theorists, including libertarians who had influenced his own thinking, but his primary objective was moving the system closer to a parliamentary model from the current presidential system.

Article I began with a declaration of rights. The first was the right to expression, which included limits on governmental ownership of media and provisions for academic freedom. The declaration included a provision that "the expectation of privacy in the body, the home and its surroundings is absolute." This right also included confidentiality of conversations with lawyers, doctors and other professionals, made provisions for "the dignity of all persons," and limited governmental denials of passports. Durst's "rights of noninterference" included the right to private consensual sexual conduct, the rights "to grow, possess in reasonable quantity, and use any psychoactive substance," and the "right to work in any lawful profession." Durst's provisions for "freedom of religion and culture" exempted conscientious objectors from military service and guaranteed all individuals "the right to participate in their culture and to enjoy and preserve their cultural heritage." Property and corporate rights included not having taxes levied on savings and the rights to form corporations and unions. Durst balanced these rights with eight duties of citizenship. These obligations included obedience to law, participation in government, voting, seeking to change laws with which one disagrees, protecting the republic, being informed, paying taxes, and honoring contracts.

Article II outlined a government of three branches consisting of "a Republic Council who execute the laws, a judiciary which interprets them, and a Parliament which causes [laws] to be made and approves them." The republic council was similar to a legislative body discussed in the New Jersey Plan, an alternative to the Virginia Plan that was proposed at the Constitutional Convention of 1787. It would establish a plural executive, and its 12 members would serve three-year terms and be presided over by the prime minister. Parliament would be a unicameral body consisting of 100 members elected yearly. A Supreme Court of from three to seven members would head the judiciary. The prime minister, elected by parliament, would "serve as liaison between the Council, the Parliament, and the ministers."

Durst provided elaborate detail about elections and voting, which could be extended to those as young as 15 who demonstrated "the ability to make an informed and reasoned political choice." Individuals would be limited to 10 years of service in national offices, with candidates selected in "partisan caucuses" and subject to election according to systems that take voters' top three choices into account. Durst would replace states with a set of 20 geographically contiguous but shifting districts, each with five seats in parliament.

Trial judges would serve three-year terms, appellate judges would receive ten-year terms, and members of the Supreme Court would have lifetime appointments "during good behavior." Courts would maintain the power of judicial review, but the parliament could overrule decisions dealing with the interpretation of statutes by a three-fifths vote. The Supreme Court would have the power to decide on the constitutionality of wars.

In Durst's constitution, the parliament and the council could call consensus committees on topics of their own choosing and on topics about which voters had petitioned. Omnibus bills would be forbidden. The council would have the power to impose taxes, but the total tax on any given item or income would be limited to 30 percent. A new common currency, designated the "shilling," would be established initially to be "worth .07 of a Swiss Franc," a standard for which Durst provided no explanation. The Council could declare war, but the parliament would make laws regarding the military and would be able to adopt emergency laws when needed.

Cabinet ministers would serve four-year terms. All ministries would be similar to those of the ministry of justice/police. Created by the council, the justice/police ministry would be based on "a uniform police force and prosecutor throughout the republic, divided geographically into departments, with oversight by the legislative and judicial branch and control by the executive." A chief prosecutor would head each police department. The prosecutor and other heads of local ministries could "form a local cabinet, to govern and coordinate the actions of the executive branch in their area of mutual geographical jurisdiction with the advice and consent of the citizen's advisory board."

Article III listed 24 separate powers of government. These included the protection of workers and consumers, the regulation of businesses, the protection of property and civil rights, environmental protection, "fair distribution of inheritances," care "for idiots and the insane," education, "access for all citizens to food, housing, and other necessities," and the like. Only a few felonies would carry a penalty of more than one year in prison.

Article IV further described the judiciary and due process rights. Durst would vest the judiciary with the right to "insure that children within the republic have access to safe, modern schools, which provide knowledge relevant to their futures and useful as citizens." Durst specifically recognized the government's obligation to provide counsel for indigent criminal defendants, and he called for compensating all persons illegally arrested. This section specifically incorporated the standard of "beyond a reasonable doubt" in criminal cases and set the jury size at 12. It also outlawed capital punishment and provided each prisoner "with a rulebook . . . which shall be strictly and unerringly enforced." Durst would guarantee broad powers to individuals to enter into contracts and outlaw discrimination by law on the basis of "a. Race, color, ethnicity, or genetic makeup; b. Condition of current or former drug use; c. Gender, marital status, gender or sexual preference; d. Religion; e. Political beliefs; [or] f. Physical disability." This provision also provided that "this constitution is to be broadly construed in such a manner that the greatest liberty is afforded the citizens, the least power and the greatest obligation consistent with that power to the government and to incorporate the longstanding traditions developed under it."

Article V authorized council members to propose amendments after receiving petitions from 10 percent of the voters. A two-thirds majority of the council would then send the amendment to a consensus committee, and the amendment, if proposed by a two-thirds majority vote of parliament, would then have to be approved by three-fifths of the people. A new amendment would go into effect for 10 years, after which it could be made permanent or extended for another 10 years. The constitution specified, however, that "no amendment may be made to this constitution which substantially alters the form of the government or the powers of its branches except by singular addition or subtraction of powers, nor may any amendment be made which addresses more than one basic topic." After 10 years under the new constitution, voters would decide whether to keep it or return to the previous document.

Ross Nordeen Proposes a Libertarian Rewrite of the Constitution

Ross Nordeen, a Floridian who identified himself as an engineer, is the creator of a Web site called the Amateur Economist (www.amatecon.com), which includes Nordeen's suggested revisions to the U.S. Constitution. Nordeen reproduced the Constitution in its entirety, but used underlining and other formatting tools to indicate the wording he would add or delete.

In revising Article I, Nordeen proposed eliminating all indirect references to slavery. He would also limit members of the House of Representatives to three terms and members of the U.S. Senate to two. Neither body would be permitted to meet for more than 60 days a year, except by a two-thirds vote that would provide for an additional 60 days. Nordeen proposed requiring a two-thirds vote for levying new taxes; deleting the provision granting Congress the power to create a post office and post roads; making the necessary and proper clause more restrictive; and providing that all congressional laws expire after 10 years. He further called for a prohibition on all retroactive taxes and approval of three-fourths majorities from both houses of Congress for deficit spending. Nordeen left Articles II and III relatively intact but proposed adding a provision to Article IV specifying that a "state may secede from the union by a two-thirds vote of its citizens." Nordeen also altered Article V so that states could select senators as they chose.

Nordeen advocated a number of changes to the Bill of Rights. These included changing the word "abridging" in the First Amendment to "infringing." Other provisions essentially codified existing case law. Nordeen proposed eliminating the preface to the Second Amendment and expanding the Third Amendment to prohibit compulsory military service. He added a preface to the Fourth Amendment specifying that "Congress shall make no law infringing on the right of the people to privacy." He further proposed strengthening the takings clause of the Fifth Amendment by providing that the government shall not take property "except for a substantial, explicit public use and with full compensation therefore paid to each owner." He added a provision to the Sixth Amendment specifying that "the jury shall have the power to judge the law in all instances in which the government or any of its agencies is an opposing party." Nordeen proposed extensive changes to the Eighth Amendment, beginning the amendment with the words "Congress shall make no law," and adding provisions to strengthen property rights:

> Forfeiture of estate, indefinite imprisonment, and unreasonable detention of witnesses are forbidden. There shall be proportionality between magnitude of felony and the severity of forfeiture of property. No person charged with a crime shall be compelled to pay costs before a judgment of a conviction has become final. A person not found guilty of a crime shall not be assessed fees or costs to recover property seized as evidence or otherwise held, impounded, or stored by the government.

Nordeen proposed strengthening the Tenth Amendment so as to rein in federal powers:

> Relative to the people, no branch of government has inherent or reserved powers, implicit or assumed prerogatives, or presupposed attributes of sovereignty. Powers must be expressly granted to government by the people, and the extent and range of such powers shall be strictly, narrowly construed.

Nordeen did not propose changes to the remaining amendments.

"Jack Rabbit" Proposes a U.S. Constitution Featuring Parliamentary Government

On March 20, 2006, a self-described poet and essayist writing under the *nom de plume* of Jack Rabbit posted on an online journal called DemocraticUnderground .com a proposed constitution for a parliamentary government, which he designated as the "Second Constitution of the United States of America." Most parts of the proposed constitution follow the existing language of the current document.

The proposal, which did not have a preamble, was divided into five articles. Article I dealt with the states, citizenship, census, and voting. The section dealing with the states specifically repudiated the idea of secession. It also bestowed statehood on the District of Columbia. The provisions for citizenship were similar to those in the current Fourteenth Amendment, but expanded parameters to include individuals born abroad of one or more U.S. citizens. Each citizen would have equal rights, and no one could strip citizens of their rights. The census would be taken every 12 years, and representation had to be drawn so that the populations of districts did not vary by more than 10 percent. The section on voting recognized the right as "inalienable," specifically guaranteed secret ballots, provided that 24-hour Election Days would be holidays, and allowed individuals to rank candidate preferences in elections featuring three or more candidates. The section on the rights of citizens included the current provisions within the Bill of Rights as well as an additional guarantee that individuals could form labor unions.

Article II outlined the new parliament, which would remain bicameral. The Senate would select the president (the head of state) from among its members with the advice and consent of the House of Representatives. The president would, in turn, appoint the prime minister (the head of government) from among the ranks of the House.

Each state was to be guaranteed at least two seats in the House, which would be presided over by a speaker recommended by the prime minister. One third of the members would be chosen according to proportional representation among parties gathering over 10 percent of the vote. All bills would originate in the House. In addition to its current powers, the House could form "an independent board of directors for state-sponsored media to assure news and information" would be balanced and professional. The Senate would have half the number (unspecified) of representatives, with some being selected on a district basis. The House could override Senate vetoes by a two-thirds vote.

The prime minister and the minister's cabinet would wield executive power. The prime minister could select members of the cabinet, which would include ministers of foreign affairs, finance, defense, and justice, from either house of parliament. The prime minister would make treaties and nominate ambassadors and judges with the advice and consent of both houses of parliament. The prime minister would also be commander in chief of the armed forces.

The system included provisions for a vote of no confidence. In the case of a "no confidence" vote by the House, the president would have the option of appointing a new prime minister or calling a new election. Elections for the House would have to take place at least once every four years. Article II also recognized the right of the opposition to introduce bills on select days and to engage in a weekly question hour. Article III did not vary significantly from the current judicial article. Neither did the remaining two articles, which dealt with miscellaneous matters and the amending process.

Robert Struble, Jr., Proposes a "Twelve Code" Combining Liberal and Conservative Ideas

In the late 1990s, Bob Struble, Jr. (1943–), a schoolteacher active in the Washington State Republican Party, posted an online work called "Redeeming U.S. Democracy." This work introduced what Struble called a "Twelve Code," a set of constitutional revisions that he hoped to propose through a constitutional convention. The document was a unique blend of proposals. Some of them would likely find favor with today's cultural conservatives, while other provisions, especially in the area of employment, seem more likely to be welcomed by liberals. Interestingly, one-time presidential candidate Eugene McCarthy wrote an introduction to the site.

Struble dedicated his work to Jesus's mother Mary, and began his preface by asking that God "forgive us the offenses and help us to turn, individually and socially, from license to liberty." In the preamble to his Twelve Code, Struble further noted that "the authority of government is the people's from God." Unlike Strittmatter's constitution based on the Ten Commandments, however, most of Struble's proposals deal with secular matters.

The first section of Struble's proposal called for limiting members of the U.S. House of Representatives to one term in the hope of making that body more democratic. Struble thought that the Senate should have more "expertise and institutional memory." He thus did not favor imposing term limits on the latter body, although he was willing to allow states to do so.

The second section of Struble's Twelve Code clarified the first by indicating that members of the House would begin their first two years of service as tribunates, during which time they would perform functions as ombudsmen, investigators, and assistants to the vice president. The vice president, in turn, would have power to veto existing regulations subject to veto by either the U.S. president, both houses of Congress, or the "Committee of Cuts" (a body designed to keep the budget under control). After the Representatives served as tribunates for two years, they would then become regular House members whose salary would be set at "twice the median income of the American household." Representatives would be subject to recall, and ex-representatives would serve as a local advisory body to the president. Their duties would also include proposing nominees for the office of "Tenth Justice," which Struble described later.

The third section of the Twelve Code was devoted to "Checks against Judicial Usurpation." Struble would clarify the power of Congress to trim the appellate jurisdiction of federal courts, in which cases decisions of state courts would become final on such matters. Struble would further allow Congress to implement Supreme Court decisions more slowly and provided automatic "sunset provisions" on court-stripping actions.

Sections 4 and 5 of the Twelve Code dealt with congressional procedures. They would limit the influence of congressional committees by subordinating their deliberation to the will of the majority. Committees would be divided into fortnight committees (in which members could serve for a maximum of two weeks), half tribute committees (where tributes or volunteers would make up at least half of the membership), and joint Senate-House committees. Members would have greater choice over the selection and removal of committee chairs.

Sections 6 through 8 dealt with problems of unemployment and underemployment. Section 6 would allow Congress to equalize work by "reducing the duration of the work-week, workmonth, or workyear." Section 7 would grant Congress the power to generate jobs by working with private businesses to create "Private Enterprise Projects" (PEPs). Section 8 would further authorize tax incentives for employers, setting a tax rate of 0 percent for those businesses that were most labor intensive and establishing a 10 percent rate for those that used the least.

Sections 9 through 12 dealt with cultural and religious issues and tied civil rights to duties and responsibilities. Section nine attempted "to counter the commerce in lewdness which undermines human dignity and degrades the culture in which we must live." To this end, Struble would create a Tenth Justice of the U.S. Supreme Court, elected by the voters from among five women, and with power to issue injunctions against the importation, exportation, dissemination, or broadcast of "sexually licentious or pornographic phenomena," abbreviated as SLOPP. Consistent with a principle of current First Amendment law, Struble would provide for "subsequent punishment" on enjoined materials rather than for "prior restraint." Work consisting of "only the written word shall never qualify as SLOPP."

Section 10 provided for a place for scripture in schools. Teachers could read such passages in public schools for up to 12 minutes a day. Similarly, teachers would be permitted to post the Ten Commandments and up to 10 other scripture verses. Section 11 provided that pupils who dissented from such readings should "practice silent [and inconspicuous] nonparticipation." States would also be permitted to give money to religious schools or to parents paying tuition to the same, but never in a way so as to "undermine or modify a school's moral and religious character, or to change its religious exercises."

Section 12 explicitly provided for prayers, including the Lord's Prayer, in public schools, as long as they were "initiated in the classroom by the respective teacher." Struble ended with a benediction that included a number of scriptures. Struble noted that his amendments were only 20 percent shorter than the Constitution they were amending, but observed that "a few brief sentences will not suffice to streamline today's Capitol City apparatus."

A revised version of Struble's constitutional reforms, now called a Treatise on Twelve Lights, is available online at the author's Tell-usa.org Web site. According to the site, Struble's proposed reforms were last updated in 2010.

An Objectivist Constitution Works from the Philosophy of Ayn Rand

Objectivism is a philosophy of government that has grown out of the libertarian philosophy of Ayn Rand. According to Rand herself, objectivist philosophy held that the pursuit of one's own rational self-interest and happiness was the highest moral purpose in life. She also described laissez-faire capitalism as the ideal political-economic system for the successful pursuit of those goals.

Objectivism Wiki is a user-contributed reference Web site that focuses on Ayn Rand's objectivist philosophy. It includes an objectivist version of the U.S. Constitution with proposed additions and deletions (http://wiki.objectivismonline.net /New_constitution). Proposed changes to the preamble included deleting the general welfare clause and adding a provision to "protect property," and another "acknowledging that the proper function of government is to protect the freedom of individuals from the initiation of force."

Article I (the legislative branch) incorporated the existing Ninth and Tenth Amendments and added that "no powers delegated to the United States by the Constitution, nor powers retained by the states nor subsidiary governments or municipalities thereof shall be construed in any way inconsistent with clause 2 [the Ninth Amendment]." Clause 6 of the existing Article provided that the chief justice would preside over the Senate in the case of both presidential and vice presidential impeachment trials. Objectivists proposed major changes in the allocations of congressional powers in Article I, Section 8. In place of the power "to lay and collect" taxes, the first clause would provide that Congress has power to "charge fees for the services of the United States from those who choose to use those services; but such fees shall be uniform throughout the United States and furthermore to raise revenue through other non-coercive means such as a lottery." The proposal would delete current powers to regulate commerce, coin money, establish post offices, and the like. A clause specifically provided that "Congress shall make no law abridging the freedom of production and trade."

Article II (the executive branch) would obligate the president to "veto and negate any law which is in violation of this Constitution." Presidential pardons, like nominations, would be executed unless rejected by the Senate within 90 days. The revisions provided that "no official action of the President, Vice-President, or any civil or military Officer of the United States shall be exempt from Constitutional Review under the Judicial Power of the United States."

Article III (the judicial branch) would incorporate changes inaugurated by the Eleventh Amendment and was worded so as to prevent Congress from withdrawing judicial review over any laws. Article IV (federalism) remained intact. Article V added a seven-year deadline for ratifying amendments and provided that "no Amendment shall authorize the initiation of force by the United States or any State." Article VI further stipulated that "each State retains the option of peacefully seceding from the United States by a vote of three fourths of its citizens in a referendum, if the state on becoming a new nation adopts the protections of individual rights laid out in this constitution."

The proposed constitution specified several changes in the Bill of Rights. The First Amendment would prohibit congressional laws abridging "any action that does not harm or threaten another person." The Second Amendment would be stripped of language referring to a well-regulated militia. The Fifth Amendment would require that indictments specify "who is alleged to have been harmed or threatened, and how." The Eighth Amendment would add compensation for "any

· loss from wrongful imprisonment" and provide "the cost of defense against any criminal prosecution that does not result in valid conviction of a crime."

Provisions in the Fourteenth Amendment would apply to both the state and national governments and would apportion representation among states according to "citizens registered to vote in each State." The proposed constitution would delete the Sixteenth Amendment, authorizing the national income tax, and the Twenty-Fourth Amendment relative to poll taxes.

Constitution of the New America Offers a Constitution of Three Articles and the Liberty Proclamation

RationalWiki is the site of a posting for a "Constitution of the New America" and "THE LIBERTY PROCLAMATION," which were apparently posted in late 2007. The author of these documents, last accessed by this book's author on July 16, 2013, is unknown, but the documents are followed by an article titled "The End Time Servant," by Joan M. Veon, a self-described businesswoman and independent journalist concerned about U.S. participation in the United Nations and other international bodies.

The preamble, almost identical to the current one in other respects, established the Constitution "for the Free Republic(s) of New America." Article I, which dealt with the "Legislative Governmental Components," actually described both legislative and executive branches. The legislature would apparently be a unicameral body whose members would serve single three-year terms. Depressed areas would be permitted to send additional "Economic Representatives." The executive branch, which would apparently dominate, would consist of 12 members serving for six-year terms, the oldest two of which would rotate off every two years. Members would apparently be chosen by the Defense Department, and they would be empowered to choose the "Supreme Chief Commander." The executive branch would make laws governing the judiciary. The section also mentioned the creation of a Public Infrastructure that includes a Just Law Observance Board and a "FREE ENERGY SOCIETY," which is not otherwise explained. This section also mentioned the creation of an "Executive Overseer" and a board of education to mandate the teaching of "the Values of our Liberty, True History, and Self-reliance."

Article 1 pledged continuing adherence to "the original Bill-of-Rights from the United States of America as a Motherland heritage of the highest significance." It further stated that "New America and its Republic(s) shall NEVER submit its sovereignty to any foreign or domestic entity," including the United Nations.

Article 2 dealt with taxes and public service compensation. Taxes were to be collected on 5 to 10 percent of taxable goods and divided evenly among expenditures for defense, public infrastructure, and public health. The article further spelled out ratios of compensation for public officials. A "costless health care system" would provide suitable compensation for service providers. The executive branch could further request contributions from citizens. Section 2 also provided for using gold and silver as legal currency.

Article 3 addressed freedoms. Section 1 pointed to the origins of the United States in Protestantism and thus limited "the public display of worship of Jesus The Christ alone." While the constitution would not mandate that individuals be Protestant Christians, it would only recognize them. Section 2 required the press to correct mistaken stories and classified the publication of "subversive materials" as treasonous. Section 3 provided a similar limit on subversive speech. Section 4 prohibited national interference with the right to bear arms. Section 5 further prohibited conscription to fill the ranks of the armed forces. The provision in Section 6 on searches and seizures provided greater limits than the current Fourth Amendment, while the provisions in Section 7 on trial and punishment eliminated prisons (although it kept jails) and provided for public shaming, compensation, banishments, and capital punishment while banning all forms of torture. Permissible means of execution included lethal injection, hanging, firing squad, or public drowning. Juries were changed to consist of odd numbers of jurors and provided for majority votes to eliminate hung juries, but the constitution would encourage arbitration to settle many legal disputes.

In acknowledging privacy rights, Section 10 prohibited restrictions on alcohol and drugs consumed in private as well as pornography and prostitution. In bold letters, however, it proclaimed that "NO HOMOSEXUAL ACTIVITY, PEDOPHILIA, ABORTION, [OR] EUTHANASIA SHALL EVER BE CONDONED OR TOLERATED IN NEW AMERICA." It further defined a family as "a wedded Man and Woman and any subsequent offspring or adoptions of children."

The Liberty Proclamation that followed resembled the Declaration of Independence but was typed in all capital letters. It condemned the current government as a form of despotism, recognized the continuing legitimacy of the Confederate States of America, opposed "forced integration" and "multiculturalism," and reaffirmed America's Protestant foundations.

Another document entitled "Abridging Principles of the Constitution of New America" blamed numerous problems on the rich and powerful and reiterated that God ordained the death penalty to "rid society of "Human Predators." It outlined a role for victims and their families in deciding on criminal penalties. It further ranted about "apostate" religion, including those who use the Scofield Reference Bible.

Steve Gillman Calls for a Constitution Emphasizing Political Beliefs over Geography

Steve Gillman of Colorado writes a blog on a host of subjects ranging from the outdoors to politics. Gillman posted ideas for "A New Constitution," perhaps around September 2008, when he published an article entitled "A Better U.S. Constitution?"

Pointing in that article to antiquated features of the Constitution, Gillman recognized the danger of creating "an entirely new constitution." Nonetheless, he expressed particular enthusiasm for a system with "an electoral process that is less based on geography and more on . . . political beliefs." In a proposed preamble in

"A New Constitution," Gillman proposed limiting governmental powers to those "specified in the constitution." He argued that the government's sole function is that of protecting rights, and he believed that the government should adhere to these standards both at home and abroad.

In implementing a revised constitution, Gillman proposed voiding all existing laws within two years. He favored mandating that each law only address a single issue. Passage of laws should require a two-thirds vote of both houses and the consent of the president, who should be able to exercise a line-item veto. Individuals could run for office once they obtain a designated percentage of signatures from registered voters. They could be party members but could not run under party labels. Voters would be able to vote for multiple candidates. Gillman advocated limiting the House of Representatives to 200 members, who would serve four-year terms and would no longer be geographically based. Senators would serve terms of eight years.

Gillman was open to other ideas. He noted that he favored proposals "that create a true limit to the power of government, and a clear vision of its purpose," which he considered to be protecting "the rights of individuals" who live within it.

Kirby Palm Seeks Three Kinds of Amendments to Eliminate Career Politicians

Kirby Palm (1955–) is a Floridian who graduated from Florida Technological University in Orlando in 1977 and has since retired from engineering. He has a Web site on which he proposed adding three kinds of amendments to the U.S. Constitution.

The first concerned "Applicability," and sought to clarify and distinguish the rights of "natural-born" U.S. citizens from "naturalized" citizens, the latter of which he did not think should have the right to vote: "Immigrants should be very happy to be able to become U.S. citizens even if they don't get full rights; their children born here *will* get full rights, which is a valuable objective for immigrating." Palm also believed that the Constitution should specifically describe the rights of criminals, of children, and even of the unborn.

Palm proposed another section dealing with "Offense and Recourse." He favored making the existing Constitution much more specific. He thus proposed a textual explanation of the Second Amendment right to bear arms that would deny the government's power to require a license, outlaw ammunition, outlaw particular types of arms, or prohibit the bearing of arms in particular situations. He favored a variation of the U.S. Supreme Court with no "connections to the other branches of the federal government" and with the power "to expel elected officials from office, if necessary." Much as monarchs can call new elections in parliamentary systems, such a body would be able to expel "all the Senators, Congressmen, and the President whose signatures appeared on a piece of legislation that was in clear violation of the Constitution."

Palm proposed a third section specifying how a state could peacefully secede. He doubted that any states would choose to do so but argued that "having the threat of secession might be just what the federal government needs to keep them from usurping more and more of the states' rights." On his personal Web site, Palm has also proposed an amendment that would repeal the Twenty-Seventh Amendment and provide that "no person shall hold successive terms in an elected office." This would apply to all offices at either state or national levels. His stated goal was that of eliminating "the career politician."

Ernest Pain Seeks to Limit Governmental Powers and Make Them More Subject to Popular Will

Ernest Pain posted the draft of "A New Constitution for the United States of America" on the Internet out of concern that elites had "hijacked" all three branches of the government, and in the hope that his proposal would serve as a starting point for a constitutional convention.

Pain's proposal followed the current outline of the Constitution but incorporated current amendments in appropriate places. His preamble declared that the first purpose of the U.S. Constitution was "to protect the rights of individual citizens." It sought to do this through "a federal republic of limited powers that serves with and by the consent of the governed." It further set forth the goal of seeing that all three branches of the federal government are coequal and that each will seek to protect individual rights "without presuming to substitute the judgment of officials for the right of each person to self-determination." Pain's constitution relied strongly on appeals to the people through referenda and on the use of modern technology, and subjected all actions of the national government "to Citizen Referendum."

Article I began with a Bill of Rights, which largely tracked current amendments. Pain's equivalent of the First Amendment specifically prohibited the use of "public funds and resources to any religious institution" and extended protection "to such electronic extensions in cyberspace such as the Internet, social networks, and such other technological realms as may in future exist." An extension of the Fourth Amendment provided security in "persons, houses, papers, private communications, and effects." An extension of the Eighth Amendment barred capital punishment except during time of war. Additional provisions protected the right to die, access to medical care, and the right to an abortion during the first and second trimesters. A provision also protected voting against abridgment on the basis of "race, religion, color, gender, disability, ethnicity, sexual orientation, social or economic status, or previous conviction of a crime for which the punishment shall have been satisfied." Another guaranteed the right to "a secular public education at public expense" within one's state or territory and vested curricular matters in local authorities. Still another provided a guarantee of online access to all citizens.

Congress would remain the same size in Pain's proposed government, but House members would serve one-year terms and Senate terms would be reduced to three years. The former would be limited to 10 years of total service and the latter to 15. All elections would be publicly financed, and proceedings of Congress "will be broadcast to The People in real time." Pain elaborated the powers of Congress in greater detail than in the current document. For example, he specified that the right to raise armed forces extended to "an air force, a marine corps, a coast guard, and such other branches of the armed forces as may be necessary." One provision would prohibit members of Congress from adopting legislation that did not apply equally to them. A war powers section would require a two-thirds vote to declare war and limit voting to those who have previously served or who have children serving in the armed forces. If Congress did not approve of a presidential troop deployment within 30 days, the troops would have to be withdrawn.

Article II provided for the people to choose the president and vice president every two years by popular vote. Article III increased the number of Supreme Court justices from 9 to 11. It further provided that nominees submitted by the president to Congress would receive automatic confirmation if Congress did not act on their nominations within three months. Pain expected the Court to uphold laws approved by popular referendum, adding that it should overturn laws "only in such cases as there has been a showing of clear and convincing proof of a violation of the rights of equal protection to an identifiable minority." The people would have power to overturn judicial precedents through a referendum by two-thirds of the voters, although this vote would not affect the decision in the particular case that prompted the referendum.

Pain left Sections IV and V virtually untouched. Article VI would provide for the continuation of laws enacted under the prior document, and Article VII would provide for ratification by a popular vote of the people in 34 or more states.

George Wynne Proposes an Amendment to Put the People "Over the Law"

"An Amendment Proposal" was sponsored and posted online as part of an otherwise unidentified Equality over the Law Project. The proposal was posted by George Wynne, who identified himself only as a resident of Houston. Although the proposal is phrased as a single amendment, it contains numerous parts that focused on giving greater political power to the people.

An introduction explained the author's conviction that people should be equal not only "*under the law*" but also "*over the law*." It further argued that "our Constitution violates equality over the law in a clear manner," most notably in apportioning representation in the Senate, in the Electoral College, and in respect to constitutional amendments. The proposal, prefaced with a preamble that noted "that all women and men are created equal" and that they have an "inalienable right to alter our government," called for seven reforms, namely:

1. Ratification according to the principles of political equality
2. Future amendments by national referendum
3. Representation of the states in proportion to population in the Senate
4. The direct election of the president
5. Statehood for D.C. and the territories
6. The end of the filibuster
7. More accurate apportionment

Although most of these proposals were relatively straightforward, the two open-ing amending provisions were the lynchpin of the rest. Section 1 provided that "Article V is inoperative on the proposal and ratification of this amendment." It further specified that the amendment shall be "proposed in a biennial election upon a majority vote of the People in a group of States, Territories, and the District constituting the seat of Government of the United States, provided that this group comprises a majority of this nation's population." It made similar provision for ratification; if adopted, Section 2 specified that the amendment would repeal Ar-ticle V completely, and provided for future amendments to be proposed "by major-ity vote of both houses of Congress" or of "an Amendment Convention called by a group of States" with a majority of the nation's population and approved "upon a majority vote of the People."

Section 3 of the proposed amendment would provide that "each Senator shall have one vote for each person in his or her State, according to the last census." Section 5, in addition to providing for statehood for the District of Columbia and for U.S. territories, further stated that "every citizen of the United States shall be the citizen of a State."

Wynne also argued for the "non-exclusivity" of the current amending process in Article V. Relying in part on arguments advanced by Akhil Reed Amar of Yale, Wynne argued that "Article V does not say it is the exclusive means to amend the Constitution." He further pointed out that those who adopted the Constitution by-passed the method of amendment spelled out in the Articles of Confederation, and that the obvious complement to the Preamble of the Constitution is the proposition that "we have the power to alter or abolish it as well."

Randy Barnett Proposes a Bill of Federalism Designed to Affirm Libertarian Ideas

Randy Barnett (1952–), a professor of law at Georgetown University, has ad-vanced his libertarian ideas in a book entitled *Restoring the Lost Constitution: The Presumption of Liberty* (2004), in which he relied largely on his interpretation of the Ninth Amendment to criticize Supreme Court decisions that have expanded federal powers. Barnett believed that restoring federalism was a key to enhancing liberty, which he especially associated with property rights. He reflected further on these ideas in an article entitled "A Bill of Federalism," which was published on Forbes.com on May 20, 2009.

Barnett began with a resolution for states to convene a convention to consider amendments to the Constitution. Arguing that the Constitution was designed to enumerate a set of limited congressional powers and that the Supreme Court had upset the balance between state and national authority, he accordingly memo-rialized Congress to call a constitutional convention when receiving identically worded resolutions from two-thirds or more of the states. Barnett proposed 10 amendments, which he followed with explanatory commentary.

Barnett's first proposed amendment would, over a five-year period, elimi-nate all taxes on "incomes, gifts, or estates, or upon aggregate consumption or expenditures" but permit "a uniform tax on the sale of goods and services" (a national sales tax). It would also require a three-fifths vote of both houses of Congress to increase any "tax, duty, impost or excise." Barnett's second proposal would limit congressional powers under the commerce clause by exempting most activities that do not cross state lines, thereby reversing legal decisions that permitted congressional regulations of "wholly interstate activity that either (a) 'affects' interstate activity, (b) uses instrumentalities obtained from outside the state, or (c) is part of a comprehensive national regulatory scheme." A third proposal sought to ban unfunded federal mandates or conditions that Congress sought to attach to appropriations for the states. Barnett's fourth proposed amendment sought to prevent Congress from using its powers to ratify treaties to increase its domestic powers.

Barnett's fifth proposed amendment would extend freedom of speech and press to cover all campaign contributions and all forms of media equally. The sixth—and arguably most significant—proposed amendment would allow three-quarters of the states to repeal any act of congressional legislation (Vile 2011, 38–9). Barnett asserted that this proposed measure "provides a targeted method to reverse particular Congressional acts and administrative regulations without the risk of permanently amending the text of the Constitution." His seventh proposed amendment would impose a two-term limit on members of the Senate and a six-term limit on members of the House. The eighth proposal further sought to guarantee balanced federal budgets by giving the president the right to exercise a line-item veto over any item in the next session of Congress.

The proposed ninth amendment read more like a preamble. After declaring that "all persons are equally free and independent, and have certain natural, inherent and unalienable rights" including that of "enjoying, defending and preserving of their life and liberty, acquiring, possessing and protecting real and personal property, making binding contracts of their choosing, and pursuing their happiness and safety," section 2 proceeded to associate due process of law with the principle that the government had the burden of showing that any law or regulation was adopted in "conformity with this Constitution." A final tenth amendment sought to prevent courts from altering the meaning of the Constitution by requiring that interpretation be based on "their meaning at the time of their enactment" unless subsequently amended. A number of other advocates of constitutional change have echoed some of Barnett's proposals.

Jon Roland Posts Proposals on Behalf of the Constitution Society

Jon Roland (1944–) is a graduate of the University of Chicago who has spent most of his life in computer work and ran as a Libertarian candidate for attorney general of Texas in 2002. Roland has posted a number of proposed constitutional amendments on a Web site that he helps maintain for the Constitution Society. The Web site described the society as a private nonprofit organization founded in 1994 that is "dedicated to research and public education on the principles of constitutional republican government." To advance those goals, the organization "publishes documentation, engages in litigation, and organizes local citizens groups to work for reform." Roland said he began the site on April 13, 2009.

Roland divided his list of proposed amendments into what he called "Clarifying, Remedial, and Substantive" proposals. Clarifying amendments were "intended only to return legal practice to original understandings." Remedial amendments were designed "to correct errors and omissions." Substantive amendments proposed "some additional powers that many people might think the national government should be authorized to exercise." Roland indicated, however, that it was less important that many of the specific amendments be adopted than that they result in legal reforms.

Roland proposed 32 clarifying amendments. Many were designed to illumine constitutional terms such as right, regulate, commerce, militia, titles of nobility, piracy, trial by jury, speech, press, the general welfare, and direct and indirect taxes. One proposal specified that the necessary and proper clause in Article I, Section 8 granted Congress "to make a limited, reasonable effort strictly necessary to exercise an express power narrowly construed, and not to go beyond completion of the duty or to do whatever might be deemed convenient to get an outcome or result for which the effort might be made." The definition of commerce was similarly limiting. An amendment on "rules of construction" indicated that precedents should "be regarded as persuasive and never binding," and it also stipulated that constitutional texts be constructed on the basis of "historical evidence of the meaning and understanding of the terms for, first their ratifiers, and second, their framers." A provision on the militia indicated that they "shall be maintained in a state of readiness sufficient to overcome any regular military force it might encounter." A provision on jury trials prevented defendants from being able to waive the right and limited *voir dire* examination of jurors.

Roland listed 13 remedial amendments. These included a statement that the Sixteenth Amendment (authorizing a national income tax) "was never ratified, or if it was, is hereby repealed and rescinded retroactively." Another provision would prevent the vice president from presiding over the Senate when being tried in an impeachment trial.

Roland listed 33 substantive amendments. They included limitations on the volume of legislation that Congress could adopt; federal jurisdiction over coastal waters out to three miles; assigning greater weight to votes of members of the House of Representatives and state legislatures who represent higher numbers of people; provision for a multistage nominating process for the U.S. Senate and other bodies not specifically based on population; and the prohibition of occupational licensing, "especially of lawyers by lawyers or judges." Another provision classified violation of the constitution as "a capital offense." Yet another would require individuals participating in the Electoral College to pass examinations "in which each shall recite from memory twenty randomly selected clauses of this Constitution." Another amendment stated that if two-thirds of the states proposed identically worded amendments within a four-year period, such amendments would become part of the constitution if ratified by three-fourths of the states. An amendment providing for the "power to cancel or suspend economic activity" would allow for a *shmita* period every seven years (based on Jewish ideas of sabbatical years in which fields would lie fallow) to cancel debts, break up corporations, and cancel activities related to the extraction of minerals, harvesting, fishing, and manufacturing.

John K. Piper Calls for a Constitution for the Twenty-First Century

On November 14, 2010, John K. Piper, who described himself as "JohnnyK, an average Joe in Austin, Texas," posted what he called "A United States Constitution for the 21st Century." His proposal contained both a "'Pipe Dream' U.S. Constitution" and another set of individual amendments favored by Piper. Both were extremely detailed and discursive, with Piper adding loquacious commentary to the Pipe Dream Constitution.

The revised preamble included a number of alterations. It changed the words "promote justice" to "suppress injustice" and added a provision to "ensure governmental accountability." Part I of the constitution dealt with "Persons," which are identified as "free agents," with the right to do what they want as long as they do not harm others. Persons have the right to seek restitution for violations of their rights, which can only be fully protected within a republic. Governments would be prevented from legislating on any topics not "specifically enumerated." The constitution would guarantee rights of life, property, and liberty, including the right to suicide, to decide on personal medical treatments, to ingest various intoxicants that do not result in harm to others, to buy and sell sex acts, to terminate pregnancies up to four and a half months after conception, and to marry whom they choose. Property rights and rights to livelihood would also be guaranteed, with income taxes and other taxes on labor eliminated, along with minimum wages, business licenses or permits, and the like. Personal rights would include the right to "be free from unfair, excessive, unequal, or complicated taxation" or from paying more than 25 percent of one's income in combined federal, state, county, and municipal taxes. Individuals would retain the right of expression, although governmental censors would be permitted during times of declared war. Individuals would have the right to "Be unpopular or vile; To be a Bigot" and to travel freely. The constitution would acknowledge parental rights and responsibilities with regard to their children. It would also recognize a "Right of Scofflaw," or "Resistance to Tyranny," both of which grant rights to defy unconstitutional directives. The individual right to guns would include weapons for self-defense, hunting, and resistance to unlawful government. Provisions also stated that laws would be clearly stated and applied equally, and that civil cases would begin in mediation and arbitration. The people would also be empowered through state governments to nullify federal laws.

Article 2 addressed personal responsibilities. Piper referred to the idea of "Positive Rights" as odious, and was adamant that illegal aliens were uninvited trespassers. He would accordingly divide people into three groups—citizens, residents, and aliens. Residents would include "natural-born people who have demonstrated no knowledge of the US and no loyalty to either the US or a foreign nation." Citizenship would require education in "American, British, and Western History;

American government; Civics; Ethics: Vocabulary; Logic; Economics; Leadership; [and] Arithmetic." All schools would be private but would be expected to follow minimum state standards.

Part II of the Pipe Dream constitution was "applicable to all governments." It set minimum qualifications for holding political office and provided that "all laws need to be approved by a majority of voters." It further anticipated that political parties would continue but be "weaker and more transparent." Companies would be commissioned to build roads and receive usage fees in return. Money from fines would be directed to chartered charity or fraternal organizations. Article 3 of this part of the constitution provided that "no law or regulation shall ever be passed unless there is an absolute need for it." Governments would be prohibited from providing subsidies or otherwise foster "dependency on government, or usurping the responsibilities of Persons."

Part III of the Pipe Dream constitution would apply to nonfederal governments. States would exercise primary authority over numerous defined areas including weapons; mineral extraction; the environment; marriages, unions, and divorces; abortion; and drug use. States unable to pay their portion of the federal budget for two of three years would go into receivership, and three-fifths of the states could nullify federal laws.

Part IV outlined the primary branches of the federal government. It would vest legislative powers in the Senate, the House of Representatives, and the Citizens Ballot Initiative. Members of the House would serve nonconsecutive two-year terms and be nominated either by "self-promotion, or by random-promotion." Senators would be appointed by state governors and the speaker of the state's most numerous legislative branch. All legislation would require a three-fifths vote in the House, and the Senate would have the right to veto but not initiate legislation. Ballot initiatives would enable people to repeal laws, restore laws, close governmental departments, change or eliminate fees, and the like. Federal spending would be limited to 15 percent of the gross domestic product, and the federal government would be prohibited from providing subsidies to the states. Congress would lose its ability to enact taxes except in times of declared war, or to borrow for more than 25 years. The nation would rely on sales taxes, user fees, and the Fair Tax. Its existing powers over interstate commerce would be restricted. Regulatory agencies would be grandfathered in but would require greater congressional direction and oversight. Congress would create a standard labor contract for companies to follow, and the redeemable value of the dollar would be pegged at 25 milligrams of gold. Congress would provide means for individuals to protect their reputations and a "Chamber of Repeal" would handle cases of impeachment.

The president would execute the will of Congress and the authority of that office would be balanced by an elected attorney general from another party or coalition. The president would serve nonconsecutive four-year terms. Supreme Court justices would be selected from federal judges by lottery. A military council would guide wartime operations, and both houses of Congress would concur in treaties. A Secretary of Epidemics and Subsistence would be authorized to mandate inoculations to prevent the spread of diseases. The president could target foreigners overseas for assassination. The United States would have to make a five-year commitment to any allies in war and use "all means fair and foul to win." Laws would be subject to judicial review, but could be overturned by the president and three-fifths majorities in Congress, which could remand them for binding decisions by an inferior court.

Part V of the Pipe Dream constitution outlined custodial branches of the federal government. These would include the Integrity Branch with an Inspector General, a Legislative Repeal Branch with a Chamber of Repeal, and an Administrative Review Branch with a Supreme Administrative Review Court. Part VI provided for an easier amending process, including ratification by "500 citizens randomly selected" from each state. It further provided for conventions every 20 years to consider each part of the constitution so that each would be reviewed within 100 years. The author listed 13 provisions—including those related to rights and revenues—that would be unamendable.

Another section of the Web site considered 13 proposed amendments and a final unnumbered amendment. These included a balanced budget amendment; a fair tax amendment; a clarification of the commerce clause; an amendment prohibiting omnibus bills and providing for a line-item veto; a prohibition of public sector unions; a clarification of the Fourteenth Amendment limiting birthright citizenship; an amendment making those on the losing side of cases pay legal fees; an amendment providing for the election of a comptroller, attorney general, and inspector general; strengthened provisions to protect against eminent domain; an amendment to count members of congress as part of a quorum when they purposely absented themselves; an amendment to forestall congressional corruption; provisions for a runoff election for the presidency; codification of the right of self-defense; and an amendment to rescue state governments that went bankrupt.

A Minarchist Proposal for a Return to Confederal Government

On January 31, 2011, an individual identified only as Anarchist420 posted a "minarchist replacement for the Constitution" on the AnandTech Forum Web site. It includes 10 very short articles and did not include commentary—aside from some fairly critical comments posted by other participants on the site. Its most notable provisions, including the preamble, include a reference to "a firm league of friendship," and a statement in Article II that mimicked that of the Articles of Confederation. This statement asserted that under the proposed constitution, "each state retains its sovereignty, freedom, and independence, and every Power, Jurisdiction, and right, which is not by this confederation expressly delegated to the United States."

Article IV excluded "paupers, vagabonds, and fugitives from justice" from "the privileges and immunities of free citizens in the several States." Article V listed the powers of Congress, which dealt chiefly with foreign affairs, but permitted the use of "private property for the public good." It also required "100% reserve commercial banking" and approved "intrastate secession," with a minimal size requirement for the seceding area to be determined later. This article further limited the ability of Congress to send conscripts abroad or to collect taxes "in anything other than in the form of gold and silver."

Article VI provided that each state would provide its U.S. representatives "due compensation." According to Article VII, state legislatures would appoint such representatives, each of which would "have one vote per every 750,000 people living in the state." Article VIII further prohibited states from allowing direct election of such individuals. It also prohibited states from issuing patents or copyrights, setting "interstate commerce barriers," or allowing slavery. Article IX provided that "this document is not supreme to the States, nor are the States Supreme to it, and the Confederation shall never use force against the States." An incomplete Article X was to provide for the regulation of oaths and debts. The constitution did not provide for a separate executive or judiciary branch, nor for provisions like those in the Bill of Rights. Presumably, as with the Articles of Confederation, Congress would exercise any executive powers and states would provide their own judges.

Billy Rojas Proposes 100 Amendments to Explain His Centrist Vision for the Future

In 2011, Billy Rojas, who has identified himself as a former lecturer of history and comparative religion, posted "A Radical Centrist Vision for the Future: 100 New Constitutional Amendments for the 21st Century" on the Web site Radical centrism.org.

Rojas began by outlining a "Radical Centrist" position between those who advocated originalism and those who favored a living constitution. He argued that it was necessary to offer a large number of amendments rather than to allow the task to be performed by unelected judges. Rojas called for an amendment to alter current Article V requirements so that amendments could be ratified by states with three-fourths or more of the population (rather than three-fourths of the 50 states) as long as they constituted more than half of the states. He also proposed giving each state three senators, so that each would have at least one such election every two years.

Rojas arranged his amendments under 11 categories, many of which included multiple pages of arguments and explanation. The opening section, on the presidency, called for such changes as opening access to presidential papers within 10 years after the chief executive leaves office; providing for succession in cases of presidential and vice presidential disability; requiring all recipients of presidential pardons to fully disclose their criminal wrongdoing; limiting recess appointments; providing for a line-item veto; making the president responsible for covert actions; and limiting secrecy restrictions.

The section on Congress contains 12 sections, the first of which has seven subdivisions. Provisions relative to Congress include requiring that all laws apply equally to members of Congress, who would have to provide for their own retirement, pensions, and health care coverage; penalizing members of Congress who failed to read legislation before they adopted it; removing convicted felons from office; assigning committee chairpersons between the parties through a new plan; devising more competitively drawn districting schemes; providing 20 at-large seats for members of minor parties; providing two or three nonpartisan tributes who would serve as national ombudsmen; capping the number of legislators from any single profession at 33 percent; limiting legislation to a clearly stated subject stated in its heading and providing for the expiration of the legislation in 20 years; mandating term limits of 12 consecutive years; and providing for updates of all federal laws and allowing two-thirds of state legislators to annul existing laws.

The section on the judiciary and criminal justice contained 15 sections. These included a provision for direct nonpartisan election of Supreme Court justices for eight-year terms while considering religious and ethnic balance; an admonition to take original intent seriously (including distinctions between homosexuals and "normal Americans"); changes in the amending process; stated constitutional justifications for all new laws; authorization for three-fourths of the state legislatures to rescind congressional laws; requirements for justices to explain their opinions; invalidation of decisions (Rojas cited *Roe v. Wade*) based on faulty evidence; provisions for removal of judges for due cause and for filling vacancies; requirements that seven of nine justices concur in overturning the result of any referenda or prohibitions against the use of any foreign law; punishments for those who knowingly adopt unconstitutional laws; provisions for equality of treatment regardless of wealth; implementation of speedy trial provisions; limits on legal fees and settlements; and limits on the costs of incarceration.

Section 4 dealt with elections, voting, and citizenship, and had nine parts. They included provisions to add one electoral vote for the at-large winner in the Electoral College for each state; a schedule for primaries and caucuses; limits on campaign spending; the establishment of voting standards; provisions for instant runoff elections; use of the Athenian Boule system (random assemblies of approximately 480 people) for approving ballot initiatives; overturning elections secured through fraud (including that of President Richard Nixon in 1972); limitation of citizenship to those with at least one citizen parent; and limitations on the rights of noncitizens.

Section 5, on governance, had 12 sections. They provided for replacing the civil service system with one that emphasized "competence and achievement"; redefining treason to include "the abusive assumption or issuance of knowingly unpayable debt"; establishing a national budget deadline; segregating of Social Security monies; prohibiting of unfunded state mandates or conditions on state expenditures of federal funds; establishing a high legislative bar to enact tax increases; means testing for all entitlements; increasing tax rates on the extremely wealthy; limiting regulations and government secrets; approving profiling as a law enforcement and security tool, especially of Muslims; providing state enforcement of immigration requirements; and adopting state bills of rights. As examples, Rojas included a workers' and employers' bill of rights, a consumer bill of rights, and a patients' bill of rights.

The section on foreign policy and foreign relations contained four parts. These parts called for encouraging democracy by limiting trade with nondemocratic nations; limiting participation in international organizations that included non-democratic members; requiring ambassadors to know the language of their host countries; and offering U.S. statehood to foreign nations. The last provision would prohibit any state from having more than 10 percent of the nation's total population and sought to balance the addition of new nations so as to continue to provide ethnic balance. Rojas favored immediate overtures to Canada, Australia, New Zealand, Israel, and Greenland.

The section on economics, trade and business contained eight subdivisions. The first, adapted from Randy Barnett, would limit the scope of federal power over commerce. Other provisions called for prohibitions on treating homes and real estate as derivatives; limiting usury (interest rates); allowing for unions but with open shops; permitting employees to own stock in the companies for which they worked; requiring construction companies to build affordable housing for those with low incomes; limiting the percent of the economy that could be devoted to financial services; and protections for "Economic Security, Trade Agreements and Corporate Policies." The latter would include prohibitions on hostile takeovers, and technology transfers and requirements for balanced trade with foreign countries.

The section on the environment and energy was designed to encourage legislation to protect the environment. It also prevented mountaintop removal and called for governmental repurchases of mineral rights. Provisions related to education were particularly detailed. The first provided for the teaching of "All Essentials." A second provided for a bill of rights and responsibilities for parents and teachers. A provision entitled the "Academic Bill of Rights," partly borrowed from David Horowitz, would eliminate academic tenure in all institutions supported by the federal government. The section also provided for electronic rights for students and teachers.

Section 10, dealing with social issues and values, provided for a "Right to Truth," which included access to government data. It also mandated enforcement of the Communist Control Act of 1954, which outlawed the Communist Party and affiliated organizations. The section would further eliminate the category of hate crimes, allow for the suppression of child pornography, and provide for cost/benefit accounting and foresight in federal legislation and for the recriminalization of homosexuality. The latter provision went into particular detail about the perceived immorality and ill consequences of homosexual practices.

The final section focused on the subject of religion. It required the teaching of comparative religion in public schools and declared Islam to be "incompatible with the US Constitution." This section provided for deporting all foreign-born Muslims, stripping U.S. citizenship from native-born citizens who were Muslims, punishing advocates of jihad with death; and dismissing all Muslims from the U.S. military. It also included language stating that Muslims could escape these punishments by renouncing their faith.

Thomas Wright Sulcer Proposes Making the State Department a Separate Branch of Government

On December 21, 2011, Thomas Wright Sulcer posted "The Second Constitution of the United States: A New and Improved Draft for the 21st Century," on Participedia. Sulcer described himself as a nonpartisan "handyman" in New Jersey who favored calling a new constitutional convention to institute parliamentary mechanisms while preserving a system of separation of powers.

Sulcer's posted constitution contained seven articles, the first of which dealt with Congress. Additions included provisions mandating "transparency," providing that "tax rules must be simple, straightforward and clear," and requiring senators to explain deficits of over 3 percent of the gross domestic product to state legislatures to receive either a vote of confidence or no confidence. Members of the House would serve two-year nonconsecutive terms and would be required to have served in a state legislature for at least one year before being eligible for the national body. Senators would be chosen by state legislatures from among those with training in the law.

Article II outlined the powers of the president, who would be selected by members of the House of Representatives from among members of the Senate. The president would have to appear before the House to answer questions and would be subject to a vote of no confidence. The president's powers would be limited to matters of domestic policy.

Article III described a supreme court of nine members who would serve 16-year terms. Article IV described a new Department of State, which would be responsible for the conduct of foreign policy. It would consist of three branches composed of foreign policy advisors, the head of state, and a military court.

The Senate would appoint 100 foreign policy advisors younger than age 40 who would serve for life. They would make treaties, determine immigration policies, and appoint the head of state, who would be commander in chief of the national armies. The military court would consist of 11 justices who "will have the final word in interpreting and judging all matters relating to foreign policy, including foreign relations, treaties, acts by citizens or soldiers abroad, or by foreigners in the United States."

Article V dealt with state governments, which would have full authority over intrastate commerce and matters involving "business, education, the professions, health care, insurance, taxation, and transportation." A majority of states could apply for Congress to make uniform regulations within these areas. Article VI dealt with citizenship. Individuals would not qualify until they turned 18, took a loyalty oath, pledged to support individual rights, and signed a copy of the Constitution in the presence of witnesses. They would be required to attend governmental meetings, vote, and comply with reasonable governmental requirements, including national defense. They would be protected by the existing Bill of Rights and by a right of privacy. Article VII dealt with miscellaneous issues. Sulcer ended with the pessimistic observation that "so far, this project has had no influence whatsoever."

A "Christian Prophet" Posts a Libertarian Constitution
Designed to Promote Moral Government

An author who identified himself as a "Christian Prophet" and a member of the Holy Instant Christian Church of Utah posted a proposed constitution, called a "21st Century Constitution for Moral Government," on Sunday, November 18, 2012. His blog postings, which sometimes quoted Mormon leaders, indicated that he was a libertarian. One such posting, "Libertarians to Conservatives: 'Wake Up! It's about Dictatorship,'" was posted on March 23, 2013. It asserted that "the fatal flaw of the U.S. Constitution" was that it permitted "three enemies of liberty: taxation, the legislation of man-made laws, and voting."

An abbreviated preamble cited "the blessings of life, liberty, and property ownership" as preconditions "for a peaceful, joyous, and loving society." Article I addressed the function and intent of governance. The author asserted that such governance is based on natural laws, which are clarified in Article II. They involved minimal government designed solely to outlaw murder, kidnapping, theft, and other evils. To this end, the government would not create a legislature to adopt additional laws, would not levy taxes, and would not permit voting. The author specifically outlawed "majority rule." Article III further specified that all funding of government would be voluntary, although it could charge for services it provided.

Article IV outlined the structure of government. It included an executive branch to enforce natural laws; a judicial branch to adjudicate disputes; and a monitoring branch to serve as a watchdog. Interim chiefs would be established for each, to be aided by five organization leaders or "consensors." They would select successors by "a 100% consensus." The chief executive would serve for 4 years, the chief justice for 7, and the chief monitor for 10. Despite praise for the Bill of Rights in his blogs, the author did not include a bill of rights with the proposed constitution, presumably because it would be unnecessary in the absence of a legislature. The constitution did not mention state or local governments.

Ian Pubman Posts a U.S. Constitution 2.0

On April 17, 2011, Ian Pubman, who identified himself as a former able seaman who studied law at the University of San Francisco School of Law and lived in Manhattan Beach, California, used a Facebook account to post headings of 22 constitutional amendments. Pubman designed his proposals "to restore the balance of power in government and to reaffirm the rights of the individual," and he dubbed his series of amendments "Constitution 2.0."

Pubman favored provisions to specifically acknowledge that individual rights took precedent over government, budget, and administrative agency controls; give greater power to the states; establish a tricameral House of Representatives; and formally incorporate the Declaration of Independence into the Constitution. It is difficult, however, to ascertain precisely what he wanted to do when he proposed an "Executive Branch Revision Amendment" (his sixth proposal), a "National Currency Reform Amendment" (his tenth), a "Firearms Amendment" (his twelfth), a

"Privacy Amendment"; or a "Level of Judicial Scrutiny Amendment" (his twenty-first) without specifically describing their purpose, function, or aims.

Ward Ricker Proposes a Modified Constitution for the United States

Ward Ricker, an antiabortion activist and songwriter, posted a "Modified Constitution for the United States of America," probably in 2011. Ricker's Web site contained a "five-point plan for democracy" that included electing good people, keeping them accountable, spreading word of government abuses, having mechanisms to fix the problems, and having a population that demanded that such fixes take place. Ricker was particularly critical of the two-party system and wanted to establish a system of "Instant Runoff Voting."

Although he believed that it would be better to create a new constitution from scratch, Ricker decided to integrate new materials and cross out sections that he thought should be deleted. His proposal included a preamble and nine articles. His preamble began with the statement that "it is the role of government to serve the people." The preamble further identified democracy as the "best guarantee" that it would do so and indicated that the revised constitution was being established to further democratic processes. An introductory article 0 further indicated that the new government would be divided into legislative, administrative, and judicial branches.

Article 1 would eliminate the U.S. Senate and allow the House to have up to 600 members. The House would assume most duties currently exercised by both houses. Two-thirds majorities of the House could override presidential vetoes and confirm ambassadors and other presidential appointees.

Ricker would eliminate the Electoral College and require the president to give information to Congress on the state of the union at least once every three months. Judges of the Supreme Court would be elected to 10-year terms, subject to five-year extensions with the consent of Congress. The authority of the Court would extend only to cases that it had directly considered, and a vote of two-thirds of the Congress could force the Court to reconsider any decision it had made during the previous year. Ricker did not significantly change Article IV of the Constitution, but he would empower a two-thirds majority of the House to propose amendments; these would be ratified according to current processes. His Article 6 provided for continuity in governments.

Article 7 revised existing amendments. Section 1 provided that Congress should "make no law promoting or restricting any religion," but it specified that protections for speech and press should not prevent government from prosecuting "libel, inciting violence, and speech intended to defraud or endanger." Section 2 permitted controlling guns "in order to protect the people from violence." Section 5 defined "Person" as "any human being, that is, any member of the species homo sapiens." Section 12 institutionalized the principle of "one vote per one person." Section 14 provided limited citizenship to "all persons legally born or naturalized in the United States." Section 28 provided that "no person's right to vote, hold office, travel freely, work, own property, . . . [and] be secure from threats of violence" would be "denied or restricted due to race, color, ethnicity, gender, sexual orientation, religious or other beliefs, stage of development or other personal characteristics."

Article 8 added seven sections relative to domestic politics. Specific provisions prevented the government from deporting citizens or denying them entry into the country; provided for greater transparency in government through creation of a "Secrecy Classification Board" and a "Secrecy Classification Commission"; prevented deficit spending and initiated progressive taxes of from 0 to 50 percent; authorized free public education to citizens through the twelfth grade as well as health care to all; mandated recycling and reuse programs at all levels of government; held governmental officials liable for wrongdoing; and authorized a plebiscite whenever 5 percent or more of the public demanded it.

A final Article 9 prohibited the nation from attacking, invading, or carrying out covert actions against nations except when under attack by them. It further prevented the nation from supplying aid to dictatorships or to nations possessing nuclear weapons or engaged in human rights abuses.

The *Slate Magazine* Pastiche

In 2012, the online magazine *Slate* invited a number of scholars to propose ways of "fixing the Constitution," and also solicited ideas from its readers. Chris Kirk of *Slate* subsequently posted a constitution that incorporated the ideas it found most worthy. Larry Sabato at the University of Virginia contributed a revision to Article I, Section 3 providing that larger states would have greater representation in the U.S. Senate. Richard L. Hasen proposed changing Section 4 so that a U.S. election commission would establish the time, place, and manner of holding elections. A reader further proposed that instead of assembling each year, members of Congress would rarely convene in the capitol but would "vote from home, host public committee meetings on Face Time [videotelephony technology] and share legislative drafts in an open forum." Michael McConnell added a provision to Section 5 providing that the rules of each house of Congress would not take effect until three years after they were enacted. With a view to the dormant commerce clause doctrine, Theodore Ruger proposed rephrasing the commerce clause so that it no longer voided state legislation except "in instances of direct conflict, or where the preemptive force of such enactment is made explicit by statute, or is based on a considered finding by an agency to whom Congress has delegated the authority to make such determination."

Michael McConnell proposed changing Article II by providing that the president would serve a single six-year term. David S. Law called for presidential nominees to be selected through a series of four regional primaries, and to prohibit such primaries from excluding individuals on the basis of party affiliation. Garrett Epps contributed an extensive addition on the office of attorney general, elected by the people to four-year terms. Larry Sabato recommended placing limitations on presidential commitments of troops in a fashion similar to the provisions contained in the War Powers Resolution of 1973.

Moving to Article II, Sabato joined with Linda Greenhouse to propose a non-renewable term of 18 years for Supreme Court justices. Jed Shugerman suggested requiring a two-thirds vote or more before the Supreme Court could void a federal statute as unconstitutional (two *Slate* readers suggested setting the bar even higher, at seven votes). Rachel E. Barkow proposed adding a provision forbidding prosecutors from seeking higher penalties for individuals who chose jury trials.

Under Article IV, *Slate* included a provision submitted by one reader that provided that "Congressional Districts shall be determined regionally, across State Lines." Bruce Ackerman proposed in Article V that a second-term president be empowered to propose amendments that, if approved by Congress, would appear on the ballot in the next election. These amendments would become part of the Constitution if approved by 60 percent or more of the voters.

Michael Meyerson provided that government could not burden religion without an important governmental interest. A reader, meanwhile, wanted to see that corporate rights did not override individual rights. Adam Cohen called for modifying the Fourth Amendment specifically to cover "the people's right to privacy in their data and communications." Ethan J. Leib and Dan Market recommended extending the double jeopardy provisions of the Fifth Amendment to charges that ended in hung juries.

Rachel Barkow proposed adding a limit on "excessive terms of incarceration" to the Eighth Amendment, while Judith Resnik and Jonathan Curtis-Resnik recommended eliminating the death penalty and "prolonged solitary confinement." Dan Market and Eric J. Miller called for further limits on pretrial detention, an end to mandatory punishments, and efforts to eliminate the influence of race on sentencing.

Richard Thompson Ford would add to Section 5 of the Fourteenth Amendment a provision requiring a unanimous decision by a three-judge panel to void acts of Congress enforcing the amendment. Sanford Levinson would alter the Twentieth Amendment to provide for a runoff in presidential elections in which no candidate got an absolute majority.

Other proposals included a Victims' Rights Amendment offered by Paul G. Cassell, an amendment guaranteeing the right to participate in primary elections by Heather Gerken, a campaign finance amendment offered by Laurence H. Tribe, a right to health care by Kevin L. Cope and Mila Versteeg, a national service amendment by Larry Sabato, a balanced budget amendment by Michael McConnell, a "Constitution in Modern Language Plain Language Amendment" by a reader, and another, also by a reader, providing that "The Constitution shall never be rewritten."

Roger Copple Proposes to Create Proportional Representation in a Unicameral Congress

Constitutional reformer Roger Copple has identified himself as a public school teacher from Indianapolis who moved to Florida upon retirement. On February 7, 2012, Copple posted the text of what he called "The Third Constitution of the United States." This document consisted of a preamble, a section on human rights with 22 sections, an overview of the document, and 22 articles. The goal of the document, according to the preamble, was to promote "human rights, social justice, ecological wisdom, peace, and egalitarianism." The section on human rights stressed the need for governments built from "the bottom-up," for freedom to practice or not practice religion, the right to grow hemp, and a number of social and economic rights including jobs, food, housing, medical care, and "a good public education from preschool to as far as he or she can advance." The constitutional overview provided a complicated explanation of bottom-up government, using Indianapolis as an example.

Article I, which had 14 sections, described a reconstituted legislative branch consisting of a unicameral Congress of 435 members selected to four-year terms through a system of proportional representation in elections involving the top seven political parties. These elections would be held without benefit of financial contributions, which would be outlawed. The people would have the right to cast electronic votes to advise their representatives or replace them by a two-thirds vote. The president would retain veto power over legislation, but the legislature could override such vetoes by a two-thirds vote.

Article II outlined the powers of the president in seven sections. The president would be selected through an instant run-off system. The president would remain commander in chief but would be unable to declare war without approval by two-thirds of Congress. Existing executive orders would be simplified and become law only if approved by majorities in Congress. Article III described the judiciary in nine sections. Congress would choose justices for nine-year terms, and could remove them by a two-thirds vote.

Article IV prohibited secession, while article V required Congress to protect states against attack. Article VI provided for paying off the national debt in 10 years by cutting military spending by 75 percent and imposing a progressive tax of up to 90 percent on high incomes. Article VII allowed for the continuation of data collection through the census, and article VIII permitted counties to grant charters for, and impose taxes upon, corporations.

Article IX proposed eliminating the Federal Reserve System. Congress would regulate banks, at least some of which will be public. Article X further announced that "the primary role of government is the protection of its citizens," and it provided for the abolition of privately owned prisons and for reducing the incarceration of nonviolent individuals.

Article XI proposed abolishing the North American Free Trade Agreement (NAFTA), while Article XII called for a "non-interventionist" foreign policy. Copple hoped to create a "democratic world federal government using the systems of Proportional Representation and Instant Run-off voting." Article XIII would further abolish the Central Intelligence Agency (CIA), while Article XIV called for enforcing the Posse Comitatus Act of 1878 so as to allow state-directed National Guards "to intervene in domestic issues."

Article XV asserted the need for habeas corpus protection and article XVI did the same for Social Security. Article XVII called for decentralizing the federal government, and article XVIII asserted the vital role of parents in raising children and made them "primarily responsible for their children's education." This same article authorized public schools to "suspend and expel" students, empowered individual neighborhoods to decide on the curriculum; and outlawed forced busing.

Article XIX called for simplifying current laws, regulations, and taxes, and article XX called for an "independent investigation" into the tragedy of the September 11, 2001, terrorist attacks on America, specifically referencing "authors such as David Ray Griffin and organizations such as the Architects and Engineers for 9/11 Truth." Article XXI further called for greater honesty and transparency in government, while article XXII explained how to replace the constitution. It stipulated that two-thirds majorities of Congress and state legislatures could adopt ordinary amendments. In addition, if 51 percent or more of the voters in a presidential election so specified, a constitutional convention would be called. This convention would feature a single delegate from each state.

Copple also referenced the need to adopt a twenty-eighth amendment to spell out procedures. One year later, on June 19, 2013, he posted, "Why a New Constitution Is Our Best Hope," which explained the elements of a proposed twenty-eighth amendment that he hoped would prepare the way for a convention to replace the existing Constitution, in part by allowing the people to vote in every presidential election as to whether they would like to call a new constitutional convention.

Ralph Bass Proposes the Bill of Freedom

Dr. Ralph Bass, Jr., a Christian pastor, counselor, and school administrator with a ThD in Theological Studies from Greenville Presbyterian Theological Seminary, posted what he called "The Bill of Freedom" on his personal Web site in 2012. After asserting that the nation "has been taken over by a committed group of Socialists and Marxists," Bass presented 10 proposed constitutional amendments.

The first called for limiting everyone in public office to two terms. The second amendment concerned tax and budget issues. It proposed limiting all taxes to sales taxes and tariffs, typically set no higher than 5 percent but capable of going up to 10 percent for nonrecurring budget items. At least half the tax would be used to fund the U.S. military. No federal taxes could be used to aid states, to fund private enterprises or charities, or for foreign aid. The government would have to balance its budget each year.

Bass's third proposed amendment required that all laws expire after seven years, granted a majority of states the right of nullification, and gave the president a line-item veto. The next amendment proposed to limit the pay of Congress to two sessions, one in March/April and the other in September/October.

The fifth proposal concerned citizenship and voting. It would limit birthright citizenship to those with two citizen parents, but would allow "voting citizenship" for legal immigrants. The right to vote would require individuals to pass a civic test "proving that they possess an adequate knowledge and understanding on how political and economic process [sic] of our constitutional republic functions."

The proposed sixth amendment would require that all executive orders follow the Constitution and be subject to judicial review. The seventh would prevent treaties from invalidating parts of the U.S. Constitution, would limit the nations where the United States could garrison troops, would prevent the United States from participating in actions of the United Nations, and would prohibit the United Nations from maintaining its world headquarters in the United States.

The proposed eighth amendment would set a term of five years and two terms for Supreme Court justices. It also required that they "interpret the U.S. Constitution in terms of its original meaning by its original authors." The proposed ninth amendment outlawed abortion and euthanasia, and the tenth defined marriage as "a union of two people, one male and one female."

Chandrashekar (Chandra) Tamirisa Posts an Alternative Constitution Based on a Council of Mayors of City-States

Chandraskekar (Chandra) Tamirisa, a naturalized citizen from India who is a global sustainability consultant and founder and CEO of a consulting and lobbying firm, is the author of "A Revised Constitution of the United States," which he appears to have conceived as part of a proposed dissertation entitled *Alternative Constitutionalism* for a PhD in political science at the University of Hawai'i at Manoa. Tamirisa's constitution contains a preamble and six articles, most of which follow the outline of the existing document.

The preamble begins with the words "We the People Together as One Nation under God." Article I vests all legislative powers in "voting citizens," consisting of all who have attained puberty. Section 2 suggests that the only test for public office will be a "merit test," while Section 3 vests the power of impeachment in the people. Section 4 calls for organizing the nation into city-states, each of which would be limited to 500,000 people, including the unborn. According to Tamirisa, "a Council of Mayors of City-States shall be responsible for acting as Legislators on behalf of their Citizens" in a legislative body called the "Assembly." His constitution vested most powers currently exercised by Congress in the Assembly, but prohibited the creation of weapons of mass destruction.

Article II continued to vest executive powers in a president, who would have to be native born or have been naturalized for at least 20 years. Apparently having transposed a section for an almost identical constitution that Tamirisa posted for Egypt on July 5, 2013, the constitution forbids the president from receiving "any other Emolument from Egypt" or from providing any "security detail for any employee of [the] Egyptian government." The president would continue to be the commander in chief of the armed forces and nominate ambassadors and judges with the advice and consent of two thirds of the Assembly. The president could also "Coin and Retract Money."

Article III vested judicial power in a supreme court and in one inferior court within each city-state. Section 2 provided that "No City-State of United States of America shall enter two or more Persons in a Bigamous or Polygamous or Polyandrous or Polyamorous Marriage or Divorce. The state shall have no jurisdiction over marriage." The United States would take responsibility for "Orphaned and Endangered Children."

Article IV substitutes city-states for existing states. Article V provided that two-thirds or more of the mayors of city-states "shall propose In-Line Amendments and Overwrites to this Constitution" without explaining whether such additions would require further ratification. Article VI contains the supremacy clause and states that all citizens "upon Oath or Affirmation, shall owe their Allegiance to this Constitution." Tamirisa followed the document with a request for readers to pay $1.50 for reading the document, $5,000 per article for one-time reproduction/syndication, and $50,000 for the copyright.

Constitution-21 Proposes a 21-Member U.S. Senate

A Web site entitled Constitution-21 contains an analysis of perceived problems in the current constitutional system. It includes a summary, a table of contents, a proposed constitution of thirteen articles, a schedule of nominations and elections under the new system, and essays on health care and radical Islam. The unidentified author of these reforms describes himself as someone whose career involves "designing commercial applications for computers." He adds that he is neither "a politician nor an academic," but mentions having been a member of the Plato Society of UCLA.

The author blamed many of the current problems in government on political primaries dominated by the extremes of both parties. The author further asserted that the current Congress involves excessive duplication, and that the federal system is malfunctioning. The author presented his constitution not in anticipation of another constitutional convention but "to inspire ideas about how to reorganize the government to meet current and future conditions."

Article I of the proposed constitution consists of a number of declarations, including a reference to the United States as a "republic," and the proposed addition of an electoral branch of the national government. In describing the legislative branch, Article II called for creating a senate with 21 members and a house with 900 to 1,000 lawmakers. Most of the power would be lodged in the former body, whose members would be drawn from multistate districts of approximately 14 million people each. Members of both branches would be elected in odd-numbered years; age requirements would be higher than current ones, and districts would be drawn on a nonpartisan basis. Primary legislative power would reside in the senate. Members of the house would serve at national nominating conventions, to which state legislatures would select about four times as many members (in anticipation of conventions of about 4,800 delegates).

Article III outlined the executive branch. The president would continue as commander in chief, but a vote of approval from 14 or more senators would be required to declare war or station U.S. troops abroad. The president would have "full and exclusive control over covert intelligence and counter-intelligence activities." The president would make government appointments—and fire officials—with senate consent.

Article V outlined the new electoral branch, which would consist of an electoral college and an election board. The former would consist of individuals who had retired from governmental service, and the election board would be a subset of 10 members from the electoral college, selected by caucuses in the house of representatives. This branch would also include the Census Bureau.

Article VI would require each state to establish a unicameral legislature with two-year terms. States would be entitled to select four times the number of its representatives to federal nominating conventions. The conventions would divide into caucuses of at least 26 percent of their membership and nominate senators and presidents. The president would be the one who won the highest number of representative districts or (in cases of a tie) a plurality of overall votes.

Article VIII dealt with "Elected and Appointed Federal Service." One provision required Congress to establish a school of public administration to train public servants. Article IX further described provisions for federal finance. It included a prohibition on payroll taxes, the institution of a value-added tax, a progressive income tax, presidential authority to raise and lower certain taxes, and estate taxes.

Article X outlined governmental responsibilities. Federal powers would include enacting business regulations, safety standards, agricultural regulations, and financing arts and sciences. States would oversee single-payer plans for medical care. Both sets of government would have authority to protect the environment.

Article XI outlined citizenship qualifications, including a "working knowledge of English." It would abrogate existing treaties with Native Americans and give them full citizenship rights and responsibilities. Article XII provided for limits on governmental power and citizen rights similar to those found in the current Constitution and the accompanying amendments. It specifically recognized "the right of privacy," and prohibited price fixing. Article XIII would enable a majority of the house or the electoral college to propose amendments to the U.S. Constitution. Amendments receiving support from 65 percent or more of the house, the electoral college, and the president would have to be approved by 60 percent or more of the voters in a referendum.

Summary and Analysis

The Internet resembles a town meeting in which participants do not necessarily have to reveal who they are. Any member of "We the People" with basic computer knowledge can post remarks. However transitory such postings may be, they have the potential to reach people who would never buy scholarly books or articles on the subject. Any future attempts to stir up grassroots support to call an Article V Convention are likely to have an Internet component. In considering a new constitution for Iceland, that nation's constitutional council assembled 950 randomly selected citizens to discuss the document, and it has regularly posted draft clauses on the Internet for public comment (Siddique 2011).

Given its relatively low cost and broad access, the Internet will likely continue to be a forum for visionaries, eccentrics, and patriots to propose new constitutions and major constitutional revisions. Alternatively, the Internet may be superseded by others forms of communication in years to come.

References

Anarchist420. 2011. "Minarchist Replacement for the Constitution." January 31. http://forums.anandtech.com/showthread.php?t=2139696 (accessed December 17, 2013).

Barnett, Randy. 2009. "A Bill of Federalism." *Forbes.com*, May 20. http://www.forbes.com/2009/05/20/bill-of-federalism-constitution-states-supreme-court-op (accessed June 29, 2013).

Barnett, Randy. 2004. *Restoring the Lost Constitution: The Presumption of Liberty*. Princeton, NJ: Princeton University Press.

Bass, Ralph. "The Bill of Freedom." http://www.livinghopepress.com/Faith-and-Freedom.thml (accessed August 4, 2013).

Brothers, Kirk. "Libertarian Writings." http://www.mega.nu/ampp/kirkbros/index.html (accessed December 17, 2013).

"Christian Prophet." 2012. "21st Century Constitution for Moral Government." November 18. http://21stcenturyconstitution.blogspot.com/ (accessed December 17, 2013).

"Constitution-21." N.d. http://www.constitution-021.com/ (accessed December 17, 2013).

"Constitutional Topic: Rewriting the Constitution." N.d. http://www.usconstitution.net/consttop_newc.html (accessed May 21, 2013).

Copple, Roger. 2013. "A New Constitution and Marijuana/Hemp Legalization." June 19. http://www.democracychronicles.com/new-constitution-marijuana-hemp/ (accessed December 17, 2013).

Copple, Roger. 2012. "The Third Constitution of the United States." February 7. http://disinfo.com/2012/02/the-third-constitution-of-the-united-states/ (accessed December 17, 2013).

Durst, Jack. 2000. "Constitution of the Republic." http://spynx_jd.tripod.com/constitution/CS-1-A.html (site discontinued).

Gillman, Steve. N.d. "A Better U.S. Constitution?" http://ezinearticles.com/?A-Better-US-Constitution?&id=1433026 (accessed December 15, 2013).

Gillman, Steve. c.2008. "A New Constitution." http://www.999ideas.com/new-constitution.html (accessed December 17, 2013).

"Jack Rabbit." 2006. Second Constitution of the United States of America." March 20. http://journals.democraticunderground.com/Jack%20Rabbit/3 (accessed June 17, 2013).

Kirk, Chris. 2012. "We the People of Slate . . ." http://www.slate.com/articles/news_and_politics/the_hive/2012/07/u_s_constitution_as-rew . . . (accessed July 1, 2013).

Nordeen, Ross. N.d. "Improving the Constitution." http://www.amatecon.com (accessed December 17, 2013).

"Objectivism Wiki: Reality, Reason, Rights." http://wiki.objectismonline.net/wiki/New_constitution (accessed December 17, 2013).

Pain, Ernest. N.d. "A New Constitution for the United States of America." http://usreconstitution.net (accessed December 17, 2013).

Palm, Kirby. N.d. "The U.S. Constitution: Formal Additions." http://www.nettally.com /palmk/ConstitutionSections.html (accessed December 17, 2013).

Palm, Kirby. N.d. "Proposed Constitutional Amendment." http://www.nettally.com/palmk /terms.html (accessed December 17, 2013).

"A Petition for a Constitutional Convention." http://www.abesindignationleague.org/peti tion1.html/ (site discontinued) (accessed June 23, 2008).

Piper, John K. 2010. "A United States Constitution for the 21st Century." http://www.pipe -dream-constitution.info/ (accessed June 7, 2013).

Platt, L. Henry, Jr. 1972. "DarkHorseCandidate.com." http://www.darkhorsecandidate.com /constitution.html (accessed December 17, 2013).

Pubman, Ian. "Constitution 2.0" (web).

Ricker, Ward. N.d. "Modified Constitution for the United States of America." http://ward ricker.com/constitution.php (accessed December 17, 2013).

Ricker, Ward. c.2011. "Five-Point Plan for Democracy." http:/wardricker.com/fivepointplan .php.

Rojas, Billy. 2011. "A Radical Centrist Vision for the Future: 100 New Constitutional Amendments for the 21st Century." http://radicalcentrism.org/resources/vision/ (accessed December 17, 2013).

Roland, Jon. 2009– . "Draft Amendments to U.S. Constitution." http://constitution.org /reform/us/con_amend.htm (accessed December 17, 2013).

Siddique, Haroon. 2011. "Mob Rule: Iceland Crowdsources Its Next Constitution." *The Guardian* (UK), June 9. http://www.theguardian.com/world/2011/jun/09/iceland-crowd sourcing-constitution-facebook (accessed December 17, 2013).

Struble, Robert, Jr. "Redeeming U.S. Democracy." http://tcmnet.com/~rusd/ (accessed July 11, 1997). Tell-usa.org.

Sulcer, Thomas Wright. "The Second Constitution of the United States: A New and Improved Draft for the 21st Century." Participedia. http://participedia.net/en/cases/second -constitution-united-states-new-and-improved-draft-21st-century (accessed December 17, 2013).

Tamirisa, Chandrashekar (Chandra). N.d. "Alternative Constitutionalism: A Revised Constitution of United States of America." http://ctamirisa.wordpress.com/2012/09/19 /alternative-constitutionalism-revising-the-constitution-of-united-states-of-america-2/ (accessed December 17, 2013).

VanSickle, John. http://enphilistor.users4.50megs.com/index.htm (accessed June 8, 2002).

Vile, John R. 2011. "The Case against a 'Repeal Amendment.'" *National Law Journal*, January 3: 38–9.

Wynne, George. N.d. "An Amendment Proposal/The Equality over the Law Project." http:// amendmentproposal.com/.

CHAPTER 13

Constitutional Reform
and Constitutional Archetypes

This book has recorded and detailed more than 170 proposals for significant revisions to the U.S. Constitution—or for an entirely new Constitution—spread out over more than 200 years. It is helpful to compare such proposals by looking at the issues that the Constitution sought to address. Because the Constitution itself resulted from numerous plans and compromises, proponents of rival views can seek to change the document from many directions. These perspectives provide conflicting answers to a series of 15 somewhat overlapping questions that American founding fathers and their successors have continued to ask throughout the nation's history.

Does the Government Require Institutional Reform
or a Change in Leadership?

In Federalist No. 51, James Madison noted that "if men were angels, no government would be necessary. If angels were to govern men, neither external nor internal controls on government would be necessary" (Hamilton, Madison, and Jay 1961, 322). Recognizing that men were not angels, he sought to create a structure that would pit ambition to counter ambition and interest to counter interest.

Although this book concentrates on constitutional, or systemic, reforms, another approach to political change, which is evident in election cycles, is simply to replace leaders who are believed to have been ineffective or who are thought to have strayed from the constitutional path with another group of leaders that voters hope will express greater fidelity to constitutional norms. A variant of this theme is to replace Supreme Court justices with individuals who will interpret the Constitution in what is perceived to be a better manner. In *An Essay on Man* (epistle 3, 1), Alexander Pope observed:

> For forms of Government let fools contest;
> Whate'er is best administered is best.

A number of important changes in American history, perhaps most notably the "Revolution of 1800," centered on replacing one set of leaders with another (in this case Federalist John Adams with Democratic-Republican Thomas Jefferson). Many attributed similar qualities to Andrew Jackson's election in 1828. The presidential election of 1860, in which Abraham Lincoln succeeded a number of ineffective presidents, was a similar watershed. The election of Franklin D. Roosevelt in 1932 seemed not only to signal a new party coalition but to herald the way out of an economic morass (Burnham 1971). In more recent memories, opinion seemed to shift from a general consensus during the presidency of Jimmy Carter that the presidency was too weak to the perception under Ronald Reagan that the institution was quite powerful.

Although he introduced some structural reforms in *A True Republic* (1879), Albert Stickney sought to create a government that chose the "best men" to give "their best work." Similarly, H. Wentworth Eldredge's call for *The Second American Revolution* (1964) focused not so much on how to change existing institutions as on how to cultivate an aristocracy of talent and virtue that would be able to solve modern problems. In 2006, William S. Field proposed creating new curricula that combined law, political science, and other disciplines to train aspiring public servants. In 1989 and 2013, Sam Carr Polk sought to create six categories of "Guardians" to guide modern policymaking, while others have suggested guidance from other groups of wise individuals.

Should It Be Easier or Harder to Amend the U.S. Constitution?

Article V of the U.S. Constitution provides two primary routes for amending the Constitution. The only route utilized to date is the one allowing two-thirds majorities of both houses of Congress to propose amendments, which are then ratified by the states. Writing about Article V in *Federalist* No. 43, James Madison argued that the Constitution "guards equally against that extreme facility, which would render the Constitution too mutable; and that extreme difficulty, which might perpetuate its discovered faults" (Hamilton, Madison, and Jay 1961, 278).

The constitutional amending process still has articulate defenders who point out that if the process errs on the side of caution, the Framers did so intentionally (Guerra 2013). The Framers had resisted the English system under which Parliament proclaimed itself to be sovereign; they had worked through a long summer to grind out compromises that might be difficult to put back together again; and they did not want amendments made without due consensus and deliberation. They thought that requiring supermajorities in both Congress and in the states for amendments would effectively address the latter concern.

Members of Congress have proposed more than 11,500 amendments throughout U.S. history, and yet the necessary majorities of Congress have only proposed 33 amendments, and, of these, states have only ratified 27. Moreover, states have never mustered the required two-thirds majority to force Congress to call a constitutional convention, and the nation thus continues with the longest-such continuously functioning document for a *nation* in the world (the constitution of the state of Massachusetts is slightly older). By comparison to other nations, the United States consequently has one of the most difficult amending processes (Lutz 1994). Many individuals advocated making the Constitution easier to amend. Individuals who favor replacing or making major modifications of the Constitution are hardly a random sample of Americans and, as expected, are often frustrated by the difficulty of the current process and want to liberalize it.

The Majoritarian or Periodic Review Alternatives

There are numerous ways in which the amending process could be made easier. The most obvious would be to decrease the majorities needed either for Congress to propose amendments or for the states to ratify them. One increasingly popular alternative dates at least as far back as 1896, when Frederick Upham Adams proposed allowing a majority of the people to amend the Constitution through initiative, referendum, or both. Proponents of such liberalization sometimes seek to assure that it nonetheless will consider proposed amendments over an extended period of time or that passage at least require a majority of people in a majority of the states.

A number of proponents of major constitutional changes have followed Thomas Jefferson and early state constitutions that included Councils of Censors in proposing to review the Constitution at periodic intervals. The author of the Anarchist Constitution of 1903 proposed that the people vote every four years on the document he proposed. Alexander Hehmeyer (1943) favored allowing presidents to call conventions every 30 years, Rexford Tugwell (1974) favored a referendum on the subject every 25 years, and Barry Krusch (1992) recommended consulting the people every 35 years about whether to have another convention. Bruce E. Tonn proposed a "Futures Congress" (1991) and a "Futures Administration" (1996) and George Kennan (1993) proposed a Council of Elders that could consider long-term governmental and constitutional needs. Malcolm R. Wilkey favored giving the president the right to call a national referendum and provide for a constitutional convention every 20 years. Roger Copple (2012) wanted voters to decide whether to replace the Constitution every time they participated in a presidential election, and Kirk Brothers (1996) proposed plebiscites on the constitution every seven years. Mark R. Levin (2013) wanted to allow two-thirds of the state legislatures to adopt amendments by proposing identical texts. Sam Carr Polk favored convening a new constitutional convention every time two consecutive bimonthly polls established that the people had lost faith in the existing document.

The John Randolph or Entrenchment Clause Alternatives

Although some reformers have called for eliminating the convention option, few have called for making the amending process more difficult. A number have introduced a variant on the current Constitution, which continues to prohibit states from being deprived of their equal votes in the Senate without their consent, by seeking to entrench one or another proposed provisions. John K. Piper (2010) actually listed 13 provisions of his proposed constitution that he thought should be unamendable.

Congressman John Randolph often argued against change on principle. At the Virginia Constitutional Convention of 1829, he observed that "governments are like revolutions. You may put them in motion, but I defy you to control them after they are in motion" (quoted in Johnson 2012, 219). So too, there are some who seek an impregnable Constitution, lest allowing needed reforms might lead to other far more undesirable consequences. The last recommendation in *Slate Magazine*'s 2012 list of possible constitutional changes was called the "DON'T FIX THE CONSTITUTION AMENDMENT," and read simply, "The Constitution shall never be rewritten." In proposing a new constitution, Roderick Long (1994) advocated not only an amending process that required support by four-fifths of both houses and ratification by four-fifths of his proposed canton and two-thirds of the people, but also one stipulating that this process be included in the section of his constitution that was unamendable.

Should the Nation Be Further Unified or More Decentralized?

The Framers of the U.S. Constitution were familiar with two models relative to centralization. Great Britain, France, and other nations had a unitary system in which the central government operated directly on individual citizens and in which there were no permanent entities that correspond to U.S. states. By contrast, the Articles of Confederation vested sovereignty in the states, which alone could operate directly upon individuals.

The Framers formulated a hybrid federal system that divided powers between the national government and the states, each with their own constitutional foundations and each with the power to operate directly upon individuals. This system, however, also left itself open to criticisms from two directions. On a worldwide basis, the percentage of nations with a federal system has fallen from a peak of 22 percent early in the twentieth century to about 12 percent in 2012 (Law and Versteeg 2012, 785).

James Madison argued in *Federalist* No. 10 that a system of representation permitted a federal government to encompass much larger land areas than prior direct democracies. Consistent with that view, the nation has expanded from 13 states that once hugged the Atlantic Coast to 48 contiguous states that reach from coast to coast as well as Alaska and Hawaii. Proponents of federalism have often touted the Constitution's ability to absorb new states as an advantage, while critics have on occasion argued that the system has led to imperialism, most notably during the Mexican-American War (1846–1848) and Spanish-American War (1898). However, most discussions in this area continue to center on the relative powers that should be exercised by the national authority and by the states.

The Articles of Confederation and the Calhounian Alternative

Defenders of the previous government under the Articles of Confederation continued to think that it would have been sufficient to vest Congress with greater powers over taxation and commerce, without invading other areas of policymaking then provided by the states and without providing federal checks on state judiciaries. Anti-Federalists thus remained jealous of state powers and, armed with a jaundiced view of congressional powers to tax and spend and the necessary and proper clause, they became convinced that the new government was unnecessarily consolidated (unitary), or was becoming so. The Virginia and Kentucky Resolutions of 1798 were premised on the idea that the Constitution was a compact among the states.

Although the Hartford Convention demonstrated that this sentiment was not confined to a single section of the nation, in time the extreme states' rights position became chiefly associated with the Southern cause and its dubious claims to nullification and secession. No individual provides a better exemplar of this philosophy than South Carolina's John C. Calhoun, whose theory of concurrent majorities was incorporated into the Confederate Constitution in 1861. An increasing number of individuals are following Thomas Naylor and William H. Willimon (1997) in advocating either the decentralization or the secession option; they have included Hans-Hermann Hoppe (2001), Kirby Palm, William Niskasen (2005), and Robert F. Hawes, Jr. (2006). Although he does not appear to have offered a full-blown plan for constitutional change, and hence is not otherwise covered in this book, Marshall L. DeRosa (2007) is among current scholars who specifically commend features, including secession, of the Confederate Constitution as a way of resisting both national and international consolidation. A. Hines (2009) has been among those who favored repealing the Seventeenth Amendment so that state legislatures once again select U.S. senators.

Throughout American history a number of individuals have believed that the federal center is destroying the state branches, and have accordingly sought greater state or regional autonomy. The proposals by the Council of State Governments (1992) resisted pressure to reapportion state legislatures. William B. Lawrence (1880), Thomas Brennan (1982), Malcolm R. Wilkey (1995), Floyd Wynne (2006), Robert F. Hawes (2006), Ross Nordeen, Randy Barnett (2009), Kirby Palm, Paul Antinori (2010), and John B. Miller and his pseudonymous associates (2012) have all stressed the need for greater state influence under the current system. The Constitution of the New America (2007) wanted to recognize the legitimacy of the Confederate States of America. The Rebirth Constitution (Dahlberg and Kaardal 2013) sought to revive state militia as a way of checking unconstitutional exercises of power by federal officials. Payne Edwards (2012) sought to rewrite the Tenth Amendment more clearly to reserve essential rights to the states. Kirk Brothers (1996) would allow state legislatures to perform the legislative functions currently exercised by the U.S. House of Representatives. Hans-Hermann Hoppe (2001) envisioned free cities asserting their sovereignty and covenant groups that would set standards for their own communities. Randy Barnett (2009), Marty Piatt (2012), and Mark R. Levin (2013) would grant states the right to repeal federal legislation. John Médaille (2010) wanted to further the principle of subsidiarity by allowing states to exercise most of the functions currently exercised by the national government; Robert R. Owens (2010) and Anarchist420 (2011) suggested returning to the confederal model; and Rick Sirmon (2011) wanted regional groups of states to resume regulation of interstate commerce. Roderick Long's provisions (1993, 1994) called for multiplying the existing 50 states into 500 or more cantons.

The Recolonization Option

The United States began as a confederation of 13 colonies. Some proponents of change have viewed the situation as so dire that they called for establishing a new nation in a new place. Like ex-Confederates who emigrated to South America after the Civil War (Harter 1985), Michael Oliver (1968) sought to find uninhabited land where he could create a government based on libertarian principles. He ended up settling for an atoll in the Pacific. Jim Davidson (1994) sought to create a constitution for a new floating island republic. The hero of a 1999 novel by Michael Marx fled to Mexico to avoid nuclear catastrophe and create a new government. William Wilson (2013) wrote his constitution for a nation that he did not think would adopt it until it was chastened by calamities from God.

The Hamiltonian Unitary Alternative

Of all those who spoke at the Constitutional Convention, none seemed less firmly attached to existing states than Alexander Hamilton, who had been born abroad. But he was not alone. At one point during the critical deliberations about representation of the states within Congress, Delaware's David Brearley, who was supporting the New Jersey Plan, suggested spreading out a map and dividing the nation into 13 equal (presumably he meant by population) states (Farrand I, 1966, 177). Since then many individuals have suggested that states create unnecessary barriers to national objectives. Some proposals have suggested either abolishing, or significantly reorganizing, existing state and local authorities. More commonly, a number of proposals have included specific provisions indicating that states do not have the right to secede.

Simon Willard, Jr., called for reorganizing the states into more rational units in 1815, and Edward Bellamy (1887) and Alan Benson (1914) thought they were dispensable. Others who have called either for redrawing or eliminating states have included Charles Merriam (1931), William Kay Wallace (1932), William Y. Elliott (1935), Hugh Hamilton (1938), H. Wentworth Eldredge (1964), Leland Baldwin (1972), Rexford Tugwell (1974), Arthur S. Miller (1987), John Mertens (1990), Dick Formichella (2005), William S. Field (2006), William Wilson (2013), and Sam Carr Polk (2013). Uldis Sprogis (2011) would completely eliminate the states and the U.S. Senate. Chandra Tamirisa apparently envisioned a unitary system in which city-states of 500,000 people or less would replace current states.

William Gardiner (1973) has been among those who envisioned a rewritten Constitution that would reorganize state governments. Some, like William Yandell Elliott (1935) and William S. Field (2006), have specifically called for unicameral state legislatures. Perhaps because the general trend throughout U.S. history has been to increase the powers of the national government at the expense of the states, there have been more recent proposals to protect state powers or devolve powers to the states than to increase national powers still further. Had the situation been reversed, there might have been as many—or even more—proposals to seek greater national powers.

Should the Nation Further Accent Separation of Powers and Checks and Balances or Should It Seek to Unify the Legislative and Executive Authorities?

The U.S. Founding Fathers believed in separation of powers, which they designed to serve as checks and balances to protect freedom. James Madison provided one of the most succinct summaries of this doctrine in Federalist No. 51:

> the great security against a gradual concentration of the several powers in the same department consists in giving to those who administer each department the necessary constitutional means and personal motives to resist encroachments of the others. The provision for defense must in this, as in all other cases, be made commensurate to the danger of attach. The interest of the man must be connected with the constitutional rights of the place. (Hamilton, Madison, and Jay 1961, 322)

Madison explained that while "it may be a reflection on human nature that such devices should be necessary to control the abuses of government," men were not angels and that "in framing a government which is to be administered by men over men," it was important first to "enable the government to control the governed; and in the next place oblige it to control itself" (Hamilton, Madison, and Jay, 1961, 322).

Despite their defenses, Anti-Federalists criticized the Framers of the Constitution in part for failing adequately to honor this principle, and F. H. Buckley (2012) has argued that they attempted to come far closer to a parliamentary system than is generally recognized. Although the incompatibility clause in Article I, Section 6 of the U.S. Constitution prohibited members of Congress from serving in any other civil office, the Constitution sometimes permitted mixed powers. It thus enabled the vice president to preside over the U.S. Senate. Because of the president's veto power, the adoption of legislation typically required the cooperation of both the legislative and executive branches. Moreover, the Senate could act as a court when trying cases of impeachment. James Madison insisted, though, that he and other Framers had not violated the principle of separation of powers. Madison argued in *Federalist* No. 47 that "he did not mean that these department[s] ought to have no partial agency in, or no control over, the acts of each other" (Hamilton, Madison, and Jay 1961, 302) but only that no set of hands should wield the whole power both of his own and another department of government.

The Anti-Federalist Complete Separation of Powers Alternative

Nonetheless, some of the Anti-Federalist criticism vis-à-vis separation of powers continued in the early republic. Augustus B. Woodward (1825) argued that congressional corruption had resulted from inadequate attention to separation of powers. Abel Upshur criticized the presidential veto by observing, "There is something incongruous in this union of legislative and executive powers in the same man" (Upshur 1840, 120). Most modern-day proponents of separation of powers have been content to argue for the perpetuation, rather than the expansion, of this concept within the current system as they have faced an increasing number of proponents of the parliamentary alternative. Steven G. Calabresi (1998) wanted to extend additional checks on all three branches of the national government. Thomas Wright Sulcer's Web site (2011) attempted to combine a more parliamentary structure with an additional branch (a new Department of State) of government. John K. Piper (2010) and the self-identified Christian Prophet (2012) both favored additional checks and balances, as did Chip Downs (2012). Although the unidentified author of "Constitution-21" in cyberspace expressed concerns over separation of powers, he added an Electoral Branch to the existing three branches of the national government. A number of writers have favored eliminating the vice presidency, but they did not necessarily do so because they were concerned about its effect on the separation of powers.

The Hamiltonian/Wilsonian Parliamentary Alternative

As the nation's first secretary of the treasury, Alexander Hamilton emulated another aspect of the emerging British system when he sought to convert his job into that of a virtual prime minister. As the powers of the British monarchy were largely transfigured into ceremonial duties of a head of state, the governing powers were transferred to the prime minister as head of government, and the British parliamentary model emerged as the chief alternative to the American model of separated powers.

Under this plan, which Walter Bagehot explained to the American people in *The English Constitution* and which Woodrow Wilson so admired, the majority party or coalition within the more powerful branch of parliament (if it is bicameral) chose the premier or prime minister, who drew his cabinet from within parliament and who expected the support of his party. When that support failed to materialize and there was a vote of no confidence, the head of state called a new election either to vindicate the power of the existing prime minister and his party or provide for the election of a new one. Other prominent elements of modern parliamentary democracies include: the question hour, during which members of parliament query the prime minister about his policies; the shadow government, or opposition party in waiting, in which the head of the opposition party is easily identified and stands ready to assume governmental responsibility if needed; collective cabinet responsibility for decisions; and concurrent terms of office for members of the lower house of parliament and the prime minister. Such a system is arguably far more "efficient" and responsive to popular wishes than the system of separated powers in the United States, and it remains far and away the most popular alternative favored by those who would seek to replace the existing American system of government. This alternative is sometimes (albeit rarely) raised in conjunction with Hamilton's relative disregard for federalism and occasionally in conjunction with hopes for an actual monarchy.

The advocates of an American version of parliamentary government compose a diverse group. It began with the provision in the Confederate Constitution of 1861 that allowed cabinet members to appear on the floor of Congress and later attracted such advocates as William B. Lawrence (1880), Isaac Rice (1884), Goldwin Smith (1898), Yandell Henderson (1913), Lewis Mayers (1918), William MacDonald (1921), Henry S. McKee (1933), William Y. Elliott (1935), Henry Hazlitt (1942/1974), Herbert Agar (1942), Alexander Hehmeyer (1943), Thomas Finletter (1945), C. Perry Patterson (1947), Herman Finer (1960), H. Wentworth Eldredge (1964), Dwight Macdonald (1968), Leland Baldwin (1972), Charles Hardin (1974), Michael Novak (1974), George Reedy (1970), Theodore Becker (1976), Lloyd Cutler (1980, 1986), Robert Shogan (1982), James Sundquist (1986), Arthur S. Miller (1987), J. William Fulbright (1989), Daniel Lazare (1996), Roderick Long (1994), Malcolm R. Wilkey (1995), Rodney Scott (1999), Paul Christopher Manuel and Anne Marie Cammisa (1999), Jack Durst (2000), Patrick J. McGrath (2000), William S. Field (2006), Thomas Wright Sulcer (2011), and Sam Carr Polk (2013). This list suggests that the momentum for such proposals steadily gained from the 1880s through the 1980s and then began to decline. In assessing reform sentiments, David R. Mayhew likened the sentiments for a parliamentary system to "static" (Mayhew 2011, 166).

A number of individuals who do not necessarily want to unify the legislative and executive branches have nonetheless sought to make Congress more democratic and efficient. Roger Copple (2012) is among those who have proposed eliminating the U.S. Senate. Other proponents of change have advocated reducing the powers of the Senate in relation to those of the House. Most proponents of a parliamentary system anticipated that it would help unify the legislative and executive branches and thus overcome gridlock. Proponents of parliamentary government sometimes disagree about whether such a system would create responsible political parties or be dependent upon them. In recent years, advocates of such responsible parties have been somewhat balanced by those who believe that the more ideologically oriented parties of the last two or three decades may have actually contributed to the gridlock rather than overcoming it.

Administrative Changes
Although it has not featured prominently in this book, another solution to perceived issues of governance would be to use the Constitution to initiate various changes in public administration. William Yandell Elliott (1935) included some such reforms among his proposals. Donald F. Kettl further argued in *The Next Government of the United States* (2009) that it was time for further administrative reorganization to deal with problems that resulted from greater governmental complexity and from greater reliance on governmental/private partnerships. Reviewing earlier innovations like the rise of the civil service system, new budget processes, and greater executive oversight, he suggested that much of the standard "vending-machine" type administration was a carryover from Progressive Era reforms and that it was necessary to come up with "rocket science" type solutions to more complex problems. Although he did not specifically propose that the Constitution institute such changes, it is certainly possible to imagine a constitution that sought to do so.

Alterations in the Size of Congress

The size of the House of Representatives grew exponentially from its initial 65 members until Congress capped it at 435 in 1911. Even with this growth, individual members represent far more individuals than when the nation was less sparsely populated. Reformers have yet to agree on an ideal size for this body, although most probably lean to increasing size (Frederick 2010).

Proponents of constitutional change who have addressed the subject have alternated between those who have sought to reduce the size of the House in order to save money versus those who have sought to increase its size so as to increase representation or, as in the case of Robert Shogan (1982), to increase the size of the majority party. Charles Hardin (1974) and Arthur S. Miller (1987) favored a unicameral Congress of only 100 members, Sam Carr Polk (2013) of 400, and William S. Field (2006) of 700. Edwin Lee Wade (1995) favored a House of only 225 members, Malcolm R. Wilkey (1995) of 250 members, and John Mertens (1990) of 300. By contrast, Theodore Becker (1976) favored a House of from 500 to 1,000 members; Barry Krusch (1992) favored one with 1,000 or more members, and Patrick J. McGrath (2000) favored one of from 625 to 650 members.

Marcia Lynn Whicker, Ruth Ann Strickland, and Raymond A. Moore (1987) proposed a multicameral Congress with a minimum of four specialized Houses of Representatives, with members of each district voting for at least one such representative a year. This plan would also have strengthened the role that the Senate would play in respect to the House.

Many critics of the current system have suggested apportioning the Senate to better represent state populations, often by adding members to represent larger states. Few appear to have directly considered how such an increase in numbers might affect deliberations in that body, which is known for the filibuster and other rules that give members wide latitude and opportunity to express themselves.

Should the President Be Stronger or Weaker?

Although delegates to the Constitutional Convention of 1787 initially feared reestablishing an office that might come to acquire the kinds of tyrannical powers that George III had wielded, Pennsylvania's James Wilson helped persuade the delegates of the need for energetic government, which a strong unitary executive could provide. Ultimately, the Framers divided powers among three branches, but enough ambiguities remained that the scope of presidential powers has remained a bone of continuing contention throughout U.S. history.

Such controversies often center on presidential powers relative to foreign affairs. During George Washington's administration, Alexander Hamilton and James Madison engaged in the Pacificus/Helvidius debate, during which they discussed whether the president had the right to declare neutrality between the United States and France (to which it had been bound by treaty) or whether such a declaration also required congressional approval. As Pacificus, Hamilton argued for the former position, and as Helvidius, Madison advocated the latter.

The Hamiltonian Presidency Alternative

Hamilton was a strong proponent of presidential power, especially in foreign affairs. Hamilton believed that it was significant that Section I, of Article II of the Constitution vested "the executive power" in the president, while Section I of Article I specifically referred to "all legislative powers herein granted." The presidency profited from being the only one of the three branches to be headed by a single individual and was therefore always on call. The presidency also profited from America's increased engagement with foreign governments.

Perhaps as a consequence, after Hamilton few proponents of constitutional change have favored increasing presidential powers still further. Although he began as an advocate of parliamentary government, Woodrow Wilson viewed the presidency as an appropriate platform from which to initiate reforms. H. Wentworth Eldredge (1964) wanted to vest almost all the power of the national government in the executive branch. Edwin Lee Wade (1995) argued that the presidency needed to be strengthened. Moreover, some advocates of the parliamentary system have asserted that it would both strengthen the office of the presidency and make it more responsible. Hans-Hermann Hoppe (2001) believed that monarchies preserved what he considered to be the natural order of things better than did democracies, but he did not call for the reinstitution of monarchy in America. The author of the *Constitution of the New America* (2007) clearly saw the proposed 12-person executive branch as a dominant force over the proposed unicameral legislature. John Médaille (2010) favored a more monarchical presidency, which he hoped to accomplish in part by doubling the president's term.

Creating a Separate Head of State

In renouncing hereditary monarchy, the United States made the elected president both the head of the government and the head of state. As such, the president not only executes domestic laws and serves as commander in chief of America's armed forces but also receives foreign dignitaries. The president, rather than a king or queen, hosts visitors from foreign countries and makes trips abroad on behalf of the nation.

France has renounced its monarchical past while maintaining a presidential head of state separate from the premier who heads the government. One way of lessening both the prestige and the burdens of the presidency would be to divide the current office in two. C. Perry Patterson (1947), Michael Novak (1974), Patrick J. McGrath (2000), and Sam Carr Polk (2013) have been among those who have called for dividing the responsibilities of the president between a head of government and a head of state, and H. Wentworth Elredge's discussion of the institution suggested that he favored the same (1964).

The Whig or Multiple-Presidencies Alternative

University of Indiana law professor David Orentlicher has called for implementing a two-person, two-party presidency (Orentlicher 2013). Similarly, numerous reformers dating back to Abel Upshur (1840) have been convinced that the constitution has vested the president with too much power, particularly in the area of foreign affairs. A few critics, including John C. Calhoun, William B. Lawrence (1880), John Mertens (1990), Roderick Long (1993, 1994), and Jack Durst (2000) have called for making the presidency plural. Others have urged abolishing it altogether (such as Henry Lockwood in 1884); for making it into a figurehead (Dick Formichella in 2005), or for rotating it among members of Congress (Charles O'Conor in 1877 and 1881). James L. Sundquist (1986) has been among those who advocated incorporating provisions of the War Powers Resolution of 1973 into the Constitution. Under Michael Noah Mautner's proposed direct democracy plan (1992), citizens would be chosen at random to serve as head of state. Other critics of presidential power have included James Hillhouse (1808), the Hartford Convention (1815), and Sanford Levinson (2006). Robert M. Hinkelman (2012) appears to have been the only individual who proposed a plural executive for the specific purpose of increasing the powers of this branch. In formulating a new nation, Michael Oliver (1968) contemplated a plural executive of from 7 to 10 people.

The No Independent Executive Alternative
Congressional committees carried out all executive functions under the Articles of Confederation. Although this bears some resemblance to parliamentary systems, an executive of such a confederation is considerably weaker than a prime minister. Notably, in posting a constitution modeled on the Articles of Confederation, Anarchist420 (2011) provided for neither a national executive nor a national judiciary. It is not clear whether Robert Owens (2010), who also favored a confederal government, would also have considered an independent executive to be unnecessary.

Should the Government Be More Direct, More Representative, or More Aristocratic?
The United States Constitution created a "republican," or representative, government, and eliminated hereditary privileges. Still, James Madison explained in *Federalist* No. 10 that the government was not a pure democracy. Madison emphasized not only that the young nation's political system would rely upon representatives who would "refine" the public view, but also that such representatives would be drawn from larger districts, which he anticipated would neutralize the effects of factional disputes.

The Jacksonian/Populistic/Progressive More Direct Democratic Alternative
Critics continue to question whether the U.S. Constitution is as successful as Madison hoped in neutralizing the impact of factional differences. Indeed, as Madison witnessed the rise of Hamilton and the Federalist Party, he himself began to have doubts! Madison and other Framers wanted to base the new nation on accountability, and they often stressed the power of "public opinion" (Vile 2005, II,

633–6), but the Constitution was far less egalitarian than it might have been. As generations of critics have pointed out, it allowed states to establish voting rights rather than setting a single national standard. It did not free African Americans or enfranchise women or 18-year-olds. It provided for an indirect method of electing the president, which gave weight to states as states; it allowed state legislatures to appoint members of the Senate; and it apportioned that body, not according to population but on the basis of state equality.

Constitutional critics have often advocated more democracy—although sometimes the bureaucracies such movements have spawned have been less than successful in achieving it (Morone 1998). Like Jefferson before him, Andrew Jackson appealed to the "common man." Jackson further thought that such men were capable of administering the government without significant training or the help of outside experts (Mashaw 2008, 1614). Abraham Lincoln advanced the dream of "government of the people, by the people, and for the people." Populists contrasted the interests of ordinary workers and farmers against those of corporations and economic elites, and Progressives advanced a vision of remedying perceived defects within democracy through more democracy.

Unlike Madison, leaders of the latter movement increasingly began to see representatives not as the embodiment of electoral mandates but as obstacles to the will of the people as reflected in more direct mechanisms such as the initiative, the referendum, the recall, and political primaries. All of these mechanisms were designed to replace decisions made by elites in so-called "smoke-filled rooms." Progressives like Woodrow Wilson and Theodore Roosevelt eventually viewed the president as the embodiment of a national will that transcended that of party or region.

When Alexis de Tocqueville visited the United States in 1831, he believed that democracy was already ascendant. Of all the movements in U.S. history, probably no movement has had more influence on the direction of American institutions. It was the motive force behind the Seneca Falls Convention and many constitutional amendments. The Fifteenth, Nineteenth, and Twenty-Sixth Amendments expanded voting rights against discrimination based on race, sex, and age, and the Twenty-Third Amendment provided representation within the Electoral College for residents of the District of Columbia. The Seventeenth Amendment provided for direct election of senators. In practice, the Electoral College is far more democratic than the Framers intended for it to be, but it allocates votes to states based on their representation in Congress, which includes the Senate, where states are represented equally rather than according to population.

Advocates of making the Constitution more democratic have included Victoria Woodhull (1870), James C. West (1890), Frederick Upham Adams (1896), Walter Clark (1906), Edward House (1912), Alan Benson (1914), the Socialist Party (1932), Malcolm Eiselen (1941), Thomas Upham (1941), P. G. Marduke (1970), Theodore Becker (1976), Roderick Long (1993), Jim Davidson (1994), the Virginia Vanguard (1995), Kenneth Dolbeare and Janette Hubbell (1996), Michael

Marx (1999), Frederick Ellis and Carl Frederick (2000), David Jeffs (2000), Richard Labunski (2000), Robert Dahl (2001), Martin J. Bailey (2001), Dick Formichella (2005), Sanderson Beck (2005), Sanford Levinson (2006), Larry Sabato (2007), Ernest Pain, and George Wynne (2006). An increasing number of proponents of constitutional change, including Victoria C. Woodhull (1870), Malcom Eiselen (1937, 1941), James L. Sundquist (1986), Herbert C. Kirstein (1994), the Virginia Vanguard (1995), Kenneth Dolbeare and Janette Hubbell (1996), David Jeffs (2000), Sanford Levinson (2006), Daryl Lloyd Davis (2011), and Ward Ricker have called for applying the initiative, the referendum, and/or the recall, which Progressives succeeded in adopting within many states, to the national level. Robert E. Beasley (1864) and Alan L. Bensen (1914) favored requiring a referendum before the nation committed itself to war, while others sought to put brakes on war-making by requiring prior approval by congressional supermajorities.

No one has drawn a starker contrast between what they considered to be the shortcomings of representative democracy when compared to direct democracy than Michael Noah Mautner (1992) and Ted Aranda (2010). The former would have created a system consisting of National Proposal Banks, Proposals Bank Juries, Debates Agencies, Issue Panels, and Public Ombudsmen. The latter favored replacing all three branches of government with assemblies and randomly selected Councils of Five Hundred, Committees of Fifty, and Boards of Five. Ethan J. Leib (2004), whom this book does not otherwise discuss because he did not propose a new constitution or a series of amendments, provided a variant plan advocating a fourth branch of government built upon requiring randomly selected citizens to participate in deliberative panels.

The Twenty-Second Amendment provided for presidential term limits, and a number of reformers have advocated term limits for members of Congress and justices of the Supreme Court. Such advocates have often argued that individuals with short or limited terms would be more responsive to popular wishes. Those who oppose such limits on popular choice often express fear that instead of returning power to the people, term limits would simply vest greater power within congressional staff or other bureaucrats.

The More Representative Alternative
Bruce E. Tonn (1991, 1996) and George Kennan (1993) both suggested creating new institutional mechanisms, respectively designated as a Court of Generations and a Council of Elders, or State, to institutionalize wisdom, especially in planning for the future. Although far more critics have called for eliminating the Senate or for basing it more closely on population, Rick Sirmon (2011) and Payne Edwards (2012) are among those who have called for repeal of the Seventeenth Amendment, which provided for direct election of Senators. Others, like the author or authors of "Constitution-21," have favored greater reliance upon, or restructuring of, national nominating conventions. This stance stems from a fear that the existing system of selecting members chiefly through political primaries appeals

to extremes within both parties and permits too little deliberation and input from existing officeholders.

The Mixed Government Alternative

The doctrine of separation of powers had roots in ideas of mixed government (Vile 2005, I, 488), which sought to create stability by balancing the rule of one (monarchy), the few (aristocracy), and the many (democracy). A number of delegates to the Constitutional Convention wanted to limit membership in the Senate to individuals with a certain amount of wealth.

The idea of using institutions to represent various classes has rarely been popular in the United States but was arguably reflected in a proposal by Caspar Hopkins (1885) that would have allowed the Senate to represent the wealthy; by Ralph Cram (1937), who favored both association representation and the establishment of a monarchy; and by Thomas Wright Sulcer (2011), who favored a Department of State consisting in part of 100 advisors who would serve for life. Hans-Hermann Hoppe (2001) believed that a monarchy would have better preserved freedom than democracy, although he favored substituting voluntary insurance arrangements for all forms of government. William Wilson (2013) sought to reintroduce an aristocratic element within government by restoring the Electoral College to its original function of exercising good judgment. Kirk Brothers (1996) would limit voters to individuals with IQs of 100 or higher and mandate that federal public officials possess IQs of 130 or higher. John Médaille (2010) sought both to make the U.S. Senate more aristocratic and the presidency more monarchical.

Should the Constitution Specifically Enumerate Individual Rights or Leave Their Protection to Institutional Protections?

The Constitution contained some explicit protections for individual rights, most notably in Article I, Sections 9 and 10, which limited the powers of Congress and of the states. Delegates, however, rejected George Mason's suggestion on September 12 of the Convention to add a bill of rights, and Federalist supporters of the new document initially argued that such a mechanism was unnecessary. In time, Madison and other supporters of the Constitution agreed to add a bill of rights that would convert the natural rights that Thomas Jefferson had identified in the Declaration of Independence into civil rights for which the people could seek vindication in courts. The Thirteenth and Fourteenth Amendment have subsequently extended the protection of such rights to new classes of citizens.

The Increased Written Protections for Individual Rights Alternative

Following in the legacy of Mason and Jefferson, a number of proponents of revamping the Constitution have called for expanding the number of rights that the Constitution protects. Some individuals have sought to accomplish this either by reversing or freezing existing judicial understandings of individual rights within the current constitution.

Reformers whose plans have called for an expanded list of rights have included Henry O. Morris (1897), William MacDonald (1921), Alexander Hehmeyer (1943), Rexford Tugwell (1974), Joseph Clark (1982), Jeremy Miller (1987), Cornelius Murphy (1988), Roderick Long (1993), Jim Davidson (1994), Chester Antieau (1995), A. R. Adams (1996), John VanSickle (1998), Jack Durst (2002), Ross Nordeen, Robert F. Hawes, Jr. (2006), William S. Field (2006), Joseph F. Coates (2007), Daryl Lloyd Davis (2011), and John B. Miller (2012). Some advocates of increased rights have focused specifically on recognizing the right to an education; they include Simon Willard, Jr. (1815), William B. Wedgwood (1861), E. L. Godkin (1864), Barry Krusch (1992), and Jesse Jackson, Jr., and Frank Watkins (2001). William K. Wallace (1932), Alexander Hehmeyer (1943), the Black Panthers (1970), Cornelius Murphy (1988), Chester Antieau (1995), A. R. Adams (1996), Jackson and Watkins (2001), Mary Becker (2001); the Revolutionary Communist Party (2010), C. Earl Campbell (2011), Uldis Sprogis (2011), Sam Carr Polk (2013), Ward Ricker, and Roger Copple (2012) are among those who have also sought the inclusion of additional social and economic rights. Many of these are similar to, if not patterned after, the proposals that Franklin D. Roosevelt advanced in his January 11, 1944, State of the Union Address as "a second Bill of Rights." Cass R. Sunstein (2004) has called for a revival of such rights and has even proposed a reworked version, albeit not one that he thinks needs to be specifically incorporated in the U.S. Constitution; Joseph F. Coates (2007) specifically concentrated on revising the Bill of Rights rather than the Constitution as a whole. Conversely, although Kirk Brothers (1996) wanted the powers of his proposed constitution to be construed narrowly, he wanted the provisions for rights to be interpreted expansively.

The Decreased Written Protections for Individual Rights Alternative

A number of proponents of constitutional change have either omitted or reduced the number of rights that they would include. Most were writing before the Bill of Rights attained its current prominence or before the Supreme Court applied most of its provisions to the states via the due process clause of the Fourteenth Amendment. They thus appear to have largely omitted such rights inadvertently. Others, who stressed social rights, believed that the current list of rights was too individualistic. Some have specifically targeted rights like the Second Amendment right to bear arms or the Fifth Amendment protection against self-incrimination. Others have sought to modify the Eighth Amendment specifically to approve or outlaw capital punishment.

Still others appear to have accepted the Constitution's original premise that the protections of federalism, separation of powers, and other internal constitutional mechanisms would provide sufficient protection to individual citizens. The self-identified Christian Prophet sought to curb abuses of rights by abolishing Congress and the laws that it would enact. William Wilson proposed expanding rights for the unborn while limiting unwholesome speech or unfair press accounts. In proposing a constitution, Anarchist420 (2011) omitted a bill of rights, presumably because he thought such protection should be provided by the states. Keith B. Anderson (2013) also omitted a bill of rights in proposing a semi-socialist constitution.

Should the Constitution Increase Protections for Private Property or Become More Socialistic?

The Constitution contains a number of protections for property rights. These included the provision in Article I, Section 9 prohibiting states from abridging contracts; the due process protections for "life, liberty, and property" in the Fifth and Fourteenth Amendments; and the takings clause of the Fifth Amendment, which guaranteed "just compensation" for property that the government takes for "public use." Over time, however, and especially with the advent of the New Deal, the government has increased its regulation of businesses, and recent Supreme Court opinions, most notably *Kelo v. City of New London*, 545 U.S. 469 (2005), have articulated an expansive judicial interpretation of public use.

The Free Market Alternative

The laissez-faire conception of capitalism is based on the notion that the "invisible hand" of the marketplace will often prove to be far more fair and efficient than the directing hand of government. The apogee of this ideal, evident in the late nineteenth century rise of Social Darwinism, was best symbolized by the British sociologist Herbert Spencer and others who opposed almost all governmental regulations of the economy. They believed that both governmental aid and private charity conspired to allow for the survival of weaker individuals and races who would otherwise benefit civilization by dying out through the process of natural selection.

Advocates of such a hands-off policy have left a number of proposals for major constitutional reforms. Although Bruce Ackerman has argued that the New Deal, which increased economic regulation and the social safety net, ushered in a new American regime, the lack of official constitutional sanction for such policies arguably makes them vulnerable. Libertarians believe that most economic matters, even those involving the provision of schools, roads, and other services, should be accomplished through private contracts.

Numerous individuals have favored increasing protections for private property or otherwise making the Constitution more capitalistic. They have included Michael Oliver (1968), Bernard H. Siegan (1992), Roderick Long (1993), Jim Davidson (1994), John VanSickel (1998), Michael Marx (1999), Martin J. Bailey (2001), Hans-Hermann Hoppe (2001), James M. Buchanan (2005), the Objectivist Constitution, Randy Barnett (2009), the libertarian posting by the self-identified Christian Prophet, A. Hines (2009), Chip Downs (2012), Tom Green (2013), and Mark R. Levin (2013). William Wilson (2013) wanted to transfer most governmental welfare programs to private charity. Kirk Brothers (1996) wanted to renounce responsibilities for governments to provide for education or health care. Rick Sirmon (2011) favored withdrawing powers from Congress to regulate any existing economic activities.

The Increased Regulatory Alternative

Congress did not have a huge regulatory role in the early republic, and most powers that it now exercises are based on expansive interpretations of the commerce clause, the general welfare clause, and/or the war powers provisions of the Constitution. While some have sought to limit the scope of these constitutional grants, others have called for adding constitutional provisions more specifically justifying congressional regulation of farming, industry, mining, and other economic activity. Despite its uneasy fit within the doctrine of separation of powers and this system's relatively clear distinctions between legislative and executive powers, Congress created the Interstate Commerce Commission in 1887, the first of many independent agencies. Some proponents of change have wanted the Constitution specifically to recognize, or rein in, such institutions. Walter Tuller (1911) proposed to give Congress power "to regulate corporations or monopolies in any form." Henry S. McKee (1933) favored increased national regulation, and Rexford Tugwell (1974) and Herbert C. Kirstein (1994) proposed new congressional powers and regulatory governmental agencies and departments. By contrast, in commenting on proposed amendments by James M. Buchanan, William Niskasen (2005) proposed delaying the application of all independent agency rules for 60 days, during which members of Congress could repeal them. Steven G. Calabresi (1998) advocated a similar change.

The Marxian Socialist Alternative

Karl Marx believed that the capitalist system was inherently inefficient, alienating, and exploitative. More importantly, he believed that the system resulted in major class differences that led to conflict. Communists and socialists who have followed in Marx's footsteps, have emphasized the need for governmental ownership of the major means of production, the former by violent means if necessary and the other through more democratic mechanisms.

A number of advocates of change have favored incorporating a system of socialism into the Constitution. The Anarchist Constitution (1903) proposed eliminating private ownership of property and allowing governments to create businesses; local governments would provide health care, the right to counsel, and even pay for burial expenses. Individuals who have directly advocated socialism have included Edward Bellamy (1888), Henry O. Morris (1897), Edward House (1912), Alan Benson (1914), Bouck White (1917), the Socialist Party Platform (1932), William Kay Wallace (1933), Thomas Upham (1941), the Black Panthers (1970), Joseph Church (1982), John Mertens (1990), Frederick Ellis and Carl Frederick (2000), the Revolutionary Communist Party (2010), and Keith B. Anderson (2013). Several proponents of change would limit the income of the highest paid individuals to some multiplier of the lowest. Huey P. Long (1935) proposed a drastic plan for redistributing wealth without advocating constitutional change. Bill Strittmatter (1970s) proposed the return of land in the Year of Jubilee, and Jon Roland called for a shmita period every seven years that would have similar consequences.

Amendments to Deal with Federal Fiscal Matters

Numerous Populists and Progressive era reformers favored adoption of the Sixteenth Amendment, which permitted a national income tax. In recent years, an increasing number of individuals have identified federal deficits either as a major problem in and of themselves or as an indication of greater systematic issues within government, such as an appetite for unbridled spending and tensions between the legislative and executive branches. Paul Fisher (1988), Bernard H. Siegan (1992), Malcolm R. Wilkey (1995), the Virginia Vanguard (1995), Kirk Brothers (1996), Martin J. Bailey (2001), James M. Buchanan (2005), Jon Roland (2009), Tom Green, Rick Sirmon (2011), John B. Miller (2012), Robert M. Hinkelman (2012), Payne Edwards (2012), Ward Ricker (2011), Thomas Wright Sulcer (2011), and Ralph Bass (2012) have all called for balanced budgets or other budget controls. Some such proposals would require congressional supermajorities to raise taxes, debt ceilings, or both. Other reformers have called for repealing the Sixteenth Amendment or for instituting or prohibiting a national sales tax, a value added tax, the inheritance tax, or other taxes. Jesse Jackson, Jr. (2001), sought to mandate that income taxes would be more progressive. Tom Hopper (2011) sought to prevent politicians from pledging to enact new taxes.

Should the Constitution Protect Political Parties, Multiply Them, or Seek to Foster Nonpartisanship?

Although Madison and his compatriots believed that they had largely transcended partisan politics when they gathered together in Philadelphia to write a new document, they did not expect such principled behavior from their successors (Smith 1992, 42–3). The Framers hoped that the system of representation would refine public views, but they did not expect representatives to fully transcend their own self-interests. The Framers never mentioned political parties in the U.S. Constitution and were initially quite wary of their development. The closest that their successors came to recognizing parties was in crafting the mechanism in the Twelfth Amendment to prevent ties within the Electoral College and the elimination of poll taxes by the Twenty-Fourth Amendment in both general and primary elections. Although David Mayhew (2011) has recently provided a strong defense of the operations of political parties within Congress, there are many who believe the current system requires fundamental change.

The Nonpartisan Government Alternative

A number of reform proponents have relied fairly heavily on establishing a system that will select elites and trust them to direct and manage affairs of state on behalf of the public. Albert Stickney's plan to get the "best men" to do their "best work" is a good example. An even more vivid example may be Edward House's fictional portrayal of an "Administrator" who was so certain of his own righteous intentions that he was willing to use military force to attain power and set the ship of state aright. In contrast to the Jacksonian belief that public administration was not the preserve of the experts, some reporters have asserted that the key to effective government is to entrust elites—whether designated as monarchs, administrators, senators, or judges—with greater power to act on behalf of the common good.

Individuals who have called for reducing the role of political parties in government have included James Hillhouse (1808), Robert E. Beasley (1864), Albert Stickney (1879), Thomas Carlton Upham (1941), William Gardiner (1973), David B. Jeffs (2000), Patrick McGrath (2000), Martin Bailey (2001), Steve Gillman (2008), Ward Ricker (2011), Marty Piatt (2012), and William Wilson (2013). A. R. Adams (1996) and Lawrence Lessig (2011) have also sought to limit the role of money in politics, which would undoubtedly affect party influence. Kirk Brothers (1999) and Payne Edwards (2012) both proposed that states select members of unicameral legislatures on a nonpartisan basis, while other reformers have called for drawing legislative boundaries on a nonpartisan basis. Sam Carr Polk (2013) proposed that "Guardians" be selected on a nonpartisan basis and given life tenure, while Keith B. Anderson (2013) proposed that members of the House of Provincial Senators be selected from a single party.

The Party Government Alternative

The Committee on Political Parties of the American Political Science Association called in 1950 for strengthening political parties without proposing constitutional change. Proponents of parliamentary government typically envision that the leader of the legislative party will also be the chief executive, and most favor more powerful and more responsible parties. Even apart from such models, some advocates of constitutional change believe that the Constitution would strengthen the political system if it specifically acknowledged and/or supported political parties. These have included Leland Baldwin (1972), Charles Hardin (1974), Robert Shogan (1982), the Committee on the Constitutional System (1987), Rodney Scott (1999), and Larry Sabato (2007). Malcolm R. Wilkey (1995) seemed to equivocate between a system that strengthened political parties and one that relied more on citizen legislators.

The Multiparty Alternative

The system of single-member districts in the U.S. House of Representatives contributes to the current two-party system, and having a single presidency rather than a coalition government rewards the top two political parties. Kenneth Dolbeare and Janette Hubbell (1996) called for establishing or facilitating the creation of a multiparty system to give voters more choices. Sanderson Beck (2005) wanted to make it easier for minor parties to get at least some representation through a system of proportional representation, which would reward parties that could get a consistent percentage of votes across a state or the nation even if they did not win a plurality of any individual districts. Steven Hill (2006, 2012) offered voting reforms that he thought would be fairer to minor parties. Roger Copple (2012) proposed proportional representation based on participation by seven political parties.

Should the Constitution Acknowledge the Divine or Seek to Enforce Biblical Law?

The Constitution created a secular state, but it neither disestablished state churches nor expressed contempt for religion. The First Amendment confirmed this stance by guaranteeing the free exercise of religion. A few years after the creation of the U.S. Constitution, French revolutionaries introduced a more rigid system of separation of church and state. Later, Russian revolutionaries tried to exterminate religion altogether. In light of America's strong religious pluralism, the Supreme Court has specifically outlawed religious exercises in public schools and other public spaces. Critics have interpreted these rulings as expressions of hostility to religion rather than as efforts to treat the subject neutrally.

The Puritan/Rushdoony Reconstructionist Alternative

Some Americans thought that a central flaw in the U.S. Constitution was its failure specifically to acknowledge the Divine (1984). Ever since Pilgrims came to America with the hope of founding a "city upon a hill" that would serve as a beacon to mankind, some have looked to America as the embodiment of Christian ideals. The New England Body of Liberties of 1642 is an early example of an agreement designed to combine scriptural and secular laws. Thomas Jefferson and Joseph Story later argued about whether American common law embodied principles of Christianity (Vile, Hudson, and Schultz 2009, II, 1028).

Some proponents of constitutional revision have focused on embodying various scriptural principles into the Constitution. John Brown's religious convictions led him to seek slave emancipation (1858), but his proposed constitution sought to preserve the Sabbath and outlaw swearing. The authors of the Confederate Constitution (1861) referenced God in their preamble. William B. Wedgwood (1861) called for a "theocratic Democracy," Bill Strittmatter (1970s) sought to build a national constitution on the scaffolding of the Ten Commandments, and Robert Struble, Jr., thought it was important for the government to support morality. The Constitution of the New America posted on RationalWiki (2007) wanted to limit recognition to Protestant religions. The Web posting by the self-proclaimed Christian Prophet thought the best way to encourage moral government was to make it as voluntary as possible and allow it to focus on the protection of natural rights. Paul R. Heim (2009) wanted to recognize the United States as a Christian nation by allowing states and localities to legislate on religious matters even as it enforced First Amendment provisions prohibiting the national government from so doing. Rick Sirmon (2011) favored altering the First Amendment to protect traditional public acknowledgements of religion and affirm "In God We Trust" as the national motto. Chip Downs (2012) indicated that the nation was courting God's judgment, and William Wilson (2013) viewed his Constitution of New America as an alternative to the existing document, which he expected would bring down God's wrath on the nation. Thomas Dahlberg and Erick Kaardal (2013) began their constitution with an acknowledgment of God (as did Chandra Tamirisa) and expressed hope that the church would set the personal values that they believed governments were illegitimately attempting to impose.

The Radical Separation or Hostility Model

Some reformers have sought to further restrict the influence of religion in the United States. In some cases, these provisions may have stemmed from unusually close historical connections between the government and the dominant Protestant theology of the day. Thus, as a Roman Catholic, Charles O'Conor (1877, 1881) expressed concern over Protestant religious indoctrination in public schools. The author of the Anarchist Constitution (1903) sought to prevent individuals from being paid to broadcast their religious faith. John Piburn (1932) sought to prohibit religious schools. Joseph Church (1982) recommended replacing the current national motto with "In Humankind We Trust." John Mertens (1990) favored greater regulation of churches. Marty Piatt (2012) advocated embodying the wall of separation language directly into the current First Amendment. Kirk Brothers called for stricter separation of church and state. Uldis Sprogis (2011) advocated making churches responsible for the health care and retirement of their employees. A dystopian novel published under the name of Dawn Blair entitled *America 2014: An Orwellian Tale* was set in "God's United States," which had prohibited the establishment of any religion other than "the state-sanctioned religion of Christianity" (Blair 2004, 219).

Should the Constitution Be Closer to an Outline or More Like a Code?

The U.S. Constitution is a relatively concise document, the original of which was less than 5,000 words. Bernard Shaw once observed that Americans had "perfected a Constitution of negatives to defend liberty" (Shaw 1933, 33), and a recent analysis of the document establishes "minimalism" as a key feature of the document (Greve 2013, 25–7). The U.S. Constitution established three branches of government, and recognized the continuing existence of states, without even initially listing many of the rights to which the people would be entitled under the new government. Those who have proposed substitutes have sometimes sought to continue this broad outline, while others have proposed far more detailed and prescriptive alternatives.

The Technologically Updated Alternative

Related to the desire to update constitutional language is the desire to bring the Constitution in line with modern technology. Few changes to American society have been more profound than those brought about by advances in transportation, communication, data collection and storage, and the potential for large numbers of people to be able to convey their views on matters of public policy. A number of proposed calls for new constitutions would allow masses of individuals to participate in the initiation, ratification, and amendment of constitutions and the election, instruction, and recall of elected representatives. Several have suggested that the people could directly take the place of members of Congress or that the members would no longer need to meet in person but could instead conduct legislative business electronically. Dick Formichella (2005) and Ian Pubman (2011) both referred to their proposals for reengineering America in "constitution 2.0" terms, and Robert M. Hinkelman (2012) entitled his novel *America 2.0*. Sam Carr Polk (2013) believed that computers could transform the way that individuals are represented and the way that Congress is organized.

The Up-to-Date Translation Alternative

Some advocates of changing the Constitution have had the relatively modest aim of bringing the current language and structure of the constitution up to date so that it is clearer and more understandable. Much like proponents of modern biblical translations, these reformers believe that constitutional language needs to be clarified to make it more accessible.

Those who seek such updates typically advocate rearranging existing articles, incorporating amendments in appropriate places within the text, eliminating archaic or confusing language, or simply recognizing extra-constitutional practices and institutions (political parties, national nominating conventions, and primaries, for example) without which it is impossible to understand the operation of the written constitution. Charles Coleman's proposed constitution (1938) and those of Holler (2008), A. Hines (2009), and Bain (2013) are the quintessential examples in this book, but most proponents of rewriting the Constitution undoubtedly anticipate that constitutional rewrites would not only correct obvious faults but bring the language up to date. Paul Lillebo has similarly proposed incorporating existing amendments within the document and deleting texts that are "clearly moot or superannuated" (Lillebo 2012). James Schmitendorf wanted to consolidate constitutional language for easier reading.

The Legal Code Alternative

State constitutions are typically far longer and more prescriptive than the U.S. Constitution. Many resemble legal codes, and, partly as a consequence, they tend to be amended and replaced far more frequently than the national document (Cornwell 1981). Some advocates of constitutional change have sought to incorporate similar specificity within the U.S. Constitution. Some of their proposals tout the inclusion of a wider set of social and economic rights, but others are driven by their authors' penchant for nailing down all the details.

Simon Willard Jr.'s proposed constitution (1815) epitomized his precision as a clockmaker, but others have also been quite lengthy. Ironically, the Anarchist Constitution of 1903 contained 225 sections and described the organization of local governments in great detail. John Piburn (1932) wanted an Education Department to specify the size of college diplomas. Michael Oliver (1968) argued that one of the flaws of the existing U.S. Constitution was that it omitted details and definitions that would have restricted governmental powers. Joseph Church (1982) was as interested in using his proposed constitution to raise consciousness and reflect changed sexual mores as he was in developing constitutional structures. The

Revolutionary Communist Party (2010) clearly regarded its proposed constitution in part as an instrument of propaganda. John K. Piper (1999) multiplied governmental agencies and described various rights and duties in sometimes near-excruciating detail. Although Chip Downs (2012) only proposed six amendments, all had multiple sections, and many would be longer than the current Fourteenth and Twenty-Fifth Amendments. A. R. Adams (1996) prescribed the content of chapel services for members of Congress, whereas Michael Marx's constitution (1999) would have made masturbation by minors unconstitutional. Keith B. Anderson (2013) listed numerous new governmental departments and agencies, including provisions dealing with alcohol, tobacco, and gambling.

How Should the Constitution Be Interpreted?

The ink had barely dried on the U.S. Constitution before those who had joined forces in writing and ratifying the document split over how it should be interpreted (Powell 1985). The Federalist and Democratic-Republican Parties were basically born over as the result of a dispute over whether Congress had authority under the new Constitution to establish a national bank. They also parted ways over the division of power between Congress and the president in the area of foreign affairs, on the degree to which the new republic should pursue an agrarian or commercial future, and on issues relative to judicial review, which while unstated, could be understood to have been implied in the Constitution.

The "Living Constitution" Model

Individuals' views on constitutional interpretation often influence whether they favor adoption of new amendments. Advocates of a "living constitution" may well be content with expansive judicial interpretations that, for example, call for expanded welfare rights. Cass Sunstein (2004) has thus joined President Franklin D. Roosevelt in suggesting that the primary way to enact a second bill of rights is through congressional legislation rather than by amendment. Mary Becker (2001) has suggested that the United States might be able to liberalize its policies by adopting various international treaties.

The Strict Constructionist Model

Advocates of original intent often suggest bad faith on the part of those who have employed more liberal interpretative methods. John O. McGinnis and Michael B. Rappaport have argued that more faithful adherence to originalism would lead to the adoption of more constitutional amendments (2013). Some advocates of constitutional change including Martin J. Bailey (2001), Randy Barnett (2009), and Jon Roland (2009) have proposed amendments embodying some form of original intent within the Constitutional text, or enjoining the Supreme Court against considering other factors. These proposals parallel Karl Spence's advocacy in a 2006 book for a "Fair Construction Amendment" (for a similar proposal see H. M. Person's *Amendment: Restoring the Plain Meaning of the Constitution and the Rule of Law*, 2011). Robert R. Owens (2010) wanted to return to the Constitution that the Federalists had originally promised in the wake of Anti-Federalist criticisms. A number of critics have proposed amendments that would either prohibit provisions of any treaty from overriding existing constitutional provisions or specifically enjoin justices from consulting foreign legal sources.

Should Citizenship Be Widened or Restricted?

The U.S. Constitution's failure to define citizenship led in part to *Dred Scott v. Sandford* (1857), in which the U.S. Supreme Court decided that blacks were not and could not become citizens. Four years later, the Confederate Constitution sought to affirm this position. Section 1 of the Fourteenth Amendment, which declared that "all persons born or naturalized in the United States are citizens thereof," eventually reversed this legal decision, but it has not ended controversy over whether the Fourteenth Amendment intended to include people born in the United States to noncitizen parents.

The Greater Inclusivity Alternative

Michael C. Dorf has observed that "the history of constitutional change in the United States is in substantial part a history of expanding the political community" (Dorf 2011, 499). The Fourteenth Amendment extended citizenship to former slaves, while other amendments have extended rights to women and 18-year-olds who, while previously regarded as citizens, did not have all the rights of citizenship. E. L. Godkin (1865) and Francis Lieber (1865) presaged the inclusion of African Americans, while numerous individuals, including delegates to the Seneca Falls Convention (1848), had called for the expansion of women's suffrage prior to the adoption of the Nineteenth Amendment in 1920. Richard Labunski (2000) has called for ratification of the Equal Rights Amendment. C. Earl Campbell (2011) advocated extending prohibitions against voting discrimination on the basis of both "species" and sexual orientation. William B. Wedgwood (1861), P. G. Marduke (1970), and Frederick Ellis and Carl Frederick (2000) have proposed allowing other nations to join the Union. Sanderson Beck (2005) proposed allowing states to accept new citizens without interference from the national government. Uldis Sprogis (2011) proposed that the United States might simply purchase foreign nations, while Roger Copple (2012) looked forward to a possible world federation.

The Decreased Inclusivity Alternative

A number of proponents of constitutional change, including some Populists and Progressives, argued for narrowing the breadth or scope of U.S. citizenship. In addition to those who favored recognizing slavery to preserve the union and advocates of various secessionist movements, some writers have sought to restrict citizenship to Anglo-Saxons, to exclude homosexuals or non-Christians from the polity, or to make it more difficult to add new states.

The author of the Anarchist Constitution (1903) sought to restrict Chinese ("Mongolians") from entering U.S. territories without presidential permission.

Walter Clark (1906) favored repeal or inapplication of the Fourteenth and Fifteenth Amendments. Ralph Cram (1937) sought to restrict suffrage, while Caspar Hopkins (1885) wanted to limit immigration and restrict suffrage to those who were native born. Hugh Hamilton (1938) advocated denying citizenship to criminals or the insane. H. Wentworth Eldredge (1964) expressed general contempt for nonelites who he believed voted with little information. Henry O. Morris (1897) voiced concern over Jews and foreigners, while Strittmatter (1970s) called for limiting citizenship to Christians (and stoning those who participated in intermarriage). Goldwin Smith (1898) sought to preserve the Anglo-Saxon heritage, the Virginia Vanguard (1995) sought to deny citizenship to those who were born in the United States to noncitizen parents, and John Mertens (1997) sought to encourage recent non-European immigrants to leave and convince African Americans to move to South Africa. Kirby Palm endorsed limiting the right to vote to native-born citizens. Paul R. Heim (2009) wanted to prohibit gays from receiving special benefits from the national government, while A. Hines (2009) heightened the distinction between state and national citizenship and would in part base the latter on "a demonstrated knowledge in, and record of adherence to, this constitution." Thomas Wright Sulcer (2011) would require an oath by 18-year-olds to uphold the Constitution before they could become citizens, while Marty Piatt (2012) sought to clarify the Fourteenth Amendment to exclude from citizenship individuals born to parents who were not legally in the country. Anarchist420 would exclude "paupers, vagabonds, and fugitives from justice" from the polity. Chip Downs (2012) would limit citizenship to individuals with adequate civic knowledge, who pledged to uphold the Constitution, and participated in some kind of universal service, while Thomas Dahlberg, Erick Kaardal (2013), and Billy Rojas (2011) would limit birthright citizenship to individuals who had at least one parent who was a citizen. Rojas further wanted to recriminalize homosexual practice and strip citizenship from and/or deport all Muslims who did not renounce their faith. Mark R. Levin would enshrine requirements for voter identification in the Constitution. Daryl Lloyd Davis (2011) was among those advocating making English the official language of the nation.

Should the Judicial Branch Be Stronger or Weaker?

Although the Framers did not specifically vest the federal judiciary with the power to void laws that it considered to be unconstitutional, many of the delegates to the Convention anticipated that it would do so, and it was not long before the Supreme Court asserted and exercised such authority when adjudicating cases and controversies (Law and Versteeg point out than an increasing number of foreign nations limit such review to specific courts or provide for what they call "abstract review" in which courts can examine laws before they go into effect [2012, 795–6]). Although the method for selecting the president has become more democratic in practice, and state citizens now choose senators, the judiciary has remained an appointed branch.

The Stronger Judiciary Alternative

In part because the judiciary has been so powerful, few advocates of constitutional change have proposed increasing its powers. Some, like John Piburn (1932) and William MacDonald (1921), favored specifically recognizing judicial review within the Constitution. Albert Stickney (1879) thought that judges, rather than members of Congress, should make and revise laws. Arthur S. Miller (1987) lauded judicial activism.

Some proponents of change have advocated specifically setting the number of Supreme Court justices at nine. The New York Bar Association (1948) proposed amendments to protect the U.S. Supreme Court from further political attacks. Others have proposed incorporating existing expansive judicial interpretations of rights into the actual constitutional text or extending the power of the judiciary to issue advisory opinions—in some cases even while Congress is considering the legislation in question. Michael Oliver (1968) wanted judges to assess the constitutionality of laws *before* they were adopted. In devising a constitution for newly emerging nations, Bernard H. Siegan (1992) proposed confining the exercise of judicial review to a single national court.

The Weaker Judiciary Alternative

By contrast, other proponents of change have sought to restrict the powers of the Court, change methods of judicial selection, and introduce new accountability provisions. Walter Clark (1906) wanted judges to be elected. Henry Lockwood (1884) and Isaac Rice (1884) thought that Congress should be the judge of the constitutionality of the laws that it passed. Edward House (1912), the Socialist Party Platform of 1932, Alan Benson (1914), and at least two contributors to the *Constitutional Commentary* symposium in 2011 also proposed to eliminate judicial review. The Council of State Governments (1962) proposed changes that would have significantly clipped the power of the federal judiciary, and H. Wentworth Eldredge (1964) suggested that the federal judiciary was interfering with the proper execution of governmental powers. A number of writers including William Y. Elliott (1935) have proposed requiring judicial supermajorities to invalidate legislation. Yandell Henderson (1913) favored giving voters the means to repeal exercises of judicial review. In addition to seeking to cut the administrative powers of the chief justice, Steven Hill (2006, 2012) wanted to limit terms of Supreme Court justices and set a mandatory retirement age. Mary Becker (2001) and Sam Carr Polk (2013) favored restricting the scope of judicial review. Paul R. Heim (2009) proposed giving state chief justices the power to initiate impeachments against U.S. Supreme Court justices. Thomas Dahlberg and Erick Kaardal (2013) called for allowing citizens to appoint and recall judges. Kirk Brothers (1996) favored limiting federal judicial review to a single court; Mark R. Levin (2013) endorsed giving supermajorities either in Congress or among the states the authority to override decisions, at least within a 24-month window, while Jon Roland wanted to require justices to base their decisions on the original intent of the framers and ratifiers of the Constitution. Still other proposals, such as those set forth by Henry Hazlitt (1942), and the New York Bar Association (1948), provided for mandatory retirement ages, specific judicial terms, or for more flexible means of removing sitting judges.

Should Voting Mechanisms Be Changed?

Republican government rests firmly on the existence and integrity of electoral mechanisms. Although the right to vote has been progressively expanded throughout United States history, some have questioned whether existing methods of voting are fair or democratic. John C. Calhoun advanced his idea for concurrent majorities because he was concerned that numerical majorities did not always protect minority interests—which for him meant state and regional minorities rather than racial minorities. Numerous proposals have, of course, favored altering the Electoral College and replacing it with alternatives. These alternatives have typically taken the form of direct election, but some of these proposals have included requirements for runoff elections in cases in which no candidate receives an actual majority (Tom Hopper wanted presidents to have to secure a majority of congressional districts). The Seventeenth Amendment altered the method for selecting Senators, and a number of critics have called for its repeal. Members of the U.S. House of Representatives, like most other offices in the United States, are selected through winner-take-all single-member districts, which some reformers have called for replacing.

Creation of an Electoral Branch of Government and/or Regulations of Primaries

Voting regulations are currently scattered throughout the Constitution and its amendments, while most nomination decisions are made by political parties, which the Constitution does not even mention. Proponents of change in the Progressive era sought to replace back-room political dealmaking at caucuses and national nominating conventions with more open political primaries. Individuals who have proposed documents that more closely resemble legal codes than the current Constitution of seven fairly sparse articles have proposed adding a new article or section specifically delineating an electoral branch. Proponents of such a branch have included Rexford Tugwell (1974), who wanted it overseen by someone selected by the U.S. Senate, and the author or authors of Constitution 21, who envisioned that an electoral branch would consist both of an electoral college and an election board.

Other individuals have called for various reforms of the current nominating system. Herman Finer (1960) wanted national nominating conventions to nominate presidential and vice presidential candidates without any instructions from primary voters. Theodore L. Becker (1976) favored creating both a "National Presidential Primary" (NPP) and a "Presidential Election Tournament" (PET). William S. Field (2006) favored entrusting voting oversight to a national Electoral Commission. Larry Sabato (2007) has called for the creation of regional primaries, and Marty

Piatt (2012) favored a nominating system that would not advantage any states over others. James L. Sundquist (1986) and the Committee on the Constitutional System (1987) called for straight-ticket voting in which the president would run on a ticket with members of Congress. Sam Carr Polk (2013) favored eliminating all primary elections and providing for public financing of all elections.

Limiting Partisan or Racial Gerrymandering

The Council of State Governments (1962) unsuccessfully fought the Supreme Court's decision in *Baker v. Carr* to subject apportionment issues subject to judicial scrutiny, but this ruling has not stopped partisan or racial gerrymandering. Political scientists continue to express concern over this issue (Miller and Walling, 2013). Malcolm R. Wilkey (1995), Larry Sabato (2007), William Wilson (2013), and George Wynne are among those who have called for less partisan drawing of districts for the U.S. House of Representatives.

Proportional and Second-Choice Alternatives

A number of proponents of new constitutions have advocated replacing or supplementing the current system of winner-take-all single-member districts in the U.S. House of Representatives with systems of proportional representation. Such systems would reward minorities who might have meaningful support without being able to gain a majority or plurality within any single district. Frederick Ellis and Carl Frederick (2000) favored proportional voting, cumulative voting, preference voting, and referendums. Steven Hill (2006, 2012) favored instant runoff voting (IRV), increased use of proportional representation, direct popular election of the President, enfranchising ex-felons, and other voting reforms. Jesse Jackson, Jr. (2001), also advocated both proportional representation and instant runoff voting; and Billy Rojas (2011) favored the latter. Mary Becker (2001) advocated at-large voting for districts with seven or more seats. The Revolutionary Communist Party (2010) called for electing members of Congress from workplaces, organs of government, districts, and designated party nominees. Roger Copple favored providing such representation for up to seven parties. Sam Carr Polk (2013) proposed granting each district two representatives in Congress, each with weighted votes reflecting the number of votes that they had received.

Voter Identification and Protection

Recent years have witnessed the development of voter identification requirements in a number of states. Some proponents of these identification requirements want to incorporate them within the Constitution. Other reformers have sought to assure that felons or ex-felons are no longer permitted to vote—or to make sure that voting privileges lost during periods of incarceration are returned to people after they serve their time. Billy Rojas (2011) proposed overturning elections that he thought had been secured through fraud (including that of President Nixon in 1972).

Voting as an Affirmative Right

Constitutional amendments prohibit discrimination in voting based on race (Fifteenth Amendment), sex (Nineteenth Amendment), ability to pay a poll tax (Twenty-Fourth Amendment), or age above 18 (Twenty-Sixth Amendment), but all these provisions are phrased as negative rather than as positive rights. Jesse L. Jackson, Jr. (2001), and Steven Hill (2006, 2012) have specifically called for making voting a positive right, and a few have even proposed penalizing those who fail to exercise their right to vote.

Changes in Campaign Financing

The U.S. Supreme Court has extended First Amendment protections both to giving and spending money on political campaigns. The Committee on the Constitutional System (1987), Malcolm R. Wilkey (1995), Steven Hill (2006, 2012), Lawrence Lessig (2011), and Sam Carr Polk (2013) have called for public funding of congressional campaigns and/or for reduction of campaign expenditures. Richard Labunski (2000) favored overturning the Court's decision in *Buckley v. Valeo* in order to limit both campaign contributions and expenditures, and Billy Rojas (2011) called for limits on campaign funding. Tom Green (2013) favored limiting external funding of elections. By contrast, Randy Barnett (2009) has specifically favored extending explicit First Amendment protections to all campaign contributions.

Where Are We Now?

Those who wrote the U.S. Constitution were convinced that the British system of customs and usages had left them bereft of rights, but as much as they attempted to replace that system with specific grants and prohibitions, it was impossible to use language that did not come with historical baggage. Legislative, executive, and judicial powers all came with a history. One cannot protect "freedom of speech" without knowing what it entails. Although precedents rarely prove to be definitive, English and colonial history help illuminate what kinds of searches are "unreasonable" and what kinds of punishments are "cruel and unusual." Terms like habeas corpus, the executive power, impeachment, cases in law and equity, and treason, to name but a few, all have a preexisting history.

Darren Patrick Guerra has argued that the Framers designed the amending processes—including the convention mechanism—as the exclusive means of purely constitutional changes, suggesting the importance of distinguishing constitutional amendments from the broader category of constitutional change (Guerra 2013). Still, history suggests that numerous changes in constitutional understandings, if not in constitutional language, have come through judicial interpretation and legislative and executive actions rather than through amendments (Vile 1994).

The current constitutional amending process is so difficult to execute that it serves as a strong guardian of the actual constitutional text. The difficulty of these processes, though, also encourages evasion and the development of extra-constitutional institutions and interpretations that ultimately work against those who seek the kind of straightforward changes advocated by authors that this book has identified. Donald Kyvig thus bemoaned a state of affairs that law scholar Bruce Ackerman seemed to celebrate; namely, that Franklin D. Roosevelt brought about a fundamentally new understanding of the role of government in modern life through changes in constitutional interpretation rather than through constitutional amendments (Kyvig 1996, 314). Kyvig believed that had major elements of the New Deal been incorporated into the text, they would have been less subject to continuing dispute.

Although the author is not a partisan of *any* of scores of proposals that he has discussed in this book, he has an innate respect for most of their authors because he believes they value written constitutionalism and what it can do. According to the biblical book of Genesis, God literally spoke the world into existence. This author believes in the power of words and thoughts. Although he realizes that it sometimes takes generations for words to be embodied in concrete actions, he believes that the endeavor of preserving, and proposing changes, in the fundamental written document is significant, and he admires all those who have proceeded in the spirit of the Founding Fathers to try their own hands at such a task.

References

Bain, Henry, ed. *The Constitution of the United States of America, Modern Edition. Rearranged and Edited for Ease of Reading*. Rockville, MD: Montgomery Books.

Blair, Dawn. 2004. *America 2014: An Orwellian Tale*. Oakland, CA: Council Oak Books.

Buckley, F. H. 2012. "The Efficient Secret: How America Nearly Adopted a Parliamentary System, and Why It Should Have Done So." George Mason University Law and Economics Research Paper Series 12–05, January 16.

Burnham, Walter Dean. 1971. *Critical Elections: And the Mainsprings of American Politics*. New York: W.W. Norton & Company.

Cornwell, Elmer E., Jr. 1981. "The American Constitutional Tradition: Its Impact and Development." In *The Constitutional Convention as an Amending Device*, edited by Kermit L. Hall, Harold M. Hyman, and Leon V. Sigal. Washington, DC: American Historical Association.

DeRosa, Marshall L. 2007. *Redeeming American Democracy: Lessons from the Confederate Constitution*. Gretna, LA: Pelican Publishing Company.

Dorf, Michael C. 2011. "The Constitution and the Political Community." *Constitutional Commentary* 27 (Winter): 499–506.

Farrand, Max, ed. 1966. *The Records of the Federal Convention*. 4 vols. New Haven, CT: Yale University Press.

Frederick, Brian. 2010. *Congressional Representation & Constituents: The Case for Increasing the U.S. House of Representatives*. New York: Routledge.

Greve, Michael S. 2013. *The Constitution: Understanding America's Founding Document*. Washington, DC: AEI Press.

Guerra, Darren Patrick. 2013. *Perfecting the Constitution: The Case for the Article V Amendment Process*. Lanham, MD: Lexington Books.

Hamilton, Alexander and James Madison. 2007. *The Pacificus-Helvidius Debates of 1793–1794*, edited by Morton J. Frisch. Indianapolis, IN: Liberty Fund Inc.

Hamilton, Alexander, James Madison, and John Jay. 1961 [1787–88]. *The Federalist Papers*. New York: New American Library.

Harter, Eugene C. 1985. *The Lost Colony of the Confederacy*. Jackson, MS: University Press of Mississippi.

Holler, Michael, ed. 2008. *The Constitution Made Easy: The United States Constitution Compared Side-by-Side with the United States Constitution in Modern English*. Woodland Park, CO: Friends of Freedom.

Jacoby, Steward O. 1984. *The Religious Amendment Movement: God, People and Nation in the Gilded Age*. 2 vols. PhD dissertation, University of Michigan.

Johnson, David. 2012. *John Randolph of Roanoke*. Baton Rouge: Louisiana State University Press.

Kettl, Donald F. 2009. *The Next Government of the United States: Why Our Institutions Fail Us and How to Fix Them*. New York: W.W. Norton & Company.

Kyvig, David E. 1996. *Explicit and Authentic Acts: Amending the U.S. Constitution, 1776–1995*. Lawrence, KS: University Press of Kansas.

Law, David S., and Mila Versteeg. 2012. "The Declining Influence of the United States Constitution." *New York University Law Review* 87 (June): 762–858.

Leib, Ethan J. 2004. *Deliberative Democracy in America: A Proposal for a Popular Branch of Government*. University Park: Pennsylvania State University Press.

Lillebo, Paul. 2012. "Updating the Sacred (?) U.S. Constitution." *Blue Ridge Journal*. http://www.blueridgejournal.com/brj-constitution.htm (accessed December 17, 2013).

Lutz, Donald S. 1994. "Toward a Theory of Constitutional Amendment." *American Political Science Review* 88 (June): 355–70.

Mashaw, Jerry L. 2008. "Administration and 'The Democracy': Administrative Law from Jackson to Lincoln, 1829–1861." *Yale Law Journal* 117: 1568–1693.

Mayhew, David R. 2011. *Partisan Balance: Why Political Parties Don't Kill the U.S. Constitutional System*. Princeton, NJ: Princeton University Press.

McGinnis, John O., and Michael B. Rappaport. 2013. *Originalism and the Good Constitution*. Cambridge, MA: Harvard University Press.

Miller, William J., and Jeremy D. Walling, eds. 2013. *The Political Battle over Congressional Redistricting*. Lanham, MD: Lexington Books.

Morone, James A. 1998. *The Democratic Wish: Popular Participation and the Limits of American Government*. Rev. ed. New Haven: Yale University Press.

Orentlicher, David. 2013. *Two Presidents Are Better Than One: The Case for a Bipartisan Executive Branch*. New York: New York University Press.

Person, H. M. 2011. *Amendment: Restoring the Plain Meaning of the Constitution and the Rule of Law*. H. M. Person.

Powell, H. Jefferson. 1985. "The Original Understanding of Original Intent." *Harvard Law Review* 98 (March): 885–948.

Shaw, Bernard. 1933. *The Political Madhouse in America and Nearer Home*. London: Constable & Co.

Spence, Karl. 2006. *Yo! Liberals! You Call This Progress?: Crime, Race, Sex, Faith, Law and the Culture War*. Converse, TX: Fielding Press.

Sunstein, Cass. 2006. *The Second Bill of Rights: FDR's Unfinished Revolution—And Why We Need It More Than Ever*. New York: Basic Books.

Vile, John R. 2005. *The Constitutional Convention of 1787: A Comprehensive Encyclopedia of America's Founding*. 2 vols. Santa Barbara, CA: ABC-CLIO.

Vile, John R. 1994. *Constitutional Change in the United States: A Comparative Study of the Role of Constitutional Amendments, Judicial Interpretations, and Legislative and Executive Actions*. Westport, CT: Praeger.

Vile, John R. 1991. "Proposals to Amend the Bill of Rights: Are Fundamental Rights in Jeopardy?" *Judicature* 75 (August/September): 62–7.

Vile, John R., David L. Hudson Jr., and David Schultz. 2009. *Encyclopedia of the First Amendment*, 2 vols. Washington, DC: CQ Press.

CHAPTER 14

Analysis and Conclusions

Most studies of proposed constitutional change have focused on the more than 11,500 proposed amendments that members of Congress have introduced in that body. Although it is possible to aggregate such proposals, most were directed— like most amendments that have been ratified—at a single issue or problem. The 27 amendments that states have ratified have, of course, significantly altered the original document, but many are more akin to tinkering than wholesale reform. In addition, proponents of one amendment, or series of amendments, might or might not agree to the addition of provisions championed by others. The current constitution, though refined and democratized, still very much reflects the architectonic vision of the Founding Fathers and the structures that they created to implement it.

An Ever-Expanding Pool of Proposals at an Increasing Pace

The author's first published book on proposed constitutional alternatives was *Rewriting the United States Constitution: An Examination of Proposals from Reconstruction to the Present* (Vile 1991), which covered approximately 40 proposals. In addition to laying out a number of the plans that preceded and laid the foundation for the current document, this book covers more than 170 sets of proposals for altering or replacing the current document. These proposals date from the earliest days of the national party system to e-book publications and recent posts on the Internet. This book thus provides a significantly larger pool of proposals from which to draw inferences and conclusions about America's evolving relationship with (and treatment of) the Constitution.

Moreover, the proposals in this book reflect a diverse array of political and philosophical perspectives. Early proposals reflected the views of American colonial settlers, revolutionaries, Federalists, Anti-Federalists, and Democratic-Republicans. Subsequent plans have been offered by Democrats, Republicans, independents, Radical Centrists, Populists, Progressives, Socialists, semi-socialists, Communists, Black Panthers, minarchists, advocates of Public Choice, Agrarians, liberals, conservatives, libertarians, feminists, futurists, pacifists, Christians (both Catholics and Protestants), Distributists, skeptics, postmodernists, futurists, members of the Tea Party movement, advocates of states' rights, and even anarchists!

Occasions for Reform Proposals

Most proposals for structural constitutional change have occurred either during periods of crisis or during constitutional or millennial commemorations or anniversaries. Crises that have elicited proposals for change have included the War of 1812, the Civil War, both world wars, the Great Depression, the Watergate crisis, and the perceived crisis generated by America's current budget deficits. Ironically, while the bicentennials of the Declaration of Independence in 1976 and the Constitution in 1987 stimulated scholarly reflection on possible constitutional changes, these events also reinforced the importance of the two documents and glorified the role of the Founders in formulating them—thus potentially dimming overall prospects for reform. Many reform proposals were also stimulated by the anticipated arrival of a new century and a new millennium, and the momentum for change has continued to increase since then.

The Pace of Reform Proposals

Factoring out individuals like John C. Calhoun and Woodrow Wilson, who chiefly provided theoretical models without directly formulating constitutional proposals, or people like Huey Long and Franklin D. Roosevelt, who did not specifically call for *constitutional* change, the author has identified the following proposals by decade: two proposals from 1800 to 1810 (Pendleton and Hillhouse); two from the 1810s (Willard and Hartford Convention); one from the 1820s (Woodward); none from the 1830s; two from the 1840s (Upshur and Seneca Falls); one from the 1850s (Brown); six from the 1860s (Peace Convention, Wedgwood, Confederacy, Beasley, Lieber, and Godwin); three from the 1870s (Woodhull, Stickney, and O'Conor); five from the 1880s (Lawrence, Lockwood, Rice, Hopkins, and Bellamy); and four from the 1890s (West, Adams, Morris, and Smith), during which time some Populists also favored calling another constitutional convention. There were three additional sets of proposals from 1900 to 1910 (Sturber, Allen, and Clark); three from the 1910s (House, Benson, and Reynolds); one (MacDonald) from the 1920s; nine from the 1930s (Merriam, Piburn, Socialists, Wallace, McKee, Elliott, Eiselen, Cram, Hamilton, and Coleman); seven from the 1940s (Upham, Hazlitt, Agar, Hehmeyer, Finletter, Patterson, and the New York Bar); none from the 1950s; six from the 1960s (Finer, Council on State Governments, Eldredge, Pei, Oliver, and Macdonald); 10 from the 1970s (Black Panthers, Marduke, Baldwin, Gardiner, Stittmatter, Tugwell, Hardin, Novak, Dillon, and Becker); 13 from the 1980s (Cutler, Shogan, Church, Brennan, Robinson, Sundquist, Committee on Constitutional System, A. Miller, J. Miller, Murphy, Fisher, and Fulbright, as well as coauthors Whicker, Strickland, and Moore); and more than 20 from the 1990s (Mertens, Tonn, Krusch, Mautner, Long, Kennan, Wilkey, Davidson, Kirstein, Mautner, Antieau, Virginia Vanguard, Wade, Adams, Dolbeare and Hubbell, Lazare, Naylor and Willimon, Calabresi, Marx, Manuel and Cammisa, and Scott).

The first decade of the new millennium brought proposals from Ellis and Frederick, Jeffs, Becker, Labunski, McGrath, Bailey, Hoppe, Dahl, Jackson, Becker,

Beck, Buchanan, Formichella, Field, Hill, Wynne, Hawes, Levinson, Sabato, Coats, Heim, and Hines. Proposals from 2010 through 2013 have included those of Antinori, the Revolutionary Communist Party, Aranda, Owens, Médaille, Schmitendorf, Davis, Campbell, Sprogis, *Constitutional Commentary*, Sirmon, Hopper, Lessig, Miller et al., Piatt, Hinkelman, Davis, Edwards, Anderson, Wilson, Green, Dahlberg and Kaardal, Levin, and Polk.

The following chart summarizes these printed proposals by decade:

Table 14.1.

Decade	Number of Proposals
1800s	2
1810s	2
1820s	1
1830s	0
1840s	2
1850s	1
1860s	6
1870s	3
1880s	5
1890s	4
1900s	3
1910s	3
1920s	1
1930s	9
1940s	7
1950s	0
1960s	6
1970s	10
1980s	13
1990s	21
2000s	22
2010–2013	24

An additional 28 proposals have been located on the Internet. Although these proposals are not always easy to date, most of them seem to have been posted since 2000. They include proposals by Platt, Brothers, VanSickle, Durst, Nordeen, "Jack Rabbit," Struble, Objectivists, Constitution of the New America, Gillman, Palm, Pain, Wynne, Barnett, Roland, Piper, Anarchist420, Rojas, "Christian Prophet," Sulcer, Pubman, Ricker, Slate, Copple, Bass, Tamirisa, Roland, and Constitution-21. Of the more than 170 proposals included in this book's overall count, well over half have been written in the last 25 years.

Only two decades (the 1830s and the 1950s) from the beginning of the nineteenth century to the present appear to have been barren of major proposals. The 1860s witnessed an uptick in numbers that reflected the Civil War years, but prior to the 1930s (which witnessed the Great Depression and the rising threat of war in Europe and the Far East), the 1880s (roughly marking the birth of Populism) was the only decade in which five or more constitutional reform proposals emerged. Through the 1980s, the gradually growing volume of proposals likely reflected the rise in population, increasing educational levels, and possibly decreased costs of print technology. Since then, even taking into account the role of the Internet in facilitating the creation and distribution of proposals, there appears to have been a virtual explosion of proposals that shows no sign of abating.

When he began writing this book, the author did not recognize that he was working at a time when the pace of such proposals was accelerating so rapidly. The large rise *might* signal increasing dissatisfaction with one or more aspects of the current Constitution, with the document as a whole, or with the time that has expired since the last amendment was adopted. Many proposals have undoubtedly been generated by concerns over specific issues like deficit spending and the proper relationship between state and national powers, and they will likely be stimulated anew by events like the late 2013 government shutdown. The increased number of proposals might reflect increased ideological divisions that have evidenced themselves in presidential elections, in conflicts within Congress, and in clashes between the legislative and executive branches. Proposals undoubtedly generate counterproposals, and as the number of plans increase, so does knowledge of the genre and the acceptability of proposing them. Notably, few of the published proposals from the last four years came from major publishing houses. The rise of self-publishing may be increasing the absolute number of proposals generated, even if individual proposals do not reach as large an audience as proposals distributed through established publishing houses.

Collective Proposals

The Articles of Confederation, which preceded the U.S. Constitution, emerged from the Second Continental Congress, while the U.S. Constitution was the product of a convention held in Philadelphia in 1787. Most state constitutions emerged from state legislatures (early practice) or state conventions.

Of the proposals to replace or make major changes in the current U.S. Constitution, more than a dozen were collective products that emerged from conventions or other group deliberations. These include proposals by the Hartford Convention of 1815; the Seneca Falls Convention of 1848; the Peace Convention of 1861; the convention that drew up the Confederate Constitution in 1861; the Socialist Platform of 1932; proposals by the New York Bar Association in the 1940s to protect the U.S. Supreme Court; the set of proposals that emerged from the Council of State Governments in 1962; the meeting of the Black Panthers in 1970; the proposals by Whicker, Strickland, and Moore (1987); the deliberations of the Committee on the Constitutional System (1987); the constitution proposed by the Revolutionary Communist Party (although it may have been the result of a single individual); the online article on constitutional change posted by *Slate*; and the symposiums held by *Constitutional Commentary*. A number of individuals who have formulated reform proposals—and a number who have not done so—have also called for meetings or conventions to revise or replace the current Constitution. Kenneth Dolbeare and Janette Hubbell, Jesse L. Jackson, Jr., and Frank Watkins, Paul Christopher Manuel and Anne Marie Cammisa, and Frederick Ellis and Carl Frederick are among the pairs of individuals who have offered proposals.

Occupations of Proponents of Change

Most of the proposals that this book has discovered can be linked to specific individuals with the exception of the pseudonymous Virginia Vanguard, the individuals who helped John Miller advance concerns raised by the larger Tea Party Movement, and a number of unspecified authors of Web sites. The author has not always been able to identify the background or occupations of those who have advanced such proposals, and the Internet has made the process of proposing constitutions a far less elite enterprise than it once was. Nonetheless, the majority of proposals to reform or overhaul the U.S. Constitution are clearly the work of elites. Most authors of these proposals were college graduates, and many hailed from leading institutions of higher learning.

More than 50 of the reformers studied in this work were college professors. Political scientists, law professors, and historians dominated. Political scientists have included Woodrow Wilson, J. Allen Smith, Charles Merriam, Herman Finer, C. Perry Patterson, Rexford Tugwell, Carl B. Swisher, Charles Hardin, Conley Dillon, members of the Committee on the Constitutional System, the Whicker, Strickland, and Moore threesome, Paul Christopher Manuel and Anne Marie Cammisa, Theodore Becker, Robert A. Dahl, Donald Robinson, James L. Sundquist, Larry Sabato, and Ted Aranda. Historians have included Francis Lieber, Malcolm Eiselen, William Yandell Elliott, Charles Coleman, Herbert Agar, Leland Baldwin, and Kenneth Dolbeare. Law professors (most of whom were trained as lawyers) have included Lewis Mayers, Mary Becker, Theodore Becker, Bernard H. Siegan, Cass R. Sunstein, Sanford Levinson, Arthur S. Miller, Jeremy Miller, Cornelius F. Murphy, Chester Antieau, Randy Barnett, and Lawrence Lessig. Other academics included professors of journalism (Richard Labinski), economics (Thomas H. Naylor, Martin J. Bailey, James M. Buchanan, and Hans-Hermann Hoppe), philosophy (Roderick Long), Christian ministry (William H. Willimon), engineering (John B. Miller), sociology (H. Wentworth Eldredge), and romance languages (Mario Pei). Other figures associated with academia included a college librarian (Isaac Rice), a professor of physiology (Yandell Henderson), a chemist (Michael Noah Mautner), and an adjunct professor of theology (John Médaille).

Lawyers—some of whom also served as politicians or law professors—are the next leading group of those who have proposed major constitutional changes. Lawyers have included Edmund Pendleton, James Hillhouse, Abel Upshur, William B. Wedgwood, Albert Stickney, Henry Lockwood, Charles O'Conor, Walter Tuller, Alexander Hehmeyer, Lewis Mayers, Thomas Finletter, Lloyd Cutler, Steven G. Calabresi, Paul Antinori, and Sam Carr Polk.

Governmental officials have included members of Congress (James Hillhouse, John C. Calhoun, J. William Fulbright, and Jesse Jackson, Jr.). They have also included presidential advisors (Edward House, Rexford Tugwell, George Reedy, and Lloyd Cutler); judges (Augustus B. Woodward, Walter Clark, Malcolm R. Wilkey, and Thomas Brennan), who were, of course, also lawyers; diplomats or former diplomats (William B. Lawrence, Edward House, William K. Wallace, and George Kennan); a former foreign service officer (Edwin Lee Wade); a former speech writer (Michael Novak); bureaucrats like Herbert C. Kirstein and Floyd Wynne; and David B. Jeffs, who identified himself as a police officer. Abel Upshur served as secretary of state, John C. Calhoun as secretary of state and vice president, Victoria Claflin Woodhull as a presidential candidate, and Woodrow Wilson as both a state governor and a U.S. president.

Journalists and/or editors have proposed 10 or more constitutional reform proposals. They have included E. L. Godkin, Edward Bellamy, James C. West, Frederick Upham Adams, William MacDonald, Henry Hazlitt, Herbert Agar, Dwight Macdonald, Michael Novak, Robert Shogan, and Daniel Lazare. Mark R. Levin is chiefly known as a conservative radio talk show host. Many of the individuals who have posted proposals on the Internet might also consider themselves to be journalists. Americans from the ranks of business have also offered proposals for major change. These individuals have included Caspar Hopkins, Henry S. McKee, Michael Oliver, Paul Fisher, Edwin Wade, Janette Hubbell, Frederick Ellis and Carl Frederick, John Médaille, and possibly C. Earl Campbell.

Proponents of change have also included social activists (Victoria C. Woodhull, Bouck White, the Black Panthers, Sanderson Beck, Steven Hill, Ward Ricker, and Ted Aranda), preachers (Bouck White, the "Christian Prophet," Bill Strittmatter, and Ralph Bass), a clock-maker (Simon Willard Jr.), a medical doctor (John Piburn), a former practitioner of homeopathic medicine (Kirk Brothers), a psychologist (Joseph Church), architects (Ralph Cram and Marty Piatt), a filmmaker (Michael Marx), a public relations specialist (Patrick J. McGrath), bloggers (Steve Gillman and the pseudonymous "Jack Rabbit"), a potter (Bouck White), engineers (Ross Nordeen, Kirby Palm, James Schmitendorf), a social worker (Rodney Scott), a researcher (Bruce E. Tonn), futurists (Bruce Tonn and Joseph F. Coates), a Web designer (Barry Krusch), a CIO (Dick Formichella), specialists in information technology (Robert F. Hawes, Jr., and Tom Hopper), a former employee of AT&T and Lucent Technologies (Robert M. Hinkelman), a former businessman (William S. Field), a retired individual who worked in the energy industry (Paul Heim), a software programmer (James R. "Chip" Downs), a career military veteran (John VanSickle), a writer and consultant (Payne Edwards), a former able seaman (Ian Pubman), and a poet and essayist who went by the name "Jack Rabbit." The Internet has widened the field of contributors still further to at least one individual (John K. Piper) who called himself "an ordinary Joe," another who identified himself as a handyman (Thomas Wright Sulcer), a retired public school teacher (Roger Copple), a self-described "craftsman, amateur writer, and part-time whatever-else" (Keith B. Anderson), and a global sustainability consultant (Chandra Tamirisa).

Other Factors Relative to Proponents of Change

Although women have made progress in many of the above fields, they have historically had only limited involvement in campaigns to change the U.S. Constitution. Were it not for the female participants in the Seneca Falls Convention, Victoria C. Woodhull, Janette Hubbell, Senator Nancy Landon Kassebaum (who participated on the Committee on the Constitutional System), Marcia Lynn Whicker, Ruth Ann Strickland, Anne Marie Cammisa, and Mary Becker, they would be completely missing from this survey (it is also possible that Joan M. Veon authored the Ayn Rand–inspired Constitution of the New America). To this point, women scholars have been more likely to introduce their views in conjunction with others rather than on their own.

Jesse Jackson, Jr., the Black Panthers, and C. Earl Campbell are the only proponents of major constitutional change that the author has been able to identify as African Americans. Billy Rojas is the only individual covered by this book who appears to have an Hispanic surname. Kirk Brothers and Mark Becker are the only two that the author remembers as specifically identifying themselves as gay. Michael Oliver appears to have formed his views of government in part from the atrocities that dictators have committed against Jews during various periods in world history.

The youngest proponents of change (Simon Willard, Jr., and Jack Durst) appear to have been in their early twenties when they unveiled their reforms. The oldest included William Gardiner and Paul R. Heim, both of whom were over 80, Tom Hopper, who was 90, and Sam Carr Polk, who was 94 when he released his constitutional reform proposals. Henry Hazlitt published his proposals during two pivotal time periods, as did Polk. Probably no one was as compulsive on the subject as Rexford Tugwell, who penned over 40 versions of a new constitution. Several advocates of major constitutional change, including Edward Bellamy (1887), Frederick Upham Adams (1896), Edward House (1912), Kenneth Dolbeare and Janette Hubbell (1996), Michael Marx (1999), Frederick Ellis and Carl Frederick (2000), Dick Formichella (2005), Floyd Wynne (2006), and Rick Sirmon (2011), advanced their ideas in novels, an increasing number have published their plans on the Internet, and at least three such proposals only remain available as e-books.

Individuals Who Actually Wrote Constitutions

Those who wrote the current Constitution had a number of models from which to draw, including colonial documents, the Albany Plan of Union, the Articles of Confederation, and state constitutions. When Steven Boyd collected the texts of proposed constitutional alternatives in 1992, he found 10. He explained that he did not include the proposal by John Brown or the Confederate Constitution (both of which this book treats) because neither would have applied to the entire nation

(Boyd 1992, 2–3). The proposals that he identified were by William B. Wedgwood (1861), Victoria C. Woodhull (1870), James C. West (1890), Frederick Upham Adams (1896), Henry O. Morris (1898), Eustace Reynolds (1915), Hugh L. Hamilton (1938), Thomas Carlton Upham (1941), Leland D. Baldwin (1972), and Rexford Tugwell (1974).

Delegates to the Seneca Falls Convention chose to phrase their goals in terms of a declaration rather than a constitution, and William Wilson and Uldis Sprogis later rewrote both the Constitution and the Declaration of Independence. This still leaves almost 40 other people or groups of people who actually drafted new constitutions, about half of whom have done so since the publication of Boyd's book. They are Simon Willard, Jr. (1815); D. I. Sturber (1903); Edward House (1912); John L. Piburn (1932); Charles Coleman (1938); L. Henry Platt, Jr. (1972); William Gardiner (1973); Bill Strittmatter (1970s); Jeremy Miller (1987); John Mertens (1990); Barry Krusch (1992); Roderick Long (1993, 1994); Herbert Kirstein (1994); the Virginia Vanguard (1995); A. R. Adams (1996); Robert Struble, Jr. (1997); Rodney Scott (1999); Jack Durst (c2000); Kirk Brothers; the Objectivist Constitution; the author(s) of the Constitution of the New America on the Rational-Wiki Website; Sanderson Beck (2005); A. Hines (2009); the Revolutionary Communist Party (2010); John K. Piper (2010); the self-described Christian Prophet, Thomas Wright Sulcer; Daryl Lloyd Davis (2011); C. Earl Campbell (2011); Anarchist420 (2011); Marty Piatt (2012); Ernest Pain (current); Ward Ricker; Roger Copple (2012); Chandra Tamirisa; Keith B. Anderson (2013); William Wilson (2013); and Thomas Dahlberg and Erick Kaardal (2013).

In addition, journalist H. L. Mencken drafted a satirical "Constitution for the New Deal," Michael Oliver (1968) wrote "Constitution for a New Nation" and Jim Davidson did the same for his "Oceania" (1994); Bernard H. Siegan (1992) used the U.S. Constitution as a model for emerging nations; Michael Marx authored a constitution for a utopia (1999); and Martin J. Bailey (2001) developed a model for what he called "a once and future country." Michael Noah Mautner (1992) drafted a constitution that could be adopted by almost any representative democracy, and eventually by the world. William Wilson anticipated that his constitution would be for a post-apocalyptic America. Other individuals, while not authoring new constitutions, presented specific wording for amendments, sometimes fairly elaborate.

Randy Barnett's proposed Bill of Federalism (2009) is a good example of this approach, as are the amendments that Richard Labunski (2001) and James R. "Chip" Downs (2012) proposed and the 53 amendments offered by Paul R. Heim (2009). Franklin D. Roosevelt (1944), Cass R. Sunstein (2004), Robert F. Hawes (2006), and Joseph F. Coates (2007) are among those who have proposed texts of a second Bill of Rights. Many individuals who have proposed new constitutions while choosing to follow the existing organization of the U.S. Constitution have listed such rights as amendments appended to the end of the document, rather than incorporating them into the document itself. Others, who are not the primary subject of this book, have drafted constitutions for the world.

Proposed Methods of Effecting Change

Not all proponents of change have indicated how they anticipated initiating such changes. The only individuals covered in this book who have mentioned violence were Kirk Brothers (who believed it would occur after social and economic collapse), the individual or individuals who wrote the Revolutionary Communist Party Constitution, and novelists, who typically portrayed such violence almost as an abstraction.

Advocates of peaceful means of reform have typically anticipated use of the existing process by which two-thirds majorities of both houses of Congress propose amendment and three-fourths of the states ratify them. Conley Dillon advocated creating a constitutional commission, and Joseph F. Coates wanted to create a National Commission on the Bill of Rights. Lloyd Cutler favored creating a bipartisan presidential commission to analyze issues and propose constitutional changes. Richard Labunski favored beginning with a series of state meetings and conventions to demonstrate the feasibility of such an approach. Paul R. Heim hoped to initiate a constitutional convention by substituting calls from state referendums rather than from the state legislatures. William S. Field anticipated the rise of a "Parliamentary Party" that would call for a constitutional convention. Steven Hill recommended using randomly selected "citizens' assemblies" to bypass partisanship and garner support for initiatives. David B. Jeffs and Dick Formichella imagined that a national plebiscite might prompt Congress to call a convention. Michael Noah Mautner thought the transition from republican to direct democracy might be facilitated if individuals were to run direct democracy campaigns in which they pledged, if elected, to cast votes in accordance with public polling. Hans-Hermann Hoppe anticipated establishing free cities that would spread throughout the country.

Proponents of calling a special constitutional convention have included Walter Tuller, Yandell Henderson, Bouck White, Lewis Mayers, William MacDonald, William Yandell Elliott, Malcolm Eiselen, Thomas Upham, Alexander Hehmeyer, the Council of State Governments, Carl B. Swisher, Mario Pei, Leland Baldwin, Theodore Becker, Thomas Brennan, Barry Krusch, Malcolm R. Wilkey, Edwin Lee Wade, Robert R. Owens, Joseph F. Coates, Richard Labunski, Floyd Wynne, Sanford Levinson, William S. Field, Larry J. Sabato, Paul Antinori, Rick Sirmon, Lawrence Lessig, James R. "Chip" Downs, James Schmitendorf, Marty Piatt, Roger Copple, and Sam Carr Polk.

Heroes and Villains

Proponents and opponents of constitutional change tend to elevate and gain inspiration from some individuals while denigrating others. Those who oppose change in general can, of course, cite James Madison's hopes that the existing document would be venerated. By contrast, proponents of reforms that are progressive or liberal in nature often quote Madison's friend, Thomas Jefferson. He stated that "'*the earth belongs in usufruct to the living*'; that the dead have neither powers nor rights over it" (quoted in Vile 1992, 63). He also observed:

Some men look at constitutions with sanctimonious reverence, and deem them like the arc of the covenant, too sacred to be touched. They ascribe to the men of the preceding age a wisdom more than human, and suppose what they did to be beyond amendment. I knew that age well; I belonged to it, and labored with it. It deserved well of its country. It was very like the present, but without the experience of the present; and forty years of experience in government is worthy a century of book-reading; and this they would say for themselves were they to rise from the dead. (Quoted in Vile 1992, 66)

Jefferson likened being bound to the past as requiring a man to wear the clothes that fit him as a child (Vile 1992, 66). Proponents of changing the Constitution to promote social and economic rights also often quote from Franklin Roosevelt's "Four Freedoms" speech.

By contrast, those who favor changing the U.S. Constitution to return to earlier understandings often quote Anti-Federalist predictions that the government under the Constitution would become too powerful, aristocratic, or too centralized. Many further excoriate Woodrow Wilson, the Progressive movement, and other proponents of a "living constitution" for what they consider to be inattention to—or erosion of—existing constitutional prohibitions. Others blame socialists, communists, or liberals for current ills. Curiously, advocates of the most drastic changes, from both right and left, often portray the Constitution and the convention that composed it in conspiratorial terms. The former, however, are more likely to emphasize what they believe to have been the centralizing tendencies of the convention with regard to states' rights, whereas the latter are most likely to emphasize what they consider to have been their personal economic interests.

Prospects for Change

The formal requirements for changing the U.S. Constitution remain authorization by two-thirds majorities of both houses of Congress and approval of three-fourths of the states. Two-thirds of the states can also request Congress to call a constitutional convention to propose amendments. Few of the framers probably anticipated that the document they drafted would last more than 225 years or that it would have relatively few amendments.

Every day brings word of a crisis or perceived crisis. Having weathered industrialization, a Civil War, two world wars, and the rise and fall of major political parties, it is difficult to imagine that a sense of crisis alone will result in a new document. Indeed, there may well be a "rally round the Constitution" effect during crises that mirrors the "rally round the flag" effect that political scientists have discovered in their study of support for the presidency during international crises (Baum 2002). Although the age of the Constitution and the paucity of its amendments suggest that it might need changing, its antiquity furthers its veneration by the public.

Most Americans likely regard the current Constitution as the best currently attainable. Many would likely agree with John O. McGinnis and Michael B.

Rappaport's assessment that the current Constitution is a "good constitution" and that "the U.S. Constitution's existing defects are less costly than the burden of dispensing with the document and attempting to create one of greater desirability" (McGinnis and Rappaport 2013, 17, 28).

As the last chapter revealed, proponents of change have arrayed themselves on opposite sides of a variety of issues. Proponents of greater protections for existing property rights may be somewhat outnumbered by those calling for socialism, but that is probably because the existing system already leans toward the former direction. Similarly, more proponents of change have advocated trimming judicial review than expanding it, but that is likely because judicial review is already fairly extensive. Similarly, many critics have targeted presidential powers, but that stems in large part from the manner in which such powers have grown. From time to time, individuals have advocated plans for nonpartisan government, but others continue to think the nation needs highly responsive political parties. Proponents of greater national unity have been roughly balanced by those who would tilt in the direction of greater state powers, although calls for decentralization (and even for the right of states to secede) appear to become more numerous in recent years. Those who favor formally acknowledging religion have been balanced by those who advocate for greater separation between church and state, although the latter may have typically proceeded through litigation rather than by proposing a new constitution. Calls for making citizenship more restrictive have been balanced by calls to extend citizenship rights to larger classes.

Two trends have been obvious throughout the course of amending history. The trend toward greater democracy has been evident in the adoption of the Seventeenth Amendment, which provided for direct election of U.S. senators, and in a series of amendments that have prohibited discrimination in voting on the basis of race (Fifteenth Amendment), sex (Nineteenth Amendment), and age above 18 (Twenty-Sixth Amendment). A second trend, which overlaps with the first and has been most evident in the adoption of the Bill of Rights and the Fourteenth Amendment, has focused on adding more protections for individual rights and liberties. Both such trends have lent themselves well to the adoption of individual amendments.

Among democratic options, the most likely alternative to the U.S. system of checks and balances is the parliamentary option, which does not as easily lend itself to such piecemeal reform. The nation could, of course, amend the Constitution to allow members of the cabinet to appear before Congress. They might even adopt amendments to allow the president or Congress to call new elections; create a separate head of state; provide for a question hour for the president; or change congressional terms to correspond more closely with those of the president. It is difficult to imagine grafting the latter mechanisms onto the current constitution, however, rather than simply changing the overall structure. Although it is a recurring proposal, sentiments for a parliamentary system seem largely to have dissipated. It appears that most reformers would prefer to work within the existing system of checks and balances rather than outside of it. Or perhaps they simply cannot conceive that existing mechanisms could bring about so drastic a change.

Absent a world catastrophe, a domestic revolution, or a foreign invasion, it seems most likely that any new constitution will emerge from a constitutional convention featuring delegates chosen from individual states, probably on the basis of combined representation in the House and Senate. If it followed the current form proscribed in Article V, Congress would likely specify that the constitution be ratified by state conventions rather than by state legislatures.

When the delegates to the Constitutional Convention of 1787 met, they provided that the new constitution would go into effect when ratified by nine or more states. Significantly, however, the Constitution applied only to those states that agreed to join, and it is highly doubtful that smaller states would have joined had the Constitution not guaranteed them equal representation within the U.S. Senate. Moreover, had key states like Virginia, New York, Pennsylvania, and Massachusetts failed to ratify, it is unlikely that the new government could have effectively taken charge, whether nine states had joined or not. Given the current geographical distribution of states, it would appear that a new constitution would somehow have to apply to all (at least of the 48 contiguous states) or none. This suggests that the most obvious way to bring about change would be to introduce the change in the form of a single amendment, or series of amendments, that three-fourths or more of the states could then ratify.

The author continues to be concerned by pronouncements by leading scholars, most notably Akhil Reed Amar (1988; for author's critique, see Vile 1991, 97–125), that a majority of the people have the right to ratify amendments, and thus, presumably, a new constitution. However democratic it would be to allow "We the People" to engage directly in such constitution-making, the existing constitution simply does not provide for such a mechanism, and putative adoption of such an amendment could lead to great confusion over the content of the document, especially in times of crisis. Unless the people of the United States use existing Article V mechanisms to amend the Constitution to provide for such an initiative or referendum mechanism, this author would regard the effects of any such referendums as a nullity and would hope that courts would do likewise.

Choices among Existing Peaceful Means

This book is one of analysis rather than advocacy, and the author did not write it with the idea of recommending a particular series of constitutional amendments or a new constitution. Indeed, he doubts that he would have had the necessarily scholarly objectivity if he had begun it with this purpose.

Having significantly widened the earlier search, however, it seems at least appropriate to consider various options for future developments with respect to the U.S. Constitution. Recognizing that there are some advocates of change, such as the Revolutionary Communist Party, that endorse violence as a means for realizing their goals, he will limit the discussion here to peaceful constitutional means.

Follow or Liberalize Current Amending Processes

The U.S. Constitution has achieved the status of an icon or sacred relic. Although one might decry the fact that many individuals who seek to preserve the Constitution do not adequately understand it, James Madison was among those who thought it would be good to have the sentiments and prejudices of the people on the side of the status quo rather than itching for constant change. Madison's advocacy of the Bill of Rights in the first Congress shows that he was willing to adopt some changes, but clearly preferred incremental changes where possible.

To date, all 27 amendments that the nation has adopted have followed the procedure whereby two-thirds majorities in both houses of Congress propose amendments and three-fourths of the states ratify them. Although the states ratified the last such amendment in 1992, members of Congress continue to introduce new proposals in each session of Congress, and they seem available especially in cases of unanticipated emergencies. Moreover, as discussed below, despite strong reasons for suggesting that Article V outlines the only formal route for changing the Constitution, numerous other reforms have and may be adopted through extra-constitutional means.

One obvious emendation to the current system would be to reduce the majorities by which amendments could be proposed and/or adopted. To date, the states have adopted 27 of 33 amendments that Congress has proposed (for texts of the failed amendments, see Anastaplo 1995, 298–9), so modifying congressional majorities would likely prove most effective in increasing the overall number of proposed amendments that are adopted.

Adopt a System That Effectively Incorporates Legislative Sovereignty

The American colonists resisted the idea, which predominated in England, that parliament was sovereign. In fact, they adopted a written constitution partly to instantiate their opposition to this predominate English view. At the time of the Civil War, however, Sidney George Fisher introduced the idea in *The Trial of the Constitution* that Congress, as the most representative branch, should simply declare and enforce its own view of the Constitution. Like modern writers who doubt the efficacy of the amending process, he argued that Article V had become an "iron fetter" rather than a safety valve (Vile 1992, 99). He also argued, again like some modern writers, that the processes that Article V outlined for formal constitutional changes were not intended to be exclusive and that Congress could go beyond them. This author knows few proponents of reform who, like Fisher, believed that such a power should rely exclusively on Congress, however, and so does not regard his position as particularly viable.

Utilize the Constitutional Convention Model to Bring About Significant Changes

Although the Articles of Confederation were drafted in Congress and approved by the states, the current Constitution was both written in a special convention held in Philadelphia and ratified by special conventions called within individual states. Moreover, this Constitution specifically provides a mechanism whereby two-thirds of the state legislatures can require Congress to call a convention to propose further amendments, presumably including a substitute for the current document.

Although many questions remain as to how such a convention would be organized and how states would be represented in it, numerous proponents of constitutional change favor calling a convention. The Convention of 1787 stands witness to the idea that there are some contingencies that call for comprehensive rather than piecemeal changes and that, if the sense of crisis is great enough and the delegates are wise enough, such conventions can succeed. In the current political environment, it would be difficult to hold a convention that could avoid polarizing issues or find a way to reconcile them. Larry Sabato has been among those who advocate keeping divisive social issues off the agenda of any future constitutional convention, but it is not clear that individuals of strong views would necessarily heed this advice.

It is worth noting that an Article V Convention need not follow the Philadelphia example of 1787 and propose a new constitution. Indeed, many proponents of such a convention make a point of indicating that it could propose individual amendments and that, if Article V is followed, such amendments would be subject to the same supermajorities in the state as amendments proposed by Congress itself. In addition to those who genuinely fear a gathering, those who emphasize fears of a "runaway convention" may well be using such arguments because they essentially prefer to leave the Constitution as it is.

Rely Chiefly on Judicial Review and Extra-Constitutional Methods of Change

A number of scholars (Harris 1993; Eskridge and Ferejohn 2010) sometimes distinguish between the written Constitution (capital C) and the unwritten constitution (lower-case c), or the written and unwritten Constitution (Tiedeman 1890). They explain that while America's framers thought they were enacting significant innovations by setting down basic principles in a single written document (the written constitution), many subsequent changes in our understanding of the Constitution have taken place through customs and usage (the unwritten constitution) (Young 2007). Judicial review has recognized rights to privacy, travel, family rearing, and equal protection, which are arguably consistent with the document without being required by it. Congress has enacted "super-statutes" that rise in importance above the general run-of-the-mill legislation (Eskridge and Ferejohn, 2010). In fact, Congress has created a variety of administrative agencies that are neither legislative fish nor executive fowl. Executives have sometimes pushed the limits of their own authority to bring about change. Cass R. Sunstein has observed that, despite its widespread influence, "the New Deal did not alter one word of the founding document" (Sunstein 2004, 121–2). Keith E. Whittington has argued that throughout U.S. history, courts and other institutions have supplemented constitutional interpretation with what he calls "constitutional construction." Whereas the former approach "attempts to divine the meaning of the text," the latter builds meanings where they can no longer be simply discovered (Whittington 2010, 119–21).

The Constitution does not provide explicit guidance on many aspects of American governance. Writing in 1913, Secretary of State Elihu Root, who was especially skeptical of the initiative, referendum, and recall mechanisms that were being adopted by many states, observed:

> We need not trouble ourselves very much about the multitude of excited controversies which have arisen over new methods of extra constitutional-political organization and procedure. Direct nominations, party enrollments, instructions to delegates, presidential preference primaries, independent nominations, all relate to forms of voluntary action outside the proper field of governmental institutions. (Root 1913, 23)

More recently, Professor David R. Mayhew has identified six major developments in constitutional interpretation, only one of which involved an amendment. Democrats working from the left were thus able to initiate legislative reapportionment, limit the Senate filibuster in civil rights debates, rein in the House committee system, and reform the presidential nominating system (Mayhew 2011, 170–4). Likewise, working from the right, Republicans were able to limit the president to two terms and bring about significant turnover in the House (Mayhew 2011, 175–6). Mayhew speculates that the two most obvious candidates for future reform involve altering the Electoral College and/or the Senate filibuster (Mayhew 2011, 179–80). He points out, however, that neither institution seems at present to give a decided advantage to one party or the other, thus giving neither an incentive to make this a major initiative (although the Democratic-controlled Senate did end the filibuster with respect to judicial nominations in 2013).

Advantages and Disadvantages of Rival Approaches

Sticking with the status quo gives the current system great stability, but it may do so at the cost of ignoring areas that might be improved. Conversely, allowing Congress to use alternate methods of proposing formal constitutional amendments would change the existing balance of power among the branches in potentially unpredictable ways. Relying largely on extra-constitutional mechanisms for change overcomes the inertia of the present system but brings some of the ambiguities that the American framers criticized in the British unwritten constitution. Calling a convention could lead to a period of great uncertainty, with murky prospects for success. Changes initiated either through well-used constitutional amending mechanisms or through a constitutional convention are difficult to alter if they later prove to have undesirable consequences; the Twenty-First Amendment repealing national alcoholic prohibition is the only amendment to date that has overturned a previous one.

In recent years, scholars like Dahl, Sabato, and Levinson have all called for making the Constitution more democratic. These calls have elicited responses from other authors. Although the authors chiefly address the specific reforms suggested by Dahl, Sabato, and Levinson, some of the arguments they make have implications for other changes as well.

Perhaps the unifying theme of these responses is the charge that these reforms might have unintended consequences. Professor Heather K. Gerken argued that directing attention to the convention mechanism might actually retard the use of current extra-constitutional mechanisms for change, which she believes provide for "a dialogic process that involves popular mobilization and interinstitutional debate" (Gerken 2007, 934). Professor Adrian Vermeule argued that a balanced system might be far more democratic than its component parts, and that making one part of the system (for example the Senate or the judiciary) more democratic might make the system as a whole not only less democratic but also less deliberative and consensus oriented (Vermeule 2009). While largely agreeing with Gerken and providing justifications for some mechanisms like equal suffrage in the Senate that are frequent subjects of criticism, Professor Stephen Macedo believed that the most important changes necessary for democratic reform—nonpartisan apportionment of legislatures and reforms of the winner-take-all aspect of the current electoral college—can largely be effected without changes in the constitutional text (Macedo 2009).

Testifying in 1982 before the Joint Economic Committee of the Congress of the United States, historian Arthur Schlesinger, Jr. remarked:

> Experiment through statute is comparatively harmless. If the law does not work, there is no great difficulty in repealing it. Experiment through constitutional amendment is a very different matter. Once something is in the Constitution, it's hard to get it out. . . . And, once impeded in the Constitution, "reform" may have unpredictable and far-flung consequences. (Schlesinger 1982, 224)

Such voices suggest that any proponents of change will have inertia working against them.

Comparing the Convention Alternative to the Role Played by Minor Political Parties

One way to regard the current system is to compare it to the existing party system. This system has helped aggregate voters over large areas to select and staff members of three branches of government that the Framers created, and yet much of the party system has grown up outside the written Constitution. Two parties have dominated through most of American history, but the system has permitted participation by other parties. The current Republican Party actually emerged from the collapse of the Whig and Federalist Parties that preceded it, and minor parties have often contributed new institutions like the national nominating convention and influenced the platforms of the two major parties. Perhaps the convention mechanism and the threat of a new constitution itself are like third parties.

Petitions for a convention, like the calls for new constitutions that this book has examined, can raise new issues and point to possible deficiencies within the current political system. They may further prompt individual calls for amendments (the Sixteenth Amendment providing for direct election of U.S. senators is the most frequently cited example), much like the presence of third parties may pressure existing parties to take specific stands on public policy issues. If support is there and existing amending mechanisms, like the two major political parties, fail to respond appropriately, these mechanisms and the system that supports them may in turn be replaced.

The Continuing Value of Studying Proposals for Constitutional Revision

American constitutional principles have been copied throughout the world (Billias 2009). The author takes special pleasure in knowing that many of the proposals that he has discussed here have been long buried or, because they have been proposed outside of academia, received little if any scholarly attention. The more he has written, the more convinced he has become that the book presents a kind of alternate constitutional history of the nation centered not so much on familiar Supreme Court decisions, but on areas in which contemporaries, often from political parties or persuasions that are out of power at the time, have diagnosed issues and problems.

This account serves not only to illumine past constitutional controversies but also to increase understanding of the current U.S. Constitution. Examinations of alternatives to the Constitution, which are subject to debate by supporters of the status quo, point to both perceived strengths and weaknesses of the current Constitution. It is one thing to talk generically or abstractly about change in the Constitution as though one were participating in a college seminar and yet another to examine individual proposals and specifically worded amendments.

It often takes a crisis to concentrate the public mind, but when crises come, it helps to have thought about possible solutions beforehand. James Madison spent years prior to the Constitutional Convention of 1787 examining ancient confederacies and attempting to diagnose the weaknesses of the Articles of Confederation. The economist Milton Friedman observed that "only a crisis—actual or perceived—produces real change. When the crisis occurs, the actions that are taken depend on the ideas that are lying around. That, I believe, is our basic function: to develop alternatives to existing policies, to keep them alive and available until the politically impossible becomes politically inevitable" (Friedman 1962, Introduction).

A free press enables citizens and scholars to consider alternate constitutional arrangements even before Congress or a constitutional convention proposes them. Whether these proponents of reform are visionaries, eccentrics, or patriots, this author remains grateful to those who have advanced ideas that allow for reconsideration of both the strengths and weaknesses of the current constitutional document. This study has increased the author's own appreciation for the wisdom of the Founding Fathers and the document that they bequeathed to posterity. But whether citizens and scholars come away from this book with greater faith in the current document and its authors or with greater resolution to change it, he hopes that they will proceed with greater knowledge of the criticisms that others have offered.

References

Amar, Akhil Reed. 1988. "Philadelphia Revisited: Amending the Constitution outside Article V." *University of Chicago Law Review* 55 (Fall): 1043–1104.

Anastaplo, George. 1995. *The Amendments to the Constitution: A Commentary.* Baltimore: Johns Hopkins University Press.

Baum, Matthew A. 2002. "The Constituent Foundations of the Rally-Round-the-Flag Phenomenon." *International Studies Quarterly* 46 (June): 263–98.

Billias, George Athan. 2009. *American Constitutionalism Heard Round the World, 1776–1789.* New York: New York University Press.

Boyd, Steven R. 1992. *Alternative Constitutions for the United States: A Documentary History.* Westport, CT: Greenwood Press.

Eskridge, William N., Jr., and John Ferejohn. 2010. *A Republic of Statutes: The New American Constitution.* New Haven, CT: Yale University Press.

Eskridge, William N., Jr., and John Ferejohn. 2001. "Super-Statutes." *Duke Law Journal* 50 (March): 1215–76.

Fisher, Sidney George. 1972. *The Trial of the Constitution.* New York: Da Capo Press. Reprint of 1862 edition by J.B. Lippincott & Co.

Friedman, Milton. 1962. "Introduction." *Capitalism and Freedom.* Chicago: University of Chicago Press.

Gerken, Heather K. 2007. "The Hydraulics of Constitutional Reform: A Skeptical Response to our Undemocratic Constitution." *Drake Law Review* 55 (Summer): 925–43.

Harris, William F., II. 1993. *The Interpretable Constitution.* Baltimore: Johns Hopkins University Press.

Macedo, Stephen. 2009. "Toward a More Democratic Congress? Our Imperfect Democratic Constitution: The Critics Examined." *Boston University Law Review* 89: 609–28.

Manuel, Paul, and Anne Marie Cammisa. 1998. *Checks and Balances? How a Parliamentary System Could Change American Politics.* Boulder, CO: Westview Press.

Mayhew, David R. 2011. *Partisan Balance: Why Political Parties Don't Kill the U.S. Constitutional System.* Princeton, NJ: Princeton University Press.

McGinnis, John O., and Michael B. Rappaport. 2013. *Originalism and the Good Constitution.* Cambridge, MA: Harvard University Press.

Root, Elihu. 1913. *Experiments in Government and the Essentials of the Constitution.* Princeton, NJ: Princeton University Press.

Schlesinger, Arthur. 1982. Testimony at *Political Economy and Constitutional Reform.* Hearings before the Joint Economic Committee of the Congress of the United States, 97th Congress, 2nd Session.

Smith, Steven D. 1998. *The Constitution and the Pride of Reason.* New York: Oxford University Press.

Sunstein, Cass R. 2004. *The Second Bill of Rights: FDR's Unfinished Revolution and Why We Need It More Than Ever.* New York: Basic Books.

Tiedeman, Christopher G. 1890. *The Unwritten Constitution of the United States.* New York: G.P. Putnam's Sons.

Vermeule, Adrian. 2009. "The Supreme Court, 2008 Term: Forward: System Effects and the Constitution." *Harvard Law Review* 123 (November): 4–72.

Vile, John R. 1992. *The Constitutional Amending Process in American Political Thought.* New York: Praeger.

Vile, John R. 1991. *Rewriting the United States Constitution: An Examination of Proposals from Reconstruction to the Present.* New York: Praeger.

Whittington, Keith E. 2010. "Constructing a New American Constitution." *Constitutional Commentary* 27: 119–37.

Young, Ernest A. 2007. "The Constitution outside the Constitution." *The Yale Law Journal* 117 (December): 408–73.

Select Bibliography

Discussions of Proposals to Rewrite the Constitution

Boyd, Steven R., ed. 1992. *Alternative Constitutions for the United States: A Documentary History*. Westport, CT: Greenwood Press.

"Constitutional Topic: Rewriting the Constitution." http://www.usconstitution.net/const top_newc.html. Accessed May 21, 2013.

Vile, John R. 2010. *Encyclopedia of Constitutional Amendments, Proposed Amendments, and Amending Issues, 1789–2020*. 3rd ed. 2 vols. Santa Barbara, CA: ABC-CLIO.

Vile, John R. 1993. "The Long Legacy of Proposals to Rewrite the U.S. Constitution." *PS: Political Science and Politics* 26 (June): 208–11.

Vile, John R. 1991. *Rewriting the United States Constitution: An Examination of Proposals from Reconstruction to the Present*. New York: Praeger.

Proposals to Rewrite the Constitution

Adams, A. R. 1996. *The Fourth Constitution of the United States of America*. Salt Lake City, UT: A. R. Adams Publishing.

Adams, Frederick U. 1896. *President John Smith: The Story of a Peaceful Revolution*. Chicago: Charles H. Kerr & Company. Reprint New York: Arno Press, 1970.

Agar, Herbert. 1942. *A Time for Greatness*. Boston: Little Brown.

Anarchist420. 2011. "Minarchist Replacement for the Constitution." January 31. http://forums.anandtech.com/showthread.php?t=2139696 (accessed December 17, 2013).

Anderson, Keith B. 2013. *Semi-Socialism: An Alternative Government and Economic System*. Bluefield, WV: Privately printed.

Antieau, Chester J. 1995. *A U.S. Constitution for the Year 2000*. Chicago: Loyola University Press.

Antinori, Paul. 2010. *A Modest Proposal to Amend the U.S. Constitution*. http://www.amendusconstitution.com (accessed December 17, 2013).

Aranda, Ted. 2010. *The Racket and the Answer: The Representative System and the Democratic Alternative*. http://democracyfortheUSA.org (accessed December 17, 2013).

Bailey, Martin J. 2001. *Constitution for a Future Country*. New York: Palgrave.

Baldwin, Leland. 1972. *Reframing the Constitution: An Imperative for Modern America*. Santa Barbara, CA: ABC-CLIO.

Barnett, Randy. 2009. "A Bill of Federalism." Forbes.com, May 20. http://www.forbes.com/2009/05/20/bill-of-federalism-constitution-states-supreme-court-op (accessed July 29, 2013).

Beasley, Robert E. 1864. *A Plan to Stop the Present and Prevent Future Wars: Containing a Proposed Constitution for the General Government of the Sovereign States of North and South America.* Rio Vista, CA: Robert Beasley.

Beck, Sanderson. 2005. "Reforming the US Constitution." http://www.san.beck.org/BFA5 =ReformingUSConst.html (accessed July 25, 2013).

Becker, Mary. 2001. "Towards a Progressive Politics and a Progressive Constitution." *Fordham Law Review* 69: 2007–56.

Becker, Theodore L. 1976. *American Government: Past—Present—Future.* Boston: Allyn and Bacon.

Bellamy, Edward. 1888. *Looking Backward.* New York: Magnum Books, 1968.

Benson, Allan L. 1914. *Our Dishonest Constitution.* New York: B.W. Huebsch.

Blair, Dawn. 2004. *America 2014: An Orwellian Tale.* Oakland, CA: Council Oak Books.

Brennan, Thomas. 1982. "Return to Philadelphia." *Cooley Law Review* 1: 1–72.

Brothers, Kirk. N.d. "Libertarian Writings." http://www.mega.nu/ampp/kirkbros/index .html (accessed December 17, 2013).

Buchanan, James M., et al. 2005. *The Living Constitution: Amendments for the 21st Century* (e-book). Washington, DC: Cato Institute.

Campbell, C. Earl. 2011. *The Revised Amended Constitution for the United States of America for the 21st Century.* Privately printed.

"Christian Prophet." 2012. "21st Century Constitution for Moral Government." http://21stcenturyconstitution.blogspot.com/ (accessed December 17, 2013).

Church, Joseph. 1982. *America the Possible: Why and How the Constitution Should Be Rewritten.* New York: Macmillan and Company.

Clark, Walter. 1906. "Some Defects of the Constitution of the United States." In *The Papers of Walter Clark*, vol. 2, edited by Aubrey L. Brooks and Hugh T. Lefler. Chapel Hill: University of North Carolina Press.

Coates, Joseph F. 2007. *A Bill of Rights for 21st Century America.* Washington, DC: Kanawha Institute for the Study of the Future.

Coleman, Charles. 1938. *The Constitution Up to Date.* Bulletin No. 10. Cambridge, MA: National Council for Social Studies.

Committee on the Constitutional System. January 1987. "A Bicentennial Analysis of the American Political Structure." Report and Recommendations of the Committee on the Constitutional System.

Committee on Federal-State Relations. 1963. "Amending the Constitution to Strengthen the States in the Federal System." *State Government* 10 (Winter): 10.

Copple, Roger. 2012. "The Third Constitution of the United States" February 7. http:// disinfo.com/2012/02/the-third-constitution-of-the-united-states/ (accessed December 17, 2013).

Cram, Ralph. 1937. *The End of Democracy.* Boston: Marshall Jones Company.

Cutler, Lloyd N. 1986. "To Form a Government." In *Separation of Powers—Does It Still Work?*, edited by Robert A. Goldwin and Art Kaufman. Washington, DC: American Enterprise Institute for Public Policy Research. Original essay was published under the same title in *Foreign Affairs* (Fall) 50: 126–43.

Dahl, Robert. 2001. *How Democratic Is the American Constitution?* New Haven, CT: Yale University Press.

Dahlberg, Thomas, and Erick Kaardal. 2013. *The Rebirth Constitution: A Whole New Constitution for the Freedom Loving People of the United States.* Lexington, KY: Privately printed.

Davidson, Jim, with Eric Klien, Norm Doering, and Lee Crocker. 1994. *The Atlantis Papers.* Houston, TX: Interglobal Paratronics Inc.

Davis, Daryl Lloyd. 2011. *New American Democracy: A Direct Democracy Alternative.* Privately printed.

Dillon, Conley. 1974. "Recommendation for the Establishment of a Permanent Commission of Constitutional Review." *Bureaucrat* 3 (July): 211–24.

"The Direct Democracy Center." www.realdemocracy.com (accessed December 17, 2013).

Dolbeare, Kenneth, and Jannette Hubbell. 1996. *USA 2012: After the Middle-Class Revolution.* Chatham, NJ: Chatham House Publishers.

Downs, Chip (James R. Downs III). *United Once More: Balanced Change through Constitutional Reform.* Church Hill, MD: Consocio Media Associates.

Durst, Jack. 2000. "Constitution of the Republic." http://spynx_jd.tripod.com/ (accessed December 17, 2013).

Edwards, Payne. 2012. *Gridlock: Why We're In It and How to Get Out.* Kissimmee, FL: Signalman Publishing.

Eiselen, Malcolm R. 1937. "Dare We Call a Federal Convention?" *North American Review* 244 (Autumn): 27–8.

Elliott, William Yandell. 1935. *The Need for Constitutional Reform: A Program for National Security.* New York: Whittlesey House.

Ellis, Frederick, with Carl Frederick. 2000. *The Oakland Statement: A Political Adventure Novel.* Miami, FL: Synergy International of the Americas, Ltd.

Eskridge, William N., Jr., and Sanford Levinson. 1998. *Constitutional Stupidities, Constitutional Tragedies.* New York: New York University Press.

Field, William S. 2006. *Why America Needs Parliamentary Government.* Baltimore, MD: Gateway Press, Inc.

Finer, Herman. 1960. *The Presidency, Crisis and Regeneration: An Essay in Possibilities.* Chicago: University of Chicago Press.

Finletter, Thomas K. 1945. *Can Representative Government Do the Job?* New York: Reynal and Hitchcock.

Fisher, Paul. 1988. *The Plan to Restore the Constitution and Help Us All Get out of Debt.* Boulder City, NV: Paul Fisher Campaign for Scientific Government.

Formichella, Dick. 2005. *Reengineering America.* New York, iUniverse, Inc.

Fulbright, J. William (with Seth P. Tillman). 1989. *The Price of Empire.* New York: Pantheon.

Gardiner, William. 1973. *A Proposed Constitution for the United States of America.* Summerfield, FL: William Gardiner.

Goldsmith, John Francis. 1935. *President Randolph as I Knew Him.* Philadelphia: Dorrance & Company.

Green, Tom. 2013. *A Simple Plan*. N.p.: Ugly Books.

Hardin, Charles M. 1989. *Constitutional Reform in America: Essays on the Separation of Powers*. Ames: Iowa State University Press.

Hardin, Charles M. 1974. *Presidential Power and Accountability: Toward a New Constitution*. Chicago: University of Chicago Press.

Hines, A. 2009. *An Informal and Unauthorized Proposition*. Bloomington, IN: Author House.

Gillman, Steve. N.d. "A New Constitution." http://www.999ideas.com/new-constitution.html (accessed December 17, 2013).

Godkin, E. L. 1865. "The Constitution and Its Defects." *North American Review* 99 (July): 117–45.

Hamilton, Hugh L. 1938. *A Second Constitution for the United States of America*. Richmond, VA: Garrett and Massie.

Hazlitt, Henry. 1942. *A New Constitution Now*. New York: Whittlesey House.

Hehmeyer, Alexander. 1943. *Time for Change: A Proposal for a Second Constitutional Convention*. New York: Farrar and Rinehart.

Heim, Paul R. 2009. *Second American Revolution: Change You Really Want*. Charleston, SC: BookSurge.

Henderson, Yandell. 1913. "The Progressive Movement and Constitutional Reform." *Yale Review* n.s. 3: 78–90.

Hill, Steven. 2012. *10 Steps to Repair American Democracy: A More Perfect Union*. 2012 Election. 2nd ed. Boulder, CO: Paradigm Publishers.

Hillhouse, [James]. 1808. *Propositions for Amending the Constitution of the United States Submitted by Mr. Hillhouse to the Senate on the Twelfth Day of April, 1808, with his Explanatory Remarks*. U.S. Senate.

Hopkins, Caspar T. 1885. "Thoughts toward Revising the Federal Constitution." *Overland Monthly* n.s. 6 (October): 388–98.

Hoppe, Hans-Hermann. 2001. *Democracy: The God That Failed; The Economics and Politics of Monarchy, Democracy and Natural Order*. New Brunswick, NJ: Transaction Publishers.

Hopper, Tom. 2011. *USGOV.FIX: Fixes for a Failing Government*. Lexington, KY: Privately printed.

House, Edward Mandell. 1912. *Philip Dru: Administrator*. Reprint. Appleton, WI: Robert Welch University Press, 1998.

Jackson, Jesse L., Jr., with Frank E. Watkins. 2001. *A More Perfect Union: Advancing New American Rights*. New York: Welcome Rain Publishers.

Jeffs, Daniel B. 2000. *America's Crisis: The Direct Democracy and Direct Education Solution*. Amherst Junction, WI: Hard Shell Word Factory.

Kettl, Donald F. 2009. *The Next Government of the United States: Why Our Institutions Fail Us and How to Fix Them*. New York: W.W. Norton & Company.

Kirk, Chris. 2012. "We the People of Slate." *Slate*, July 29. http://www.slate.com/articles/news_and_politics/the_hive/2012/07/u_s_constitution_as_rewritten_by_slate_legal_experts_and_readers_.html (accessed December 17, 2013).

Kirstein, Herbert C. 1994. *U.S. Constitution for 21st Century and Beyond*. Alexandria, VA: Realistic IDEALIST Enterprise.

Krusch, Barry. 1992. *The 21st Century Constitution: A New America for a New Millennium*. New York: Stanhope Press.

Labunski, Richard. 2000. *The Second Constitutional Convention: How the American People Can Take Back Their Government*. Versailles, KY: Marley and Beck Press.

Lawrence, William B. 1880. "The Monarchical Principle in Our Constitution." *North American Review* 288 (November): 385–409.

Lazare, Daniel. 1996. *The Frozen Republic: How the Constitution Is Paralyzing Democracy*. New York: Harcourt Brace & Company.

Lessig, Lawrence. 2011. *Republic, Lost: How Money Corrupts Congress—And a Plan to Stop It*. New York: Twelve.

Levin, Mark R. 2013. *The Liberty Amendments: Restoring the American Republic*. New York: Threshold Editions.

Levinson, Sanford. 2006. *Our UnDemocratic Constitution: Where the Constitution Goes Wrong (And How We the People Can Correct It)*. New York: Oxford University Press.

Lieber, Francis. 1865. *Amendments of the Constitution Submitted to the Consideration of the American People*. New York: Loyal Publication Society.

Lockwood, Henry C. 1884. *The Abolition of the Presidency*. New York: R. Worthington. Reprint, Farmingdale, NY: Darbor Social Science Publications, 1978.

Macdonald, Dwight. 1968. "The Constitution of the United States Needs to Be Fixed." *Esquire* 70 (October): 143ff.

MacDonald, William. 1922. *A New Constitution for a New America*. New York: B. W. Huebsch.

Manuel, Paul, and Anne Marie Cammisa. 1998. *Checks and Balances? How a Parliamentary System Could Change American Politics*. Boulder, CO: Westview Press.

Marduke, P. G. 1970. *The CASCOT System for Social Control of Technology*. Silver Spring, MD: Citizens' Association for Social Control of Technology.

Marx, Michael. 1999. *Justus—A Utopia: Formation of a Tax Free Constitutional Democracy*. Flat Rock, IL: Marx & Marx.

Mautner, Michael Noah. 1992. *A Constitution of Direct Democracy: Pure Democracy and the Governance of the Future, Locally and Globally*. Christchurch, NZ: Legacy Books.

Mayers, Lewis. 1918. "Should We Remake the Constitution?" *The New Republic* 16 (August 17): 73–4.

McGrath, Patrick J. 2000. *The Way to Responsible Government: The Constitutional Re-Structuring America Needs*. San Jose, CA: Writer's Showcase.

McKee, Henry S. 1933. *Degenerate Democracy*. New York: Thomas Y. Crowell.

Médaille, John. 2010. "Monarchy and the American Constitution." *The Distributist Review*, December 6. http://distributistreview.com/mag/2010/12/monarchy-and-the-american-constitution/ (site discontinued).

Merriam, Charles. 1931. *The Written Constitution and the Unwritten Attitude*. New York: Richard R. Smith.

Mertens, John. 1997. *The Second Constitution for the United States of America*. Cottonwood, CA: Gazelle Books.

Miller, Arthur S. 1987. *The Secret Constitution and the Need for Constitutional Change.* Westport, CT: Greenwood Press.

Miller, Jeremy. 1987. "It's Time for a New Constitution." *Southwestern University Law Review* 17: 207–37.

Miller, John B., ed. 2012. *The Second Bill of Rights & The New Federalist Papers: Eleven Amendments to the United States Constitution and Fifty Papers That Present Them.* Arlington, MA: The New Federalism.

Morris, Henry O. 1897. *Waiting for the Signal, a Novel.* Chicago: Schulte.

Naylor, Thomas H., and William H. Willimon. 1997. *Downsizing the U.S.A.* Grand Rapids, MI: William B. Eerdmans.

Novak, Michael. 1974. *Choosing Our King: Powerful Symbols in Presidential Politics.* New York: Macmillan.

"Objectivism Wiki: Reality, Reason, Rights." N.d. http://wiki.objectismonline.net/wiki /New_constitution (accessed December 17, 2013).

"Oceania—The Atlantis Project." N.d. http://www.oceania.org/indexgif.html (accessed December 17, 2013).

O'Conor, Charles. 1877. *Address by Charles O'Conor, delivered before the New York Historical Society at the Academy of Music. May 8.* New York: Anson D. F. Randolph.

Oliver, Michael. 1968. *A New Constitution for a New Country.* Revised ed. Reno, NV: Fine Arts Press.

Owens, Robert R. 2010. *The Constitution Failed: Dispatches from the History of the Future.* Maitland, FL: Xulon Press.

Pain, Ernest. N.d. "A New Constitution for the United States of America." http://usrecon stitution.net (accessed December 17, 2013).

Palm, Kirby. N.d. "The U.S. Constitution: Formal Additions." http://www.nettally.com /palmk/ConstitutionSections.html (accessed December 17, 2013).

Palm, Kirby. N.d. "Proposed Constitutional Amendment." http://www.nettally.com/palmk /terms.html (accessed December 17, 2013).

Pendleton, Edmund. 2004 [1801]. "The Danger Not Over." In *Liberty and Order: The First American Party Struggle*, edited by Lance Banning. Indianapolis, IN: Liberty Fund.

Patterson, C. Perry. 1947. *Presidential Government in the United States: The Unwritten Constitution.* Chapel Hill: University of North Carolina Press.

Pei, Mario. 1967–68. "The Case for a Constitutional Convention." *Modern Age* 12: 8–13.

Piatt, Marty. 2012. *If I Was President . . . My Blueprint for America.* Bloomington, IN: Author House.

Piburn, John L. 1932. *A Constitution and a Code.* San Diego: Bowman Printing Company.

Piper, John K. 2010. "A United States Constitution for the 21st Century." http://www.pipe -dream-constitution.info/ (accessed June 7, 2013).

Platt, L. Henry, Jr. 1972. "DarkHorseCandidate.com." http://www.darkhorsecandidate .com/constitution.html (accessed December 17, 2013).

Polk, Sam Carr. 2013. *Dethroning King Money by Re-Forming Uncle Sam* (e-book).

Rabbit, Jack. 2006. "Second Constitution of the United States of America." March 20. http:// journals.democraticunderground.com/Jack%20Rabbit/3 (accessed June 17, 2013).

Reedy, George. 1970. *The Twilight of the Presidency.* New York: World Publishing Co.

Revolutionary Communist Party, USA. 2010. *Constitution for the New Socialist Republic in North America.* Chicago, IL: RCP Publications.

Reynolds, Eustace. 1915. *A New Constitution: A Suggested Form of Modified Constitution.* New York: Nation Press.

Rice, Isaac. 1884. "Work for a Constitutional Convention." *Century Magazine* 28 (August): 534–40.

Ricker, Ward. c.2011. "Modified Constitution for the United States of America." http://wardricker.com/constitution.php (accessed December 17, 2013).

Robinson, Donald. 1989. *Government for the Third American Century.* Boulder, CO: Westview Press.

Roland, John. 2009–. "Draft Amendments to U.S. Constitution." http://constitution.org/reform/us/con_amend.htm (accessed December 17, 2013).

Sabato, Larry J. 2007. *A More Perfect Constitution: 23 Proposals to Revitalize Our Constitution and Make America a Fairer Country.* New York: Walker and Company.

Schmitendorf, James M. 2011. *Lex Ferenda: We the People.* Lexington, KY: Privately printed.

Scott, Rodney D. 1999. *The Great Debate: The Need for Constitutional Reform.* Chicago: Rampant Lion Press.

Shogan, Robert. 1982. *None of the Above: Why Presidents Fail—And What Can Be Done about It.* New York: New American Library.

Siegan, Bernard H. 1994. *Drafting a Constitution for a Nation or Republic Emerging into Freedom.* 2nd ed. Fairfax, VA: George Mason University Press.

Sirmon, Rick. 2011. *In Search of George Washington (The Story of the 28th Amendment).* Bloomington, IN: Xlibris.

Smith, Goldwin. 1898. "Is the Constitution Outworn?" *North American Review* 166 (March): 257–67.

Smith, J. Allen. 1965. Reprint of 1907 edition. *The Spirit of American Government,* edited by Cushing Strout. Cambridge, MA: Belknap Press of Harvard University Press.

Somin, Ilya, and Neal Devins. 2007. "Can We Make the Constitution More Democratic?" *Drake Law Review* (2006–7): 971–1000.

Sprogis, Uldis. 2011. *New Constitution of the United States* (e-book).

Stickney, Albert. 1879. *A True Republic.* New York: Harper and Brothers.

Strauss, Erwin S. 1979. *How to Start Your Own Country.* Boulder, CO: Paladin Press.

Strittmatter, Bill. N.d. "A Christian Constitution and Civil Law for the Kingdom of Heaven on Earth." Lakemore, OH: Privately printed.

Struble, Robert, Jr. "Redeeming U.S. Democracy." http://temnet.com/~rusd/ (site discontinued) (accessed July 11, 1997).

Sturber, D. I. 1903. *The Anarchist Constitution.* San Francisco: Radical Publishing Company.

Sulcer, Thomas Wright. "The Second Constitution of the United States: A New and Improved Draft for the 21st Century." http://participedia.net/en/cases/second-constitution-united-states-new-and-improved-draft-21st-century (accessed December 17, 2013).

Sundquist, James L. 1986. *Constitutional Reform and Effective Government.* Washington DC: Brookings Institution.

Sunstein, Cass. 2006. *The Second Bill of Rights: FDR's Unfinished Revolution—And Why We Need It More Than Ever*. New York: Basic Books.

"Supreme Court of the U.S.: Amendments of the Constitution Are Proposed." 1948. *American Bar Association Journal* 34 (January): 1–3.

Tamirisa, Chandrashekar (Chandra). "Alternative Constitutionalism: A Revised Constitution of United States of America." http://ctamirisa.wordpress.com/2012/09/19/alternative-constitutionalism-revising-the-constitution-of-united-states-of-america-2/ (accessed December 17, 2013).

Tonn, Bruce E. 1996. "A Design for Future-Oriented Government." *Futures* 28 (June): 413–31.

Tugwell, Rexford. 1974. *The Emerging Constitution*. New York: Harper and Row.

Tuller, Walter K. 1911. "A Convention to Amend the Constitution—Why Needed—How It May Be Obtained." *North American Review* 193: 369–87.

Upham, Thomas C. 1941. *Total Democracy: A New Constitution for the United States. A Democratic Ideal for the World*. New York: Carlyle House.

Upshur, Abel P. 1863. *A Brief Enquiry into the True Nature and Character of Our Federal Government: Being a Review of Judge Story's Commentaries on the Constitution of the United States*. Philadelphia: John Campbell Publisher. Reprinted from the original Petersburg Edition of 1840.

"U.S. Constitution for the 21st Century and Beyond." http://www.newusconstitution.org/usc21a.html (accessed December 17, 2013).

The United States Constitution (Rev. Ed.). 2011. "How Would You Rewrite the United States Constitution?" (Symposium). *Constitutional Commentary* 27 (Winter 2011): 499–589.

Virginia Vanguard. 1995. *The Populis: A Draft Constitution for a Political New Age*. Brentsville, VA: The Wingspread Enterprise.

Wade, Edwin L. 1995. *Constitution 2000: A Federalist Proposal for the Next Century*. Chicago: Let's Talk Sense.

Webster, Noah. 2008 [1785]. *Sketches of American Policy*. Introduction by John R. Vile. Clark, NJ: The LawBook Exchange, Ltd.

Wedgwood, William B. 1861. *The Reconstruction of the Government of the United States of America: A Democratic Empire Advocated and an Imperial Constitution Proposed*. New York: John H. Tingley.

Whicker, Marcia Lynn, Ruth Ann Strickland, and Raymond A. Moore. 1987. *The Constitution under Pressure: A Time for Change*. New York: Praeger.

White, Bouck. 1917. "Shall We Call a Constituent Assembly as Provided by the United States Constitution?" *Outlook* 116 (August 22): 613–15.

Wilkey, Malcolm R. 1995. *Is It Time for a Second Constitutional Convention?* Commentary by Walter Berns, et al. Washington, DC: National Legal Center for the Public Interest.

Willard, Simon, Jr. 1815. *The Columbian Union, Containing General and Particular Explanations of Government, and the Columbian Constitution, Being an Amendment to the Constitution of the United States: Providing a Yearly Revenue to Government of about Forty Millions of Dollars, and the Inevitable Union of the People by a Rule of*

Voting, and Exemption from Unnecessary Taxation, Consequently Their Permanent and Perpetual Freedom. Albany, NY: Printed for the author.

Wilson, Woodrow. 1961. *Constitutional Government in the United States.* New York: Columbia University Press. Reprint of 1908 edition.

Woodward, Augustus B. 1825. *The Presidency of the United States.* New York: J & J. Harper

Wynne, Floyd. 2006. *Saving Our Constitution.* Bloomington, IN: Author House.

Additional Proposals for Re-framing the Constitution Discovered or Published as This Book Was Being Produced

Cunning, John N. 1890. *The New Constitution: How the Farmer May Pay Off His Mortgage and the Working-Man Become His Own Master.* Chicago: Donohue, Henneberry & Co.

Fruth, William H. 2010. *10 Amendments for Freedom.* Palm City, FL: POLICOM.

Hirschhorn, Joel S. 2006. *Delusional Democracy: Fixing the Republic without Overthrowing the Government.* Monroe, ME: Common Courage Press.

Howard, Philip K. 2014. *The Rule of Nobody: Saving American From Dead laws and Broken Government.* New York: W.W. Norton & Company.

Kacprowicz, Charles. 2010. *Reclaiming America through Single Issue Federal Conventions.* Spruce Pine, NC: Markets Global Publishing.

Lawhon, George Enice. 2012. *A Citizens Manual for Amending the United States Constitution in 2012.* CreateSpace Independent Publishing Platform.

Naglee, John F., Sr. 2011. *Our New Constitution: Conceived by Citizens Determined to Restore their Nation.* Shelbyville, KY: Wasteland Press.

Oregon Physician. "Common Sense: A Booklet on How Simple It Is to Make Our Country Even Better." Accompanying Web site: http://commonsensebooklet.com/letter.htm.

Schouler, James. 1908. *Ideals of the Republic.* Boston: Little, Brown, and Company.

Stevens, John Paul. 2014. *Six Amendments: How and Why We Should Change the Constitution.* New York: Little, Brown and Company.

Of Additional Interest

Tsai, Robert L. 2014. *America's Forgotten Constitutions: Defiant Visions of Power and Community.* Cambridge, MA: Harvard University Press.

The Constitution of the United States

*Note: The following text is a transcription of the Constitution in its **original** form. Items that are italicized have since been amended or superseded.*

We the People of the United States, in Order to form a more perfect Union, establish Justice, insure domestic Tranquility, provide for the common defence, promote the general Welfare, and secure the Blessings of Liberty to ourselves and our Posterity, do ordain and establish this Constitution for the United States of America.

Article. I.

Section. 1.

All legislative Powers herein granted shall be vested in a Congress of the United States, which shall consist of a Senate and House of Representatives.

Section. 2.

The House of Representatives shall be composed of Members chosen every second Year by the People of the several States, and the Electors in each State shall have the Qualifications requisite for Electors of the most numerous Branch of the State Legislature.

No Person shall be a Representative who shall not have attained to the Age of twenty five Years, and been seven Years a Citizen of the United States, and who shall not, when elected, be an Inhabitant of that State in which he shall be chosen.

Representatives and direct Taxes shall be apportioned among the several States which may be included within this Union, according to their respective Numbers, which shall be determined by adding to the whole Number of free Persons, including those bound to Service for a Term of Years, and excluding Indians not taxed, three fifths of all other Persons. The actual Enumeration shall be made within three Years after the first Meeting of the Congress of the United States, and within every subsequent Term of ten Years, in such Manner as they shall by Law direct. The Number of Representatives shall not exceed one for every thirty Thousand, but each State shall have at Least one Representative; and until such enumeration shall be made, the State of New Hampshire shall be entitled to chuse three,

Massachusetts eight, Rhode-Island and Providence Plantations one, Connecticut five, New-York six, New Jersey four, Pennsylvania eight, Delaware one, Maryland six, Virginia ten, North Carolina five, South Carolina five, and Georgia three.

When vacancies happen in the Representation from any State, the Executive Authority thereof shall issue Writs of Election to fill such Vacancies.

The House of Representatives shall chuse their Speaker and other Officers; and shall have the sole Power of Impeachment.

Section. 3.

The Senate of the United States shall be composed of two Senators from each State, *chosen by the Legislature* thereof for six Years; and each Senator shall have one Vote.

Immediately after they shall be assembled in Consequence of the first Election, they shall be divided as equally as may be into three Classes. The Seats of the Senators of the first Class shall be vacated at the Expiration of the second Year, of the second Class at the Expiration of the fourth Year, and of the third Class at the Expiration of the sixth Year, so that one third may be chosen every second Year; *and if Vacancies happen by Resignation, or otherwise, during the Recess of the Legislature of any State, the Executive thereof may make temporary Appointments until the next Meeting of the Legislature, which shall then fill such Vacancies.*

No Person shall be a Senator who shall not have attained to the Age of thirty Years, and been nine Years a Citizen of the United States, and who shall not, when elected, be an Inhabitant of that State for which he shall be chosen.

The Vice President of the United States shall be President of the Senate, but shall have no Vote, unless they be equally divided.

The Senate shall chuse their other Officers, and also a President pro tempore, in the Absence of the Vice President, or when he shall exercise the Office of President of the United States.

The Senate shall have the sole Power to try all Impeachments. When sitting for that Purpose, they shall be on Oath or Affirmation. When the President of the United States is tried, the Chief Justice shall preside: And no Person shall be convicted without the Concurrence of two thirds of the Members present.

Judgment in Cases of Impeachment shall not extend further than to removal from Office, and disqualification to hold and enjoy any Office of honor, Trust or Profit under the United States: but the Party convicted shall nevertheless be liable and subject to Indictment, Trial, Judgment and Punishment, according to Law.

Section. 4.

The Times, Places and Manner of holding Elections for Senators and Representatives, shall be prescribed in each State by the Legislature thereof; but the Congress may at any time by Law make or alter such Regulations, except as to the Places of chusing Senators.

The Congress shall assemble at least once in every Year, and such Meeting shall *be on the first Monday in December,* unless they shall by Law appoint a different Day.

Section. 5.

Each House shall be the Judge of the Elections, Returns and Qualifications of its own Members, and a Majority of each shall constitute a Quorum to do Business; but a smaller Number may adjourn from day to day, and may be authorized to compel the Attendance of absent Members, in such Manner, and under such Penalties as each House may provide.

Each House may determine the Rules of its Proceedings, punish its Members for disorderly Behaviour, and, with the Concurrence of two thirds, expel a Member.

Each House shall keep a Journal of its Proceedings, and from time to time publish the same, excepting such Parts as may in their Judgment require Secrecy; and the Yeas and Nays of the Members of either House on any question shall, at the Desire of one fifth of those Present, be entered on the Journal.

Neither House, during the Session of Congress, shall, without the Consent of the other, adjourn for more than three days, nor to any other Place than that in which the two Houses shall be sitting.

Section. 6.

The Senators and Representatives shall receive a Compensation for their Services, to be ascertained by Law, and paid out of the Treasury of the United States. They shall in all Cases, except Treason, Felony and Breach of the Peace, be privileged from Arrest during their Attendance at the Session of their respective Houses, and in going to and returning from the same; and for any Speech or Debate in either House, they shall not be questioned in any other Place.

No Senator or Representative shall, during the Time for which he was elected, be appointed to any civil Office under the Authority of the United States, which shall have been created, or the Emoluments whereof shall have been encreased during such time; and no Person holding any Office under the United States, shall be a Member of either House during his Continuance in Office.

Section. 7.

All Bills for raising Revenue shall originate in the House of Representatives; but the Senate may propose or concur with Amendments as on other Bills.

Every Bill which shall have passed the House of Representatives and the Senate, shall, before it become a Law, be presented to the President of the United States: If he approve he shall sign it, but if not he shall return it, with his Objections to that House in which it shall have originated, who shall enter the Objections at large on their Journal, and proceed to reconsider it. If after such Reconsideration two thirds of that House shall agree to pass the Bill, it shall be sent, together with the Objections, to the other House, by which it shall likewise be reconsidered, and if approved by two thirds of that House, it shall become a Law. But in all such Cases the Votes of both Houses shall be determined by yeas and Nays, and the Names of the Persons voting for and against the Bill shall be entered on the Journal of each House respectively. If any Bill shall not be returned by the President within ten Days (Sundays excepted) after it shall have been presented to him, the Same shall be a Law, in like Manner as if he had signed it, unless the Congress by their Adjournment prevent its Return, in which Case it shall not be a Law.

Every Order, Resolution, or Vote to which the Concurrence of the Senate and House of Representatives may be necessary (except on a question of Adjournment) shall be presented to the President of the United States; and before the Same shall take Effect, shall be approved by him, or being disapproved by him, shall be repassed by two thirds of the Senate and House of Representatives, according to the Rules and Limitations prescribed in the Case of a Bill.

Section. 8.

The Congress shall have Power To lay and collect Taxes, Duties, Imposts and Excises, to pay the Debts and provide for the common Defence and general Welfare of the United States; but all Duties, Imposts and Excises shall be uniform throughout the United States;

To borrow Money on the credit of the United States;

To regulate Commerce with foreign Nations, and among the several States, and with the Indian Tribes;

To establish an uniform Rule of Naturalization, and uniform Laws on the subject of Bankruptcies throughout the United States;

To coin Money, regulate the Value thereof, and of foreign Coin, and fix the Standard of Weights and Measures;

To provide for the Punishment of counterfeiting the Securities and current Coin of the United States;

To establish Post Offices and post Roads;

To promote the Progress of Science and useful Arts, by securing for limited Times to Authors and Inventors the exclusive Right to their respective Writings and Discoveries;

To constitute Tribunals inferior to the supreme Court;

To define and punish Piracies and Felonies committed on the high Seas, and Offences against the Law of Nations;

To declare War, grant Letters of Marque and Reprisal, and make Rules concerning Captures on Land and Water;

To raise and support Armies, but no Appropriation of Money to that Use shall be for a longer Term than two Years;

To provide and maintain a Navy;

To make Rules for the Government and Regulation of the land and naval Forces;

To provide for calling forth the Militia to execute the Laws of the Union, suppress Insurrections and repel Invasions;

To provide for organizing, arming, and disciplining, the Militia, and for governing such Part of them as may be employed in the Service of the United States, reserving to the States respectively, the Appointment of the Officers, and the Authority of training the Militia according to the discipline prescribed by Congress;

To exercise exclusive Legislation in all Cases whatsoever, over such District (not exceeding ten Miles square) as may, by Cession of particular States, and the Acceptance of Congress, become the Seat of the Government of the United States, and to exercise like Authority over all Places purchased by the Consent of the Legislature of the State in which the Same shall be, for the Erection of Forts, Magazines, Arsenals, dock-Yards, and other needful Buildings;—And

To make all Laws which shall be necessary and proper for carrying into Execution the foregoing Powers, and all other Powers vested by this Constitution in the Government of the United States, or in any Department or Officer thereof.

Section. 9.

The Migration or Importation of such Persons as any of the States now existing shall think proper to admit, shall not be prohibited by the Congress prior to the Year one thousand eight hundred and eight, but a Tax or duty may be imposed on such Importation, not exceeding ten dollars for each Person.

The Privilege of the Writ of Habeas Corpus shall not be suspended, unless when in Cases of Rebellion or Invasion the public Safety may require it.

No Bill of Attainder or ex post facto Law shall be passed.

No Capitation, or other direct, Tax shall be laid, *unless in Proportion to the Census or enumeration herein before directed to be taken.*

No Tax or Duty shall be laid on Articles exported from any State.

No Preference shall be given by any Regulation of Commerce or Revenue to the Ports of one State over those of another; nor shall Vessels bound to, or from, one State, be obliged to enter, clear, or pay Duties in another.

No Money shall be drawn from the Treasury, but in Consequence of Appropriations made by Law; and a regular Statement and Account of the Receipts and Expenditures of all public Money shall be published from time to time.

No Title of Nobility shall be granted by the United States: And no Person holding any Office of Profit or Trust under them, shall, without the Consent of the Congress, accept of any present, Emolument, Office, or Title, of any kind whatever, from any King, Prince, or foreign State.

Section. 10.

No State shall enter into any Treaty, Alliance, or Confederation; grant Letters of Marque and Reprisal; coin Money; emit Bills of Credit; make any Thing but gold and silver Coin a Tender in Payment of Debts; pass any Bill of Attainder, ex post facto Law, or Law impairing the Obligation of Contracts, or grant any Title of Nobility.

No State shall, without the Consent of the Congress, lay any Imposts or Duties on Imports or Exports, except what may be absolutely necessary for executing it's inspection Laws: and the net Produce of all Duties and Imposts, laid by any State on Imports or Exports, shall be for the Use of the Treasury of the United States; and all such Laws shall be subject to the Revision and Controul of the Congress.

No State shall, without the Consent of Congress, lay any Duty of Tonnage, keep Troops, or Ships of War in time of Peace, enter into any Agreement or Compact with another State, or with a foreign Power, or engage in War, unless actually invaded, or in such imminent Danger as will not admit of delay.

Article. II.

Section. 1.

The executive Power shall be vested in a President of the United States of America. He shall hold his Office during the Term of four Years, and, together with the Vice President, chosen for the same Term, be elected, as follows:

Each State shall appoint, in such Manner as the Legislature thereof may direct, a Number of Electors, equal to the whole Number of Senators and Representatives to which the State may be entitled in the Congress: but no Senator or Representative, or Person holding an Office of Trust or Profit under the United States, shall be appointed an Elector.

The Electors shall meet in their respective States, and vote by Ballot for two Persons, of whom one at least shall not be an Inhabitant of the same State with themselves. And they shall make a List of all the Persons voted for, and of the Number of Votes for each; which List they shall sign and certify, and transmit sealed to the Seat of the Government of the United States, directed to the President of the Senate. The President of the Senate shall, in the Presence of the Senate and House of Representatives, open all the Certificates, and the Votes shall then be counted. The Person having the greatest Number of Votes shall be the President, if such Number be a Majority of the whole Number of Electors appointed; and if there be more than one who have such Majority, and have an equal Number of Votes, then the House of Representatives shall immediately chuse by Ballot one of them for President; and if no Person have a Majority, then from the five highest on the List the said House shall in like Manner chuse the President. But in chusing the President, the Votes shall be taken by States, the Representation from each State having one Vote; A quorum for this purpose shall consist of a Member or Members from two thirds of the States, and a Majority of all the States shall be necessary to a Choice. In every Case, after the Choice of the President, the Person having the greatest Number of Votes of the Electors shall be the Vice President. But if there should remain two or more who have equal Votes, the Senate shall chuse from them by Ballot the Vice President.

The Congress may determine the Time of chusing the Electors, and the Day on which they shall give their Votes; which Day shall be the same throughout the United States.

No Person except a natural born Citizen, or a Citizen of the United States, at the time of the Adoption of this Constitution, shall be eligible to the Office of President; neither shall any Person be eligible to that Office who shall not have attained to the Age of thirty five Years, and been fourteen Years a Resident within the United States.

In Case of the Removal of the President from Office, or of his Death, Resignation, or Inability to discharge the Powers and Duties of the said Office, the Same shall devolve on the Vice President, and the Congress may by Law provide for the Case of Removal, Death, Resignation or Inability, both of the President and Vice President, declaring what Officer shall then act as President, and such Officer shall act accordingly, until the Disability be removed, or a President shall be elected.

The President shall, at stated Times, receive for his Services, a Compensation, which shall neither be increased nor diminished during the Period for which he shall have been elected, and he shall not receive within that Period any other Emolument from the United States, or any of them.

Before he enter on the Execution of his Office, he shall take the following Oath or Affirmation:—"I do solemnly swear (or affirm) that I will faithfully execute the Office of President of the United States, and will to the best of my Ability, preserve, protect and defend the Constitution of the United States."

Section. 2.

The President shall be Commander in Chief of the Army and Navy of the United States, and of the Militia of the several States, when called into the actual Service of the United States; he may require the Opinion, in writing, of the principal

Officer in each of the executive Departments, upon any Subject relating to the Duties of their respective Offices, and he shall have Power to grant Reprieves and Pardons for Offences against the United States, except in Cases of Impeachment.

He shall have Power, by and with the Advice and Consent of the Senate, to make Treaties, provided two thirds of the Senators present concur; and he shall nominate, and by and with the Advice and Consent of the Senate, shall appoint Ambassadors, other public Ministers and Consuls, Judges of the supreme Court, and all other Officers of the United States, whose Appointments are not herein otherwise provided for, and which shall be established by Law: but the Congress may by Law vest the Appointment of such inferior Officers, as they think proper, in the President alone, in the Courts of Law, or in the Heads of Departments.

The President shall have Power to fill up all Vacancies that may happen during the Recess of the Senate, by granting Commissions which shall expire at the End of their next Session.

Section. 3.

He shall from time to time give to the Congress Information of the State of the Union, and recommend to their Consideration such Measures as he shall judge necessary and expedient; he may, on extraordinary Occasions, convene both Houses, or either of them, and in Case of Disagreement between them, with Respect to the Time of Adjournment, he may adjourn them to such Time as he shall think proper; he shall receive Ambassadors and other public Ministers; he shall take Care that the Laws be faithfully executed, and shall Commission all the Officers of the United States.

Section. 4.

The President, Vice President and all civil Officers of the United States, shall be removed from Office on Impeachment for, and Conviction of, Treason, Bribery, or other high Crimes and Misdemeanors.

Article III.

Section. 1.

The judicial Power of the United States shall be vested in one supreme Court, and in such inferior Courts as the Congress may from time to time ordain and establish. The Judges, both of the supreme and inferior Courts, shall hold their Offices during good Behaviour, and shall, at stated Times, receive for their Services a Compensation, which shall not be diminished during their Continuance in Office.

Section. 2.

The judicial Power shall extend to all Cases, in Law and Equity, arising under this Constitution, the Laws of the United States, and Treaties made, or which shall be made, under their Authority;—to all Cases affecting Ambassadors, other public Ministers and Consuls;—to all Cases of admiralty and maritime Jurisdiction;— to Controversies to which the United States shall be a Party;—to Controversies between two or more States;—*between a State and Citizens of another State,*— between Citizens of different States,—between Citizens of the same State claiming Lands under Grants of different States, and between a State, or the Citizens thereof, and foreign States, Citizens or Subjects.

In all Cases affecting Ambassadors, other public Ministers and Consuls, and those in which a State shall be Party, the supreme Court shall have original Jurisdiction. In all the other Cases before mentioned, the supreme Court shall have appellate Jurisdiction, both as to Law and Fact, with such Exceptions, and under such Regulations as the Congress shall make.

The Trial of all Crimes, except in Cases of Impeachment, shall be by Jury; and such Trial shall be held in the State where the said Crimes shall have been committed; but when not committed within any State, the Trial shall be at such Place or Places as the Congress may by Law have directed.

Section. 3.

Treason against the United States, shall consist only in levying War against them, or in adhering to their Enemies, giving them Aid and Comfort. No Person shall be convicted of Treason unless on the Testimony of two Witnesses to the same overt Act, or on Confession in open Court.

The Congress shall have Power to declare the Punishment of Treason, but no Attainder of Treason shall work Corruption of Blood, or Forfeiture except during the Life of the Person attainted.

Article. IV.

Section. 1.

Full Faith and Credit shall be given in each State to the public Acts, Records, and judicial Proceedings of every other State. And the Congress may by general Laws prescribe the Manner in which such Acts, Records and Proceedings shall be proved, and the Effect thereof.

Section. 2.

The Citizens of each State shall be entitled to all Privileges and Immunities of Citizens in the several States.

A Person charged in any State with Treason, Felony, or other Crime, who shall flee from Justice, and be found in another State, shall on Demand of the executive Authority of the State from which he fled, be delivered up, to be removed to the State having Jurisdiction of the Crime.

No Person held to Service or Labour in one State, under the Laws thereof, escaping into another, shall, in Consequence of any Law or Regulation therein, be discharged from such Service or Labour, but shall be delivered up on Claim of the Party to whom such Service or Labour may be due.

Section. 3.

New States may be admitted by the Congress into this Union; but no new State shall be formed or erected within the Jurisdiction of any other State; nor any State be formed by the Junction of two or more States, or Parts of States, without the Consent of the Legislatures of the States concerned as well as of the Congress.
The Congress shall have Power to dispose of and make all needful Rules and Regulations respecting the Territory or other Property belonging to the United States; and nothing in this Constitution shall be so construed as to Prejudice any Claims of the United States, or of any particular State.

Section. 4.

The United States shall guarantee to every State in this Union a Republican Form of Government, and shall protect each of them against Invasion; and on Application of the Legislature, or of the Executive (when the Legislature cannot be convened), against domestic Violence.

Article. V.

The Congress, whenever two thirds of both Houses shall deem it necessary, shall propose Amendments to this Constitution, or, on the Application of the Legislatures of two thirds of the several States, shall call a Convention for proposing Amendments, which, in either Case, shall be valid to all Intents and Purposes, as Part of this Constitution, when ratified by the Legislatures of three fourths of the several States, or by Conventions in three fourths thereof, as the one or the other Mode of Ratification may be proposed by the Congress; Provided that no Amendment which may be made prior to the Year One thousand eight hundred and eight shall in any Manner affect the first and fourth Clauses in the Ninth Section of the first Article; and that no State, without its Consent, shall be deprived of its equal Suffrage in the Senate.

Article. VI.

All Debts contracted and Engagements entered into, before the Adoption of this Constitution, shall be as valid against the United States under this Constitution, as under the Confederation.

This Constitution, and the Laws of the United States which shall be made in Pursuance thereof; and all Treaties made, or which shall be made, under the Authority of the United States, shall be the supreme Law of the Land; and the Judges in every State shall be bound thereby, any Thing in the Constitution or Laws of any State to the Contrary notwithstanding.

The Senators and Representatives before mentioned, and the Members of the several State Legislatures, and all executive and judicial Officers, both of the United States and of the several States, shall be bound by Oath or Affirmation, to support this Constitution; but no religious Test shall ever be required as a Qualification to any Office or public Trust under the United States.

Article. VII.

The Ratification of the Conventions of nine States, shall be sufficient for the Establishment of this Constitution between the States so ratifying the Same.

The Word, "the," being interlined between the seventh and eighth Lines of the first Page, the Word "Thirty" being partly written on an Erazure in the fifteenth Line of the first Page, The Words "is tried" being interlined between the thirty second and thirty third Lines of the first Page and the Word "the" being interlined between the forty third and forty fourth Lines of the second Page.

Attest William Jackson Secretary

done in Convention by the Unanimous Consent of the States present the Seventeenth Day of September in the Year of our Lord one thousand seven hundred and Eighty seven and of the Independance of the United States of America the Twelfth In witness whereof We have hereunto subscribed our Names,

G°. Washington
Presidt and deputy from Virginia

Delaware
Geo: Read
Gunning Bedford jun
John Dickinson
Richard Bassett
Jaco: Broom

Maryland
James McHenry
Dan of St Thos. Jenifer
Danl. Carroll

Virginia
John Blair
James Madison Jr.

North Carolina
Wm. Blount
Richd. Dobbs Spaight
Hu Williamson

South Carolina
J. Rutledge

Charles Cotesworth Pinckney
Charles Pinckney
Pierce Butler

Georgia
William Few
Abr Baldwin

New Hampshire
John Langdon
Nicholas Gilman

Massachusetts
Nathaniel Gorham
Rufus King

Connecticut
Wm. Saml. Johnson
Roger Sherman

New York
Alexander Hamilton

New Jersey
Wil: Livingston
David Brearley
Wm. Paterson
Jona: Dayton

Pennsylvania
B Franklin
Thomas Mifflin
Robt. Morris
Geo. Clymer
Thos. FitzSimons
Jared Ingersoll
James Wilson
Gouv Morris

Source: National Archives.
http://www.archives.gov/exhibits/charters/constitution_transcript.html

Amendments to the U.S. Constitution

The Bill of Rights: A Transcription

The Preamble to The Bill of Rights

Congress of the United States
begun and held at the City of New-York, on
Wednesday the fourth of March, one thousand seven hundred and eighty nine.

THE Conventions of a number of the States, having at the time of their adopting the Constitution, expressed a desire, in order to prevent misconstruction or abuse of its powers, that further declaratory and restrictive clauses should be added: And as extending the ground of public confidence in the Government, will best ensure the beneficent ends of its institution.

RESOLVED by the Senate and House of Representatives of the United States of America, in Congress assembled, two thirds of both Houses concurring, that the following Articles be proposed to the Legislatures of the several States, as amendments to the Constitution of the United States, all, or any of which Articles, when ratified by three fourths of the said Legislatures, to be valid to all intents and purposes, as part of the said Constitution; viz.

ARTICLES in addition to, and Amendment of the Constitution of the United States of America, proposed by Congress, and ratified by the Legislatures of the several States, pursuant to the fifth Article of the original Constitution.
Note: The following text is a transcription of the first ten amendments to the Constitution in their original form. These amendments were ratified December 15, 1791, and form what is known as the "Bill of Rights."

Amendment I
Congress shall make no law respecting an establishment of religion, or prohibiting the free exercise thereof; or abridging the freedom of speech, or of the press; or the right of the people peaceably to assemble, and to petition the Government for a redress of grievances.

Amendment II

A well regulated Militia, being necessary to the security of a free State, the right of the people to keep and bear Arms, shall not be infringed.

Amendment III

No Soldier shall, in time of peace be quartered in any house, without the consent of the Owner, nor in time of war, but in a manner to be prescribed by law.

Amendment IV

The right of the people to be secure in their persons, houses, papers, and effects, against unreasonable searches and seizures, shall not be violated, and no Warrants shall issue, but upon probable cause, supported by Oath or affirmation, and particularly describing the place to be searched, and the persons or things to be seized.

Amendment V

No person shall be held to answer for a capital, or otherwise infamous crime, unless on a presentment or indictment of a Grand Jury, except in cases arising in the land or naval forces, or in the Militia, when in actual service in time of War or public danger; nor shall any person be subject for the same offence to be twice put in jeopardy of life or limb; nor shall be compelled in any criminal case to be a witness against himself, nor be deprived of life, liberty, or property, without due process of law; nor shall private property be taken for public use, without just compensation.

Amendment VI

In all criminal prosecutions, the accused shall enjoy the right to a speedy and public trial, by an impartial jury of the State and district wherein the crime shall have been committed, which district shall have been previously ascertained by law, and to be informed of the nature and cause of the accusation; to be confronted with the witnesses against him; to have compulsory process for obtaining witnesses in his favor, and to have the Assistance of Counsel for his defence.

Amendment VII

In Suits at common law, where the value in controversy shall exceed twenty dollars, the right of trial by jury shall be preserved, and no fact tried by a jury, shall be otherwise re-examined in any Court of the United States, than according to the rules of the common law.

Amendment VIII

Excessive bail shall not be required, nor excessive fines imposed, nor cruel and unusual punishments inflicted.

Amendment IX

The enumeration in the Constitution, of certain rights, shall not be construed to deny or disparage others retained by the people.

Amendment X

The powers not delegated to the United States by the Constitution, nor prohibited by it to the States, are reserved to the States respectively, or to the people.

AMENDMENT XI

Passed by Congress March 4, 1794. Ratified February 7, 1795.

Note*: Article III, section 2, of the Constitution was modified by amendment 11.*

The Judicial power of the United States shall not be construed to extend to any suit in law or equity, commenced or prosecuted against one of the United States by Citizens of another State, or by Citizens or Subjects of any Foreign State.

AMENDMENT XII

Passed by Congress December 9, 1803. Ratified June 15, 1804.

Note: A portion of Article II, section 1 of the Constitution was superseded by the 12th amendment.

The Electors shall meet in their respective states and vote by ballot for President and Vice-President, one of whom, at least, shall not be an inhabitant of the same state with themselves; they shall name in their ballots the person voted for as President, and in distinct ballots the person voted for as Vice-President, and they shall make distinct lists of all persons voted for as President, and of all persons voted for as Vice-President, and of the number of votes for each, which lists they shall sign and certify, and transmit sealed to the seat of the government of the United States, directed to the President of the Senate;—the President of the Senate shall, in the presence of the Senate and House of Representatives, open all the certificates and the votes shall then be counted;—The person having the greatest number of votes for President, shall be the President, if such number be a majority of the whole number of Electors appointed; and if no person have such majority, then from the persons having the highest numbers not exceeding three on the list of those voted for as President, the House of Representatives shall choose immediately, by ballot, the President. But in choosing the President, the votes shall be taken by states, the representation from each state having one vote; a quorum for this purpose shall consist of a member or members from two-thirds of the states, and a majority of all the states shall be necessary to a choice. [And if the House of Representatives shall not choose a President whenever the right of choice shall devolve upon them, before the fourth day of March next following, then the Vice-President shall act as President, as in case of the death or other constitutional disability of the President.—]* The person having the greatest number of votes as Vice-President, shall be the Vice-President, if such number be a majority of the whole number of Electors appointed, and if no person have a majority, then from the two highest numbers on the list, the Senate shall choose the Vice-President; a quorum for the purpose shall consist of two-thirds of the whole number of Senators, and a majority of the whole number shall be necessary to a choice. But no person constitutionally ineligible to the office of President shall be eligible to that of Vice-President of the United States.

Superseded by section 3 of the 20th amendment.

AMENDMENT XIII
Passed by Congress January 31, 1865. Ratified December 6, 1865.

Note: A portion of Article IV, section 2, of the Constitution was superseded by the 13th amendment.

Section 1.
Neither slavery nor involuntary servitude, except as a punishment for crime whereof the party shall have been duly convicted, shall exist within the United States, or any place subject to their jurisdiction.

Section 2.
Congress shall have power to enforce this article by appropriate legislation.

AMENDMENT XIV
Passed by Congress June 13, 1866. Ratified July 9, 1868.

Note: Article I, section 2, of the Constitution was modified by section 2 of the 14th amendment.

Section 1.
All persons born or naturalized in the United States, and subject to the jurisdiction thereof, are citizens of the United States and of the State wherein they reside. No State shall make or enforce any law which shall abridge the privileges or immunities of citizens of the United States; nor shall any State deprive any person of life, liberty, or property, without due process of law; nor deny to any person within its jurisdiction the equal protection of the laws.

Section 2.
Representatives shall be apportioned among the several States according to their respective numbers, counting the whole number of persons in each State, excluding Indians not taxed. But when the right to vote at any election for the choice of electors for President and Vice-President of the United States, Representatives in Congress, the Executive and Judicial officers of a State, or the members of the Legislature thereof, is denied to any of the male inhabitants of such State, being twenty-one years of age,* and citizens of the United States, or in any way abridged, except for participation in rebellion, or other crime, the basis of representation therein shall be reduced in the proportion which the number of such male citizens shall bear to the whole number of male citizens twenty-one years of age in such State.

Section 3.
No person shall be a Senator or Representative in Congress, or elector of President and Vice-President, or hold any office, civil or military, under the United States, or

under any State, who, having previously taken an oath, as a member of Congress, or as an officer of the United States, or as a member of any State legislature, or as an executive or judicial officer of any State, to support the Constitution of the United States, shall have engaged in insurrection or rebellion against the same, or given aid or comfort to the enemies thereof. But Congress may by a vote of two-thirds of each House, remove such disability.

Section 4.
The validity of the public debt of the United States, authorized by law, including debts incurred for payment of pensions and bounties for services in suppressing insurrection or rebellion, shall not be questioned. But neither the United States nor any State shall assume or pay any debt or obligation incurred in aid of insurrection or rebellion against the United States, or any claim for the loss or emancipation of any slave; but all such debts, obligations and claims shall be held illegal and void.

Section 5.
The Congress shall have the power to enforce, by appropriate legislation, the provisions of this article.

Changed by section 1 of the 26th Amendment.

AMENDMENT XV
Passed by Congress February 26, 1869. Ratified February 3, 1870.

Section 1.
The right of citizens of the United States to vote shall not be denied or abridged by the United States or by any State on account of race, color, or previous condition of servitude—

Section 2.
The Congress shall have the power to enforce this article by appropriate legislation.

AMENDMENT XVI
Passed by Congress July 2, 1909. Ratified February 3, 1913.

Note: Article I, section 9, of the Constitution was modified by amendment 16.
The Congress shall have power to lay and collect taxes on incomes, from whatever source derived, without apportionment among the several States, and without regard to any census or enumeration.

AMENDMENT XVII
Passed by Congress May 13, 1912. Ratified April 8, 1913.

Note: Article I, section 3, of the Constitution was modified by the 17th amendment.

The Senate of the United States shall be composed of two Senators from each State, elected by the people thereof, for six years; and each Senator shall have one vote. The electors in each State shall have the qualifications requisite for electors of the most numerous branch of the State legislatures.

When vacancies happen in the representation of any State in the Senate, the executive authority of such State shall issue writs of election to fill such vacancies: *Provided*, That the legislature of any State may empower the executive thereof to make temporary appointments until the people fill the vacancies by election as the legislature may direct.

This amendment shall not be so construed as to affect the election or term of any Senator chosen before it becomes valid as part of the Constitution.

AMENDMENT XVIII
Passed by Congress December 18, 1917. Ratified January 16, 1919. Repealed by amendment 21.

Section 1.
After one year from the ratification of this article the manufacture, sale, or transportation of intoxicating liquors within, the importation thereof into, or the exportation thereof from the United States and all territory subject to the jurisdiction thereof for beverage purposes is hereby prohibited.

Section 2.
The Congress and the several States shall have concurrent power to enforce this article by appropriate legislation.

Section 3.
This article shall be inoperative unless it shall have been ratified as an amendment to the Constitution by the legislatures of the several States, as provided in the Constitution, within seven years from the date of the submission hereof to the States by the Congress.

AMENDMENT XIX
Passed by Congress June 4, 1919. Ratified August 18, 1920.

The right of citizens of the United States to vote shall not be denied or abridged by the United States or by any State on account of sex.

Congress shall have power to enforce this article by appropriate legislation.

AMENDMENT XX
Passed by Congress March 2, 1932. Ratified January 23, 1933.

Note: Article I, section 4, of the Constitution was modified by section 2 of this amendment. In addition, a portion of the 12th amendment was superseded by section 3.

Section 1.

The terms of the President and the Vice President shall end at noon on the 20th day of January, and the terms of Senators and Representatives at noon on the 3rd day of January, of the years in which such terms would have ended if this article had not been ratified; and the terms of their successors shall then begin.

Section 2.

The Congress shall assemble at least once in every year, and such meeting shall begin at noon on the 3d day of January, unless they shall by law appoint a different day.

Section 3.

If, at the time fixed for the beginning of the term of the President, the President elect shall have died, the Vice President elect shall become President. If a President shall not have been chosen before the time fixed for the beginning of his term, or if the President elect shall have failed to qualify, then the Vice President elect shall act as President until a President shall have qualified; and the Congress may by law provide for the case wherein neither a President elect nor a Vice President shall have qualified, declaring who shall then act as President, or the manner in which one who is to act shall be selected, and such person shall act accordingly until a President or Vice President shall have qualified.

Section 4.

The Congress may by law provide for the case of the death of any of the persons from whom the House of Representatives may choose a President whenever the right of choice shall have devolved upon them, and for the case of the death of any of the persons from whom the Senate may choose a Vice President whenever the right of choice shall have devolved upon them.

Section 5.

Sections 1 and 2 shall take effect on the 15th day of October following the ratification of this article.

Section 6.

This article shall be inoperative unless it shall have been ratified as an amendment to the Constitution by the legislatures of three-fourths of the several States within seven years from the date of its submission.

AMENDMENT XXI

Passed by Congress February 20, 1933. Ratified December 5, 1933.

Section 1.

The eighteenth article of amendment to the Constitution of the United States is hereby repealed.

Section 2.

The transportation or importation into any State, Territory, or Possession of the United States for delivery or use therein of intoxicating liquors, in violation of the laws thereof, is hereby prohibited.

Section 3.

This article shall be inoperative unless it shall have been ratified as an amendment to the Constitution by conventions in the several States, as provided in the Constitution, within seven years from the date of the submission hereof to the States by the Congress.

AMENDMENT XXII

Passed by Congress March 21, 1947. Ratified February 27, 1951.

Section 1.

No person shall be elected to the office of the President more than twice, and no person who has held the office of President, or acted as President, for more than two years of a term to which some other person was elected President shall be elected to the office of President more than once. But this Article shall not apply to any person holding the office of President when this Article was proposed by Congress, and shall not prevent any person who may be holding the office of President, or acting as President, during the term within which this Article becomes operative from holding the office of President or acting as President during the remainder of such term.

Section 2.

This article shall be inoperative unless it shall have been ratified as an amendment to the Constitution by the legislatures of three-fourths of the several States within seven years from the date of its submission to the States by the Congress.

AMENDMENT XXIII

Passed by Congress June 16, 1960. Ratified March 29, 1961.

Section 1.

The District constituting the seat of Government of the United States shall appoint in such manner as Congress may direct:

A number of electors of President and Vice President equal to the whole number of Senators and Representatives in Congress to which the District would be entitled if it were a State, but in no event more than the least populous State; they shall be in addition to those appointed by the States, but they shall be considered, for the purposes of the election of President and Vice President, to be electors appointed by a State; and they shall meet in the District and perform such duties as provided by the twelfth article of amendment.

Section 2.

The Congress shall have power to enforce this article by appropriate legislation.

AMENDMENT XXIV

Passed by Congress August 27, 1962. Ratified January 23, 1964.

Section 1.

The right of citizens of the United States to vote in any primary or other election for President or Vice President, for electors for President or Vice President, or for Senator or Representative in Congress, shall not be denied or abridged by the United States or any State by reason of failure to pay poll tax or other tax.

Section 2.

The Congress shall have power to enforce this article by appropriate legislation.

AMENDMENT XXV

Passed by Congress July 6, 1965. Ratified February 10, 1967.

Note: Article II, section 1, of the Constitution was affected by the 25th amendment.

Section 1.

In case of the removal of the President from office or of his death or resignation, the Vice President shall become President.

Section 2.

Whenever there is a vacancy in the office of the Vice President, the President shall nominate a Vice President who shall take office upon confirmation by a majority vote of both Houses of Congress.

Section 3.

Whenever the President transmits to the President pro tempore of the Senate and the Speaker of the House of Representatives his written declaration that he is unable to discharge the powers and duties of his office, and until he transmits to them a written declaration to the contrary, such powers and duties shall be discharged by the Vice President as Acting President.

Section 4.

Whenever the Vice President and a majority of either the principal officers of the executive departments or of such other body as Congress may by law provide, transmit to the President pro tempore of the Senate and the Speaker of the House of Representatives their written declaration that the President is unable to discharge the powers and duties of his office, the Vice President shall immediately assume the powers and duties of the office as Acting President.

Thereafter, when the President transmits to the President pro tempore of the Senate and the Speaker of the House of Representatives his written declaration that no inability exists, he shall resume the powers and duties of his office unless the Vice President and a majority of either the principal officers of the executive department or of such other body as Congress may by law provide, transmit within four days to the President pro tempore of the Senate and the Speaker of the House of Representatives their written declaration that the President is unable to discharge the powers and duties of his office. Thereupon Congress shall decide the issue, assembling within forty-eight hours for that purpose if not in session. If the Congress, within twenty-one days after receipt of the latter written declaration, or, if Congress is not in session, within twenty-one days after Congress is required to assemble, determines by two-thirds vote of both Houses that the President is unable to discharge the powers and duties of his office, the Vice President shall continue to discharge the same as Acting President; otherwise, the President shall resume the powers and duties of his office.

AMENDMENT XXVI
Passed by Congress March 23, 1971. Ratified July 1, 1971.

Note: Amendment 14, section 2, of the Constitution was modified by section 1 of the 26th amendment.

Section 1.
The right of citizens of the United States, who are eighteen years of age or older, to vote shall not be denied or abridged by the United States or by any State on account of age.

Section 2.
The Congress shall have power to enforce this article by appropriate legislation.

AMENDMENT XXVII
Originally proposed Sept. 25, 1789. Ratified May 7, 1992.

No law, varying the compensation for the services of the Senators and Representatives, shall take effect, until an election of representatives shall have intervened.

Source: National Archives
http://www.archives.gov/exhibits/charters/bill_of_rights_transcript.html and
http://www.archives.gov/exhibits/charters/constitution_amendments_11-27.html

Index

Dates within parentheses in main headings indicate the date the discussed plan or document was proposed. Page numbers in **bold** indicate main discussion of the topic.

About the Author

Dr. John R. Vile is a professor of political science and Dean of the University Honors College at Middle Tennessee State University, and the author of numerous books on the U.S. Constitution, including *The Men Who Made the Constitution: Lives of the Delegates to the Constitutional Convention* and *The Encyclopedia of Constitutional Amendments, Proposed Amendments, and Amending Issues*.